The Oxford Guide to **Writing and Speaking**

The Oxford Guide to
Writing

and Speaking

John Seely

OXFORD UNIVERSITY PRESS

1998

Oxford University Press, Great Clarendon Street, Oxford OX2 6DP

Oxford New York

Athens Auckland Bangkok Bogota Bombay Buenos Aires
Calcutta Cape Town Dar es Salaam Delhi Florence Hong Kong Istanbul
Karachi Kuala Lumpur Madras Madrid Melbourne Mexico City
Nairobi Paris Singapore Taipei Tokyo Toronto Warsaw
and associated companies in
Berlin Ibadan

Oxford is a trade mark of Oxford University Press

Published in the United States
by Oxford University Press Inc., New York

© John Seely 1998

The moral rights of the author have been asserted

First published by Oxford University Press 1998

British Library Cataloguing in Publication Data
Data available

Library of Congress Cataloging in Publication Data
Data available
ISBN 0-19-863144-8

10 9 8 7 6 5 4 3 2 1

Designed and typeset by Jane Stevenson

Printed in Spain by
Mateu Cromo Artes Graficas S.A.
Madrid

Acknowledgements

A book like this, which covers a wide range of topics, has to draw on the knowledge and experience of many different advisers. I have been fortunate to receive the help of readers who have given great time and care to commenting on early drafts of the manuscript and advising how it might be improved. In particular, I should like to thank Brigid Avison, Alison Baverstock, Tim Cracknell, David Elsmore, Jacky Hart, Caroline Hartnell, Andrew Heron, and Samantha Manning in the UK, while Dr Nelson Ong of New York offered an American perspective. They will probably recognize where their advice and comments have produced changes in the final text. For this I am deeply grateful, but, of course, the final responsibility is my own.

I should like to thank the staff at Oxford University Press who have patiently supported this project, in particular Kate Wandless and Kendall Clarke, for their encouragement and advice.

Closer to home, Katherine and Timothy Seely gave excellent and critical 'consumers' comments', especially about the communication needs of students and those seeking and gaining their first jobs. (I knew those long years of parenting would pay off eventually!) My debt to my wife, Elizabeth, is immeasurable. Although we have both worked as writers and editors for many years, I can only say that this time I was even more vague and abstracted than usual, but she bore it with great good humour. As ever, she read the manuscript with a critical eye and made many trenchant and invaluable comments, and it is with gratitude that this book is dedicated to her.

Contents

How to use this book

Book structure

The *Oxford Guide to Writing and Speaking* is divided into four main sections, plus a Reference Section:

Section A: Communicating in everyday life

If you are looking for detailed information and advice on a specific topic such as writing a business letter, applying for a job, organizing a meeting, making a presentation, writing a press release, or preparing a report, then this section should contain the information you need.

Section B: Getting the message across

When we communicate with others we should match our language to the situation. Many people are less effective communicators than they could be because they fail to do this. This section shows you how to understand the demands of audience, subject, situation, and purpose and to tailor your message accordingly.

Section C: The English language

This section contains detailed and extensive coverage of the technicalities of using English: vocabulary, grammar, spelling, punctuation, and speech.

Section D: The process of writing

If you want further guidance about how to plan, draft, and edit an extended piece of writing, this section provides it, as well as advice on related topics such as writing a summary and making effective notes.

Reference Section

If you want a brief definition or explanation of a particular term or concept, then look in the alphabetical reference section. Each entry is cross-referenced to the relevant page(s) in the main part of the *Guide*.

Chapter pattern

Each chapter in the book follows a similar pattern:

■ **A summary of the main points to be covered**
This appears in a blue tinted box immediately after the title.

■ **The body of the chapter**

■ **Cross references**
Where a topic is mentioned that is also covered elsewhere in the book, you will see a blue 'See also' box to the left of the main text.

■ **'You try' boxes**
Many chapters contain one or more of these. They give you an opportunity to check your understanding and knowledge of the points covered.

■ **Guidelines**

At the end of the chapter the main practical points covered are summarized in a series of numbered points, which are useful for quick reference.

■ **Key to 'You try' boxes**

Some 'You try' boxes have answers. If so these are given. In other cases there is comment or advice.

Section A

Communicating in Everyday Life

1: Speaking and writing
How we speak and write is affected by: the people involved; the subject matter and the language required to discuss it; where and when communication is taking place; and our purpose in communicating. This chapter introduces these ideas and explains how they affect the way in which we communicate.

2: Business letters
The structure and presentation of formal and informal business letters. How to make sure that you control the all-important element of **tone** in your letters.

3: Fax and email
How to present and make effective use of the two electronic messaging systems most commonly available.

4: Applying for a job
How to research and construct a CV that is designed to meet the requirements of a particular job application. How to write a letter of application to accompany it.

5: Interviews
The importance of proper preparation for a job interview. How to analyse your strengths and weaknesses as a candidate and prepare for the awkward questions. Tackling the interview itself; dealing with problems; and reviewing your performance afterwards.

6: Organizing a meeting
The aims, competences, and constitution of formal meetings. How to prepare an agenda, chair a meeting, and control the proposing and seconding of motions and the votes on them. How minutes should be prepared and ratified. How to run an informal meeting.

7: Presentations
Preparing a successful presentation: thinking about your audience; organizing the structure; making effective use of visual and other aids. Delivering the presentation, using prompts, making sure that you address your audience directly, and dealing effectively with questions and interruptions.

8: Reports Brainstorming, researching, and planning a business report. The structure of a report: executive summary, introduction, body of the report, conclusions, recommendations, appendices, and bibliography. Other organizational devices. Addressing your readership.

9: Essays, papers, and dissertations Preparing an extended piece of writing for school, college, or university: generating ideas, doing research, ordering your material. Writing style and the use of quotations and references. The particular requirements of the dissertation.

10: Meeting the media Writing a press release: studying how newspaper reports work; organizing your material in the right order and format to ensure maximum effect. How to prepare for and undertake an interview with press, radio, and TV interviewers.

1 Speaking and writing

All communication, whether it is written or spoken, has certain features in common. We have to be aware of the **situation**:

- the **people** involved
- the **subject matter** and the language required to discuss it
- **where** and **when** the communication is taking place
- our **purpose** in communicating

In addition, all communication has a **format**, whether it is a telephone conversation, a letter, or an annual report. Each format has its own conventions and rules.

A kind of conversation

A lot of the guidance in this book concerns written expression. This is because people seek advice and information about written English far more often than they do about spoken English. We all use speech apparently fairly naturally and usually without any obvious problems. Also, most of the time, spoken words disappear as soon as they have been uttered, so it is difficult for them to come back to haunt us. Writing, on the other hand, is more permanent. Other people can pick up what we write, examine it, and pull it to pieces. So we often feel more vulnerable about what we write than about what we say.

Yet there is a sense in which all communication is a kind of conversation. Compare these two items:

Dialogue   *A coffee stall. A* BARMAN *and an old* NEWSPAPER SELLER. *The* BARMAN *leans on his counter, the* OLD MAN *stands with tea. Silence.*

MAN: You was a bit busier earlier.
BARMAN: Ah.
MAN: Round about ten.
BARMAN: Ten, was it.
MAN: About then.
            Pause
            I passed by here about then.
BARMAN: Oh yes?
MAN: I noticed you were doing a bit of trade.
            Pause

> BARMAN: Yes, trade was very brisk here about ten.
> MAN: Yes, I noticed.

Postcard

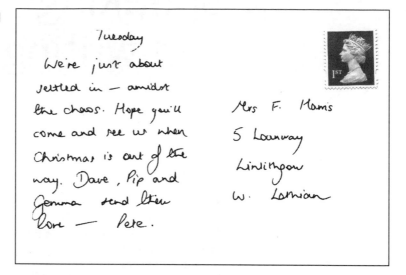

Both these examples show a dialogue in progress. In the first it is a conversation; in the second the writer, Pete, is presenting one side of a continuing 'conversation' with a close friend or relative, Mrs Harris. In both cases the two know each other quite well—there are no real preliminaries and the dialogue gets going straight away. Although there is some kind of communication going on, not a lot of hard information is being exchanged; clearly transmitting facts from one person to another is not the main aim. It is what some writers call *phatic communion*: 'speech communication as used to establish social relationships rather than to impart information' (*OED*). A lot of background information is taken for granted; for example, Pete assumes that Mrs Harris knows who 'we' are and understands the situation which involves them 'settling in'.

Such situations are common in everyday life, especially in conversation. They also occur in written communication. Not only postcards, but other greetings cards, and notes we leave at home for other members of the household, are typical occasions for this kind of easy-going, personal communication, where there appear to be few rules provided that those involved understand each other.

A little further along the scale of formality come situations like these:

Informal telephone conversation

> A: Hullo, 597421.
> B: Hullo Martin, it's Peter.
> A: Hullo Peter, how are you?
> B: Very well, thank you, yes. Just a very quick call. I've had a letter from Beasdale and Williams, to say they're going to reprint 'Journey Home'.
> A: Yes I had that . . .
> B: Oh you've had it. Right. I just wasn't sure whether they'd written to you as well.

A: . . . and they want some information by Monday . . .

B: Yes.

A: . . . which is . . . very nice!

B: *(laughs)* Yes.

A: I don't think there's anything, but if I get time I'll have a look, and ring them up, which is the only way I can get the information to them now.

email

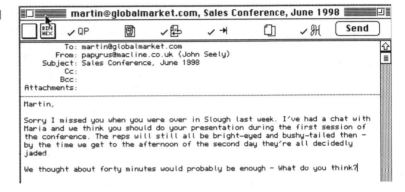

The people involved in both these two situations know each other well and can take a lot for granted: they don't have to stand on ceremony; the situation they are discussing is understood by both, so they don't have to do a lot of explaining and they have some shared technical terms (e.g. 'presentation', 'reps'). As a result they can cover a lot of ground in a brief space.

Sometimes, however, we have to communicate with people we don't know very well—if at all—in situations that are more complex:

More formal telephone conversation

A: Good afternoon, Celtic Water, Pat speaking.

B: Good afternoon. The name is Williams; we live at Mordegrave, and for about five weeks now we've been promised a filter on our water supply, because the quality is not up to standard.

A: Right. Can I have your postcode, please, Mrs Williams?

B: JR1 4ZQ.

A: And the house number or name?

B: The Larches.

A: Right.

B: Now can I just fill you in?

A: Yes.

B: Four weeks after this was promised—a week ago last Friday—I rang your office—

A: Right.

B: I rang on Friday morning. I was told that someone would either ring me on Friday afternoon or Monday morning. Now when that didn't happen, I rang last Tuesday afternoon— exactly a week ago—

A: Yes.

B: —and I was told that the people in Bangor would by then have had the message and that I would hear by the end of the week. Now once again there's been a deafening silence and

             I'm beginning to lose patience, I'm afraid.

A: Yes, I can appreciate that. I'll get on to the depot myself. Now I'm looking to see if we've got a date for you. There is a job on this—

B: Yes, a date would help.

A: I'm just going to have a look on the job now to see if they have got anything on this.

B: Right. Thank you very much.

and so the conversation continues, with both participants making sure that they have understood clearly what is going on and behaving to each other with polite formality. A has gone through the opening routine of all such calls: establishing the caller's name, postcode, and address. B has identified herself and set out the reasons for her call with clarity and brevity. They have then moved on to try to work out what ought to be done. Although B is probably in fact annoyed that the company have not done anything, she uses a formal tone and approach calculated to achieve her ends, keeping A on her side, rather than starting in a confrontational way.

Compare the telephone conversation with this letter:

Formal letter

Dear Mr & Mrs Grayson,

RE: THE LARCHES, DUNSCOMBE ROAD, POOLE

Further to our recent inspection of your property I write to confirm that if placed on the open market I would recommend an asking figure in the region of £120,000–£130,000 (max.).

Whilst writing I confirm that our sale fee, for Sole Agency, is 1.50% plus VAT.

In the event of our being instructed and the property subsequently being withdrawn from the market an administration charge of £120 plus VAT would be made.

Should you require additional coverage in Bournemouth we are able to provide this as although we do not directly have a Bournemouth Office, we have a link up with Mandel Price whereby we are able to offer a Joint Agency at a special rate of 1.75%. You may not feel that this is necessary but it is an option worth considering.

Should you have any further queries please do not hesitate to contact me.

Yours sincerely,
Peter March

This is a different kind of communication. Peter March and the Graysons have already met and discussed the subject. Peter March is writing to confirm what was said and to put it on the record. The letter forms part of any future business relationship between them. This recording function is a very important feature of written communications.

So all our uses of speech and writing can be placed on a spectrum from informal chat through to legal documents. A lot of the time we are perfectly comfortable with the way in which we express ourselves, and it is only in a number of specialized or unusual situations that we have to think carefully about how to communicate. This is not, usually, because we are incapable of expressing ourselves in those situations, but rather that we are unsure of where to place them on the scale of situations we have experienced and feel confident about.

What is going on?

In all forms of communication there are a number of constants: features that we have to pay attention to if we are to get our message across effectively. We have already seen most of them in action in the examples quoted in this chapter.

The situation

As we have seen, participants need to be aware of the situation in which they are trying to communicate. This involves:

■ People

The two or more people who are involved. Here we have to think about how well we know our audience and so how informal we can afford to be, as well as how much we can take for granted about their knowledge and language skills.

See also:
■ **Chapter 11** *Audience* (p. 89)

■ Subject matter

We have to choose the right language to deal with the subject matter we are discussing. The letter quoted had to use the correct terminology for dealing with property sales, for example. At the same time, the language chosen has to be appropriate for the audience. If the listener or reader doesn't understand the terminology—even if it is correct—then communication will fail.

See also:
■ **Chapter 12** *Subject* (p. 102)

■ Time and place

The actual setting in which we are communicating can affect the way in which we do so. Imagine two young colleagues in an office setting, taking part in a meeting with an older person who is their section manager. Now imagine the same two discussing the meeting together in a café as they take their lunch break. Very probably the way in which they address each other and the language they use will be different on the two occasions. Some businesses require their employees to use language in special ways when preparing reports or making presentations.

See also:
■ **Chapter 13** *Time and place* (p. 108)

■ Purpose

Every communication has a purpose, and many have more than one. It is important to keep your purpose in mind if you wish to communicate effectively. Caller B in the telephone conversation about the water filter had her purpose clearly in mind right from the start of that conversation. As a result, although A was being given a number of things to do (possibly time-consuming and tiresome), her task was made much easier.

See also:
■ **Chapter 14** *Purpose* (p. 113)

Format

The features mentioned so far are all present in all the examples in this chapter. But as we have seen, we have a great range of different forms of communication available to us. The illustrations given so far cover:

- face-to-face conversation
- postcard
- telephone conversation
- email
- letter

And, of course, there are many others. Each format has its own 'rules'. An email, for example, does not work in quite the same way as a letter. You *can*, it is true, write a conventional letter and send it by email, but many people would probably find it a little over-formal to do this. Similarly, if you were to send a letter couched in the more informal style of many email messages, it would probably raise a few eyebrows.

In this section of the book, the focus is on formats, but inevitably a lot of attention will be paid to the situation, the 'who', 'what', 'where', 'when', and 'why' of communication. These features will be covered as needed. There is a more analytical and thorough discussion of them in Section B.

Guidelines

1 When you feel that a particular piece of communication is likely to cause problems, try to work out where it fits into your own range of experience.

2 Think about the person(s) you are dealing with. Find situations in the past that are similar and recall how you tackled them. Focus on those in which you felt that you communicated effectively: try to remember the 'tone of voice' you used—even if it was a written communication. If you find that you are remembering a number of situations in which you did **not** communicate effectively, analyse where things went wrong.

3 Think about the subject matter and consider the language you are using: is it suitable for this subject and this audience?

4 Think about your purpose in communicating. What are you trying to achieve and what is the best way of setting about it?

5 Finally, be aware of the format you are using. Are you following the conventions of this particular format? If you are not sure, then check in the rest of this section or look in the **Reference Section** on pages 285–96.

2 Business letters

Structuring the letter
The key to writing an effective business letter is to have a clear definition of your purpose in writing. This should then be reflected in the structure of your letter. This normally contains three parts:

1 An **introduction** which sets out briefly the subject matter and purpose of the letter.

2 The **body of the letter** in which you develop and explain your purpose. This is normally divided into a number of paragraphs, ordered so that each covers a different aspect of your subject and each follows on logically from the one before.

3 The **conclusion** in which you re-emphasize your purpose, possibly spelling out what you would like to be done about it.

Getting the tone right
It is important to consider carefully the person who will read your letter—even if they are unknown to you—and write in a suitable **tone**. This should be neither casual nor too formal. In particular it is important to avoid pomposity and jargon.

Letter layout
Letter layouts vary considerably, but all have the same key features.

Greeting and ending
For most business letters there is a limited choice of greeting and ending, according to the degree of formality you wish to present.

In this book, letters are placed before telephone calls, faxes, and email messages. This ordering probably does not reflect the frequency with which we use these different media, but although most of us use letters less than we did, especially for social and personal communication, they still have a key role to play in many areas of life.

That role may be partly symbolic. For example, I recently consulted my general practitioner (GP) about a minor but tiresome medical problem. He decided that I should consult a local specialist and, as I sat in his consulting room, wrote a letter to the specialist describing the symptoms. He could have communicated the same information by phone, fax, or email, but a GP's letter is both traditional and symbolic: it indicates a particular relationship. The doctor writes his colleague a letter which is then sealed and secret—its contents are often not revealed to the patient. The specialist then opens and reads the letter, usually in the presence of the patient, and again frequently does not reveal its exact contents. What could be better designed to show patients their status?

Letters have an importance and permanence that are comforting and reassuring. Even when we transact business by phone, we like to 'have something in writing' to confirm what we have agreed, and employers often lay great stress on the letters written by those applying for jobs—even to the extent of sometimes demanding that these be handwritten rather than word-processed.

See also:
■ Chapter 4 *Applying for a job* (p. 27)

The result of this special status of letters is that they can prove quite difficult to write. Some writers, faced with having to write a job application, freeze up and cannot even think of a first sentence. So much seems to hang on what we write—our whole personality, career, life so far will be judged when the letter is opened and read!

Yet there is nothing inherently 'special' about letters. They are just another technology of communication, outdated, expensive, and rather time-consuming. The general rules we apply when using any other form of communication still hold. We still have to consider:

- our purpose in writing
- our audience
- the conventions which govern the ways in which letters are usually set out (and which our audience will expect)

See also:
■ Chapter 11 *Audience* (p. 89)
■ Chapter 13 *Time and place* (p. 108)
■ Chapter 14 *Purpose* (p. 113)

The conventions of letter-writing are placed last in this list because they are often given undue importance; it would be mistaken to believe that once you have mastered them, you know how to write a good letter. Knowing how to structure the body of the letter and being sure that you have adopted the right tone are far more important.

In this chapter the focus is on what are often called 'business' letters, letters we write to people we do not know or to those whom we know but with whom we have a business relationship rather than a personal one. They are usually letters written 'to get something done'.

Structuring the letter

If you find a particular letter difficult to write, it may well be because you have not worked out clearly in your mind what its purpose is.

Begin by asking yourself these questions:

1 Why am I writing this letter—what has led up to it?
2 What do I hope to get out of it (my maximum aims)?
3 What do I expect to get out of it (my realistic aims)?
4 What is the best way to achieve this?
  – What information do I need to provide?
  – What arguments do I need to use?

Leaving aside for a moment the precise way in which the letter should begin, most business letters have a clear three-part structure:

1 An introduction in which you outline what the letter is about.

2 The body of the letter in which you explain step by step the detail of your 'argument'.

3 A conclusion in which you set out what you want to achieve.

Introduction

The introduction to a letter has to fulfil these requirements:

■ **It must state clearly what the letter is about.**
This enables the recipient to make an initial decision about what to do with it. (Deal with it quickly, put it in a heap of mail to be dealt with at an appointed time, pass it on to someone else . . .) One way of doing this is to give the letter a heading immediately after the salutation:

```
Dear Mr and Mrs Green,
   Personal Overdraft. Account No: 12345678
```

■ **It should indicate why the writer is writing it.**
A heading such as the one quoted only gives a general idea of the subject matter. The introduction should go on to spell out the writer's purpose:

```
I am pleased to confirm the renewal of your Personal
Overdraft of £1000.
```

These two functions can be expressed in a simple sentence or two. In fact in the example given, the heading is not strictly necessary because the following sentence repeats most of the information it contains. It could be rephrased to read:

```
I am pleased to confirm the renewal of your Personal
Overdraft of £1000 on account number 12345678.
```

And that, essentially, is all the introduction has to do. When you have read it, you should have a clear idea of what the letter is going to be about and enough information to be able to decide how to tackle the rest of it.

Body

The letter now has to move steadily and convincingly towards the conclusion (in which you will explain what you want done, or reinforce the significance of the information you have set out). The more clearly information is expressed, and the more tellingly different items are linked, the better the letter. To see how this can work, we will look at a sequence of letters about the same subject. First, here is the body of the letter we have already quoted:

```
You can overdraw up to your limit whenever you want,
but you should not be permanently overdrawn by the
whole amount. Please remember that personal overdrafts
are repayable on demand. Details of interest and
charges that apply to this overdraft are enclosed.
   Personal Overdraft Protection has been arranged for
Mr Green, and a monthly insurance premium of £8.00 will
be collected from your account on the first working day
```

of each month. Your protection certificate, which includes details of cover, is also enclosed.

Each of these paragraphs has a clear topic. The first is about using the overdraft facility and the second concerns overdraft protection, an insurance protecting the user against being unable to repay the overdraft in the event of illness or unemployment.

Unfortunately Mr and Mrs Green hadn't requested this insurance and didn't want it. Their letter of reply followed a similar pattern:

Dear Mrs White,

Personal Overdraft on account number 12345678

Thank you for your letter of 1st October, in which you say that Personal Overdraft Protection has been arranged at a rate of £8 per month.

We don't recall asking for this protection. If we did, it was by an oversight and we do not wish to have it. We shall be grateful if you will arrange to stop it and make sure that no deductions are made for it.

If this protection is a condition of the overdraft facility, then we do not wish to have the overdraft facility. It certainly isn't worth £96 p.a. before use. We only ever use it by accident when we forget to transfer money from our Deposit Account. It would be much more satisfactory if you offered the service of automatically topping up one account from another when it gets below a certain level.

Here the heading and first paragraph introduce the subject matter and link it to Mrs White's previous letter. The second paragraph deals with the subject of the unrequested insurance. The third moves the discussion on to a related but different topic. It introduces what is clearly the writer's main complaint.

Of course, such letters can have considerably more material in the body than is the case here. But the approach should be similar. Each paragraph is about a separate topic, or aspect of the main topic, and leads logically on to the next.

Conclusion

The main point of the conclusion is to underline the purpose of the letter and, sometimes, to spell out the action the writer would like taken. In the bank's letter, the final paragraph read:

If you require further information regarding your Personal Overdraft, please contact me and I will be happy to answer any queries you may have.

This isn't necessarily asking for any further action, but it is intended to leave the reader feeling positive towards the writer, which is always a useful aim. The Greens, however, had other uses for the conclusion to their letter:

We look forward to receiving your confirmation that the Overdraft Protection has been cancelled.

No doubt about that!

You try

Some time later in the negotiations between Mr and Mrs Green and the bank, an assistant manager wrote them a letter apologizing for what had happened:

```
Dear Mr & Mrs Green,
Your letter of 13th October has been referred to
me.
    I take this opportunity to apologize,
unreservedly, for our error in this connection.
    Upon examination it would appear that our letter
of the 1st October, referring to insurance cover
on your overdraft, was sent in error.
    I can assure you that at no time have insurance
premia been debited to your account.
    I believe a colleague has now sent an amended
renewal letter to you, confirming your facility
has been marked forward at its existing level.
    You mention that you would like to explore the
possibility of our setting up an automatic trans-
fer between your Current Account and your Deposit
Account.
    I can confirm that such a facility is,
occasionally, extended to our customers.
    This facility would need to be agreed by a
member of the Bank's management and should you
wish to pursue this option I would suggest that
you contact a member of our Customer Facing Staff.
    I again apologize for any inconvenience caused
to you following the issue of our letter of the
1st October and look forward to hearing from you
if I may be of any further assistance in this or
any other matter.
    Yours sincerely,
```

This letter differs from the two quoted so far. It is not divided into paragraphs; instead each sentence is separated out as if it were a paragraph in its own right.

- Does this make it easier or harder to follow?
- If you wanted to organize it into three or four paragraphs, how would you do so?

Getting the tone right

See also:
- **Chapter 11** *Audience* (p. 89)

So far the writing of letters has been treated as if business letters were directed to, and received by, anonymous 'recipients'. Of course they are not; they are received and read by individual human beings with thoughts and feelings. What makes such letters difficult to write at times is that although one is aware of this obvious fact, one has no idea of who will actually read the letter.

This is why business letters sometimes fall back on jargon, over-formality and even pomposity. There is a touch of this in the bank's second letter quoted on page 13. Here are some of the expressions it uses, with 'translations' alongside:

See also:
■ **Chapter 19** *Vocabulary* (p. 179)

Expression	**'Translation'**
our error in this connection	the mistake we made
your facility has been marked forward at its existing level	your overdraft arrangement has been renewed
This facility would need to be agreed by a member of the Bank's management and should you wish to pursue this option I would suggest that you contact a member of our Customer Facing Staff.	You would need to arrange this with one of our Managers. If you would like to do this, please ask one of our staff.

Some writers are afraid of becoming too informal and offending the reader. But this should not be a real risk. The gap between writing and speaking is not so large. Imagine that instead of writing the letter, you are communicating the same subject matter face to face, speaking to a complete stranger. It is unlikely that you would offend by being too informal. You would adopt a neutral tone, and take care to explain clearly and simply what you had to say. A letter should do exactly the same thing. If you wouldn't normally say to a customer, 'should you wish to pursue this option I would suggest that you contact a member of our Customer Facing Staff', then don't write it either!

To avoid excessive formality and pomposity:

■ **Avoid using the passive.**
(e.g. 'Our letter was sent in error.') Use a personal pronoun and the active form instead. ('We sent you that letter by mistake.')

■ **Avoid jargon whenever possible.**
Terms like 'Customer Facing Staff' and 'your facility has been marked forward at its existing level' may mean something to the writer, but they are likely to alienate the general public.

■ **Use shorter sentences rather than longer ones.**
(It is difficult to be pompous in short sentences!)

To avoid unsuitable informality:

■ **Don't let your own feelings get the better of you.**
It is easy—especially when you are making a complaint and/or feel that you are in the right—to cause offence. You may wish to do so, but if you do, you are less likely to get satisfaction.

■ **Don't try to be too clever.**
Some writers get carried away with their own sentences and don't know when to stop. It is very easy for them to cause offence just because they like to 'hear the sound of their own voice'. For example, they start sounding off about how the recipient's organization ought to be managed. Such gratuitous 'advice' is likely to cause offence and very unlikely to further your cause.

■ **Be clear and to the point, but don't be too blunt.**

Letter layout

There is a considerable choice of how to set out a formal letter. Different organizations have different styles governing:

- the positioning of the recipient's address
- the punctuation of the address
- the spacing and alignment of paragraphs
- the spacing and alignment of the ending ('Yours sincerely/Yours faithfully' and signature)

The examples on pages 16 and 17 are only two of many different possible styles, therefore, and are presented as illustrations. The numbers in them refer to the list below.

1 Your address
2 The name, title, and address of the recipient
3 The date
4 Reference(s)
5 The greeting
6 The first paragraph
7 Other paragraphs
8 The ending

Greeting and ending

In British English there is a fairly simple choice of greeting and ending for business letters. Presented in descending order of formality it is:

Greeting	Ending
Dear Sir, Dear Madam, Dear Sir or Madam,	Yours faithfully, A. B. Capstick
Dear Mr Green, Dear Mrs Green, Dear Miss Green, Dear Ms Green,	Yours sincerely, Alan Capstick (or Alan)
Dear Alan,	Yours sincerely, Moira (or, commonly, With best wishes, Yours sincerely, Moira)

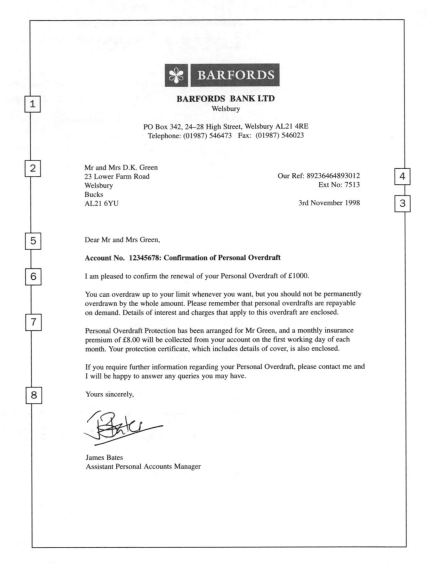

Increasingly the 'Dear Sir . . . Yours faithfully,' formula is being abandoned in favour of the less formal 'Yours sincerely,' versions. 'Dear Sir . . . Yours faithfully,' is retained for very formal occasions: threatening letters from government departments, banks, and lawyers, for example. In the past it was acceptable to address an unknown correspondent as 'Dear Sir', regardless of gender, but not today. So unless you know the gender of the person you are addressing (in which case you probably know them well enough to use their name and 'Yours sincerely') you are forced to use the rather awkward 'Dear Sir or Madam'.

The drawback of the 'Yours sincerely' formula is that you have to have a name to address it to. Here three problems can arise:

1 You do not know the recipient's name. In this case, you are forced back on to using a job description, real or invented: 'Dear Personnel Manager', 'Dear Fellow-sufferer', or whatever. If you are happy with

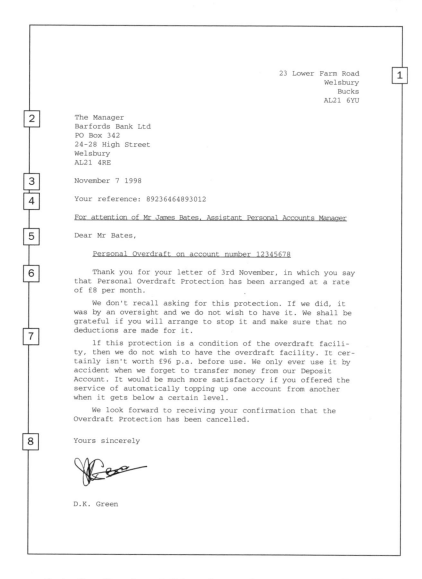

```
                                              23 Lower Farm Road
                                                       Welsbury
                                                          Bucks
                                                       AL21 6YU
```

2

```
The Manager
Barfords Bank Ltd
PO Box 342
24-28 High Street
Welsbury
AL21 4RE
```

3   November 7 1998

4   Your reference: 89236464893012

    For attention of Mr James Bates, Assistant Personal Accounts Manager

5   Dear Mr Bates,

        Personal Overdraft on account number 12345678

6   Thank you for your letter of 3rd November, in which you say
    that Personal Overdraft Protection has been arranged at a rate
    of £8 per month.

        We don't recall asking for this protection. If we did, it
    was by an oversight and we do not wish to have it. We shall be
    grateful if you will arrange to stop it and make sure that no
    deductions are made for it.

7   If this protection is a condition of the overdraft facili-
    ty, then we do not wish to have the overdraft facility. It cer-
    tainly isn't worth £96 p.a. before use. We only ever use it by
    accident when we forget to transfer money from our Deposit
    Account. It would be much more satisfactory if you offered the
    service of automatically topping up one account from another
    when it gets below a certain level.

        We look forward to receiving your confirmation that the
    Overdraft Protection has been cancelled.

8   Yours sincerely

    D.K. Green

that, all well and good. Otherwise you have to resort to 'Dear Sir or Madam . . . Yours faithfully'.

2 You have a surname but no first name, only initials. So you do not know whether you are addressing a man or a woman. Unless you are happy with 'Dear A. B. Capstick . . .', you have to use a job description, or use 'Dear Sir or Madam . . .', as above.

3 You know that the recipient is a woman but do not know how she likes to be addressed. (Not, incidentally, the same as knowing her marital status—some married women prefer to be addressed as 'Ms——'.) Here it is best to play safe and use 'Ms'.

The other awkwardness that can arise is whether to address the recipient as 'Dear Mrs Green', or as 'Dear Lynda'. If you have met or spoken to them, then generally there is no problem: use a first name. For many people, however, this is not acceptable if they have never met or spoken to the person concerned, although for others, especially younger writers, this is not a problem. If, when addressing a person you do not know at all, you feel that a first name is too informal and a title plus surname is too formal, you can try the intermediate position of 'Dear Lynda Green', although for some that is a rather artificial compromise.

Guidelines

1   Before you begin writing a business letter, define clearly your purpose in writing. Make sure that you have a clear idea of:

- the events that have led to your writing the letter
- your maximum aims (the most you can hope to achieve)
- your realistic aims (what you expect to achieve)
- the information you need to explain in the letter
- the arguments you need to deploy

2   The **first paragraph** of the letter should introduce the subject matter and either state or imply your purpose in writing.

3   The **body** of the letter should consist of one or more paragraphs. It should develop clearly and logically the argument and facts of the case. If there is more than one paragraph, each paragraph should focus on a separate aspect of the subject matter and there should be clear links between the paragraphs.

4   The **final paragraph** should leave the reader in no doubt about your attitude towards the subject of the letter. It may, for example, spell out what you would like to see happen. It should be positive and unambiguous.

5   Although the reader of your letter may be unknown to you, it is important to achieve a suitable **tone** in your writing. So, as far as possible, **avoid**:

- jargon
- too many long sentences
- using the passive
- letting your feelings get the better of you
- trying to be too clever
- being too blunt

6   Adopt a letter layout that is clear and consistent.

7   If you are writing to someone whose name and title you do not know, use the greeting *Dear Sir or Madam*, and the ending *Yours faithfully*, signing yourself with your initials and surname.

8   If you are writing to a named person, address them as *Dear Mr/Mrs/Miss/Ms——*, and end *Yours sincerely*, followed by your first name and surname.

9   If you have met them or spoken to them by phone, or otherwise feel that you have some acquaintance with them, address them by their first name and sign yourself *Yours sincerely*, using your first name.

You try: key

page 13   It would be difficult to argue that this letter is a success. It is expressed in an awkward, pompous, and jargon-ridden way. Using a layout in which each sentence is presented as a separate paragraph makes it difficult to read. It would be much more successful if it were rewritten along these lines:

Dear Mr & Mrs Green,

Your letter of 13th October has been referred to me. I should like to apologize unreservedly for the mistake we made.

It seems that our letter of the 1st October, about insurance cover on your overdraft, was sent by mistake. I can assure you that your account has not been charged with any insurance premium. You should by now have received an amended letter, confirming that the overdraft arrangement has been renewed.

You mention that you would like to explore the possibility of our setting up an automatic transfer between your Current Account and your Deposit Account. This is sometimes arranged for our customers. You would need to arrange it with one of our Managers. If you would like to do this, please ask one of our staff.

I apologize again for any inconvenience caused by our letter of the 1st October. Please do not hesitate to contact me if I may be of any further assistance in this or any other matter.

Yours sincerely,

3 Fax and email

Fax

The fax was the first of the 'written' electronic media to become widely available. Its advantages are that:

- it is quick
- it can contain pictures as well as words
- the recipient does not have to be there to receive it
- it is generally cheaper than a telephone call

Because it is relatively recent and widely used, the fax has fewer formal conventions than, for example, the letter. Message faxes can be:

- informal and handwritten
- based on the letter
- based on the memo

Email

Email is even more recent than the fax. Its chief advantages are:

- it is quick
- it is cheap
- replying to messages is easy
- messages can be copied to others and re-routed
- the receiver can incorporate an email message into a computer program (e.g. a word-processed text)
- you can 'attach' computer files to an email message (e.g. a graphics file)

Fax

See also:
- **Chapter 2 *Business Letters*** (p. 9)

Like a letter, a fax, short for 'facsimile', is a technology, a way of passing a message from one person to another. It is different from the letter because it is relatively new. Letters have been used for centuries, so traditions and conventions of letter-writing have developed. It is true that you can ignore these conventions, if you wish, but they are still there, and they affect people's attitudes towards what you write. Because the fax is new, there are fewer fixed rules or conventions about how it should be written.

But there are some. At the very least, a message that is going to be transmitted by fax must carry certain information if it is to reach the person for whom it is intended. At its simplest this information can be carried by a stick-on fax label:

```
┌─────────────────────────────────────────────────────────────┐
│ ▐TELEFAX▌ TO:  H. WOOD (ROMFORD) LTD                         │
│ FAX NO:    01708  873645          NO OF PAGES:    1          │
│ ATTENTION OF:  SIMON ERICSON                                 │
│ FROM:   JEANETTE ARNOLD          DATE:  14/5/98              │
│ COMPANY:  BECKENHAM  PLASTICS    FAX NO: 0181 299 3872       │
└─────────────────────────────────────────────────────────────┘
```

Essential information

- The company or organization to which the fax is addressed.
- The person within that organization for whom the fax is intended.
- Their fax number (because often the writer of the fax is not the person who is going to transmit it).
- The number of pages (so that the recipients can check that they have received the whole fax).
- The sender's name.
- The sender's company or organization.
- Their fax number (and possibly their phone number in case there have been problems about transmitting or receiving the fax).
- The date.

Handwritten fax

For transacting everyday business, quickly, with someone you know well, a simple handwritten note with a fax label attached may be all that is needed:

```
┌─────────────────────────────────────────────────────────────┐
│ ▐TELEFAX▌ TO:  H. WOOD (ROMFORD) LTD                         │
│ FAX NO:    01708  873645          NO OF PAGES:    1          │
│ ATTENTION OF:  SIMON ERICSON                                 │
│ FROM:   JEANETTE ARNOLD          DATE:  14/5/98              │
│ COMPANY:  BECKENHAM  PLASTICS    FAX NO: 0181 299 3872       │
└─────────────────────────────────────────────────────────────┘

Embossed plastic wallet envelopes

Order no: 1837965

Thanks for your fax. The order was despatched two
days ago (12 May) via Matheson Haulage. I've
contacted them and they say they had problems
yesterday due to the storms, but the goods
will definitely be with you tomorrow pm at
the latest.

Sorry for the delay,

JA
```

More often, however, you will want something that is word-processed, more formal, or both.

Letter fax

For many informal or semi-formal situations, it is useful to send a fax that is really a letter in disguise:

| | TRAVEL AGENTS & TOUR PLANNERS | Lower House Farndon Lane Chiselhampton DK21 3RG Phone: 01361 568194 Fax: 01361 568195 |

BY FAX

TO: Jane Hargreaves, Customer Services, Ranger Adventure Travel

FAX NO: 0891 34019

FROM: Peter James

NUMBER OF PAGES: 1

DATE: 18th June

Dear Jane,

Thanks for the latest information and schedules for the Republic of Congo. I'm not sure just how viable this is going to be. Our clients still seem rather vague about exactly what they want to do. (So what's new!)

We've had another odd query, this time about Kenya and travel to Lake Turkana. Apparently this client wants to take her family, including some young children, and is worried about how they will tackle the journey. Have you got any information about timings, stops, etc., on that trip?

Look forward to hearing from you.

All the best,

Pete

In this case, once you have included the essential information listed on page 21, it is a letter like any other. (Remember, however, that a fax—even more than any other communication to an organization— can be read by anyone in an office, so it is not the best way to send information that is confidential or sensitive.)

Memo fax   For more formal situations, or where it is a matter of company policy, it is common practice to model the fax on a memo:

TRAVEL AGENTS & TOUR PLANNERS	Lower House Farndon Lane Chiselhampton DK21 3RG Phone: 01361 568194 Fax: 01361 568195

BY FAX

TO:	Andrew Wilkinson
COMPANY:	Hellenika Books
FAX NO:	0891 34019
FROM:	Peter James
NUMBER OF PAGES:	1
DATE:	18th June
SUBJECT:	**The Hellenika Guides to the Greek Islands**

1   As in previous years we should like to supply customers travelling to the Greek islands with a complimentary copy of the relevant island guide.

2   We estimate that this year we shall require copies as follows:

Island	Copies
Corfu	50
Crete	100
Mikonos	60
Naxos	30
Rhodes	40

3   As you can see, this is an increase of about 25% on last year. We would suggest, therefore, that an increased discount (of, say, 30%?) would be in order.

4   We assume that as in previous years, goods will be supplied on a sale or return basis.

We look forward to hearing from you.

Email

Electronic mail, or email as it is commonly known, is increasingly used instead of letters or faxes. Any two computers that are connected by wire can communicate using an electronic mail program. So, within any organization that has computers linked to a network, internal email is a simple way of passing information and ideas around the office. If you have a modem connected to a telephone line, then you can communicate in a similar way with computers many miles away. The disadvantage of this is that you have to pay to use the phone line, just as for any other call. So long-distance and international communication can be expensive if this approach is used.

There is, however, a cheap and readily available alternative. If your modem is connected to the Internet, via an Internet service provider, then you can send and receive email for the same cost as any other Internet usage. Most Internet provision now costs the same as a local call, so sending email to anywhere in the world is very cheap. Typically you compose and key in 'offline' (i.e. before connecting to the network) any messages you want to send, dial up the Internet service provider (which is normally done automatically via the software), and, once you are 'online' (connected), send your messages and 'download' (collect and save) any that have been sent to you. You then disconnect and read your mail. The whole operation takes a few minutes and costs a matter of pence. 'Writing' the messages is done at your computer keyboard; there is no need for paper and no need to get up, dictate a letter, pick up the phone. It is as near instant as it is possible to get.

Other advantages   Email has a number of other advantages which don't take long to discover:

- The messages you send are in the form of text. This means that your correspondents can include them in computer documents of their own.
- Because they are just text, you don't have to spend a lot of time worrying about layout, typefaces, paper quality, or print quality, so you can focus on the words.
- A by-product of this is that email is uncluttered and unstuffy. A typical email message is short and informal.
- Email is in many ways even more convenient than the telephone. But it is a written message, so the technology is leading to the rebirth of the personal letter.
- As well as sending simple messages you can 'attach' computer files—for example, desk-top publishing (DTP) pages, graphics, or spreadsheets—which others can then use in their own work.
- The software allows you to send the same message to a number of recipients, for the cost of one message, which is particularly useful when you are a member of a work group or interest group.

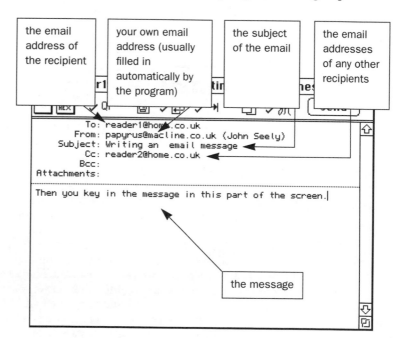

- When you receive an email and wish to reply to it, you can attach your reply to the message. This keeps the correspondence together, which is useful when checking back what has already been said.

    When you use this facility, you will probably find that the 'form' you are offered to use for your reply begins with the text of the message you are replying to. Since your correspondent doesn't need to re-read this, it is best either to delete the whole message except for its heading, or to delete selectively, just leaving relevant headings or extracts of text to provide a context for your own message.

Technicalities

When you use an email program you have to provide a certain amount of information in order to send a message. The screen provides prompts showing what is required. It is similar to filling in a form.

Popular email programs also offer a number of other facilities, including:

- the automatic addition of a 'signature', which can be anything you like, but might, for example, include your name, postal address and telephone number
- the option of keeping a copy of emails you send out
- various options about the electronic format in which messages are sent
- an address book for keeping email addresses of regular correspondents
- a filing system for sorting and storing messages

Using email

See also:
- **Chapter 11** *Audience*
  (p. 89)

Email is quick, easy, and cheap to use. Replying to messages takes but a moment—so it is all the more important to reply to messages promptly (and, preferably, briefly).

The medium invites informality, but this can be abused or mistaken and it is important to remember that an email message, like any other message, may well be read by someone other than the person to whom it was originally addressed. So verbal or other indiscretions can let you down when you least expect it! On the other hand, as noted earlier, email is a great opportunity to correspond easily, clearly, and without stuffiness.

Guidelines

Fax   Every fax should have a header which contains this information:

1 The name of the person and/or organization to which it is addressed.

2 Their fax number.

3 The number of pages including the header sheet.

4 The name of the sender and/or organization.

5 Their fax number.

6 Their telephone number (in case of transmission problems).

7 The date.

Faxes can take various forms of which the commonest are:

1 A handwritten message.

2 A message set out like a letter.

3 A message set out like a memo.

Email   The mechanics of sending a message by email are generally looked after by the software, which will prompt you about essential information. Email messages can be—and usually are—informal and to the point.

4 Applying for a job

The traditional CV

The *Shorter Oxford Dictionary* defines a curriculum vitae, or CV, as:

> A brief account of one's life and career, especially as required in an application for employment.

Traditionally the CV was a bald recital of basic information, which probably included the following:

1 Full name.
2 Address and telephone number.
3 Age, date, and place of birth.
4 Nationality.
5 Marital status.
6 Number of children.
7 Dates and places of primary, secondary, and tertiary education.
8 Educational qualifications (public examinations taken and grades/degrees achieved).

9 Employment record, to include details of each period of employment:
 – company/organization
 – position held
 – dates

10 More detailed information about current position held, including salary.

11 Interests.

12 Names of two people who will provide references (often: one as a character reference, and one as a professional/work reference).

An example of this type of CV is shown below.

Name:	James Michael Brown	
Address:	76, Lower Green Road, Newbury, Berks, RG23 5RT	
Telephone:	01892 293478	
Born:	23rd February 1964, Liverpool, England	
Age:	34	
Nationality:	British	
Marital status:	Divorced	
Children:	None	
Education:	1969–1975	St Francis' Primary School, Huyton
	1975–1980	Gondersfield High School
	1980–1982	Huyton Sixth Form College
	1982–1985	Trent Polytechnic, Nottingham
Qualfications:	1980	GCE 'O' level English Language (B), Maths (C), Geography (B), Chemistry (A), Physics (B), Biology (A), French (D)
	1982	GCE 'A' level Maths (C), Physics (D), Chemistry (B)
	1985	BA Honours Class 2/2 Chemical Engineering
Employment:	1985–1990	Graduate trainee with Myersons-Chemco Ltd, Nottingham
	1990–1994	Assistant Sales Manager, Alders & Green, Leicester
	Current Position from 1994	Sales Manager, Brown-Petlow, Solihull Responsible for department of 12 and sales team of 24 representatives Current salary £17,500
Interests:	Golf, swimming, scuba diving Member Solihull Round Table Member St James, Edenlow, Parochial Church Council	
Referees:	Mrs Mary Hayling 23 Orchard Close Graystoke Essex CM23 8YH (Telephone: 01287 203785)	Mr Peter Smithson The Meadows Peterlee Reading RG12 8BV (Telephone: 01824 538467)

It is true that most, if not all, of this information is of importance to a potential employer. But the layout and ordering are not particularly helpful, and the document does little to 'sell' the person concerned. Traditionally this was done in the accompanying letter, in which the applicant explained what was attractive about the job and why he or she was suitable for it.

There are, however, disadvantages to this approach. The accompanying letter needs to be quite substantial, since it has to do all the work of promoting the applicant's case. It can only do this in conventional prose, so the employer is faced with the task of reading a considerable amount in order to determine whether this is the right person for the job—or at least is worth calling to interview. The CV is not designed to help here, since, as we have seen, it is a bald recital of facts with little guidance as to which are the important ones.

A solution to this dilemma is to make the CV a 'selling document', a kind of prospectus in which the applicant's virtues are set out, together with supporting details. The letter then becomes a reinforcement of the CV (and a proof that the applicant can write satisfactory English). It is this approach which is detailed in the rest of this chapter.

New approaches

A successful CV is the product of careful thought and planning. The employer is looking for an applicant who has the right experience, skills, and personal qualities for the job. The person appointed is likely to be the one who not only possesses all these but also presents them in the most attractive way. The only way in which you can achieve this is by thinking very carefully about yourself and what you have done in the past and believe you could do in the future, given the right opportunity.

Preparation

Begin by thinking about these three areas:

- experience
- skills
- personal qualities

There are various ways in which you can do this. What follows is only one possibility. Whichever approach you choose, however, make sure that you make detailed notes of your ideas—even if you think they may not be relevant. Also, keep all your lists and sheets of notes 'open'; go back to them from time to time and make sure that you haven't missed anything out. This preparation stage is essentially one of brainstorming. Selection and ordering come later.

Experience

Many people find it easiest to start with this, because it is the most concrete. Begin by thinking of your life as divided into a number of stages.

What these are depends on you—the divisions between the stages may be marked by changes of job, moves from one place to another, or by key events in your life—marrying, having children, buying a house, and so on. Your notes on your experience should certainly include:

- education
- any professional training
- periods of employment—include part-time jobs and those which didn't last very long, as well as 'proper' jobs
- other extended periods in which your life focused on a particular activity (for example, periods of foreign travel)
- any voluntary work you have done

Skills   Your notes on your experience should provide you with useful prompts when it comes to listing your skills. Look at each of the different stages of your life and ask yourself:

- Which skills did I use here that I already had?
- Which skills did I improve on or consolidate?
- What new skills did I learn?

Make sure that you include not only skills related to your trade or profession, but also personal skills, for example:

organizing events	training staff
interviewing	giving advice
chairing meetings	making presentations
supervising	trouble-shooting
meeting the public	

Don't be too concerned at this stage about whether the skills you list are relevant. That can come later. For now write them all down.

When you have finished, look back through the list and consider whether each item is one separate skill, or, in fact, a bundle of skills that should be separated out. For example, you may have written 'communicating', when it might be preferable to list 'simplifying technical subject matter and communicating it to non-specialist workers'.

Personal qualities   This is the area that many people find most difficult; they are unhappy talking about themselves and their qualities because they feel it is big-headed or 'pushy'. They may also find it quite difficult to step back and look at themselves objectively. On the other hand, if you don't tell a potential employer about your personal qualities, who will?

It is sometimes difficult to begin such a list, so here are some qualities to start you off. Write down any which you think apply to you, and then add others of your own. For each one you choose, make sure that you can think of incidents in your own life and work experience that bear them out.

accurate	competent
adaptable	cooperative
astute	courteous
can work under pressure	decisive
careful	dedicated
committed	energetic

extrovert	orderly
flexible	organized
friendly	positive
get on well with other people	practical
good communicator	receptive
good sense of humour	relaxed
good time-keeper	reliable
hardworking	self-confident
imaginative	self-motivated
independent worker	sensitive
lively	thorough
logical	thoughtful
loyal	vigilant
methodical	work well with others
meticulous	

Constructing your CV

You should by now have three sets of rough notes. (It doesn't matter how rough they are, provided they are as detailed as possible.) The next stage is to decide how you want to order your CV. This can be done in one of two ways:

- chronologically
- functionally

Chronological

A chronological CV presents your education and work experience either in the order in which they happened, or in reverse order, with your most recent experience first. Since recent experience is probably of most interest to an employer, this latter method is now widely used.

The advantages of a chronological CV are that it emphasizes the companies or organizations you have worked for (and the periods of time involved) and your continuity of employment. The disadvantage is that if your career has had ups and downs, especially if it includes periods of unemployment, these show up very clearly. The employer who is looking for a steady and reliable employee will probably favour this approach.

There is an example of a chronological CV on page 32.

Functional

A functional CV is organized by skills and qualities. If, for example, your experience is in motor-parts sales, both as a representative and in head office, the functions you could use as headings might be:

- presenting the product range
- customer care
- information technology

Under each one you can provide further details of specific experience. The advantage of this approach is that you can focus on your strengths without having to spell out relative inexperience or periods of unemployment. The disadvantage is that it may not make clear important periods of employment with impressive employers. The employer who is looking for applicants with particular skills and capabilities will find the functional CV more helpful than the chronological.

There is an example of a functional CV on page 33.

Mary J. Morris

'The Larches'
Spottonham Road
Larswick
Lincs
SP12 5MS

tel: 01854 658194

Experience

1994–present

Education and Publications Officer, Boston Museum. Responsible for organizing annual programme of school visits, lectures, and holiday courses. In charge of liaison with primary and secondary schools. Preparing and publishing a range of leaflets and 'mini-guides' to the Museum's collections. Managing an annual budget of £10,000.

1989–1994

Head of Humanities, Larswick Middle School. Responsible for department of four teaching history, geography, religious education. Preparing and administering departmental policy documents. Member of School's Senior Management Team. Pastoral care tutor to 35 pupils. Responsible for school magazine.

1985–1989

Teacher of History at St Wulfstan's High School, Scunthorpe. Teaching pupils across full ability and age range (11–18). Preparing classes for GCE 'O' level and GCSE examinations, GCE 'A' levels and university entrance. House tutor.

Qualifications and training

Postgraduate Certificate in Education, University of Hull
BA Honours 2nd class, History and Economics, York University
'A' level English, History, French
'O' level English Language, English Literature, Maths, French, History, Geography, Biology

Interests

Mountain walking and rock climbing
Foreign travel
Voluntary social work with local women's refuge

Referees

Dr P. J. Cleary,   Mrs S. P. Greenwick,
Director,   34, High Street,
Boston Museum,   Brentham,
Boston,   Surrey,
Lincs,   GU23 9BV
B01 2RF

Katherine Hardwick

22 Redden Road
Hartwell
North Yorkshire
YO7 4PQ

Tel/Fax: (01301) 653801

Profile
Enthusiastic, responsible graduate with a Post-graduate Printing and Publishing Diploma and good organizational skills. Able to work independently using initiative and as part of a team to tight deadlines. With editing, desktop publishing, and keyboarding skills.

Training
Has recently completed the Post-graduate Diploma in Printing and Publishing at the London Institute.

Skills gained
- Design
- Desktop Publishing
- Costing & Estimating
- Letter Assembly
- Graphic Reproduction
- Screen Printing
- Printing Processes
- Data Processing & Information Systems
- Publishing Administration
- Print Finishing & Bookbinding
- Technology of Printing Materials
- Technology of Colour Reproduction

Experience
- Three months' work experience with Quantum Publishing, a company involved in writing, editing, and publishing business and information technology texts.
- Word processing, research, and general office administration.
- Work with an Apple Mac using ClarisWorks and QuarkXpress.
- Work experience at Reed Professional Publishing and Cambridge University Press.
- Currently working with Quantum Publishing as a paid employee with increased responsibility.

Education
Degree   BA (Hons) with major in English (2.2), Nottingham Trent University
A levels   English Literature
           Art & Design
GCSEs   Eight Grade C or above, including English and Maths

Interests
Music: playing the saxophone.
Riding a mountain bike.
Cinema and theatre-going.

Referees
Dr J.M. Barker, B.Sc., PhD   Mrs J.W. Pawsey
The Publishing Institute   29, Lower Redhill Lane
Castle Street   Downham
London SE1 6SB   MN21 7ST

Tailoring your CV

So far, the CV has been considered in a vacuum. In fact when you are applying for a job, it should be adjusted to suit the particular post you are applying for. Once you have written the original CV, this is not difficult, especially if you have word-processed it and stored it as a computer file. A word of caution, however: make sure that you check, and if necessary update it, before sending it off. Print out a file copy of the particular version you use for each application.

The letter of application

See also:
■ **Chapter 2** *Business letters* (p. 9)

Your CV should be accompanied by a letter of application, and these two items form a package. The letter has a number of purposes:

■ It allows you to sell yourself by pointing out key features of your CV.
■ It gives you the opportunity to include material that is not in the CV, especially personal qualities that you listed when making your preparations.
■ It shows a prospective employer that you know how to write a letter. While this may be of decreasing importance in an electronic age, many employers still value it highly, both as a skill in its own right and as a test of your ability to communicate clearly and effectively.

What should go in it?

The letter of application should follow the general guidelines for all business letters. It should have an introduction, a body, and a conclusion.

The introduction

In the introduction you should detail the job you are applying for, and, if relevant, the circumstances that have led to this (for example an advertisement, or the recommendation of an agency).

The body

The body of the letter provides you with an opportunity to present yourself to the employer. You should make use of the list of personal qualities you made while preparing, and should re-emphasize the skills you have which make you particularly suitable for the job. You can also highlight periods of employment or other experience that are particularly relevant.

It is important not to write too much, however. Two, or at most three, short punchy paragraphs are much more effective than two sides of rambling prose.

The conclusion

The conclusion should round the letter off, leaving with reader with a positive image. It should sum up **briefly** the selling points made in the body of the letter, mention any items (including the CV) you are enclosing, and express willingness to provide any further information that the reader may want.

JAYNE SAUNDERS

143 Farndon Street, Blackstock, Essex CM21 8BG

TEL/FAX (01402) 546091

Ms Cath Harries
Editorial Manager
Harper Books Ltd
The Old Fire Station
Clapton Street
Poole
Dorset
SP19 8GS

29th August 1997

Dear Ms Harries,

Assistant Editor/Desk Editor

I wish to apply for the above post, advertised in *The Bookseller.*

Currently I am working in a new small publishing company, *Notions,* that specializes in highly designed, high-quality non-fiction books. Since I started here I have been the only full-time employee working on all editorial aspects of the books. Answering directly to the Publishing Director and the Editorial Director, I have a very wide range of responsibilities including: editing on screen in Quark and Microsoft Word, liaising with the designers and freelance editors, checking manuscripts at the film stage, managing the stationery budget, Americanizing text, as well as signing off books, having checked the ozalids.

I have been at Notions for over a year, and I have learnt a great deal, but there is no longer the scope to use all my knowledge and experience. I am seeking a position that offers responsibility for the full range of publishing and editorial skills, as well as the opportunity to meet and work with a range of people. I like to think that I bring enthusiasm and adaptability to my work.

I would welcome the opportunity to discuss this letter and my enclosed curriculum vitae. The telephone number I have given is my home one and all calls are answered.

I look forward to hearing from you.

Yours sincerely,

Jayne Saunders

Guidelines

The CV

1 Begin by mapping your experience. Divide it into significant blocks—by work or personal experience.

2 List your education, training, and work experience. Add other significant experience. Give dates for each item.

3 Analyse and list all your technical and personal skills.

4 Analyse and list important personal qualities. You can begin this process by looking at the list on pages 30 and 31

5 Decide whether you wish to construct your CV on a chronological or functional basis.

Advantages of chronological
- shows continuity
- emphasizes key periods of employment

Disadvantages of chronological
- does not easily highlight skills
- shows up inexperience and periods of unemployment

Advantages of functional
- highlights skills
- helps to conceal inexperience and periods of unemployment

Disadvantages of functional
- does not easily highlight key periods of employment
- does not highlight continuity of employment and reliability

6 Word-process your CV so that it is clear and uncluttered and the eye is led to the key features.

7 Try to keep it to one side of A4. Certainly make sure that all the important information is on the first side. Never go beyond two sides of A4.

The letter of application

8 Use the letter of application to emphasize your selling points and to include key personal qualities that do not appear in the CV.

9 Begin with a brief explanation of what you are applying for and why.

10 Use the body of the letter to highlight exactly why the job attracts you and why you think you are very suitable for it.

11 Write a brief conclusion designed to leave the reader with the best possible impression.

Presentation

12 Both documents should be word-processed and printed on a good printer, using high-quality paper. Layout and typefaces should be chosen with care.

See also:
- **Chapter 25 *Getting it on the page*** (p. 268)
- **Chapter 26 *Using technology*** (p. 277)

5 Interviews

The most challenging interview most people face is the job interview, which is the focus of this chapter. Much of what it contains, however, is also applicable to interviews in other work situations. Media interviews are covered in Chapter 10.

Preparation

The key to a successful interview is good preparation. However apprehensive or nervous you may feel about the interview itself, if you have prepared thoroughly you will gain considerably in confidence and will give a good interview.

The job

See also:
- **Chapter 23 *Planning and research*** (p. 239)

It should go without saying that you need to know as much as possible about the company or organization to which you are applying. You may have been sent some briefing information when you applied for the job—but then so will all the other candidates for interview. Further information about many companies and other organizations is available at your local public library. In addition you may have personal contacts who can give you information or tell you where to find it. Compile a dossier of the information you collect.

Now look at whatever information you received about the job. Remember that this is part of an advertisement for the company or organization which is thinking of employing you. Just as your application puts your experience, skills, and qualities in the best possible light, so this job description puts the best possible gloss on the job.

Examine it from every angle: what are the hidden snags and unanswered questions? You know what is desirable and attractive about the job: that is why you have applied for it. What are the less attractive features of it? Is there likely to be anything about it that might make you regret having taken it on? Make a list of questions you need to ask about the job, phrasing them in a positive or, at least, neutral way.

Now imagine that you have been successful and it is your first day with the company. What do you see yourself doing and what questions do you need to ask? Write them down on a sheet of paper. Use them as a starting point for a list of questions that you want to put about the job and the organization. Use these questions as a stimulus to further questions. Then organize your questions by theme: questions about the company's structure, questions about your own responsibilities, and so on.

There will be a section of the interview during which you are told more about the company and the job and are invited to ask questions. This is when you should use your list of questions. It shows that you have made a thoughtful preparation for the interview and are serious about the job.

The candidate

For the next stage of preparation, you need:

- your letter of application
- your CV
- a copy of your application form, if you had to complete one
- any job description you have been given

For the company, the purpose of the interview is to find out how suitable you really are for their purposes. They have summarized these purposes in the job description you have in front of you. When they read the information you have sent them they will want to ask two types of question:

- those which seek further information, giving you an opportunity to enhance your attractiveness as a candidate
- those which probe the gaps and weaknesses in the information you have given and which may detract from your attractiveness as a candidate

You can prepare for the first group of questions using your CV as a memory-jogger. The second group contains questions that are harder to answer and to prepare for.

Preparing for difficult questions

Good interviewers ask difficult questions not out of some inborn sadism, but because they have to establish the weaknesses as well as the strengths of each candidate. This is the best way for them to work out who is the strongest candidate overall.

Begin by placing yourself in the interviewer's shoes. Look again carefully at your CV. Make a list of gaps, weaknesses, and other 'problem areas' in it. Make a list of questions that you as an interviewer would want to ask this candidate. Take each question in turn and work out the best way of answering it:

■ **Be positive**

There are usually two ways of answering difficult questions: positive and negative. For example, you might have left a job after only a short time in it and then had a period of unemployment before finding another post. If asked, 'Why did you leave that job after such a short time?' you could answer, 'Because I had a row with my boss.' That is the negative response. Another reply might be: 'There was an unfortunate conflict of personalities between me and a senior manager and we agreed that it was better if I left the company.' That is really a longer way of saying the same thing, but it has the advantage of putting the two people concerned on an equal footing—it was as much the manager's fault as yours. A better answer might be, 'My boss would not accept my professional judgment on a key issue so I was forced to resign'—but only if it's true, because you will certainly be asked what the issue was.

■ **Make sure you answer the question**

Don't try to sidetrack or to put up a smokescreen, because a skilled interviewer will not be impressed. In many jobs you have to face hard questions and the way in which you answer such questions in an interview is thus a useful indication of how you will answer them in the job.

■ **Be honest**

Similarly, there is little point in lying. Leaving moral considerations on one side, there is a strong probability that you will be found out. Also there is a merit in frankly admitting that you made a mistake. Everyone does from time to time, and saying that you were wrong or mistaken, and that you have learned from it, is often to your credit in an interview rather than the reverse.

If you have someone who can help you in your preparation for the interview you may find it useful to get them to role-play the interview with you. Give them the list of hard questions and let them put them to you—together with any others they may think of themselves. Ask afterwards how they thought you tackled the questions. This not only gives you practice, but it also helps to fix some of the key ideas in your mind.

Yourself

The preparation listed earlier should be completed in plenty of time and not left until the night before. Better to have a relaxed evening and a good night's sleep than to go to bed late with all the possible questions and problems buzzing around inside your head.

In any conversation we receive messages not only from the words a person speaks, but also from their appearance and body language. It is unfortunately true that we begin to make judgements about a person even before we hear them speak; their face, build, posture, and clothing all contribute to that first impression. Candidates at interview are judged in just these ways, and it is important to think about the impression you want to create and to present yourself accordingly. Generally it is better to err on the side of dressing too formally rather than not formally enough.

Take with you to the interview the papers you have been using in your preparation. Place the list of the questions you would like to ask about the company and the job in a clean file together with some writing paper so that you can make notes during the interview if necessary. Take this folder into the interview with you so that you can refer to the papers as necessary.

Give yourself plenty of time to get to the place where you are being interviewed, but avoid arriving too early, since it will only mean that you have a long wait which only serves to build up the tension.

The interview

In the interview itself, you may not be feeling particularly confident, but it must appear that you are.

Preliminaries

You will probably be collected for interview from the room in which you have been waiting, and escorted by a member of staff, who may well be one of the interviewers. So as soon as you are called, the interview has begun.

As you enter the room, look round and make eye contact with the people there. Smile and greet them when introduced. Shake hands if that is expected, and sit when invited to do so. If you find that the chair you are offered is placed so that it is difficult for you to see the people interviewing you comfortably without having to keep moving around, then by all means alter its position.

The early questions will probably be 'ice-breakers'—about the sort of journey you had and so on. Answer them politely but not at too great length. Use this period to settle yourself and take stock of the situation.

Nuts and bolts

A common strategy is for the interviewer(s) to move on to explain about the company and the job. Some of this information may already be known to you and some will answer questions on your list. Pay careful attention to this, because at some point in the interview—either now or, more commonly, at the end—you will be asked if you have any questions you wish to put. This is where you can make use of your prepared questions.

The interview will probably then move on to your experience and skills. Assuming you have prepared carefully, much of this stage of the interview should progress fairly smoothly—until you reach the stage of difficult questions.

Dealing with difficult questions

The thing to remember here is that the interviewer has a set of questions he or she wishes to ask and you have answers you want to give. These may not match perfectly. Part of the art of being interviewed is to say what you want to say while appearing to be answering the question—or at least not to seeming to evade it. Experienced politicians have to do this every day and it is educational to observe how they do it.

Even when you are dealing with a gap or a problem in your CV, your aim should be to turn this to your advantage. Answer the question, deal briefly with the negative aspects, and move on to a detailed account of the positive aspects of the situation. Compare these two dialogues:

A

INTERVIEWER: You only worked at Parker-Brown for two years and then you left. Why was that?

CANDIDATE: Unfortunately the company was going through a difficult patch and I was made redundant.

INTERVIEWER: Why?

CANDIDATE: I've just explained. The company—

INTERVIEWER: No, why you? Why you and not someone else?

B

INTERVIEWER: You only worked at Parker-Brown for two years and then you left. Why was that?

CANDIDATE: Unfortunately the company was going through a difficult patch and I was made redundant. That was how I was able to do a refresher course on spreadsheet construction which I found invaluable in my next job.

INTERVIEWER: At Myersons?

CANDIDATE: Yes.

INTERVIEWER: Tell us about that.

In Dialogue A the candidate is forced onto the back foot, having to explain why she was the one made redundant, and not someone else. In Dialogue B she is able to turn the question so that she can tell the interviewer that she has additional skills in spreadsheet construction.

Problems

When you are being interviewed, you are under a certain amount of stress. Things can go wrong. The commonest is that you suddenly just dry up. Your mind goes blank and you don't know what to say. The temptation in such situations is just to talk, to say anything to cover the silence and to hide your confusion. This is a mistake, because you will probably find yourself talking nonsense. It is much better to pause for a moment and try to relax. Then either ask the interviewer to repeat the question, or—if you have dried up because you cannot answer a difficult question—admit that you don't know.

From time to time you may encounter an interviewer who is aggressive, or who irritates or annoys you for some other reason. Be polite, but not cringing. If you believe in what you are saying, stick to your guns. But don't answer rudeness or aggression with similar behaviour—unless you have already decided that you don't want the job, in which case it probably doesn't matter.

Concluding

As already suggested, you may well be asked whether you have any questions you would like to put to the interviewer. This is often a signal that the interview is drawing to a close. Use your list of questions and draw from it one or two questions which have not already been answered and which you really need to have an answer to. Don't ask too many questions. This is the section of the interview in which you are most obviously in control and if you bore the interviewer, or hold up the day's timetable, you will not be popular.

As the interviewer brings the interview to a close, rise, say your thanks, shake hands if this is expected, and turn to leave. At the door, turn and smile, thank the interviewer again and say goodbye. Remember that last impressions are nearly as important as first ones.

Later, when you have had time to relax, go through the interview in your mind and analyse how it went. There will have been good features and bad. Analyse the bad to see how they can be avoided in future—and remember the good.

Guidelines

Preparation

1 Research the company so that you know as much about it as possible. Make notes.

2 Think carefully about the job description. In particular look for gaps in the way it is written and make a list of the questions they raise.

3 Look at your CV and letter of application. Make a list of 'straight' questions you expect to be asked. Make sure that you can answer them fluently.

4 Look again and think of the 'awkward' questions you could be asked. Make sure that you can answer them positively.

5 If possible, get a friend to interview you, using your lists of questions plus any others that come up during this rehearsal.

The interview

6 Enter confidently and greet the interviewer(s) politely.

7 Use the introductory questions to settle yourself and take stock of the interviewer(s).

8 When asked difficult questions, try to turn them so that your answer ends positively.

9 If you are thrown by a question, don't waffle. If you don't know the answer, say so. If you are confused, gain valuable time for thinking by asking the interviewer to repeat the question (but don't do this too often!).

10 When invited to ask questions, select one or two from your prepared list, but don't go on too long.

11 Leave the interview confidently and pleasantly, remembering that this last impression is very important.

12 Later, take stock of how the interview went and make a note of lessons you have learned from it.

6 Organizing a meeting

Formal meetings

When preparing a formal meeting you need to consider:

- Your **aims**: what you hope the meeting will achieve.
- The **competence** of the meeting: what it can practically and legally achieve.
- The **agenda**: the list of items to be considered.

When running the meeting:

- The role of the **chair** is very important.
- The organization of **motions and voting** should be clearly defined.
- Accurate **minutes** should be kept (and ratified at the subsequent meeting).

Informal meetings

Many meetings, especially in the workplace, do not need such a formal organization, but there is still a need for sensible **planning** and **organization**.

Most people at some time in their lives have to attend meetings of one kind or another: from parish councils to the committees of local organizations, from a board meeting to a works council. Such organizations all have their own special rules and customs, but they also have many things in common. In this chapter we look primarily at what are loosely called 'formal meetings'. By this is meant any meeting which is big enough or 'official' enough to require formal chairing and organization.

At the end of the chapter there is a short section on informal meetings. This deals with those ad hoc meetings which are set up, often at short notice, to discuss specific points and decide upon a course of action: in the workplace, or as part of the work of a social grouping of some kind.

Preparing for a formal meeting

One of the secrets of successful meetings is careful preparation. Obviously this is particularly important for the person chairing the meeting, but good preparation is important for other participants as well. Frequently participants are not well prepared—they don't have time, or it doesn't seem necessary—and this results in meetings that take longer than they need and achieve less than they could.

Aims

To begin with it is important to define what the meeting is for. Most of us have attended meetings which seemed rambling and interminable just because those involved had no clear idea of exactly what they were there for. The person responsible for chairing the meeting should:

- Write a brief and clear definition of the purpose of the meeting.
- Distribute it to those invited to the meeting (or publish it in a suitable place if the meeting is a public one).
- Remind the meeting of that purpose at the start (or make sure that it is expressed in the agenda which is distributed to participants).
- Keep it clearly in mind as the meeting proceeds.

Competence

Meetings of committees and other constituted bodies frequently have a clearly defined competence: what they can and cannot do is set down in their constitution and/or standing orders. For example, at the annual parish meeting at which an English parish council reports to the electors, the public can ask questions of the councillors through the chair. They cannot, however, propose and vote on motions; that is the prerogative of the council itself.

It is essential that the chair and the participants know clearly the competence of the meeting. This may require an understanding of the constitution of the organization and a knowledge of the standing orders set down to govern meetings of its members or committee. Some participants may have only a hazy grasp of the 'small print' of these, or may, in the heat of debate, forget them, but the chair must always have them clearly in mind. In practice it often falls to the secretary to have a copy of any rules and to refer members to them if they are in danger of breaking their own rules.

The competence of a meeting defines what it can and cannot do. If there is no constitution to refer to then it is up to those organizing the meeting to define in their own minds what the meeting's competence is. This should be made clear to those taking part and then kept to. The chair of a public meeting might begin by saying:

This meeting has been called by the Sports Field Committee to consult local people about their plans for the field. We have already made a detailed planning application, but we are aware that there is some local opposition. We should like to find out in more detail what that opposition is. Then we shall—if necessary—apply to the District Council to amend our plans accordingly. I should point out that this is only a consultation meeting. It can't decide anything and there will be no votes.

Agenda

Most meetings should have an agenda, a list of topics to be covered, presented in the order in which they should be tackled. In the case of any official meeting, the form the agenda takes may well be laid down, but this is a fairly common form of agenda:

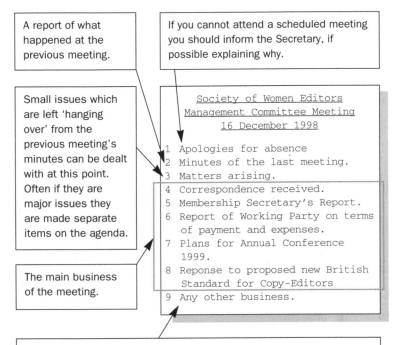

A report of what happened at the previous meeting.

If you cannot attend a scheduled meeting you should inform the Secretary, if possible explaining why.

Small issues which are left 'hanging over' from the previous meeting's minutes can be dealt with at this point. Often if they are major issues they are made separate items on the agenda.

The main business of the meeting.

```
        Society of Women Editors
      Management Committee Meeting
            16 December 1998

1  Apologies for absence
2  Minutes of the last meeting.
3  Matters arising.
4  Correspondence received.
5  Membership Secretary's Report.
6  Report of Working Party on terms
   of payment and expenses.
7  Plans for Annual Conference
   1999.
8  Reponse to proposed new British
   Standard for Copy-Editors
9  Any other business.
```

Sometimes referred to as 'AOB', this allows members to raise issues not on the agenda. Some committees do not allow this item, on the grounds that it can lead to major issues being raised for which committee members are not prepared (and at a time when most people want to close the meeting and go home).

Agendas can be much longer and more detailed than this, but their form is normally similar. They are essentially a list. If it is necessary for those attending the meeting to have more details these can be supplied as separate documents to which the agenda refers.

Running a formal meeting

Constituted bodies like council committees and those that run recognized charities have constitutions which determine their powers. They may also have standing orders which determine how their meetings should be run. These usually cover matters such as:

- Frequency and duration of meetings.
- How many members make up a quorum (the minimum number required for a meeting).

- Officials and when and how they should be elected.
- If and how members can be co-opted.
- Which matters may and may not be included in the agenda.
- How items for the agenda of a meeting should be tabled.
- How the meeting should be chaired and the rules governing individual speakers.
- How motions should be tabled and seconded.
- How amendments should be tabled and seconded.
- The order in which votes should be taken and the procedures for doing so.
- How points of order should be put and dealt with.
- The creation and use of sub-committees.

Even in less formally organized meetings, a number of these points are very important.

The chair

It is the job of the chair to manage the meeting and to ensure that:

- all present have a fair chance to express their views
- only one person speaks at a time
- speakers are not interrupted
- the agenda is followed and items are discussed in the correct order
- if votes are to be taken, this is organized properly and everyone present knows exactly what is being voted on and in what order.

Those present should address their remarks to the chair and not directly to each other. This may seem pedantic, but it is a useful device for maintaining order within the meeting. If two participants at a meeting start addressing each other directly, it becomes very difficult for the chair to maintain control of what is going on, or for others to make their own voice heard.

Chairing is a skilled matter. You have to balance the ideal of fairness with an awareness of how much time is available for the meeting and what it is reasonable to expect to achieve. Some speakers have a much better grasp of the subject matter than others and can speak clearly and concisely. Some may have a far weaker grasp or a greater desire to speak at length (sometimes at great length). Others may have valuable points to make but may be reticent or unable to make themselves heard. A good chair will not only balance the demands of the subject matter and the speakers, but also try to make sure that everyone has a chance to be heard. This will be done with patience and good humour so that, even when determined speakers are interrupted and asked to give way, they do not feel aggrieved or irritated.

Voting

Some meetings have to have votes; others never do. It depends on the competence of the meeting. If you are an advisory body, you may well not wish to vote, but prefer to achieve consensus, or—if you cannot agree—an agreed description of the balance of views expressed:

```
There was general agreement that a new pavilion should
be built. A clear majority of the committee felt that
the existing plans should be retained, but a
```

```
significant minority expressed the view that these
plans should be reduced in scale and expense.
```

If you do have votes, it is important to make sure that everyone knows exactly what they are voting on. This may sound self-evident, but it is easy for confusion to arise, especially if there are both a motion and amendments to be voted on. The procedure usually runs along these lines:

1 There is a motion to be voted on. This may have been tabled before the meeting or at the meeting. (The word 'tabled' is commonly used in British English (Br. E.), as it is in this chapter, to mean that an item is placed 'on the table' for the consideration of the meeting. Rather confusingly it can also mean 'put aside, taken out of consideration'. This is the sense in which it is used in the USA.) Tabling a motion (Br. E.) generally requires a proposer and a seconder.
2 The chair places the motion before the meeting for debate and then speakers—at the invitation of the chair—express their views.
3 Anyone who is not happy with the motion can propose an amendment. This takes the form of a change to part of the wording of the motion, or an addition to it. (It is important that the chair gets a precise wording for the amendment and makes sure that, with it, the motion still makes sense.) The amendment must be seconded.
4 Other views are expressed and possibly other amendments are tabled.
5 A vote is taken on the amendments first. Those which are carried then become part of the motion.
6 A vote is then taken on the motion incorporating any amendments that have been carried.
7 If any vote is a tie, the chair has the casting vote. The convention is that this is normally cast in favour of the status quo (i.e. no change), although this is not necessarily always done.

Minutes

See also:
■ **Chapter 23** *Planning and research* (p. 239) for advice on how to make notes.

The secretary of the committee is required to make a record of what happens at the meeting—the minutes. At a public meeting called for a specific purpose there may not be a secretary, but it is useful to appoint one to make such a record, if only to supply those who enquire—and the local press—with information.

The minutes of a meeting summarize the main points which are debated and the main views expressed. They should go into sufficient detail to make the substance of the meeting clear, but should not be too detailed, unless there is an important reason for this:

```
3. AGM
James McDonald suggested that a possible subject for
the talk at the AGM would be Public Lending Right.
The Secretary said she would contact the Chair of the
PLR Advisory Committee and report back at the next
meeting.
4. Dates of Meetings for 1996
The summer seminar would be held on 27th April. There
would be Committee meetings on Wednesday 5th June and
```

```
22nd October (subject to checking with those members
of the Committee who were not present at the meet-
ing). 22nd October would also be the date of the AGM.
5. P.S. Bowman's survey of Educational Science
Publishers
Peter Bowman had submitted an article for possible
publication in 'The Author'. It was the result of a
survey he had conducted with members of the
Association for Science Education, grading publishers
in various categories. There was very little time in
which to discuss the survey but the Committee felt
that it should be published in 'The Author', if the
Editor ageed, and it was hoped that it would generate
interesting responses from Science writers...
```

Tabling the minutes   Usually the minutes are distributed to members of a committee along with the agenda for the next meeting. At that meeting the chair tables the minutes so that the committee can check their accuracy and, if necessary, correct them, before they are signed by the chair as a true record of what took place at the meeting.

Informal meetings

By their nature, it is difficult to make generalizations about informal meetings—those occasions that fall somewhere between a formal meeting and a conversation between acquaintances. Some of the points that have been made about formal meetings, however, can be adapted to informal meetings.

Aims and competence   If you call a meeting, it is useful to have in your mind an idea of what you would like to cover and what you can realistically expect to achieve. The word 'realistically' is important here: it is easy to imagine that more can be achieved in the time available than is actually the case.

Agenda   While it may not be necessary to have a published agenda, it is very useful to jot down a list of the main points you want to cover—and the best possible order in which to tackle them. Not only does this mean that you don't forget important points, but also it helps you keep an eye on how you are getting on, especially if time is limited.

It is also useful to make sure that those invited to attend an informal meeting know what it will be about; if they need to prepare for the meeting, they obviously need sufficient warning.

Procedure   Again, while the informal meeting probably does not need any kind of set procedure, it is important to make sure that it is orderly and that everyone gets a fair chance to speak.

In the case of meetings that have no clear leader, it is often a good idea to begin by discussing how you will proceed and possibly electing someone to act as chair for the duration of the meeting.

Minutes Decisions at informal meetings are often recorded—for example, in the form of an internal memo, or a letter to those who attended. This provides a useful record of the meeting to go on file.

If there is no pre-arranged way of doing this it is often useful to appoint an ad hoc secretary for the meeting to keep a note of what happens.

Guidelines

If you are chairing or organizing a formal meeting, these points are worth remembering:

Preparation

1 Have a clear idea of the aims of the meeting.

2 Make sure that you understand the competence of the meeting.

3 Work out a clear and logical agenda.

Chairing the meeting

4 You are in command; others present depend on you to make sure that the meeting is fairly organized.

5 Make sure that everyone has an equal chance to express their views. (It may be necessary to suggest or even impose time limits to achieve this.)

6 Keep speakers to the point firmly but pleasantly.

7 Keep to the agenda, or—if necessary—make it clear that you are proposing it should be altered and why. (If necessary, put this to a vote.)

8 Try to keep the meeting good-humoured but to the point. (Don't let it descend into irrelevant chat.)

Votes

9 Make sure that any motion for debate is clearly worded and understood by the meeting.

10 Motions and amendments should be formally proposed and seconded.

11 The process should be as follows:
   – a motion is proposed and seconded
   – it is debated
   – any amendments are proposed and seconded
   – amendments are debated
   – amendments are voted on
   – any amendments that are carried are applied to the wording of the motion
   – the (amended) motion is put to the vote.

7 | Presentations

Preparation

When preparing for a presentation it is important to think about:

- **Purpose**

  Is your primary aim to inform, to persuade, to entertain, or to interact?

- **Audience**

  Consider their knowledge, education, ability to follow what you have to say; their expectations; their needs—practical, intellectual, personal.

- **Structure**

  This includes thinking about: content, priorities, ordering.

- **Communication aids**

  These include whiteboard, flipchart, overhead projector, slide projector, audio and video recordings, film.

Delivery

- Most speakers need some form of prompt to make sure that they follow their pre-planned line or argument. This needs careful management.

- A number of strategies are available to make sure that you address the audience directly and maintain their attention.

- Questions and interruptions need to be handled firmly and skilfully.

Spoken presentations to an audience can come in a variety of forms. For example:

- a company sales team offering a range of goods or services to a potential client
- a training session for new employees
- a college lecture

All have these key features:

- one or more speakers presenting information and ideas
- a clearly defined purpose
- an audience

Preparation

The key to a successful presentation is careful and intelligent preparation. Without this, the presentation may be hopelessly disorganized.

Even professionals can and sometimes do fail to make proper preparation, whether out of over-confidence, lack of time, or even laziness, as this real-life example demonstrates.

> The scene is a large teaching space in a college arts faculty. The occasion is a lecture on the history and theory of photography. At the time the lecture is due to begin, about forty students are assembled, waiting for something to happen. They are sitting on chairs arranged in no particular order. After a few minutes the lecturer staggers in carrying a slide projector, two slide carousels, and a pile of handouts. He looks round at the room, realizes that there is no blackout, and decides to move the lecture to an adjoining space. He spends the next ten minutes setting up projector, stand, and screen, trying to work out how the focus and remote control work, and alternating apologies for the delay with complaints about the fact that the college hasn't got proper facilities for his lecture. Eventually everything is ready and the lecture begins.
>
> If lecture it can be called. It is more a kind of rambling chat linking the slides, some of which are projected back to front or even upside down. Towards the end the lecturer passes round some handouts, but there aren't enough to go round because he left copying them until the last minute and the copying machine broke down. He promises more copies next week, but these never materialize. He finishes and shambles off, leaving the students feeling bored, possibly confused, and certainly dissatisfied.

Unfortunately such performances are not uncommon and not only in the educational world. We cannot all be brilliant, witty, or elegant public speakers, but anyone can turn in a polished and professional performance—if they want to. The key is in the organization.

Think of your purpose

See also:
- **Chapter 14 *Purpose*** (p. 113)

Begin by thinking about **why** you are making the presentation. It may be:

- to inform
- to persuade
- to entertain
- to meet and get on with your audience

Frequently it will be a mixture of some or all of these.

To inform

Most presentations provide information, often considerable amounts of it. It is not uncommon for members of an audience to go away with the feeling that 'there was a lot of good stuff there, but it was far more than I could take in at one sitting'. With this in mind, it is valuable to break 'information talk' down into different kinds:

See also:
- **Chapter 15 *Different ways of communicating*** (p. 123)

- **straight facts (data)**
  While these are undoubtedly important, they are often the most difficult to digest. A string of unrelated figures, dates, names, and events is very difficult for most of us to remember, so the speaker has to provide as much help as possible by putting such data into contexts, patterns, and pictures.

■ **stories**

People find stories much easier to remember. There are two reasons for this. First, a story has its own built-in pattern, and patterns make facts easier to remember; and secondly, stories fulfil a very primitive need in human beings—the love of a beginning, a middle, and an end, and the desire to 'know what happens next' are strong in almost everybody. 'Story' may sound rather a childish name; in the 'grown-up' world, stories are often called 'reports'.

■ **descriptions and explanations**

Descriptions of what things or people look like are easy to remember in the same way that stories are. More often, however, it is necessary to explain the functioning of organizations, machines, or institutions. Here it is important to make sure that the description creates clear patterns to help the audience visualize what is being described, for example by using images or analogies.

To persuade   Many business presentations have as their chief purpose to persuade the audience to do something: buy your product, sign up for a different way of doing things, agree to a particular course of action. Even apparently factual presentations such as a college lecture may involve persuasion: for example, the lecturer may wish to persuade students to take a subject more seriously than they currently do, or to open their minds to a new and challenging way of thinking.

To entertain   Sometimes—as in the case of an after-dinner speech—the speaker's main aim may be to entertain. Even when it is not the primary aim of a presentation, however, it is very often an important secondary aim. If you can entertain your audience it often makes your primary aim of informing or persuading very much easier.

To meet and get on   Occasionally the primary purpose of a presentation may be to meet
with your audience   and get on with the members of the audience; for example, a new manager may set up such a meeting with those he or she will be working with. Any presentation to a new audience must have this as a secondary aim, especially if you are dealing with potential clients; and if your presentation is to people whom you meet on a regular basis—students or members of your company—then you need to keep in mind your continuing relationship with them.

Much of this is fairly obvious, but it is important to be aware of **all** your purposes in making a presentation and not just the primary or most obvious one.

Think of your audience

See also:
■ **Chapter 11** *Audience*
(p. 89)

The lecturer we met on page 51 would probably have argued that he **was** thinking of his audience. 'I made the slides and prepared the handout,' he would argue. 'That took me a long time.' What he had forgotten is that the audience sees the whole event as a package that begins when they arrive and ends when they leave. Everything that happens between those two times is part of the presentation as far as they are concerned. So the waiting around, the need to move to another venue, the confusion, the incompetence with the slides were all part of it. The lecturer's preparation time was not.

This may make the preparatory need to think of your audience appear rather daunting, but if it is approached step by step it need not be.

Where they are now The starting point should be a clear idea of 'where the audience are now': what they currently know and understand about the subject matter of the presentation:

- their theoretical knowledge
- their practical knowledge
- their intelligence
- their level of education
- the terminology they are confident about handling
- how quickly they can pick up new ideas
- their concentration span

This information may not be easy to establish and you may have to make assumptions and deductions about it. It is also important to remember that your audience may contain a wide range of experience, education, and expectations.

Their expectations The audience have come for a reason. They may be enthusiastic volunteers bursting to hear your words, or they may be unwilling conscripts who can think of many things they would rather be doing. More likely they will be somewhere between these two extremes. Whatever their attitude to the event, they will have a bundle of expectations and hopes about it. The students at the lecture, for example, were there because it was a compulsory part of their course. Since it took place first thing on a Monday morning, some, at least, may have been unwilling conscripts. This lack of enthusiasm will have been tempered by a willingness to learn and a belief that the lecture would be useful—if only to help them pass one of the modules on the course. Notice how the lecturer's behaviour both reinforced their negative feelings ('We've got to be here and he can't even be bothered to turn up on time.') and damaged their positive ones ('This could be really useful, but he can't even project the slides the right way round.').

If you have delivered a presentation on the same subject once or more in the past it is very tempting to churn out exactly the same material again. This can, however, lead to a dull and uninspiring performance. The subject matter may not be new to you, but it is to this particular audience, and it is important to assess them and their needs afresh each time and to adapt your material accordingly.

Their practical needs It is also important to remember the practical needs of your audience:

- Where you will place a screen and projector(s), flipchart, or whiteboard?
- How you will arrange the seating so that
  - everyone can see without straining?
  - everyone can hear?
  - the participants are in the best relationship with you and with each other?

- Where will you place yourself, and do you want to be able to move around?
- What lighting (or blackout) do you need?
- Do you need a microphone and loudspeakers and, if so, how should these be placed?

All this requires thought and preparation. If you are operating on home ground, this is more straightforward, but even if you are a visiting speaker, most of these points can be organized in advance.

Their intellectual needs

You should already have some idea of this, having considered the list of points under 'Where they are now' (p. 53). You need a strategy for structuring your presentation to make it as effective as possible. This should include:

- **the order in which you present material**
- **the communication aids you will use:**
  - visual aids such as overhead or slide projection, charts, and the use of a whiteboard
  - audio or video tape or film
  - verbal aids such as stories and anecdotes, images and analogies, and mnemonics
  - handouts
- **the use of rhythm and variety to keep your audience interested and alert**

Their personal needs

Consider also the personal needs of your audience. If a presentation session goes on too long, without opportunities for the audience to relax physically and mentally, then it will become increasingly ineffective. In the course of a long session there should be periods for such relaxation: chances for a chat, to stretch your legs, have a coffee, and so on.

Build a structure

How you structure your presentation will depend on the particular circumstances, but there are a number of general rules which apply to most situations.

Content

How much should you try to get through? This depends on three variables:

See also:
- **Chapter 23 *Planning and research*** (p. 239)

- what you want to include
- how much time you have
- how much your audience can tackle

This may seem obvious, but people often forget that these three generally pull in conflicting directions and so try to include more material than is really possible. This may result in the audience being detained for longer than envisaged, or in the presentation only covering part of the intended ground. It is always better to err on the side of caution when deciding how much material to include, and to develop a structure that has sufficient flexibility so that you can adapt as you see how the time is going.

Priorities It is as well to be realistic. Much of what you have to say will be forgotten soon after you have said it, and frequently the things that are remembered are not necessarily the most important. (An audience may come away from a presentation remembering the two or three jokes the speaker made but forgetting the three or four key points that were made—just as one can say after a TV advert, 'That was good', but not remember what it was advertising.)

You should have a small number of key points that you consider it is essential your listeners should take away with them at the end of the presentation. The main part of your presentation should be devoted to making sure that these key points are understood and remembered.

More detailed information that you want your audience to retain should be communicated in the presentation, preferably using whatever aids are available, but should also be distributed in the form of a handout.

Ordering A number of factors will help you decide on the order in which material is presented. First and most obviously:

- **the logic of the subject**
  Frequently there isn't a lot of choice; the subject matter will largely dictate the ordering.

- **the logic of learning and understanding**
  It is essential to move from the known to the unknown, and from the easy to the difficult.

- **the need for variety**
  Wherever possible the strictly logical order should from time to time be broken in order to provide variety.

Other points to bear in mind are:

- Try to start with a 'bang'—a lively and memorable statement or question to catch the listeners' attention.
- Give yourself time to size your audience up, to develop some rapport, before launching into the main substance of your presentation. If the occasion is one which allows a to-and-fro of questions between speaker and audience, it is helpful to warm them up and find out about them by questioning them about their experience of the subject and what they hope to gain from the presentation.
- Make the structure of your presentation clear early on. The old adage of 'Tell 'em what you're going to do; do it; then tell 'em you've done it' is a good one here. An audience feels much more comfortable if they 'know where they are' throughout a presentation.
- After the detailed presentation of each key point allow time to recap not just that point but its relationship to what has gone before. This not only helps to clarify the material but also reinforces the listeners' sense of the structure of the whole presentation.
- End memorably, summing up what has been said and giving the audience something to take away with them.

Communication aids

A brilliant speaker can communicate effectively without using aids, and a disastrous one can make a bad presentation even worse by mismanaging them. Most of us fall somewhere between 'brilliant' and 'disastrous' and need to make effective use of the best aids available.

Each aid has its particular advantages and problems.

Whiteboard

For quick ad hoc use, the modern successor to the school blackboard has a lot of advantages. Particular uses include:

- Building up a summary of key points as you proceed with the presentation.
- Collecting ideas from participants in a brainstorming session.
- Demonstrating links between ideas collected in this way.
- Quickly showing the spelling of important technical terms and names.

Its disadvantages are:

- Permanence: once you have written something up, it stays there until you remove it.
- Not everyone can write neatly and clearly on a whiteboard.
- The amount of space is limited so you may have to remove important material to make way for more.
- When you write on it you have to turn away from your audience, so talking and writing require careful management.
- In some work spaces the whiteboard is fixed and not easy for everyone to see clearly.

Flipchart

One step on from the whiteboard, the flipchart can be used for the same purposes, but has a number of advantages:

- There is no need to erase unwanted material; you simply flip to the next sheet.
- Important material, including diagrams, can be prepared in advance.
- Even when you want the apparent spontaneity of writing up new material as you speak, it is possible to 'cheat' by writing a small pencil version of your text in one corner of the sheet beforehand, as a memory-jogger. Alternatively, the main lines of a diagram can be lightly pencilled in to guide your drawing.

The main disadvantages of a flipchart are that you have to turn away to write on it, and that in a large space it may not be easy to see.

Overhead projector

The overhead projector or OHP is a widely used—and misused—aid. When it is used well, it has several important advantages:

- It puts the image where everyone can see it easily.
- Transparencies can be used for a wide range of pre-prepared material from quite lengthy texts to complex diagrams involving several different colours.
- Transparencies can be prepared using a normal computer printer. There are specialist computer presentation programmes to help you do this and many word-processing programmes and business

packages also facilitate transparency preparation.

■ Empty and pre-printed transparencies can be written on without the speaker having to turn away from the audience.

■ Transparencies can be overlaid so that a complex diagram or text can be built up stage by stage.

■ You can mask a transparency, only revealing its contents a bit at a time, a useful way of focusing the audience's attention.

■ Once a set of transparencies has been prepared for a presentation it can be stored and re-used.

The main problems arise from inefficient use of the projector:

■ Faulty alignment of the projector and screen leads to the 'keystone' effect, where the top of the projected area is considerably wider than the bottom and as a result text and graphics are distorted and partly out of focus. Either the projector needs to be raised, or the screen needs to be angled to avoid this.

■ Faulty focusing.

■ Text or diagrams that are too small to be comfortably read.

■ Mismanagement of transparencies so that they are badly aligned, or get knocked onto the floor.

These can, of course, be overcome, but this requires preparation, practice, and thought.

Slide projector   The slide projector is a somewhat more specialized aid than the OHP, over which it has a small number of advantages which can be very important:

■ The image projected is of a higher quality.

■ It is the best way to project detailed pictures and photographs.

■ Images and sound can be co-ordinated into a comprehensive and complex audio-visual programme.

On the other hand, to use a slide projector effectively you need a darkened room and you need to make sure that you are proficient at using it, or have an operator who is. (Focus, in particular, can be tricky—and it helps if you get the slides the right way round!)

Other aids   These include audio and video tapes and film. It is also possible to project from a computer display, which allows for a wide range of text, still images and even video clips to be integrated into a complete programme that has been prepared in advance, but which can still be controlled by the speaker. All have considerable advantages and require considerable resources. In general, the more sophisticated the equipment, the more likely it is to go wrong at a vital moment. So it is very desirable to arrive in plenty of time so as to check that everything is working properly and to have a backup of some kind in case the worst happens.

Delivery

Giving a presentation can be a worrying prospect. Faced by nerves about the audience's reaction and anxiety not to miss out anything important, some speakers resort to reading a prepared text. Such occasions are rarely a success. A reader finds it difficult to engage with an audience in the way that an unscripted speaker can. When you read, your eyes are, much of the time, turned down towards your script and thus away from the audience. You do not make eye contact and cannot be properly aware of the way in which your listeners are responding to your words. For them it is like listening to the radio with a not very animated puppet miming to the words.

At the other extreme, it is very difficult to sustain a presentation of any duration without some kind of written prompt. It is too easy to lose the thread of your discourse and either flannel, or be led down some tempting but irrelevant by-road. So it is a question of what form of written preparation to make.

Prompt cards A popular solution is to use a set of cards, about the size of postcards, on which the main points of the presentation are written. Each card is numbered and one key point to be made is written on each, with any additional details that it is important to remember. It is preferable to write on only one side of each card so that after you have used it you can turn it over to indicate that it has been used.

The other advantage of this system is that if you find you are running short of time, you can quickly skip over cards carrying less important points and move on to the more important topics. It is even possible to mark on the cards the approximate time at which you should reach that point so that you have a check on how things are progressing.

Other methods If you are using a lot of OHP transparencies, it is possible to use them as the basis of a set of prompt cards. You keep them in their box, interleaved with sheets of white paper, so that you can read what is on them. In between the transparencies you place further sheets of paper, each of which carries a summary of the main points you wish to make between transparencies. As you finish with each transparency or sheet of notes you place it face downwards in the lid of the transparency box, so that the order is not destroyed.

You may feel that you really do need to write the whole of your presentation out in full. This is certainly a good way of ensuring that all the details and arguments are fully worked out. The danger is that written prose and speech are different. If you read written prose aloud it sounds like a reading and not a speech. One solution is to write the whole thing out . . . and then ignore it! Type it out using good spacing and a fairly large typeface, on one side of the paper only. Go through it and underline the key phrase or phrases on each page in red. Then, instead of reading it, use it as a set of prompt cards, talking directly to the audience and only referring to the script to remind yourself of the points you wish to make. If you have spent some time working on what you want to say, you may be surprised just how much of your original phrasing and detail you remember without having to make lengthy references to the typescript.

Talking to your audience

See also:
■ **Chapter 22** *Speech* (p. 228)

However you tackle the question of remembering what to say, it is essential to address your main attention to the audience. If your listeners do not feel that you are talking to them personally, then they might just as well have stayed at home and listened to a tape recording of your talk. What gives a live presentation its interest is just that: it is live. The audience are hearing it as it happens, and **how** it happens is affected by the way they respond, or it should be.

So speak to them directly. Look at them. Early on, try to locate one or two friendly faces in the crowd, people whose eyes—or, even better, their smiles—tell you that they are favourably disposed towards you. Remember where they are so that from time to time you look at them and address remarks to them personally. That does **you** some good, by boosting your confidence. The rest of the time your attention should be divided fairly evenly between your other listeners. Let your eyes move over the audience as you speak, focusing briefly on individuals and addressing that part of your speech to them, before moving on again. The purpose of this is that every member of the audience should feel that your words are intended for them personally.

Dealing with interruptions and questions

Speakers sometimes invite the audience to interrupt them to ask questions or even to challenge what is being said. This can be a useful way of engaging with your listeners and providing a lively discourse. It has a number of disadvantages, however. For one thing, your audience do not know what you are going to say and so may ask questions that will be answered later. Secondly, it can drag you away from the sequence of points you wish to make down a number of blind alleys. And it is an invitation to the bore, the crank, and the attention-seeker to monopolize your attention, to the irritation of everyone else present. A presentation is a presentation, and not primarily a discussion or a public meeting.

It is generally better to offer one or more slots for questions and discussion at moments in the presentation selected by **you**. If people interrupt without being invited to, you can then ask them, politely, to hold their fire until you reach the chosen moment. If they insist, then try to deal with the point briefly and then move on to your next point.

Question-and-answer sessions can be tricky to handle. The rest of the time you are, or should be, firmly in control; here you are to some extent at the mercy of events. Begin by allocating a set period of time—even if you are actually prepared to spend longer than the stated time on questions. That way if one person threatens to monopolize the session you can point out that others, too, have questions they wish to ask and the time is limited—and then hope that someone else **does** have a question!

Things that have to be read

Any text that your audience can see needs careful handling. If you project a text using an OHP or slide projector, you must allow sufficient time for it to be read—and some people are slow readers. Some speakers get round this by reading the text aloud, but audience members may find this irritating. On the other hand if the projected text is at the limits of legibility because of the size of the room, then it is advisable to read it out.

The question of handouts is more complicated. The trouble is that if you distribute handouts before or during your talk, people tend to read them and not listen to what you are saying. So unless there is a good reason to do otherwise, only distribute them at the end of the presentation. It is also helpful to advise your audience that you will be doing this, and to tell them roughly what the handout contains, so that listeners are saved the trouble of taking unnecessary notes. (Also, during the presentation, when you refer to important details it is helpful to say, 'Those details are in the handout which you will receive at the end.')

Guidelines

Preparation Careful and thorough preparation is the key to a successful presentation.

1 Think carefully about your purpose. Is it to inform, to persuade, to entertain, to interact with your audience? Or if, as is likely, it is a mixture of these, what is the balance?

2 If you have the provision of information as a primary aim, think in detail about how you will achieve your aim. How will you combine factual information, narrative, description, and explanation?

3 Make a careful analysis of the audience you expect to address. Begin by considering how well equipped they will be to handle the information and ideas you wish to communicate. How can you make their task of understanding easier?

4 Think also about the expectations and needs they bring to the occasion. If you do not satisfy these—at least in part—they will go away feeling that their time has been wasted.

5 Analyse the content that you wish to communicate, bearing in mind that the amount you can do is limited by the time available and what the audience can take in. It is better to underestimate how much you can do than to be overambitious.

6 Set yourself priorities to make sure that the most important points are grasped **and remembered** by your audience, even if it means reducing the total amount covered.

7 Think carefully about the order in which material should be covered, bearing in mind the logic of the subject, the need to move from the known to the unknown, and the value of variety.

8 Decide which communication aids are most suitable for your purposes. (The advantages and disadvantages of each are listed on pages 56 and 57.) Prepare accordingly (e.g. OHP transparencies).

9 Prepare your prompt cards or other notes.

10 Prepare any handouts you intend to distribute.

Delivery

11 Aim to have every member of your audience going away with the impression that you were talking directly to them.

12 Identify one or two members of the audience who are clearly favourably disposed to you and use them as 'home bases' to return to regularly when speaking. This helps maintain and develop your sense of confidence and rapport.

13 From them let your gaze cover the rest of the audience regularly, coming to rest on individuals and staying on them for a few moments, before moving on. Try to make each person you look at feel that you are talking to them personally.

14 Allocate one or more definite slots for questions and/or discussion and try to confine audience participation to these. If people ask questions at other times, or otherwise interrupt, answer them politely but firmly and return to your line of argument as quickly as possible.

15 Remember that if you display or distribute text, people will want to read it. Build in time for your audience to read the text you display (e.g. on OHP transparencies) and try to delay distributing handouts until the end of the presentation.

8 Reports

Modern life depends on the flow of information. For managers this can seem a mixed blessing, as their in-trays overflow with the stuff: reports on this vie for their attention with proposals about that and all clamour for a response. It seems that 'of making many reports there is no end'.

Yet management, along with many other aspects of life, is impossible without information. Before you can make a decision you need to have at your disposal all the relevant facts, and these often come in the form of a report. It is important, therefore, that such documents are prepared and constructed in the most useful possible way.

Most documents designed to provide information leading to action can be placed on a spectrum.

The report At one end is what might be called the 'pure' report, intended to provide accurate and unbiased information about a situation. If it deals with possible courses of action, it presents all the possibilities and their likely outcomes without favouring one above another. An example of this type of report might be described in this way:

Foreign Language Needs of Business
The study was conducted to identify business needs for languages and the methods by which companies resourced such needs.

The proposal   At the other extreme is the proposal, which is, from the outset, openly and unashamedly biased. Its purpose is to promote a particular course of action. Like the report it provides information and judgements about that information, but it uses these to further its own ends. If other possibilities are considered, it is only to show why they are wrong and the favoured one is right. An example is the proposals that authors prepare to convince publishers that they should publish their books. These often contain considerable detail, spelling out not only what the book contains but also where in the market it is placed and how it compares (favourably, of course) with the competition.

The range   Most reports and proposals fall somewhere between these two extremes. They are designed to be read by decision-makers. They survey a range of information, make judgements about it, and come to conclusions, often in the form of recommendations. Some of these documents will tend towards the objective end of the spectrum, while others will take a more committed stance, but all tend to follow similar patterns and to be prepared in similar ways—which is the subject matter of this chapter.

Preparing a report

Objective   It is impossible to write a clear and cogent report without a clear objective, or set of objectives. So it is important to formulate this as precisely—and briefly—as possible at the outset. For example:

> To survey the present practice of the teaching of mental arithmetic in the authority's secondary schools, to assess present standards, and to make recommendations about what can be done to improve them.

Audience   It is also very important to have a clear idea of the audience for the report. The example above could be aimed at a number of different audiences:

See also:
■ **Chapter 11** *Audience*
(p. 89)

- local authority inspectors
- head teachers
- subject teachers
- parents of children at local schools
- governors of local schools

Each of these audiences has

- a different understanding of the subject
- different concerns

So while it is relatively easy to work out what to say and how to say it to one of these audiences, addressing your report to all five is much more difficult.

Planning your research

See also:
- **Chapter 23** *Planning and research* (p. 239)

Doing the necessary research for a report is much easier if you begin by making two lists:

- questions you need to ask
- people and places where you hope to find the answers

The second list may well not be as complete as the first. It may be necessary to do preliminary research in order to complete it. In the example we are following, you might ask this question:

> What is the current classroom practice?

and then, on reflection you might decide to break it into two:

> **1** What do teachers say they do in the classroom?
> **2** What do they actually do?

Clearly, question 1 is fairly easy to get answered, but question 2 is much more tricky. If time does not allow a personal inspection of a representative sample of lessons, you must look for secondary sources of information, research data and other publications. But where? In this situation the local authority schools inspectorate would clearly be a logical starting point. The person who can answer questions directly is an important resource, but so is the person who can direct you to where you can find out answers to the questions that are left.

Sources of information

Given the very diverse nature of all the reports that people are asked to write, it is impossible to provide a useful detailed list of sources of information. The following list is intended to cover the general areas that need to be considered:

- **Direct observation**
  possibly the most dependable, but also the most time-consuming, source of information

- **People**
  using personal contacts (via email, telephone, fax), questionnaires, meetings, focus groups

- **Publications**
  books, journals, government publications including legislation

- **Research findings**
  a wide range of commercial, government, academic, and other independent organizations sponsor and carry out research and publish their findings

- **Documents and data within your own organization**

Scheduling research

Your list of questions and sources of information can be used to generate a list of things to do. Some of these may be easy and informal, like asking a colleague for an opinion or a piece of information. Others will be more complex and time-consuming, such as contacting a provider of commercial information, acquiring a list of publications, discovering which are relevant, acquiring and reading them, finding relevant information, and making notes on it.

So it is important to make a research plan:

1 Group similar activities together, especially those which involve contacting the same people.
2 Identify those topics which are going to take a long time and so need to be started as early as possible.
3 Work out whether any aspects are interdependent and decide the order in which they must be tackled.
4 Calculate approximately how long each part of the research is likely to take.
5 Order the actions logically, using all this information.

Writing the report

Structure The structure of a report is determined by its content and the needs of its readers. While the following structure is not the only one, it is a popular one and contains all the features that would be expected in a fairly lengthy report. Those in bold type should appear in all reports, regardless of length.

1 Contents list
2 **Executive summary**
3 **Introduction**
4 **Body of the report**
5 **Conclusions**
6 Recommendations
7 Appendices
8 Bibliography

Examples in this section are taken from a number of real-life reports.

If the report is any more than a few pages long it needs a contents list detailing the main sections and the pages on which they appear.

Contents list

CONTENTS

Executive summary The readers of a report are usually busy people. They haven't got time to wade through page after page of text just to find out which parts of a report may be of value to them—if any. The purpose of the executive summary is to set out the substance of the report briefly and in such a way that busy readers can see at a glance whether the report is relevant to them and, if so, which aspects of it are of most interest. Ideally it should not exceed one side of A4. Executive summaries that run to several pages can be self-defeating.

The study was conducted to identify business needs for languages and the methods by which companies resourced such needs. The study was based on a survey of nearly 2000 companies and case studies of 14 companies. Fieldwork took place between March and June 1991.

LANGUAGE NEEDS
The study showed extensive language needs amongst business:
• over 60 per cent of companies conducted business with foreigners whose first language was not English;
• language needs were highly concentrated in a few language areas: predominantly French and German speaking countries, followed by Spanish and Italian; these were the countries where both business was most often conduct-

Introduction   This should contain the following information:

■ **The origins of the report**
   The background and events leading to the need for the report.

■ **Its terms of reference**
   The scope (and limitations) of the report and its purpose.

■ **How it was conducted and by whom**
   This can also include acknowledgements of help received.

■ **Other introductory information**
   It is important to think of the readers of the report and to include at this point any other background information they will need in order to understand the material in the body of the report.

INTRODUCTION

Banks and building societies have been characterized by stable, regulated internal labour markets. However, internal labour markets have been subjected to changes following deregulation in the 1980s, diversification of financial products, and increased use of technology.

   It is perceived that these events, together with a tendency towards flatter organization structures, have greatly changed the nature of employment in banks and building societies.

   The purpose of this study of [*client name*] has been to discover the extent to which that organization conforms to the model which has been traditionally associated with employment in banking. This traditional

Body of the report   The main part of the report contains:

- a detailed account of what your research discovered
- the conclusions that you draw from it
- references to sources that you have quoted. The sources should be listed in the bibliography, and the references should follow a standard pattern (see 'References' below).

A report of any length will be divided into a number of main sections, each on a separate topic or theme. These in turn will probably be subdivided into subsections. All sections and subsections will need headings and, to avoid confusion, it is very desirable to use a numbering system. A commonly used one is decimal: the first main section is numbered 1; subsections are then numbered 1.1, 1.2, etc., and their subsections become 1.1.1, 1.1.2, and so on.

> 5.12 Some companies expect their future senior managers to have as wide a range of job experiences as possible. Others put more weight on an individual's proven track record. ——'s senior man-

> 5.13 Nonetheless, most companies are grappling with the problem of fast-stream staff moving out of jobs too quickly. This issue was raised in the interviews with —— and —— where the

The body of the report will consist of the details of the research—often in the form of tables, charts, and figures, with relevant quotations.

Occupational Pattern of Training

Where training was provided for employees with a business need, training was most often provided for managers, 89 per cent, and least often for secretaries, receptionists and telephonists, less than 60 per cent, Table 7.2.1. This pattern matches the pattern of jobs which companies identified as needing languages, see Chapter 4. Where training was less directed at business needs, the case-study evidence suggested that training was likely to be available for staff in all types of jobs.

Table 7.2.1:   **Training Provision for those with a Business Need**

	Percentage of Companies Providing Training
Managers	89
Professional	78
Technical	71
Sales/Purchasing Staff	71
Secretarial	58
Receptionists/Telephonists	57

N = 226

The argument may be presented in continuous prose, and/or as a series of bullet points:

TRAINING PROVIDERS
Public-sector providers were used by fewer companies than private or in-house. Privately provided training was considered better on grounds of quality, standard, tailoring to business use, range, and availability when needed. Public-sector-provided training fared badly on two counts: its tailoring to business use and its availability when needed. However, where the public sector provided company in-house courses, these criticisms disappeared.

Cultural Training
Apart from the cultural and business training included in many language courses, the extent of cultural training appeared to be low.

ENCOURAGING LANGUAGE ACQUISITION
Companies encouraged language learning in a number of ways:
- employees had to learn a language to conduct their job;
- through career enhancement;
- by easy access and subsidized (usually free) access to training;
- by making language acquisition more fun or challenging, including through encouraging trainees to sit exams.
Financial incentives, other than the above, were rare.

If the material you are handling is detailed, there is a danger that the main thrust of your argument will become obscured by details. In such situations it is better to place highly detailed material in appendices and to refer to it in the body of the report in numbered notes. While the reference number appears at the relevant point in the text, the note itself can either be placed at the foot of the page or at the end of the section or chapter. If there are not too many notes, it is better to put them at the bottom of the page, since it is irritating for the reader to have to keep turning pages to find the relevant note. If there are a lot of notes, however, they are better placed at the end of the chapter, since to place them at the foot of the page will make the pages look messy and unbalanced.

It is essential that when published or unpublished textual sources are referred to, they are clearly identified and readers are enabled—should they so wish—to check the original. In the case of books, the following information should be given:

- the name(s) of the author(s)
- the full title
- the name of the publisher and place of publication
- the year of first publication or, if it is a subsequent edition, the number of the edition and the date of its publication

A common style for doing this is:

Seely, J. (1998): <u>The Oxford Guide to Writing and Speaking</u> Oxford: Oxford University Press

This information should appear in the bibliography at the end of the report. References to the book in the text should simply use the author's name and date followed by the page(s) referred to:

Seely (1998), pp. 34–5

References to periodicals and journals should appear in the bibliography in this style:

Haywood, K. T. (1997): 'Teaching mental arithmetic to 11-year-olds' <u>Modern Maths Quarterly</u> 15, pp. 34–7

Conclusions Each section of the report should lead to a number of conclusions. At the end of the section these are spelled out and the reasoning behind them explained. If there is a separate *Conclusions* section these conclusions are pulled out and presented as an ordered sequence.

> The findings show that [*client name*] does not conform to the model of the flexible firm. If the managerial group constitutes an internal labour market and the non-managerial group does not because it is peripheral, we should expect to see differences in the following characteristics: entry points, attachment to the organization, and career development of the two groups.
> As far as entry points are concerned, our figures so far fail to indicate any

Recommendations Not all reports present recommendations; some are merely required to present a set of information based on research. Where there are recommendations, these may be presented as part of the report's conclusions, or in a separate section which may be placed towards the end of the report, after the conclusions, or immediately after the executive summary. Indeed, some writers prefer to make their recommendations part of the executive summary, since they are an important part of what the busy reader wants to know first.

Appendices The value of placing certain lengthy detailed information in a series of appendices (sometimes called *annexes*) has already been mentioned. The type of information that may go in appendices includes:

- a detailed description of the research method, including the questionnaire(s) used and how the sample was selected
- the research brief and the members of the team producing the report
- detailed research data
- case studies

Addressing your readership

The importance of thinking carefully about your readers has already been mentioned when considering the content and structure of the report. It is equally important to remember your readers when drafting the report itself.

Normally a report should be written in a fairly impersonal and formal style. Reports are formal documents and, even if you have a very

See also:

■ **Chapter 24** *Writing, drafting, and revising* (p. 256)

good idea of who will read what you write and know them all quite well, you cannot know for certain who will read it at some point in the future. Reports are usually stored for later reference and may be passed to anyone with a legitimate interest in the subject, so it is unwise to write them in too relaxed or informal a style.

On the other hand this is not to suggest that you should imagine that you are a nineteenth-century civil servant. In particular, try to avoid writing sentences that are too long or involved. On the whole the reports quoted in this chapter were examples of clear writing. An exception is this sentence quoted earlier:

> If the managerial group constitutes an internal labour market and the non-managerial group does not because it is peripheral, we should expect to see differences in the following characteristics: entry points, attachment to the organization, and career development of the two groups.

This is difficult to follow, because it sets up a fairly complicated hypothesis and then follows through its implications all in one sentence. It would be better to recast it as two sentences:

> It could be argued that the managerial group constitutes an internal labour market whereas the non-managerial group does not because it is peripheral. If so, we should expect to see differences between the two groups in the following characteristics: entry points, attachment to the organization, and career development.

This says the same thing but, because it forms two sentences, the logic of the argument is easier to follow.

Guidelines

Preparation

1   Begin by defining clearly your objective(s) and your readership.
2   Plan your research. Begin by making two lists:
    ■ questions you want to ask
    ■ the people and places where you can expect to find an answer (or where you can get advice on relevant sources of information)
3   Use your lists to help you schedule your research.

Writing the report

The main items a report can contain are:

4   **A table of contents**

5   **An executive summary**. Use this to state clearly and concisely what the report is about and what it discovered. You may also wish to include your principal recommendations here. (But see 9, below.)

6   **An introduction**. Use this to explain the history of the commissioning of the report, its terms of reference, how it was conducted, and any other important background information.

7   **The body of the report**. Here you should set out the main information

which your research uncovered and the conclusions that you draw from it. If the material is dense and/or detailed, you may prefer to place the detail in one or more appendices and refer to it through footnotes.

8 **The conclusions**. It is often a good idea to repeat the conclusions you reached again in a separate section, referring back to relevant sections of the report as necessary.

9 **The recommendations**. You can list these separately after the *conclusions*, or place them in or after the *executive summary*.

10 **Appendices**. Use these for material such as detailed research data, a description of the research methodology, and case studies.

11 **Bibliography**. This should contain details of all published and unpublished texts quoted or referred to, following one of the conventional styles.

9 Essays, papers, and dissertations

Preparation
- Defining the subject and analysing questions
- Generating ideas
- Research
- Ordering your material

Writing
- Style
- Using quotations and references

Dissertations
- Structure
- Writing approach
- Other considerations

What the report is to the business world, the essay, paper, and dissertation are to the academic community. From the sixth-form essay to the Ph.D. thesis, the writing of an extended piece of prose is used to demonstrate and measure the writer's grasp of a given subject.

There is, however, a major difference between these two types of writing. A manager normally reads a report in order to learn new information about a topic—the writer knows more about the subject than the reader. A university lecturer reads a paper or dissertation in order to judge how well the writer has understood the subject; here the reader probably knows more about the subject than the writer.

This is one of the reasons why some students have writing problems. It seems artificial to be telling the reader something that he or she already knows. In addition, the dissertation is almost certainly by far the longest piece of writing the student has ever undertaken; the task seems daunting. It seems impossible to prepare, initiate, and then control such an extended piece of prose, even leaving aside the additional difficulties caused by one's uncertainty about the purpose and audience of such a text.

Such a view is not uncommon and can be crippling, but there is a positive side to each of the negatives it contains. The fact that the reader already has a good knowledge of the subject means that there is no need to provide a lot of low-level explanation at the outset. The academic context means that there are well-established conventions for structuring and composing this type of writing—and readily available research material. The situation in which it is written means that plenty of time is allowed for writing it. Most important of all, extended writing of this type allows the writer really to get to grips with a substantial subject and come to understand it fully.

This chapter goes through the process of writing an essay, paper, or dissertation step by step. For convenience it refers to an 'essay' throughout, but this should be taken to refer to the whole range of writing of this type. The main differences between an essay on the one hand and a dissertation on the other are that the dissertation is much longer and has a more elaborate formal structure. This is dealt with at the end.

In this chapter the various stages of writing are covered fairly briefly. Readers who wish to study the subject in more depth should turn to Section D of this book, *The process of writing*, where four chapters are devoted to it.

Preparation

It is difficult to write at any length without some form of preparation. Nevertheless it is surprising how many writers do just launch themselves into writing straightaway, only to find that after a page or two they come to a halt, uncertain as to how to proceed. Planning may be a lengthy process, but it need not be. How much you do depends on the subject, how well you know it, and how much research you need to do.

Defining the subject

Some of the problems a writer may face arise because the subject of the essay has not been clearly defined or understood. Sometimes teachers set topics that are imprecise or vaguely worded. But if students just go along with this and write the essay without trying to define the subject more precisely, then they only have themselves to blame. It is better either to tackle the person who set the subject and ask them to clarify it, or, failing that, to redefine it yourself. (If you do this, you should, of course, make it clear that you have done so.)

'Not answering the question' *may* be the fault of the questioner. More often, however, it is the fault of the writer, who has not thought carefully enough about what the question means. A good starting point is to ask yourself, 'What is the question asking me to *do*?' Essay questions often provide helpful clues to what is expected. For example:

1 What is the likely impact of the Internet on British business?
2 What is meant by 'factoring'?
3 In *King Lear*, Gloucester and Lear both learn through suffering. In what other ways are they similar and how might their circumstances be said to be different?
4 'In 1997 Britain was in danger of becoming a one-party state.' Discuss.
5 What were the main events leading up to the Hundred Years' War?

Each of these questions asks the writer to perform a different task:

■ **Analyse**
   Question 1 asks the writer to examine a particular phenomenon and analyse its likely effects. Analytical questions ask the writer to

See also:

■ **Chapter 15** *Different ways of communicating* (p. 123)

tease out the significant features of a situation, to describe them, and to explain why they are significant.

■ **Define**

Question 2 asks for a definition of an economic term. The writer is required to list its defining features and to support this definition by reference to good examples from the real world.

■ **Compare and contrast**

Question 3 refers to two characters from a play who have similarities and differences and asks the writer to set these out. The question does not ask the writer to describe one character, describe the other, and then compare them. Instead the writer has to find key features of similarity and difference and build the essay up around these.

■ **Argue a case**

Question 4 puts a challenging interpretation of a piece of recent history and asks the writer to examine the two sides of the argument and evaluate them.

■ **Narrate**

Here the writer is being asked to tell a story. The danger of narrative is that writing it seems easy: anyone can tell a story and many people enjoy doing so. As a result writers often fall back on narrative, when they should be analysing, defining, or arguing.

Each of these types of question has its own distinctive structures and approaches. Sometimes questions are 'pure' examples of one type, as in the examples quoted. Often they are hybrids, combining two or more types in one question.

Generating ideas

See also:

■ **Chapter 23** *Planning and research* (p. 239)

Once you have analysed the wording of the question and decided what kind of question it is, you can begin to develop your ideas. It is a good idea to 'think on paper'. In its simplest form this just involves jotting down a **list** of ideas as they occur to you:

> Main events leading up to Hundred Years' War
>
> growth of nationalism
> competing economic interests
> increasing contradictions of feudalism and growth of royal power

Some questions lend themselves to putting ideas into two or more columns:

> | Lear/Gloucester similarities | Differences |
> |---|---|
> | both 'blind' about children | At start of play Lear has absolute power, Gloucester doesn't |
> | both deceived and then humiliated by favoured child(ren) | |

An alternative is the 'web' or 'spider' diagram:

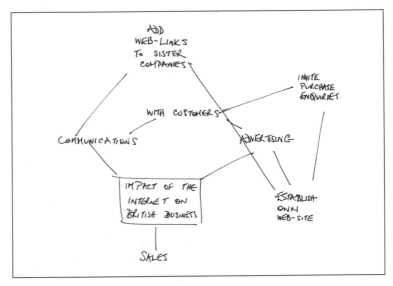

Research

See also:
■ **Chapter 23 *Planning and research*** (p. 239), where this subject is covered in much more detail.

Three key points to remember about effective research are:

- Make effective notes. (Although taking notes is more laborious than making photocopies, notes are often more useful because they force you to focus on the text and determine its key points.)
- Keep a careful record of the source of all material, including full bibliographical details.
- Distinguish carefully between information and ideas that you have abstracted from a source and direct quotations. Otherwise you risk using someone else's words as if they were your own (plagiarising).

Ordering your material

See also:
■ **Chapter 23 *Planning and research*** (p. 239)

Once your ideas and material have been developed, you can begin to order them into a logical sequence. How you do this will be determined by the demands of the question and how you have decided to respond to it.

1 You need to decide first how many main sections there should be, apart from an introduction and a conclusion. There should be enough to encompass all the ideas you have generated, but few enough for the pattern of the essay to be clear to the reader.
2 You should decide how best to order these sections so that your material can be presented in a logical and interesting way.
3 You can then arrange your material, fitting all your ideas into the relevant sections.
4 Now decide how you will introduce your essay and conclude it. The introduction needs to indicate the approach you propose to take, but should avoid giving the game away right at the start. If you tell the reader everything that you are going to say in the course of the first paragraph, there is little incentive to read on. Similarly the conclusion should refer to the main points you have made without being repetitive; but if possible you should save up a telling, interesting, or amusing point for the conclusion, so that the reader's interest is held until the very last sentence.

Writing

See also:
- **Chapter 11** *Audience* (p. 89)
- **Chapter 24** *Writing, drafting, and revising* (p. 256)

The process of writing is covered in detail later in this book. Here two key points are worth stressing.

1   It is important to achieve the right 'tone of voice' in your writing. The convention is that essays, papers, and dissertations are written in a fairly impersonal and formal style. This convention is worth respecting unless there are good reasons for doing otherwise. Among other things it usually means that you should write in normally paragraphed prose rather than using bullet points or other similar devices.

2   If your essay is going to be cogent and coherent, it needs to be built up of carefully constructed paragraphs. In particular you need to look carefully at the way in which paragraphs are linked. The reader should be led naturally and easily from one key point to the next without sudden leaps or unexplained changes of topic.

Quotations and references

See also:
- **Chapter 8** *Reports* (p. 62)

Make sure that it is clear when you are quoting directly from another person. Short quotations can go into the body of your text, marked off by quotation marks. Longer quotations should be separated and indented.

All quotations should be properly attributed. In an essay of any length it is better to list all works referred to separately at the end. They can then be referred to briefly, as described on pages 68–9.

Dissertations

In essence, a dissertation is an extended essay, but saying this can be misleading. Once a piece of writing reaches a certain length a number of problems arise—mainly because the reader finds it increasingly difficult to keep a grasp of what is going on. The writer, therefore, needs to keep checking that the reader is still following the argument. This is partly a question of structure and partly one of writing approach.

Structure

Readers need as many structural devices as possible to help them keep track of the argument. These can include:

- **A table of contents**
- **An introduction** explaining the nature of the subject, the treatment, and the reasons for choosing this approach.
- **Division of the text into sections or chapters**. Each should be treated as an essay in its own right with:
  - an introduction which introduces the subject matter and explains its link to what has gone before
  - a conclusion which sums up the main points and leads on to the next section.

- **A conclusion** which sums up the entire argument, referring back, where necessary, to specific sections of the main text.
- **A bibliography** and list of other sources used.

It is worth pointing out, however, that different universities and other institutions have their own 'rules' about how a text should be structured. Some, for example, say that sub-headings are unacceptable, while to others bullet points are not to be used.

Writing approach

See also:
- **Chapter 24** *Writing , drafting, and revisng* (p. 256), where this subject is covered in much greater detail.

A dissertation can be anything up to 10,000 words long. Inevitably you will need to write more than one draft. Some sections will probably go through several drafts before you are satisfied with them. Many colleges that require a dissertation as part of a final assessment require students to submit a full first draft for comment by a supervising tutor before the final draft is begun.

As you write, you should try to carry in your mind the structure of the whole dissertation, being aware of how what you are writing at this particular moment relates to what has gone before and what is yet to come. When you are working on a first draft this is difficult to achieve, but it is certainly something you should remember when you come to redraft a section. As you read the first draft through, keep checking how the parts relate to each other and asking yourself whether you are providing sufficient signposts for your readers as they travel with you from the beginning to the end.

Above all, make use of whatever help other people can give you. All writers, however skilful and experienced, depend on constructive criticism from people whose judgement they trust.

Other considerations

See also:
- **Chapter 25** *Getting it on the page* (p. 268),
- **Chapter 26** *Using technology* (p. 277), where this subject is covered in much greater detail.

As was noted above, many institutions provide detailed guidelines on how to prepare a dissertation, which must, of course, be followed. These will almost certainly include the question of presentation. Any set of dissertations submitted for assessment will almost certainly divide into three categories:

- those which fail to observe the presentation guidelines given to students
- those which do the minimum required
- those whose writers have used the guidelines and have done everything in their power to make their work as clear and reader-friendly as possible

Given the pressures of time and workload under which the assessors have to work, there are no prizes for guessing which dissertations will receive the most favourable treatment.

Guidelines

Note

There is more detailed guidance on the processes of writing in Section D:
Chapter 23: Planning and research (p. 239)
Chapter 24: Writing, drafting, and revising (p. 256)
Chapter 25: Getting it on the page (p. 268)
Chapter 26: Using technology (p. 277)

1 Begin by analysing the question to make sure that you understand not only the **content** of your writing, but also the **approach** and **type of writing** that are required.

2 Generate ideas on paper, using lists, columns, or web diagrams.

3 Do your research, making sure that:
   - you make detailed notes
   - you distinguish carefully between quotations and your own words
   - you keep a detailed record of books and articles you refer to

4 Produce a written plan ordering your material into a small number of main sections, giving the essay an introduction and a conclusion.

5 When you write the text, use an impersonal and fairly formal style.

6 Make sure that your paragraphs are carefully constructed, with 'hooks' linking them to the paragraphs which precede and follow them.

7 Mark off short quotations with quotation marks and longer ones by starting a new line and indenting the whole quotation. Make sure that all quoted material is correctly attributed, using a bibliography at the end of the essay and a brief textual reference at the point of quotation.

Dissertations

8 Use structural devices such as a table of contents, separate sections, an introduction, and a conclusion to make your text as 'transparent' as possible to the reader.

9 Be aware of the needs of your readers as you write and redraft.

10 Present the final draft in as polished and reader-friendly a way as possible.

10 Meeting the media

There are two common ways in which one may expect to encounter the media in everyday life and work:

- the press release
- the interview

These are the subject matter of this chapter.

Writing a press release

If you have something you wish to publicize, then you should aim to have it reported in local, regional, or national press, radio, or TV. It is always possible, of course, to buy advertising space and put your message across in that way. But getting a report in the press or on the air has the distinct advantage of being free. Reports are also—sometimes at least—given more attention and credence.

You might wonder why a newspaper or local radio station should be interested in the news you wish to promote. They may well not be particularly interested, but they almost certainly need it. The media have a voracious appetite for material; the radio or television station has so many hours of airtime to fill, and the newspaper so many column inches to occupy. Their resources for collecting material are limited, so ready-made news is a godsend—provided that it is interesting to their audience (or can be made so) and is in a form that is easy to use.

The commonest way of contacting the media with a story that you would like them to publish is to issue a press release. This can either be distributed to the newsdesks of the outlets you wish to contact (preferably preceded by a personal contact to make sure that the right person gets the release and knows what it is about), or it can be issued at a press conference to which reporters are invited.

Before constructing a press release, it is worth studying how news reports are put together. If you can pattern your text on actual report style you will make the journalist's job a lot easier and so increase the chances of getting the story published. The report that follows is taken from a regional newspaper and could well have originated in a press release. The main features of the story's structure are shown alongside.

See also:
■ **Chapter 8** *Reports*
(p. 62), where the other common type of report is described—very different, of course, from the press report.

Heading

LEE'S A HIGH FLIER

Subhead

His career is taking off and now at 20 he's teaching others to be pilots

Lead paragraph

PILOT Lee Bayliss is reaching new heights of expertise in his soar-away career.

Main story

He has become Britain's youngest flying instructor at the age of 20. Lee had his first flying lesson for his 13th birthday, earned his pilot's licence at 17 and got a commercial licence a year later.

Now Lee, from Twyning, near Tewkesbury, whose ambition is to become an airline pilot, has become an instructor at the South Warwickshire flying school at Stratford upon Avon.

'I decided I wanted to fly when I was four,' he said. 'My mother worries about me. She stopped my father flying because she thought it was too dangerous, but I wouldn't stop.'

Interesting details

Lee worked in a flour factory and took other temporary jobs to raise the £18,000 needed to finance his high-flying career.

He caught the flying bug while jetting off with his parents Tony and Heather on family holidays.

Background information

Mr Bayliss, aged 47, works as a civil engineer while Lee's brother, also called Tony, 22, runs the family's smallholding.

'My husband never took his pilot's licence because I was unhappy about him flying,' said Mrs Bayliss.

'I went up with him in a light-aircraft once and didn't like it one bit.

Comments by people involved

'I tried to talk Lee out of it but he was determined that it was something he wanted to do.

'I still worry about him and I make sure that he always rings me after going up to put my mind at rest.'

Flying-school principal Rodney Galiffe said Lee flew through his exams and got first-time passes in all of them.

'We've checked it out and he definitely is the youngest instructor,' he said.

'He did everything as quickly as possible and qualified as an instructor in the shortest possible time.'

At first sight the ordering of information in a news story like this seems rather wayward. It appears to jump around in time so that a lot of events that happened at the beginning of the real story (like Lee working to earn money for his lessons) come nowhere near the beginning of the news report. There is a good reason for this, however. Most people do not read a newspaper like a novel, beginning on page 1 and working steadily through until they reach the end. They dot around, scanning a page until something interesting catches their eye. Then they may read just part of the report before moving on again.

The structure of the story about Lee Bayliss is based on this habit of reading. It begins with a **heading** and **sub-heading** designed to catch the eye. The **lead paragraph** continues this approach before the succeeding two or three paragraphs tell the **main story** briefly and clearly. At this point some readers will opt out, but others will be more interested and will have the patience to read on. So the remainder of the report offers more **interesting details** about the main story, **background information** and, if available, **comments by people involved**. This has the added advantage of extending the human interest of the story.

Constructing a press release

When you construct a press release, you should bear all this in mind:

1 Give it a **heading** designed to inform readers what the story is about but which also catches their interest.
2 If appropriate add a **sub-heading** and/or a **lead paragraph** which develops interest and leads into the main story.
3 Tell the **main story** in two or three *short* paragraphs.
4 Follow this with one or two paragraphs containing **interesting details** and another two or three which provide **background information**.
5 If you have any useful **quotations or comments**, use these to round the story off.

Whenever possible, give the story a human-interest angle. For example your press release may be about the company's success in doubling its overseas sales of portable crop sprayers; but if your sales director has just returned from an interesting and unusual trip to remote parts of East Africa, use this as a key feature of the story to attract interest.

Two other key features should always appear in a press release. At the beginning the reader should be told when the story can be used. If it is **for immediate use**, then this should be stated. Otherwise it should be made clear that the story is **embargoed until . . .** followed by the time and date when it can be used.

At the end of the story should be stated the name of the person who can be contacted for further information and their contact details.

The media interview

The interview with press, radio, or TV may come about as a result of a press release, it may be deliberately set up by the organization of which you are a member, or it may come out of the blue.

FOR IMMEDIATE USE

MIKRON SALES REACH NEW RECORD

ORDER BOOK DOUBLES AFTER ADVENTUROUS FOREIGN SALES TOUR BY
PIONEERING MIKRON TEAM

Mikron Sales Director Andrew Bruce found himself face to face
with an elephant on a lonely Tanzanian road while promoting sales
of the company's revolutionary new knapsack crop sprayer.

The two-month journey to Kenya, Uganda, and Tanzania was part of
Mikron's 1997 drive to top 2 million sales overseas by the end
of the year. Andrew Bruce travelled over 5000 miles on dusty
tropical roads, visiting regional agricultural advisers,
government officials, and leading farmers.

His tour was a triumphant success and the company now has full
order books for the rest of the year. It is planning to take on
10 new fulltime staff at its Wolverhampton factory.

But the trip had its worrying moments, as the Mikron Sales
Director found when his Landrover broke down in central Tanzania.
He was just figuring out what to do, when he turned round and saw
he was being approached at some speed by an inquisitive elephant.

'Fortunately he saw that I wasn't a threat and made off,' said
the 33-year-old Birmingham man. 'But I have to admit I was a bit
worried at the time.'

Mikron Crop Sprayers opened on the Langford Road Industrial
Estate in 1991 with a workforce of just three. The last six years
have seen the company grow until it now has a turnover of £10
million and employs 23 staff.

Its main products are knapsack-style sprayers with a simple
battery-operated pump, which are robust, easy to use and repair,
and have an average lifetime of five years. These are
particularly effective against the many insect pests that
threaten crops of coffee, tea, and cotton in tropical Africa.

'We have a very healthy pattern of investment and technical
development,' said Managing Director George Green. 'There is no
reason why 1998 should not see even further rapid growth.'

----15TH JANUARY 1998------------ENDS------------------

For further information, please contact:

Jennie Haswell, Press Officer
Mikron Crop Sprayers Ltd
Phone: 01873 467590
Fax: 01873 467591

See also:
■ **Chapter 5** *Interviews*
(p. 37), which covers
job interviews.

As remarked earlier, the media have a hunger for new material. This does not mean, however, that if you agree to an interview they will necessarily give you an easy time. You may well find that your agenda and that of the person interviewing you are radically different. In fact, as likely as not you will. This is not surprising. Journalists are entertainers; if they fail to keep the interest of their audience, they fail totally. This means that every interview involves a search for the unusual, the entertaining, the controversial . . . anything that keeps the reader reading, the listener listening, and the viewer watching.

So you may find that the interview you agreed to give on the economics of farming in North Herefordshire suddenly turns into a heated debate about the ethics of factory farming, or the measured discussion of the merits of secondary-school selection develops into a harangue about falling standards in our schools.

The answer is to be prepared. This may sound paradoxical in the case of the unexpected interview, but it isn't really.

As far as possible it is important to keep control of the terms of the interview. Unless you are desperate to be interviewed and the interviewer is less than enthusiastic, you can normally achieve quite a lot simply because you have got something that the interviewer wants: a slice of your time. So you can make demands and bargain. In particular you should give thought to the advice that follows.

Where and when the interview takes place

Journalists like to keep control of when and where an interview takes place. A press reporter or a radio journalist will often prefer to do the interview by phone; it is easier and saves time. Telephone interviews are also frequently used by TV. If you are happy about that, fine; otherwise insist on a face-to-face meeting at your convenience.

Telephone interviews have the advantage that you can do them at home or in the office, and so have any necessary notes and other documents to hand. They have the disadvantage—especially in the case of radio and TV—that ultimate control tends to rest with the interviewer, who can always switch you off with ease and poise, whereas unless you are very experienced you will probably just sound petulant if you put the phone down.

If you are literally or metaphorically buttonholed by a reporter—in the street, or by telephone—refuse to give an interview unless you are sure you want to. Find out what the interviewer wants and arrange a meeting so that you have time to prepare yourself.

For a face-to-face interview, try to ensure that it is arranged at a time and place to suit you, so that you are relaxed, in familiar surroundings and not under pressure of time.

The terms of the interview

As noted earlier, your agenda and that of the interviewer may well be different. Ask the interviewer to explain the kind of questions that will be asked. Think carefully about what you are and are not prepared to discuss in public. Explain the guidelines you wish to be observed and make it clear that you mean business. If the journalist goes outside these—and you can be sure that if it does it won't be accidental—point this out and, if necessary, terminate the interview.

Preparing for the interview

However well you lay down your own guidelines, the interview may well develop into a battle for the agenda. You therefore need to have a clear idea of:

- the topics you want to talk about
- any topics that are off limits
- topics the interviewer may want to raise which you think are less important, or wish to avoid

Suppose, for example, you are the representative of a group promoting traffic-calming measures in your locality. The dangers caused by the pressure and speed of traffic in the area, and the advantages of different traffic-calming schemes are the topics you wish to discuss. Recently, however, the chair of your group resigned after an acrimonious row, news of which soon became public. This is human interest that a journalist might wish to question you about but which you, reasonably, do not wish to discuss, so it is something you should place off limits. On the other hand the questioner may also want to ask you about your career as a rally driver—more human interest. This is an irrelevance as far as you are concerned, but you can expect questions about it and should look to turn them back to your chosen topics. You could point out, for example, that rally drivers are highly trained and drive on roads that are closed to the general public but that many drivers have a fantasy that they are rally drivers when they are driving along the B4224, which is what causes the danger to pedestrians.

If you need to quote facts and figures in the interview, it is a good idea to prepare notes to which you can refer while it is in progress. For a press or radio interview on home ground there is no problem about referring to these, as long as you don't make it too obvious and—in the case of radio—make too much noise rustling paper. In other situations, such as the live TV interview, you will have to use them to refresh your memory before the interview and hope to keep the information clear in your mind that way.

It is a good idea to practise giving answers that are pithy and, if possible, striking, but above all *short*. This is the age of the sound-bite and there are two good reasons for accepting this situation and working within it. First, your interview may well be heavily edited and you will help that process considerably if you provide plenty of 'quotable quotes'. Secondly, even if the whole interview is broadcast, many listeners will find it much easier to grasp if you concentrate the information and ideas you are giving into neat and digestible 10–15 second 'bites'.

The interview itself

Interviews can be stressful occasions. You probably only do interviews very occasionally, while the interviewer is doing this sort of thing every day of the week. However carefully you have prepared, it is difficult to control what will happen. The interviewer is the professional and has immediate control of what happens in the interview as well as, in many cases, ultimate control of how it will be edited and used. (If you are seriously concerned about being misrepresented, it is a useful idea to make your own recording of the original interview as a check on the way in which it is edited.)

Even if you are feeling stressed about the situation, it is important to appear as relaxed and confident as possible. Don't be rushed into the interview; sometimes radio journalists interviewing by phone launch into their questions after the briefest of introductions. Slow them down by greeting them; take your time.

As the interview progresses, you will probably find that your confidence increases. This should be good for the authority with which you respond to questions, but avoid the dangers of overconfidence. It is easy to say something which you later regret. If in doubt, shut up.

Many interviewers on radio or TV make use of silence as a way of getting their subjects to say more than they originally intended:

> Silence is a wonderful prompter. People—if you don't say anything when they've finished—think, 'Oh, I'd better go on.' So they say something else and very often the thing that they say after that silence is the very thing that you wanted them to say all the time. That's the way to get the last thing out.
>
> **Jenni Mills, broadcaster and writer**

It is difficult to let a silence just hang in the air without feeling you have to break it, but if you have said everything you want to, that is what it is best to do.

During the interview, remember that the interviewer has an agenda and will be constantly guiding the interview so that that agenda is covered. You too have an agenda; if it is not being covered, seek out opportunities to redirect the conversation towards it. (If you want to see how this is done, listen to interviews with politicians; they are experts in this field.)

Above all, don't lose your temper. If you feel that the line of questioning is becoming too personal or is, in some other way, impertinent, remain polite and simply decline to answer. If the journalist persists, turn the questions against your questioner:

A: So how much does a top writer like yourself get paid for an article like this?

B: I'm sorry, I don't answer questions about my private business affairs.

A: Oh come on. I mean this is a matter of public interest. How much would you get for it?

B: Probably no more than you do for doing this interview. How much does the BBC pay you for a day's work?

And, of course, the journalist won't answer that one!

Assessing the result Finally, when the interview is over, it is useful to weigh up how it went and seek to learn from what you did. Read the newspaper report based on a press interview; watch or listen to the recording of the broadcast interview. Look out for points where you could have expressed yourself more clearly, and occasions where you could have steered the conversation on to more useful ground. Don't, however, be too self-critical if you don't think you have completely succeeded. Many interviews are compromises. The journalist gets some of the answers he or she wants, while you make some but not all of the points on your list. An interview that you are dissatisfied with is much more likely to be an honourable draw than an out-and-out defeat.

Guidelines

Press release

1 Bear in mind the needs of the journalist when writing your press release.

2 Give it a heading designed to inform readers what the story is about but which also catches their interest.

3 If appropriate add a sub-heading and/or a lead paragraph which develops interest and leads into the main story.

4 Tell the main story in two or three short paragraphs.

5 Follow this with one or two paragraphs containing interesting details and another two or three which provide background information.

6 If you have any useful quotations or comments, use these to round the story off.

7 At the head of the first page state when the story can be used.

8 At the end give the name and contact details of a person who can provide further information.

Media interview

1 Remember that normally the interviewer needs the interview as much as or more than you.

2 Try to organize the time and place of the interview so that they suit you. At least make sure that you are not interviewed at a time and place that you find difficult or inhibiting.

3 Discuss the terms of the interview and make clear any topics that are off limits.

4 Make sure that you have clear in your mind the points that you want to make.

5 Think about topics that the interviewer may wish to pursue and how you can use them to your advantage.

6 Make notes of any facts, figures, or quotations that you wish to use. If possible have these available during the interview.

7 During the interview, relax as much as possible and try to impose your own pace on it, rather than being hurried.

8 Remember the dangers of overconfidence and don't be led to say things that you will later regret.

9 Don't be pressured by silence into saying more than you intended.

10 Keep your temper and, if necessary, refuse to answer improper questions or deflect them back on to the interviewer.

11 Afterwards assess your performance and note points to remember for future interviews.

Getting the Message Across

11: Audience   We need to be aware of the needs of our audience when writing and speaking. We need to consider their language skills, education, and level of comprehension; their knowledge and understanding of the subject matter; and the relationship we have with them. These three factors will help us choose the best vocabulary, sentence structures, and general style for our purpose.

12: Subject   The subject matter we are writing or speaking about has important effects on the language we use. We need to be precise, and to use the correct terminology required by the subject. On the other hand, we have to try not to use language that is too difficult for our audience; to confuse or irritate them with jargon; or to offend them by being too blunt or too coy. We also need to avoid excessive use of clichés.

13: Time and place   Time and place affect the language we use and the messages we give to each other. We need to be aware of this—especially of how particular situations and institutions tend to determine what we feel we can and cannot say and write.

14: Purpose   All communication takes place for a purpose. Is it to inform, to enquire, to interact, to influence, to regulate, to entertain, to record, or some combination of these? Being aware of our purpose can help us decide our overall approach and select the most suitable vocabulary, sentence structures, and style.

15: Different ways of communicating   Traditionally people believed that there were four ways of writing and speaking: narrative (story-telling), description, exposition (explanation), and argument. This fourfold approach is still a useful way of looking at the process of communication, especially when we are required to write at any length.

11 Audience

When we communicate we should be aware of our audience.

Language skills and intelligence

This involves considering:
- age
- education
- intelligence

Assessing the readability of a text includes a consideration of:
- sentence length
- vocabulary

Knowledge and understanding

It is important to:
- be aware of how much the audience is likely to know about the subject
- check their understanding, or give them opportunities to plug gaps in their knowledge as necessary

The relationship between speaker/writer and audience

We need to consider:
- how well we know them
- how formal we wish to be

This affects:
- vocabulary
- sentence grammar

Communication takes place in social situations. When you speak or write you need to think about your audience. You need to consider:

- their language skills
- their knowledge of the subject
- your relationship with them

Language skills and intelligence

You should begin by assessing how skilfully the reader or listener can use the language. For example, it would be unwise to assume that a five-year-old will be able to cope with long and complicated sentences containing many long and unusual words. On the other hand highly educated adults will not take kindly to being addressed as if they had the understanding of five-year-olds.

The three factors we need to bear in mind are:

- age
- education
- intelligence

Writing for children

You can see the importance of readability very clearly if you look at writing for young children. Experienced writers in this field know that they must use:

- a controlled vocabulary
- a limited range of sentence structures

This is illustrated by these two extracts from information books describing how the human eye works:

A   In the middle of each eye there is a small black hole covered by clear skin. It is called your pupil.

Your pupils are like windows. They let in the light rays from everything you look at.

If it is quite dark your pupils get bigger to collect more light. If it is very bright, your pupils get smaller to let less light in.

B   An image of what you are looking at is focused on the retina, which contains about 126 million light-sensitive cells. These cells are divided into two types—rod cells and cone cells. They get their names from their shapes. The brain gets a constant stream of messages from the rods and cones. These messages are transmitted to the brain along the optic nerve.

Rod cells only make a black and white image, so they send black and white messages to the brain. The good thing about rods is that they need only a little light to work. Because there is so much light during the day, the rods are permanently activated. When you first enter a darkened room, you have difficulty seeing things. This is because it takes the rods a few minutes to become dark-adapted.

The child for whom 'A' is suitable will struggle with 'B'. It contains difficult words such as *focused*, *retina*, *light-sensitive* and the sentences are longer and more complicated. Conversely, the child for whom 'B' is suitable will find 'A' boring and childish. Both writers have worked hard to make their texts suitable for their intended audience. We can see this by comparing them with a text on the same subject written for adults:

C   The amount of light entering the eye is restricted by the aperture in the iris, the pupil.

When a person is in a dark room, his pupil is large, perhaps eight millimetres (0.3 inch) in diameter, or more. When the room is lighted there is an immediate constriction of the pupil, the light reflex; this is bilateral, so that even if only one eye is exposed to the light both pupils contract to nearly the same extent. After a time the pupils expand even though the bright light is maintained, but the expansion is not large. The final state is determined by the actual degree of illumination; if this is high, then the final state may be a diameter of only about three to four millimetres (about 0.15 inch); if it is not so high, then the initial constriction may be nearly the same, but the final state may be with a pupil of four to five millimetres (about 0.18 inch).

Here there are far more difficult words, but what really makes the text harder to read is the length and complexity of the sentences. Many adults would struggle to follow this text at a first reading.

Writing for adults

A very common mistake made by those who write for adults is that they underestimate the problems their audience may have in reading their text. Journalists, whose livelihood depends on effective written communication, are very aware of their audience. Newspapers provide a good example of how writers approach different audiences. Compare these two reports of the same news story:

D

ROCK TURNS TO GOLD FOR 1M INVESTORS

MORE than a million building society customers are heading for handouts of up to £1,475. They'll cash in when Northern Rock launches on the stock market in October.

Free shares worth a maximum £1,475 go to all 900,000 savers and borrowers with the Newcastle-based firm. But around 100,000 people with mortgages and savings accounts receive TWO handouts.

And the 2,500 staff qualify for THREE windfalls as workers are being rewarded with a payout on top of money from home loans and savings. Another 150,000 people who miss out on the £1.25 billion shares handout will share £4 million in cash bonuses.

Reward

Director David Baker says: 'The vast majority of our members will do well out of this.'

Bosses, headed by £330,000-a-year chief executive Chris Sharp, won't take the staff payout.

But they won't have to wait long for a reward—the firm plans a share perks scheme next year.

Customers had to have £50 in their account before April 2 last year and £100 by December 31 1996 to qualify. They now need to keep just £1 in their account until October to share in the bonanza.

Charities benefit under plans for the Northern Rock Foundation which will receive five per cent of profits a year.

That would have been £8 million this year with cash going to charities for the homeless.

But at least £1 million will be handed to organizations for the disabled this year.

It's being given because many disabled people are missing out in the windfall because they are not the first-named person on savings accounts.

E **Northern Rock to pay £1,500 in shares**

Retailers in the North-east are anticipating a mini-boom after Northern Rock Building Society floats on the stock market in the autumn and distributes free shares worth almost £1,500 to each of its members. Northern Rock, based in Newcastle, is the smallest of the societies which plan to convert to banks this year but is paying out the greatest windfall to its 900,000 members, half of whom are in the North-east of England. The flotation is scheduled for 1 October. The transfer document, published yesterday, unveiled a 'flat' distribution scheme similar to the controversial one chosen by Alliance & Leicester. Regardless of the balance in their accounts, all eligible savers and borrowers with Northern Rock will receive 500 shares.

David Baker, executive director of Northern Rock, said this distribution scheme for the shares was the most suitable for members. In a bid to avoid controversy caused by the inability of other converting societies to distribute free shares to some disabled members, Northern Rock intends to give a £1m donation to charities for the disabled and their carers. One in three households in the North-east is expected to receive the shares, which are forecast to be worth between 260p and 295p. The total value of the allocation will be worth between £1,300 and £1,475. The exact value of the shares will be known on 1 October when the society expects its stock market flotation to go ahead. Members must vote on the flotation plans by post by 12 April or at a meeting at Newcastle Arena on 15 April.

Readability

'D' is from a tabloid, while 'E' comes from a broadsheet. Analysing why 'D' is easier to read than 'E' will help to highlight some of the issues involved in readability.

Sentence length

Both texts are the same length, yet 'D' has 15 sentences while 'E' only has 10. So the sentences in 'E' are one and a half times as long as those in 'D'. Compare:

D But at least £1 million will be handed to organizations for the disabled this year.

It's being given because many disabled people are missing out in the windfall because they are not the first-named person on savings accounts.

(2 sentences, one of 15 words and one of 22 words)

E In a bid to avoid controversy caused by the inability of other converting societies to distribute free shares to some disabled members, Northern Rock intends to give a £1m donation to charities for the disabled and their carers.

(1 sentence of 38 words)

See also:
- **Chapter 17** *Introduction to grammar* (p. 153)
- **Chapter 18** *More about grammar* (p. 167)

Advocates of 'Plain English' usually recommend that average sentence length in a text should not exceed 15–20 words. In 'D' the average is 16, while in 'E' it is 26.

Another thing that can cause problems for the reader is the use of too many long words.

What is a 'long' word? Any word of three or more syllables, but excluding:

- personal names and place names
- verbs which are over two syllables because they have had -*ing*, -*ed*, or -*es* added
- plural nouns which are over two syllables because they have had -*es* added

Using this definition 'D' contains 18 long words, while 'E' has 29.

The Fog Index A simple mathematical way of assessing readability is the Fog Index. It was devised by the American Robert Gunning, who considered that the more a writer uses long sentences and long words, the more the clarity of the text is 'fogged'. It is calculated like this:

1 Take a sample of about 100 words, ending with the end of a sentence.
2 Count the number of sentences and divide the number of words by the number of sentences to produce the average sentence length (ASL).
3 Count the number of long words (NLW).
4 Perform this calculation:
Fog index = (ASL + NLW) × 0.4

Using this formula a figure is produced on a scale of readability:

5   easy
10   more difficult
15   difficult
20   very difficult

A commonly used guideline is that the average 15-year-old can cope with texts with an index of 10 while the average level for university students is 14–16.

Extract 'D' has a Fog Index of 8.8, while that of 'E' is 14.4.

Length is not everything While calculations like the Fog Index are a handy short way of looking at a text (and certainly direct our attention to important features of readability) they do not give the full picture. Shorter sentences are not always easier to read. Compare these two:

1 What figure of us think you he will bear? (9 words)
2 How well do you think he will do when he acts as my representative? (15 words)

Also, not all long words are difficult to read, any more than all short ones are easy. Anyone who has helped a small child learn to read will know that it is not just the length of a word that causes problems. Children can sometimes read quite long words at a very early age. If a word is part of a child's spoken vocabulary and has a distinctive shape—like *elephant,* for example—then it may be recognized quite easily.

Similar considerations apply to adult readers. Extract 'D' contains few difficult long words. Most of the three-syllable words are in common use—like *customers* and *majority*. While 'E' has its share of such words, it also includes more demanding vocabulary like *distribution* and *flotation*. Clearly the more common a long word is the fewer problems it will cause the average reader.

The frequency with which words occur in normal use is another guide to difficulty; the less common a word, the more likely it is to cause problems. There are word lists which provide information on word frequency for use when writing texts for specific audiences; for example, when preparing textbooks for teaching English as a foreign language. The *Cambridge English Lexicon*, for example, lists a basic vocabulary for teachers of English as a foreign language. It grades words from 1 to 7, with level 1 being 'at beginner, or post-beginner level' and level 5 containing items that are 'approaching or at First Certificate in English level'. Levels 1 to 5 contain 4470 words. Where a word has more than one meaning or use, the *Lexicon* lists them separately:

> 5 **homeless** *adj.*
> 3 **home-made** *adj.*
> 2 **honest**
> 2 *adj.* not telling lies: *an honest man*
> 4 *adj.* showing character: *an honest face*
> 5 **honesty** *n.*
> 4 **honey** *n.*
> 3 **honour**
> 3 *n.* great respect: *in honour of the dead*
> 5 *n.* person bringing credit: *he is an honour to his family*
> 6 *v.* respect highly
> 7 *n.* good personal character: *on my honour*

> Roland Hindmarsh: *Cambridge English Lexicon*

Using a list like this can be fairly laborious and at times misleading. It is more generally useful to read reasonably widely in the general subject area about which you wish to write, and to write with an imaginative insight into the needs of your audience.

You try

These three extracts are all about the same subject, but are at different levels of difficulty. What kind of audience do you think each would be suitable for, and why?

A Mummies are the first things most people think about at the mention of Ancient Egypt, but what exactly are they and how and why were they made? Although the term 'mummy' is associated with Ancient Egypt, it is also applied to preserved bodies from many other cultures. The word itself comes from the Arabic name for 'bitumen', and was used to describe these bodies because their black appearance suggested that they had been coated in pitch. Most of the bandaged mummies that have survived date from the New Kingdom or the later half of Egyptian history. By this time, the embalming process, which had previously been reserved for royalty, became available to all who could afford it.

B The Ancient Egyptians were firm believers in life after death. But first you had to make sure your soul survived in the next world. This wouldn't happen if your body was left to rot away. And so you were mummified to make you last!

C Traditionally, the royal body was first washed and anointed, after which mortuary priests removed the viscera by way of a small incision in the left side of the abdomen. By the 18th dynasty, the removal of the brain was also common—usually through the nostrils, but occasionally in other ways (the cranial tissue of King Amosis was removed through an incision at the back of the neck). The liver, lungs, stomach and intestines were extracted, treated and stored in canopic containers and the body packed with absorbent materials which hastened the process of desiccation. The body was then placed on a slanted bed and covered with powdered natron. After 40 days the body would have lost some 75 per cent of its weight through the dehydrative action of this salt-like compound and it was then rewashed, dried, bandaged and adorned with protective amulets—each stage of the process being carried out with the recitation of appropriate spells and incantations.

Knowledge and understanding

Some audiences are self-defining. If you are preparing copy for an automotive parts catalogue, for example, it is reasonable to assume that your reader knows quite a lot about cars and how they work. On the other hand, the writer of 'The reluctant car mechanic' could not make such an assumption, but could safely expect that his readers were interested in the subject and willing to make the effort to understand what he was telling them.

These two texts about growing roses clearly assume very different audiences:

A   **Roses**
Preparation and Planting
All types of rose do best in a sunny well-drained area, but they are tough and will survive fairly unfavourable conditions. As always, make sure the ground is well prepared with animal manure, especially on light sandy soils, and the bottom of the planting hole broken up to ensure good drainage. The roots should be well spaced. Standards and half standards will need staking.

B   Culture of Dwarf Roses: Soil, deep, rich loam well enriched with decayed manure. Add clay and cow dung to light soils, road grit, leaf-mould, burnt refuse, horse dung and lime to heavy soils. Do not mix lime with manure but apply to surface after manure has been well dug in. Position, sunny beds or borders. Plant, Nov.; or Feb. to March, average distance apart 18 in. to 2 ft. Depth of soil over roots should be 4 to 6 in. on heavy and 7 to 8 in. on light soils. Prune end of March or early in April. Hybrid Perpetuals should have damaged and weak shoots removed and others shortened to dormant bud to 18 in. from base according to strength. . . .

Other situations are not so simple. Any writing done for 'a general audience' can be much more problematic. It is safest to assume little or no prior knowledge of your subject, unless you have good reason to believe otherwise. Far more people have been put off reading a text because they could not understand it than because they were offended at being treated like idiots. The latter can, in any case, be avoided by allowing for different levels of knowledge and making the structure of your text clear: 'The first part of this text is introductory and can be skipped by those who have some knowledge of the subject . . .'.

Checking the channel   In conversations, we can check that the assumptions we have made about another person's knowledge are correct. I can tell from my audience's facial expressions and other non-verbal signals (gestures, nods, grunts, and so on) whether my subject matter is one which is familiar and whether I am tackling it at the right level. In a written text this is more difficult, although sometimes it may be done quite explicitly. A letter may say, 'Please contact me for further details.' An instruction book can suggest, 'If you are not sure how to . . . , turn to page . . .'.

> **You try**
>
> These two texts both come from the introductions to instruction booklets for computer users. What level of knowledge do you think each assumes in its readers?
>
> **A Moving the monitor**
> Handle the monitor with care. Carry the monitor with its screen facing you (most of its weight is near the screen). If you have to bend to lift it, bend at your knees, not your waist. Leave a few inches behind the monitor clear when you position it so you can tilt and swivel it freely on its base.
>
> **B** The preparation of a drive or cartridge for use by Macintosh is done at three levels. The low level format writes over the entire disk, erasing all data. The partition operation divides the space on the drive into separate areas, or partitions, including one (or more) areas to hold your files. It also sets aside an area for a table of partitions, and an area for the software which operates the drive. Partitioning or re-partitioning your drive effectively erases any data held on it. The third layer . . .

What is the relationship?

Our relationship with our audience affects the way in which we frame even the most casual message. The better you know people, the more relaxed you can be about the way in which you express yourself to them. This works at many different levels. With a person you know very well, for example, you can use words that carry a special meaning which only they will understand. Some people have a complete private language reserved for a particular relationship. At the other end of the scale, we have to be much more careful when addressing people we do not know at all.

The choices speakers and writers make are often subtle and complicated and usually take place without conscious thought. But it is useful to set out some of the more obvious features of them.

One way of looking at the effects of relationship on language is to ask two simple questions:

- How well do we know each other?
- How close or distant do I want to be?

We can represent this on a simple diagram:

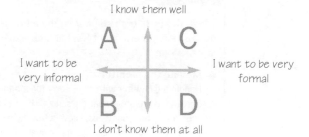

It might seem strange to think of communicating very formally with someone whom you know very well, but such situations can occur: for example, a letter about the distribution of family property from a husband to his wife following an acrimonious divorce.

Effects on language

How we view the relationship can affect:

- choice of vocabulary
- use of short forms in writing
- choice of pronouns
- choice of standard or non-standard grammar

Vocabulary

Some words are considered by many people to be informal, colloquial, slang, or even obscene. Dictionaries often indicate this by abbreviations, for example:

See also:
- **Chapter 19 _Vocabulary_** (p. 179)

colloq.   colloquial
inf.   informal
sl.   slang

Such definitions can be misleading, however. It is very difficult to draw a clear line between what is 'formal' and what is 'informal' language. Language is constantly developing as society changes; words come and go, and yesterday's slang is often acceptable today. For example, in Shakespeare's day, if you called someone _naughty_ it was a serious accusation of moral depravity. Today it is normally reserved as a term of mild reproof for children and if applied to adults is used ironically or archly. By contrast, Chaucer did not consider the word _shit_ unsuitable for a poem to be read aloud in mixed upper-class society, whereas it would not be acceptable in some social settings today.

Use of contractions in writing

With people we know and can relax with, it is quite acceptable to use contractions like _can't_ and _shouldn't_ in writing. In more formal settings this is still frowned on, although here usage is clearly on the move.

Choice of pronouns in writing

In this book I have made use of _I_ and _you_, when referring to the writer and the reader. This is considered by some people to be rather informal; they would prefer that the writer remained anonymous and the reader was referred to in the third person. Instead of writing:

If you are consulting this book, it probably means that you have a particular problem in mind.

they would prefer:

> Most people who consult a book like this do so because they have a particular problem in mind.

Dialects often use grammatical forms that are different from those of Standard English. A former leader of the Liberal Democrats when explaining the problem of his party's credibility gap in general elections told the story of a conversation he once had with a Devonian while he was out canvassing. He was told:

> Oh yes. Us do be proper Liberals, but us int goin to vote for they till they do come top of the polls, see?

Standard or non-standard grammar

Many people, including children, commonly switch between dialect and a more standard form of English according to their audience. For children, standard English is more suitable when talking to school-teachers, for example. On the other hand their peers might laugh at them if they used it in the playground. Similar shifting is done by many adults as they move from one social setting to another.

You try

There are certain situations in which people find it difficult to address their audience using the right tone. One of these is when writing letters to newspapers. The following letter was sent to a local newspaper shortly after the announcement that the local cathedral had accepted a donation from a company that processes battery-farmed chickens. What is wrong with it?

Cathedral support for Sun Valley?

How ennobling of Hereford Cathedral to broiler breeders as the presumed epicentre for our community's future new spiritual and ethic values, to be seen through your columns (intentionally or otherwise) as seeming to confer recent 'blessing' upon those involved in the trade's intensive factory-farming methods by accepting local charity from the profits of same to restore a part of its permanently crumbling edifice.

Nowadays, the 'established Church' desires to be perceived as 'Being-All Things-To-All-Men', a self-delusion by which she considers it 'Good-for-God's Business' and often AN Other's too!, the latter view relating to our cathedral's acceptance of charity from Hereford's (reported) 'largest employer'. That company will now doubtless be 'over-the-moon' as a result of the report of October 17.

Somewhat ironically, the very nature of that article could not avoid affording the donor great satisfaction in being given publicity (always eagerly sought) when involved in its chosen philanthropy.

At present, the company basks in its warm relationship with the Hereford Cathedral authorities.

This seems tantamount to it believing that our cathedral condones, even if it does not perhaps tacitly support, the ethics of intensive factory-farming, which Sun Valley Foods cannot deny that it is directly involved in.

I therefore call on the Dean and Chapter of Hereford to now publicly clarify and confirm, through the columns of The Hereford Times if possible, their stance on this highly emotive subject. Caring people are utterly disgusted by these factory farming practices. The church, by reason of locally associating itself with Sun Valley Foods, now has an urgent duty to explain its attitude.

Guidelines

Language skills and education

1 Think carefully about the audience's language skills, especially when writing or speaking:
- for children
- for speakers of English as a second or foreign language
- for a general audience who may include a wide range of readers
- about subjects where it is vital that every word is clearly understood—for example in matters of public safety

2 Make written text more readable by keeping sentence length down. 15–20 words per sentence is often considered to be a good average to aim for.

3 Difficult and 'long' words (three syllables or more) contribute to the difficulty of a text. When aiming for simplicity, either use shorter words or make sure that difficult words are explained or set in a context which helps the reader.

Knowledge and understanding

4 Make a careful assessment of:
- how much your audience is likely to know about the subject
- what background information you need to provide

5 In speech, check that you have got the knowledge level right by monitoring the reactions of your audience. In writing, consider the possibility of providing additional background information in a 'skippable' introduction or an appendix to which readers can refer.

Relationship with the audience

6 Decide how well you and your audience know each other and how close or distant you wish to be when you address them. This will determine how formal or informal your tone should be.

7 Make sure that your
- vocabulary
- use of long or contracted forms (e.g. *is not/ isn't*)
- choice of pronouns (e.g. *I* or *one*)
- standard or non-standard grammar

support the decision you have made about tone.

You try: key

page 95 Extract 'A' is from an introduction to Egyptology for the general (adult) reader. Extract 'B' is from a book for children aged 7–11, and Extract 'C' is a more specialized book for adults.

page 97 Extract 'A' is clearly aimed at a very low level of knowledge—not just about computers, but about life! (For example, most adults *should* know that it is safer to lift heavy objects by bending at the knees, rather than the waist.) Extract 'B', on the other hand, assumes quite a high level of knowledge. For example, the reader is expected to know what *drives*, *files*, *data*, and *software* are.

page 99　This writer has a good vocabulary, using words such as *ironically*, *epicentre*, and *philanthropy*. Unfortunately he is under the impression that in order to make his point he has to sound pompous and write long sentences which run away with him. The first sentence, for example, is so convoluted that it is impossible to work out what it means. The moral is clear: imagine that you are talking to one or two people of a similar intelligence to yourself, and address them in straightforward sentences that are not too long. If in doubt, try reading your text aloud to yourself and check that it sounds right. Writers such as the author of this letter fail to have the effect they would like and just make themselves look foolish.

12 Subject

The subject matter we wish to communicate affects the language we use. A number of considerations affect our final choice:

- The need to use language precisely.
- Avoiding confusing the audience by using words and expressions they do not understand.
- Making sure not to exclude them by the use of jargon.
- The risk of causing emotional offence and the dangers of euphemism.
- Problems caused by hackneyed expressions and clichés.

Naturally the subject we are talking about has a powerful influence on the language we use. For example, it is difficult to describe the working of a 35mm camera without using words like *focus*, *shutter*, and *exposure*, or expressions such as *wind the film on to the next frame*.

Choosing the best words is thus an important part of effective communication. There are five factors that affect this process and determine how effectively you communicate:

- precision
- confusion
- exclusion
- emotion
- style

Precision

See also:
- **Chapter 19 *Vocabulary*** (p. 179)

Language should always be as precise as possible. So, for example, if you wish to refer to a *split-image rangefinder* when talking about a camera, then that is the phrase you must use.

Or is it? The use of such 'technical terms' is fine if your readers know and understand them. But what if they don't? Sometimes it doesn't matter too much if the reader does not know the precise meaning of all the words in a passage. Consider, for example, this short text:

> The music the children provided was exciting, colourful, and exotic. They used a wide range of instruments. The younger ones had fun playing simple percussion instruments like timbales and bongos. Others played ocarinas, maracas, and guiros, while the melody was provided by two older students playing a zither and a balalaika.

Many readers will not know *exactly* what all these instruments are or what kind of sound they make, but it doesn't really matter; the overall impression is clear and ignorance of what a *guiro* is does not spoil it.

On the other hand, consider these sentences:

The disadvantage of the Leica is that it is not an SLR, so the user has to get used to focusing with a split–image rangefinder. If that doesn't worry you, then you have at your disposal an excellent camera.

If readers don't know what a split-image rangefinder is, they are lost. The writer could argue that they will just have to look the words up in a dictionary:

split-image, an image in a rangefinder or focusing system that has been bisected by optical means, the halves of which are displaced when the system is out of focus, used esp. in various types of camera

rangefinder, a device used for the estimation of the distance separating the observer from an object; spec.
(a) Mil., usu. attached to a weapon, to estimate the range of a target;
(b) Photogr., as an aid to focusing a camera, freq. coupled to the lens

But this is laborious and even the meaning of the dictionary definition takes some untangling!

So precision is desirable, but not if it leads to confusion.

Confusion

Confusion is caused when the writer or speaker assumes a higher level of expertise than the audience actually possess. This has already been touched on in Chapter 11, but the point is worth pursuing.

Essentially you can do one of three things:

- avoid using words your audience may have difficulty with
- use them and explain them at the time, or in a glossary
- use them and not explain them

The first approach is suitable for some kinds of writing and speaking for children (although if they never hear the 'difficult' words for things they have no chance of ever learning them). This approach can also be used when presenting simple (or simplified) material for adults, but it is important to be sure that you are not talking down to your audience, which quickly gives offence.

The second approach is more useful for a wide range of writing and speaking for adults. Care is needed to make sure that too many explanations and definitions do not obscure the main thread of what is being explained.

The third approach might seem rather off-putting, but it depends on the situation. Many general readers, for example, might find the following text fairly impenetrable:

Every lens projects a disc of light, the base of a right circular cone whose apex is at the centre of the exit pupil of the lens (page 48). The illumination of this disc falls off towards the edges, at first gradually and then very rapidly. The limit to this circle of illumination is set by the rapid fall–off due to natural vignetting (page 52) as distinct from any concomitant mechanical vignetting. Also, owing to the presence of residual lens aberrations, the definition of the image within this disc deteriorates from the centre of the field outwards, at first gradually and then more rapidly. By defining an acceptable standard of image quality, it is possible to locate an outer boundary defining a circle of acceptable definition within this circle of illumination.

The text is intended for professional photographers. If the authors were to explain every single term used, the book would become impossibly long and most of its intended readers would be irritated by being told things they already knew.

So it is a matter of judgement. When you are speaking to an audience you can work out from their reactions whether you are getting it right. In a book this is impossible, but it underlines again the importance of giving very careful thought to exactly who your audience are.

You try

These two extracts are about similar subjects. How do they differ, and could either be written more clearly and/or contain more explanation?

A　Benefit Value

(a) At the Pension Date, Investment Units allocated to each Arrangement to be vested will be cancelled and the value calculated in accordance with Condition 27(b). The amount so calculated is the 'Benefit Value'.

The Benefit Value will be applied at GA Life's immediate annuity rates (taking account of any relevant charges) current at the date Investment Units are cancelled to secure an annuity payable during the Member's lifetime by monthly payments in arrear from the Pension Date without proportion to the date of death.

B　The pensions timebomb

TALKING of pensions and grim warnings, Dresdner Kleinwort Benson has chosen a good day to point to what could be the next mis-selling scandal, the growing switch to money-purchase plans or defined contribution pensions. The shift from traditional final-salary schemes, whereby employers promise to pay an eventual fixed proportion of employees' salaries, to such plans has been accelerating over the past five years, and it is making many observers uneasy.

In a traditional pension, any shortfall in the sum promised must be made up by employers, which leaves their risk uncapped. By contrast, money-purchase plans throw the responsibility firmly on the employee. If the investment performance of his or her pension fails to keep pace, then hard luck.

All very well in these times of self-reliance, but large numbers of people may not be competent to look after their own pensions, patronizing though it may seem to suggest it. This is why final-salary schemes have always put the onus on their employers.

Exclusion

A text that is confusing because of the technical language it uses excludes readers or listeners who cannot understand it. It is also possible to exclude an audience—deliberately or unintentionally—by using 'insider' language:

Does your bandwidth need a boost?

If you want to deliver your files at warp speed, add a little rocket fuel to your workflow with iSDN Manager™ Primary Rate.

Utilizing all 30 channels, iSDN Manager™ Primary Rate delivers even a 100MB file anywhere on earth in just 10 minutes; or up to 15 simultaneous transfers makes iSDN Manager™ Primary Rate the obvious solution for even the busiest of pre-press departments.

Boldly delivering your files with the simplest drag & drop, iSDN Manager™ comes in many guises: single or multi user, internal or external ISDN hardware devices, portable or desktop machines, MacOS, Windows 3.1, '95 or NT. And if ISDN 30 at 12.5MB per minute is too far into hyperspace, there's always ISDN 2 or ISDN 8 to choose from.

See also:
■ **Chapter 19** *Vocabulary* (p. 179)

This is computer **jargon** and is designed to appeal to potential purchasers who use or are entertained by such language. If it puts off other people because they find it irritating, that doesn't matter, because it was not intended for them anyway.

There are occasions, however, when it is possible to exclude people with whom you wish to communicate by using language they regard as irritating jargon. It is often said that one person's technical term is another's jargon. This is a little extreme; in many fields there are certain technical terms which cannot be avoided, as we have seen. But excessive use of technical terminology and certainly use of 'insider talk' *is* jargon and *does* put people off. So it should be avoided.

You try

The writer of this report probably did not think he was using jargon. What do you think? If it is jargon, how could it be made more 'reader-friendly'?

These principles underpinning effective performance appraisal have wider relevance than simply improvements in individual performance. They are also concerned with the development of a participative organizational culture by contributing to the broader goals of creating satisfying, effective jobs, encouraging the involvement of people in the organization, and the development of people.

Failure to view the performance appraisal strategically as an important element in an involved organizational culture committed to the development of its individual members has resulted in problems. The early emphasis on the feedback principle, i.e. letting people know how they are performing, neglecting the involvement of the individual in the process, cast appraisers in the uncomfortable role of judge and often resulted in damage to individual development and involvement and commitment to the organization.

Emotion

See also:
- **Chapter 19** *Vocabulary*
  (p. 179)

There are situations in which we may not wish to use the most technically accurate language because it could hurt or offend our audience. For example, when breaking the news of a death to a close friend or member of the family, many people avoid blunt words such as *died* and prefer expressions such as *passed away*. This use of language is referred to as **euphemism**.

Euphemistic language is commonly used by people when talking about death, certain kinds of illness (e.g. cancer), sex, and other bodily functions such as excretion. It even affects the language used to describe certain parts of the body. For example, that part which is most accurately referred to as the *belly* is much more frequently called the *stomach* (inaccurate) or *tummy* (euphemistic).

We should, however, be wary of excessive use of simple or childish language. Doctors are sometimes accused of underestimating the linguistic maturity of their patients and of using unnecessarily euphemistic language. ('Any problems with the waterworks, Mrs Green?') This can not only be insulting, but may simply lead to further confusion, as in the famous story of the doctor who was explaining to a patient how to use a suppository and told him to 'place it in the back passage'. 'I did as he said,' the patient told a friend, 'and put it just outside the back door, but I might as well have stuck it up my arse for all the good it did.'

Once again, it is a question of balancing the requirements of the subject matter with the needs of our audience. It is desirable not to cause unnecessary offence, but it is important to make sure that the message is communicated accurately. If the message is essentially one of sympathy, then we can speak sensitively and avoid hurtful bluntness. If it is essentially factual, then it is important to use words that leave no room for confusion, and any concern about the emotional impact of what is said has to come second.

Style

There is another way in which you can unintentionally offend your audience, and that is by exhibiting linguistic 'tics' and using hackneyed phrases, or tired once-fashionable expressions, known as **clichés**:

> In the good old days it was all down to the private individual to earn an honest penny and make ends meet, but in this day and age all that's gone by the board. Life's a lottery and when push comes to shove, it's every man for himself.

Everybody uses clichés from time to time. They are formulae that save time and thought. Usually they either add nothing to what we are saying, or just give a general impression of the line we are taking or the attitude we are presenting. They have little or no real meaning and if we use them too much we not only diminish the content of what we are trying to say, but run a severe risk of alienating our audience. Indeed, many people have a personal list of clichés they hate; if they hear another person use one of them, then that person immediately goes down in their estimation.

Guidelines

1 Choose language carefully to convey the precise meaning required.

2 Be aware of the problems your audience may have with technical terminology.

3 Don't use jargon or insider language unless you are sure that your audience will appreciate it.

4 By all means avoid hurting people's feelings or giving offence, but avoid relying on euphemism. It is better to speak plainly and communicate clearly even at the risk of causing offence than to fail to communicate at all.

5 Watch out for over-reliance on clichés: hackneyed expressions and other tired, once-fashionable turns of phrase.

You try: key

page 104 Extract 'B' is certainly much easier to understand; it is journalism and journalists who fail to communicate clearly are soon out of a job. Extract 'A', on the other hand, is part of a pension policy, a legal document. The writer decided to choose what could be defended in a court of law in preference to what might be easily understood by the lay person. As the Plain English Campaign has shown, however, these two need not be so obviously in conflict. Extract 'A' *could* be written more clearly. The sentence beginning 'The Benefit Value. . .', for example, is clearly too long and needs punctuation to make it clearer. It could be rewritten like this:

> The Benefit Value will be applied to secure an annuity. GA Life's immediate annuity rates current at the date Investment Units are cancelled will be used (taking account of any relevant charges). The annuity will be paid during the Member's lifetime by monthly payments in arrear from the Pension Date without proportion to the date of death.

page 105 There is an element of jargon here. Some of the expressions used would certainly put off many general readers and some professional ones: *organisational culture* and *the feedback principle*, for example. This is made worse by the length of some of the sentences, especially the last one quoted, which is convoluted and difficult to disentangle.

13 Time and place

Time and place affect the language we use and the messages we pass to each other.

- Many situations in life are like scenes in a play, scripted by one or more of the people taking part.
- Some institutions take advantage of this to control the way in which people behave.
- A major element of this control is their use of language.
- Understanding how this works can help us to communicate with more confidence and success.

It may seem unlikely, but time and place affect what we say or write and how we do it. The physical setting determines what we can and cannot say.

An example: selling clothes

- The time: mid-morning on a wet weekday.
- The place: an open-air market in the centre of Birmingham.
- A crowd of people are gathered around the open side of a long lorry piled high with clothing and household linen. In the centre a small stage provides room for an energetic market trader and his two assistants. The trader is in full flow. He shows his audience a page in a mail-order clothing catalogue:

Will you just raise your hand in the audience if you like that dress, I'm not asking you to buy it, if you like it. You can all see it there in the picture, with the price, 24.99. Yeah? What I'm going to do with you, is this: if you buy that dress, there is another one on that page, I'm gonna have a right little deal with you if you buy that dress. OK? Hands in the air if you said you liked it. Then put your hands back up if you could afford a fiver . . . You could? Well I'll tell you what I'm going to do with you. You know who I am don't you? I'm Mick and I work on Birmingham Market on a Tuesday, Friday, and Saturday and I'm the cheapest in the country, OK? Get your money out—have a look in your pockets, have a look in your bra, in your knickers wherever you keep your money—shoot your hands up as fast as you can and give me 2 pounds 99 . . .

> 25 pounds that dress my price 3 quid and on the top I'm going to do something now that is totally immoral and against all good trading practices and I'll do it and get away with it. It's only me who could. Did I say to you I always keep my promise? Did I say to you that there was another dress on that page that I was gonna give you free of charge? Yes? All those people who can show me a dress they've already bought is in for that.

This text could only exist in this particular setting. Mick can only use the words and sentences he does in this particular place and time.

If the women in his audience went round the corner to a large department store at Sales time, they would not expect the shop assistant to speak to them in this way. They might well have a conversation about price and value for money, but it would be in very different terms. By the same token, if one of the couples from the audience met Mick in a market pub at lunchtime they would not expect him to address them with the same familiarity or use similar language.

The setting allows Mick a number of 'liberties' with his audience, some of whom are regulars, but many of whom are hearing him for the first time. He can joke with them, speak in his highly individual, racy style, and even use language which some of them might, in other settings, find mildly embarrassing or even offensive. The context gives him his licence to do this—and if anyone doesn't like it they have only to walk away to another stall and another trader.

Theatres of life

See also:
- **Chapter 5** *Interviews* (p. 37)
- **Chapter 10** *Meeting the media* (p. 79)

Mick has set up his own theatre in which he is not only lead actor but scriptwriter and director as well. The rest of us are both audience and bit-part players. We can, admittedly, take it or leave it, but we would find it difficult to change the script of the drama. You might argue that this is an extreme case, but it isn't really. There are many much more ordinary situations which work in a similar way: in a job interview, for example, the script is largely written by the person(s) conducting the interview and the interviewee has little choice but to accept the role allotted to him or her in the drama.

Institutions

Sometimes we are so weak that 'the scriptwriters' take advantage of their power and use it to control all our behaviour. It is a common complaint about hospitals that they deliberately cast patients in a very subordinate role so that they will behave in ways that are convenient to the staff. This is satirized in the following extract from an American novel. The narrator is in a private ward, recovering from a car crash:

> A middle-aged nurse nurse popped her head through the door, 'How are we doing?'
> 'Some of us are doing better than others. Do you know when Dr Herschel is coming back?'

'Probably around seven.' The nurse came in to feel my pulse. If there isn't anything else to do, make sure the patient's heart is still beating. Gray eyes twinkled with meaningless jollity in her red face.

'Well, we're certainly a lot stronger than we were a few hours ago. Is the shoulder giving us any pain?'

I looked at her sourly. 'Well, it isn't giving me any—I don't know about you.'

The writer picks up the nurse's use of *we* instead of *you* as part of the way in which some medical experts attempt to depersonalize the interaction. (If the nurse can thus avoid having a 'you and I' conversation, she can avoid becoming personally involved with the patient's suffering.) The use by Health Service workers of the patient's first name, rather than title plus family name, can also diminish the individual's status. The practice is not, significantly, common in private hospitals. A similar set of institutional pressures is often at work when the individual visits a large government or local authority office, or a large company.

Telephone calls

It might be objected that all this is well known but that the knowledge that the individual is likely to be weak and manipulated when up against a large institution is of little practical use. But this is not so.

First, it is important to remember that the main means used to achieve and control these situations are linguistic. So it is helpful to pick up the ways in which language is being manipulated—such as the use of 'we' in the extract quoted earlier. Secondly, if one can observe the ways in which the script of the situation has been written, it may be possible to take it over and rewrite it to one's own ends. A common trick used by companies dealing with telephone complaints goes like this:

CALLER: Could you put me through to the Customer Services Department, please?

SWITCHBOARD: Who shall I say is calling?

CALLER: Jane Pershore.

SWITCHBOARD: And what company is it?

CALLER: Well, it isn't a company, it's just—

SWITCHBOARD: Putting you through . . .

The caller is made to feel inferior because she isn't calling on behalf of a company, but is 'just' a private individual—and when she starts to explain is cut off by the switchboard in mid-sentence.

It is important to understand what is being done and the way in which the switchboard operator's language has—or can have—the effect of diminishing the caller's confidence and effectiveness. If you remember this, then it can help you to remain confident and focused on the task in hand. It is also helpful to have found out the name of the person who deals with the type of enquiry you are making.

Of course you can always go one step further and make up a company name—preferably as long and impressive-sounding as possible:

CALLER: Could you put me through to Mark Wood, please?

SWITCHBOARD: Who shall I say is calling?

CALLER:	Jane Pershore.
SWITCHBOARD:	And what company is it?
CALLER:	(*Speaking very quickly*) Amalgamated Inshore Biotechnology Computer Services
SWITCHBOARD:	Amalgamated Inshore Bio—Sorry what was that again?

Written texts

One of the commonest ways in which institutions manipulate individuals in written texts is the use of forms. If you want to apply for a job, apply for a payment of some kind, or even tell a company what you think of their products, you have to fill in a form. Forms manipulate individuals by inhibiting their freedom of expression:

- They control what you can write about. If there isn't a question about a topic, you cannot write about it.
- They decide the structure and sequence of your writing. Having to present information in a particular order can sometimes change the complete message.
- They determine how much you can write on a given topic.

On the other hand, forms are a convenient way for organizations to collect information in a format that enables them to process it quickly and efficiently. So how you respond to being asked to fill in a form depends on:

- the message you wish to communicate
- your judgement of how the reader will react
- how much this reaction matters to you

It is easy enough to overcome all the restrictions and subvert a form: you can ignore questions, add more information than has been allowed for (by pasting on flaps of paper), and give information that has not been requested. You can even redesign the form and produce your own 'reconstructed' version. More conventionally, you can refer the reader to an additional sheet of information enclosed with the form itself.

With something like a customer satisfaction form you can do whatever you like. All you risk is that your form will be thrown away and you will not be entered for the prize draw—if there is one. A job application is rather different. By demonstrating your independence you may go up in the estimation of your prospective employer; or you may be marked down as a potential troublemaker.

Working on the inside

Institutions can also put linguistic pressure on those who work within them. They can require the individual to speak in a particular way when addressing others. The army requires other ranks to use particular language when addressing officers; nurses are expected to speak to doctors in an 'acceptable' way; schools require the same of pupils and teachers. Similar expectations may apply with written texts. The institution may produce its own forms which have to be completed by employees; reports and memos may have to be written using a specific vocabulary and sentence style.

Often these expectations are made clear when the individual joins the institution. It does not take long to work out the extent to which you have to adhere to the rules, and how far you can bend and use them for your own purposes. Sometimes, however, there are no clear guidelines. The institution appears to operate a kind of code but what this is and the rules which govern it are not made clear to the newcomers. They have at first to operate like anthropologists meeting a completely unknown tribe, noting behaviour patterns without initially knowing what they mean.

Guidelines

1 Whenever you are in a new language situation—even if it only involves one other person—try to assess how far it is being 'scripted' by someone else, and how this is being done.

2 If it is being scripted, decide how happy you are about this, whether you want to change the script, and how this can be done.

3 When contacting an organization or institution as a member of the public, be aware of how language may be used to control the situation.

4 Again, decide whether you want to go along with this, or to seek to change the situation. But also be aware of the risks involved. (You can, for example, make hospital staff address you in the way you want, but the cost may be that you are labelled as 'difficult'.)

5 As a new member of an institution take trouble to find out what 'the rules' governing language are and how well they are kept. Then assess how you will respond.

14 Purpose

It might seem obvious why people write or speak to each other: they do so to communicate. Communication involves conveying information, feelings, and ideas from one person or group to another. The more precisely and clearly we do this the more effectively we are communicating.

Everyday experience, however, suggests that things may be rather less simple. This is the beginning of a very ordinary telephone conversation between two neighbours:

> A: John—Anthony here.
> B: Hullo.
> A: How are you?
> B: I'm fine.
> A: Good. I've got your keys which I must remember to bring round.
> B: Yes . . .
> A: Er, they're spare keys are they?
> B: Yeah . . . er, yes . . . they're . . . sorry, there's no problem. There's no need for you to bring them round—I'll pop over.
> A: Or I'll pop them through or something . . .

The conversation contains about sixty words. It is true that some information and ideas are communicated: 'Anthony here' is essential information at the beginning of the conversation, unless B is to be left to work out who the speaker is. It might seem, too, that 'I've got your keys' is useful information, too, until we reflect that presumably B knows that A has got his keys. And what information or ideas are conveyed by this exchange?

> B: . . . I'll pop over.
> A: Or I'll pop them through or something . . .

It really does not matter to either of them exactly what is done about a spare set of keys and indeed the whole purpose of the phone call is something of a mystery until A gets to the point:

A: Or I'll pop them through or something . . . um, what modem
have you got?

He wants to discuss computers, so why did he begin by talking about
keys? In fact the beginning of the conversation is not about communicating information or ideas at all, but is to establish (or re-establish)
the channel of communication between two people. The language is a
kind of code; A and B are really saying to each other: 'Look, we are two
people who know each other fairly well and last time we met it had to
do with keys. This conversation continues from there.'

You might ask 'Why do it?' If we remove the 'chat' from the conversation, we see why:

A: John.
B: Hullo.
A: What kind of modem have you got?

While this would achieve A's purpose in calling, it would seem abrupt
and even rude. Social intercourse often requires a more leisurely
approach.

The seven purposes

We use language for a wide variety of purposes, which include communicating information and ideas, and when we speak or write—especially in more formal situations—it is helpful to reflect on what our
main purposes are. This chapter examines the more common purposes for speaking and writing.

To interact

As we have seen, an important function of language is to help us get
on with other people, to interact. In the example above this formed
part of a larger purpose: the caller A wanted to enquire about types of
computer modems. He was using language to find out.

Sometimes language is used primarily to interact:

> Near Ely.
> Mon. before Sat. 23rd!
>
> Dear Elizabeth & John,
>
> A very, very belated letter to thank
> you very much indeed for a much enjoyable stay.
> Sorry I've been so remiss about writing but in all
> this walk-about period, letter writing & phoning haven't
> been easy. At the moment I'm staying with an

> I've just realised that you will be in
> France by the time this reaches Founhope.
> Hope you have a really enjoyable, refreshing
> stay – and that all goes well till I see you
> again. Some time after 3rd Sept. !!!
>   Love,

Even here information and ideas are being communicated as well. Normally this use of language takes place between people who have met or had some kind of contact even if only by letter or telephone. But it can also take place when the speaker and the listener are completely unknown to each other, as in many local radio phone-in programmes.

This kind of language use is sometimes referred to—dismissively—as small talk: 'I'm afraid I'd be no good at that; I've got no small talk.' Yet interacting with others forms an important part of most people's lives and the ability to talk to people one does not know (or, perhaps, to those whom one has no reason to like) is a valuable social skill. Of equal value is the ability to write in a variety of social situations. As W. H. Auden put it:

> Letters with holiday snaps to enlarge in,
> Letters with faces scrawled on the margin,
> Letters from uncles, cousins and aunts,
> Letters to Scotland from the South of France,
> Letters of condolence to Highlands and Lowlands,
> Written on paper of every hue,
> The pink, the violet, the white and the blue,
> The chatty, the catty, the boring, the adoring . . .

To inform

Every day of our lives we communicate information and ideas to other people. Sometimes such communication is official, formal, businesslike:

The new Self Assessment tax return
In April 1997, you will get
• an eight-page, easy-to-follow, new-look tax return
• supplementary pages to fill in if they are relevant to you
• a separate section where you can calculate the tax due, if you wish.
If you do not want to do so, we will still do it for you.

It will be a combined tax return for all your sources of income and gains, and your reliefs, deductions and allowances, for one year.

It has been extensively researched with taxpayers and tax advisers to make it as easy to follow as possible. It will come with clear instructions telling you exactly what you have to do and how to fill it in. And we will provide free advice to help you.

But this text contains more than a 'straight' communication of facts. The writer is 'selling' something to the reader. If the new tax return won't exactly be fun, it will, apparently, be very user-friendly. It will be 'new-look' and 'easy-to-follow'. The tax man is there to help: if you do not wish to calculate the tax due 'we will still do it for you . . . And we will provide free advice to help you.'

Although we may be suspicious of the tax man, 'even bearing gifts', at least his communication of this information is clear and to the point. Some people find it difficult to convey a clear and simple message, as in the following transcript of a telephone conversation. A representative of a mail-order company is answering a query from a customer who has not received the whole of an order. A parcel containing a computer scanner has gone missing.

> Apparently on the discrepancy report that scanner hasn't actually come up so what Business Post are doing—they are chasing this still and they want to work out whether it was stolen from us to them or whether or not it went out from their hub . . . uum . . . so they are looking into this. What we're going to be doing is that we're obviously waiting till they get some feedback to us—or whether or not it's gone off to another hub by mistake. Normally what would happen is that this would be on the discrepancy report but obviously it's only been a day I understand . . . that um . . . it could've been that . . . um . . . it still hasn't been received by another hub as yet so they won't know until the end of the day before we can find out what the situation is with that . . . uuh what we're going to be doing is that as soon as we get from some report from them we'll get in touch with you. If we don't hear anything by the weekend we'll be chasing this ourselves.

The speaker is clumsy and difficult to follow. When you boil his message down it is that he does not know where the goods are and is still trying to find out. His secondary purpose is to calm the customer down and persuade him to wait a little longer so that the company can sort things out. (You could even argue that his very incoherence and use of technical terms like 'hub' are intended to contribute to this. The message is certainly so mind-numbingly confusing as to inhibit further enquiries.)

At least in a telephone conversation it is possible to question a speaker who is confused or confusing. In a radio talk or television commentary, as well as in most written texts, this is not possible and it is vital to consider the needs of the listener or reader. When a writer fails to do this, there is little the reader can do. Writing or speaking to inform needs to be clear and this means not only knowing the facts, but also being aware of the needs of your audience.

To find out

Not only do we use language to inform, we also use it to find out information. The ability to ask questions and then follow them up with further enquiries is very important in both work and leisure. Its importance in human development is shown by the behaviour of young children who, as soon as they can frame questions, bombard their parents with enquiries about—literally—everything under the sun.

For adults too, the ability to ask the right question is essential. Often it is just part of the everyday business of living:

A: I've managed to get a glassless neg. carrier for you to have a look at . . . I borrowed one from Birmingham . . .

B: So I need to come in and have a look at it.

A: Yes please, yes.

B: How long do you reckon you can hang on to it?

A: I'll probably send it back on Monday.

B: Monday . . . so I need to come in by the end of the weekend, in other words by the end of Saturday.

A: Yes.

B: OK. What time are you open to in the evenings?

A: Half-past five.

In this brief conversation B speaks four times. Only two of these utterances are framed as questions, specifically asking for information, but the other two are also in effect requests for information—or at least confirmation that he is thinking along the right lines ('. . . so I need to come in . . . by the end of Saturday . . .').

There are other occasions when the pattern of question-and-answer is part of a more formalized situation. When you fill in a form, for example:

See also:

■ **Chapter 13** *Time and place* (p. 108)

Even when the subject matter is more light-hearted, the situation may still be 'formalized':

See also:
- **Chapter 5** *Interviews* (p. 37)
- **Chapter 10** *Meeting the media* (p. 79)

RADIO INTERVIEWER:	Are you at all concerned about hair loss?
A:	Er . . . no, not really. I think it's something I can't avoid, so I try not to worry about it.
RADIO INTERVIEWER:	Do you do anything to try and ease the situation?
A:	No.
RADIO INTERVIEWER:	But have you lost—you've obviously lost a little bit of hair . . .
A:	Just a little bit, yes!
RADIO INTERVIEWER:	What does your wife or partner think about that?
A:	She doesn't mind. No, she still loves me.

By answering the interviewer's first question, the respondent is agreeing to take part in the 'game' of being interviewed and to play according to the rules. This may seem an odd way of describing it, but imagine what might happen if the person being interviewed did not play according to the interview rules:

| RADIO INTERVIEWER: | Are you at all concerned about hair loss? |
| A: | No. Are you? |

or

| RADIO INTERVIEWER: | Are you at all concerned about hair loss? |
| A: | Don't you think you're rather overweight to be asking me questions like that? |

or

| RADIO INTERVIEWER: | Are you at all concerned about hair loss? |
| A: | Tell you what, why don't we just slip down to my place and I'll give you a full and frank run-down on my hair loss situation. |

Of course such responses may occur, but if they do, they tend not to be broadcast.

To influence

See also:
- **Chapter 15** *Different ways of communicating* (p. 123)

Whether I look at life as a private individual, as a worker, or as a citizen, it is important that I should be aware of when others are trying to influence me, and of how they are trying to do it. This covers a wide spectrum of writing and speaking. At one end of this we are fully aware that different points of view are being expressed and are free to make up our own minds. Sometimes a writer or speaker may even express two contrasting viewpoints without offering his or her own opinion. Frequently, however, the writer chooses to put an argument as strongly and persuasively as possible:

Just think about it.
Nuclear power involves splitting atoms to create some of the deadliest materials on Earth, then using the water they heat to drive a turbine. And when these lethal materials are removed from the reactor—what then? What do you do with this poisonous waste?

Nobody's ever worked out a safe way to deal with these 'spent' fuel rods, which are now even more dangerous than they were to start with. The result? Since the first commercial nuclear power station opened at Calder Hall at Sellafield in 1956, there has been no way of getting rid of any of the fuel rods or other dangerous radioactive waste. It has simply been stockpiled and will be left for future generations to clean up.

Isn't it time to say 'enough is enough'?

Don't you think it's time to close these death traps down now, before there's another 'accident'?

At the other end of the scale language is used to influence without the audience being conscious of it. This often happens in advertising. Consider the way in which the text of this advertisement uses words:

LOOKS CAN BE DECEIVING

It isn't just the sleek design that makes the BeoCenter 9300 so satisfying to own. It's also the way it's constructed to be at the forefront of technology to give you the very best in sound quality. The way it functions is equally impressive too. Take the CD and cassette doors. Watching them glide back and forth is a pleasure in itself. Touch 'play' with your fingertip and the real beauty of the 9300 will be revealed to you. The very sound of the CDs, tapes, and even radio broadcasts will reach out to you more profoundly than ever before. Would it be going too far to describe the sensation as sensual? Perhaps. Perhaps not. So why don't you experience it for yourself at one of our dealers—seeing is believing.

See also:
■ **Chapter 19 *Vocabulary***
(p. 179)

Here words are chosen not simply for their meaning, but for their connotations, their emotional effect. 'The way it functions' (rather than 'works') is '*impressive*'. The 'very sound of the CDs . . . will reach out . . . *profoundly*'. The writer's aim is not to persuade by argument but to carry the reader along on a magic carpet of words which are on analysis rather meaningless. Politicians often use language in a similar way when addressing the public.

To regulate

Advertisers and politicians may try to persuade us of the rightness of a particular course of action; legislators tell us what to do. They use language to regulate our actions. So do school teachers (at times), doctors, and many others:

1 Remove the red mouthpiece cover and check that the mouthpiece is clean. If the inhaler is cold, warm it in your hand before use.
2 Shake the inhaler well (at least 5 times). If the inhaler has not been used for a while or you are using it for the first time, release one puff into the air to make sure that it works.
3 Holding the inhaler well away from your mouth breathe out gently but not fully, to avoid condensation and blockage of the spray. DO NOT breathe out through the inhaler.

To entertain

Fortunately language isn't all work. There is also play. And the playful use of language is both important and widespread. The way in which we use language in entertainment also varies widely, from simple jokes:

A famous Washington columnist, dining in the old quarter of Montreal, raved over the trout Marguery. He summoned the proprietor of the restaurant and said, 'I'd like to have the recipe for this dish.' The proprietor smiled and answered suavely, 'I'm sorry, m'sieur, but we have here the same policy as you journalists. We never reveal our sauce.'

to poetry:

Shall I compare thee to a Summer's day?
Thou art more lovely and more temperate:
Rough winds do shake the darling buds of May,
And Summer's lease hath all too short a date:
Sometime too hot the eye of heaven shines,
And often is his gold complexion dimm'd;
And every fair from fair sometime declines,
By chance or nature's changing course untrimm'd:
But thy eternal Summer shall not fade
Nor lose possession of that fair thou owest;
Nor shall Death brag thou wanderest in his shade,
When in eternal lines to time thou growest:
   So long as men can breathe, or eyes can see,
   So long lives this, and this gives life to thee.

These two examples may differ in their profundity, but both make playful use of language and draw attention to the fact that they are doing so. Even in more practical applications of language we may sometimes wish to do this.

To record

The previous six purposes all presuppose an audience other than the speaker or writer. There is one use, however, that does not. It is predominantly a purpose for writing, although it can be spoken. In many different situations we need to make a record of something. From a shopping list to a school attendance register, from Domesday Book to a ship's log: the primary intention of such texts is get something down on paper so that it is not forgotten. If we have an audience in mind when we write to record, then that audience is often unknown to us, and usually at some distance in the future.

Diaries are a rather specialized form of this. Many diarists write purely for themselves and to keep a record. Most of the diaries we get to read, however, have either been written with an audience in mind or have been 'tidied up' for an audience:

Ministry of Defence   Wednesday 23rd January

We're five days into the air war, but I am unhappy about the strategy. Attacking missile sites is always wasteful, has very little tactical effect and occurs mainly in response (as most obviously now) to political demands. We lost another Tornado last night. That's now five. I can't help noticing that traditions (ancient and revered) of Bomber Command are reasserting themselves. From the Tabuk mission last night, out of ten sorties six either aborted for technical reasons, or 'jettisoned ordnance while manoeuvring to avoid (sic) SAMs', or took targets of opportunity. (Uh? At night?) The sad thing is that it's always the brave ones, the true grit, who press on regardless (the contravening tradition) and get killed. Of the Italian flight of six, five turned back and only one brave boy went ahead. They got him. It's the difference between James and Andrew. But I want James to survive, don't I?

MGO has been here for an hour and a half. There's a potential ammunition crisis in some calibres. Unbelievably our NATO 'partners' are being most reluctant to pool their stockpiles, even though we're paying cash. The smelly little Belgians, who would never fire a shot at anyone and never have, and who did their best to shaft the BEF in 1940, have actually refused to let us have anything, except 'humanitarian supplies'—bandages and general past-its-sell-by-date detritus we don't need.

You try

What would you say was the main purpose of each of these texts?

Checklist

- to inform
- to find out
- to interact
- to influence
- to regulate
- to entertain
- to record

A Don Quixote was enraged, when he heard such blasphemies uttered against his mistress Dulcinea, and lifting his lance, without speaking a syllable, or giving the least notice of his intention, discharged two such hearty blows upon the squire, as brought him instantly to the ground, and had not Dorothea called aloud and begged him to forbear, would certainly have murdered poor Sancho on the spot.

B The study showed that foreign business activity was important to industry: over 60 per cent of the survey companies conducted some form of business with foreign-speaking clients and this was of major importance to over 40 per cent of respondents. Such business was highly concentrated in a few language areas: about two-thirds each of companies with foreign business dealt with French or German speakers, about one-third each with Spanish and Italian speakers. Otherwise Japanese, Arabic, and Dutch were the only languages of clients of 10 per cent or more of companies.

C To install the application software:
1 Switch on your computer and wait for the desktop to be displayed.
2 Check that the CD driver is correctly installed.
3 Insert the floppy disk into the floppy disk drive slot.
4 Drag the contents of the floppy disk to your hard disk.

D Within minutes of the shelling of the UN base near Tyre in Southern Lebanon, the Red Cross was on the spot providing vital medical care to the injured.

The Red Cross is currently the only international aid agency providing assistance throughout Southern Lebanon. We are distributing supplies to medical centres and clinics. We are giving mattresses, blankets, and vital food aid to people who have left everything behind. And we are deploying 32 ambulances and 25 mobile Red Cross clinics to the areas of greatest need.

Now we need your help to ensure aid continues to reach those who need it desperately. Please give as much as you can today. Your donation can save lives. Thank you.

Guidelines

1 When writing and speaking it is often useful to remember that you almost certainly have a primary purpose, which will usually come from this list:

- to interact
- to inform
- to find out
- to influence
- to regulate
- to entertain
- to record

2 You will often find that you have more than one purpose; other, secondary purposes will run alongside your main purpose.

3 When writing, check that the language you have used—especially your tone—contributes to your purpose rather than detracts from it.

4 When you are listening to a speaker or reading what someone else has written, it is often useful to analyse their purposes, especially if they are seeking to influence you in some way.

You try: key

page 121   A: to entertain
B: to inform
C: to regulate
D: to influence (although it also informs)

15 | Different ways of communicating

There are four main ways of communicating:

Narrative

A narrative is a sequence of events recounted either in the order in which they happened, or in an order chosen to emphasize certain aspects of the story.

Description

Descriptive writing deals with appearances: what things look, sound, feel, taste, or smell like. Observation and selection are key skills in effective descriptive writing.

Exposition

Exposition involves explanations: it may require the description of patterns, accounting for how things work, how processes take place, or a more theoretical analysis of a situation.

Argument

Argument requires the expression of one or more points of view, often to persuade or influence others. It usually requires the writer or speaker to give an explicit or implicit explanation for the views expressed, based on evidence and/or reasoning.

It is often the case that a written text or a piece of speech will involve a mixture of two or more of these **modes of discourse**.

Much of what we say or write is composed of four 'building blocks', known traditionally as modes of discourse:

Mode	Example
narrative	telling a story
description	saying what something looks like
exposition	explaining how something works
argument	expressing an opinion and giving the reasons for it

Narrative

See also:
■ **Chapter 8 *Reports***
  (p. 62)

A narrative deals with a sequence of events in time. Typical formats for narrative are:

■ novel and short story
■ biography and autobiography
■ diary
■ newspaper, radio, and TV news report
■ other forms of report
■ conversational anecdote

In this extract from an autobiography, the writer remembers an incident from his schooldays.

> One night, as I slunk along Church Hill in Harrow, dodging from the mouth of one alleyway to the next, I noticed something which had escaped my attention before. At the back of the Old Schools, one of the original buildings, dating in part from 1615—lay an expanse of lawn. Between the back of the Old Schools and the retaining wall across the end of the garden there was a gap about two feet wide, running away into the hillside at right angles to the street. Although this gap was closed by a cross-wall along the pavement, I spotted a small opening in it, two feet high by one wide, some four feet off the ground. A man's body would not have fitted through the aperture, but I was small and slim.
>
> In a flash I had jumped up and wriggled through the gap. I found myself in a tunnel with an arched brick roof, separating the Old Schools from the garden. Suddenly my adrenaline ran faster. In the wall of the school building was another small opening, blocked by an iron grille. Inside the building, I knew, was the Armoury, where all the Corps rifles were kept. This second opening appeared to lead straight into the Armoury. If only the grille were loose . . .
>
> It was. In a second I had lifted it clear and was wriggling through the aperture. Sure enough, I was in the heart of the Armoury.

Writing narrative Telling stories is one of the commonest modes of speaking and writing. Because it 'comes naturally' it is easy to take it for granted and to write narrative without giving it sufficient thought, but there are important choices to be made and if the writer is unaware of these, the writing will be the poorer.

The story you have just read continues with the following information:

1 In the nights that followed he made more visits to the armoury.
2 He decided to 'borrow' a .22 rifle.
3 He already had illicit .22 ammunition taken from practice sessions on the rifle range.
4 As an experiment he took a shot at the window of a room belonging to one of his fellow pupils at the school.
5 No one heard the shot or realized what had happened.

6 On the last day of term he repeated the exploit. He chose the window of a room being used for an illegal party by sixth formers.

7 The curtains were open and the light on. He fired two rounds at the light bulb, but missed. The people in the room realized what was happening and put the light out.

8 Shortly afterwards the police arrived and he escaped to the armoury to return the rifle.

9 The school authorities took it as the work of outsiders and nothing was done. He later realized that his actions had been very foolish.

Order These events could be narrated in a number of different ways. Unless there are strong reasons for changing things, it makes sense to tell the story in the order in which it happened. As the King told the White Rabbit in *Alice in Wonderland*:

> 'Begin at the beginning, and go on till you come to the end: then stop.'

Filling in the background In the sequence above the events are listed in the order in which they happened with the exception of number 3, which is necessary at some point to explain why he had ammunition for the rifle he took. This need is a common one in narrative—since many stories are not entirely 'freestanding'. The problem is how to integrate such background information without interrupting the flow of the narrative too much.

One solution is to begin with this information:

> Before I begin I should explain that the school cadet corps used to go to the firing range regularly to do target practice with .22 rifles. There was little proper control over ammunition on these occasions . . . , etc.

This can be satisfactory, although it tends to give a narrative a rather flat beginning. An alternative is to weave such explanations into the narrative itself—as was done by the original writer:

> . . . But I told nobody that I had conceived an ambitious plan. Whenever we had a shooting practice on the .22 range, control of ammunition was slack, and I found it easy enough to carry off a few spare bullets each time. I had already amassed a stock of these, and used to amuse myself by dropping into a boy's room for an apparently casual visit in the evening, surreptitiously scattering a few bullets on to his coal fire, and then taking my leave; a few minutes later, sudden explosions would shower red-hot coal all over his floor. Now I had a better use for this smuggled ammunition.

Skilfully handled, as here, this technique works well, but if there are too many interruptions to the flow of the story, or if the teller appears to be going off at a tangent, it can ruin the impact of the narrative.

Subverting the order Sometimes it is useful to subvert the sequence and present events in a different order from that in which they occurred. A common reason for this is to achieve a dramatic effect. By plunging into the middle of the story with a startling, amusing, or dramatic event we hope to grab the reader's or listener's attention. This approach is popular with newspaper journalists, who rarely 'begin at the beginning':

> **PLAYING WITH FIRE**
> **Stupid prank at public school**
> A teenager fired two shots at sixth formers at Harrow School last night. In an extraordinary incident a fifteen-year-old boy broke up an illicit party by firing live rounds at the room where it was taking place.
>
> **Stolen rifle**
> Earlier the boy—whose name is being withheld—broke into the armoury belonging to the school cadet corps . . .

See also:
- **Chapter 10** *Meeting the media* (p. 79)

A common pattern for such reports is:

1 Lead paragraph
This tells the key part of the story in brief.

2 Story
The details of the story following the main sequence of events.

3 Background
Further background information.

4 Comment
Selected comments from people involved, 'experts', politicians (and anyone else who can be persuaded to say something eye-catching).

Since newspaper readers often only read the beginning of a report, this approach ensures that they can grasp the essentials of a story by reading a few paragraphs. Those who wish for further detail can read the remainder at their leisure.

Special formats   A similar alteration of the order of events is found in other kinds of report. If the head of the school had made a report of the incident to the governors, he might have begun with a brief summary of the main events:

> Events of Tuesday 14th July
> At 11.15pm on 14th July, the last day of the Trinity Term, two shots were fired at a study window in New Block. No one was injured and no serious damage was done. The shots were fired by a fifth former using a rifle he had stolen from the armoury that evening and ammunition taken on a normal cadet firing day at the indoor range.
> Theft from the armoury
> Earlier in the term the fifth former, . . .

Emphasis   Even when writers keep the same sequence of events, they can give the story a very different emphasis, and therefore meaning, by putting greater weight on some incidents and less on others. This can be seen any day of the week by comparing reports on the 'same' event by different daily newspapers.

You try

These two reports of the same event come from different daily newspapers. What would you say are the chief differences in the ways the two papers have treated the story?

Driving ban for nine-in-car son of millionaire MP

THE son of a multi-millionaire Tory Minister was banned for drink driving yesterday after being arrested with eight other people in his car, including two in the boot.

Alexander Bonsor, 20, spent the night in police cells and had to call his father—Foreign Office Minister Sir Nicholas—to tell him what had happened.

Bonsor, whose father is said to have a £13 million fortune, was banned for 14 months and fined £600 with £40 costs. The money will not unduly trouble the Bristol University politics student, full name Alexander Cosmo Walrond Bonsor.

Robert Davies, defending, told the city's magistrates: 'He has money. He is not a student who lies awake at night worrying about where money for the next curry or pint of beer comes from. He does not have to mark his milk to stop his friends taking it out of the fridge. He is given £500 a month to cover all his expenses.'

The court heard Bonsor and his friends had spent the evening in a Bristol pub watching the England v Italy World Cup qualifying match. Afterwards eight people climbed into his Ford Sierra—two in the boot, two in the front passenger seat and four in the back—and he drove off. Police stopped the car because it was so low on the ground that sparks were flying from it. Bonsor was breath-tested and found to be more than twice the limit.

He admitted driving with excess alcohol and using a vehicle where the number of passengers carried was such that it would cause danger of injury.

Mr Davies said when Bonsor and his friends left the pub he had no intention of driving home, but 'the red or blue mist descended on all nine of them'.

Sir Nicholas, who was in court, said afterwards: 'It was a very fair verdict and I hope he will learn a lesson from this.'

Eton-educated Sir Nicholas, a father of five, lives in a 14-bedroom mansion on an 800-acre Bedfordshire estate with Nadine, his wife of 25 years.

▶

9-IN-CAR TORY SON BANNED OVER BOOZE
The student son of Foreign Office minister Sir Nicholas Bonsor was yesterday banned for drink-driving with eight pals in his car—two in the boot.

Alex Bonsor, 20, boozed as he watched the England v Italy World Cup soccer qualifier on TV in a pub. Then he drove off in his J-reg Ford Sierra, which was so weighed down that sparks flew from the back of it.

His father was in court at Bristol to see him get a 14-month disqualification and £640 fine after admitting drink-driving and carrying too many passengers.

Magistrates were told that the Bristol University politics student had no money worries because he was paid a £500-a-month allowance by his dad, who is worth £13 million.

Young Bonsor's lawyer Robert Davies said: 'He is from a thoroughly decent and respectable family.'

Mr Davies added: 'The incident has caused embarrassment to himself, his father and his family.'

Sir Nicholas, 54-year-old Tory MP for Upminster Essex, said afterwards: 'I think it was a very fair verdict and hope he will learn a lesson from this.'

Description

Descriptive writing is used in many different situations. For example:

- travel writing
- biography, autobiography and other writing about people
- diary and personal letter
- technical and scientific works

Personal and impersonal

In some contexts, like scientific writing, the personality of the writer may hardly appear:

Mebnoleuca cognata: rather yellowish or tan coloration; stem tall; gills ochre-tan

In conifer woods on paths and clearings. Autumn. Uncommon. Cap 10 cm (2 in), convex then expanded and umbonate; smooth, ochre-yellow to tan, paler when dry. Gills becoming clearly pale ochre or tan when mature; sinuate-adnate, crowded. Stem tall, straight, slightly bulbous, colour as cap with darker fibrils . . .

In other situations, the writer's personality may be quite intrusive:

Ag Roumeli (60km from Chania) Tel. prefix 0821. There was an ancient settlement here, as long ago as the 5th century BC, as evidenced by archaeological excavations to the left (Fsw) of the

Gorge. In an attempt to hold down the locals the Turks built a fort (surprise, surprise).

Ag Roumeli continues to resemble a hot, Alaskan shanty town, the only 'establishments' missing being John Wayne and a bordello! The rustic, doo-hickey ambience is accentuated by the wandering, foraging chickens, goats and sheep. Other animal life in situ include mosquitoes, and the dawn chorus of the village's stray dogs will doubtless wake the heaviest sleeper.

The inhabitants ('Sfakiots') have had a pretty hard life for the last 1000 years or so, what with tending and skinning goats, and sheep, in order to earn a crust. But now they are engaged in tending and skinning the tourists . . .

Writing description

Clearly it is essential to have the necessary information available before beginning to write descriptively. Preparation may range from careful research (as in the case of the technical description of a fungus), a mixture of research and memory (as with the travel-book extract) or pure memory and reflection. Even where the writer is relying heavily on memory it is useful to make preparatory notes, which will help with the ordering of the material and will enable the writer to see where problems are likely to arise.

Key decisions

How you structure a description and the tone and style you adopt depend heavily on the answers to these questions, already tackled in this section of the book:

See also:
■ **Chapter 11** *Audience* (p. 89)

■ **Who?**
You must think carefully about the background knowledge and needs of your audience. For example, the description of *Mebnoleuca cognata* is of no use to a reader who has no botanical knowledge and cannot cope with words like 'sinuate-adnate' and 'fibrils'. By the same token a reader who wants a straight factual account of a place will find the description of Ag Roumeli irritatingly jokey.

See also:
■ **Chapter 14** *Purpose* (p. 113)

■ **Why?**
All description has to some extent the purpose of providing information. This may, however, take place within a broader setting. The fungus text is nothing—indeed, is downright dangerous—if it does not inform fully and accurately. The guidebook is clearly intended to provide a large measure of entertainment. The description of fungi, on the other hand, is intended to convey information succinctly and impersonally.

Pattern and emphasis

The writer of the text about fungi had few problems to overcome when planning. His description of each fungus follows a certain pattern:

■ brief description of appearance
■ habitat and season of appearance
■ distribution ('common', 'uncommon', etc.)
■ cap

and so on.

The writer of the guidebook, for all the apparent spontaneity of his style, also follows a pattern:

- location/telephone code
- history
- general impressions
- the people
- a walk through the town

As with much writing, the ordering of a description is crucial. Once you have found the right pattern and emphasis for the text, your writing can proceed with greater confidence and facility.

You try

These two descriptions are both about the same place. In what ways are they different?

The greatest disappointment was Chandni Chowk. In the poems and travelogues, the Moonlight Bazaar is praised as a kind of Oriental Faubourg St Honoré, renowned for its wide avenues, its elegant caravanserais and its fabulous Mughal gardens. Having read the descriptions of this great boulevard, once the finest in all Islam, as you sit on your rickshaw and head on into the labyrinth you still half-expect to find its shops full of jasper and sardonyx for the Mughal builders, mother-of-pearl inlay for the pietra dura craftsmen; you expect to see strings of Bactrian camels from Kashgar and logs of cinnamon from Madagascar, merchants from Ferghana, and Khemer girl concubines from beyond the Irrawaddy; perhaps even a rare breed of turkey from the New World or a zebra to fill the Imperial menagerie and amuse the Emperor.

But instead, as you sit stranded in a traffic jam, half-choked by rickshaw fumes and the ammonia-stink of the municipal urinals, you see around you a sad vista of collapsing shop fronts and broken balustrades, tatty warehouses roofed with corrugated iron and patched with rusting duckboards. The canal which ran down the centre of the bazaar has been filled in; the trees have been uprooted. All is tarnished, fraying at the edges. On the pavement, a Brahminy cow illicitly munches vegetables from the sack of a vendor; a Muslim ear-cleaner squats outside the Sis Ganj gurdwara and peers down the orifices of a Sikh nihang (gurdwara guard). A man grabs your arm and stage-whispers: 'Sahib, you want carpets hashish smack brown sugar change money blue film sexy ladies no problem!'

▶

You try continued

Old Delhi (Shahjahanabad)

Although it's not in fact the oldest part of Delhi, the seventeenth-century city of Shahjahanabad, built by the Moghul emperor, Shah Jahan, is known as OLD DELHI. The original city walls spread for seven miles, enclosing the sprawling fort, Lal Qila, and the formidable Jami Masjid, or 'Friday Mosque'. Old Delhi's main thoroughfare, Chandni Chowk, a seething mass of hooting, pushing cars, tempos, cycle rickshaws and ox carts, was once a sublime canal lined with trees and some of the most opulent bazaars of the East. Today the city walls have crumbled, and houses and shops have long since spilled beyond the remaining five of the fourteen old gates.

On the west bank of the River Yamuna northeast of the modern centre, Old Delhi resembles an overgrown village of tight-knit communities, alive with intriguing contradictions and contrasts. Photographers huddled at the east end of Chandni Chowk using rickety equipment left over from the days of the Raj are overlooked by garish film boards and advertisements for sex clinics, while the bazaars in the back alleys have changed little since the eighteenth and nineteenth centuries. It's a fascinating area, but you'll need stamina, patience and time to endure the crowds and traffic, and pursue a rewarding exploration of the city's streets, mosques, temples and guradwaras.

Exposition

Exposition is concerned with:

- the pattern of things
- how things work
- how to do something
- the underlying reality of a situation

At its simplest—and most practical—exposition deals with the physical world:

MULTIGRADE IV RC Deluxe is available in glossy, pearl, and new satin finishes. Choice of surface influences the density range of a print, and affects how good it looks on display. Glossy paper gives slightly richer blacks, and is therefore the first choice if your print is going to be reproduced in a book, newspaper or magazine. For display, the choice is more difficult. Glossy prints pick up reflections more easily and, in a shop window for example, a satin finish print might be easier to see at certain angles. The high sheen of glossy paper also shows up fingerprints and other marks, so if prints are to be handled a lot, satin or pearl paper might be a better answer.

Often such writing is impersonal and formal in tone. But it need not be. Here a writer explains a practical subject in a more relaxed and personal way:

The Victorians were extremely frugal and parsimonious, watching every halfpenny. The staggering waste of anything and everything which we see today was the exact contrary to their world. It was because of this parsimony that they could afford to buy a thousand solid silver fishknives—and pay in gold napoleons—and get something that would be polished daily for fifty years without wearing out. For this they had a system; in the kitchen called the System. Its exact French title—for the French were the most frugal of all Victorians—is 'Rien se Perd' which is translatable as 'Waste does not Exist'.

Exposition is either outside time, or—as in the extract above—covers a period of time. This type of writing and speaking to expound and explain occurs in many different situations, especially in areas of life that are practical and useful. For example:

- home decorating, gardening and other household books and radio and TV programmes
- the features pages of newspapers and magazines
- books, articles, and programmes about countries, institutions, organizations, and developing situations

Good exposition is clear, logically ordered, and hits exactly the right level for the reader; it provides the information required, but does not assume knowledge and understanding that the reader does not possess.

Writing exposition

It is not easy to write good expository prose. Most people can work their way through a story with considerably greater confidence than they can through an explanation. This is probably linked to the important part storytelling plays in the lives of most people from an early age. By contrast, for many of us explaining is something we learned to do when things went wrong and we were in some kind of trouble!

It will help considerably if you focus on a few key areas.

Background knowledge

See also:
- **Chapter 11** *Audience* (p. 89)

It is important to have a clear idea of:

- what background knowledge you can assume that your audience already has
- what additional background information they need before the main exposition can begin. This will include not only general information, but also the language needed to discuss the topic.

This information can be presented in different ways:

- **all at the beginning**
  This has the advantage that it gets it over with all at once, but if this introduction is extended, it may prove rather daunting so that the audience may be tempted to 'switch off'—which can be counter-productive.

- **in stages as required**
  This places the necessary background information at the point where it is needed and avoids an over-long introduction. It has the

disadvantage that those who already know this material may find it rather trying.

- **in a supplement or annexe to which readers are referred**
  In a written text, this leaves the main exposition clean and uncluttered, but some readers may not bother to turn to the back for information that they need.

Taking your audience with you

Closely related to this are the twin questions of clarity and pace. Probably more so than in narrative and description, the elements of an exposition are closely linked and interdependent. If the audience fails to grasp one component it may well prove fatal to their understanding of the whole.

It is important to ensure that:

- you have not assumed knowledge that does not exist
- each part of your exposition is properly 'keyed in' to what has gone before and there are no gaps
- you have got the pace right, so that all members of your audience can grasp what you are saying, but you are not going so slowly that some are bored or insulted

Argument

The key features of argument are that:

- an opinion or point of view is expressed—with which others may or may not agree
- the reasons for that point of view are stated—or at least implied

An argument may also seek to persuade—often we want other people to agree with us—but it doesn't have to. The following text does not seek to persuade. It presents both sides of a longstanding disagreement and leaves it to the reader to decide.

Foxhunting

For: hunts help protect wildlife

1

Foxes are vermin which need controlling—the Royal Society for the Protection of Birds has to shoot them to protect endangered bird species at some reserves. There are about a quarter of a million foxes before the start of each breeding season and their numbers appear to be rising. They kill huge numbers of game birds reared for shoots and also slaughter some new-born lambs.

Against: cruel, divisive sport

1

Foxhunting is the least effective way of controlling the fox population, probably accounting for less than one-tenth of foxes killed by humans. While the pro-hunting lobby argues that it is helping to curb rising fox numbers, across much of lowland England the hunts themselves effectively admit that this is not the reason they hunt when they say that a lower fox population would

2

Foxhunting is one of the main reasons why the traditional, diverse landscape of hedgerows, copses, and spinneys has been preserved across much of England. Farmers who enjoy or support the hunt plant or maintain woodlands to provide cover for foxes and hedges for horses to jump. This is good for other wildlife as well as the scenery.

3

The sport is an important plank in the rural economy. According to a consultants' report commissioned by the hunting lobby, the hunts directly employ 9,500 people, while there are 7,000 jobs in associated trades such as grooms and stable staff. The report suggests a further 23,200 rural jobs would disappear if hunting were banned—in veterinary surgeries, feed merchants, saddle-makers, etc.

4

Hunting is a key part of rural society and recreation. Up to 250,000 people take part each year, most of them as on-foot followers. It brings a variety of professions and classes together and is adrenalin-boosting, traditional, fresh-air fun.

harm their sport. The Ministry of Agriculture says foxes may take large numbers of lambs on some farms but they are not 'a significant factor in lamb mortality nationally'. And foxes help to keep down the numbers of rabbits, a destructive farm pest.

2

Hunting is becoming less of a force in conserving hedgerows and spinneys, according to an Oxford University fox expert, Dr David Macdonald. Farmers have a more general interest in conservation, and a variety of state incentives now encourage them to protect landscapes and wildlife.

3

Hunting's opponents do not question that the bloodsport maintains large numbers of rural jobs but they say the hunts should switch to drag hunting, in which the hounds follow an artificial scent trail and no foxes are involved.

4

Hunting is a divisive issue in the countryside as well as between town and country; many farmers and rural dwellers oppose it. It may be fun but it is unacceptably cruel. The fox may be killed swiftly, but it suffers extreme stress and fear during the chase. A fox which has gone underground and is pursued by terriers, dug out and shot endures further anguish. Pre-season cub-hunting in the autumn, when the hounds are familiarised with fox scent and kill cubs, is especially cruel.

It is possible to use this 'ammunition' in a number of different ways.

Expressing a point of view

An important use of argument is to present one's point of view and the reasons for it:

> I find it bizarre that in the closing years of the twentieth century men and women dressed up in funny clothes should ride across farmland on expensive horses with a lot of tame dogs, chasing one wild dog.
>   If you ask them what they are doing and why . . .

In expressing this point of view, the writer is not seeking primarily to persuade others to agree. It is the expression of a point of view. The vigour with which the view is expressed and the tone adopted may have that effect incidentally, but that is not the prime aim.

'Come and join us'

A step further is to take one point of view wholeheartedly and to try to sell it to anyone you can persuade to listen. This approach is used in posters and advertisements for organizations opposed to or in favour of hunting.

Sitting on the fence or near it

The old truism tells us that 'there are two sides to every argument' and sometimes we may genuinely have mixed feelings about an issue, perhaps because the arguments for and against are very evenly balanced, or because they are are very complex. In such a situation the speaker or writer may prefer to present both sides of the argument, much as was done in the text quoted earlier, and explain the weight which he or she attached to the different strands.

If you are writing or speaking in a personal context—explaining your thoughts and feelings to a friend, for example—this approach has much to recommend it. If on the other hand you have been asked to come up with a recommended course of action—in a business context, for example—then you not likely to find it helpful.

Presenting an argument

A successful argument, whether spoken or written, depends on three things:

Purpose

You need a clear idea of why you are presenting this argument. The commonest purposes are:

- **to inform**
  the text on pages 133 and 134 informs the reader of the key arguments for and against hunting

- **to persuade or influence others**
  the text on page 135 sets out to persuade the reader that hunting is wrong

- **to interact**
  you may wish to express a personal viewpoint and the reasons for it as part of your relationship with someone else

Pros and cons

1 You must have a clear idea of the reasons for and against the viewpoint(s) you are presenting.
2 Reasons can be either:
   - factual evidence which most people will accept:

There are about a quarter of a million foxes before the start of each breeding season and their numbers appear to be rising . . . so they . . . need controlling.

■ a logical progression from a starting point that those who hold a different opinion should find it difficult to reject:

While the pro-hunting lobby argues that it is helping to curb rising fox numbers, across much of lowland England the hunts themselves effectively admit that this is not the reason they hunt when they say that a lower fox population would harm their sport.

3 You must somehow take account of contrary arguments. You can:
■ present both sides of the argument and then come down on one side or the other, explaining why (or sit on the fence, if that is what you have decided)
■ state your own opinion and the reasons for it. State the contrary arguments as you go and explain clearly why they are wrong.
■ state your own opinion and the reasons for it. Do not refer to contrary arguments directly but 'rubbish' anyone who does not agree with you.

Tone and style   The way in which your argument is presented will be largely decided by the two preceding considerations. It is very important to adopt a tone that is suitable for your purpose and for the style in which you have decided to present your case. If you are addressing a group of senior managers on the argument in favour of purchasing an important piece of capital equipment, it is not advisable to adopt the tone of someone arguing about football in a pub—and vice versa.

How it works

The four modes that have been described are sometimes used separately, but often they are combined, as in this illustration:

Description
the writer sets the scene and describes what he could see

The narrow street was crowded with people. Old men leant on sticks side by side with mothers holding babies; teenagers chatted in a relaxed way, and above them the balconies were crowded with spectators. Vendors of sweets, soft drinks and peanuts made their way through the throng.

Narrative
now he begins to tell the story of what happened

A murmur began to work its way through the crowd. All heads turned towards the the church of St John the Baptist at the end of street. Suddenly silence fell as the great doors of the church began to swing open.

Behind me someone spoke and all around a sibilant hushing demanded silence. We all craned towards the doors and then it began. A great procession of black-hooded figures, all wearing the tall conical hats of the penitents, made their way out of the church and into the street.

Behind them, high above our heads, came a gigantic statue of Christ on the cross. It stood on a platform covered with blue irises and was carried on the shoulders of perhaps as many as a hundred men, moving slowly in step along the street. As they approached we could see that some were blindfold and many were barefoot: a strange and moving sight.

Exposition

he explains why this procession is taking place

This was Semana Santa in Malaga. In the week leading up to Easter there are processions all over Spain and other Catholic countries, to commemorate the events leading to Christ's Crucifixion. Those in Malaga are particularly elaborate. From four o'clock every afternoon until the early hours of the morning, the whole of the city centre is taken over by these massive processions.

Argument

he considers the different arguments people give to explain the continuing popularity of these celebrations

It is difficult for an agnostic from a protestant and undemonstrative culture like ours to understand why people should behave in this way. I was told that many of these people, especially the men, never enter a church from one year's end to the next. Some say that they do the procession to atone for this. Cynics add that, like all Latins, they love a show. Whatever the reason, you have to accept that there is more to Semana Santa than a petrified relic of a dead belief. It still has meaning.

You try

What is the main mode of each of these texts?

A In Africa universities were seen, with some accuracy, as focal points for all the malcontents and ideamongers in the country. Along with the television station, they were the first to go in times of trouble.

B It had a rather insubstantial rear, which later models moulded into extravagant fish tails of chrome and steel. The driver rested one delicate arm, as muscled but fine as an antelope's, on the sill.

C I watched him pull the stick towards him and down for first gear. We drove smoothly along Victoria Road and turned into Zwane, past the church. The driver glanced at me from time to time.

D He is a remarkable broadcaster and someone I have admired since I was a child. Despite the fact that millions of people are listening to him, he always sounds as if he is having a one-to-one conversation; there is an intimacy there which, as a listener, whatever you are doing, you respond to without thinking. He also makes his broadcasts sound effortless.

Guidelines

Narrative

1 Make sure you have a clear idea of the order in which events happened.
2 Think about:
   - audience
   - purpose
3 Decide what background information—if any—the audience need.
4 Decide on the order in which to present the background information and the events:
   - chronological order is simplest to use and easiest to follow
   - starting in the middle can be dramatic but needs careful handling
   - different situations and formats may demand a particular ordering
5 Think carefully about audience and tone when presenting the narrative.
6 You can change the emphasis you give a story by giving more weight to some events than to others.

Description

1 Before beginning a piece of description think about:
   - purpose
   - audience
2 Then decide how personal or impersonal your writing should be.
3 Your preparation may involve research, memory, reflection, or a combination of these.
4 You should also give careful thought to the order and pattern of your description. This may be strictly logical or it may be more creative or intuitive. It must lead the reader through so that the relationship between the parts of your description is clearly seen.
5 Try to appeal to your audience's senses of sight, sound, smell, touch, and taste.

Exposition

1 Consider your audience carefully to work out what background material they will need:
   - information
   - terminology
2 Decide how this should be introduced:
   - at the beginning
   - as you go along
   - separately—e.g., in the appendix of a piece of writing.
3 Use your knowledge of your audience to make sure that you take them with you. Try to imagine the problems they may have in following different elements of your exposition, and allow for these.
4 Build in revision and consolidation as you go, especially where the topic is large-scale or complex.
5 Use visuals to support your text and even to replace parts of it.

Argument

1 Decide on your approach:
   - a statement of your view with reasons
   - an attempt to persuade others to your point of view

- a statement of the arguments on each side with a clearly stated preference and the reasons for it
- a statement of the opposing sides without any final judgement

2 Support the planks of your argument with:
  - evidence
  - reasoning from an agreed position, or evidence and arguments already presented

3 Think about audience and purpose when deciding on the style and tone of your text.

You try: key

pages 127–8 Clearly the first paper has given a lot more space to the story than the second, so it must believe that it is of greater interest to its readers. The headlines already suggest a difference of emphasis, with the second account making use of the derogatory word 'booze' to ensure that its readers know what was involved—and what to think of it. The same word is then repeated in the story. The first account uses the more neutral phrase 'banned for drink driving' and keeps it out of the headline.

The first account carries a lot more detail about Alexander Bonsor's lifestyle and we get the impression that the whole affair was a bit of a prank and not to be taken too seriously. The second story does not appear to take such a lenient view of the affair, although it does not go so far as to openly criticize the subject of the story.

The first extract is taken from the *Daily Mail*, the second from the *Mirror*.

pages 130–1 The first extract is from a travel writer's account of a stay in Delhi. The second comes from a guidebook. The first pulls no punches and gives us a personal account of the writer's earlier preconceptions and later disillusion. The second account does not attempt to pretend that the romantic view of Chandni Chowk is entirely true to life, but it does still give a qualified recommendation: 'It's a fascinating area, but . . .'

As might be expected from a guidebook, the second extract contains a mass of detailed information. The first piece, on the other hand, is more concerned to paint a picture and so selects detail with this in mind.

page 137 A, although historical, is essentially exposition. B is description. C is narrative. D presents an argument.

The English Language

16: Talking about English

This section is about how English works. But our language is very varied and always in a state of change, so before we can begin to look at the elements of English—grammar, vocabulary, and so on—we need to understand about dialects and standard English, and the ways in which English has developed and continues to change. It is also important to understand that there are two opposed approaches to grammar: the traditional, which seeks to lay down rules about what we should and should not do; and the modern, descriptive approach, which sets out to describe the ways in which language is actually used.

17: Introduction to grammar

This chapter sets out the main levels of language that grammar describes: words, phrases, clauses, and sentences. It then focuses on simple (one-clause) sentences and analyses their possible component parts: subject, verb, object, complement, and adverbial.

18: More about grammar

This chapter continues the analysis by looking at multiple sentences (sentences with more than one clause). Compound sentences contain two or more clauses of equal status joined by conjunctions like *but* and *or*. In complex sentences, one clause is more important, the main clause, while other clauses are subordinate to it. Such sentences can be constructed in a very large number of ways and some of the most important of these are analysed. The chapter concludes with an examination of some of the problems associated with multiple sentences.

19: Vocabulary

We all have a range of words we use in speech and writing, and there are many more words which we understand when we come across them. Our vocabulary can be extended by the skilful use of suitable word books such as dictionaries and thesauruses. It also helps to understand how words are constructed, with a stem, prefix, and suffix. Words are not just 'bundles of meaning'; people have attitudes to them and their use in particular situations. Some words are regarded as slang, or informal, while others are 'taboo'. We need to be sensitive to this aspect of vocabulary.

20: Spelling An analysis of why and how spelling can be a problem, followed by advice on tackling difficulties. The main spelling rules are then set out, followed by lists of problem words, grouped by type.

21: Punctuation This chapter lists all the punctuation points, giving detailed advice on their use.

22: Speech Although speech seems perfectly natural, it is helpful to have a basic understanding of how it is produced and the ways in which our voices can express subtle shades of meaning. The introductory analysis of the individual speech sounds of English is followed by a consideration of stress, intonation, accent, and pronunciation.

Talking about English

Which English are we talking about?

Talking about the English language is complicated by two important facts:

- **English is constantly changing**
  English is the product of 1500 years' development and is continuing to grow and change.

- **There is more than one version of English**
  English is not one monolithic language but a large number of dialects. Each major English-speaking country has its own version of the language and within countries there are regional dialects, too. Fortunately there is a **standard English**, which is widely used in writing and formal speech. In addition to dialects, we have to be aware of important differences between written and spoken English.

How are we talking about it?

There are two opposed views about how we should talk about language:

- **Traditional grammar**
  Based on the grammar of Latin, this view prescribes how language should be used; believes that language is static not dynamic; and only focuses on formal English.

- **Descriptive grammar**
  Modern linguists concentrate on how English is used by real people and do not set out to prescribe how it should be used. An understanding of the elements of grammar can be very useful to users of English.

Which English are we talking about?

The way in which people use their own language is the subject of much debate and disagreement. Some people become very angry about the way in which others, especially those in the media and public life, speak and write. The linguist David Crystal invited listeners to his radio series about language to write to him describing language usage they liked or disliked. Hardly anyone wrote about usage they liked, but many—especially listeners over fifty—wrote at length about 'pet hates'. Crystal noted that the language his correspondents used was frequently intemperate. They referred to expressions they disliked as *abominations* and said they were *appalled* and *driven wild* by the way in which English was being *prostituted*.

There are three reasons why people disagree about language usage and why, as a result, the debate about English will continue to be heated:

1 English is not static but dynamic; its vocabulary and grammar continue to develop and change, as they have done for centuries. People who are innately conservative feel threatened by changes in 'their own' language.
2 There isn't just one version of English but many; in different geographical regions people use different vocabulary and grammar, and there are also variations according to social groupings. Language can be a sign of group membership, and some people are tempted to see others who use it differently as inferior in some way.
3 While academic students of language, linguists, insist on **describing** the ways in which English is used, many others who write and speak about it insist on **prescribing** how it should be used. The ways in which these two groups develop their arguments are completely different.

It is useful to look at these three points in a little more detail before we begin to examine how English works.

Our changing language

Without going into a detailed survey of the history of English, it is worth pointing out that the origins of the language we speak today go back over 1500 years. When the Angles, Saxons, and Jutes invaded Britain in the 5th century, they effectively imposed their language on their new territories. Much the same happened at the Norman Conquest 600 years later, and the first version of English that is recognizable to the modern reader developed out of this fusion of the Germanic language of the Anglo-Saxons with the French spoken by the Normans. But even that English is a long way from the language we speak today. When Chaucer writes,

> Whilom ther was dwellinge at Oxenford
> A riche gnof, that gestes heeld to bord,
> And of his craft he was a carpenter.
> With him ther was dwellinge a poure scoler,
> Hadde lerned art, but al his fantasie
> Was turned for to lerne astrologie . . .

> (There once lived in Oxford a wealthy lout who took in lodgers. He was a carpenter by trade. He had living with him a poor scholar who had studied for his degree but was obsessed with the idea of learning astrology . . .)

we can recognize it as English—but only just.

By the time we get to Shakespeare, some 200 years later, the language being used is much more obviously like modern English, but it still isn't the language we speak today. In this brief extract from *Twelfth Night*, Malvolio has been woken up by the drunken singing of Sir Toby and his friends:

MALVOLIO: My masters, are you mad? Or what are you? Have you no wit, manners, nor honesty, but to gabble like tinkers at this time of night? Do ye make an alehouse of my lady's house, that ye squeak out your coziers' catches without any mitigation or remorse of voice? Is there no respect of place, persons, nor time in you?

SIR TOBY: We did keep time, sir, in our catches. Sneck up!

While a modern reader can understand much of what is going on, some of the words are strange. For example, most readers will have a very good idea of what Sir Toby means when he tells Malvolio to 'sneck up', but they are unlikely to have come across the word 'sneck' before.

Since Shakespeare's day some words have disappeared from use, while others have changed their meanings. New words have come into the language. It would be a mistake to assume that this process has come to an end, but a mistake that is commonly made. As long as people have discussed language usage, there have been those who deplore the ways in which it is changing, just as there have been people who want to be in the forefront ('on the cusp', 'at the cutting edge', to use two relatively recent expressions) of that change.

Where you place yourself in relation to this process of change is a personal choice, made—as many other choices are—after a consideration both of how you feel about the ways in which the language is changing and of how other people will regard you. If, for example, you are a barrister arguing a detailed and complex civil case, then the use of a lot of 'fashionable' expressions may well not be appreciated. On the other hand, if you are an advertising executive you would probably not speak to your clients in language suitable for the barrister. Language choice and expression are matters of awareness and sensitivity to the situation you are in.

You try

The words and expressions in the list below all appear in *The Longman Register of New Words* 1989 edition. Try dividing them into three categories:

A: still 'new' or 'fresh'
B: current common usage, and so unremarkable
C: stale and dated

bratpack	card swipe
networker	pressing the flesh
dork	crumbly
moral majority	infomercial
des res	mega

Just as English vocabulary continues to change, so does English grammar, although at a slower pace. In the past, for example, it would have been frowned on to begin a sentence, *If I was you* . . . Now this is increasingly heard, even from the mouths of educated speakers. Some will argue that there is an important difference between

> If I *were* captaining the team, I'd . . .

and

> If I *was* captaining the team, I'd . . .

The first, they say, means that the speaker believes that there is not the remotest possibility of the situation arising, while the second regards it as unlikely, but possible. If language is developing towards the abandonment of *If I were*, however, it means that more and more people will simply not pick up this difference—so we shall have to find other ways of communicating the same meaning.

People who discuss language use take up one of three positions about the way in which English is changing:

1 They disapprove of change and hark back to a golden age when English was in some way purer. This is the spirit that made the French set up their Academy and later even pass laws banning the use of English words where there were French words that would serve.
2 They simply describe the changes without any comment about whether they are good or bad.
3 They describe the change and attempt to judge how far it has progressed and how people are reacting to it. The purpose of this is to help people to judge which usage they should adopt themselves.

The first group cannot, ultimately, win; their campaigns to 'defend the language' may give them some satisfaction but will not make any difference. The second group are safe but unhelpful to the everyday user. It is only the third group that can give the everyday user of English helpful advice: a mixture of factual information and balanced judgement. Here, for example, is Godfrey Howard in *The Good English Guide*:

> **-related**   In the fast lanes of the 1990s there is a constant drive to speed up communication. As a word joined on with a hyphen, *-related* is a short cut. Instead of 'illnesses caused by stress', 'crimes caused by drink', 'negotiations about money', we have stress-related illnesses, drink-related crimes, money-related negotiations. It would be a pity to overdo this or, like any other useful linguistic device, it would degenerate into jargon.

How many 'Englishes'?

Most people are aware that people in the United States and people in Britain speak the same language but with important differences of vocabulary and grammar. An English reader would probably pick up that this message was written by an American:

> I would be happy to meet with you while I am in Oxford. Mornings are best because I will be teaching in the M.B.A. program in the afternoon . . .

Both *meet with* (for British *meet*) and *program* (for *course*) give the game away.

American English has a powerful influence ('impacts heavily') on British usage. Many people are fairly relaxed about this, but some purists resent this Americanization of English. It tends to be new words, especially technical and social ones, that transfer most readily. Despite the close contacts between the two countries a number of common words remain steadfastly different. Britons still speak of *taps*, *cupboards*, and *lifts* rather than *faucets*, *closets* and *elevators*, for example.

Many other English-speaking countries, such as Australia and India, also have distinctive versions of the language, and even within Britain and the other countries there are important variations of dialect. To the academic linguist, no one dialect is better than any other; they are simply different. For the user, social attitudes are important and if you ignore them, you risk alienating those who hold different attitudes from yourself.

Standard English

Ever since the invention of printing there has been pressure to standardize English. When Caxton set up his printing press in the fifteenth century, he was aware of the problems caused by the variety of different dialects spoken in England. He had to choose which dialect and which spellings to adopt when publishing books in English. The period since then has seen the evolution of standard English, which may be only one more dialect of the language, but which has far more social prestige than the others and which is normally used in writing as well as being used in all formal or semi-formal speech situations.

Standard English is not, however, something fixed. When people who write about language describe a usage as 'non-standard', they are making a judgement based on experience, rather than a statement of scientific fact. This is perhaps easier to understand if one compares the possible alternatives.

See also:
■ **Chapter 11: *Audience***
(p. 89)

standard English:	*very frightened*
informal English:	*scared stiff*
regional dialect:	*frit*
taboo slang:	*shit scared*

The formal phrase will always work and will offend no one. The informal expression is acceptable in many situations and is on the edge of being standard English. Until the 1970s *frit*, on the other hand, would not have been heard in formal situations, being a dialect word—until it was used by the then prime minister, Margaret Thatcher. Now it would be regarded as acceptable informal usage—which is certainly not the case with the fourth item in the list.

You try

Which of the following, if any, would you describe as standard English?

1 Let's get this show on the road.

2 He got down on his hunkers.

3 It happened in the dead of winter.

4 She had just argued herself into a corner.

5 Most of the women were only working there to earn some pin money.

6 When we got home my wife wrote them a bread-and-butter letter.

Speech and writing

The way in which we use language when we speak need not be different from how we use it when we write, but it often is. When we use speech in face-to-face conversation, our audience is present and we can adjust what we say according to their response. We can use gesture, facial expression, and vocal tone in order to help us communicate. On the other hand, speech, unlike writing, takes place in 'real time'. A written text can be revised and rewritten until we are satisfied with it. Spoken language, on the other hand, is—apparently at least—spontaneous and made up as we go along. As a result we have to revise and recast our sentences even as they are being uttered. Alternatively we have to add other sentences which revise or clarify the meaning of what has gone before. Here, for example, are two students discussing how we judge people by the way they speak:

> A: A lot of people—as soon as you open your mouth they judge you by what comes out.
>
> B: My mother's from Birmingham and my dad's from Leicester— my mother especially is—is—it's obviously not deliberate—but because she works in the university she's got . . . she's—like— adopted over the years this quite stuffy accent really.

The standard English version of what A says would be written as:

> As soon as you open your mouth a lot of people judge you by what comes out.

In what B says, we can see the process of 'instantaneous revision' going on, with false starts and rephrasing as she sorts out what she wants to say.

This is not to say that spontaneous speech is just sloppy language. In ordinary conversation we cannot work out carefully in advance exactly how each sentence is going to be constructed. If we did, conversation would become boring and stilted. Instead of careful formal constructions we rely on the listener's goodwill and on our own ability to reconstruct and explain as we go along.

In situations where we cannot be sure of that goodwill, or where it is important to sound confident, prepared, and unhesitant, then some form of preparation is required and this produces speech that is less spontaneous and more like written standard English.

See also:
■ **Chapter 13** *Time and place* (p. 108)

How are we talking about it?

We have already seen that different attitudes towards language affect the way in which we talk about it and the conclusions we draw.

Traditional grammar

In the past, many scholars attempted to describe the grammar of English in terms of Latin. They worked on the assumption that this was a standard grammatical structure which could be applied to all languages, including English. Since all languages work in different ways and their grammars have to reflect this, the attempt to impose a Latinate grammar on English was not a success. It led to a number of important side effects:

■ Traditional grammarians tried to prescribe how the language should be used. Where the flexibility of English meant that it did not fit the imposed Latinate grammar very well, they said that this was because language was being used sloppily.
■ They believed that language should be fixed and unchanging. Where changes occurred they were for the worse.
■ They believed that only the standard form of the language should be used and that all other forms were inferior. Pushed to its extreme this meant that American English was inferior to British English.

Some of these attitudes still linger on, as we have seen, but during the twentieth century a new approach to grammar has developed and been broadly accepted.

Modern descriptive grammar

The modern approach is to take a large selection of language, to study it scientifically and then to describe exactly how it actually works. Grammars of this kind also produce 'rules', but they are rules which explain how things work—just as the law of gravity does in physics—rather than telling people what to do. For example, traditional grammarians would object to splitting an infinitive. They would argue that the form *to go* constitutes a grammatical unit (since in Latin the infinitive *ire* [to go] is one word) so no words should come between *to* and *go*. To write *to boldly go*, therefore, is wrong. A modern grammarian, on the other hand, would say something like this:

> Infinitival *to* is a separate word, and therefore adverbials (especially single adverbs) sometimes intervene between it and the infinitive. The interruption results in what is traditionally known as the split infinitive.
>
> **Sidney Greenbaum:** *The Oxford English Grammar*

The writer does not say whether he considers it right or wrong, but explains, technically, that it happens and how it works.

Modern descriptive grammar, therefore, deals in facts. The conclusions it draws may be more or less accurate, depending on the skill of the practitioner. But this is in stark contrast to traditional prescriptive grammar which deals in opinions, many of which are based on false information or false reasoning.

The need for guidance

All of this is of little help to the person who wants advice on how to speak and write. Traditional grammarians are too narrow and unyielding in the advice they give, which is often unscientific and unreliable; modern grammarians do not offer advice. It would be tempting to assume that as a result anything goes.

Tempting but wrong. This can be shown by three simple examples. Each of these sentences has something 'wrong' with it, but the reasons for that 'wrongness' are different.

1 Who was that girl I saw you with?
2 Several of my friends, including Jamie, has decided to have a holiday together this year.
3 I'll see her when I shall go to Bristol.

Number 1 is disapproved of by some traditionalists, who say that you should not end a sentence with a preposition. This a matter of stylistic prejudice and is not based on grammar at all. Number 2, on the other hand, is an error of grammar. The subject of the sentence is 'Several of my friends', so the verb should be 'have decided'. The speaker has presumably been confused by the fact that the singular 'Jamie' comes immediately before the verb. Sentence 3 is not one that is likely to be constructed by a native speaker of English, but contains an error often made by foreign learners. It is a literal translation of what might be said in French, for example. In English, even if a *when* clause refers to the future we use the present tense ('I'll see her when I go to Bristol') or the present perfect ('I'll see her when I've finished the shopping').

So some knowledge of grammar would help explain the mistake in sentence 2 to a native speaker and the mistake in sentence 3 to a foreign learner. A basic understanding of the general structure of English and a handful of technical terms with which to describe its main features are useful tools for any user of the language. They can be used to analyse writing and speech, and to help develop a sense of style.

A simple grammatical grounding, and the necessary technical terms, are the subject matter of the next two chapters. The grammatical content is kept to an absolute minimum and all the terms used are explained in the glossary on pages 285–96, to which readers who need to can refer for guidance.

> ### You try
>
> Each of the following sentences would be objected to by some people. What are your feelings about each of them?
>
> 1 The car I have just bought is totally different to the last one I had.
> 2 I was trying hard to fully understand his problems.
> 3 Peter Davies was the person I sold my last car to.
> 4 I will send you the invoice next week.
> 5 None of my friends like Tom Cruise films.
> 6 The British media is dominated by a small number of wealthy men.
> 7 We hope to be able to finalize the deal in the next few days.
> 8 There are less Spaniards living in some sections of the Costa del Sol than expatriates.
> 9 I am really interested of impressionist paintings.
> 10 Her latest film is centred around the last earthquake to strike San Francisco.

Guidelines

1 When thinking about language, remember that it is living, not dead. It continues to develop and change. To use English well, you need to be aware of how it is being used in different situations and for different purposes. Some changes don't 'take', but others last a long time, so it is impossible to have one single attitude towards all new words and expressions. How you react to change depends on who you are and the social contexts in which you write and speak.

2 Remember, too, that English exists in many different dialects. The 'official' form, **standard English**, is suitable for nearly all writing and for formal occasions when you are addressing people whom you do not know well, or in situations when people expect formality. At other times the use of a regional or social dialect may well be more suitable. But if in doubt, use standard English.

3 Do not expect modern grammatical writers to tell you how to speak and write; their function is to describe how English *is* used, rather than how it *should* be. Guides to usage can help you here, but they are based on the writer's judgement, so some are better than others. Look around in libraries and bookshops before selecting one that answers the questions you have in a way that you find helpful.

You try: key

page 145   Your response to this will depend on who you are and when you make it. This chapter was written late in October 1996. At that time, and for the writer, it looked like this:

bratpack	slightly dated
card swipe	current
networker	current
pressing the flesh	dated but usable in a slightly ironic way
dork	not my generation, but probably passé
crumbly	in the sense of 'an older person', slightly dated
moral majority	a useful historical term
infomercial	reasonably modern
des res	only in ironic use, anyway
mega	slightly dated

page 148   Again these are personal judgements:

1 informal
2 informal
3 standard
4 standard
5 informal
6 informal

page 151   1 People disagree about whether *different to* and *different than* are acceptable. They have been widely used by many famous writers for centuries. The argument is that if you can say *similar to* there is no reason why you can't say *different to*. The use of *different than* tends to be American. If you don't want to be criticized by people who fuss about things like this, use *different from*.

2 A split infinitive. Nothing wrong with it. If you put *fully* anywhere else in the sentence it sounds awkward.

3 Some people object to a preposition at the end of a sentence, but for no good reason. If you avoid it by saying . . . *to whom I sold* . . . it sounds a bit strained.

4 Some people say that it should be 'I shall . . . ' for normal future time and that 'I will' is emphatic, but this is clearly dying out, especially in speech.

5 The *Oxford English Dictionary* states that 'none' means 'no persons', so this sentence is correct. Some people, however, argue that 'none' is a shortened form of 'no one' and so is singular.

6 Technically 'media' is a plural and should be followed by 'are', but few people follow this rule these days, except in very formal writing.

7 Some people object to -ize forms like 'finalize'. Certainly, 'finalize' says nothing that 'complete' or 'conclude' does not.

8 'Spaniards' is a countable noun, so 'fewer' would be better.

9 Standard English is 'interested in'.

10 The centre is the mid-point of something, so 'centred on' is correct.

17 Introduction to grammar

Grammar analyses language at different levels. In particular it is concerned with:

- sentences
- clauses
- phrases
- words

There are four sentence types:

- statements
- questions
- directives
- exclamations

Simple sentences contain one finite verb. The five elements they can contain are:

- subject
- verb
- object
- complement
- adverbial

Sentence length and variety are important when writing. Verbless ('minor') sentences can have their place but need to be used sparingly.

Introduction

To many people grammar appears threatening and even impossible to understand. This is often because of the way in which it has been presented to them, whether at school or later in their lives. The purpose of this chapter is to provide a simple introduction to what grammar is and how a basic understanding of it can be used to see how simple sentences are constructed. Chapter 18, *More about grammar*, as its name suggests, goes into more detail.

Grammar is a set of rules which describe how a language works. These are rules in the sense that scientific laws are rules: general statements that describe how things are, not moral regulations like the Ten Commandments. Grammar can be divided into two:

- The rules which describe how words are arranged to make sentences. The technical name for this is **syntax**. Syntax explains why these two sentences have different meanings:
  The cat sat on the mat.
  The mat sat on the cat.
- The rules which describe how words are changed to fit into sentences. Linguists call this **morphology**. Morphology explains why these two sentences have different meanings:
  The cat sat on the mat.
  The cat sits on the mat.

Levels

One of the difficulties of grasping grammar is that there seem to be so many things going on at the same time: are we supposed to be looking at the whole sentence, or bits of it? And if the answer is, 'Bits of it,' how do we know which bits to look at?

Grammar answers this by working at a number of different levels. They can be illustrated by this sample sentence:

The cat sat on the mat, while the dog ate its dinner.

We can divide this **sentence** into two **clauses**

The cat sat on the mat	*while the dog ate its dinner.*
MAIN CLAUSE	SUBORDINATE CLAUSE

Each clause is composed of different **clause elements**:

The cat	*sat*	*on the mat*
SUBJECT	VERB	ADVERBIAL

Each of these can be considered as a **phrase**:

The cat	*sat*	*on the mat*
NOUN PHRASE	VERB PHRASE	PREPOSITIONAL PHRASE

Each phrase in the sentence is made up of words and each word belongs to a particular **word class**:

The	*cat*	*sat*	*on*	*the*	*mat*
ARTICLE	NOUN	VERB	PREPOSITION	ARTICLE	NOUN

So there are all these different levels to think about when talking about grammar:

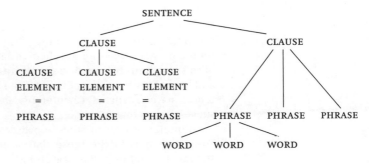

Definitions

It would seem reasonable at this stage to proceed to a simple definition of each of these levels: 'A sentence is . . . ' and so on. Unfortunately the experts find it difficult (many would say impossible) to give a clear simple definition of what a sentence is. This can give writers about grammar a slightly shifty air, as they try to avoid answering that 'big question'.

The approach in this chapter is as follows. Most people who speak English have in fact got a fairly good working understanding of sentences. Much of the time they have no difficulty in telling you what is and what is not a sentence. Problems arise when they write a sentence that they think may be suspect and they want advice about how it should be put right. The focus in this book is on just such problem situations. Usually they can be resolved by understanding how the components of the sentence work together. For example, a large proportion of such sentence problems have to do with the relationship between the subject and the verb. So it is important to be able to identify the subject and the verb and to understand a number of key features about them.

In this chapter we concentrate on simple sentences. These are sentences that consist of one clause, with one subject and one verb. Chapter 18 then looks at more complicated constructions and their related problems.

Types of sentence

The sentences we use can be divided into four types, according to their purpose:

- **Statements**
  Mr Sanderson is leaving the company next month.

- **Questions**
  Why is Mr Sanderson leaving the company next month?

- **Directives** (sometimes called commands or requests):
  Clear your desk before leaving.

- **Exclamations**
  What a worker that man was!

All simple statement sentences contain **one subject** and **one verb**.

The subject

Position and meaning

In a statement sentence, the subject normally comes before the verb. It often (but not always) gives information on what the sentence will be about, or where its focus will be, as in these sentences:

Success drives many managers.
Many of my friends are unhappy in their work.

This is not always true, however. Sometimes the subject gives little away:

It is not always easy to spot a successful product.

The subject of a sentence may be:

- **A noun**
People are strange.

- **A noun phrase**
This is a group of words based on a noun:
The people in our department will miss Mr Sanderson.
The noun phrase marked is based on the noun *people*.

- **A pronoun**
This is a word which 'stands for' a noun, a noun phrase, or some other group of words which has recently been mentioned.
They say the strangest things.

Warning   The subject does not always come first in the sentence. It is often preceded by other words, placed in brackets in these examples:

[During the whole of last year] **I** only went fishing twice.
[Fortunately for the fish] **my luck** was out.

The subject does not always come before the verb, although this is uncommon:

Standing in the corner was **my old friend Mrs Isaacs**.

The verb

The grammatical term 'verb' can be used to refer to a class of words, like *be, happen,* and *kill.* It is also used to refer to one part of a clause or sentence (when it is sometimes referred to as the **verb phrase**). This is how it is being used in this section.

Position   In a statement sentence the verb usually comes after the subject:

Mrs Hart **hates** ice cream.

It does not necessarily come immediately after the subject. In this sentence the words in brackets come between the *subject* and the **verb**:

She [only recently] **started to eat** yogurt again.

In exceptional cases, as we have seen, the verb may come before the subject:

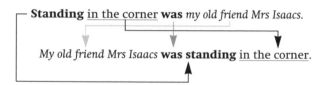

Standing <u>in the corner</u> **was** *my old friend Mrs Isaacs.*

My old friend Mrs Isaacs **was standing** <u>in the corner</u>.

Meaning The verb provides important information about the subject. It usually refers to:

- **an action**
  The volcano **destroyed** the village.

- **a state or condition**
  I **hate** American football.

Or it may act as a **link** between the subject and the rest of the sentence:

My father's first name **is** Peter.

The form of the verb phrase

The verb in a sentence may be one word or several:

I **visited** Paris last week.
I **should have been visiting** my grandfather today.

When the verb phrase consists of several words, these are all verbs. They are either:

- **full verbs**
  These are verbs that can stand on their own in a sentence, without reference to any other verb. They are mostly words with a 'dictionary meaning'. For example:
  collect   make   send   suggest

- **auxiliary verbs**
  These are verbs which work with the full verb. They are:
  shall   should   will   would   may
  might   can   could   must

- In addition there are three verbs which can work either as full verbs or as auxiliaries:
  be/is/am/was, etc.   have/has/had   do/does/did, etc.
  These are called **primary verbs**.

Parts of a verb Verbs exist in these forms:

- **the infinitive**
  This is the 'to' form of the verb:
  *to **sleep**, perchance to **dream***
  If you remove the *to*, you are left with the verb **stem**, which—in regular verbs at least—is used to form:

- **the -ing form**
  describing   laughing

- **the -ed form**
  described   laughed

This is used in a number of different **tenses**:

I described   I have described   I have been described

Many common verbs are irregular, however:

to walk	she walked	she has walked
to sing	she sang	she has sung
to go	she went	she has gone

Tense

English has a wide variety of tenses, which give information about **when** something happened, and also the **aspect** of the action we wish to focus on. For example:

SIMPLE PAST   *I **walked** to the office this morning.*
(Action in the past, attention focused on the fact that it is a single completed action.)

PAST CONTINUOUS   *As I **was walking** I saw a swan.*
(Action in the past, attention focused on the continuing nature of the action—it was going on when something else happened.)

Agreement

The verb has to agree with the subject in number and person:

SINGULAR	FIRST PERSON	I walk
	SECOND PERSON	you walk (*thou walkest*)
	THIRD PERSON	he/she/it walks
PLURAL	FIRST PERSON	we walk
	SECOND PERSON	you walk
	THIRD PERSON	they walk

Sentence problems

One of the causes of problems when writing sentences, especially long sentences, is the verb.

Finite verb

A sentence must contain a complete, or **finite** verb. This is a verb that shows **tense**, **number**, and **person**. If a sentence does not contain a finite verb, then it isn't a sentence:

In late September in Herefordshire, during those last magic days of summer, **walking** through the fields down by the river Wye!

It is typical of sentences like this, that the reader is left waiting for something to happen, but nothing does and then the sentence ends. We want to know **who** the sentence is about and exactly **what they were doing**. It might mean, for example:

In late September in Herefordshire, during those last magic days of summer, **I used to love walking** through the fields down by the river Wye!

But we cannot know what the writer meant, because the sentence does not contain a finite verb.

Lack of agreement

Another possible reason why sentences sometimes don't work is that the subject and verb fail to agree. As we have seen, they should agree in number and person. If the subject is short and simple, there is usually no problem, but when the subject is complicated it becomes more difficult to keep track of exactly what the whole subject is:

> Several members of the Royal Family, including the Prince of Wales, **has visited** the region in the past year.

The trick is to ask yourself 'How many: one, or more than one?' In this case the answer is 'More than one', so the verb should be *have visited*.

The question of agreement is particularly vexed where **either** or **neither** are used in the subject. If both items are singular, then there is no problem; the verb is singular:

> Either the sales manager or his assistant **is** the person to take charge of this assignment.

If one of the two is plural, then the verb should agree with the one that comes immediately before it:

> Either the prime minister or his ministers **are** to blame.

The same applies to the *person* of the verb:

> Either Peter or I **am** going to look after it.
> Either you or Peter **is** going to look after it.

You try

Pick out the subject and the verb in each of the following sentences:

1 Making good coffee is an art.

2 The occasion of my last visit to see my Great Aunt Annie could have been a disaster.

3 This time next month I shall have been living in Australia for ten years.

4 During the last years of his reign, the king had become increasingly eccentric.

In each of the sentences that follow, the verb is in brackets. Put it into the correct form so that it agrees with the subject of the sentence.

1 Both James and I (*be*) members of the local golf club.

2 After some time, all the members of the board of management, including our latest recruit, Mrs Greene, (*be*) happy about the decision.

3 Either your brother-in-law, or you (*have*) to decide what to do next.

4 Neither I nor my sisters (*be*) present when the will was read.

Other sentence elements

Some sentences only consist of a subject and a verb:

SUBJECT	VERB
Mrs Howard	has left.
Most of our long-term problems	are being overcome.
This question	would have been foreseen.

Many sentences have one or more elements after the verb.

Object

One definition of the object is that it describes 'what is affected by the action of the verb' and in this example that is clear enough:

The dog bit **our visitor**.

Often, however, there isn't much 'action' involved:

I like **ice cream**

so it is more accurate, if more complicated, to say:

An object is a noun, a preposition, or a noun phrase that follows the verb and usually refers to a different person or thing from the subject.

Some sentences have two objects: direct and indirect:

Our visitor	gave	the baby	a rattle.
SUBJECT	VERB	INDIRECT OBJECT	DIRECT OBJECT

To distinguish these two kinds of object, remember that this kind of sentence can normally be turned round, with the addition of *to*:

Our visitor gave   the baby   a rattle.

Our visitor gave   a rattle   **to** the baby.

The commonest problem for writers concerns the **case** of the object. Some pronouns in English change according to whether the word is the subject or the object of the sentence:

SUBJECT	VERB	OBJECT
(SUBJECTIVE CASE)		(OBJECTIVE OR ACCUSATIVE CASE)
I	told	**him**.
He	told	**me**.

The pronouns concerned are:

I/me   he/him   she/her
we/us   they/them   who/whom (and whoever, etc.)

Problems can arise when there is a double object:

After the accident the chairman visited **my wife and I/my wife and me** in hospital.

If you are in any doubt about which is correct, remove the other part of the object and see if it sounds right.

After the accident the chairman visited **I** in hospital.

This can never be correct in standard English (although it is in some dialects); the objective or accusative case, **me**, is what is required:

After the accident the chairman visited **my wife and me** in hospital.

You should also use the objective or accusative case after prepositions:

The chairman paid several warm compliments **to** my wife and **me**.

Complement

A small number of verbs are followed not by an object but by a complement. The verbs, sometimes called **linking verbs**, include:

to be   to seem   to appear   to become

In sentences containing these verbs, the subject and the complement refer to the same person or thing:

SUBJECT	VERB	COMPLEMENT
My uncle	became	Mayor of Sidmouth.

The complement of a sentence can be a noun, preposition, or noun phrase (just like the object), but it can also be an adjective or adjective phrase:

SUBJECT	VERB	COMPLEMENT
My uncle	is	very happy.

Grammatically the complement should be the same case as the subject; hence the problem people have with:

Who's there? It is I.

Technically this is correct and, in formal written English, this is what you should use. But if you use 'It is I', rather than 'It's me' in everyday conversation people will probably think you are being a bit finicky.

Adverbial

Adverbials are much more varied. They provide information that answers these questions:

- **when/how long?**
  *I met her **yesterday**.*
- **(to) where?**
  *He placed a book **on the table**.*
- **why?**
  *They did it **for my sake**.*
- **how?**
  *The trick was performed **very very skilfully**.*
- **how much?**
  *I helped them **as much as possible**.*

As these examples show, the adverbial can be:

- a single word, an adverb: *yesterday*
- an adverb phrase (a group of words built up on an adverb): *very very skilfully*
- a prepositional phrase (a group of words that begins with a preposition): *on the table*

Position The other sentence elements are fairly predictable; there isn't much choice about where you put them in the sentence. Adverbials can pop up anywhere. There is often a choice about where you put them. Both these sentences are possible:

> He placed a book on the table.
> On the table he placed a book.

The difference is one of emphasis.

Normally the adverbial should come as close as possible to the verb it modifies, though not between the verb and its object. There are, however, occasions when to follow this rule may itself cause confusion. If the object is longer and we place the adverbial after it, the adverbial may become attached to the wrong part of the sentence: This sentence:

> *The bricklayer explained his reasons for leaving the site angrily*

clearly does not mean the same as this one:

> *The bricklayer explained angrily his reasons for leaving the site.*

Warning Some common adverbials can cause ambiguity when wrongly placed. All these sentences have different meanings:

1 **Even** the scientists are concerned about traffic fumes.
2 The scientists are **even** concerned about traffic fumes.
3 The scientists are concerned about **even** traffic fumes.

1 means that **everyone including scientists** is concerned
2 means that scientists are **concerned about lots of things**, including traffic fumes
3 means that scientists are **concerned about all fumes**, including traffic fumes

To avoid ambiguity or wrong emphasis, *even* should be placed next to the word it refers to.

There are sometimes similar problems with *only*, but they are not so great and much of the time it is possible to place *only* in its natural place, next to the verb, without causing confusion:

> I **only** *read his letter last week.*

clearly means 'It was only last week that I read his letter.' No one is likely to understand it to mean 'I could have torn it up or burned it, but all I did was read it.' Particularly in speech we can make our meaning clearer by tone of voice and emphasis, so normally *only* takes its natural place next to the verb and our voices do the rest. In writing, if there is any possibility of confusion, *only* should be placed next to the word(s) it refers to.

You try

Each of the following sentences has one part printed in bold. Is it subject, verb, object, complement, or adverbial?

1 The mechanic placed the new carburettor **on the workbench**.

2 Later that year she became **leader of the local council**.

3 Our only daily local paper has just ceased **publication**.

4 **I should have preferred** a more interesting approach.

5 In a few years' time **everyone except us old folk** will be computer literate.

Is there any difference in meaning between the sentences within these groups?

1a Harry forgot even his grandfather's birthday.

1b Even Harry forgot his grandfather's birthday.

2a Originally I concentrated on black and white photographs.

2b I concentrated originally on black and white photographs.

2c I concentrated on black and white photographs originally.

3a Happily Peter gave Maria back her book.

3b Peter gave Maria back her book happily.

4a Only the Sales Department wants the new product painted pink.

4b The Sales Department wants only the new product painted pink.

4c The Sales Department wants the new product painted only pink.

Sentence length and variety

Of course, most writing does not consist entirely of simple sentences, containing only one subject and one verb, but there are certain things it is useful to say at this point about written style.

Short sentences

A real strength of simple sentences is that they can be short and punchy. In the right place they can be very powerful. This paragraph contains one short simple sentence right in the middle:

> I had seen the collision coming, but when it happened the impact was so abrupt and stunning that it shocked the sense out of me, and for a while I sat quietly among the broken glass of the jeep as though I had been sitting there forever. In any case I found I could not move because of the dead weight of the soldiers on either side of me. **We had hit the bus head-on.** The front of the jeep was embedded under its bonnet, and the crash must have somehow distorted the wiring apparatus because the first thing I became aware of was a continuous metallic howl from the horn that nobody tried to stop. It seemed as though the machinery itself was screaming in pain, while all the people involved were spellbound and silent.

The first two sentences introduce the situation but by the end of the second we are still not clear exactly what has happened. Then the writer tells us, simply and brutally.

It is important not to overdo it, however. Too many short sentences can make a text seem jerky or immature (young children often write in this way).

Minor sentences

In this chapter, a sentence has been partly defined as having a finite verb. We often encounter 'sentences' that break this rule. They are particularly common in public notices:

> One-way street.
> Parking for residents only.
> Fresh stock now in.

They also occur in speech:

> Lovely weather this morning!
> Oh well, easy come, easy go.

They make complete sense, but they are grammatically incomplete. Linguists sometimes call them minor sentences. They can be used in continuous writing for a particular effect. A good idea? Possibly. Definitely capable of overuse, however. Like most things.

Sentence punctuation

Normally, of course, written sentences are marked off by punctuation, beginning with a capital letter and ending with a full stop. Occasionally writers fail to do this, running sentences together, or separating them with a comma, rather than a full stop:

> This type of of writing can be difficult for readers, their eyes are trained to see a comma as marking off parts of one sentence, when

they come across writing where this is not done they become confused, it is important to remember this when writing.

This error is sometimes called the comma splice, because a comma is used to splice, or join, two sentences. There is, however, a punctuation mark which can be used for this purpose, the **semicolon**.

If you have two sentences which are closely related in meaning, they can be linked in this way:

Writing clearly and simply is not easy; it requires practice.

This sentence reads slightly differently from:

Writing clearly and simply is not easy. It requires practice.

In the first example we see that the two ideas are closely linked together. In the second they are offered as separate thoughts, one after the other, and the reader is left to make the link from the sense.

Guidelines

Subject 1. The subject of a sentence can be quite extended. Make sure that your readers do not lose track of the subject before they even reach the verb. This is particularly likely to happen if you put a participle before the subject:

Walking down Exhibition Road, just by the old Alhambra Theatre, my old and trusted friend from the good old days and now a wealthy property developer, James McVity, saw . . .

Verb 2 Make sure that the verb is finite and agrees with the subject in both number (singular/plural) and person (*she is/we are*, etc).

3 Agreement is particularly tricky in these situations:
■ where there is a multiple subject, joined by *and*
■ where you are using *either* or *neither*

Object 4 Make sure that pronouns used as objects are in the correct, objective, case (*me*, not *I*, *him* not *he*, etc.).

Complement 5 In formal writing, pronouns used as complements should be in the subjective case (*It is I*).

Adverbial 6 Make sure that you have placed any adverbials in the best position in the sentence. Often this is next to the verb, but sometimes the adverbial must be placed to make the precise meaning clear. This applies particularly to *even* and *only*.

Style 7 Use short sentences sparingly for maximum impact.

8 Minor sentences can be used in written texts, but again only sparingly and for a particular effect.

9 Make sure that sentences are correctly separated by punctuation, normally a full stop and following capital letter. If two sentences are closely linked in sense they can sometimes be joined by a semicolon.

You try: key

page 159

SUBJECT	VERB
1 Making good coffee	is
2 The occasion of my last visit to see my Great Aunt Annie	could have been
3 I	shall have been living
4 the king	had become

page 163

1 are
2 were
3 have
4 were

1 adverbial
2 complement
3 object
4 verb
5 adverbial

1 a means that Harry forgot everyone's birthday
  b means that everyone forgot grandfather's birthday
2 little difference
3 a means that it was fortunate that Peter gave the book back
  b means that he was happy to give it back
4 a means that Sales is the only department to want this
  b means that Sales want every other product painted a different colour from pink
  c means that they want pink to be the only colour to be used on the new product

18 More about grammar

In the last chapter simple sentences were defined as having only one verb. Technically such sentences consist of one **finite clause**. A finite clause is a grammatical unit that contains a finite verb; it can stand alone as a simple sentence, or be combined with other clauses into compound or complex sentences.

Compound sentences

The simplest way of joining clauses is by bolting them together like this:

> Maybrick Ltd supplies bearings   and   ERICO fits them.
> CLAUSE   +   CLAUSE

The two clauses are of the same status in the sentence (they are described grammatically as 'coordinated'—of the same level) and each could stand on its own as a simple sentence.

Coordinating conjunctions

The commonest conjunctions used to link clauses in this way are:

> and   but   or   nor   then   yet

It is important to remember that although they all do the same job grammatically, they have very different meanings.

Then

Then is straightforward: the event described by the second clause must follow that described in the first:

> Maybrick Ltd supplies bearings, then ERICO fits them.

Clearly it wouldn't make sense to have the clauses the other way round.

But/yet

In the example above, *and* simply joins the two clauses, but if it were replaced by *but*, the meaning of the whole sentence would be changed:

> Maybrick Ltd supplies bearings, but ERICO fits them.

On its own, the sentence does not make clear why the speaker has said 'but', and this is sometimes true even when we know the context. *But* does imply some sort of contrast, conflict, or contradiction, however, even when its exact meaning is unstated. For example, if the speaker is the managing director of Maybrick Ltd he may be implying that once the bearings have left the factory his company has no responsibility for what ERICO does with them.

     Yet is used in a similar way to but.

Or/nor

These two conjunctions only make sense when the two clauses they link are genuine alternatives. It would, for example, be nonsense to say:

> Maybrick Ltd supplies bearings, or ERICO fits them.

On the other hand you could say:

> Maybrick Ltd supplies bearings, or ERICO purchases them from a company in the States

where it is understood that the first clause means ' . . . supplies bearings *to ERICO* . . . '.

Nor works in a similar way to *or*, but as a negative:

I have never met Dominic McGhee, *nor* do I want to.

Beginning a sentence with *and*

It is sometimes said that you should not begin a sentence with a co-ordinating conjunction, because, as its name implies, it must come between the two things it is coordinating and should not, therefore, be separated from one of them by a full stop. This 'rule' may appear to be logical but it has cheerfully been ignored by writers across the centuries. Separating the two items being linked by *and* or *but*, for example, can be an effective way of giving additional emphasis to the item that is thus separated. But you should not do it too frequently. Or people will find it irritating. Then they will stop reading.

Complex sentences

You can only go so far by using compound sentences. Often we need to show more sophisticated relationships between two clauses. Each of the sentences that follows uses the same two clauses, but each expresses a different meaning:

1 If Maybrick Ltd supplies bearings, ERICO fits them.
2 Maybrick Ltd supplies the bearings that ERICO fits.
3 ERICO fits the bearings that Maybrick Ltd supplies.
4 Maybrick Ltd supplies bearings so that ERICO can fit them.

Which version is chosen depends on the context and the meaning you wish to convey. In this section of the chapter some of the main kinds of link between clauses are examined.

In grammatical terms, one clause in a complex sentence is more important than the others and is described as the **main clause**. The other clauses, the **subordinate clauses**, are grammatically less important and are nearly always introduced by a **subordinating conjunction**.

A complex sentence works in much the same way as a simple sentence. It contains similar elements: subject, verb, adverbial, object, and complement. In a simple sentence these elements may be single words or phrases. In a complex sentence some of them may also be clauses.

Adverbial clauses

Adverbial clauses are very useful and perform a wide range of different functions. They answer a number of different questions.

When?

It is often important to show the relationship in time between two events. Perhaps one was completed before the other began; or one occurred during the period that the other was going on. English is particularly well supplied with ways of showing this.

The commonest conjunctions are:

after   as   before   since   until   when   while

These words do not do their work on their own, however. They work closely with the verbs in the sentence to convey their meaning. Each of the following sentences uses *when*, but each conveys a very different meaning:

1 When she makes the cake she will listen to the radio.
2 When she was making the cake she listened to the radio.
3 When she had made the cake she listened to the radio.

Where?

Time clauses are very common; those indicating place may be less common but can be very important—in instructions and descriptions, for example:

- Turn right where the speed limit ends.
- We parted where three roads meet.

The conjunctions used are *where* and *wherever*.

There is one special use of *where* which is worth remembering. It can be used to define conditions under which certain things can happen:

- Where it can be shown that the company is negligent . . .
- Where there is shade and moisture, these plants will flourish.

What if?

Often we want to say that one thing depends on another happening. We frequently do this by using *if* or *unless*:

1 If he comes to the office, the manager will explain the situation.
2 If the company was to blame, then it would pay compensation.
3 If the cheque had bounced, the bank would have told us.

These three sentences all deal with 'one-off' situations: a single event and its possible results. Each suggests a different degree of possibility. Number 1 is open: the 'if' event may or may not happen. In number 2 the 'if event' is unlikely, but if it did happen, then the consequences would follow. These two sentences deal with something that has not yet happened. Sentence 3 is about something in the past and clearly the speaker believes that it has not happened. (But the bank hasn't told us, so the cheque hasn't bounced.)

There is a different kind of conditional sentence which does not deal with a single event, or a definite number of events, but which concerns 'things in general':

- If the company makes a profit, it pays a dividend to the shareholders.
- If babies are unhappy they cry.

As these examples show, it is important to use the correct form of the verb when using *if*. Failure to do so may mean that you do not communicate correctly your own view of the likelihood of the 'if' event—and when dealing with difficult situations, that could cause problems. So, for example, you may want to tell a client in a completely open way that you will help if she has a problem. You mean to say,

If your computer plays up, phone me and I'll come and put it right.

Company policy, however, says you should be more formal than this, so you end up saying:

If the product failed to operate properly during the first six months, then the purchaser would be entitled to free on-site service.

Not only does this lapse into unnecessary jargon ('on-site service'), but it makes the customer feel that the events described are extremely unlikely. Now that is fine if the machine is very reliable, but it may leave a lingering suspicion in the customer's mind that the home visit is very unlikely—*even if it turns out to be needed*.

Sentence 2 above can be expressed in two ways that are similar but significantly different:

- If the company **was** to blame, then it would pay compensation.
- If the company **were** to blame, then it would pay compensation.

The second of these uses a relatively uncommon form of the verb, the **subjunctive**. Its effect is to make the condition *impossible*, rather than just improbable, which is why it is used in sayings such as 'If I were you . . .' (which is clearly impossible). Many people, however, do not observe this distinction; increasingly people say 'If I was you . . .' and it may be that this use of the subjunctive is dying out.

You try

Each of these groups of sentences looks at the same possible event in two or three different ways. Can you explain the differences between them?

1 a If I need to see you, I'll phone.
  b If I needed to see you, I'd phone.
  c If I had needed to see you I would have phoned.

2 a He'd have told us if he'd wanted to come.
  b He tells us if he wants to come.

3 a Please let us know if the party includes children.
  b Please let us know if the party is going to include children.
  c Please let us know if the party included children.

4 a If you experience difficulty cashing the cheque it is because the bank is in the process of transferring our account.
  b If you experienced difficulty cashing the cheque, it was because the bank was in the process of transferring our account.
  c If you had experienced difficulty cashing the cheque it would have been because the bank was in the process of transferring our account.

For what purpose?   Two common conjunctions enable us to explain the purpose behind an event: *in order that* and *so that* (sometimes abbreviated to *so*):

- The man was executed so that others would be discouraged from imitating him.

- We changed the design in order that health and safety regulations would not be broken.

Why? 'Never apologize; never explain' may be a popular saying, but we often *do* need to explain the reasons for an event. We do so using *because*, *since*, and *as*:

- As I'm going to be in New York anyway, I thought I'd drop in on her.
- We made it of wood because that is the most suitable material.
- Since she is responsible for this project, she should be the person to make the presentation.

With sentences like these, you can often choose in which order to place the two clauses:

1 Since she is responsible for this project, she should be the person to make the presentation.
2 She should be the person to make the presentation, since she is responsible for this project.

The only difference is one of focus. Sentence 1 focuses on the reasoning process; sentence 2 focuses on 'her' and uses the reason as 'backup'.

With what result? Typical conjunctions here are: *so that*, *so*, and *and so*:

Some of them have no qualifications in engineering so that they are looked down on by senior management.

Sometimes *so* and *that* are separated, with *so* referring to an adjective or adverb. The 'that clause' still describes a result:

- It all happened so quickly that I didn't realize what was going on.
- He was so fat that he could not get through the door to the dining room.

Making concessions When reasoning or presenting an argument, we may wish to deal with alternative views or other possibilities. We do so using *although*, *though*, *even if*, *whereas*, and *while*:

- Although a pony and trap is an entertaining form of transport, a car is more reliable.
- While gas bills may have fallen during the past quarter, our general running costs have remained the same.

Noun clauses

Noun clauses can stand as subject or complement in a sentence:

What I cannot understand is *how she got away with it.*

Here both subject and complement are noun clauses.
The object of a sentence can also be a noun clause:

He told the Board **that he wished to resign**.

In these examples, noun clauses are introduced by *what*, *that*, and *how*.

There are several other words which can introduce them, including *where, why, whether,* and *when.*

Relative clauses

Relative clauses act like adjectives or adjective phrases:

- I gave her a *red* scarf. (ADJECTIVE)
- I gave her a scarf *with a red pattern on it.* (ADJECTIVE PHRASE)
- I gave her a scarf **that I bought in Amsterdam**. (RELATIVE CLAUSE)

Relative clauses can be introduced by the **relative pronouns** *who, whom, which, that, where, when* and, confusingly, nothing at all. Sentence 3 above could be:

I gave her a scarf **I bought in Amsterdam**.

The relative pronoun is 'understood'.

Defining and non-defining

Relative clauses do not normally give rise to many problems for the writer. There is, however, one important distinction it is important to make. These two sentences are apparently the same:

1 Teachers who work long hours should be paid more.
2 Teachers, who work long hours, should be paid more.

In Sentence 1 the writer has two groups of teachers in mind: those who work long hours and those who do not. The former group should be paid more. In Sentence 2 the writer is making a statement about **all** teachers: they work long hours and so should be paid more. In the first sentence the relative clause **defines** or **restricts** the group (a 'defining—or restrictive—relative clause'); in the second it does not (a 'non-defining—or non-restrictive—relative clause'). When we speak we can make the difference in meaning clear by timing and intonation; in writing the difference is made by the punctuation.

It is also argued by some that the relative pronoun *which* normally introduces a non-defining clause. If we want to introduce a defining clause we should use either *that* or nothing. Like other such 'rules' this is quite often ignored, but the following guidelines may be of help:

- Use *which* rather than *that* to introduce a non-defining relative clause.
- Normally use *that* rather than *which* to introduce a defining relative clause.
- Only use *which* to introduce a defining relative clause to avoid repetition or for emphasis.
- Always use *which* rather than *that* after a preposition. (e.g. *The bank in which I placed my trust has gone bust.*)
- Use commas before and after a non-defining relative clause to emphasize what it is.
- Don't use a comma before a defining relative clause.

Who or whom?

The other problem area with relative pronouns is the question of when to use *who* and when to use *whom.* The traditional rule is simple—deceptively so:

1 who is used as the subject of the verb
I had a word with the manager who is looking after the Neasden account.
2 whom is used as the object of the verb
I spoke to our Neasden manager, whom I think you have met.
3 whom is used after prepositions
I spoke to Peter, from whom I received that interesting letter.

Modern usage, however, inclines more and more to the use of *who* in all three cases:

2 *I spoke to our Neasden manager, who I think you have met.*
3 *I spoke to Peter, who I received that interesting letter from.*

On the other hand, there are still traditionalists out there who object to this and certainly most people would still find:

I spoke to Peter, from who I received that interesting letter

rather strange. A sensible rule would be:

USE	FORMAL SITUATIONS	INFORMAL SITUATIONS
subject of verb	who	who
object of verb	whom	who
with preposition	whom, preceded by preposition[1]	who, with preposition at end[2]

1 ... from whom I received ...
2 ... who I received that interesting letter from.

Problem areas

Coordinating

Many problems associated with conjunctions are linked to the fact that when we use coordinating conjunctions they must link two items that have the same grammatical status (i.e., both clauses—including a finite verb—or both phrases). When writers fail to remember this, they make mistakes:

He told us about the trip and that he had managed to make a number of important new contacts.

If you break the sentence down diagrammatically, it is easy to see what is wrong:

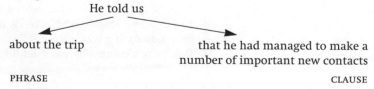

He told us

about the trip   that he had managed to make a
                                  number of important new contacts

PHRASE   CLAUSE

The sentence needs to be re-cast so that the two items joined by *and* have the same status:

He told us about the trip and the important new contacts he had made.

Here *and* is joining two noun phrases:

> *the trip*
> *the important new contacts*

Both *Both* is used to join two items and not more than two. It is wrong, therefore, to use expressions such as *Both Eleanor and the two girls . . .* If it works with another conjunction, that conjunction should be *and*, so that this sentence is unsatisfactory:

> The company produces both PVA products as well as PVC.

It should be:

> The company produces both PVA and PVC products.

Again, it is important to remember that . . . *both . . . and . . .* should only be used to join items of equal status.

> *He both plays in the orchestra and as a soloist*

should be rephrased as:

> *He plays both in the orchestra and as a soloist.*

Finally, in expressions involving figures, *both* can produce ambiguities like this:

> *Both books cost £20.*

Did each book cost £10 or £20? Better to write either *Each book cost £10* or *The two books together cost £40.*

Either/or & Like other coordinating conjunctions, *either/or* and *neither/nor* must
neither/nor join items of equal status. It is poor style to write:

> *This argument neither explains what went wrong nor how it should be put right.*

It should read:

> *This argument explains neither what went wrong nor how it should be put right.*

A simple check is to remove the section of the sentence that begins with *either/neither* and ends with *or/nor*. If the rest of the sentence still works grammatically, then you have got it right. (The sense will have changed, of course.)

> *This argument explains ~~neither what went wrong nor~~ how it should be put right.*

Other problems with these conjunctions concern the agreement between subject and verb. The comments that follow all use *either* but apply equally to *neither*:

1 *Either* is singular when it acts as the subject of the verb:

> *I have looked at both the Ford Escort and the Peugeot 305; either is suitable for my purposes.*

2 When *either/or* link two singular items, then the verb should be singular:

Either the Ford Escort or the Peugeot 305 is suitable for my purposes.

3 When *either/or* link a singular and a plural item, the verb takes its number from whichever is nearest:

Either oranges or ice cream is my choice for pudding.
Either ice cream or oranges are my choice for pudding.

4 The same rule applies when there is a change of person:

Either you or she has the best chance of winning.
Either she or you have the best chance of winning.

5 Informally this 'rule of proximity' also operates when *either* is used without *or* to indicate a choice of plurals:

Either of the cars are suitable for my purposes.

but this is still frowned on in more formal situations.

The above rules also apply to *or* when it is used on its own.

Subordinating conjunctions

Subordinating conjunctions can cause problems, too, frequently because of ambiguity. Some of the commonest are listed here.

As
This small word can be tricky. It can work as a conjunction or as a preposition. As a conjunction it has a range of meanings, including:

1 while/when
2 because/since

The first two can sometimes be confused. For example:

As I was going to the shops, I decided to buy some onions.

Does the writer mean 'I made the decision on the way to the shops' or 'Because I was going to the shops'? If the former, then it could be made clearer by writing 'While . . . '; if the latter, then starting the sentence with 'Because . . . ' would be clearer.

Another common use of *as* is paired: *as . . . as*. This construction can produce ambiguities, too:

I have visited Peter as often as Mary.

This could mean:

- I have visited Peter as often as I have visited Mary.
- I have visited Peter as often as Mary has.

Because
When it follows a negative statement, *because* can lead to ambiguity, as in this sentence:

He didn't take up the option because he was hard up.

This has two possible meanings so it should be rephrased:

- *Because he was hard up he didn't take up the option.*
- *It wasn't because he was hard up that he took up the option.*

Another possible cause of ambiguity occurs when the reason for coming to a particular conclusion comes **after** the conclusion:

I knew he was lying because I'd spoken to his wife.

Here there are two possible meanings:

■ As I'd spoken to his wife I knew he was lying.
■ I'd spoken to his wife and I knew he was lying because of that.

So   *So* can produce ambiguities similar to those of *as*, because it can mean:

■ 'as a result'
■ 'in order that'

This sentence, for example, is ambiguous:

He left home so his parents could get some peace.

To make the meaning clear it should be rephrased:

■ *He left home in order that his parents could get some peace.*
■ *He left home and as a result his parents could get some peace.*

Guidelines

1 When you use compound sentences, coordinated with conjunctions like *and, or, but, nor, then, yet*, be aware of the limited range of meanings these can convey.

2 Remember that although complex sentences can convey a much wider range of meanings, they require more careful construction.

3 When you write *when* clauses make sure that the order of events you are describing is clear.

4 Remember that conditional (*if*) sentences require careful handling. Check on pages 170–1 for the range of possible meanings.

5 Relative clauses may be defining or non-defining, and you need to be clear which is which. Check on pages 173–4 for advice on when to use *which, that, who,* or *whom*.

6 Take care with coordinating conjunctions like *both . . . and*: they need to link items that are grammatically similar. (pp. 174–5)

7 Make sure that *either/neither* and *or/nor* are correctly placed and that the verb agrees with the subject. (pp. 175–6).

8 Subordinating conjunctions *as, because,* and *so* also need careful use. (p. 176 and above)

You try: key

page 171   **1a** describes a possible situation in the future. **1b** describes a situation in the future that could happen but is unlikely. **1c** describes a situation in the past that did not happen.

2a describes a situation in the past that did not happen. **2b** describes a general situation that already exists and will continue to do so.

3a and **3b** describe much the same situation, although **3b** is clearer. **3c** refers to a situation in the past.

4a describes a possible situation in the future. **4b** describes a possible but unlikely situation in the past. **4c** describes a situation in the past that could have happened but is improbable.

19 Vocabulary

All language users have an **active** and a **passive** vocabulary.

Getting help
In order to find words, and to understand their meanings and how to use them, we can use:
- dictionaries
- thesauruses
- other word books

Word formation and structure
A knowledge of word formation often helps in the understanding of unfamiliar words.

Word structure
- All words have a stem.
- Some also have affixes: a prefix and/or a suffix.
- A knowledge of prefixes helps in understanding the meaning of a word.
- Suffixes are used:
  - grammatically, to modify certain words before using them in a sentence
  - in word formation

Compounding
- Classical compounds are derived from Greek and Latin words, or parts of them.

Words and their connotations
- Social attitudes also have an important impact on which words can and cannot be used in different social contexts, especially in the areas of:
  - taboo
  - slang
  - informal language
- Caution is also required when using language that can be described as jargon.
- Our use of language can also betray social attitudes and bias, especially towards defined and vulnerable social groups.
- Even in more general situations language often carries emotional attitudes or 'colour'.

Most of the time we use words without conscious thought . . . until we are stumped either for the right word to use or for the precise meaning of a word we have read. While it is true that we all have a vocabulary of so many thousand words, our ability to use the words we know varies considerably. In my own experience I am aware of the following groups of words:

1 Those I know and use every day in conversation and casual writing.
2 Those I use with confidence when doing 'more serious' writing.
3 Those I use but need to think about a bit before committing myself to using—even to the extent of checking their meaning in a dictionary.
4 Those I understand clearly when I read them (and could define fully if challenged), but which I do not recall ever having used in speech or writing.
5 Those I understand well enough (I think!) not to hesitate over when I read them.
6 Those I have come across before, but the meaning of which I am very hazy about (and which, if it mattered enough, I would look up in a dictionary).
7 Those I have never encountered before.

Groups 1 and 2 are often combined and described as a person's active vocabulary. This includes all the words that person knows and can use confidently in speech and/or writing. Groups 4 and 5 are the person's passive vocabulary, the words that person can understand when listening or reading. Group 3 includes the words that are in the process of moving from being passive to being active (or possibly vice versa), while Group 6 includes those words that are beginning to enter the passive vocabulary.

You try

1 Look at the list of words below. Divide them into three groups:

- those you would feel confident to use in a sentence
- those you understand but would hesitate to use in a sentence
- the rest

contract	compact	covenant	transaction	pledge
concordat	indenture	bond	undertaking	

Words in the first group form part of your active vocabulary, while those in the second group are part of your passive vocabulary.

2 Now do the same with this list:

fraction	fractionate	fractostratus	fraenum	fragile
fragment	fragrance	frail	fraise	frame
franchise	francium	francolin	frangible	frank

Fortunately we do not usually encounter words in isolation; they are normally in the context of a sentence and often in a paragraph or longer text. The context frequently gives sufficient clues to help the reader with the meaning of a difficult word.

You try

Determining the size of your vocabulary

It is difficult to say just how many words a person knows, but it is an interesting experiment to try to assess the size of your own vocabulary. This is one way in which it can be done:

1 Take a dictionary of between 1000 and 2000 pages.

2 Select 1 per cent of the total number of pages evenly distributed throughout the dictionary. (So, for example, if you were using a 1500-page dictionary you would need to choose 15 pages.)

3 Go through each page counting:

- how many words you recognize and think you know the meaning of (your passive vocabulary)

- how many words you think you have used in speech or writing (your active vocabulary)

4 Multiply each figure by 100 to get an approximate idea of the size of your active and passive vocabulary.

Getting help

If you go into a large bookshop or reference library, you will find a bewildering array of reference books offering information and advice about words. The easiest way to describe word books is to break them down into three groups:

- dictionaries
- thesauruses
- the rest

Dictionaries

A large dictionary, such as the *New Shorter Oxford English Dictionary*, can provide a wealth of information, as this extract shows:

Headword
The word which the entry is about, and on which any derivatives listed at the end of the entry are based.

Pronunciation
This may use a phonetic alphabet, as here, or some other system. This will be explained in the introduction to the dictionary. With words of more than one syllable, the word stress is also shown.

Word class
(part of speech)
This gives information on how the word is used in sentences.

sage /seɪdʒ/ a¹ ME. [(O)Fr. f. Proto-Gallo-Romance, f. L *sapere* be wise.] **1** Of a person: wise, discreet, judicious, now esp. through experience. ME. **b** Of advice, behaviour, etc.: characterized by profound wisdom; based on sound judgement. M16. **c** Of an expression, bearing, etc.: exhibiting profound wisdom. Now freq. *iron.* E19. †**2** Grave, dignified, solemn. M16–M17.
  1b P. G. WODEHOUSE The venerable old man was whispering sage counsel. **2** SHAKES. *Haml.* We should profane the service of the dead To sing sage requiem to her.
  sagely *adv.* LME **sageness** *n.* the quality of being sage; profound wisdom: E16.

Etymology
Information about the origins and development of the word.

Meanings
Many words have more than one meaning and here these are numbered and lettered.

Quotations
Selected quotations illustrating a particular meaning of the word in use.

History
The dates or periods shown tell you when the word was first used in this way.

Derivatives
Other words that are derived from the headword.

Usage
Comments on the way in which the word may be used. Here we are told that this usage is often 'ironic', rather than 'straight' or 'serious'.

Smaller dictionaries provide correspondingly less information:

sage (1) noun
  an extremely wise person
  Word Family: **sage**, *adjective*, wise; **sagely**, *adverb*; **sageness**, *noun*
  [Latin *sapere*, to be wise]

Heinemann English Dictionary (for schools)

There are also specialist dictionaries that can be used for specific purposes. Some provide more detailed information about usage and are particularly useful for foreign learners and others who are uncertain about this aspect of language:

sage /seidʒ/, **sages**, 1 A **sage** is a person, especially an old man, who is regarded as being very wise; a rather literary use EG *Homage was paid to the great sages buried in the city* ...... *the Sage of Chelsea, Thomas Carlisle.*	N COUNT = guru
2 A **sage** person is wise and knowledge-able, especially as a result of age and experience; a rather literary use. EG *They became sage parents anxious to dispense their wisdom* ◊ **sagely** EG *He nodded his head sagely, a smile of amusement appearing on his face*	ADJ QUALIT ◊ ADV WITH VB

Collins Cobuild English Language Dictionary

The key question to ask any dictionary before relying on it is, 'Who says?' In other words: 'On what basis is the information provided?' Most dictionaries of any size are the work of teams of lexicographers working over a period of many years. They rely on a corpus of printed and spoken texts from which they define the ways in which the word in question is used at the time they are writing. Some, like the *Shorter Oxford Dictionary*, also provide information about how the word was used at different points in the past.

In all of this, lexicographers have to exercise judgment. This is even more true when it comes to making comments on usage. For example, the *Shorter Oxford* describes one usage of 'sage' as 'now frequently ironic', while the *Collins Cobuild* says it is 'literary'. Such divergences of opinion are frequently even greater when the word discussed is informal, slang, or taboo.

See also:
■ *Taboo, slang, and informal* (pp. 190–2)

So dictionaries are time-bound and, to some extent at least, based on the personal opinions of those who construct them. As a result, simply having recourse to a dictionary to resolve some dispute about a word's meaning or usage may not of itself be enough. We also have to consider just how far we trust the lexicographer's judgement. And, of course, the bigger the dictionary, the more information it will provide to help us make up our minds.

Using a thesaurus

If you have an idea and want to find the exact word, a thesaurus *may* be what you need. The word *thesaurus* derives from the classical Greek word for 'storehouse or treasury', which describes it well. It is a storehouse of words. Some thesauruses follow the US pattern and are arranged alphabetically, providing lists of synonyms (words of similar meaning) and antonyms (words of opposite meaning) for any word you look up. The traditional arrangement, however, is thematic. The original concept was developed by an English doctor, Peter Mark Roget, who developed a hierarchical classification which is still used (and explained) in contemporary versions of *Roget's Thesaurus*. Other thesauruses, such as Bloomsbury's, follow the same principle but have devised their own classification system.

A typical thematic thesaurus consists of two parts:

- the thematic presentation of synonyms and antonyms
- an index in which words can be looked up.

Index   The index is necessarily lengthy and detailed. It normally provides more than one reference for a word:

> **sage 45** Herbs and Spices, 4,
> 277.7 *deep thinking*, 413.5 *herbs*, 459.8 *intellectual person*, 459.10 *intelligent*, 501.6 *knowledgeable person*, 507.3 *wise man*, 517.8 *oracle*, 611.4 *bigwig*, 654.4 *adviser*, 655.4 *skilled person*, 688.10 *person of authority*, 696.9 *educational leader*, 849.14 *awe-inspiring*

Each of these references leads to a list in the thematic section:

> 459.8
> **intellectual person**, intellectual, scholar.
> academic, academician, thinker, genius, wise man, sage, savant, master, guru, elder statesman, oracle, pundit, polymath, litterateur, illuminati, bookman, bookworm, bibliophile, bluestocking, highbrow, egghead (Inf), intellect (Inf), boffin (Inf), brainbox (Inf), know-all (Inf), know-it-all (US inf), clever clogs (Inf), swot (Inf), smart aleck (Inf), smarty pants (Inf), smartarse (Inf)

In the search for the *exact word*, you may strike lucky first time, or you may have to follow up several references in the index. When it comes to the moment of choice, however, you often find that what the thesaurus is doing is reminding you of words that you already knew. If so, then more likely than not you know how they should be used and when they are appropriate. Occasionally, however, the thesaurus will suggest words that you have never met before, or about which you are rather unconfident (possibly, in the list above, *illuminati* or *bluestocking*). Then it is necessary to follow up with a dictionary.

Other word books

Most reading and writing needs are fulfilled by a good dictionary and thesaurus. There are, however, other specialist word books which may be needed from time to time:

- **Reference dictionary**
  In addition to definitions of words, reference dictionaries provide information about a wide range of topics, and usually include geographical place names and biographical information.
- **English usage**
- **Quotations**
- **Synonyms and antonyms**

- **Spelling**
- **Idioms**
- **Proverbs**

My own bookshelves also contain dictionaries of 'Troublesome words', 'Low speak', and 'Clichés', as well as a 'Slang thesaurus' and 'The Official Politically Correct Dictionary and Handbook'.

Word structure

One way of gaining a better understanding of English words is to look at how new words are formed. Some knowledge of word structure, compound words, and other types of word formation is particularly helpful when one is faced with a previously unknown word.

Some words are simple and cannot be broken down into parts. For example:

grasp   settee   hippopotamus

Many words, however, are composed of identifiable parts:

un	comfort	able
PREFIX	STEM	SUFFIX

Stem

The stem (or *base form*) of the word is what is left when any affixes (prefixes and suffixes) have been removed. Words like *grasp* consist of just a stem. *Uncomfortable* has the stem *comfort*, the prefix *un-* and the suffix *-able*.

Prefixes

Prefixes add meaning to the stem. A knowledge of how prefixes are used can be a great help when working out the meaning of unfamiliar words. Common prefixes include the following.

PREFIX	MEANING	EXAMPLE
a-	not, not affected by	amoral
ante-	before	antecedent
anti-	against	anti-pollution
arch-	chief	archpriest
auto-	self	autobiography
bi-	two	bipartisan
bio-	(from biology)	biodiversity
circum-	around	circumference
co-	joint, together	coordinate
contra-	opposite	contradiction
counter-	against	counteract
crypto-	hidden	crypto-fascist
de-	making the opposite of	demystify

PREFIX	MEANING	EXAMPLE
demi-	half	demigod
di-	two	dialogue
dis-	making the opposite of	disagree
du-/duo-	two	duologue
eco-	(from ecology)	eco-tourism
Euro-	(from European)	Eurodollar
ex-	former	ex-husband
	out of	extract
fore-	in the front of, ahead of	forerunner
hyper-	very big	hypermarket
in-	not, opposite of	inexact
	in, into	insert
inter-	between	inter-state
intra-	inside	intravenous
mal-	bad(ly)	maladministration
mega-	very large	megastar
mid-	middle	midlife
midi-	medium-sized	midi-length
mini-	small	minimarket
mis-	wrong, false	misadventure
mono-	one	monogamy
multi-	many	multi-layered
neo-	new	neolithic
non-	not, opposite of	non-partisan
out-	beyond	outreach
over-	too much	overreach
para-	ancillary	paramedic
	beyond	paranormal
poly-	many	polymath
post-	after	post-election
pre-	before	pre-election
pro-	for	pro-gun
	deputy	proconsul
pseudo-	false	pseudo-intellectual
re-	again	rerun
	back	reverse
retro-	backwards	retrograde
self-	self	self-sufficient
semi-	half	semi-serious
sub-	below	sub-zero
super-	more than, special	superhuman
supra-	above	suprasensuous
sur-	more than, beyond	surreal
tele-	at a distance	telematics
trans-	across	trans-Siberian
tri-	three	tripartite
ultra-	beyond	ultraviolet
	very much indeed	ultra-careful
un-	not, opposite of	unnecessary
under-	below, less than	underachieve
uni-	one	unitary
vice-	deputy	vice-chancellor

Suffixes

Suffixes have two functions:

- to inflect words for grammatical purposes (for example, -s and -ed added to verbs, and -s added to nouns)
- to form new words from other words, often, but not always, by changing its part of speech (so the noun *beauty* can be made into a verb *beautify*)

Suffixes are used to form verbs, adverbs, adjectives, and nouns.

Verb suffixes

-ify	beautify
-ise/-ize	idolize

Adjective suffixes

-able/-ible	excitable
-al/-ial	adverbial
-ary	stationary
-ate	insensate
-ed	flat-roofed
-esque	picturesque
-ful	fateful
-ic	Icelandic
-ical	economical
-ish	childish
-ive	destructive
-less	childless
-like	blood-like
-ous	analagous
-y	dozy

Adverb suffixes

-ly	happily
-ward(s)	westwards
-wise	counterclockwise

Noun suffixes

-age	acreage
-al	referral
-ant/-ent	inhabitant
-ation/-ion	examination
-dom	kingdom
-ee	addressee
-eer	auctioneer
-er	abstainer
-ess	tigress
-ery/-ry	effrontery
-ette	leatherette
-ful	handful
-hood	neighbourhood
-ing	mooring
-ism	impressionism
-ist	pianist
-ity	chastity
-ment	postponement
-ness	happiness

-ocracy	meritocracy
-or	escalator
-ship	directorship
-ster	trickster

Derivation families

As a result of the possibilities created by the use of prefixes and suffixes, one stem can be the 'parent' of a whole family of derived words:

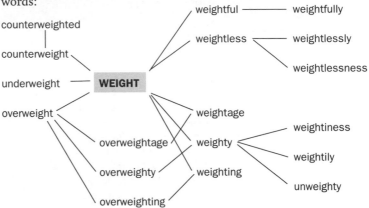

One or two of these words may look slightly strange (although all are recorded in the *Oxford English Dictionary*). Nevertheless, an understanding of affixes makes it possible to work out the meanings even of these. For example, *overweighting* is not a particularly common word, but, even if you did not know it, you could work out its meaning. The stem *weight*, as a verb, means *to load with a weight*; knowledge of suffixes will tell us that one effect of adding *-ing* is to change it into a noun meaning *the process of loading with a weight*. The prefix *over-* adds the meaning of *too much*; hence *overweighting* means *the process of loading with excessive weight*.

You try

1 This is a list of words derived from the stem ***clean***. Use it to construct a diagram similar to the one above.

clean	cleanable	cleaner	cleaning
cleanish	cleanlily	cleanliness	cleanly
cleanness	over-clean	reclean	self-cleaning
unclean	uncleanable	uncleanliness	uncleanly
uncleanness			

2 Make similar diagrams based on these stems:

large	sail	wait

Classical derivations

There is a large group of words that come from Greek and Latin stems. Many of these are to be found in the fields of science and other academic specialisms. A knowledge of the common classical stems from which many of these words are drawn can help in gaining at least a rough idea of what an unknown word may mean. Although you may not feel that you know anything about classical Greek and Latin, you will find that words you already know which derive from them provide a useful starting point. For example, if you know the meaning of *geography* and *biology*, it isn't too difficult to work out the meaning of *biogeography*:

> The science of the geographical distribution of living things, animal and vegetable. (*OED*)

You try

Use your knowledge of words derived from Greek and Latin to work out as many of these meanings as you can.

geocentric	geochemistry	geochronology	geodynamic
hydrogeologist	geophysicist	theogeological	geometrize
geoscopy	bioclimatic	bioluminescence	biomechanics
biosphere	bioscope		

More than just a meaning

See also:
- **Chapter 11** *Audience* (p. 89)
- **Chapter 13** *Time and place* (p. 108)

The decision about which word goes with which is, of course, a matter of experience—hence the problems encountered by foreign learners. Our experience of language is not, however, purely a matter of words and sentences. Linguistic knowledge is enmeshed with social experience. Words have dictionary meanings but they also have a range of social contexts in which they are habitually used and, in many cases, a range of contexts in which they are not used. This is what makes thesauruses and many dictionaries so difficult for foreign learners to use. A native speaker would probably not have much difficulty in knowing which of the following words and phrases would be acceptable in different social situations:

> unintelligent, stupid, dense, foolish, . . . empty-headed, . . . obtuse, . . . witless, . . . dim-witted, . . . thick, thick as two short planks, . . . daft, . . . soft in the head, not all there, . . . two sandwiches short of a picnic, . . . out to lunch.

> (*Bloomsbury Thesaurus*)

On the other hand, there are situations in which even the most sophisticated user of English has to think very carefully about the exact implications of using one word rather than another. This section of the chapter examines some of the ways in which words have 'more than just a meaning'.

Taboo, slang, and informal

See also:
■ **Chapter 11** *Audience*
(pp. 97–9)

If the list above, extracted from a thesaurus, had been printed more fully, it would have appeared like this:

> unintelligent, stupid, dense, foolish, . . . empty-headed, . . . obtuse, . . . witless, . . . dim-witted (Inf), . . . thick (Inf), thick as two short planks (Inf), . . . daft (Inf), . . . soft in the head (Inf), not all there (Inf), . . . two sandwiches short of a picnic (Inf), . . . out to lunch (Sl).

The list could also have included *thick as shit* (Tab Sl).

By using the abbreviations in brackets, the compilers of the thesaurus can give simple guidance about usage:

> Inf = informal
> Sl = slang
> Tab = taboo

Most people have a general idea of the meanings of these three. The difficulty is in applying them.

Taboo

Taboo subjects and the words and expressions associated with them are those which are prohibited for use in general social intercourse, either because they are too holy to be discussed, or, more commonly, because they deal with topics considered to be too vulgar, notably sex and excretion. If you ask, 'Prohibited *by whom*?', the answer is usually 'by most people'. It is not of course a matter of a legal or even a formal religious ban, but rather one of general social agreement. Such agreement is constantly challenged and redefined, and works differently in different social strata.

People respond to it in different ways:

■ Some take the topics themselves as taboo and always avoid talking about them.

■ Some apply the taboo to the words rather than what they denote and move away from simple 'coarse' words like *shit* and *fuck* to longer, frequently latinate, words like *defecate* and *copulate*.

■ Others—often people who still find the topics a little difficult to talk about—go in a different direction and use euphemisms like *do number twos* and *make love*.

■ A small number of people, usually because of a deliberately adopted social stance, insist on both talking openly about the topics and on using the most explicit language.

Clearly each of these approaches has its drawbacks. What you do and in what social settings depends both on what you feel comfortable with yourself and on your perception of how your audience is likely to respond. How people will respond is always difficult to judge, but never more so than in the area of taboos, because here both language and attitudes are constantly shifting.

Slang   Slang is:

- **language that is less socially acceptable than standard English**
  It is generally less formal and is unsuitable for formal writing and speech. So, from the examples quoted earlier, whereas *dim-witted* is simply an informal usage, *out to lunch* is clearly slang.

- **constantly changing**
  Expressions like *out to lunch*, meaning ; 'unintelligent', have both a history and a limited lifetime. The phrase probably started life in the 1950s and at some stage in the future will drop out of use (it is already beginning to sound rather dated).

- **often connected with membership of a particular social group**
  The word *slang* was originally used to refer to the language of thieves and other criminals. Now the specialist language of such groups is more correctly referred to as *cant* or *argot*. But particular slang words or expressions are still frequently the preserve of particular groups. As one writer puts it:

  The aim of using slang is seldom the exchange of information. More often, slang serves social purposes: to identify members of a group, to change the level of discourse in the direction of informality, to oppose established authority. Sharing and maintaining a constantly changing slang vocabulary aids group solidarity and serves to include and exclude members.

  Connie C. Eble in the *Oxford Companion to the English Language*

Informal   Informal language is any language that is casual, familiar, colloquial, 'unofficial'. It is not an absolute; any use of language can be placed on a continuum:

FORMAL ←————————————————————————→ INFORMAL

Not everyone will necessarily rank different language uses in the same way. For example, these words taken from the thesaurus list quoted earlier could be ranked in more than one way:

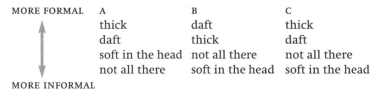

MORE FORMAL	A	B	C
	thick	daft	thick
	daft	thick	daft
	soft in the head	not all there	not all there
	not all there	soft in the head	soft in the head
MORE INFORMAL			

This kind of judgement is, in any case, difficult to make entirely in the abstract. If possible, it is better to think of the particular audience you have in mind before deciding on a choice of language. It is better to amuse by being over formal than to offend by being too informal.

> **You try**
>
> How would you rank each of these groups of words on a scale of formality/informality?
>
> 1 intellectual, clever clogs, egghead, guru, intellect, boffin, smartarse, highbrow, knowall
>
> 2 insolvent, strapped, short of money, boracic, skint, hard up, in difficulties, cleaned out
>
> 3 relax, kip down, rest, take five, have forty winks, snooze, hit the hay, take a nap, take a breather
>
> 4 hurry off, scarper, run away, skedaddle, flee, vamoose, decamp, beat it, split

Jargon

See also:
■ **Chapter 12 *Subject***
(p. 102)

Like slang, jargon is connected with group membership. The *Oxford English Dictionary* defines it as:

> Applied contemptuously to any mode of speech abounding in unfamiliar terms, or peculiar to a particular set of persons, as the language of scholars or philosophers, the terminology of a science or art, or the cant of a class, sect, trade, or profession.

(Which some might argue is itself verging on jargon!) It is true that the word *jargon* is widely used to indicate disapproval. In fact, as the definition implies, it has two related elements:

1 It is specialist language used by members of a group of people with a common interest.

2 This language is often difficult, off-putting, or incomprehensible to others.

We could add a third feature which is often present:

3 People often use jargon, unthinkingly or deliberately, to confirm their own 'expertise' by one or more of the following:
   - showing off
   - sounding more knowledgeable or intelligent than they are
   - deliberately obscuring the subject matter and confusing others

For example:

> This Spring we persuaded the chief winemaker of the award-winning village cellar of Kientzheim—my old friend from the early days, Jean Petitdemange—to dig deep for a prime example of his art. What a tasting! Despite the tiny volumes available, we couldn't resist *two* of his 'special reserve' offerings.
>
> **1 Gold-medal-winning Alsace classic—a subtle explosion of aroma and flavour**
>
> Truly excellent Gewürztraminer—the spicy aromatic grape that is Alsace's great speciality. Jean's 1994 'Gewürz' is characteristically dry with intense floral aromas, and a rich spicy flavour.
>
> 'mid-depth golden-yellow colour. Classic Gewürztraminer aromas of rose

petals and lychees. Dry and weighty—beautifully rich and mouthfilling, but with a light minerally hint. Exceptionally long-lasting, rich flavours . . . '

This is an example of what might broadly be described as 'foodie jargon', that form of over-writing typical of pretentious restaurant menus. (You know the kind of thing: 'Crisp nuggets of chicken with farm-fresh mushrooms, and just a hint of mint'.) It does not achieve incomprehensibility, but in its excessive enthusiasm and desire to sell it will tend to put off all except those who are, or would like to be, wine buffs.

This raises a key feature of jargon. There is nothing wrong with it in its own place. Wine tasting has developed its own vocabulary (jargon)— 'long in the nose', 'plenty of tropical fruit on the palate', and so forth. If you are a wine enthusiast speaking to fellow enthusiasts then such language is not just accepted but expected. Others, however, can find it irritating. Civil servants and other state functionaries have developed a variety of jargons which enable them to communicate with each other speedily and, presumably, efficiently. So have doctors, academic sociologists, and a wide range of trades, businesses, and professions. As long as they keep their jargon 'between consenting adults in private', all well and good. It is when they require the rest of us to read or hear their jargon *and respond to it* that the trouble starts.

You try

This extract comes from a notice put up near a minor landslip on the sea front at Lyme Regis.

. . . *Surveys indicated that restabilization schemes could involve either short-term or long-term solutions, although the latter, notwithstanding the inherent costs, was to be preferred.*

The funding factor being crucial therefore and the magnitude of the problem beyond the immediate resources of the Town Council, West Dorset's offer of assistance was welcomed and the stabilization project was subsequently included in an application to the Ministry of Agriculture, Fisheries and Food for funding as part of the Coastal Defence Programme.

J. M. Amesby, Town Clerk, June 1996

What do you think it means—in simple English?

Jargon can be widened to deliberately confuse the listener or obscure unfortunate facts. This happens in warfare, state welfare, and business, for example. The following examples of 'official-speak' give the flavour. They are all taken from *Jargon: its Uses and Abuses* by Walter Nash:

acceptable/unacceptable Adjectives denoting what politicians and financiers think they can or cannot get away with; or what we, the public, are prepared or not prepared to put up with—always supposing we know what is going on.

collateral damage   Militarese or General Staffspeak for 'civilian casualties'; as when a missile hits the wrong bunker, or a computer demolishes a hospital.

open government   Politicians' shop talk. Open government, the noblest article of democratic faith, is actually a condition of utmost secrecy, based on the need to know and the right to know, which members of the general public . . . do not have.

and we might add:

downsize   To reduce the running costs of a company by sacking a large number of staff. (Synonyms include: letting staff go, destaffing, rationalization, vocational relocation.)

You try

How would you define the use and real meaning of each of these jargon terms?

hidden agenda   ballpark figure   cold calling   de-skilling   hands-on

---

Language and discrimination

See also:
- **Chapter 11** *Audience* (p. 89)
- **Chapter 13** *Time and place* (p. 108)

Another set of baggage that words carry around with them is that they frequently imply that the user has certain social, personal, or political attitudes. When words are combined into well-known phrases, those attitudes, or prejudices, can become even more apparent. A not-uncommon expression illustrates this well:

Well, you know what Peter's like when faced by a problem—he's a bit of an old woman, isn't he?

Sexism *and* ageism in one short phrase!

Language used to refer to social, physical, or gender groups can display prejudice, bias, thoughtlessness, or neutrality, but what makes words acceptable or unacceptable is not fixed but moves with changing attitudes and even fashion. For example, in the United States at different periods of history and in different social groups, people have referred to:

niggers, negros, blacks, African Americans

Similarly, people of a particular sexual orientation in Britain have been called:

poofters, queers, homos, homosexuals, gays

Everyone has to choose their own position on this question, if not word by word, certainly issue by issue. Most people will probably not want to go as far as using 'sobriety-deprived' for 'drunk', or 'involuntarily undomiciled' for 'homeless'. On the other hand you need to be aware that unthinking use of language that some people regard as discriminatory can alienate the very people with whom you wish to communicate. If you want to make a particular point by deliberately flouting these sensibilities, that is a matter of choice, but you should avoid doing it accidentally.

He, she, it, or they?

One problem that will not go away is the lack of a neuter personal pronoun in English. We can refer to animals of either sex, or even babies, as 'it', but not older children and adults. One can avoid gender-specific terms like chairman (chair), foreman (supervisor), and so on. But how do you avoid choosing between 'he' and 'she' in sentences like this?

Every writer knows that —— should avoid sexist language.

Various possibilities have been explored, including the use of s/he, which is rather ugly and does not solve the problem of him/her and his/her(s). Three solutions are now commonly adopted:

1 Use *he or she, him or her, his or her(s).*
    In less formal situations these can be shortened to *he/she, him/her, his/her(s)*. This is an effective way of getting round the problem but can be cumbersome if used excessively.

2 Recast the sentence so that it is in the plural.
    All writers know that they should avoid sexist language.
    This is always acceptable, but not always possible. Some sentences do not lend themselves easily to such conversion.

3 Use the plural pronoun as a neuter pronoun.
    Every writer knows that they should avoid sexist language.
    This is always possible but not always acceptable, especially to those, often older people, who were brought up in the traditions of prescriptive grammar, which teaches that a plural pronoun can only refer back to a plural noun or noun phrase. It is, however, widely used and increasingly accepted.

Other solutions which some writers prefer include:

4 Using *he/him/his* throughout and explaining in a preface that you are not a sexist and that these words refer equally to *she/her/her(s)*. This is still done but increasingly it is not accepted by large numbers of readers.

5 Doing the same thing, but using the feminine pronouns. Objected to for similar reasons.

6 Using *he/him/his* and *she/her/her(s)* alternately. This can have some rather bizarre effects and is not to be recommended.

You try

What terms would you use to avoid these gender-specific words?

clergyman   craftsman   layman   man-made   policeman   salesman

---

Words and connotations

As much of the foregoing material has shown, the meaning of words is not confined to their dictionary meanings. We have seen how they can be acceptable or unacceptable in a wide range of situations, and for many different reasons. More than that, however, very many of the words we use have *connotations*. Imagine, for example, that you wanted to describe a person's physical appearance. If the person is below average height and weight, you could choose between these words and phrases:

> short, diminutive, petite, compact, squat, dwarfish, elfin, dainty, midget, knee-high to a grasshopper, stunted

Of these some are relatively neutral, 'short', for example (although some would argue that this is is 'heightist' and should be replaced by 'of below average height'). Others imply criticism or hostility, such as 'stunted' and 'knee-high to a grasshopper'. Others again are more favourable: 'compact', and 'petite'.

You try

Divide these words to describe personal appearance into three categories:

A those which are favourable to the person described

B those which are unfavourable

C those which are neutral

heavy	well-built	fat
stocky	thickset	burly
brawny	beefy	chunky
hefty	elephantine	obese
gross	comfortable	paunchy
well-endowed	well-upholstered	lumbering

Guidelines

Getting help

1 Make use of a good (and up-to-date) dictionary—the best you can afford. For everyday use a large single-volume dictionary such as the *Oxford Concise* or the *Collins English Dictionary* is practical. Use it regularly, not only to check spellings and meanings, but also to browse in—an excellent way of improving and developing your vocabulary. It is also very valuable to have access to a larger dictionary such as the *Shorter Oxford Dictionary*.

2 Use a thesaurus as an active guide to finding the best word and developing your vocabulary.

3 As you read, and listen to people speaking, be alert for new words, or words that you have heard before but are not sure about. (Some radio programmes are particularly articulate in their use of language and worth listening to for this, as well as their entertainment value.) Use a dictionary to check new words you encounter and look for opportunities to use them yourself.

4 Be alert, too, to the contexts in which words are used. Try to grade them in your mind according to the criteria that have been used in this chapter (formal/informal, slang, taboo).

Word structure

5 Develop an awareness of how words are constructed. Use your existing knowledge of stems and affixes to help you 'decode' words that are unfamiliar. Use the list of prefixes on pages 185–6 to help you in this.

6 Develop an awareness of how words can be changed in their use by the addition of suffixes. Use the list of suffixes on pages 187–8 to help you in this.

7 Use your existing knowledge of words that have been derived from classical Greek and Latin to help you work out the probable meanings of other words similarly derived.

More than just a meaning

8 It is important to be sensitive to other people's responses to taboo language and slang.

9 All of the words and expressions we use in everyday life can be placed on a scale running from formal to informal. You can learn how this works only by being constantly aware of people's attitudes towards language.

10 Jargon is common in many walks of life but it can confuse people or put them off. Again, you need to be aware when you are using jargon and of the effect its use has on others.

11 As readers and listeners we need to recognize when jargon is being used to obscure the truth.

12 Similarly, we need to be aware of the effects discriminatory language can have on others, especially in the areas of gender, race, and disability.

13 It is possible and desirable to avoid gender bias in the use of nouns and pronouns.

14 Many words imply that the user has favourable or unfavourable attitudes towards the subject under discussion. We need to be aware of this when writing and speaking.

You try: key

page 188

Words that could be included in each of the other diagrams are:

large	sail	sailor	wait
larger	boardsailing	sailoress	await
enlarge	cross-sail	sailoring	awaited
enlarged	disailment	sailorizing	dumb-waiter
enlargement	fore-sail	sailorless	outwait
enlarger	fore-spritsail	sailorly	overwait
largely	fore-topsail	sailorship	quarter-waiter
largemost	gaff-topsail	sailplane	unawait
largeness	head-sail	sailsman	wait-list
over-large	lug-sail	sailworthy	waiter
re-enlarge	mainsail	sailyard	waitership
unenlarged	main-topsail	spreet-sail	waiting
unlarge	outsail	spritsail	waiting-maid
	plain sailing n.	sprit-topsail	waiting-man
	sailable	square sail	waiting-room
	sailage n.	staysail	waiting-
	sailcloth	topsail	woman
	sailboard	under-sail	waitress
	sailed	unsailable	
	sailer	unsailed ppl.	
	sail-fish	unsailorlike	
	sailful	unsailorly	
	sailing	windsail	

Page 189   The definitions that follow are taken from the *Oxford English Dictionary*

geocentric   Referred to the earth as centre; considered as viewed from the centre of the earth.

geochemistry   The chemistry of the earth; the study of the chemical composition of the earth.

geochronology   The chronology of the earth; the measurement of geological time and the ordering of past geological events.

geodynamic   Of or pertaining to the (latent) forces of the earth.

hydrogeologist   An expert in, or student of, hydrogeology, that part of geology which treats of the relations of water on or below the surface of the earth.

geophysicist   An expert in, or student of, geophysics, the science or study of the physics of the earth, esp. of its crust.

theogeological   Of or pertaining to geology as accommodated to theological tenets.

geometrize   To work by geometrical methods, to form geometrically.

geoscopy   A kind of knowlege of the nature and qualities of the ground, or soil; gained by viewing and considering it . . .

bioclimatic   Pertaining to the study of climate in relation to the seasonal activities and geographical distribution of living organisms.

bioluminescence   The emission of light by living organisms; also, the light so produced.

biomechanics   The study of the mechanical laws relating to the movement or structure of living organisms.

biosphere   The regions of the earth's crust and atmospherc that are occupied by living organisms; occas., the living organisms themselves.

bioscope **1.** A view or survey of life. Obs. **2.** An earlier form of cinematograph (cf. biograph n. 2); retained in South Africa as the usual term for a cinema or a moving film.

page 192 This is, to some extent, a matter of personal experience and opinion, but this is one possible grading. In each case the lists run from formal to informal.

intellectual	insolvent	relax	flee
guru	in difficulties	rest	run away
highbrow	short of	snooze	hurry off
intellect	money	take a	decamp
boffin	hard up	breather	split
egghead	cleaned out	take a nap	beat it
knowall	strapped	have forty	skedaddle
clever clogs	skint	winks	scarper
smartarse	boracic	take five	vamoose
		kip down	
		hit the hay	

page 193 A simpler version of the text might be:

Surveys showed that it was possible to stabilize the land in a temporary or a long-term way. The Town Council preferred a long-term solution, although it would cost more.

The Town Council did not have enough money to undertake the work, so it welcomed an offer of help from West Dorset District Council. We then applied to the Ministry of Agriculture, Fisheries and Food to receive additional funding as part of the Coastal Defence Programme.

page 194 The definitions that follow are quoted—for both enlightenment and entertainment—from *Jargon* by Walter Nash. The author does not necessarily follow the suggestions about language use contained in this Guide.

agenda, hidden In the political mode, the hidden agenda means the complex of sensitive issues that make up the potentially unacceptable items of someone's ideology—meaning what they don't tell you about what they intend to do if they get half a chance. Old phrases like 'ulterior motive' or 'concealed purpose' might do at a pinch, but somehow lack the clout. This is a very modish expression. Do not say 'Some parish councillors are trying to get rid of the old fish-and-chip shop on the sly'; say 'The progressive streamlining of local catering facilities is evidently an item of high priority on the council's hidden agenda'.

ballpark figure Book-keepers' and statisticians' shop: a general, round figure estimate of a large number. Originally used to denote the probable size of the crowd at a baseball game, this American expression was subsequently extended to any estimate of population, expenditure, budgetary outlay, etc. 'How much is this project going to cost?—I don't want it down to the last penny, just give me a ballpark figure.' Britons tend to confuse 'ballpark' and 'ballgame'—but that is a whole new ballpark.

cold calling Salesman's jargon: the practice of calling on a prospective client or entering a potential market without a preliminary introduction or recommendation. 'Before arriving' (at the Cannes Film Festival) 'she researches the trade papers, discovers who will be here and what projects they are keen on. Then she braces herself for some "cold calling" at the luxury Majestic and Carlton hotels'—*Independent*.

de-skilling In industry, through technological advances, rendering the skilled worker unnecessary. 'It is now in the US and UK, where the implementation of the style [= the technology] is proving difficult, that it is doing most to increase inequality; destroying whole industries, de-skilling occupations, weakening unions . . .'—*Guardian*.

hands-on Adjective, meaning 'practical', 'direct', as in hands-on experience. The original hands-on experience was the trainee's first touching of the computer keyboard; now the expression can apply more diversely—for example to a medical student's first attempts at the clinical examination of a patient, or a learner-driver's practical training in handling the controls of a car. The epithet hands-on may also be used in application to persons; 'The question hardly anyone dare ask in Washington . . . was whether the crisis could have been averted in the first place by a more hands-on president'—*Observer*. From hands-on follows hands-off: 'Mr Lilley . . . has traditionally taken a hands-off approach to industry'—*Guardian*.

Page 195   **clergyman**: *priest, minister*
craftsman: *craft worker*
layman: *lay person* (in religious contexts), *non-expert*, or *ordinary person* (where the word is meaning 'someone without special knowledge or qualifications')
man-made: *synthetic, artificial, manufactured*
policeman: *police officer* (or give rank)
salesman: *sales representative, sales assistant*

Page 196   This is another occasion where the choice is based on personal experience. One possible grading would be:

A	B	C
stocky	brawny	heavy
well-endowed	gross	hefty
well-built	elephantine	thickset
beefy	well-upholstered	obese
comfortable	fat	
burly	paunchy	
chunky	lumbering	

20 | Spelling

Why *is* English spelling so much of a problem for so many people? There are two answers to this question. The first is that actually it is not as much of a problem as many people think. Wrong spelling rarely leads to mistakes of understanding; much more frequently it just annoys sticklers for accuracy. This is not, however, to justify a deliberate policy of letting things slip. It is much easier for everyone if we all spell words in the same way.

The second answer is a matter of linguistic history. Unlike Italian and other so-called 'phonetically spelled' languages, English cannot easily have a direct correspondence between sounds and letters. There are over forty sounds in English, far more than in Italian, and we only have the same twenty-six letters in the alphabet. So we have to combine letters in different ways to represent the 'missing' sounds. To do this we rely on a series of conventions. These developed over a period of history during which the vocabulary of English and its pronunciation were both also developing. Words came into English from many other languages and many retained their original spelling but changed their pronunciation. Other imports came from languages with a different writing system and were written down by travellers and merchants in the best way they could. In all this richness of vocabulary and linguistic vitality there has never been a consistent attempt to reform the whole spelling system and, given the worldwide status of English, probably never will be.

So we are stuck with a spelling system that is far from ideal and the best we can do is to devise workable strategies to help us spell better. There is no doubt that some people find spelling much easier than others. But even so it *is* possible for even the worst speller to make big strides towards much greater accuracy. There are ways of getting a grip on spelling generally and there are specific rules which can be learned.

Looking for patterns

The key to a generally more positive approach to spelling is to look constantly for *patterns*. There are two kinds of pattern which are helpful:

- patterns of sound/letter relationship
- patterns of letter/letter relationship

Sound/letter patterns

At first sight looking for correspondences between the sounds and letters of English seems a daunting task. The first sound in the name 'George' can be spelled in eight different ways:

> *j* as in *jug*
> *g* as in *gesture*
> *dg* as in *judge*
> *gg* as in *suggest*
> *dj* as in *adjust*
> *de* as in *grandeur*
> *di* as in *soldier*
> *ch* as in *sandwich* (as pronounced by some speakers)

Vowels cause even more difficulty. /i:/ is commonly spelled in seven different ways:

> *ee* as in *beet*
> *ea* as in *beat*
> *e* as in *dene*
> *ie* as in *fief*
> *ei* as in *receive*
> *ey* as in *key*
> *i* as in *routine*

In addition it occurs in these words:

> quay   people

Leaving the latter two 'exceptions' on one side, however, it is easy to see patterns of sound/letter correspondence:

beet	**beat**	**fief**
feed	heap	thief
feet	leap	piece
feel	real	field
peep	heal	siege
etc.		

When children are taught to read using by sounding letters (the 'phonic' method), this is how they are taught. *The cat sat on the mat* follows just such an approach.

Letter/letter patterns

The other broad approach to teaching children to read is often called *look-and-say*. This works on the belief that the human brain looks for visual (and other) patterns and that when children are learning to read they often perceive a whole word as a pattern. This accounts for the fact that very early on in the process children will learn to recognize quite long words, provided they have a clearly distinguishable visual pattern, with ascenders and descenders, like *elephant* or *aeroplane*.

As we learn to read we also take on board the combinations of letters that are typical of English. For example, given a small amount of time, most people could think of words that contained these letter combinations:

-IGH-
-UGH-

It is much more difficult to think of words that contain the combination -EGH-. There are some, but they are fairly obscure.

The other way in which we habitually use patterning is in the recognition of word stems, prefixes, and suffixes: once you understand and can spell *psychology* you should not have too much trouble spelling the first part of **psych**iatry and **psycho**-analysis or the endings of geo**logy** and histo**logy**.

See also:
■ **Chapter 19** *Vocabulary* (p. 179)

Developing a personal strategy

If you wish to develop a positive strategy based on this, you need to begin by analysing the nature of the mistakes you make. It is then necessary to attach your problem words to words that you *can* spell. A typical problem area is the double or single letters that occur in words like *accommodation*, *imitate*, and *professional*. You *could* try to learn the whole list of problem words by heart. An approach more likely to succeed, however, is to group the words according to a series of patterns and thus relate problem words to others that have the same pattern:

See also:
pages 208–9 where these words are listed

Words with no double letters
  pedal
  imitate
  etc.

words with one pair of double letters
  accelerate
  assist
  etc.

words with two pairs of double letters
  accommodation
  address
  etc.

You could develop a similar approach to problems of sound/letter correspondence. That is what happens in the most famous spelling rule of all:

'I before E except after C, when the sound is long EE'

This rule works, has very few exceptions (*caffeine*, *codeine*, *counterfeit*, *protein*, *seize*, *species*, plus *either*, *neither*, *inveigle* if you pronounce them with a long 'ee'), and only causes trouble when people forget the second half of it.

Finally, and most important, **write it down**. If you wish to remember a visual pattern it is important that you should see it. When you are trying to learn a spelling that causes problems, a well-known method is *look—cover—write—check*:

- **Look** at the correct spelling on the printed page so that you 'print' it on your brain. Spell the word out loud.
- **Cover** it up.
- **Write** it down from memory, spelling it out loud as you do so.
- **Check** against the printed version that you have got it right.

With a problem word this process should be repeated at increasing intervals until you are confident that it is fixed in your mind. Also, when in doubt about a spelling it is always worth trying to write down its various possible forms on scrap paper to see which looks right.

Rules based on patterns

Spelling rules and patterns fall into two broad groups:

- those that cover the spelling of certain sounds which can be written in two or three different ways
- those that explain how adding to a word changes the spelling of the original word

Sounds and letters

The rules that follow are not exhaustive, but have been chosen because they are useful and fairly easy to remember.

-ie- and -ei-

i **before** *e* **except after** *c* **when the sound is long 'ee'**

examples: *thief, receive*
exceptions: *caffeine, codeine, counterfeit, protein, seize, species* (plus *either, neither, inveigle*)

-c- and -s-

c **noun** *s* **verb**
(easily remembered because the initial letters are in alphabetical order: C-N-S-V)

examples:

noun	verb
practice	*practise*
prophecy	*prophesy*

-ise, -ize, -yse

This is an area where an old rule and a new one are in conflict. Traditionally there was a group of words derived from Greek which reflected the Greek spelling by ending *-ize*. Examples include *organize* and *realize*. Today it is permissible to spell almost any word with this sound at the end with *-ise*, except for *capsize* which must be spelled with a -z-. As ever, the important thing is to be consistent. This book, for example, follows the house style of Oxford University Press, using *-ize* where the author would normally use *-ise*. In addition, a small number of words of Greek origin end *-yse* and must be spelled that way (unless you are American and prefer to spell them *-yze*). They include *analyse*, and *paralyse*.

-able, -ible There *is* a rule, but it requires a fair amount of linguistic knowledge to apply it!

-ible is reserved for words borrowed from Latin and the list of 180 or so words spelled in this way is 'closed'—no new words spelled in this way are being created. More common words spelled in this way are:

accessible	admissible	audible
collapsible	combustible	compatible
comprehensible	contemptible	credible
defensible	destructible	digestible
divisible	edible	fallible
flexible	forcible	gullible
horrible	illegible	implausible
inaccessible	incontrovertible	incredible
indefensible	indelible	inedible
insensible	intelligible	invincible
invisible	illegible	irresistible
irreversible	ostensible	permissible
plausible	possible	responsible
reversible	sensible	susceptible
suggestible	tangible	terrible
visible		

Words derived from Old English words and all new words now created with this ending are spelled *-able*. So the list includes old words like:

affordable	laughable	washable

and new words (often ugly!) like:

networkable	unclubbable	windsurfable

A quick check, which works most of the time, is that if you remove *-able* from a word, you are usually still left with a complete word. If you do the same with *-ible*, generally you are not.

-ar, -er, -or Tricky, because there is some overlap. In most cases, when a verb is turned into a noun (meaning 'the person who does this') we add *-er* (or just *-r* to words ending in *-e*):

designer	maker	miner

All new nouns made from verbs work in this way. But verbs that end in *-ate* make nouns ending in *-ator*. There are a number of other nouns derived from verbs which also end in *-or*, of which the commonest are:

actor	contractor	contributor	defector
distributor	governor	inheritor	inspector
inventor	investor	persecutor	prosecutor
prospector	reflector	resistor	sailor
supervisor	surveyor	survivor	visitor

There are also a few that add *-ar*, of which the commonest are:

beggar	burglar	liar

Rules for changing words

The other group of rules or patterns covers how we spell words when we add bits to them.

Adding -s

We add *-s* to words for two reasons:

- to make nouns plural
- to form the she/he form of the present tense of verbs

The rules for both are the same, so the plural -s rules are given here, with a few additional rules which apply only to plurals.

1 Normally just add *-s*:
papers, hopes
2 Words that end with any of the following, add *-es*
-ch, -s, -sh, -x, -z:
branches, masses, bushes, boxes, chintzes
3 Words that end in *-f* or *-fe*, change the ending to *ves*
wives, calves
Exceptions to this:
beliefs, chiefs, dwarfs, griefs, gulfs, proofs, roofs
4 Words that end in *vowel + y*, add *-s*:
days, boys
5 Words that end in *consonant + y*, change the *-y* to *-ies*:
babies, spies
6 Words that end in *-o* normally just add *-s*:
pianos, radios
There is however a group of common words which add *-es*:

buffaloes	*cargoes* (can be *cargos*)	*dominoes*
echoes	*goes*	*grottoes*
haloes	*heroes*	*mangoes*
mosquitoes	*mottoes* (can be *mottos*)	*potatoes*
tomatoes	*tornadoes*	*torpedoes*
vetoes	*volcanoes*	

Adding *-ing* and *-ed*

When using verbs we often need to add the grammatical suffixes *-ing* and *-ed* to the stem of the verb:

As I was *walking* along the High Street I *bumped* into an old friend.

Unless the verb is covered by one of the rules that follow, you simply add the suffix. Before adding the suffix:
1 Words ending in *consonant + y*; change the *y* to *i* before *-ed*
cry → crying → cried
2 Words ending in *vowel + y*; just add the suffix:
played
Exceptions:
said, paid, laid

Words of one syllable

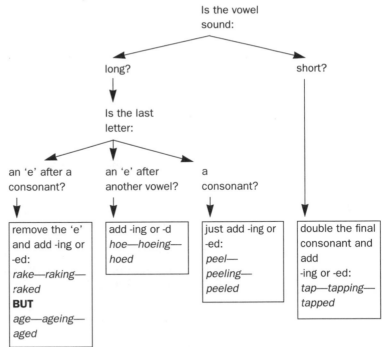

Words of more than one syllable, ending with a consonant

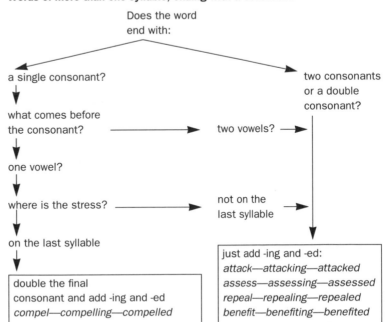

Adding *-ly*   Many adjectives can be turned into adverbs by the addition of the suffix *-ly*. Normally this is simply added to the adjective. There are a few exceptions:

1 If the word ends in *-ll*, simply add *-y*:
   fully
2 Words of more than one syllable ending in *-y*, remove the *-y* and add *-ily*:
   happily
3 Words ending with a consonant followed by *-le*, remove the final *-e* and add *-y*:
   terribly
4 Most single-syllable words ending in *-y* are regular, except for:
   daily, gaily

Adding *-er* and *-est*   The comparative and superlative forms of many adjectives are formed by adding the suffixes *-er* and *-est*:

   great, greater, greatest

The suffixes are normally added without further change. There are four groups of exceptions:

1 Words that end in a consonant followed by *-y*, change the *-y* to an *-i* before adding the suffix:
   happier, happiest
2 Words with one syllable which contain a long vowel sound and which end with *-e* (e.g., *late*); remove the *-e* before adding the suffix:
   later, latest
3 Words of one syllable containing a short vowel sound and ending in a single consonant letter (e.g., *sad*); double the final consonant before adding the suffix:
   sadder, saddest
4 Words ending in *-l* normally just add the suffix, but there is one exception:
   cruel → *crueller* → *cruellest*

Awkward customers

Double and single letters   Some words just cause problems which cannot be solved by learning rules. The only thing to do then is to learn them by heart. In this section problem words are arranged in lists, with brief comments.

This problem was referred to earlier (on p. 203). These are longer versions of the lists suggested there.

No double letters
   fulfil (fulfill in AmE)
   imitate   marvel   omit
   patrol   pedal   transmit

One pair of double letters

abbreviate	accelerate	accident	accomplish
accurate	allergy	appropriate	approximate
assist	beginning	brilliant	caterpillar
collapse	collect	commemorate	commit
corridor	desiccated	disappear	disappoint
dissatisfied	discuss	exaggerate	excellent
gorilla	happen(ed)	harass	hallelujah
illustrate	immediate	millenium*	millionaire
necessary	occasion	occur	paraffin
parallel	proceed	procession	professional
questionnaire	scissors	sheriff	succeed
sufficient	terrible	tomorrow	tranquillity

Two pairs of double letters

accommodation	accidentally	address	commission
committed	embarrass	guerrilla	happiness
mattress	millennium*	possess	successful
unnecessary	woollen		

*Either spelling is acceptable

Words sometimes confused

accept/except

I **accept** everything you say **except** your claim that you are telling the truth.

access/excess

I could not gain **access** to the building because of an **excess** of security precautions.

accessary/accessory

The accused, who wore a green dress with matching **accessories**, was found guilty of being an **accessary** to the crime of murder.

affect/effect

■ as nouns

affect is a relatively uncommon word and means 'mood, mental state, emotion'

effect means 'the result of an action', or 'belonging' as in personal effects

■ as verbs

affect means 'to alter the state of something, to have an effect on it'

effect means 'to bring something about', as in effect a change

all ready/already

'Now are we **all ready**?' she asked, **already** beginning to get flustered.

all together/altogether

If you put his mistakes **all together**, his reputation looks **altogether** different.

amend/emend

Both words have a similar meaning of 'changing something', but amend carries a meaning of 'make improvements to', while emend tends to mean 'correct a mistake in'.

amoral/immoral

*Before they reach the age of reason babies are **amoral**; their behaviour shows no knowledge of right and wrong. Those who mistreat them are **immoral**.*

apiary/aviary

Both are containers for creatures: an apiary for bees, and an aviary for birds.

appraise/apprise

*After **appraising** my work, the inspector **apprised** me of his opinion.*

ascent/assent

*After John's **ascent** of the Matterhorn, Mary gave her **assent** to his proposal and they were married.*

assay/essay

- as nouns

  assay means the process of testing something out and more technically the process of assaying precious metals

  essay is most commonly used to mean an extended piece of formal writing

- as verbs

  assay means to put something to the proof, or to test metals chemically to determine their purity

  essay means to attempt something

auger/augur

*The student's inability to use a simple **auger** to bore a hole did not **augur** well for his career as a boatbuilder.*

aural/oral

*In the French examination we had to do a dictation, which tested our **aural** ability, and also give a five-minute talk to demonstrate our **oral** skills.*

awhile/a while

awhile is an adverb; *a while* is a noun phrase. So:
'Let's rest **awhile**', she said after **a while**.

bail/bale

*After being let out of prison on **bail** he went on a parachuting course and learned to **bale** out of an aircraft. On his first descent he broke his leg landing on a **bale** of straw.*

base/bass

*In some operas the **bass** singer plays a villain or other **base** character.*

biannual/biennial

*If you're lucky you get **biannual** holidays (every six months); if you're unlucky they are **biennial** (every two years).*

born/borne

*The couple's problems seemed too great to be **borne**, especially after their sixth child was **born**.*

buy/by/bye

by is a preposition with a range of meanings; *bye* is a noun with meanings in cricket and other games; either spelling can be used in *by the by(e)* and *by(e)-law*

calendar/colander

*I must put a note on the **calendar** in the kitchen to remind me to buy a new **colander** for the vegetables.*

callous/callus

'Is that a wart on your finger or just a **callus**?' she asked **callously**.

cannon/canon

The cathedral **canon** wanted to fire a small **cannon** from the tower to scare the pigeons but he was told it was against the **canons** of the church.

canvas/canvass

When he went round the area to **canvass** votes, he carried his election literature in a **canvas** holdall.

censer/censor/censure

A *censer* is a container in which incense is burned.

A *censor* is someone who controls the content of books, newspapers, films, and other media.

If you *censure* someone, you criticize or condemn them.

cereal/serial

As he ate his breakfast **cereal** he read the comic-strip **serial** in his daily paper.

complement/compliment

A *compliment* is paid to someone you admire. The *complement* is what completes something: the ship's *complement* is its crew, without which it would be incomplete.

complaisant/complacent

Someone who is *complaisant* is accommodating and wishes to please others.

A *complacent* person is certainly easily pleased and probably pleased with himself.

confidant(e)/confident

As with all words ending with -*ant*/-*ent*, the former is a noun and the latter an adjective:

He was so **confident**, he did not need a **confidant** in whom to confide his fears.

contagious/contiguous

A *contagious* disease is one that can be passed on by physical contact. Two things that are *contiguous* are next to each other and may actually be touching.

council/counsel

At the meeting of the royal **council** the king asked his senior ministers for their **counsel** about what he should do.

credible/credulous

Although the story was so far-fetched as to be hardly **credible**, my friend was so **credulous** he believed every word of it.

crevasse/crevice

From a great height the huge **crevasses** in the ice looked like tiny **crevices** in a sheet of crumpled paper.

curb/kerb

A *curb* is something that restrains someone or something (or curbs them).

A *kerb* is the edge of a pavement.

currant/current

A *currant* is a piece of dried fruit.

A *current* is a moving stream of water in the sea.

Current also means 'happening now'.

debar/disbar

*The lawyer was **disbarred**; this meant among other things that he was **debarred** from participating in criminal trials.*

defuse/diffuse

If you *defuse* something you literally remove its fuse, so more generally it means 'neutralize, remove the danger from'.

If you *diffuse* something you spread it around.

dependant/dependent

*His father was not **dependent** on the state, although he had nineteen **dependants**.*

deprecate/depreciate

*The cricket authorities **deprecated** the batsman's bad behaviour, arguing that it would only cause the reputation of cricket as a sport to **depreciate**.*

desert/dessert

*The arrogant explorer refused to take any advice so when he perished in the **desert** he got his just **desserts**.*

detract/distract

*When politicians seek to **detract** from the merits of their opponents it is usually to **distract** attention from their own shortcomings.*

disassemble/dissemble

*The clever nine-year-old said, 'Father I will not **dissemble**. It was I **disassembled** your computer.'*

dinghy/dingy

A dirty little sailing boat could be described as a *dingy dinghy*.

emigrate/immigrate

*As a rule, those who **immigrate** into one country must first have **emigrated** from another.*

eminent/immanent/imminent

Things or people that are *eminent* stand out in some way.

If something is *imminent* it is just about to happen.

Some philosophers have believed that God is *immanent* (all-pervading) in the universe.

ensure/insure

*Before they went on holiday he **ensured** that the house and contents were fully **insured**.*

exalt/exult

If you *exalt* something you raise it up, literally or figuratively.

If you *exult*, you rejoice.

extant/extent

*I do not know to what **extent** belief in miracles is still **extant** in our society.*

factious/fractious

*The prime minister's nights were broken by the crying of her **fractious** infant son, so during the day she was not in the mood to deal with the divisions of her **factious** party.*

fatal/fateful

On that *fateful* day, just as the soothsayer had predicted, Caesar received a *fatal* injury.

faze/phase

I was completely *fazed* by her behaviour, which seemed to mark a new *phase* in our relationship.

flaunt/flout

The streaker *flouted* all the conventions of cricketing society by *flaunting* his body in front of the Test Match crowd.

foreword/forward

In her *foreword* to the book she put *forward* some new arguments.

gild/guild/gilt/guilt

At courses run by the *Guild* of Cake Decorators you can learn how to put gold icing, or *gilt*, on a cake; they call the lesson '*Gilding* the gingerbread'. The slogan 'Naughty but nice' suggests that if you eat cream cakes you should feel a pleasurable *guilt*.

grill/grille

A *grill* is something you cook on.
A *grille* is a barred opening in a wall.

human/humane

Most **human** beings who eat meat expect the treatment of the animals they consume to be **humane**; they do not want them to suffer.

impractical/impracticable

An *impractical* person, who does not have much idea of how things should be done, is likely to suggest *impracticable* (unworkable) solutions to problems.

inapt/inept

An *inapt* solution is one which is not suitable for that particular problem. It may well be suggested by someone who isn't very good at such things, who is, in fact, *inept*.

index/indexes/indices

In everyday usage the plural of *index* is *indexes*. *Indices* is reserved for the mathematical sense of *index*. (As in *The minister referred to a number of different indices to show how prices were moving.*)

ingenious/ingenuous

Ingenuous means 'Honourably straightforward; open, frank, candid' (*OED*)—often innocently so.
Ingenious means clever.
Disingenuous means deviously clever but pretending to be honourably straightforward, etc.

interment/internment

Interment means burial.
Internment means imprisonment.

junction/juncture

The transport minister said that at this *juncture* (point in time) there was nothing to be done about the dangerous road *junction*.

lightening/lightning

During a long and very dull lecture about the effects of thunder and **lightning** on pregnant moles, the only thing that was **lightening** my boredom was the thought that it could not go on for ever.

liqueur/liquor

A *liqueur* is a strong and usually sweet *liquor* (alcoholic drink) such as Cointreau or Bénédictine. A *liquor* can also be a more general term for a liquid.

loathe/loath/loth

If you *loathe* something, you hate it and are *loath* (unwilling) to have anything to do with it. *Loth* is an alternative spelling for *loath*.

lose/loose

These two are sometimes confused (because *lose* rhymes with *choose*?). You might, for example, *lose* a pet dog if you left it *loose* rather than tied up.

meter/metre

A *meter* is used to measure things. A *metre* is a distance and also the regular pattern of strong and weak syllables in *metrical* poetry.

militate/mitigate

To *mitigate* is to lessen the harmful effects of something or someone. To *militate* is to conflict with or work against someone or something.

miner/minor

A *miner* digs underground.
A *minor* is under-age.

moral/morale

The **moral** *of the story was that when an army's* **morale** *is low it loses battles.*

naval/navel

Naval means concerning the navy.
A *navel* is a belly button, or a kind of orange.

palate/palette/pallet

The *palate* is part of the mouth.
A *palette* is the range of colours used by an artist or the small tray they are placed on.
A *pallet* is a wooden platform on which goods are stacked for storage or carriage. It is also a straw bed or mattress.

passed/past

These two are sometimes confused.
Passed is the past tense and past participle of the verb *to pass*:
I have **passed** *my exam; all the students in our year* **passed**.
Past is an adjective or a preposition:
I have **passed** *all my examinations so the time for worrying is* **past**.
He walked **past** *the house.*

peninsula/peninsular

Peninsula is a noun:
Devon and Cornwall form a **peninsula**.
Peninsular is the adjective derived from it:
The **Peninsular** *War was fought in Spain against the French.*

precede/proceed

As the procession **proceeded** *along the Mall, the royal carriage* **preceded** *that of the prime minister.*

prescribe/proscribe

Prescribe means recommend or advise.
Proscribe means ban or forbid.

principle/principal

Principle is a noun and means what is central to something, a fundamental truth:

*Whenever we argued he always insisted on taking things back to first **principles**.*

Principal can be either an adjective or a noun. As an adjective it means 'main, or chief'; as a noun it means 'the head or leader of a group or organization':

*The **principal** rule, or **principle**, on which the college was run was that the **Principal** was always right.*

resister/resistor

A *resister* is someone who resists.

A *resistor* is an electronic device which reduces the flow of an electric current.

sceptic/septic

*He was always a **sceptic**, so he did not believe me when I told him that the wound had gone **septic**.*

sensual/sensuous

Sensual refers to pleasures experienced through the body, often sexual.

Sensuous refers to pleasures experienced through the mind, often artistic.

sight/site/cite

*He argued that tourism was bad for the Developing World and **cited** one example where a popular **site** had become an eyesore rather than a **sight** for sore eyes.*

stationary/stationery

Stationary is an adjective and means not moving.

Stationery is usually a noun referring to paper and other office consumables, but it can be a modifier, as in *the stationery shop*.

systematic/systemic

A person who does things in an orderly way can be described as *systematic*.

A disease that invades the bloodstream or other systems of the body is said to be *systemic*.

taught/taut

Subjects are *taught* in schools.

Taut is the opposite of loose or slack.

ton/tonne

A *ton* is 2240 pounds (UK) or 2000 pounds (USA).

A *tonne* is a metric ton: 1000 kilograms.

urban/urbane

Urban means relating to a city or cities in general.

Urbane means cultured and smooth-mannered.

vicious/viscous

Vicious means nasty, aggressive, or cruel.

A *viscous* liquid is one that is thick and slow-flowing.

waiver/waver

*She never **wavered** in her determination to get the bank to renounce their legal right to repossess her house. In the end she got the **waiver** she was requesting.*

Guidelines

1 It is important to realize that because of the complexity of English the number of people who have no problems with spelling is tiny.

2 So most people need to develop strategies for dealing with spelling problems: strategies that work for them.

3 Always look for patterns and remember that spelling is a visual matter.

4 Learn difficult spellings by the *Look—Cover—Write—Check* method.

5 Test doubtful spellings by writing down possible versions and seeing which one looks right.

6 Use the sound/letter rules listed in this chapter.

7 Use the rules for adding endings listed in this chapter.

8 Try to place problem spellings in a group of similar spellings which also includes words you *can* spell.

9 A lot of 'spelling' mistakes are actually the confusion of two words with slightly different spellings but very different meanings. These have to learned.

10 Use a good dictionary.

21 Punctuation

Punctuation marks

- Full stop
- Question mark
- Exclamation mark
- Colon
- Semicolon
- Comma
- Apostrophe
- Inverted commas
- Capital letter
- Hyphen
- Dash

Using punctuation

- Direct speech and other quotations
- Abbreviations
- Lists
- Enclosing text, including non-defining relative clauses

Punctuation is a set of conventions to make it easier to read written English. It is important to stress that the so-called 'rules' of punctuation are simply conventions—agreed ways of separating a text into sections that the reader's eye and brain can assimilate. Like any other set of conventions (table manners, for example), punctuation changes over time. There are fashions; people experiment, and as a result the 'rules' change.

Some areas of punctuation are clear-cut and straightforward. For example, no one would disagree that a sentence should begin with a capital letter. Other points are much more a matter of opinion and style: commas and semicolons, for example. So punctuating well is a combination of knowing a number of fixed 'rules', and applying a series of rather looser conventions to your own writing style.

No two people, however experienced they may be as writers, will punctuate in exactly the same way. All this guide to punctuation can do is to set out the principles and leave you to choose how heavily or lightly you wish to punctuate your own writing.

In this chapter, punctuation is looked at from two points of view:

- the punctuation marks and their functions
- the different ways in which we can use punctuation to achieve the effects we wish in our writing

Punctuation marks

In this section of the chapter, the marks are listed and the main uses for each one are set out. Examples are given where these will help understanding, otherwise not.

Full stop

See also:
■ *Abbreviations* (p. 224)

Full stops (US *periods*) are used:

1 To mark the end of a sentence.
2 At the end of 'minor' (verbless) sentences:
  Liverpool now head the Premier League. **But not for long.**
3 After some abbreviations:
  This is a complicated matter and is covered in detail on pages 224–5.
4 To show that something has been omitted.
  I suggest we delete the sentence, 'If this is not done . . . will be reduced.'
     These are sometimes referred to as ellipsis dots, or points. There are normally three of them. They are also used to show that a sentence is left unfinished:
  'It was just one of those awkward . . . ' she finished lamely.
5 As a decimal point.

Question mark

A question mark ends a sentence, as a full stop does, and is used to indicate that the sentence is a question.

1 The sentence often takes the correct grammatical form for a question:
  Have you seen the latest Pinter play?
2 If a statement sentence is intended as a question, this is indicated by a question mark:
  'You've seen the latest Pinter play?' she asked.
3 Some sentences end with what is called a tag question:
  'You've seen the latest Pinter play, **have you***?' she said.*
     If the tag question is *really* asking a question, then it should be followed by a question mark. In many cases, however, the speaker is just requesting confirmation, and then there is no need for a question mark:
  'You've seen the latest Pinter play, **haven't you***,' she said.*
     If you are not sure whether you need a question mark, read the sentence aloud. If your voice falls at the end of the tag question, then it doesn't need a question mark. If it rises, then it does.
4 You can also place a question mark in brackets after a word or phrase in a sentence that seems to you questionable:
  He said he was absolutely delighted (?) that you were coming for Christmas.

Exclamation mark

The exclamation mark is very similar to the question mark, except that, as its name suggests, it marks exclamations rather than questions.

1 It indicates that a sentence is exclamatory:
'Get out of my way!' she shouted.

2 It does the same thing in minor (verbless) sentences:
Danger! Keep out!

3 You can also place an exclamation mark in brackets after a word or phrase in a sentence that seems to you amusing, ridiculous, or otherwise causes you to exclaim:
He said he was absolutely delighted (!) that you were coming for Christmas.

The full stop (and the associated question and exclamation marks) are the strongest punctuation marks, used to divide clauses into separate sentences. If we do not want to go as far as this in separating elements, we can use a colon or a semicolon. These two punctuation marks do similar but distinct jobs.

Colon

The colon has a small number of related and clearly defined functions.

See also:
■ *Lists* (p. 225)

1 It introduces a list:
When the secret door was opened, it revealed an amazing treasure trove of unlikely items: old clothing, broken picture frames, tarnished silver cutlery, a stuffed elephant's foot, and dozens of old football-match programmes.

2 It introduces a piece of speech:
At last the old explorer spoke: 'This is the most unhappy day of my life.'

3 It introduces another section of text that the preceding words have led up to:
If I have learned one thing in life, it's this: never trust someone who says, 'I must be honest with you.'

Semicolon

The semicolon is midway between a full stop and a comma in strength.

1 It is used to separate two clauses that are related:
Sometimes it is right to forgive; sometimes it is wrong to forget.

If these two clauses were separated into independent sentences by the use of a full stop, the relationship between them would be weakened:
Sometimes it is right to forgive. Sometimes it is wrong to forget.

2 It can separate a clause and a related phrase:
To err is human; to forgive divine.

3 It can separate items in a list, when these are either clauses or extended phrases:
a *Young people today lack all reverence for the old; they live only in the present; they do not expect to reach old age themselves.*
b *There were several important reasons why the initiative was a failure: a serious lack of funds; the unwillingness of many groups to participate; and a general lack of confidence in the leadership.*

In the second example, some writers would use a comma instead of the second semicolon.

It is worth observing that when the semicolon separates two balanced or related clauses it can be replaced by a full stop. When it separates the items in a list it can be replaced by a comma. Problems can occur when the writer gets these two functions confused. The example in (1) above should not be punctuated:

Sometimes it is right to forgive, sometimes it is wrong to forget.

This 'comma splice', joining two independent clauses, is frequently confusing for the reader, who expects the comma to be doing a different job, and so should be avoided.

Comma

The comma is the most difficult punctuation mark to use well. It is essential for clear writing, but there are few hard-and-fast rules. It has been said that the person who has learned how to use commas has learned how to write.

The traditional advice used to be that you should read a text aloud and where it was necessary to make a short pause, there you should put a comma. While there is some truth in this, it does not always work. It is important to remember that most reading is silent, and the comma is as much an instruction to the eye as to the voice. It helps the reader see speedily which items in a sentence are linked and which are separated.

1 We use commas to separate items in a list:
   In her diary she itemized all the foods she most disliked: popcorn, fish and chips, anchovies, white bread, and margarine.
   It is sometimes argued that you should not place a comma before *and* in a list. As the example shows, sometimes it is essential to put a comma before *and*, to indicate the sense. If the last comma were removed, the final item on the list would be *white bread and margarine*, whereas the writer means that she disliked both white bread and margarine separately, not as a combination.

2 We use a comma to indicate a break between clauses, where this increases clarity and helps the reader:
   Although I don't like coffee, milk shakes are one of my favourite drinks.
   Remove the comma, and the reader cannot easily see how the sentence works. The eye passes over the grammatical break, to read:
   Although I don't like coffee milk shakes . . .
   and then slows down, as the reader realises that it is not clear whether the writer is referring to one kind of drink or two.

3 Commas also serve to enclose sections of a sentence. This often indicates that the enclosed section adds extra information, but is not essential to the structure and meaning of the main sentence:
   Lord Plonkett, for many years our man in Havana, is now on the board of several tobacco companies.
   The phrase *for many years our man in Havana* could be omitted and the sentence would still work effectively.

See also:
■ ***Enclosing text*** (p. 226)

Apostrophe

The apostrophe is the most abused punctuation mark in English. Everywhere—on posters, chalked up on greengrocers' slates, even in broadsheet newspapers—we see it wrongly used. So it is not surprising that many children, and adults too, have just given up. What makes it worse is the fact that, if we abandoned it completely and never used another apostrophe, it would cause almost no problems of confusion in our writing. But, for the moment at least, we are stuck with it.

Apostrophes have only two purposes:

1 To show that one or more letters have been left out. This happens most often with commonly contracted forms:

it ~~is~~	→	it's
did ~~not~~	→	didn't
can ~~not~~	→	can't

There is only one additional point to note. In these contractions you only ever use **one** apostrophe, between the *n* and the *t*, even when letters are omitted in more than one place. So

shall ~~not~~ → shan't (not sha'n't)

2 To show possession. The rule is this:

- for singular nouns, add **'s**:
  Harry's hat   the budgie's cage
- for plurals that end in **s**, just add the apostrophe:
  her parents' advice
- for plurals that do not end with **s**, add **'s**:
  children's games

The only problem area is proper nouns that end in *s*, such as *James*: should it be *James'* or *James's*? Either is correct.

It is also worth pointing out that possessive *its* meaning *of it* has no apostrophe: *The cat hurt **its** paw.*

If you add to these rules a third:

Apostrophe + s should never be used to indicate a plural

you have a complete 'Apostrophe kit'.

Inverted commas

See also:
- **Direct speech** (p. 223)

Inverted commas are used:

1 To mark off the words spoken in a passage of direct speech:
'There's no need to look at me like that!' he snarled.

2 To show that the words enclosed are a quotation:
It is not clear what is meant when the contract refers to 'other authorized persons'.

3 To indicate a book or other title:
'Gone with the Wind'
'The Oxford Guide to Writing and Speaking'
In printed matter, however, it is the convention to miss out the inverted commas and set such book, film, play, radio, and TV titles in italics.

It is also necessary to decide whether to use single or double inverted commas. This is partly a matter of individual style (although single inverted commas are now widely used), but it is important to be consistent: choose which you are going to use and then stick to it throughout a text. If a quotation contains a second quotation, or a title, within it, then this should use the form of inverted commas not so far used:

'I really don't understand,' he replied, 'why you say, "No one is to blame," when it is quite clear whose fault it was.'

Capital letter

Capital letters are used as follows:

1 For the first letters of people's names:
Virginia Woolf
2 In other proper names. (A proper name is usually the name of a place or institution, or the title of a person, play, book, film, or other work of art.) The convention is that all the main words are capitalized, while the less important words are not. So nouns, verbs, adjectives, and adverbs should have initial capital letters:
The Bishop of Bath and Wells
All's Well that Ends Well
If the proper name begins with an article, then that too should have a capital letter, but only if it is an essential part:
Have you ever been to The Hague?
but
I have never visited the United States of America.
3 In abbreviations, where the capital is the first letter of the word abbreviated and stands for the whole word:
BBC   OUP

See also:
■ *Abbreviations* (p. 224)

Hyphen

Hyphens have two purposes:

1 To show that a word has been split across a line break. If the last word on a line of text is too long to fit on the line, then part is printed at the end of that line, followed by a hyphen, and the rest appears at the beginning of the next line. There are conventions for this and medium-sized dictionaries often show how words can be split. Word-processing and page layout programs usually contain hyphenation dictionaries that do this automatically.
2 To join two or more words together and show the reader that they belong together as a grammatical unit:
medium-sized dictionaries
an eight-year-old
  Sometimes it is not clear whether two words should be printed as separate words, linked by hyphens, or printed as a single word: *paper knife*, or *paper-knife*? *semi-colon* or *semicolon*? Such compounds start life as separate words and then move through hyphenation to become single words. Some, like *paper knife* and *semicolon*, are still moving. Hence the confusion. If in doubt check in a good dictionary.
  If only the first part of a hyphenated word is printed, as part of a group of alternatives, then it should conclude with the hyphen:
mini- and midi-length skirts

3 Related to this use of the hyphen is another:
Monday-Thursday
pages 23-78
Here the two items linked by the hyphen show the extremes of a range of values. In printed matter this hyphen is generally replaced by a slightly longer unspaced dash.

Dash

The dash is like a long hyphen. It has two main purposes.

1 It indicates a sharp break in the flow of thought in a sentence:
It was an unfortunate event—in fact I'd say it was the worst thing that's ever happened to me.

2 It is used in pairs to enclose a section of a sentence, in a similar way to commas or brackets:
Mr Hindley came home to the funeral; and—a thing that amazed us, and set the neighbours gossiping right and left—he brought a wife with him.
Here the words enclosed by the two dashes could be omitted without destroying the grammar of the sentence.

It is very easy to overuse the dash and to give your writing a broken, breathless feel, so it should be used with caution.

Using punctuation

Some aspects of punctuation are best described by starting with what the writer wants to do. In this section, this functional approach is followed.

Direct speech

It is sometimes necessary to quote what someone has said or written, word for word. To do this we use a combination of inverted commas and other punctuation marks and conventions. As is often the case, there is no one 'correct' way of doing this. What follows is a description of the commonest method. It assumes throughout that it is spoken words that are being quoted, but the same approach applies to the quotation of written texts.

1 The actual words spoken are enclosed in single or double inverted commas.
2 The words spoken follow the normal rules of punctuation for sentences—**within the inverted commas**. In other words, each sentence begins with a capital letter and ends with a full stop, question mark, or exclamation mark; all other punctuation marks are used as normal:
He said, 'I don't believe a word of it. Do you?'
3 If the words, 'he said' or some similar expression precede the words quoted, then they are followed by a comma or colon, before the opening inverted comma(s).

4   If the words, 'he said' or some similar expression follow the words quoted, then there should be a comma, question mark, or exclamation mark at the end of the quoted speech and before the inverted commas. (See 5)

5   Every group of words quoted that is enclosed between inverted commas must end with a punctuation mark immediately before the closing inverted comma(s). If such a mark does not naturally occur (e.g. a full stop or question mark), then a comma should be placed in this position.

6   If there is more than one speaker then each time a new person speaks you should begin a new paragraph.

This approach is illustrated in the following text.

> On the green I saw a white man coming with a cassock on, by which and by the face of him I knew he was a priest. He was a goodnatured old soul to look at, gone a little grizzled, and so dirty you could have written with him on a piece of paper.
> 'Good-day, sir,' said I.
> He answered me eagerly in native.
> 'Don't you speak any English?' said I.
> 'French,' says he.
> 'Well,' said I, 'I'm sorry, but I can't do anything there.'

It is important to remember that inverted commas should enclose only the actual words used. It is not uncommon to see incorrectly punctuated sentences like this:

> He said that 'he was delighted with the outcome of the talks.'

What he actually said was, 'I am delighted with the outcome of the talks.' So the sentence should be either:

> He said, 'I am delighted with the outcome of the talks.'

or:

> He said that he was 'delighted with the outcome of the talks'.

Notice that because this is not true direct speech, but simply a quotation within a sentence, the final punctuation of the sentence comes **outside** the inverted commas. (Contrast it with: *He said, 'I am delighted with the outcome of the talks.'*)

Abbreviations

There is a certain amount of confusion about how abbreviations should be punctuated; some writers are not clear whether, or when, they should use a full stop. This is partly because the convention itself is in a process of change. What follows is one explanation of how it works, but it is easy to find texts that do not follow this set of 'rules'.

1   If an abbreviation is made up of individual capital letters, each one of which stands for a whole word, then each should be followed by a full stop:
   Bachelor of Arts → *B.A.*

2   Abbreviations composed of initial lower-case letters should follow the same rule:

exempla gratia (for example) → *e.g.*
In fact *e.g.* often appears as *eg.*

2 If an abbreviation forms an **acronym**, that is to say a common name by which an organization is known, composed of initial letters, then full stops are not required:
British Broadcasting Corporation → BBC

3 If the abbreviation consists of the first part of a word then it should end with a full stop:
August → Aug.

4 If an abbreviation begins with the first letter of a word and ends with its last letter, then a full stop is not required:
Monsignor → Mgr

Lists

See also:
■ *Colon, Semicolon*
(pp. 219–20)

Lists have already been touched on. If a list forms part of continuous text, then the items are normally separated by commas, or—if each is more complex, especially if it already contains commas—by semicolons.

The list can be preceded by a colon:

He quickly reviewed the options open to him: owning up to what he had done; trying to bluff his way out of it; or simply walking away before anyone noticed.

In many documents, however, we may wish to use the layout of the text to clarify the items in the list. This is something which is done frequently in this book. If you have a number of points which you wish to stand out, they can be presented like this:

Our family Christmas package offers:
■ *luxury accommodation;*
■ *all meals;*
■ *free welcome hamper on arrival;*
■ *presents under the tree.*

Here the list has been punctuated as if it were continuous prose; the items have been separated by semicolons and the last is followed by a full stop. If you find this is rather formal, then there is no reason why you should not remove the semicolons; the items are already perfectly clearly separated by the layout and the use of bullet points. It is even possible to remove the semicolons and final full stop, since the layout will make clear what is intended.

If each of the items forms a complete sentence, then they should be punctuated as such, as in the following example.

An unexpected rise in tax revenues means that the chancellor has three options available to him:
■ *He can act prudently and use the extra money to reduce the PSBR.*
■ *He can mix prudence and political benefit by reducing the PSBR appreciably **and** cutting income tax by 2p in the £.*
■ *He can bow to the demands of backbenchers and cut tax by up to 4p in the £.*

Purists might protest that this misuses the colon, arguing that you cannot follow a colon with a complete sentence that starts with a capital letter. On the other hand each of the bullet points introduces a complete sentence, which would look strange if it did not begin with a capital and end with a full stop. Most people would find the punctuation as printed acceptable, but for those who do not the best solution is probably to conclude the introductory sentence with a full stop rather than a colon.

Enclosing text

It is often necessary to enclose a section of text between two punctuation marks, so that it is separated from the rest of the sentence. This frequently has the effect of placing the enclosed text in parentheses and, indeed, parentheses are one of the punctuation marks used:

- commas: ,xxx xxxx xxx,
- dashes: —xxx xxxx xxx—
- parentheses: (xxx xxxx xxx) (sometimes called 'brackets')

The important thing to remember is that these points always come in twos:

My maternal grandfather, **a well-known traveller and early photographer,** *died in Venice and was buried there. My grandmother—* **who was understandably vexed at this arrangement—***fought to have his body exhumed and returned to Britain. The arrangements were made by Messrs Brownlow and Kemp* **(a local firm of builders and funeral directors)**, *who happened to have an employee who was fluent in the Venetian dialect.*

It is normally the case that if a section of text is enclosed in this way, the sentence would still work perfectly well if the 'bracketed' section were removed. The commonest way of enclosing text for this purpose is to use commas. Dashes have a slightly relaxed, casual feel about them, while parentheses can seem stiffer and more 'scientific'.

Relative clauses

There is one specialist use of pairs of commas which needs to be mentioned, although it is probably missed by many readers. Frequently a relative clause **defines** the noun or noun phrase to which it refers:

The person **who was standing by the window** *turned out to be a visiting professor from Australia.*

Such clauses should not be enclosed by commas or any other punctuation. Sometimes, however, a relative clause is used not to define, but just to provide additional information:

All the people at the meeting were women except one. This man, **who seemed ill at ease in such company,** *said nothing for several minutes.*

Here the relative clause is **non-defining**, and so is separated by commas. It could be omitted from the sentence without destroying its grammar or meaning.

See also:
- **Chapter 18** *More about grammar* (p. 167)

Guidelines

1 Always remember that the primary purpose of punctuation is to aid the reader. Too many punctuation marks make a text confusing; too few make it ambiguous and difficult to follow.

2 A number of punctuation marks have fairly clearly defined rules for their use, about which there is little disagreement. These are referred to below (numbers 3–6).

3 Every sentence has to begin with a **capital letter** and end with a **full stop**, **question mark**, or **exclamation mark**. Problems only occur if you are not sure whether what you have written is a complete sentence or not.

4 The rules for using **apostrophes** are not difficult and can be learned.

5 The same applies to **colons** and **hyphens**.

6 The punctuation of direct speech and other quoted matter, using **inverted commas** and other punctuation marks, is also largely defined by a number of simple rules which can be learned.

7 Other punctuation marks and situations are more complicated and depend on experience and judgement.

8 The use of **semicolons** and **commas** is complex and needs thought. Essentially they serve to **separate** items that need to be kept apart or to **enclose** sections of text—often because these contain additional, non-essential information.

9 **Abbreviations** can also cause problems, but a simple rule is that if you are in any doubt it is better to omit a full stop than insert one.

22 | Speech

1 Speech sounds

- Vocal sound is shaped by the 'organs of articulation' to make speech.
- Vowels are sounds produced with an open mouth.
- Consonants involve blocking the flow of breath in the mouth.
- Clarity of speech requires clear articulation, especially of consonants.
- The sounds of English can be transcribed using a phonemic transcription.

2 Stress and intonation

- Intonation is the 'tune' of sentences and carries an important part of the meaning.
- Words consist of one or more syllables.
- Polysyllabic words have one syllable that is stressed more than the others.
- Sentences also carry stressed and unstressed syllables and this pattern of sentence stress helps convey meaning.

3 Accent and pronunciation

- Different regions have distinctive ways of pronouncing English: regional accents.
- Received pronunciation, a social rather than a regional accent, is the socially dominant accent in Britain.

The human voice works on the same principle as any musical wind instrument. A column of air is forced over a 'reed', the vocal cords, which are caused to vibrate. This vibration is amplified in a hollow space, primarily the mouth, and sound is produced. The vocal cords can be tightened or slackened and this alters the musical pitch of the sound produced.

Essentially if you open your mouth wide and sing a musical note, this is what happens. The tone you produce is the raw material of speech. In order to speak we have to shape it and cut it up into small segments to construct the speech sounds, or *phonemes*, out of which words are built. This process is called *articulation* and the parts of the body we use for it are sometimes referred to as the *organs of articulation*.

The organs of articulation

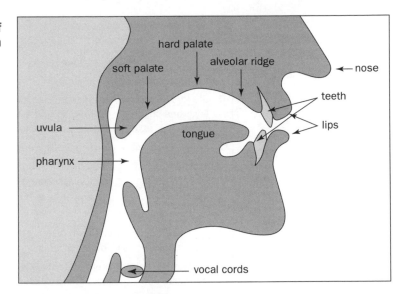

Breathing and speech

The supply of air is essential to the production of vocal sound, so there is an important connection between breathing and voice production. At the simplest level, if you don't coordinate breathing and speech properly you will find that you run out of breath in mid-sentence. Most commonly this happens when people are nervous or when they have to say a lot very quickly. More prepared and extended sections of speech, such as a public reading or an after-dinner speech, allow opportunities for pre-planning. Actors often plot precisely where in a major speech they will take breath, and radio performers have to be careful about not taking noisy breaths close to the microphone.

It is also important, when speaking to large numbers of people without the benefit of a public-address system, to make sure that breath is used efficiently. Speakers who try to produce vocal sound in the same way as is done in conversation end up shouting and will, eventually, lose their voices. In such situations it is necessary to 'project' the voice by proper use of the diaphragm, the sheet of muscle and tendon which lies immediately beneath the lungs. If the diaphragm is used to push air up (i.e. from the 'bottom' of the lungs) greater volume can be produced without straining the vocal cords. This technique can be learned and developed by practice.

You can learn how to use the diaphragm quite simply.

Locating the diaphragm:

1 Stand comfortably, feet slightly apart, and rest the backs of your fingertips on the lowest ribs, so that the upper parts of your fingers are resting lightly on the upper abdomen.

2 Breathe normally and then stop partway through breathing out.

3 Now pant in and out without taking further breath in the normal way. Feel the movement of the diaphragm as it pushes the lungs up and down.

Using the diaphragm:

4 Now take a good breath and, opening the mouth comfortably, make a continuous and fairly quiet 'er' sound.

5 Partway through the breathing-out cycle, while you are still sounding the voice, use the diaphragm to suddenly push the sound out harder—the effort involved is exactly the same as that for panting. This should produce a sudden increase in volume.

There is a range of similar exercises which can be used to develop understanding and use of the diaphragm further and which are of particular value to those involved in regular public speaking.

Speech sounds

The phonemes of English can be divided into two main groups: vowels and consonants. (It is important to remember that we are considering *sounds* here and not letters. The first sound of the word *thin*, for example, is spelled using two letters, t-h, but it is only one sound.)

Vowels

This sound/letter discrepancy becomes painfully clear when we look at vowels, for while there are five vowel letters, a-e-i-o-u, there are twenty or so vowel sounds, depending on regional accent.

Vowels are speech sounds produced with an open mouth. The sound is formed using the shape of the mouth and the position of the tongue, which does not, however, block the passage of the air.

Say the following sequence of vowels. As you do so, observe the shape of your mouth and the position of your tongue. Try to observe where in the mouth the vowel appears to be shaped.

1 *ee* as in *teeth*

2 *oo* as in *soon*

3 *ar* as in *far*

4 *u* as in *hut*

Vowels can be pure, like those listed above, or they can be combined into *diphthongs*, in which one pure vowel glides into another. The vowels in these words are diphthongs:

hate—height—soil—foul.

Consonants

When we make consonant sounds, the passage of air through the mouth is blocked or impeded in some way. Different consonants require the use of different organs of articulation. For example, the first consonant of *pin* is produced using the lips, while the first consonant of *goat* uses the middle of the tongue and the hard palate.

The quality of the consonant sound depends on the way in which the blockage of air is achieved. For example:

- **nasal**
  the mouth itself is blocked off in some way and the sound is made in the nasal cavity. For example, all the consonants of *mining*.

- **plosive**
  the air is blocked and then released with a small 'explosion'—as in the first sound of *pat*

- **fricative**
  air is forced through a narrow gap between two parts of the mouth. Examples are the first sounds of *first* and *shirt*.

You try

Pronounce the first consonant of each of these words several times. In each case work out which of the organs of articulation are used and what type of sound is produced.

1 nice	**3** sing	**5** vase	**7** kick	**9** dance
2 butter	**4** tap	**6** zoo	**8** the	**10** heart

Clarity and articulation

When speech is indistinct and difficult to hear or follow it is often because the speaker is not articulating the consonants clearly enough. The quality of the vowels will tell us a lot about where a speaker comes from (both regionally and socially). Without clearly pronounced consonants, however, we may not be able to understand what is said. For this reason, particularly when speaking in public, it is important to work at the clear articulation of consonants, especially those which fall at the end of words.

Writing speech sounds down

It is easy to forget that written English is a transcription of speech; speech is not a pronunciation of writing. You sometimes hear people say words to the effect of: 'You aren't pronouncing it right. It's written with a "c", and you aren't pronouncing the "c".' English spelling—chaotic and confusing as it may appear at times—is an attempt to put down on paper the words we say. Like the language, it has evolved over a period of time and was further confused by the efforts of 'reformers' who attempted to introduce some system into it at different points in the past. All have failed, with the result that, if we were 'logical', the word we normally spell f-i-s-h could also be spelled **ghoti**:

> **gh** as in cou**gh**
> **o** as in w**o**men
> **ti** as in commo**ti**on

Faced with such a difficulty, students of language have devised different ways of transcribing speech sounds accurately. There is an *International Phonetic Alphabet* which can be used to transcribe *any* speech sounds. As might be expected, however, this contains a vast number of symbols and is not particularly useful if all one wants to do is focus on the sound system of a single language. For this we need to look not at *phonetics*, the study of speech sounds generally, but at *phonology*, the study of the sound system of a language—how sounds are used to communicate meaning. We need a way of writing down the *phonemes*, or significant sounds of the language—a *phonemic transcription*.

The most widely used phonemic transcription system for British English is that developed by A. C. Gimson. The list that follows is based on Gimson's. Note that phonemic symbols are usually enclosed by two obliques: / /.

Consonants

/p/	as in	pin	/s/	as in	sin
/b/		bin	/z/		zeal
/t/		tin	/ʃ/		shin
/d/		din	/ʒ/		leisure
/k/		kin	/h/		hot
/g/		goat	/m/		mine
/tʃ/		chin	/n/		nine
/dʒ/		gin	/ŋ/		sing
/f/		fin	/l/		line
/v/		vineyard	/r/		right
/θ/		thin	/j/		yet
/ð/		this	/w/		wet

Vowels

/i:/	as in	beat	/ə:/	as in	hurt
/ɪ/		bit	/ə/		the
/e/		bet	/eɪ/		rain
/æ/		bat	/aɪ/		die
/ʌ/		but	/ɔɪ/		boy
/a:/		hart	/ou/		toe
/ɔ/		hot	/au/		out
/ɔ:/		fort	/ɪə/		dear
/u/		put	/ɛə/		air
/u:/		boot	/uə/		tour

Stress and intonation

Individual speech sounds are not, of course, the only way in which we use our voices to communicate meaning. This is easily seen if you look at the different ways in which the same sequence of words can be said. The sentence, *You're going out* can, for example, be spoken in these ways:

1 as a flat statement of fact, with the voice falling at the end
2 as a question, with the voice rising at the end
3 as a question which asks in effect whether 'you' or someone else is going out, with emphasis on 'you' and the voice rising at the end
4 as an emphatic statement of fact, almost an order, with the words strongly stressed and a short pause between each

In normal writing the only way in which we can show these variations is by the use of punctuation, underlining, or other typographic conventions:

1 You're going out.
2 You're going out?
3 **You're** going out?
4 (Very difficult!) You're . . . *going* . . . **out!**

Here we have used two different types of sound signal: intonation and stress.

Intonation

Intonation is the 'tune' of the language. If you listen to people speaking and pay attention to the way in which the pitch of their voices rises and falls, rather than to the individual sounds and words, you will see that this is not just a matter of statements and questions, but is essential for the communication of meaning.

You try

See how many different ways you can think of to say the single word *really*—imagining that it comes in the middle of a conversation and stands on its own. For example:

■ showing casual interest in what has been said

■ showing eager interest in what has been said

■ making it clear that you are not the slightest bit interested

■ showing that you don't believe a word of what you are being told

■ showing incredulity

You can probably think of more!

Stress

There are two different kinds of stress in English, word stress and sentence stress. Both are essential to communicate meaning satisfactorily (and both cause many foreign learners of the language severe problems).

Syllables

English words consist of one or more syllables. Each syllable must contain a vowel. This may have one or more consonants before and/or after it. In the examples that follow the letter V represents a vowel *sound* and C a consonant *sound*. Notice that sometimes one consonant sound may be represented by more than one letter ('sh' is one sound) and vice versa (the single letter 'x' requires two sounds—*ks* or *gz*—depending on where it comes in the word).

Words of one syllable

or	V
my	CV
aim	VC
bit	CVC
scratched	CCCVCC

Words of two syllables

tapers	CVCVC
matchbox	CVCCVC

Words of more than two syllables

examination   VCCVCVCVCVC (5 syllables)

Word stress

The syllables of a word can be spoken with more or less force or emphasis. Where a syllable is spoken with emphasis it is said to be stressed. Syllables that are not spoken with emphasis are unstressed. Each of these two-syllable words has one stressed and one unstressed syllable:

motor
de**tach**

In longer words there may also be a lesser, secondary stress—here marked by italics:

ex*ami***na**tion
ex**em**pli*fied*

Sentence stress

The situation is complicated by the fact that sentences, too, are stressed to underline their meaning. A sentence can carry a normal stress:

We're going to **Spain** for a *holiday.*

MAIN STRESS   SECONDARY STRESS

Sometimes, however, we may wish to change this normal pattern to provide extra information. We may, for example, want to emphasize that we are travelling to Spain for a holiday and not on business:

We're going to *Spain* for a **holiday.**

SECONDARY STRESS   MAIN STRESS

Sentence stress is very important. We use it to communicate part of the meaning of the sentence and it also determines the rhythm of our speech. However quickly or slowly you speak, the stresses in your sentences will be fairly evenly spaced in time. Since the pattern of stresses in the sentence is pre-determined (by meaning), this means that longer groups of words without any stress are apparently 'gabbled' and shorter ones appear to pass more slowly and deliberately. This **stress-timing** of English can cause serious problems for foreign learners. To the French learner, for example, it can seem that the English speak with a mixture of excessive force (stress) and a slovenly swallowing of whole words and phrases (because of stress timing). By the same token the English learner of French finds it difficult to unlearn stress timing and use a more measured and regular *syllable timing* when speaking French. While the French have word stress, they use sentence stress much less, preferring to rephrase a sentence or to add words to indicate special emphasis.

Accent and pronunciation

In different countries of the world, and in different regions of those countries, English words are pronounced differently. The most obvious differences appear in vowel sounds: compare, for example, the way in which a Londoner, someone from North Yorkshire, and a New Yorker pronounce the vowel in *bath*. But consonants, too, vary as we travel from place to place. Many Londoners, for example, would say the last consonant of *bath* as /f/. Many Scots do not use the typical 'tapped' /r/ of Southern English (in which the tongue just taps the ridge above the top teeth) preferring a longer 'trilled' sound.

Received pronunciation   In many countries regional accents are common at all levels of society, but in Britain there has grown up over a period of time one non-regional accent which is widely considered to be 'better' than others. Based on the accents of Southern England, and used by many educated and influential people throughout society, it is known technically as *received pronunciation* (or *RP*) and sometimes called 'BBC English' or 'educated English'. It is also sometimes confused with standard English. There is, however, no direct connection between the two— although many people who regularly use standard English also speak using RP. While it is possible to speak standard English with a regional accent, it would sound very strange to speak a regional dialect using RP.

It has to be said that while the use of a standard dialect makes very good sense, the 'superiority' of RP has more to do with class consciousness than clarity of communication. Unfortunately, however, it remains true that if people with strong regional accents wish to succeed in the company of people to whom these things are important they may well have to learn to play the game according to the RP rules.

Word pronunciation   Speakers are sometimes judged by the way in which they pronounce (or 'mispronounce') words. Some people even have a few key words by which they judge others. For example, do you pronounce the first vowel of *either* to rhyme with *eye* or *me*? Do you talk about a **con**troversy or a cont**ro**versy? None of this should matter very much—the purpose of a standardized pronunciation is that people understand each other—but again social judgements can and will be made. Any good-sized dictionary will provide information about both the phonemes of a word and how it should be stressed, but some use a phonetic transcription, which you need to be able to follow. (It is usually explained in the introduction to the dictionary.) Alternatively you can check tricky pronunciations in a 'guide to usage':

> **controversy** This word is now very often pronounced in Britain with the stress on the second syllable, but this pronunciation attracts criticism from some people. The traditional British pronunciation with the stress on the first syllable is normal in American English.
>
> Sidney Greenbaum & Janet Whitcut:
> *Longman Guide to English Usage*

Of course, as with other controversial matters of usage, different authorities may not necessarily agree.

Guidelines

1 Remember that good breathing is essential to good speech. If you are reading aloud or making a speech, prepare carefully so that you do not find yourself running out of breath at key points.

2 When you need to speak loudly, use your diaphragm to produce the extra force required, and so avoid shouting and straining the vocal cords.

3 Regional and social accents are largely carried through the vowels. Be aware of the social dimension of speech: many people give received pronunciation greater prestige than regional accents. If you have a strong regional accent you may have to choose between remaining 'true to your origins' and compromising by using a regional version of RP (RP with 'quieter' regional vowels).

4 Clarity of speech is greatly affected by the quality of the consonants. It is important to articulate these clearly, which requires awareness, effort, and, sometimes, practice.

5 Be aware of the impact of intonation and sentence stress on the communication of meaning. Listen to experienced speakers (for example, good broadcasters) to hear how they use these features of speech. Faulty stress and intonation, and the wrong use of pauses, are common causes of poor communication. Listen to bad broadcasters (of whom there are plenty) to hear how irritating this can be.

6 The correct pronunciation of words involves both the separate sounds of which they are composed and word stress. Some people are very aware of small variations of pronunciation. If it is important to impress such people, then be aware of the 'pitfalls' and avoid them.

The Process of Writing

This section of the book looks in more detail at the production of extended pieces of writing, beginning with the initial idea and going right through to the use of modern technology to produce the final document.

23: Planning and research

There is an interaction between developing your ideas and doing any necessary research into a subject. Both processes are examined in some detail. The chapter concludes by suggesting ways of preparing a plan which orders all the elements of your writing in the best possible way.

24: Writing, drafting, and revising

One of the keys to good writing is the paragraph. This chapter analyses what paragraphs are and how they can be used to plan and build a piece of extended writing. It proceeds to show how the writer can revise a first draft so that it expresses the original intention with greater life and accuracy.

25: Getting it on the page

The layout and appearance of a piece of writing are an important part of the way in which it communicates to the reader. Elements such as headings, spacing, typefaces and their size and spacing all contribute to this, as does the appropriate use of visuals such as diagrams and charts.

26: Using technology

Computers now form part of everyday life and offer an enormous range of aids to the writer. This chapter examines some of the most common features offered by word processing and associated software: editing, layout, spellcheckers and thesauruses, outliners, and grammar and readability checkers.

23 Planning and research

See also:
- **Chapter 8 Reports** (p. 62)
- **Chapter 9 Essays, papers, and dissertations** (p. 72)

The main stages in preparing for an extended piece of writing:

Generating ideas

- writing a statement of intent
- thinking on paper:
  - lists, web diagrams, corkboard, flowchart

Research

- where to start
- people
- print media
  - using libraries
  - newspapers, journals, magazines
- electronic information
  - CD-ROM
  - the Internet
- making notes and summaries

Planning the order

- deciding the main points
- deciding how far to go
- developing a satisfactory pattern
- introductions and conclusions

Whatever kind of writing you do, there are three stages you should go through before you begin:

- generating ideas
- research
- planning the order

Although these are presented in sequence, and do sometimes happen in that order, there is often an interaction between the three. You may, for example, begin by jotting down ideas which lead you to research one aspect of the subject. Your research may, in turn, suggest other ideas. Then, when you come to plan how you will present your material, you realize that you do not have enough information on a key point in your argument. This leads to further research . . . and so on.

The period of preparation may be as extended as this suggests, but not necessarily. For many pieces of writing, you may accomplish all three processes quickly and almost unconsciously, without ever writing anything down. But if you do not go through these processes before writing, then they have to take place while it is going on. For shorter texts this may not be a problem, but for extended writing it can lead to delay, frustration, and muddled expression. Confused writing is nearly always a product of confused thought. Very often much of the confusion can be avoided if the writing is properly prepared.

Generating ideas

Some people have a horror of sitting in front of a blank sheet of paper. Their mind goes blank and they don't know how to begin. The way to avoid this is to have a clear idea of what the text will contain and the broad outlines of how the material will be developed.

Statement of intent

A good way of starting the process of generating ideas is to write a short statement of what you are trying to achieve in your text. This statement of intent is just something you write for yourself; no one else sees it, so there are no difficulties about audience or tone. There is only one rule: what you write must be clear. Until you can produce a clear statement of what you want to write, who it is for, and why you want to write it, you are unlikely to be able to achieve a satisfying piece of writing. So it is worth spending some time trying to get this right.

> A report for internal use within the company examining the possibilities of further development of tourism in Kenya, with special reference to new areas. The purpose is to inform discussion and lead to a decision about future plans

Like this example, your mission statement should answer these questions treated in Section B:

- Who is the writing aimed at?
- What do I want to say?
- Why am I writing it?

The statement is not necessarily fixed. You may well find that as you go through the processes of generating ideas, researching, and planning, you need to add to it or change it.

Thinking on paper

If you are writing at any length, it is a mistake to try to do all your planning in your head. It is too easy to lose valuable ideas if they are not written down. Your thinking on paper may take a number of different forms.

Lists At its simplest you can just jot down ideas as they occur to you.

> Kenya as a country where 'real people live real lives'
>   eco-tourism
>   local craft manufacture
>   underdeveloped geographical features
>   Lake Victoria
>   Mount Elgon

Lists like this form a part of many writers' planning, especially in the early stages.

Columns Some topics lend themselves to planning in columns. If there is a clear argument, for example, it may be useful to collect material 'for' and 'against' in separate columns. Or there may be a small number of categories under which data and ideas can be gathered:

> Places   Features   Facilities
>
> Lake Victoria   Local crafts   Tented camps
> Mount Elgon   Farm tours?   Private flights
> Masai Mara Game   Balloon trips?
>   Reserve

Web diagram As soon as you start jotting ideas down, you often find that one idea leads to another. A very productive form of jotting, called a web or spider diagram builds on this idea.

You begin by writing the main idea in the centre of the page. You then link to it ideas that it suggests to you:

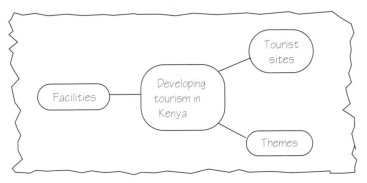

This process is then continued, with one idea leading to another:

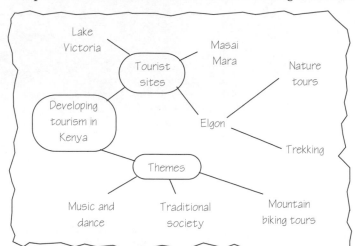

Corkboard   Another kind of 'brainstorming on paper' is the corkboard. This technique is used by film writers to create and order the elements of their plot, but works just as well for other types of writing. You write each idea on an index card or small piece of paper and pin it to a board. As ideas build and change, the positions of the cards can be shuffled around so that related ideas are placed near each other. A similar thing can be done using Post-it® notes on any surface they will stick to.

Flowchart   Certain types of writing call for a different approach. If you are writing exposition, you often need to describe a process. If that process is fairly complicated, it helps to write it down diagrammatically in the form of a flowchart. A simple flowchart represents the stages in a process in sequence.

Processes often involve choices, however, and some may require that a particular stage is repeated. More complex flowcharts can represent this and help in sorting out how best to describe both process and choices.

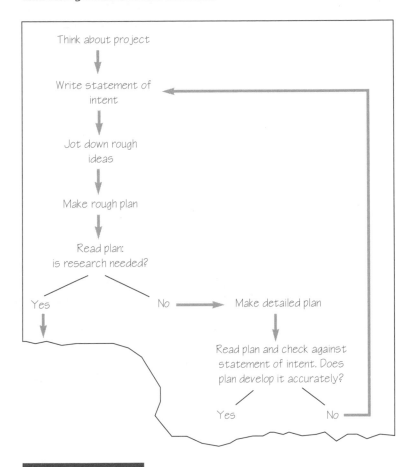

Research

How much research you do depends on the situation. If you are writing about a subject on which you are very knowledgeable, 'research' is probably a question of sorting through information which is already in your head and making sure that there are no details that you need to look up. Other subjects may require detailed research lasting several weeks or even months.

Where to start — Very often your starting point will be fairly obvious. If you are a student, for example, then you will probably have been given a reading list, or, at least, advice on where to look for information. The college or university library will also be able to give expert advice. If you are working for a business, then your company will probably have documents and research data already available, and colleagues will probably have experience and ideas they are willing to share.

It is always a good idea to begin with your own knowledge and understanding plus whatever other resources are immediately available to you personally: books and other documents in your possession, friends and personal contacts who can be easily approached.

People

One of the best ways of finding out about almost anything is to ask someone who knows. This may, however, be easier said than done.

Most public libraries carry directories of local organizations and can provide information about local institutions and businesses. They can also provide directories of national businesses and organizations. Your nearest large public library will probably have several, including these very helpful directories, published by CBD Research Ltd:

- *Directory of British Associations*
- *Directory of European Learned and Professional Societies*
- *Councils, Committees and Boards*
- *Centres and Bureaux*

These all have subject indexes, so that it is possible to find quickly the organization which specializes in the subject you are researching.

As before, however, one of the best ways to start your research is with a personal contact; your local trained librarian will be able to direct you either to the name of a person who can help, or to the directory where you can find out whom you need to consult.

Print media

The traditional resource medium is the printed word. The researcher begins with books, newspapers, magazines, and the wide range of printed and written records which are available if you know where to look for them.

Obviously where you look depends on what you are looking for, but a list of useful general sources of print information would include the following.

Public libraries

The nearest large public library is the best starting point for the researcher. For most people it is normally the nearest place to consult a qualified librarian, and a conversation at your local library may well save a lot of time later. Most public libraries also have the basic bibliographical tools to enable you to begin to list sources you will need to consult.

The library's own stock may well contain all the material you need. Books can usually be located using several different search methods in a computerized library catalogue:

- **by subject**
  this normally relates catalogue categories (for example 'Politics') to shelf marks

- **by shelf mark**
  in British public libraries usually organized on the Dewey Decimal System (e.g. 941.085)

- **by author**

- **by title**

- **by key word(s) in the title**

Many libraries also have specialist catalogues for particular subjects, for example books of local interest.

Public libraries are also the most convenient way of gaining access to books and articles that are not in your own local library system:

- new books can be requested for a small fee and, provided the book is not heavily in demand, you should not have too long to wait
- other books can be requested via the inter-library lending scheme
- .articles in magazines and journals can be requested at the library using the British Library Document Supply Centre

All these take some time, so, if you are in a hurry, you may need to travel to the nearest large city that has a specialist reference library.

Larger libraries

There are six 'copyright libraries' which are entitled to a free copy of every book published in the United Kingdom:

- the British Library in London
- the Bodleian Library in Oxford
- Cambridge University Library
- the National Library of Wales in Aberystwyth
- the National Library of Scotland in Edinburgh
- Trinity College Library, Dublin

In any of these it is possible to consult more or less anything published since the eighteenth century and a considerable volume of earlier material. It is possible for serious researchers to use these libraries upon provision of proof that they are engaged in genuine research and, in some cases, payment of a fee.

Other useful reference libraries open to the general public include:

- the Central Reference Library in central London
- Birmingham Central Reference Library
- Newcastle-upon-Tyne Central Library

It is also usually possible to use the reference sections of large public libraries in areas other than your own by applying to the librarian.

Specialist libraries

There are, in addition, many libraries devoted to specialist subjects. Further information about these can be obtained by referring to the *Aslib Directory of Information Sources in the United Kingdom*, which is available at public libraries. Many business institutions and other organizations also maintain their own libraries and research facilities. Further information about many of these is contained in the CBD Research directories listed earlier.

Newspapers and periodicals

Past copies of certain daily newspapers and weeklies are held by the larger public libraries. For more detailed research it is necessary to go to the British Library Newspaper Library in Colindale, London, which holds issues back to 1801.

Electronic information

Much information is now published electronically. For most people access to this comes in one of the following forms:

CD-ROM

For this you either need your own computer with CD-ROM player, or to go to a library or other site where you can use one. Some of the multimedia publications are excellent. A lot are dross.

The Internet Again you either need your own computer and modem or to go to a site where you can use them. The correct software will then enable you to access immense quantities of information all over the world. It is not cheap, however, since in addition to the equipment you have to pay a subscription and telephone bills. Some service providers make additional online charges of so much per hour.

Nevertheless there is an amazing amount of information to be found on the Internet. This mainly comes from these sources:

■ **Usenet newsgroups**

Usenet is a system whereby people can set up a newsgroup to share information and ideas on a subject of interest. Using a software newsreading program such as *NewsWatcher*, it is possible to participate in a chosen newsgroup . . . once you have found the newsgroups you are interested in. There are tens of thousands to choose from.

■ **Connecting to other computers worldwide**

Academic institutions, government departments and many other organizations make certain kinds of information available freely to anyone who can connect to their computers. To do this you need a suitable program; one of the most popular is *TurboGopher*. Using this program to research business and other information about Kenya produced among a host of others these two documents, both courtesy of United States government organizations:

KENYA: OVERSEAS BUSINESS REPORT
Prepared by Chandra D. Watkins, Office of Africa with the assistance of the U.S. Embassy in Nairobi, Kenya
CONTENTS
FOREIGN TRADE OUTLOOK
    Opportunities for U.S. Business--Government of Kenya's
    Development Plan
THE ECONOMY
    Agriculture--Tourism--Energy--Power--Manufacturing--
    Mining--Transport and Communication
TRADE POLICY AND REGULATIONS
    Import Licensing--Import Duties--Preferential Trade

*Kenya, Geography
Location:
    Eastern Africa, bordering the northwestern India Ocean between
    Tanzania and Somalia
Area:
    total area: 582,650 km²
    land area: 569,250 km²
    comparative area: slightly more than twice the size of Nevada
    Land boundaries: total 3,446 km, Ethiopia 830 km, Somalia 682 km,
    Sudan 232 km, Tanzania 769 km, Uganda 933 km

■ **The Worldwide Web**

The best-known source of information on the Internet is the Web. Companies, institutions, and individuals maintain websites which provide an enormous amount of information, entertainment, and other services. Some of this must be paid for, but there is a lot of free information to be found, if you know where to look. For this you need two things: a web browser program, such as Netscape Navigator or Microsoft Explorer, and access to a search engine (which both of these provide), such as Infoseek or Yahoo.

The main differences between the Web and the other Internet sources of information are that pages can be illustrated by both still and video images, they can carry sounds, and—perhaps most important of all—can be linked together. Each page can carry any number of links, short sections of text or 'buttons'. A mouse click on one of these will take you either to another page on the same site or to a completely different site. So the use can start on one site and then move on a journey from site to site, simply by clicking on key words or images.

The search engines are thus a useful way of initiating a search, but once you have found a good starting point, you often find that it will lead you further and further along the route, without your having to initiate another search. Particularly useful are the pages of 'links' which are to be found on many sites.

The 'Kenya' search on the Web produced thousands of possibilities. For example:

Making notes and summaries

An important aspect of effective research is how you record results. As we have seen, research often involves using books and other resources that are at some distance from your workplace, so that you cannot have them readily available when the time comes to write your first draft. Even if you have access to research materials as you write, you may waste valuable time searching though them to find a particular piece of information that you 'know is there somewhere'.

There are three solutions to this problem:

- photocopying
- making notes
- writing a digest or summary

Photocopying

If it is important that you have the exact wording of a document, then you have either to copy it out by hand or—if it is allowed—make a photocopy. Photocopying is normally allowed, provided you follow the rules, which are usually displayed in libraries and other places where you are likely to be doing your research.

It is tempting to rely entirely on photocopying, amassing a store of copied documents for later use when writing. This has several drawbacks. First, it may be illegal; you cannot, for example, copy (by any means, including handwriting) more than 10% of a book that is still in copyright, even though you only intend to use the copies for private research. Second, you may find that you end up with so much material that you still have difficulty locating information you need. Related to this is the temptation to photocopy sections of a book as a substitute for reading them carefully and thinking about them.

Notes

Making notes is a valuable way of not only recording information and ideas for future use, but also focusing your mind on the text you are reading; you cannot make good notes unless you have read carefully and fully understood the text. If you make clear and suitably detailed notes at the time of reading, they will both record information and remind you of its significance later.

Effective notemaking

But only if they are good notes. Your notes should:

- be easy to read and understand long after you made them
- be related in structure and content to the purposes you are likely to use them for
- both contain information and make clear its significance

Exactly how you make notes is a personal matter. We all have individual ways of shortening words, indicating links between material, and so on. The example that follows shows one approach.

The original text

Climate
Because of Kenya's diverse geography, temperature, rainfall and humidity vary widely but there are effectively four zones about which generalizations can be made.

The undulating plateau of western Kenya is generally hot and fairly humid with rainfall spread throughout the year though most of it falls in the evenings. The highest falls are usually during April when a maximum of 200 mm may be recorded, whilst the lowest falls are in January with an average of 40 mm. Temperatures range from a minimum of 14 or 18°C to a maximum of 30 to 34°C.

The central highlands and Rift Valley enjoy perhaps the most agreeable climate in the country though there's quite a variation between the hot and relatively dry floor of the central rift valley and the snow-covered peaks of Mt Kenya. Rainfall varies from a minimum of 20 mm in July to 200 mm in April and falls essentially in two seasons—March to May (the 'long rains') and October to December (the 'short rains'). The Aberdare mountains and Mt Kenya are the country's main water-catchment areas and falls of up to 3000 mm per year are often recorded. Average temperatures vary from a minimum of 10 or 14°C to a maximum of 22 to 26°C.

The vast semiarid bushlands, deserts and lava flows of

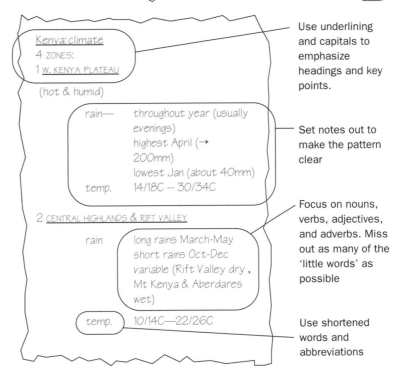

Kenya: climate
4 ZONES:
1 W. KENYA PLATEAU
(hot & humid)
rain— throughout year (usually evenings)
highest April (→ 200mm)
lowest Jan (about 40mm)
temp. 14/18C -- 30/34C
2 CENTRAL HIGHLANDS & RIFT VALLEY
rain long rains March-May
short rains Oct-Dec
variable (Rift Valley dry, Mt Kenya & Aberdares wet)
temp. 10/14C—22/26C

Use underlining and capitals to emphasize headings and key points.

Set notes out to make the pattern clear

Focus on nouns, verbs, adjectives, and adverbs. Miss out as many of the 'little words' as possible

Use shortened words and abbreviations

You can also use different colours to highlight important points or colour code different kinds of information.

Making a summary

When you are referring in some detail to a book or other source, you can either quote directly from it, or summarize what it says. The ability to write a clear and accurate summary is a valuable skill, useful not only when referring to a text produced by someone else, but also when you have to reduce the length of your own writing. This is one way of approaching it.

1 List the main points made in the text.
2 Make sure that they are in the most logical order (rearrange them if necessary) and under each one make a brief list of supporting arguments and data.
3 Without referring to the original text, make a first draft of the summary.
4 Check your draft for length and cut it if necessary.
5 Now check it against the original. Look for two things:
   ■ important points you have missed out (If there are any, make sure they are included.)
   ■ any accidental direct quotations from the original (If there are any, reword them.)
6 Write a final draft, keeping an eye on length.

Stages 1, 2, and 6 are illustrated in the example that follows.

Original text

Refugees & the Dispossessed

Kenya, being a relatively stable country with opportunities to make a living or at least working the tourists for hand-outs, is a natural magnet for refugees from strife-torn neighbouring countries. Nairobi and Mombasa and, to a lesser degree, the coastal resort towns, are the favoured destinations. You'll come across plenty of these people on your travels and it's relatively easy for them to remain anonymous if they can make enough money to stay off the streets.

There's nothing remarkable about this—it happens all over the world. What is remarkable in Kenya is the number of unattached teenage and early-20s mothers—many of them Kenyan but also quite a lot from Uganda, Sudan, Ethiopia and even Rwanda. With the break-up of many traditional communities as a result of colonial policies that were designed to bring people into the money economy, and the continuation of this system under post-colonial regimes, there has been large-scale movement of people to urban areas. Most arrive with nothing and are forced to live in overcrowded shantytowns (some 60% of Nairobi's population lives in these places) with little hope of anything resembling a steady job with reasonable pay.

As a result, all the facets of urban alienation can be found in these places with drunkenness, theft and rape (particularly of schoolgirls) being fairly commonplace. But this isn't confined to the major urban areas. It appears to be fairly widespread every where outside of traditional tribal areas.

As far as the girls are concerned, once they become pregnant they're expelled from school (in other words, it's the end of their educational prospects) and, as likely as not, rejected by their families, too. In 1986, the number of young girls who found themselves in this position (according to official figures) was 11,000 and it's been rising steadily ever since. The options for those to whom this happens are extremely limited. A few shelters do exist (usually run by Christian organizations) but it's only the lucky few who get in. For the rest, it's very poorly paid domestic work or the flesh market.

Main points

> 1 a lot of refugees in Kenya
> 2 many are young mothers
> 3 the poor gravitate to cities
> 4 leads to crime and degradation
> 5 the girls become outcasts
> 6 they can only become servants or prostitutes

Main points plus key details

1 a lot of refugees live in Kenya
   - surrounded by countries where there are problems
   Kenya prosperous and it's easy to get a job or beg
2 the poor gravitate to cities
   - breakdown of old communities
   - development of cash economy
   - not enough jobs
   - development of shanty towns
   - leads to crime and degradation
3 many of the poor are young mothers
   - Kenyans, but also refugees from surrounding countries
4 the girls become outcasts
   - pregnancy leads to expulsion from school and rejection by family
   - increasing problem—numbered in 10,000s
5 they can only become servants or prostitutes
   - no qualifications
   - lack of work

Final draft of the summary

Kenya's relative prosperity means that it attracts refugees from the troubled states that surround it. They find it quite easy to get employment or to beg in the popular tourist resorts. The break down of old, tribal society and the growth of a cash economy have led many of the poor to move to the cities, but there are not enough jobs, so shanty towns have sprung up. Here people live surrounded by poverty, degradation and crime. Many of the poor Kenyans and refugees are young mothers who have found that pregnancy has made them outcasts. Unable to continue their schooling, and often rejected by their families, they are left with little choice: they can either become servants or prostitutes.

Planning the order

One of the most important things to do when preparing an extended piece of writing is to establish its broad outline.

Deciding the main points

To do this, look at the ideas and material you have collected and pick out a small number of key points which will form the framework to which arguments, ideas, and information can be attached. This process may seem rather time-consuming, but it will almost certainly save much more time later. If this planning stage is faulty, you may find that your writing slows down and eventually stops as you discover that your original plan doesn't work; alternatively, when you finish, you may realize that the text just isn't coherent and needs to be re-written.

As an example of how this planning stage works, the web diagrams on pages 241–2 could yield this list of main topics:

- new tourist sites that could be developed
- new themes for tourism
- the facilities that exist and new facilities that may be needed

If your main topics are well chosen, each will lead to a number of sub-topics which explore it:

- new tourist sites that could be developed
    - Mount Elgon
    - Lake Victoria

These in turn will subdivide again and so on, to produce a hierarchy:

- new tourist sites that could be developed
    - Mount Elgon
        - walking and climbing
        - wildlife safaris
            - on foot
            - by 4x4
            - camping
    - Lake Victoria

and so on.

Starting with the detail

You may feel that your material does not lend itself to this approach— or, simply, that your mind 'does not work that way'. You may prefer to take a large piece of paper and a marker and jot down ideas as they occur to you. You can then link related ideas together by lines and arrows. This rough diagram can form the basis of a set of topics and sub-topics as suggested above. (This is similar to the corkboard approach described on page 242.)

How far do you go?

How far you take this process of planning depends on a number of factors:

- how complicated the subject matter is

If there is a lot of detail to communicate, or you wish to put forward a complex argument, you may well need to do quite a lot of detailed planning on paper.

- how good you are at holding ideas in your head as you write
- how spontaneous you want to be
  Some would argue that if you make a very detailed plan, with the hierarchy of ideas fully worked out, you become constricted by the rigidity of the plan and are not free to change it as you go along.

A satisfactory pattern

A successful text is one where the reader is taken along by the flow of the writing, doesn't get lost or confused, and comes away with the feeling that the ideas it contains could not have been expressed in any other way. So it is important to make a plan in which ideas are developed logically and necessary information is introduced at exactly the right point. Where it is necessary to use ideas or information that have not been referred to for some time, the reader needs a gentle reminder of what these are. If the flow of ideas needs to take a sudden new turn, this may need preparation or explanation. At every point the reader's needs, expectations, and possible difficulties must be considered.

The introduction

The introduction is often the most difficult section to write. That first sentence can often prove exasperatingly elusive. Novelists sometimes agonize for weeks over the first sentence of a new novel; it sets the tone of what is to come and fixes the reader's expectations.

You try

These are the openings of a number of full-length works. What thoughts and expectations does each arouse in you as reader?

A   The 'average Frenchman' is often known today as Monsieur Dupont or Monsieur Durand. Durand means obstinate. John Bull, according to the Larousse Encyclopaedia, is 'the nickname given to the English people to indicate their obstinacy'.

B   With the vision of a large single European marketplace unfolding before our eyes, it is inevitable that many British companies are re-considering and re-examining their investment and location strategies.

C   The sheer physical diversity of France would be hard to exhaust in a lifetime of visits. The landscapes range from the fretted rocky coasts of Brittany to the limestone hills of Provence, the canyons of the Pyrenees to the Germanic picturesqueness of Alsace, the volcanic uplands of the Massif Central to the wide grain fields of Touraine, the wooded valleys of the Dordogne to the glacier-capped peaks of the Alps.

However important the first sentence or two may be, the introduction to a text will normally consist of one or more paragraphs and may be a complete chapter or even section of a book. It has to perform these functions:

- It gives the reader an indication of what the subject matter will be.
- It persuades the reader that reading this text is going to be at least worthwhile and—if possible—enjoyable.
- It establishes a relationship with the reader by the language and tone adopted.

The conclusion Second only to the introduction in difficulty and importance is the conclusion to a piece of writing. If the introduction hopes to entice readers to sample the mouth-watering delights that are in store, the conclusion should aim to send them away with a nice taste in their mouths, rather than feeling unsatisfied or dyspeptic. It should remind readers of what they have been reading, by:

- summing up key points without being unduly repetitive
- if action is required, highlighting what it is
- rounding off the text neatly and—if possible, and appropriate—in an entertaining way

Guidelines

Generating ideas   1 Before starting to plan a lengthy piece of writing, write a short statement of intent describing its subject, audience, purpose, and format.

2 'Think on paper' so that good ideas are not lost.

3 Use lists, web diagrams, a corkboard, or flowcharts to develop ideas.

Research   4 Whenever possible use personal resources first: books, papers, documents that are readily available, and people whom you know.

5 Human resources are often accessible and quick.

6 Use public libraries for books, articles, and bibliographical and other help.

7 Use newspapers and magazines available in public libraries or at the British Library Newspaper Library.

8 Use electronic resources, including the Internet, if these are available to you.

Planning the order   9 Begin by deciding a small number of key points. Don't begrudge the time spent on this.

10 Use these as the start of a hierarchy of ideas.

11 Alternatively, start with your detailed ideas and organize your thought on paper. Then build up the hierarchy of ideas.

12 Spend time planning an effective introduction and conclusion.

You try: key

page 253 All three extracts come from books about France and the French. **A** indicates that it is going to be about people. By starting with a reference to national stereotypes it perhaps implies that it wants to dig beneath the surface and find out what the 'real people' are like. **B** clearly has a business and commercial focus, while **C** is obviously concerned with the landscape of the country and how it appears to visitors.

A comes from *The French* by Theodore Zeldin
B is from the guide *Setting up a small business in France* published by the French Chamber of Commerce in London
C comes from the *Rough Guide to France*

24 Writing, drafting, and revising

Paragraphing

Effective use of paragraphing is at the heart of good writing:

- as a means of structuring a whole text
- as a way of shaping the argument as you write
- as a technique for ensuring that the argument flows through the text and so is easy to read

So the writer should use paragraphing:

- when planning
- when writing
- when revising

Revising

Any extended text needs careful revision:

- as you write
- after you have finished the first draft

Revision includes

- changes to the structure of the text
- alterations to the choice of words and the way in which sentences are constructed
- corrections to spelling, punctuation, and grammar

The process by which thought is translated into written sentences is not easy to analyse or explain. The three words which head this chapter all describe aspects of that process, and the fact that there are three of them underlines the point that it is not a simple one. Sometimes, it is true, I write a sequence of sentences and then deliver them to their intended audience without looking through them and making changes. But such occasions are rare. As soon as I read through what I have written and even begin to consider altering it, I have moved from writing to editing. If I decide to make a second version of my text, then I am beginning to re-draft. Simple texts may receive only minor alterations, to ensure that the sense is clear; longer and more complex ones, like this book, go through several drafts before they are made public.

It could be argued that writing consists of no more and no less than adding one sentence to another, but that would be a misleading oversimplification. It is easy enough to write one sentence and then to write another. The problem is how to judge whether the two sentences you have written fit together properly, or whether you need to adjust one or both of them—or even add a third to help them out. What is missing is a guiding principle, and that guiding principle is the paragraph.

Paragraphing

To adapt the proverb: 'Look after the paragraphs and the sentences will look after themselves.' If you have a clear sense of how your text should break down into paragraphs and if you understand how to write paragraphs through which the argument of the text flows clearly and unobtrusively, then the individual sentences should cause you few problems. On the other hand, if you haven't given any thought to paragraphing, then you can write the most beautiful sentences in the English language but your text will still be difficult and displeasing to the reader. Writing a text of any length requires the writer to keep an eye on both the particular sentence being written at the moment and the whole text of which that sentence forms a small part. Paragraphing is the means by which this is done.

The best way to see how this works in practice is to examine a short text. The extract that follows comes from an introduction to geomorphology, the study of how the formation and development of rocks creates landscape.

Paragraph 1

Most of the spectacular landscapes of England and Wales are found within the rugged, higher lands of the north, west and south-west. Why is there such a striking difference between the areas of mountains and moorlands, and the gently undulating lowlands characteristic of the south and east? The answer lies in the nature of the rocks and of their susceptibility to being worn away by the elements.

The introductory paragraph not only introduces the subject matter, but indicates how it will be tackled. The words 'the nature of the rocks' tell us how the following paragraphs will be arranged.

Paragraph 2

There are three major types of rock. Igneous rocks are formed by the cooling of molten material ('magma') that escapes to the surface layers of the Earth from the interior. Metamorphic rocks are formed by baking and deformation at high temperatures and pressures. Sedimentary rocks are formed under much quieter conditions, by the accumulation of material on the sea floor or land surface. Most of the igneous and metamorphic rocks are hard and compact, and are therefore more resistant to attack at the Earth's surface than the weaker sedimentary rocks. And so it is hardly

The lead sentence follows this up and tells us what the paragraph will contain: a brief explanation of igneous, metamorphic, and sedimentary rocks. This is then linked to the original question posed in the first paragraph: why is there such a contrast between the landscapes of the north and west and those of the south and east?

surprising to discover that many of the upstanding areas in England and Wales are composed of igneous and metamorphic rocks, the moorlands of the South-West Peninsula (except Exmoor), the highlands of North Wales, and the Lake District.

Paragraph 3   Let's now fill in some of the details by looking at the different rock types to see how they are formed, how resistant they are and what sort of landscapes they give rise to in England and Wales.

This short paragraph stands as a signpost to show how the next part of the text will develop.

Paragraph 4   When the Earth came into being nearly 5000 million years ago it was made up of molten magma. This gradually cooled and solidified at the surface, forming a crust, but the interior of the Earth remained hot and molten. Today, when this molten material is pushed up under great pressure through cracks in the crust, volcanoes are formed. On reaching the air, the magma cools rapidly to form hard, compact rocks such as basalt. The exact type of volcanic rock formed depends on the chemistry of the magma. Some volcanic eruptions also produce much softer ash, which is nothing more than the shattered rock fragments that originally blocked the volcanic pipe.

This paragraph introduces the first main section in which igneous rocks are described in more detail. The lead sentence makes clear that the approach will be historical: how igneous rocks were originally formed. This topic is developed in the rest of the paragraph, ending with a reference to volcanoes . . .

Paragraph 5   Although there are no active volcanoes in Britain today, some of our older rocks were formed in this way. Particularly well known are . . .

. . . which is neatly picked up in the lead sentence of the next paragraph.

Building the argument

If we look at the way in which the paragraphs of this text are constructed and used, we can pick out a number of general points about paragraphing:

Developing the pattern

The paragraphs form a pattern which helps the writers develop their argument. Paragraphs 1–3 form an introduction to the subject:

1 leads into the subject and its two main inter-related aspects: landscape and geology
2 introduces the three main types of rock and gives a brief explanation of how each was formed
3 points forward to the main subject matter of the text and explains how it will be tackled

Paragraphs 4 onwards then go through the three main rock types in much more detail.

4 introduces the topic of igneous rocks by going right back to the formation of planet Earth
5 moves this discussion to the geographical region we are concerned with: the British Isles

The shape of a paragraph

A typical paragraph has three sections:

- **an introduction**

    Each paragraph in the quoted text has a sentence at or very near the beginning which introduces the subject matter of the paragraph:

    There are three major types of rock. (para. 2)

    When the Earth came into being nearly 5000 million years ago it was made up of molten magma. (para. 4)

- **a conclusion**

    At or near the end of the paragraph is a sentence which rounds it off:

    And so it is hardly surprising to discover that many of the upstanding areas in England and Wales are composed of igneous and metamorphic rocks, the moorlands of the South-West Peninsula (except Exmoor), the highlands of North Wales, and the Lake District. (para. 2)

- **the body of the paragraph**

    The body of the paragraph leads in an orderly and convincing way from the introduction to the conclusion. The body of paragraph 2, for example, consists of four sentences:

    - *Igneous rocks . . . interior.*
    - *Metamorphic rocks . . . pressures.*
    - *Sedimentary rocks . . . surface.*
    - *Most of the igneous and metamorphic rocks . . . sedimentary rocks.*

    The introductory sentence offered us three different types of rock. The body of the sentence delivers them, so that the concluding sentence can say, in effect: 'There you are—*that's* why the north and west are different from the south and east.'

Hooks

If the thought is to flow comfortably from paragraph to paragraph, there need to be hooks which link the paragraphs together:

> *Some volcanic eruptions also produce much softer ash, which is nothing more than the shattered rock fragments that originally blocked the volcanic pipe.*
> *Although there are no active volcanoes in Britain today, some of our older rocks were formed in this way.*

The final sentence of paragraph 4 rounds this part of the topic off by dealing with softer volcanic rocks and the reason for them. It uses the word 'volcanic' twice, which draws it to the reader's attention. The writer then makes the link to Britain by using 'volcanoes' in the first sentence—even though the statement is a negative one. A less skilful writer might have missed this opportunity. See how much weaker the link would be:

> *Some volcanic eruptions also produce much softer ash, which is nothing more than the shattered rock fragments that originally blocked the volcanic pipe.*
> *Many of the older rocks in Britain are igneous.*

There are many different ways in which the link between one paragraph and the next can be made. The main ones are:

- **subject matter and vocabulary**

    as in the case of volcanic activity in the example just given

See also:

■ **Chapter 18** *More about grammar* (p. 167)

■ **the use of conjunctions:**

. . . It seemed as though the attempt on the summit could not fail. All was in place for a successful assault.

   But we had reckoned without the weather . . .

■ **the use of what are called conjuncts**

These work in a similar way to conjunctions, but whereas conjunctions are used to join sentences and parts of sentences, conjuncts are commonly used to link paragraphs:

. . . the students were left to find their own way back to the rail terminus.

   Meanwhile their teachers were having to answer several awkward questions at the local police HQ . . .

Examples of conjuncts are:

first	secondly (*etc.*)	finally
furthermore	next	moreover
for example	therefore	as a result
in other words	however	meanwhile
on the other hand		

■ **the use of pronouns:**

. . . and it was while leading a tour round the Uffizi Gallery that she first met Berenson.

   He had, of course, been a famous figure in Florence for many years . . .

You try

The following paragraph comes from the beginning of an account of the life and psychology of a Frenchwoman. The sentences have been numbered for ease of reference. What is the subject matter of the paragraph? Which sentences form the introduction and conclusion? How do the other sentences develop the argument of the paragraph? How might the ending of the paragraph lead on to what is to follow?

1 What is Thérèse thinking, as she shows you to your table in La Vieille Alsace in Strasbourg, and helps you order your meal?

2 She gives the impression that she knows exactly what to say, what to do, all energy, a brisk walk, a direct look, friendly solicitude.

3 If you have been there before, she can remember more about you than you ever told her.

4 How are you to know that she is not a waitress waiting for better times, that she is not calculating the size of the tip you can afford to give, that she has a master's degree in the history of art?

5 Thérèse has been doing this job for fifteen years because she has a purpose in life.

Think paragraphs!

There are three stages in writing, at each of which you need to keep the principles of paragraphing clearly in mind.

1 Planning

When you make a written plan, you should remember that the paragraphs you are going to write are the way in which you will execute that plan. Each point in your plan should represent either one paragraph or a small group of paragraphs. If your argument is at all complicated it is very useful to make a separate point in the plan for each paragraph you are going to write.

2 Writing

As you write, you have to carry in your mind:

- the structure of the individual paragraph (beginning, middle, and end)
- its hooks to the preceding and succeeding paragraphs
- its position in the plan of the whole text

3 Revising

Fortunately it doesn't all have to be done at the moment of writing. When you revise you can check the structure of each paragraph, its links to the paragraphs before and after, and its placing in the overall structure of the text.

Revising

Writing normally involves more than one stage. Most people do not just go through the simple process of:

have idea ⟶ write it down ⟶ finish

For most of us the process looks more like this:

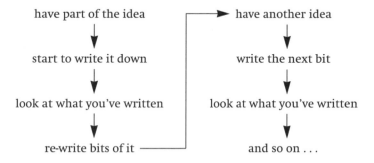

What kind of changes?

Writing is a process of refinement. We begin with a fairly rough version and gradually, by cutting, adding, and re-ordering we work towards a finished product. The changes that can be made happen at two different stages:

- as you go along
- when you have completed the first and subsequent drafts

The changes themselves are of three main types.

Changes to the structure

You may decide that even after the planning stage has been worked through, the shape of a whole section is wrong and the ordering of paragraphs needs drastic modification. Normally this kind of change should only be done when a draft of the whole text has been completed. If you find yourself making major changes before you finish the first draft, then probably your initial planning was faulty.

Revisions to the text

The commonest type of revision is to change the way in which one or more sentences are written, in order to clarify the meaning or improve the style.

Corrections to grammar, punctuation, and spelling

At some stage you have to put right errors of spelling and grammar. You may also amend punctuation, which is sometimes a matter of correctness and sometimes a question of style.

Revisions to the text

To illustrate how a text takes shape, here are extracts from two drafts of the previous page of this book.

Like many writers, I usually write direct on to a word processor, which is very convenient, but obscures the process of revising and redrafting. Knowing that I would need examples of revision, I wrote the first draft of this chapter by hand:

First draft manuscript

Writing is a process of refinement. We begin with a fairly rough version and

gradually, by a process of cutting, adding altering and so - we hope - improving, we

work towards a finished product. The changes that we make ~~fall into two groups.~~ ~~can be divided~~

happen at different stages

- ~~those we make~~ as we go along

- ~~those we make~~ when we have finished the first draft.

placed in three categories

They can also be ~~categorised in a different way.~~

- *'correcting'* - putting right errors of spelling, grammar, and, to some extent,

  puntuation

  although punctuation is also a matter of style

- *'editing'* - changing the way in which one or more sentences are written.

  This can be to improve their style - make them sound better - or, if they do

  not convey the meaning we intend, to clarify them.

  changes'

- *'structural* We may realise that, even ~~if~~ after careful planning, the shape of

  the whole section is wrong and the ordering of the paragraphs, for example,

  needs to be modified drastically. ~~Normally this~~

Normally this third kind of change should only be done when a first draft has been

completed. If you find yourself ~~chang~~ making major changes to the structure before

you finish the first draft, it suggests that your initial planning was seriously faulty.

You try

Compare the original handwritten version (i.e., before alterations were made to it) and the corrected word-processed version (on page 264).

1 What are the main changes that have been made?
2 Why do you think they were made?
3 In what other ways could the extract be improved?

You try

1 What are the main changes that have been made between the first and second drafts (on page 264)?
2 Why do you think they were made?

First draft word-processed

When this was keyed in and printed off, further changes were made:

Writing is a process of refinement. We begin with a fairly rough version and gradually, by cutting, adding, re-ordering we work towards a finished product. The changes that we make happen at two different stages:

- as we go along,
- when we have completed the first and subsequent drafts.

~~Changes~~ are of three main types:

- **Editing**:
  changing the way in which one or more sentences are written, in order to clarify the meaning or improve the style.
- ~~**Making structural changes**~~:
  we may decide that even after the planning stage has been worked through, the shape of a whole section is wrong and the ordering of paragraphs need drastic modification. Normally this kind of change should only be done when a draft of the whole text has been completed. If you find yourself making major changes before you finish the first draft, it suggests that your initial planning was seriously faulty.
- **Proof-reading**:
  putting right errors of spelling and grammar. We may also amend punctuation, although this is only ~~partly~~ a matter of 'correctness' ~~it is frequently~~ a question of style.

The changes themselves

Altering the structure

Sometimes and can often be

Second draft

When the first draft was revised, further changes were made:

What kind of changes?

Writing is a process of refinement. We begin with a fairly rough version and gradually, by cutting, adding, and re-ordering we work towards a finished product. The changes that can be made happen at two different stages:

- as you go along
- when you have completed the first and subsequent drafts

The changes themselves are of three main types.

Changes to the structure

You may decide that even after the planning stage has been worked through, the shape of a whole section is wrong and the ordering of paragraphs needs drastic modification. Normally this kind of change should only be done when a draft of the whole text has been completed. If you find yourself making major changes before you finish the first draft, then probably your initial planning was faulty.

Revisions to the text

The commonest type of revision is to change the way in which one or more sentences are written, in order to clarify the meaning or improve the style.

Corrections to grammar, punctuation, and spelling

At some stage you have to put right errors of spelling and grammar. You may also amend punctuation, which is sometimes a matter of correctness and sometimes a question of style.

Approaches to drafting

The purpose of all the changes you make in a text is to improve communication and increase its effectiveness. Weakness of vocabulary and of sentence and paragraph construction, and uncertainty of tone, will damage the impact of your text. As you work through successive versions of a text, your aim is to remove such weaknesses. Unfortunately they are *your* weaknesses; as a result you may well not be the best person to find and eradicate them.

The trusted reader

All writers, however experienced, can benefit from the comments of readers. By the time you read these words, they will already have been read and commented on by many different readers. For example:

- my wife and friends whose judgement I trust
- editorial staff at Oxford University Press
- outside advisers selected by the publishers and myself to provide expert comment on the whole text or on sections of it

Each person who reads the manuscript comments on it and I then have to decide what changes, if any, to make.

The advice of other readers is invaluable as you build and improve your text. If possible, therefore, show it to one or more people whose judgement you respect. If you cannot do this, then your second-best ally is time. If you can leave a piece of writing for a while, go away and do something entirely unconnected with it, and then return, you stand a much better chance of seeing it with fresh eyes. What seemed clear fluent prose may still read well . . . or it may be revealed as flawed and unsatisfactory.

Drafting strategies

Ultimately the responsibility for your text lies with you, the writer. You have to judge whether it successfully achieves what you set out to do. The following list of questions is designed to help you focus on this.

Structure, approach, and tone

1 Does it cover all the required aspects of my selected subject?
2 Does it contain material that is not relevant to the subject and which can be cut out?
3 Does it fulfil the original purpose(s) I had when I started writing?
4 Do I address the audience in a way that is suitable for their knowledge of the subject and ability to understand what they read?
5 Is the tone of my writing suitable for this audience?
6 Is the text organized so that it is as easy as possible for readers to make their way through it and be able to find material easily later?
7 Does the paragraphing present the argument in a clear and logical way?
8 Are the paragraphs linked so that the text flows easily?

See also:
- **Chapter 11** *Audience* (p. 89)
- **Chapter 12** *Subject* (p. 102)
- **Chapter 14** *Purpose* (p. 113)

Sentence construction

9 Are my sentences clear and easy to read?
10 Are there a large number of long sentences? (Sentences of over 40 words are generally considered 'long'.)

11 Are the sentences that are long still easy to follow?

12 Are there too many short sentences, making the text choppy and uncomfortable to read?

Vocabulary

13 Is the technical vocabulary I have chosen appropriate for my audience?

14 Is the language suitable in other ways, avoiding jargon, euphemism, and cliché whenever possible?

15 Have I avoided excessive repetition of words and phrases?

16 Are there any other quirks of style that readers may find irritating?

See also:
■ **Chapter 11** *Audience* (p. 89)
■ **Chapter 19** *Vocabulary* (p. 179)

One good way of testing your writing is to read it aloud. Very often this will highlight sentences and phrases that are unsatisfactory. They just sound 'wrong' when read aloud.

It should not be necessary to add that in addition to testing your text in the ways suggested above, you also have to check it carefully for accuracy of grammar, spelling, and punctuation.

Guidelines

Paragraphing

1 Use paragraphing as a planning tool. Remember, as you make your plan, that each point in it represents either one paragraph or a small group of linked paragraphs.

2 As you write, form your thought into paragraphs.

3 Begin each paragraph with one or two sentences that introduce the topic of the paragraph.

4 The beginning of the paragraph should also have some kind of 'hook' to the previous paragraph. (There is a list of these on page 260.)

5 Make sure that the paragraph ends with one or two sentences that round it off and lead on to the next paragraph.

6 The body of the paragraph should lead smoothly from the introduction to the conclusion.

7 When you are revising your text, it is important to check that you have got the paragraphing right.

Revising

8 Begin by thinking about the structure of the whole text. It may need re-ordering.

9 Revising the text *can* be done while you are writing and *should* be done after you have completed a draft.

10 Use the checklist on page 265 and above.

11 Check the whole text against your intentions when you started writing. In particular think about audience and purpose.

12 Check the wording of each sentence carefully for:
■ clarity
■ style

13 Look at your vocabulary, checking it for suitability, accuracy, and avoidance of jargon and cliché.

14 When you have completed structural and other editorial changes, check your work carefully for errors in:
- spelling
- grammar
- punctuation

You try: key

Page 260 Sentence 1 presents us with a situation (the waitress showing us to a table in a restaurant) and a puzzle (what is going on inside her head as she does so?). The second sentence provides an amplification both of the situation (by describing Thérèse's manner in more detail) and, by implication, of the puzzle (if she is so self-possessed and 'all energy', what is she doing waiting at tables?). Sentence 3 develops the last two words of the second, by giving an example of her 'friendly solicitude'. Now that Thérèse's situation and manner have been established, the fourth sentence returns to the puzzle by providing a key piece of information: that she has an MA in Art History. Sentence 5 provides a kind of coded solution to the puzzle. Thérèse is highly competent because she is intelligent and well-educated; she works in this apparently lowly job because she gets something special out of it. It gives her a 'purpose in life'. And thus the writer sets up the succeeding paragraphs: they will explain just what that 'purpose in life' is.

Page 263 In the first part of the **manuscript**, most attention is focused on the relation between the first paragraph and the two bullet points that follow it. The changes are intended to make this as simple and clear as possible. The later changes are mainly a question of tidying up, but in the middle of the extract an important later addition is made to the point about correcting punctuation.

In the **word-processed version** the main change is that the order of the second set of bullet points has been changed. Other changes are quite small, but there is an attempt to rephrase the last sentence so that it is more accurate.

The ways in which I thought the text still needed improvement can be seen in the final version on page 264. You may not necessarily agree with me.

Page 263 One important set of changes concerns the way in which the writer addresses the reader. In the previous draft I used 'we' throughout. This has now been changed to 'you'—in keeping with the general tone throughout the book. (There was a gap of nine months between the two drafts, during which the style and tone of the book had 'settled down' quite a lot. Revisions of material written early on had to take this into account.) The other main change is that the order of the original three bullet points ('Changes to the structure', etc.) has been rationalized by placing the biggest first and the smallest last. These three short sections of text have been upgraded from bullet points to short paragraphs, to make them easier to read.

25 Getting it on the page

The importance of good layout as a means to effective communication:
- headings
- spacing
- running heads and feet

Typefaces and sizes:
- faces
- styles
- parts of a typeface
- measurements and leading
- readability

Using visuals:
- diagrams and drawings
- charts

However good your text may be, if it is not presented to the reader with care, it will not have the impact it should. This text, for example, is so badly presented that it puts the reader off straight away:

> How we view the relationship can affect: choice of vocabulary, use of short forms in writing, choice of pronouns, choice of standard or non-standard grammar. Some words are considered by many people to be informal, colloquial, slang, or even obscene. Dictionaries often indicate this by abbreviations, for example: colloq. -colloquial; inf.-informal; sl.-slang. Such definitions can be misleading, however. It is very difficult to draw a clear line between what is 'formal' and what is 'informal' language.

Presented with care and thought, however, it becomes accessible and even welcoming:

Effects on language

How we view the relationship can affect:

- choice of vocabulary
- use of short forms in writing
- choice of pronouns
- choice of standard or non-standard grammar

Vocabulary

Some words are considered by many people to be informal, colloquial, slang, or even obscene. Dictionaries often indicate this by abbreviations, for example:

colloq.	colloquial
inf.	informal
sl.	slang

Such definitions can be misleading, however. It is very difficult to draw a clear line between what is 'formal' and what is 'informal' language.

With the widespread use of computers and word-processing and other software, a huge range of options is available to the writer who wishes to present a text effectively and attractively. The technology and software are discussed in the next chapter. Here we are concerned with the ideas behind effective presentation.

Layout

Not unreasonably, the book you are reading demonstrates the author's and publisher's ideas about how a printed text of this kind should be set out. As will be demonstrated in the next chapter, all the layout effects used in this book are now available to the user of a 'standard' computer with word-processing software. The main features that should be considered when laying out a long document are demonstrated on the following page and can be adapted to suit most texts.

A **running head** helps guide the reader through a long document. Here it carries the page number and the title of the section, but it may tell the reader the title of the chapter, or a subdivision of the chapter.

The use of simple **diagrams** and other **visuals** also helps communicate ideas and information simply and quickly.

Headings can be set in different sizes and styles to indicate their relative importance.

Displaying information and using **bullet points** helps material stand out and makes it easier for the reader to understand.

The use of **space** between paragraphs and around headings helps considerably with clarity. Paragraphs can also begin with an indented line.

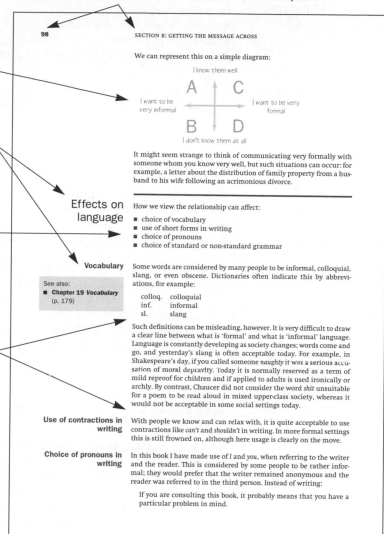

98

SECTION B: GETTING THE MESSAGE ACROSS

We can represent this on a simple diagram:

I know them well

A   C

I want to be   I want to be very
very informal   formal

B   D

I don't know them at all

It might seem strange to think of communicating very formally with someone whom you know very well, but such situations can occur: for example, a letter about the distribution of family property from a husband to his wife following an acrimonious divorce.

Effects on language

How we view the relationship can affect:
- choice of vocabulary
- use of short forms in writing
- choice of pronouns
- choice of standard or non-standard grammar

Vocabulary

Some words are considered by many people to be informal, colloquial, slang, or even obscene. Dictionaries often indicate this by abbreviations, for example:

See also:
- **Chapter 19 Vocabulary** (p. 179)

colloq.   colloquial
inf.   informal
sl.   slang

Such definitions can be misleading, however. It is very difficult to draw a clear line between what is 'formal' and what is 'informal' language. Language is constantly developing as society changes; words come and go, and yesterday's slang is often acceptable today. For example, in Shakespeare's day, if you called someone *naughty* it was a serious accusation of moral depravity. Today it is normally reserved as a term of mild reproof for children and if applied to adults is used ironically or archly. By contrast, Chaucer did not consider the word *shit* unsuitable for a poem to be read aloud in mixed upper-class society, whereas it would not be acceptable in some social settings today.

Use of contractions in writing

With people we know and can relax with, it is quite acceptable to use contractions like *can't* and *shouldn't* in writing. In more formal settings this is still frowned on, although here usage is clearly on the move.

Choice of pronouns in writing

In this book I have made use of *I* and *you*, when referring to the writer and the reader. This is considered by some people to be rather informal; they would prefer that the writer remained anonymous and the reader was referred to in the third person. Instead of writing:

If you are consulting this book, it probably means that you have a particular problem in mind.

Letters and the spaces between them

In the 'good old days' of mechanical typewriters, the writer did not have to be concerned about which typeface a typed document used. There was only the one on the machine that was being used. In many offices today, much the same applies, with one or two typefaces being used as standard, either because this is office policy, or because those using the machines have not thought of doing anything else. Increasingly, however, it is important to understand a little more about typefaces and their use.

Certainly the choice of a good typeface can considerably enhance a document, and the use of a bad one can seriously damage its impact. Most computers today come with a choice of several as standard and there are literally hundreds to choose from if you wish to acquire more. In addition to this range of choice, most word-processing software offers the user highly sophisticated control over how the chosen typeface appears when printed.

Typefaces

Originally a distinction was made between the words 'typeface' and 'font', but increasingly the words are used interchangeably. Some typefaces are very old and well established, but new ones are being designed all the time. For non-expert purposes, they can be divided into two broad groups:

- those suitable for the presentation of blocks of text
- those meant to be used in small quantities for special effects, sometimes called 'display' typefaces. In a printed document they may be used for headings, but the more adventurous fonts are more suitable for advertising and similar applications. On my own computer, for example, I can find these fonts, which are of little everyday use to me:

abcdefg

abcdefg

abcdefg

Text fonts These normally exist in a number of different versions. The commonest are:

Roman (or 'upright')

Italic

Bold

Bold italic

Italic and bold are commonly used in documents to emphasize particular words or groups of words. If this is done too much the effect is lost, so restraint is necessary. Also, it is important to be consistent about their use. If, for example, you decide to use italics for the titles of books, then this convention must be followed throughout the document.

Parts of a typeface Since some computer manuals and other publications refer to different parts of a typeface, it is useful to know the terms used:

Text typefaces fall into two groups:

serif—like this
sans serif—like this

Books and long documents are more commonly printed in a serif type-face since this is generally believed to be easier to read. Sans serif faces are often used, as in this book, to mark off different types of text. A whole book in a sans serif face can be rather trying for the reader.

Type size and leading

A word-processing program usually requires you to decide what size type you want your text to appear in. This is normally measured in points (1 point = 1/72 of one inch), abbreviated to pt. The measurement is done from the top of an ascender to the bottom of a descender:

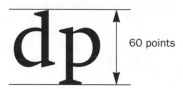

Normally the default typesize on a computer is 12 pt. It is also necessary to determine the space between the lines; this is called the leading, because in the days of metal type, thin strips of lead were inserted between the lines of type as spacers. Again the computer will do this for you, but if you wish to override this, you will often be asked to determine the leading in points. This is done by beginning with the size of type and then adding the number of points space you want between the bottom of the descenders on one line and top of the ascenders on the next. If you add none and give, for example, 24pt type 24pt leading, the ascenders and descenders will touch:

this is not usually
completely satisfactory

The main text on this page is printed in 9pt type with 11 pt leading.

Readability

Newcomers faced with such a range of typefaces, sizes, and leading are sometimes fascinated by the effects they can achieve. It is important to remember that above all a document must be readable. Any of the following can interfere with readability:

- **making lines of text too long**
  12–14 words to a line is as much as most readers can cope with.

- **making the typeface too large or too small**
  Normally this should be in the range 9pt to 12pt.

- **getting the leading wrong**

Using visuals

A document can be considerably enhanced by a number of different types of visual:

Diagrams and drawings

These can be used, for example, to illustrate physical objects and processes.

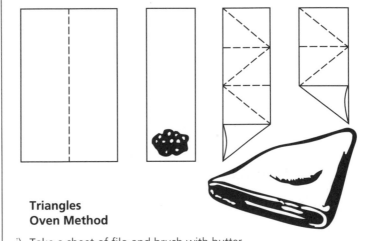

Triangles
Oven Method

i)   Take a sheet of filo and brush with butter.
ii) Fold in half lengthwise. Brush top with butter.
iii) Place filling on end of strip and fold as illustrated.
iv) Place triangles on a baking sheet and brush top lightly with butter.

Charts

Numerical information and other abstract data can be represented by a range of different charts.

Flowchart   A process, or series of actions and decisions, can be shown on a flow-chart.

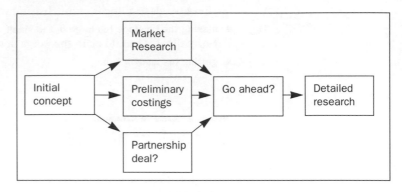

Gantt chart   If you want to set a number of activities or tasks against a timetable, a Gantt chart is an effective tool:

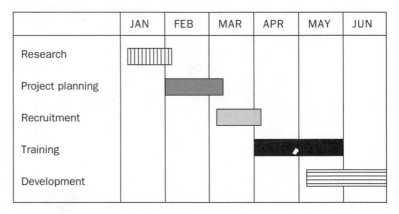

Pie chart   If you have a set of figures and wish to show their relative proportions, this can be done by means of a pie chart:

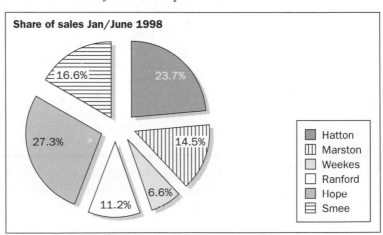

Column chart   This is a useful way of showing how a set of statistics change over time:

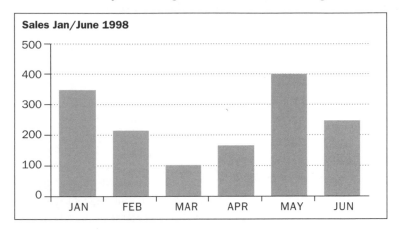

A column chart can also be used to show how two or more sets of figures develop against time or another variable:

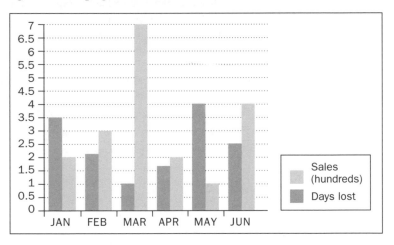

Line chart   The same data can be shown on a line chart.

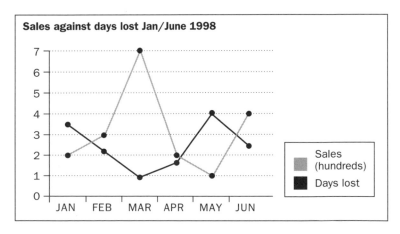

Guidelines

Layout

1 Take care that your layout makes the text as clear as possible.

2 Use headings of different weights to indicate how the text is structured.

3 Set out lists and similar data using bullet points and hanging indents.

4 Make generous use of space on the page so that it is easy for the reader to see where different sections are.

5 Use running heads and running feet to help the reader navigate through a long document.

Type

6 Choose a suitable and attractive typeface for large blocks of text.

7 Normally use a serif face for large amounts of text and reserve sans serif faces for special text.

8 Only use display typefaces for headings and special effects.

9 Select a typesize between 9.5pt and 12pt for normal text.

10 Make sure that the leading (space between lines of text) is neither too tight nor too generous.

11 Always make sure that your text is readable; in particular make sure that lines are not too long (normally not more than 14 words to a line).

Visuals

12 Whenever possible, use visuals to illustrate your text, especially when a visual representation can replace a large amount of text.

13 Use diagrams and drawings to illustrate physical objects and processes.

14 Use flowcharts and other diagrams to represent abstract ideas.

15 Use graphs, bar charts, and pie charts to point up the significance of numerical data.

26 Using technology

The range of features offered by word-processing and DTP packages is considerable. There are also desktop accessories available to help the writer. Facilities include:

- editing
- layout
- spellchecking
- thesaurus
- outliner
- grammar and readability checker
- glossary and macro

Information technology offers the writer a dazzling array of tools with which to prepare, organize, and present documents. Software is developed and updated so fast, however, that there is little point in describing individual programs. Instead it is more helpful to list and describe the different features that are available in different programs. This should make it possible for the reader to work out which features are desirable when shopping around for software.

Software features

Even the types of program seem to evolve remarkably rapidly. Not long ago it would have been logical to divide programs for the writer into:

- word processing
- desktop publishing (DTP)
- reference
- other desktop accessories

Recently the larger word-processing packages have been enlarged to include many of the features of the other groups, so that it is, for example, possible to use a word processor to carry out many functions of a DTP program. The same program may also include an electronic thesaurus and a grammar checker, which previously might have been bought as separate desktop accessories.

On the other hand, some users are opposed to these very large top-of-the-range programs. Because they are so comprehensive, they inevitably include a number of features that you will never use, and they are very demanding, taking up huge amounts of computer memory and considerable space on the hard disk. They are also expensive.

In the comments that follow, I assume that the reader has a basic familiarity with computers and has probably at least used a simple word processor.

Editing

The fundamental feature of any word-processing program is that it enables the user to key in words so that they appear on screen and can subsequently be printed out. The text can be altered, cut, and added to until the writer is satisfied with it. If necessary it can be saved on disk and re-used later. Only when all the changes have been made does it need to be printed—although many writers like the 'comfort' (and security) of printing off at regular stages in the life of a document.

The fundamental techniques involved are:

- **Insertion**
  The cursor is placed at the correct point in the text and new matter typed in. Existing text automatically moves to accommodate the new.

- **Overtyping**
  A section of text is highlighted (marked off) and then new matter keyed in to replace it.

- **Cut and paste**
  A section of text is highlighted and then cut. This text is stored temporarily in a 'clipboard'. It can then be 'pasted' elsewhere in the document. Some computer systems and software also allow what is called 'Drag and drop', whereby you highlight a section of text and drag it from one place in the text to another.

In this way the main editorial changes described in the previous chapter can be achieved on screen. The disadvantage of working in this way—as opposed to using pen and paper—is that normally the old version (i.e., before the current round of changes) is lost for ever. If you later want to use an earlier version you cannot recall it unless you take precautions:

- Some programs have a feature which enables the user to see changes which have been made. For example, deletions are shown as words struck through, and additions appear in bold. This may be useful at certain stages in the life of a text.
- More commonly, it is advisable to save different versions of a document, especially when embarking on a major revision. Then if required an earlier version can be recalled for use. Some programs will automatically save backup versions if required.

Search and replace

One of the first features of word processors to catch writers' imagination was their ability to search through a document for every occurrence of a word or words and to change them to something else. This is still a very valuable and powerful feature, although it is so powerful that it is easy to make disastrous mistakes—especially as on some programs its effects cannot then be undone!

Layout

When setting out a document for printing, it is useful to be able to see the text on screen exactly as it will appear on paper. The feature is commonly known as WYSIWYG, short for 'What You See Is What You Get'. Most recent word-processing programs either operate in WYSIWYG all the time, or allow the user to view the text in this mode before printing. If the appearance of your text is particularly important to you, it is very desirable to use a program that allows you to work in WYSIWYG all the time.

Sophisticated word-processing and DTP programs offer more or less complete control over all elements of the layout of a text.

Type

You can select the typeface you wish to use and its size. Many programs now even display the names of the typefaces in a pull-down menu as they will appear:

Amasis

Architect

Bembo

which is very useful if you are not familiar with the names of typefaces, or have a considerable number on your computer.

The computer also allows you to style the typeface you are using. For example:

plain
bold
italic
outline
shadow
underline
SMALL CAPITALS

You can also select the colour and shade in which your text is displayed and printed.

Paragraph styles

For those who were brought up on a typewriter, where applying a style to paragraphs was impossible beyond indenting the first line and altering the margins, there is a bewildering range of possibilities on a computer. For any given paragraph it is possible to set:

- the leading
- the left and right margins
- the indent of the first line
- the indent of subsequent lines
- the position of the tabs
- the space between it and the preceding paragraph
- the space between it and the succeeding paragraph
- the alignment of the lines:
  - left aligned
  - right aligned
  - centred
  - justified (left and right aligned)

With many programs it is possible to save the settings you have chosen and to give them a name, so that they can be recalled for use later in a document. You might, for example, have separate styles for:

- the first paragraph after a heading, with no indent for the first line
- succeeding paragraphs in which the first line is indented
- material set out using bullets and a hanging indent

All this may seem rather daunting, although it does not take most people long to develop a good working understanding of what they want and how to achieve it. To assist in this process, some programs have useful common styles pre-programmed for you to choose from.

Other layout features

It is also possible to achieve a range of other effects involving type-faces, backgrounds, and graphic elements.

- **headings**
  These can be set in a contrasting typeface, size, and colour and may be accompanied by a rule (line) above or below, or both.

- **boxes and tints**
  If you wish to mark off a section of text it can be surrounded by a rectangle (box), be set against a tint, or a combination of the two.

- **bullet points**
  You can use a range of bullet points to mark the beginning of each of a number of listed features. In this book we have used ■ , but there are several others available. For example :

- **flags**
  You can draw the reader's attention to an important section or sections within the text by the use of graphic symbols:

These symbols are all taken from a typeface called Zapf Dingbats, which is widely available.

More advanced layout

Writers who wish to achieve more sophisticated layouts will probably need to work in a slightly different way. Word processors normally work with a standard 'page' which is defined when you start work on the document. Some programs allow you to have several different pages defined in one document. It is possible to indent the text as described above and to have one or more columns on each page. It is even possible to have columns of different widths on the same page. It is not normally possible, however, to arrange blocks of text 'freely' on the page. Nor can you easily place graphics wherever you like and have the text flow round them.

For these effects you need to work in an approximation to a desktop publishing environment. In DTP the page is more like a layout pad on which the user places objects. These may be blocks of text or graphics.

These objects can then be moved around on the page until the user is satisfied with the arrangement. Text can be made to 'flow' from one text box to another and flow round graphics. In the larger DTP programs, you can also create master pages with text blocks and graphic spaces predetermined.

While the most sophisticated effects are the preserve of large DTP packages, word-processing programs and combined 'works' packages, like Microsoft Works and ClarisWorks, incorporate increasingly sophisticated DTP elements.

Words

There are two useful features in most word-processing programs, which work at the level of words.

Spellchecking

No word processor can do the job of checking a text for you, but the task can be made easier by the use of a spellchecker. These work by comparing all the words you have keyed in with a built-in dictionary. If one of your words is not in that dictionary, you are asked if you want to change it. Usually one or more possible alternatives from the dictionary are offered. You can add special words and proper names to a separate user dictionary to save time in subsequent checks.

Of course a spellchecker will only pick up words that do not exist in its dictionary. If you have misspelled a word so that it makes another word, this will not be corrected.

Most word processors include a spellchecker, although some are very much better than others. Some writers prefer to use a standalone checker since these often have a much bigger and better dictionary than those which are included in a package. Whichever you choose, make sure that it is a version that reflects the type of English you and your readers speak. There is nothing more frustrating for a writer of British English than to have spellings 'corrected' by an American English spellchecker, and vice versa.

Thesaurus

If you like using a thesaurus, and some writers do, then having one available on screen may be attractive. They are, however, rather limited by comparison with a good printed version, because they are much more difficult to browse through—a process which often provides unexpected discoveries, even if you do not find the word you are looking for.

On the other hand, given the word 'browse' (in the sense used just now) one word processor's thesaurus suggested *skim, scan, glance at, look through, peruse*; a second came up with *dip into, leaf through, look through, peruse, scan, skim, survey*; while a 1500-page book version (the *Bloomsbury Thesaurus*, normally very reliable) produced nothing at all!

Specialist tools

The features listed so far should be available in any middle-of-the-range word-processing package. There are, however, rather more specialized tools which many writers find useful.

Outliners and 'thought processors'

These are devices for organizing your ideas on screen. One of the disadvantages of the computer is that it is difficult to use creatively by comparison with a large sheet of paper and a few coloured markers. A normal word-processor, for example, is not a device that lends itself to jotting down a web diagram. The commonest software device for organizing ideas is the outliner. This enables you to list ideas in a hierarchical framework and then order and reorder them as the project takes shape. Without going into great detail, it enables the writer to proceed from:

```
workshops:          – UK
     –abroad
themes    wildlife
     landscape
     darkroom stuff
does cost include accommodation?
(compare like with like)
     portraits
```

to

```
■ types of photographic workshop
         photographic categories
            nature
                      landscape
                      wildlife
            people
                      portrait
                      documentary
```

without ever having to put the rough thoughts down on paper. All the 'thinking' is done on screen.

There are other 'thought processors' which operate on different principles, and there may well be one which suits you. The problem is that they are often quite expensive and certainly impossible to evaluate from descriptions, brochures, or sales talk—you have to try them out. So unless you know someone with a particular program and can try it out, buying one is something of a gamble.

Grammar and readability checkers

Many people who have to write as part of their daily work are concerned that their writing skills are inadequate and that their efforts at clear expression will lay them open to criticism and even ridicule. There are computer programs that will check a text against grammatical and stylistic criteria and comment on errors, repetitions, sentence length, and suitability. It is possible to tell the program to check the text against one of a number of stylistic criteria, for example: 'Academic', 'Business', 'Informal'.

Such programmes suffer from three major drawbacks:

■ They have to apply to a wide range of writing situations, even when a particular 'style' is chosen, and as a result their recommendations may not apply to your particular case. The more sophisticated ones allow you to build up an individual 'customized' style guide.

- In order to use one effectively, you need a relatively good knowledge of grammatical terminology. The better programs have a 'teaching mode', which will help the user overcome this.
- Their tools for analysing sentences are sometimes not sophisticated enough to cope with even quite simple sentences. For example, one grammar checker found the following 'errors' (among others) in the text of this chapter:

Sentence	Grammar checker comment
Instead it is more helpful to list and describe the different features that are available in different programmes.	Consider 'describes' instead of 'describe'. Verbs that have the same subject must agree with that subject. If the subjects (real or implied) differ, the verbs differ in number.
The text can be altered, cut, and added to until the writer is satisfied with it. **If necessary it can be saved on disk and re-used later.**	This sentence does not seem to contain a main clause. A main clause can stand alone as a sentence and usually does not begin with a conjunction.

In both these cases, the programme has been fooled by a perfectly acceptable but—to it—unusual sentence construction. On style it also proved unreliable:

Sentence	Grammar checker comment
Sophisticated word-processing and DTP programs offer **more or less** complete control over all elements of the layout of a text.	Wordy expression. Consider 'approximately' or 'somewhat' instead.
While the most sophisticated effects are the preserve of large DTP packages, word-processing programs and combined 'works' packages, **like** Microsoft Works and ClarisWorks incorporate increasingly sophisticated DTP elements.	Consider 'as' or 'as if' instead of 'like'.

Neither of these pieces of stylistic advice is at all helpful. In the first case, the suggested words won't work in that position. In the second the program has been fooled by the fact that there is a comma missing after *ClarisWorks* (which would isolate the phrase *like Microsoft Works and ClarisWorks* from the rest of the sentence).

So such programs need to be used with care. If you feel that your writing tends to be ungrammatical, by all means try one of them, but do not follow it slavishly, and use it in 'teaching mode' so that you learn the terminology it uses and understand the rules it is applying.

Glossaries   If you have to key in lengthy and complicated words or even short sections of text several times in the course of the document, time can be saved by using a glossary. This is a feature which allows the user to save the relevant words and text sections and then allocate a particular combination of keys to each one. So, for example instead of keying in Sir Fosdyke Maxwell Winterbotham every time, you simply hold down the Control and Alt keys at the same time as pressing the 'w' key.

Macros   A similar saving of time and effort can be achieved, when editing lengthy documents, by the use of macros. These are short pieces of program that you write yourself to tell the computer to carry out a sequence of operations. You can, for example, use this type of 'short cut' to find every instance of a particular word, put it into bold type, and place a carriage return before and after it, so that it functions as a subheading.

It is possible to write macros by actually keying lines of program language. Less expert computer users normally prefer to work in a different way. The macro feature is switched to 'record' and then the separate stages of the required operation are gone through. Recording is then switched off and the sequence of key strokes is given a name and saved.

Guidelines

1 If you are purchasing word-processing or DTP software, begin by making a list of features that are essential to the work you are doing now.

2 Make a second list of features that you think you might need in the foreseeable future.

3 Compare these two lists against the feature lists of possible programs.

4 When making a decision consider carefully the hardware requirements of each program (the amount of memory and hard disk space each requires, along with any other special requirements).

5 Try to find out also what quality of support each program provides:
- the manual
- on-screen help
- tutorials on disk
- telephone back-up (and whether this is free or charged)

6 Be wary of buying a program that is packed with features you will probably never use, which takes a long time to learn, and which demands masses of memory and disk space.

7 One approach to consider is buying a relatively simple word processor and adding a dictionary, a thesaurus, and other features as desktop accessories.

8 Remember that most software is upgraded regularly and if you wish to 'keep up', you will have to pay for major upgrades.

Reference

Most of the terms explained in this section concern the grammar of English. All are explained in greater detail in the main part of this book.

page 235 **accent** The ways in which two different people pronounce the same word may differ considerably, especially in the vowel sounds. If so, we say that they have different accents. A person's accent may come from the area where they were brought up, or from their social background, or a mixture of the two.

See: RECEIVED PRONUNCIATION, DIALECT

page 225 **acronym** A word formed from the first letters of a group of words, for example the name of an organization:

UNICEF

BBC

An acronym is either pronounced as a word (like UNICEF) or as a series of letters (like BBC). In either case it is used as a noun (e.g. 'The clever old BBC's latest ploy . . .').

adjective When we go to school we are taught that adjectives are 'describing words', which gives a good idea of how they are used. Grammatically they:

- modify nouns (e.g., 'the *red* house')
- act as the COMPLEMENT of a clause (e.g., 'She is *happy*.')

adverb Adverbs are a class of words with a wide range of grammatical functions. The commonest are:

- to modify verbs ('She *slowly* came round.')
- to modify adjectives ('I am *really* sorry.')
- to modify other adverbs ('I behaved *very* badly.')

page 161 **adverbial** Part of a clause which modifies the verb and provides information in answers to questions such as:

WHEN?: 'I met her *this afternoon*.'
WHERE?: 'We went *to the cinema*.'
HOW?: 'We travelled *by bus*.'
WHY?: 'She left her husband *because of her love for another man*.'

Within a clause an adverbial can be a group of words, a phrase, as in these examples, or it can be a single word—an adverb.

A COMPLEX SENTENCE may contain one or more adverbial clauses.

These work in a similar way to the adverbial phrases, but contain a FINITE VERB:

'I met her *when we had both finished work*.'

There are also 'sentence adverbials', which provide some kind of comment on the sentence as a whole:

'*Unfortunately* our team lost again.'

affix *see*: WORD STRUCTURE.

page 158 **agreement** The subject and the verb in a clause must agree:

1 IN NUMBER

'She *was* very sad and her parents *were* supportive.'

2 IN PERSON

'I *am* going, Mary *is* going, and you *are* going.'

article A small class of words consisting of 'a', 'an', and 'the'.

page 158 **aspect** The form of the verb in a sentence can tell us not only *when* an action occurred (the TENSE), but also *how*. Compare these two sentences:

A

'As I *was walking* to work yesterday, I met Mrs Pepys.'

B

'I *walked* to work yesterday because I wanted to call in on Mrs Pepys.'

In **A** the speaker wants to show that the action of walking was continuing at the moment when something else happened. In **B** the speaker sees the action as a completed, one-off event. English verbs have three aspects. In the present tense they are:

SIMPLE: 'I walk.'

CONTINUOUS OR PROGRESSIVE: 'I am walking.'

PERFECT: 'I have walked.'

auxiliary verb *see*: VERB PHRASE

page 154 **clause** A group of words (which normally contains a subject and a finite verb) that either forms a whole SIMPLE SENTENCE or part of a MULTIPLE SENTENCE.

cliché In French the word 'cliché' means an engraved plate used in the past by printers. Once you have made such a plate you can use it as many times as you like to print a picture. Of course, if you pretend that each picture is an 'original', you will soon be found out. The same is true of language. Expressions such as, 'I will leave no stone unturned' were once new, but they have been used so many times that today they seem tired and stale. On the other hand, many common idiomatic expressions are clichés—'leading light', 'let sleeping dogs lie', and 'end of the road', for example. No one would try to avoid such expressions altogether; it is a matter of balance.

pages 98, 191 **colloquial** A term usually used to refer to everyday (often spoken) language as opposed to the more formal, polite, or 'posh' language that many people feel they ought to use. The word is sometimes used as a term of criticism: 'Her language was rather colloquial for a head-teacher.' But this ignores the fact that we all use a range of different forms of language according to the situation we are in.

page 161 **complement** A clause component. One of the seven basic clause patterns is :

My wife + became + a district councillor
SUBJECT + VERB   + COMPLEMENT

where the subject and the complement both refer to the same person or thing and are joined by a LINKING VERB. Another clause pattern is:

The company + made + me   + Head of Security
SUBJECT   + VERB + OBJECT + COMPLEMENT

Here the object and the complement both refer to the same person or thing.

page 169 **complex sentence** A MULTIPLE SENTENCE which contains a main clause and one or more subordinate clauses. A main clause is one that can with little or no alteration stand alone, whereas a subordinate clause cannot, as in this complex sentence:

'We have decided + that we should close the plant.'
——MAIN CLAUSE—— + ——SUBORDINATE CLAUSE——

page 168 **compound sentence** A MULTIPLE SENTENCE which contains two or more main clauses joined by COORDINATING CONJUNCTIONS. For example:

'First she went to Woolworths, then she visited the bank, and finally she had a coffee in Fuller's.'

Here the three clauses are of equal status and are joined by the co-ordinating conjunctions 'then' and 'and'.

page 170 **conditional** A conditional sentence is one containing an 'if'. For example: 'If you don't stop making that noise, I shall go mad!' Conditionals come in different forms, according to how 'open' the condition is. Compare these four sentences:

A
If you heat water to 100°C at sea level, it boils.
B
If Martha comes, we'll open a new pot of jam.
C
If you thought about it even for a moment, you'd see that he's wrong.
D
If I were you, I'd think again.

Sentence A describes a fact that will never change—a law of nature. The event described has happened many times before and will doubtless happen many times more. Sentence B concerns something that has not yet happened, but the speaker believes that it is perfectly possible that it will. In sentence C, on the other hand, although the event described is possible, the speaker thinks it rather unlikely. Sentence D sets up an impossible condition—'I' can never be 'you'.

Although the large majority of conditionals use 'if', there are other words which can be used: 'although' and 'provided that', for example.

pages 174–7 **conjunctions** As their name suggests, these are the 'joining words' of grammar, used to combine two or more clauses into one MULTIPLE SENTENCE. They may be COORDINATING CONJUNCTIONS, like 'and' and 'but', or SUBORDINATING CONJUNCTIONS, like 'when', 'although', and 'because'.

page 260 **conjuncts** These are adverbials which help to relate one part of a text to another through a relationship of meaning. For example: 'Peter and I had planned to go into business. When it came to the crunch, *however*, he lacked the necessary capital.' Here the word 'however' shows the relationship between the second sentence and the first; in this case, there is a contrast—the first sentence sets up an expectation and the second one knocks it down. Conjuncts are a useful way of making the link between two paragraphs.

pages 230–1 **consonant** The alphabet contains 21 consonant letters:

bcdfghjklmnpqrstvwxyz

RECEIVED PRONUNCIATION has 24 consonant sounds (although some linguists classify two of them as 'semi-vowels'—the sounds at the beginning of these two words: 'wet' and 'yet'). In some cases a consonant letter is almost always pronounced in the same way and is represented by one consonant sound symbol—for example, the first sound in the word 'bet'. In other cases there are sounds for which there is no single letter equivalent. Examples are the first sound in 'this' and the last sound in 'bath'—which are spelled the same but pronounced differently!

contraction In speech we sometimes miss sounds out and squash words together, producing contracted versions of words. In writing, the omission of letters in contracted forms is partly shown by the use of apostrophes:

'I shall not' becomes 'I shan't' (not 'I sha'n't')

pages 174–5 **coordinating conjunction** A CONJUNCTION used to join two CLAUSES in a COMPOUND SENTENCE. Examples are:

and, or, but, then

defining relative clause *see*: RELATIVE CLAUSE

page 149 **descriptive grammar** The type of grammar which is based on the analysis of a body of carefully selected spoken and written texts and leads to a set of statements which describe how language actually works, rather than how the writer thinks it should. It is commonly contrasted with PRESCRIPTIVE GRAMMAR.

page 147 **dialect** English exists in a wide number of different versions, or *dialects*, spoken by different social and geographical groups. For example, the natives of Glasgow use a number of words and grammatical constructions that are not used by those of Penzance. Of course there is a large amount of overlap between these different dialects, but the question still arises: 'What is English?' Most regional dialects have an associated form of pronunciation, or ACCENT. There is one dialect of English which has more prestige than any other, STANDARD ENGLISH. It is widely used in speech in education, the professions, government, and business, and is the normal form in written texts. In this book, unless otherwise stated, comments about English are always about the standard form.

page 155 **directive** Sentences which instruct, command, or request are frequently constructed in a special way that is different from

STATEMENTS. For example:

'Keep off the grass.'

'Just leave me alone!'

The most obvious difference between a statement and a directive is that in a directive the subject is usually missed out—but not always:

'You just put that down at once!'

direct object *see*: OBJECT

page 182 **etymology** The study of the history of the words of a language. The word 'etymology' is also used to refer to the origins of a particular word.

page 106 **euphemism** A 'gentle' word or expression which is used in place of one which may offend some people. Sometimes the use of a euphemism is thoughtful and sensitive, as in the use of euphemisms for 'death' and 'died' when talking to people who are grieving the death of someone they loved. Often it is fussy, as in 'Do you want to spend a penny?' for 'Do you want to use the lavatory?' And it can even be confusing, as in 'Do you want to wash your hands?' for the same question.

page 158 **finite verb** A clause normally has to contain a finite verb. That is a verb which:

1 AGREES with the subject in number and person

2 shows tense

So, for example, this is not a proper simple sentence:

'To visit Paris in the spring,—one of the great experiences of youth.'

because the only verb in it is an infinitive, 'to visit'. It doesn't agree with the subject (because there isn't one) and it has no tense. Compare:

'I *visited* Paris in the spring—one of the great experiences of youth.'

'I *shall visit* Paris in the spring—one of the great experiences of youth.'

full verb *see*: VERB PHRASE

pages 149–154 **grammar** The study of how words are changed to fit into sentences (morphology) and how they are ordered to construct sentences (syntax). *See also*: DESCRIPTIVE GRAMMAR, TRADITIONAL GRAMMAR, PRESCRIPTIVE GRAMMAR

indirect object *see*: OBJECT

page 157 **infinitive** The 'to——' form of the verb:

to be, to go, to understand

Many languages have a one-word infinitive form (as French—être, aller, comprendre), but English does not. If you remove the 'to', you are left with the verb stem, which is used in certain tenses:

'She will be unhappy.'

The infinitive itself is used with verbs like 'want' and 'love' ('I'd love to go to Paris.') and can be used in sentences as a part of a noun phrase: '*To lose* one parent, Mr Worthing, may be regarded as a misfortune; *to lose* both looks like carelessness.'

page 233 **intonation** The 'tune' with which we speak. This sentence, for example, can be spoken in more than one way: 'You saw her yesterday.' If we say it so that the voice rises at the beginning of 'yesterday' and then falls through the rest of the word, the sentence is a statement of fact. If we say it so that the voice *rises* towards the end of 'yesterday', the sentence becomes a question and should be written with a final question mark.

pages 116, 192 **jargon** Many subjects have a specialist language, which non-specialists find difficult or impossible to understand. This means that when specialists speak to each other they may accidentally or deliberately exclude any non-specialists who happen to be present. Any such technical language can be described as 'jargon', but the term is often used as a criticism—especially when technical or specialist language is used either to show off, or to exclude other people, or both.

page 161 **linking verbs** A small group of verbs (sometimes called copular verbs) that are used to link a subject and its complement:

'Mrs Brown *is* a teacher at the local school.'

Other linking verbs are:

appear, seem, become, feel, remain, sound

page 169 **main clause** In a COMPLEX SENTENCE one clause is grammatically more important than the other *subordinate* clauses. In the sentences that follow, the main clauses are underlined:

A

'She told us that she had to go home.'

B

'When I arrived, all the food had gone.'

C

'Mr Jones was the teacher who taught me most.'

In each of these sentences, the subordinate clause can be replaced by a single word or short phrase, and the main clause will then make a grammatically complete simple sentence:

A: 'She told us *the truth*.'

B: '*By then* all the food had gone.'

C: 'Mr Jones was the *best* teacher.'

You cannot do the same with the subordinate clauses—they depend on the main clause.

page 164 **minor sentence** It is possible to construct a kind of 'sentence' without a finite verb. Such utterances have a clear and complete meaning but they are grammatically incomplete:

No entry.

Car park for customers only.

Such sentences are called 'minor sentences'.

multiple sentence A multiple sentence is one that consists of more than one clause. Multiple sentences are either COMPOUND or COMPLEX.

pages 124–8 **narrative** One of the four traditional modes (types) of discourse (writing and speaking). Any text which relates a series of events which happened over a period of time is a narrative. The simplest form begins at the beginning and relates events in the order in which they happened, but this approach is frequently not followed; newspaper reports, for example, are narratives, but they often begin with the most striking element of the story and then fill in the background later. Other examples of narratives are short stories, novels, the minutes of a meeting, the record of a legal trial, and many jokes ('There's this fellow who goes into a pub, right?').

non-defining relative clause *see*: RELATIVE CLAUSE

non-restrictive relative clause *see*: RELATIVE CLAUSE

non-standard A term used to refer to language uses that differ grammatically from standard English.

noun Traditionally nouns have been described as 'words that refer to people, places, things, and ideas'. Grammatically we can say that most nouns:
- can be modified by an ADJECTIVE ('the red *house*')
- can be preceded by an ARTICLE ('the *house*')
- preceded by an article can stand as the SUBJECT or OBJECT of a clause
  'The *house* has been sold.' (subject)
  'We have sold *the house*.' (object)
- can follow a preposition ('All the illustrations were done *in house*.')

page 172   **noun clause** A clause which forms the subject, object, or complement of a complex sentence:

SUBJECT
'What I want to know is the answer to my first question.'

OBJECT
'You still haven't told me what I want to know.'

COMPLEMENT
'That is what I want to know.'

page 156   **noun phrase** A phrase which is based on a noun. It can have words before and after the noun:

'The highest *mountain* in Scotland'

Noun phrases can form the subject, object, or complement of a sentence; they can also form part of other phrases.

page 158   **number** The subject of a sentence can be singular (one) or plural (more than one). The verb must agree with the number of the subject. *See*: AGREEMENT

page 160   **object** The object in a clause normally comes after the verb. The objects in these sentences have been underlined:

'I nearly lost my temper.'
'I nearly lost what I most treasured in the world.'

In the first example the object is a NOUN PHRASE; in the second it is a NOUN CLAUSE.

Certain verbs can have two objects, a *direct* object and an *indirect* object:

I gave the dog   a bone.
    INDIRECT   DIRECT
    OBJECT   OBJECT

These sentences can be turned round like this:

I gave a bone to   the dog.
                DIRECT   INDIRECT
                OBJECT   OBJECT

The indirect object is the one which needs 'to' placing before it.

page 158 **person** PRONOUNS can be 1st, 2nd or 3rd person:

1ST PERSON: I/we (and my/our, etc.)

2ND PERSON: you/your, etc.

3RD PERSON: she/he/it/they

The form of the verb changes according to the person:
I like/she likes.

See: AGREEMENT.

pages 228–232 **phoneme** Phonemes are the speech sounds of a language. In RECEIVED PRONUNCIATION there are 44 phonemes. See CONSONANT and VOWEL.

page 154 **phrase** A group of words which forms a part of a clause, but which, unlike a clause, does not contain a finite verb. Phrases are named after their headword. In these examples the headword is in bold type:

- a noun phrase ('the **leader** of the gang')
- a verb phrase ('would have been **going**')
- a prepositional phrase ('**to** the edge')
- an adverbial phrase ('very, very, **slowly**')
- an adjective phrase ('really rather **unusual**')

page 92 **Plain English** Literally, 'plain English' is speech or writing in English that is clear and straightforward to understand. Since 1974, it has also been the name of a movement in the UK, the Plain English Campaign, founded to persuade government and business to communicate simply and clearly with the general public. Books such as *The Plain English Guide* (Martin Cutts, OUP, 1995) set out rules which can be followed by the writer who wishes to write 'plain English'. This campaign and its establishment of the 'Crystal Mark' have achieved a great deal to make government and commercial communications clearer and more straightforward. There are, however, limitations to what such an approach can achieve. It is not possible to communicate effectively in the widest possible range of situations just by following a set of rules; you need also to be sensitive to the demands of audience, subject, and purpose, as suggested in Section B of this book.

prefix *see*: WORD STRUCTURE

preposition A class of words which are used with nouns, pronouns, noun phrases, and some verb forms. As their name suggests, they come before the word(s) that complement them. In these phrases the prepositions are underlined:

in time
with us
behind the green baize door
without thinking

Prepositions may consist of more than one word:

up to you
except for the French

page 149 **prescriptive grammar** Grammar which sets out rules about how language should be used. For example: 'You should never end a sentence with a preposition.' A large number of the rules of prescriptive grammar either have exceptions, or are just plain wrong (as with the example quoted).

primary verb *see*: VERB PHRASE

pages 98–9, 195 **pronoun** A word which refers back to a noun, noun phrase, pronoun, or another group of words or idea already mentioned in a text. Examples are:

I/me/my/mine/myself
they/them/their/theirs/themselves

page 235 **received pronunciation (RP)** An English ACCENT which used to be regarded as superior to other, regional, accents. It was also known as 'BBC English'. Until recently, and even to some extent today, people believed that you had to learn how to speak with an RP accent if you wished to advance in the professions, national government, and other areas of employment. It is certainly true that many regional accents are still widely regarded as inferior to RP.

pages 173, 226 **relative clause** A clause that modifies a noun, noun phrase, or pronoun. In these examples the relative clauses are underlined:

A
'Mrs Rowen, <u>who was born in France</u>, loved good plain cooking.'
B
'The person <u>she most admires</u> is the Duchess of St Pancras.'
Relative clauses may be introduced by a relative pronoun, as in sentence A. Other relative pronouns are 'whom'/'whose', 'which', and 'that'. Sometimes a relative clause has no introductory relative pronoun, as in sentence B.
Some relative clauses define or restrict the word or words they refer to. In sentence B, for example, 'she' obviously admires more than one person; the relative clause is there to define the person we are referring to. Such relative clauses are described as defining or restrictive relative clauses. Other relative clauses do not define, but simply add extra information, as in sentence A: there is only one Mrs Rowen in question and the clause tells us more about her. Such non-defining or non-restrictive relative clauses should be enclosed in commas, as in the example.

RP *see*: RECEIVED PRONUNCIATION

page 191 **slang** Language that is much less formal and less socially acceptable than standard English. It is subject to changes of fashion and is often connected with membership of a particular social group. Slang expressions for *eat* include:

feed your face
tie on the feed bag
grab a bite
get amongst the groceries

standard English *see*: DIALECT

stem *see*: WORD STRUCTURE

pages 234–5   **stress** In any spoken sentence, some SYLLABLES will be spoken with more emphasis than the others; they are said to be *stressed*. English has two kinds of stress. In any word of more than one syllable, there will be one syllable that is stressed more than the others. For example:

> des**pair**, **hap**py

Longer words may have two stressed syllables, but one of them will normally be stronger (primary stress) and the other weaker (secondary stress).

In addition to word stress, there is sentence stress. If you say that last sentence aloud, you see that two syllables are stressed:

> In addition to **word** stress, there is **sen**tence stress.

Sentence stress combines with INTONATION to give spoken English its distinctive rhythm and tune.

page 155   **subject** The subject of a statement clause normally comes before the verb. It frequently, but by no means always, gives an indication of what the clause will be about:

> *Our success in the match* was due to excellent teamwork.

Sometimes, however, a clause may have a 'dummy subject', with a grammatical purpose but not a lot of meaning:

> *It* is raining this morning.

subordinate clause *see*: MAIN CLAUSE

subordinating conjunction *see*: CONJUNCTION

suffix *see*: WORD STRUCTURE

page 234   **syllable** A syllable is the smallest unit into which spoken language will break down. It can be just one vowel, or a combination of consonant(s) and vowel. All these words have one syllable:

> I, my, mine, mind, dined, grind

(Notice that we are dealing with spoken language here; 'dined' may appear to have two syllables on the page, but when you say it you can see that there is only one.) These words all have two syllables:

> any, many, timid, grounded, happened

See: STRESS

page 190   **taboo** Certain informal words and expressions are generally considered to be unsuitable for 'polite society'. These are often concerned with human sexuality and excretion. They are described as 'taboo', or 'taboo slang'. Which words and expressions are taboo is a matter of opinion, and people's ideas about this shift as society changes.

page 158   **tense** One of the ways in which time can be indicated in a sentence is by the use of verb tense. Confusingly, this term is used in two different ways by people who write about language. In its strictest sense, tense means changes to the form of the verb to show a difference of time. In this sense, English has two tenses:

> PRESENT: I walk, she walks, etc.
> PAST: I walked, she walked, etc.

So it is correct to say that 'English has no future tense'. But, people argue, what about 'she will walk'? The answer is that the term 'tense' is also widely used to describe all the different forms the verb phrase can take to show time. In that meaning of tense, all the following are different tenses:

I walk, I am walking, I have walked, I walked, I was walking, I shall walk, I shall be walking, I shall have walked, and so on

See: VERB PHRASE

pages 97–9 **tone** Sometimes a person speaks in such a way that their voice makes clear what their attitude is to the person they are addressing. We may say, 'I knew she didn't like me the moment she opened her mouth; I could tell it from her tone of voice.' It is often possible to detect the same thing in the way a person writes: we can tell from the tone of their writing their relationship with and attitude towards their audience.

page 149 **traditional grammar** In the past all students of language were educated in a system that laid great emphasis on Greek and Latin language and literature. When they came to study English they based their systematic analysis of this language on what they knew of the great classical languages. The result was a grammar that often regarded English as inferior to Latin and sought to improve it, often by bringing it closer to Latin. This process involved distorting the true nature of English and imposing 'rules' which did not reflect linguistic reality.

See: PRESCRIPTIVE GRAMMAR, DESCRIPTIVE GRAMMAR

verb A large class of words which are used to refer to actions, states, and conditions. For example:

to run   to decide   to love   to be

To check whether a word is a verb add 'to' to it and see if it makes an INFINITIVE. If it does, the word is a verb.

page 156 **verb phrase** Every clause must contain a verb phrase (sometimes shortened to 'verb'). In a statement sentence, this normally comes after the subject and before the object or complement. The verb phrase may consist of one word or more than one. The verbs that make up a verb phrase are of three types:

FULL VERBS
These are verbs with a 'dictionary meaning' and they can be the only verb in the verb phrase: 'I *love* ice cream.'

AUXILIARY VERBS
These work with full verbs: 'I *should* love an ice cream.' They cannot stand as the only verb in a verb phrase, unless they are referring back to an earlier verb phrase. (As in 'Would you like an ice cream?'—'Yes, I *would*.')

PRIMARY VERBS
There are three verbs that can act as full verbs or as auxiliaries: 'to be', 'to have', 'to do'. So we can say, 'I *have* a golden labrador' (full verb use) and 'I *have taken* the dog for a walk' (auxiliary use).

pages 230–1 **vowel** There are five vowel letters in English: a e i o u.

Vowel sounds are those speech sounds made with the mouth open and the flow of air unimpeded. Each of the following words has one vowel sound sandwiched between two consonant sounds:

beet, bit, bet, bat, but, part, pot, port, put, boot, hurt, bate, bite, boil, bowl, howl

The second sound in each of these words is a vowel sound:

the, here, there, poor

The vowel sounds represented in the words listed comprise all the vowels of RECEIVED PRONUNCIATION.

page 185 **word structure** All words have a stem, and some words consist only of a stem. For example:

paper, example, comfort

Other words have a stem with a section before and/or after it:

un comfort able
PREFIX   STEM   SUFFIX

The general term for prefixes and suffixes is *affixes*. Prefixes are used to add meaning to the stem or alter its meaning. (For example, adding 'un-' to a stem gives it the opposite meaning to what it had before.) Suffixes are used to form new words from existing words. This often involves moving them from one word class to another. So the noun 'comfort' gives us the adjective 'comfortable'.

Index

Thanks are due to the following for permission to reproduce extracts from copyrighted material in this book.

ACAS: copyright © ACAS *Work Research Unit 1988.*

Ashford, Buchan, & Enright: from *Groc's Candid Guide to Crete and Mainland Ports.*

Bang & Olufsen: 'Looks can be deceiving', extract from an advertisement for the *BeoCenter 9300.*

Blackwell Publishers: from Walter Nash, *Jargon, Its Uses and Abuses* (1993).

Bloomsbury: 'Sage' from *Bloomsbury Thesaurus* (1993), edited by Betty Kirkpatrick.

The British Red Cross: extract from a newspaper advertisement, 'Urgent Appeal: Crisis in Lebanon'.

Butterworth-Heinemann Ltd: extract from R. E. Jackson, S. F. Ray, G. G. Attridge, *The Manual of Photography* (Focal Press, 1988).

Cobuild Ltd. Institute of Research & Development: definition of 'Sage' from *Collins Cobuild English Language Dictionary* (1987).

Ann Cotterrell, Christine Porter, and Valerie Mills: from *Abbey National—A Report on employment and career development.*

Daily Mail: 'Driving ban for nine-in-car . . .', *Daily Mail*, 21/3/97.

Judy Daish Associates Ltd: extract from Harold Pinter, *Pinter Plays: Two* (Eyre Methuen, 1977; orig. publ. Methuen 1961, © Harold Pinter 1961).

Driver and Vehicle Licensing Agency: extract from Vehicle Registration document.

Encyclopaedia Britannica International Ltd: 'Sensory Perception', p. 181 from *Encyclopaedia Britannica Macropedia.*

Faber & Faber Ltd: extract from 'Night Mail' by W. H. Auden, from *The Collected Poems of W. H. Auden*, edited by Edward Mendelson (1976).

Fisons plc: extract from instruction leaflet for Intal Inhaler, © Fisons plc 1989.

4-Sight UK: extract from an advert in *MacUser 7*, March 1997.

HarperCollins Publishers: extracts from William Dalrymple *A Year in Delhi* (1993); Peter de la Billière *Looking for Trouble* (1994);

Heinemann Educational Publishers, a division of Reed Educational & Professional Publishing Ltd: 'Sage' from *Heinemann English Dictionary*; extract from Anita Ganeri, *Pharaohs and Embalmers* (1997).

The Controller, Her Majesty's Stationery Office: extract from the new Self Assessment form. Crown © 1996.

Lonely Planet Publications: extracts from 'Climate' and 'Refugees & the Dispossessed', Geoff Crowther and Hugh Finlay, *East Africa—A Travel Survival Kit* (1994).

Ilford Imaging: from Richard Platt, *Ilford Multigrade IV RC DeLuxe.*

2001

CYBERARTS

Cyberarts, International Compendium Prix Ars Electronica –
Net Vision / Net Excellence, Interactive Art, Computer
Animation / Visual Effects, Digital Musics, cybergeneration –
u19-Freestyle Computing

Edition 2001

Publisher: Dr. Hannes Leopoldseder,
Dr. Christine Schöpf
Editor: Christian Schrenk, ORF, Landesstudio Oberösterreich,
Europaplatz 3, 4021 Linz
Translation: Aileen Derieg, Helmut Einfalt
Cover-Design, Layout: Arthouse, Hansi Schorn
Frontispiece: team cHmAn / Banja
Coordination/German Proof-Reading:
Ingrid Fischer-Schreiber
English Proof-Reading: Aileen Derieg
Offset Reproduction, Assembly: Typeshop, Linz
Copyright 2001 by Österreichischer Rundfunk (ORF),
Landesstudio Oberösterreich

Photo Credits
Cover. Team cl lmAn; 130 – 133: Pixar;
144, 145: Warner Bros; 156, 157: Bay Vista Productions;
214–219: Kutzler + Wimmer, Traun

Printing: Gutenberg-Werbering Gesellschaft m.b.H., Linz

Printed on acid-free and chlorine-free bleached paper.

Prix Ars Electronica 2001
International Competition for Cyberarts
Organizer: Österreichischer Rundfunk (ORF),
Landesstudio Oberösterreich
Managing Director: Mag. Kurt Rammerstorfer
Idea: Dr. Hannes Leopoldseder
Conception: Dr. Christine Schöpf
Financing/Copyright: Dkfm. Augner
Liaison Office: Prix Ars Electronica, ORF,
Europaplatz 3, A-4021 Linz
Phone: 0043/732/6900-24267
Fax: 0043/732/6900-24270
E-Mail: info@prixars.orf.at
www.prixars.orf.at

©2001 Österreichischer Rundfunk (ORF),
Landesstudio Oberösterreich

SPIN 10831479

ISBN 3-211-83628-4

Springer-Verlag Wien New York

CYBERARTS

2001

HANNES LEOPOLDSEDER · CHRISTINE SCHÖPF
PRIX ARS ELECTRONICA

SpringerWienNewYork

contents

CONTENTS

Net Vision / Net Excellence
Interactive Art
Computer Animation / Visual Effects
Digital Musics
Cybergeneration u19 –
freestyle computing

Prix Ars Electronica 2001

the GOLDEN NICAS – the DISTINCTIONS

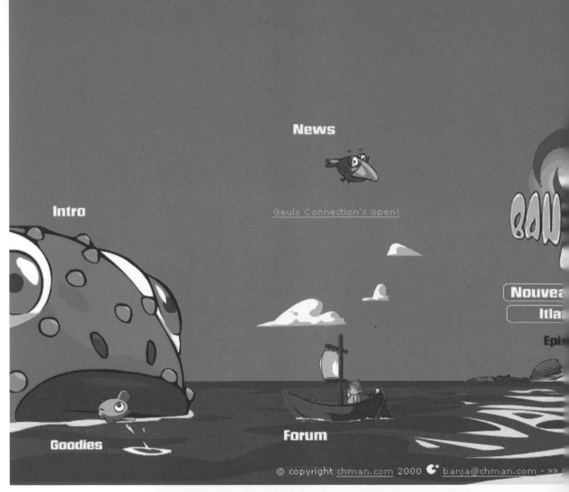

News

Geuls Connection's open!

Intro

Nouvea

Itla

Epis

Goodies

Forum

© copyright chman.com 2000 banja@chman.com - >>

DISTINCTION

Phantasy Star Online

Yuji Naka /
Sonic Team / Sega (J/USA)

http://www.sega.com/sega/
game/pso_launch.jhtml

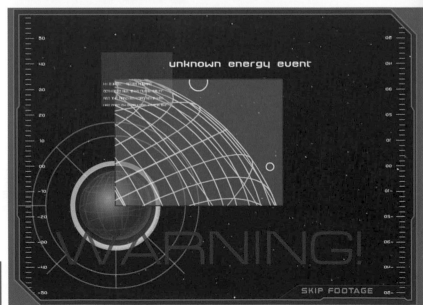

unknown energy event

WARNING!

SKIP FOOTAGE

GOLDEN NICA 2001

Banja

Team cHmAn (F)

http://www.banja.com

DISTINCTION

ImaHima

Neeraj Jhanji (India/J)

http://shiva.imahima.com

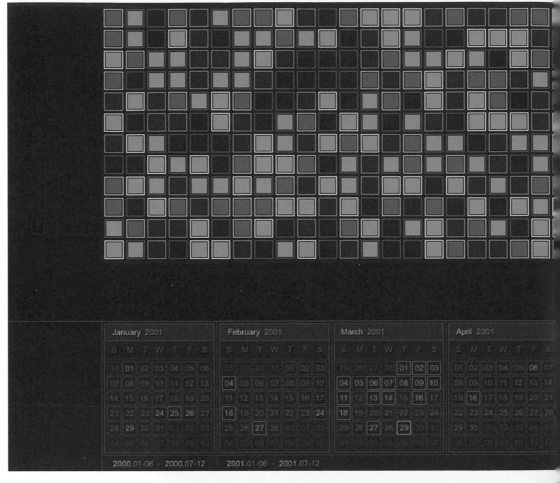

DISTINCTION

Warp Records

Chris McGrail /
Dorian Moore /
Dan Sayers / Kleber (UK)

http://www.
warprecords.com/warp

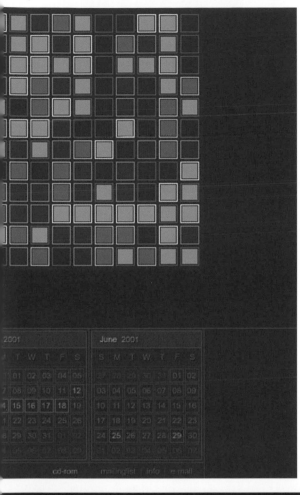

GOLDEN NICA 2001

PrayStation

Joshua Davis (USA)

http://www.praystation.com

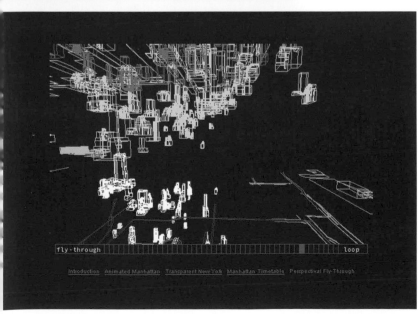

DISTINCTION

Manhattan Timeformations

Brian McGrath /
Mark Watkins (USA)

http://www.skyscraper.org/
timeformations

>

DISTINCTION

bump

association.creation (A)

GOLDEN NICA 2001

polar

Carsten Nicolai /
Marko Peljhan (D/SLO)

DISTINCTION

Remain in Light

Haruki Nishijima (J)

DISTINCTION

For The Birds

Ralph Eggleston (USA)

GOLDEN NICA 2001

Le Processus

Xavier de l'Hermuzière /
Philippe Grammaticopoulos (F)

DISTINCTION

L'Enfant de la Haute Mer

Laetitia Gabrielli /
Pierre Marteel /
Mathieu Renoux /
Max Tourret (F)

GOLDEN NICA 2001

Matrix

Ryoji Ikeda (J)

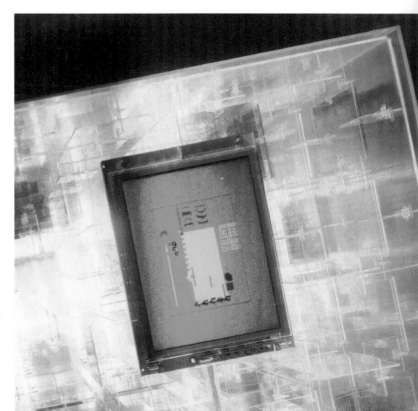

DISTINCTION

*ovalprocess /
ovalcommers*

Markus Popp / oval (D)

X

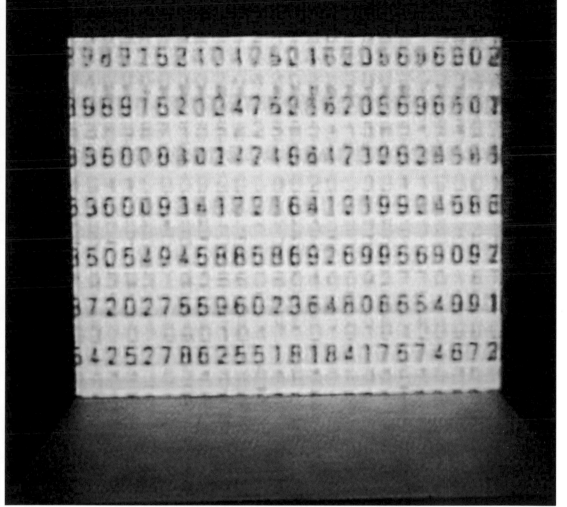

DISTINCTION

The Messy Jesse Fiesta

bLectum from bLechdom
(USA)

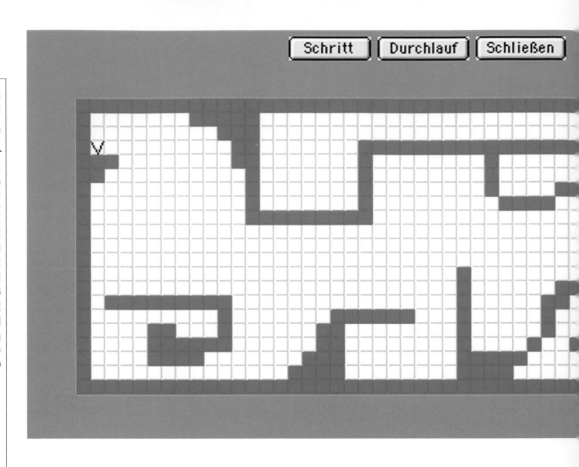

Schritt | Durchlauf | Schließen

DISTINCTION

Powersphere

Martin Leonhartsberger (A)

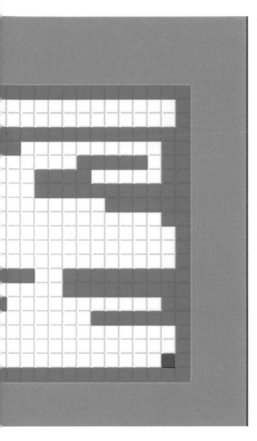

GOLDEN NICA 2001

JIND

Markus Triska (A)

DISTINCTION

Professor Brösl

Johannes Schiehsl /
Conrad Tambour /
Peter Strobl (A)

Net Vision / Net Excellence Pete Barr-Watson - Tanja Diezmann - Solveig Godeluck - Machiko Kusahara - TNC Network

Interactive Art Masaki Fujihata - Ulrike Gabriel - Peter Higgins - Hiroshi Ishii - Joachim Sauter

Computer Animation/ Visual Effects Paddy Eason - Christophe Héry - Barbara Robertson - Rick Sayre - Christian Volckman

Digital Musics Ned Bouhalassa - Reinhold Friedl - Tony Herrington - Naut Humon - Kaffe Matthew

Cybergeneration u19 Sirikit Amann - etoy.TAKI - Florian Hecker - Horst Hörtner - Robert Pöcksteiner

Chairman of the Jury *Hannes Leopoldseder*

15 YEARS PRIX ARS ELECTRONICA:
THE PRESENT OF THE FUTURE
DIE GEGENWART DER ZUKUNFT

Hannes Leopoldseder

The Prix Ars Electronica is awarded this year for the fifteenth time. The Ars Electronica Festival with its tradition since 1979 has achieved a continuity as a media festival that is unique around the world. Having been awarded fifteen times, the Prix Ars Electronica competition holds an equally unique position around the world. For this reason, the Prix Ars Electronica is justly called the Oscar of media art. Since it was founded in 1987, with both the idea and the organization embedded in critical discourse each year, the Prix Ars Electronica can point to a considerable achievement: since the inception of this competition, artists from all over the world—from over 60 countries—have sent around 20,000 digital media projects to Linz; 200 artists have received Golden Nicas, money prizes and Honorary Mentions; a total of just over ATS 20 million in prize money (approximately 1.45 million EURO, 1.23 million US dollars) have been awarded to artists from all over the world. Over the course of these fifteen years, the works by the prize-winning artists, distinguished by the international juries, mirror developments in the field of digital media since 1987.

The Prix Ars Electronica is still conducted by the Austrian Broadcasting Corporation, Upper Austrian

Der Prix Ars Electronica wird in diesem Jahr zum fünfzehnten Mal vergeben. Das Festival Ars Electronica hat mit seiner Tradition seit 1979 weltweit eine einzigartige Kontinuität als Medienfestival erreicht. Der Wettbewerb Prix Ars Electronica hält durch seine fünfzehnmalige Verleihung ebenfalls eine weltweit einzigartige Position. Aus diesem Grunde wird der Prix Ars Electronica zurecht als Oscar der Medienkunst angesprochen. Seit seiner Gründung im Jahr 1987, von der Idee und der Durchführung her jeweils im kritischen Diskurs, kann der Prix Ars Electronica eine beträchtliche Bilanz aufweisen: Seit Bestehen dieses Wettbewerbs haben Künstlerinnen und Künstler aus aller Welt – aus über 60 Nationen – an die 20.000 digitale Medienprojekte nach Linz geschickt, 200 Künstlerinnen und Künstler haben Goldene Nicas, Geldpreise und Anerkennungen erhalten; insgesamt sind etwas über 20 Millionen ATS an Preisgeldern (ungefähr 1, 45 Millionen Euro, 1,23 Millionen US-Dollar) weltweit vergeben worden.

Über die 15 Jahre hinweg sind die von den internationalen Jurys ausgezeichneten Arbeiten der Preisträger des Prix Ars Electronica ein Spiegelbild der künstlerischen Entwicklung im digitalen Medienbereich seit 1987.

Träger des Prix Ars Electronica ist nach wie vor der Österreichische Rundfunk, Landesstudio Oberösterreich – in Zusammenarbeit mit dem Ars Electronica Center und dem O.K Centrum für Gegenwartskunst –, der als öffentlich-rechtliches Rundfunkunternehmen mit dieser Initiative über 15 Jahre hinweg bewusst seinen öffentlich-rechtlichen Auftrag als Rundfunkunternehmen zum Ausdruck bringt, der sich nicht nur auf die Wiedergabe, auf Information über das kulturelle Geschehen konzentriert, sondern bewusst Initiativen setzt, die in die Zukunft weisen.

Die Preisgelder in der Höhe von rund 20 Millionen ATS stammen allerdings nicht vom Österreichischen Rundfunk, sondern über alle 15 Jahre hinweg von Sponsoren. In diesem Jahr sind es Jet2Web Internet,

Regional Studio—in collaboration with the Ars Electronica Center and the O.K Center for Contemporary Art—which as a public broadcasting company has purposely expressed its public mission as a broadcasting corporation with this initiative over the course of fifteen years. This mission does not consist of solely conveying information about cultural events, but rather purposely takes initiatives that point toward the future. However, the money prizes amounting to roughly ATS 20 million have not come from the Austrian Broadcasting Corporation, but rather from sponsors throughout the entire fifteen years. This year, these are Jet2Web Internet, Datakom Austria, VOEST ALPINE Steel, the City of Linz, the federal province of Upper Austria and the Austrian Postal Bank (PSK). At this point, the sponsors, not only this year, but all their predecessors as well, are to be sincerely thanked on behalf of all the prize-winners.

Since 1987 the world has radically changed, not only geopolitically, but also and especially technologically. In 1987 there were over 10,000 host computers in operation, today there are roughly 350 million people on the Internet. The World Wide Web had not yet been invented in 1987, yet today Tim Berners-Lee, the man who started the World Wide Web, already speaks of further development, of a "Semantic Web", in which information is more likely to be understood by machines than people. And people, he says, will talk about the Web in the same way that they talk about paper.

If the effects of computer culture were not yet predictable in 1987, the year the Prix Ars Electronica was initiated, to the same extent that they are today, the basic principles of the development could still be pinpointed. "The computer is in the process of introducing another stage in the evolution of the human

jet2web Datakom, die VOEST ALPINE Stahl, die Stadt Linz, das Land Oberösterreich und die PSK. Den Sponsoren, nicht nur in diesem Jahr, sondern auch allen Vorgängern, ist an dieser Stelle im Namen der Preisträger der Dank auszusprechen.

Seit 1987 hat sich die Welt nicht nur geopolitisch, sondern vor allem auch technologisch radikal verändert. 1987 waren über 10.000 Host-Rechner in Betrieb, heute sind an die 350 Millionen Menschen im Internet. Das World Wide Web war 1987 noch nicht erfunden, heute spricht allerdings Tim Berners-Lee, der Mann, mit dem das World Wide Web begann, bereits von der Weiterentwicklung, er spricht vom „Semantic Web", in dem Information eher von Maschinen verstanden wird als von Menschen. Und die Menschen, so sagt er, werden über das Netz in der gleichen Weise reden, wie sie über Papier sprechen („People will talk about the Web in the same way that they talk about paper").

Wenn 1987, im Entstehungsjahr des Prix Ars Electronica, die Auswirkungen der Computerkultur noch nicht in dem Maße wie heute absehbar waren, so konnten dennoch die Grundzüge der Entwicklung geortet werden. „Der Computer ist dabei, eine weitere Stufe in der Evolution des Menschen einzuleiten", schrieb ich im Katalog zum Prix Ars Electronica 87. Heute sind die Entwicklungslinien bereits klarer auszumachen als damals. Computertechnologie, Gentechnologie und Nanotechnologie entwickeln sich mehr denn je zu den tragenden Säulen unseres jungen Jahrhunderts.

Frank Schirrmacher, Herausgeber der FAZ, fasst diese drei in einer Wissenschaftsdebatte sowie in einer Publikation unter dem Begriff „Darwin-AG" zusammen. Es wird im kommenden Diskurs weniger um die Frage des Verzichtes auf

being," I wrote in the Prix Ars Electronica catalogue in 1987. Today the lines of development are more clearly recognizable than they were then. Computer technology, gene technology, nanotechnology are developing more than ever before into the central pillars of our young century.

Frank Schirrmacher, publisher of the Frankfurter Allgemeine Zeitung, summarizes these three in a scientific debate and in a publication with the term "Darwin Ltd." In future discourse, it will be less a question of renouncing the new technologies, as Bill Joy suggests, but rather of finding the appropriate ethical guidelines in this triad in the future. One thing is becoming increasingly clear: in consequence of the development of this triad nanotechnology, biotechnology and computer technology, now in our century, evolution is placed in the hands of human beings for the first time. This is the dawn we face; what is concealed behind it is ultimately unknown virgin territory. With computer culture, as I wrote in this publication on the Prix Ars Electronica in 1987, a new stage of culture will be developed. At that time, as a comparison I chose Hermann Hesse's *Glass Bead Game* as the vision of a society, in which the glass bead game players have invented a universal language and method to express all intellectual and artistic values and find a common measure for them, in the way that the computer created a new system of language and thinking with the binary alphabet.

Today, fifteen years later, Douglas Adams, the brilliant thinker, who died this year in May in Santa Barbara at the age of barely 50, picks up Hermann Hesse's glass bead game again. In an article by Claudia Riedel in the weekly newspaper *Die Zeit*, Douglas Adams said that he had long been dreaming of doing something like the glass bead game with the technology of the

neue Technologien gehen, wie es Bill Joy vorschlägt, sondern vielmehr darum, in der Zukunft auch die entsprechenden ethischen Richtlinien in diesem Dreigestirn zu finden. Eines wird immer deutlicher: Aus der Entwicklung des Dreigestirns Nanotechnologie, Biotechnologie und Computertechnologie wird in unserem Jahrhundert die Evolution zum ersten Mal auch in die Hände des Menschen gelegt. Vor dieser Morgendämmerung stehen wir, dahinter verbirgt sich letztlich noch unbekanntes Neuland.

Mit der Computerkultur wird sich, so schrieb ich 1987 in dieser Publikation zum Prix Ars Electronica, eine neue Kulturstufe entwickeln. Als Vergleich wählte ich damals Hermann Hesses *Glasperlenspiel*, als Vision einer Gesellschaft, in der Glasperlenspieler eine universale Sprache und Methode erfunden haben, um alle geistigen und künstlerischen Werte und Begriffe auszudrücken und auf ein gemeinsames Maß zu bringen, in der Art und Weise, wie der Computer mit dem binären Alphabet ein neues Sprach- und Denksystem schafft.

Heute, 15 Jahre später, greift Douglas Adams, der geniale Denker, der im Mai dieses Jahres in Santa Barbara im Alter von knapp 50 Jahren verstorben ist, das Glasperlenspiel von Hermann Hesse auf. In einer Aufzeichnung von Claudia Riedel in der Wochenzeitung *Die Zeit* sagt Douglas Adams: „Ich träume schon lange davon, so etwas wie das Glasperlenspiel mit der Technologie des Internet zu realisieren. Ein Spiel, in dem nicht Spieler die Hauptrolle spielen wie beim Schach und anderen Kriegsspielen; bei dem es nicht um Punkte geht, sondern um Ideen, Musik, Informationen, Erfahrungen, Gedichte, Literatur."

Douglas Adams hat auch bereits seine Spieler parat – unter anderem wären es gewesen Johann Sebastian Bach, Danny Hillis, Richard Dawkins und seine Frau Lalla, Schauspieler Steven Fry, die Astrophysikerin und Science Fiction-Autorin Fiorella Terenzi, um nur einige von ihnen anzuführen.

Der Magister Ludi, sagt Douglas Adams, das wäre er

Internet. A game, where it is not the players who play the main role, as in chess or other war games; where it is not a matter of points, but rather of ideas, music, information, experience, poetry, literature.

And Douglas Adams already had players in mind—these would include Johann Sebastian Bach, Danny Hillis, Richard Dawkins and his wife Lalla, the actor Stephen Fry, the astrophysicist and science fiction author Fiorella Terenzi, to name only a few.

The Master Ludi, said Douglas Adams, would be himself. The dream of a social game with tiny supercomputers remained a dream. Douglas Adams died this year on May 11, but his ideas did not. They will continue on, like his trilogy *The Hitchhiker's Guide to the Galaxy*.

At the beginning of this century, Ars Electronica 2001 poses the question "Takeover—Who is doing the art of tomorrow?" At the beginning of this new century, Ars Electronica is taking stock, not so much of the past, but rather of the new lines of development, new systems of reference, the potential of net art, of cyberculture.

The history of the Prix Ars Electronica from 1987 to 2001 reflects the developments of media, art and, most of all, technology over this period. Whereas the Prix Ars Electronica was oriented to animation, computer graphics and music in the beginning, today the net and interactivity are in the foreground, but also the youngest offspring of the Prix Ars Electronica, u19 Cybergeneration—freestyle computing, which addresses computer kids, the young generation. This is the generation growing up with computer literacy right from the start.

With the Ars Electronica, since 1979 Linz has attained a specific profile for artists and scientists in the field of digital media. Starting from Linz, the existence of the

schließlich selbst. Der Traum eines Gesellschaftsspiels mit winzigen Supercomputern ist ein Traum geblieben. Douglas Adams starb am 11. Mai dieses Jahres, nicht aber seine Ideen. Die werden weiterreichen, wie seine Trilogie *Per Anhalter durch die Galaxis*.

Ars Electronica 2001 stellt zu Beginn des neuen Jahrhunderts die Frage „Takeover – Wer macht die Kunst von morgen?"

Ars Electronica will zu Beginn des neuen Jahrhunderts Bilanz legen, weniger über die Vergangenheit, eher über die neuen Entwicklungslinien, die neuen Referenzsysteme, über das Potenzial der Netzkunst, der Cyberkultur.

Die Geschichte des Prix Ars Electronica spiegelt von 1987 bis 2001 mediale, künstlerische, vor allem aber auch die technologische Entwicklung in dieser Zeit wider.

War zu Beginn der Prix Ars Electronica auf Animation, Computergrafik und Musik ausgerichtet, stehen heute das Netz und die Interaktivität im Vordergrund, aber auch der jüngste Spross des Prix Ars Electronica, u19 Cybergeneration – freestyle computing, der die Computerkids, die junge Generation anspricht. Jene Generation, die Computerliteracy von Kindheit an mitvollzogen haben.

Seit 1979 hat sich Linz mit dem Festival Ars Electronica ein spezifisches Profil für Künstler und Wissenschafter im digitalen Medienbereich erworben. Von Linz aus hat der Prix Ars Electronica mit seinem Bestehen dazu beigetragen, dass sich ein weltweites Netzwerk von Künstlern, Wissenschaftlern und Cyberartisten entwickelt, ein Netzwerk, das durch diesen zukunftsorientierten Preis der Ars Electronica mit Linz und damit mit Österreich verbunden bleibt. Mit den Jurymitgliedern, mit den Preisträgern und mit den Wettbewerbsteilnehmern hat sich eine Community zusammenge-

Prix Ars Electronica has contributed to the development of a worldwide network of artists, scientists and cyberartists, a network that remains affiliated with Linz and thus with Austria, because of this future-oriented prize of the Ars Electronica. With the jury members, with the award-winners and with all the participants in the Prix Ars Electronica, a community has emerged that comprises roughly 13,000 artists and scientists around the world, a large number of the "digerati" and the "evangelists" of the digital age.

Yet even though the hopes and expectations of the digital revolution have not been fulfilled in many areas, even though the stock markets signal drastic setbacks in the new economy, the continuation of this development already begun is not to be stopped. On the contrary: with the breakthrough of broadband networks, miniaturization, the spread of mobile computing, computer technology will change to a degree that still seems unimaginable today. Together with gene technology and nanotechnology, the next decades will be a period of tremendous transformation. The Prix Ars Electronica will continue to follow its goal of addressing artists and creative people in this radical development to probe the artistic creative potential of the digital future.

funden, die insgesamt an die 13.000 Künstler und Wissenschafter weltweit umfasst, eine große Zahl von „Digerati" und „Evangelisten" des digitalen Zeitalters. Auch wenn sich die Hoffnungen und Erwartungen des digitalen Aufbruchs in vielen Bereichen noch nicht erfüllt haben, auch wenn die Börsen in der New Economy drastische Rückschläge signalisieren, ist der Fortgang der eingeschlagenen Entwicklung nicht aufzuhalten. Im Gegenteil: Mit dem Durchbruch der Breitbandnetze, der Miniaturisierung, der Ausbreitung von Mobile Computing wird sich die Computertechnologie in einem Masse verändern, wie es heute noch undenkbar erscheint. Zusammen mit der Gentechnologie und der Nanotechnologie werden die nächsten Jahrzehnte die große Zeit des Wandels werden. Der Prix Ars Electronica wird auch weiterhin sein Ziel verfolgen, in dieser radikalen Entwicklung Künstler und kreative Menschen anzusprechen, um das künstlerische Gestaltungspotenzial der digitalen Zukunft auszuloten.

CYBERARTS 2001
Christine Schöpf

With the year 2001, the Prix Ars Electronica, conducted by the Austrian Broadcasting Corporation (ORF), Upper Austrian Regional Studio, in conjunction with the Ars Electronica Festival, enters its 15th year.

From the start, the Prix Ars Electronica has been conceived as an open platform for various disciplines in the field of digital media design at the intersection of technology, art, science and society, and over the course of the years, it has accordingly been repeatedly renewed, in order to be able to take the rapid developments in the realm of information technologies into account. Around 13,000 artists, scientists, researchers and representatives from the entertainment branch from all over the world have entered their works in the Prix Ars Electronica, thus formulating and commenting on the media developments of the past fifteen years. In this way, they have created a public forum for a highly productive discussion. At the same time, with their works they have laid the foundation for a new, highly qualified media-theoretical exploration and investigation of computer art / cyberart within the sphere of contemporary art.

In 2001 the Prix Ars Electronica 2001 was announced internationally for the areas of Net, Interactive Art, Digital Musics, Computer Animation and Visual Effects. In addition, there is also a competition for young people under the age of 19 in Austria, the category cybergeneration - u19 freestyle computing.

2,195 works from 62 countries were submitted to this year's 15th edition of the competition. The scope of the works ranges from contemporary digital sound creations, high-end special effects in film, interactive installations and robotic applications to sophisticated, future-oriented Internet applications from the fields of art, research, science and entertainment.

Mit dem Jahr 2001 geht der vom Österreichischen Rundfunk (ORF), Landesstudio Oberösterreich, im Rahmen des Festivals Ars Electronica organisierte Wettbewerb für Cyberkunst, der Prix Ars Electronica, in seine 15. Ausgabe. Von Beginn an war der Prix Ars Electronica als offene Plattform für die unterschiedlichen Disziplinen im Bereich digitaler Mediengestaltung an der Schnittstelle von Technologie, Kunst, Wissenschaft und Gesellschaft konzipiert und hat sich dementsprechend im Verlauf der Jahre immer wieder erneuert und so der rapiden Entwicklung im Bereich der Informationstechnologien Rechnung getragen.

Rund 13.000 Künstler, Wissenschafter, Forscher und Vertreter der Unterhaltungsbranche aus aller Welt haben mit ihren zum Prix Ars Electronica eingereichten Arbeiten die Medienentwicklung der vergangenen eineinhalb Jahrzehnte formuliert und kommentiert und so das öffentliche Forum einer höchst fruchtbaren Auseinandersetzung geschaffen. Gleichzeitig haben sie mit ihren Arbeiten das Fundament für eine neue qualifizierte medientheoretische Auseinandersetzung mit der Computer-/Cyberkunst innerhalb des Bereiches der zeitgenössischen Kunst gelegt.

2001 wurde der Prix Ars Electronica international in den Bereichen Net, Interaktive Kunst, Digital Musics, Computeranimation/Visual Effects ausgeschrieben, dazu kommt als Bewerb für Jugendliche unter 19 Jahren in Österreich die Sparte cybergeneration – u19 freestyle computing.

2.195 Werke aus 62 Ländern haben sich bei der diesjährigen 15. Ausgabe beworben. Die Bandbreite der Arbeiten geht von zeitgenössischen digitalen Klangkreationen über High-End-Filmspezialeffekte, interaktive Installationen und Robotikanwendungen bis zu

The entries unite up-to-date works by top research institutions and renowned special effects studios with individual art creations and thus demonstrate the enormous spectrum of digital media creativity today.
The section Net has been significantly expanded and placed on a broader basis in 2001 with a Golden Nica and two Awards of Distinction in each of the sub-categories Net Vision and Net Excellence. With the further development of this category, that was first opened in 1995, the Prix Ars Electronica takes into account the tempestuous development of this medium and the undiminished potential for creativity in this area.
The total prize money of the Prix Ars Electronica 2001 amounts to EURO 100,000 (US$ 89,700), sponsored by jet2web Internet. Other supporters, who have made the Prix Ars Electronica possible, are VOEST ALPINE Steel, jet2web Datakom, the city of Linz and the federal province of Upper Austria. The youth category cyber-generation u19 freestyle computing is supported by the Austrian Postal Bank (P.S.K.) and conducted by ORF Upper Austria together with the Austrian Culture Service (ÖKS).
In addition to the public awards presentation during the Ars Electronica Festival and live on the European satellite program 3sat, the public presentation of the distinguished works in exhibitions, artists' discussions and performances, this edition of *Cyberarts 2001* as a book, in addition to other media such as video, DVD and CD, goes beyond the immediate occasion of the competition and the festival to remain an enduring documentation for the future.

ausgeklügelten, zukunftsweisenden Internet-Applikationen aus dem Kunstbereich ebenso wie aus Forschung, Wissenschaft und Entertainment.
Die Einreichungen vereinen aktuelle Arbeiten von Top-Forschungseinrichtungen und renommierten Special-Effects-Studios mit individuellen Kunstkreationen und demonstrieren so das enorme Spektrum aktueller digitaler Mediengestaltung.
Wesentlich erweitert und auf eine breitere Basis gestellt wurde im Prix Ars Electronica 2001 die Sparte Net mit je einer Goldenen Nica und je zwei Auszeichnungen in den Subkategorien Net Vision und Net Excellence. Mit der Weiterentwicklung dieser erstmals 1995 ausgelobten Kategorie trägt der Prix Ars Electronica der stürmischen Entwicklung dieses Mediums und dem ungebrochenen Kreativpotenzial in diesem Bereich Rechnung.
Die Gesamtdotation des Prix Ars Electronica 2001 beträgt Euro 100.000 (US$ 89,700), gestiftet von jet2web Internet. Weitere Förderer, die die Realisierung des Prix Ars Electronica ermöglichen, sind die VOEST-ALPINE STAHL, jet2web Datakom, die Stadt Linz und das Land Oberösterreich. Die Jugendkategorie cybergeneration-u19-freestyle computing wird von der Österreichischen Postsparkasse gefördert und vom ORF-Oberösterreich gemeinsam mit dem ÖKS durchgeführt.
Abgesehen von der öffentlichen Preisverleihung beim Festival Ars Electronica und live im europäischen Satellitenprogramm 3 Sat sowie der öffentlichen Präsentation der ausgezeichneten Arbeiten in Ausstellungen, Künstlergesprächen und Performances ist diese Ausgabe der *Cyberarts 2001* als Buchedition über den aktuellen Anlass des Wettbewerbes und des Festivals hinaus neben anderen Medien wie Video, DVD und CD die bleibende Dokumentation für die Zukunft.

net vision
net excellence

R E S P E C T !
Tina Cassani / Bruno Beusch (TNC NETWORK)

"It never stops... everyone jams—and it pushes us all to become better ..." (*Bradley Grosh*)

And so it has come to this: the bubble burst, dotcoms drying up, lost in a haze of burn rate, the very Internet itself returning to a quaint network of chums, and we can at last happily return to the old order ... UH UH, WRONG SCRIPT! In fact, quite the opposite: As lumbering behemoths struggle with slippery notions of profitability, small, nimble units of advanced Net players have adapted the rules of competitive cooperation, using media literacy, techno savviness, and street smarts to leapfrog to the next plateau, Yamakasi-style.

In recognition of this proliferation of innovation and creativity in digital culture, the 2001 edition of the Prix Ars Electronica Internet category has been expanded, revamped, and thoroughly redesigned from the ground up. Where once there was one, now there are two discrete categories: Net Vision and Net Excellence. Vying for these honors are 22 projects, carefully culled from the cream of Net activities by a highly committed jury team. These projects reflect many of the current developments on the Net: Internet-capable console games, location-based i-mode services, straight investigation journalism, hyperactive coder and designer platforms, broadband entertainment—a full range of ideas and concerns that are implemented in a bewildering array of forms and formats.

The projects chosen, and detailed below, should be seen as a tribute to the vitality of Net culture, to all of those creative minds devising brand new modes of entertainment, communication, business, livelihoods and lifestyles, continually remaking the Net, far beyond any short-term hype, into the place to be. RESPECT!

„It never stops ... everyone jams ... and it pushes us all to become better ..."
(Bradley Grosh)

Es ist also so weit: Mit der Dotcom-Bubble ist auch gleich das ganze Internet geplatzt, und endlich können wir getrost zur alten Ordnung zurück kehren ... STOP, WRONG SCRIPT! Das Gegenteil ist natürlich der Fall! Der Netz-Jahrgang 2001 beweist, dass avancierte Net-Player ihre Media Literacy längst souverän mit den Vorzügen einer kooperativen Wettbewerbssituation kurzgeschlossen haben und im Yamakasi-Style das nächste Level erreicht haben.

Um die aktuellen Innovations- und Kreativitätsschübe zu erfassen, wurde dieses Jahr die Internetkategorie des Prix Ars Electronica von Grund auf neu konzipiert. Ein hoch motiviertes Juryteam wählte in den beiden neuen Kategorien (Net Vision und Net Excellence) insgesamt 22 Projekte aus, die viele der gegenwärtigen Entwicklungen im Netz widerspiegeln. Internetfähige Konsolengames, ortsbezogene „iMode"-Services, straighter Investigationsjournalismus, hyperaktive Coder- und Designer-Plattformen, Broadband-Entertainment – ein breites Spektrum von Ideen und Anliegen, umgesetzt in höchst diversen Formen und Formaten. Die folgenden Zeilen verstehen sich als Tribut an alle, die dazu beitragen, dass aus dem Netz immer wieder neue und überraschende Impulse kommen, die es – jenseits von kurzfristigen Hypes – zum Hang-out erster Wahl machen. RESPECT!

Yes Papa!

Was entsteht, wenn sich ein Haufen energiegeladener Creatives, deren Referenzen zwischen Internet, Coding, Games, Anime, Hip Hop und Clubculture oszillieren, im Norden Frankreichs ein Studio einrichtet und sich Zeit und alle Frei-

Yes Papa!

What happens when a bunch of energy-charged creatives, whose references oscillate between the Internet, coding, games, anime, hiphop and club culture, set up a studio in the north of France and take every liberty to produce exactly what they find is the most fun? The result is a ground-breaking online game that pushes the envelope of sophisticated flash programming into realms unimagined. Unanimously, and very enthusiastically, the jury has nominated *Banja* for the Golden Nica in the Net Vision category. For two years, Team cHmAn has been working with unconditional dedication on this game, which is named after one of its protagonists, a cool Rasta with bound dreadlocks. Unlike most other games which regurgitate the Tomb Raider formula ad nauseum, Team cHmAn actually developed their own ideas. Players are invited to take part in the savoir-vivre of the inhabitants of an island paradise, Itland. Living by the motto "Become a Banja Star and get online glory!" players have to collect as many points as possible (so-called Yes Papas), to gain access to new content—which then enhances their reputation within the Banja community. Along the way, they gradually discover the many game modules, the Itland cinema, the elaborate communication tools that are completely integrated in the game universe, or special music events, like a beach party with the French DJ producer Laurent Garnier—all implemented with that peculiar cHmAn-ian charm and a love of detail. It's no coincidence that Team cHmAn have made a name for themselves in dealing with up-to-date vector-based animation technologies, as in the perfect use of narration techniques, or by programming one of the very first pure Flash chat environments, in which the Gallic crew joined forces with their architect friends, the "Digital Koboyz." Presented in an early phase as *the* discovery at the Electrolobby 2000 at the Ars Electronica Festival, *Banja* is now well on the way to becoming a killer application and, in the jury's view, to opening up completely new perspectives in web-based entertainment.

Wanna play with me?

The second nomination in the category Net Vision is also a game: *Phantasy Star Online*. The first massive

heiten nimmt, um genau das zu produzieren, was ihnen selber am meisten Spaß macht? Ein wegweisendes Online-Game, das die Möglichkeiten raffinierter Flash-Programmierung in bisher unerreichter Weise ausreizt und vorantreibt. Einstimmig und mit Begeisterung nominierte die Jury *Banja* für die Goldene Nica in der Kategorie Net Vision. Seit zwei Jahren arbeitet Team cHmAn mit bedingungslosem Engagement am Spiel, das nach seinem Protagonisten benannt ist, einem sympathischen Rasta mit hoch gesteckten Dreads. Im Unterschied zu vielen anderen Games, die sich zum x-ten Mal der Tomb-Raider-Schablone bedienen oder bei denen man am Ende eines Levels den „Boss" killen muss, entwickelt Team cHmAn lieber eigene Ideen. Und so werden die Spieler eingeladen, am Savoir-Vivre der Bewohner der paradiesischen Insel Itland teilzuhaben. Nach dem Motto „Become a Banja Star and get online glory!" muss man möglichst viele Punkte (so genannte Yes Papas) sammeln, um exklusiven Zugang zu neuem Content zu erhalten – was einem innerhalb der Banja-Community denn auch zu Ansehen verhilft. Dabei entdeckt man nach und nach die zahlreichen Game-Module, das Itland-Kino, die ausgefeilten, komplett ins Spiel-Universum integrierten Kommunikationstools oder spezielle Music-Events wie etwa eine Beach Party mit dem französischen DJ-Produzenten Laurent Garnier – alles mit cHmAnschem Charme und großer Liebe zum Detail umgesetzt. Nicht umsonst hat sich Team cHmAn im Umgang mit aktuellen vektorbasierten Animationstechnologien einen Namen gemacht, so zum Beispiel durch den perfekten Einsatz von Narrationstechniken oder durch die Programmierung eines der allerersten reinen Flash-Chat-Environments, für das die Frenchies mit ihren Architekten-Freunden, den „Digital Koboyz", zusammengespannt haben. Bereits im Frühstadium als *die* Entdeckung in der Electrolobby 2000 am Ars Electronica Festival präsentiert, ist *Banja* im Mai 2001 auf bestem Weg zur Killer-Application und eröffnet in den Augen der Jury dem webbasierten Entertainment völlig neue Perspektiven.

Wanna Play With Me?

Die zweite Nominierung in der Kategorie Net Vision ist ebenfalls ein Spiel: *Phantasy Star Online*. Das erste massive Multiplayer-Role-Playing-Game für Konsole (Sega Dreamcast) bestätigt den Trend zur Konvergenz von Internet und Game-Entertainment (sichtbar u. a. in der angekündigten Integration von

multi-player role-playing game for consoles (Sega Dreamcast) affirms a trend toward the convergence of the Internet and game entertainment (further confirmed in the announcement that Real and Flash players will be integrated in the PlayStation2 console). *Phantasy Star Online* also illustrates how the gaming world is picking up impulses from the Net: based on concepts of collaboration and community, the dimension of networked playing is, indeed, looming large. The global implementation of this idea has been slowed by technological bottlenecks, allowing it to be played only on a local level. A language barrier exists as well. But by integrating innovative communication modules, Yuji Naka's Sonic Team has overcome these obstacles. Gamers can interact with other players around the world by using either a set of dialogue sequences coupled with a real-time translation, or by an editable, icon-based language system. And *Phantasy Star Online* is particularly striking because of its luminous, other-worldly graphical surface, utilizing themes from high tech, science fiction and fantasy worlds, where entertainment merges into art. You'll definitely be hooked by the time you have to feed your "MAG"—a kind of virtual pet that assists you in tricky situations and whose well-being is closely linked with the development of your own character.

Game formats of the most diverse types are being used with much greater frequency—as well as being a major trend in this year's competition—to transport contents, ideas and messages effectively. *Austropolis*, a political simulation game, uses typical elements of the Net (agents and avatars) to build up a form of virtual democracy, whereas *Fuckedcompany* captures the essence of the web and the dot-com collapse using a game, in which you can bet on Internet companies (or their ruin). With rumors of collapse and horror scenarios from US Internet companies, Philip Kaplan has succeeded in establishing an insider information portal—*Anonymity is king, rumor is truth*—which is closely watched by savvy business people. Again and again, the independent New Yorker GameLab, centered around Eric Zimmerman (the mastermind behind the already legendary *Sissy Fight*), succeeds in gaining new audiences for games with novel approaches. *Netbabyworld*, a net-based game platform that has

Real- und Flash-Player in die PlayStation2-Konsole). Zudem illustriert *Phantasy Star Online*, wie die Gaming-Welt zurzeit Impulse aus dem Netz aufnimmt: Ausgehend von Aspekten wie Kollaboration und Community gewinnt die Dimension vernetzten Spielens zunehmend an Bedeutung. Die Umsetzung dieses Vorhabens scheiterte bislang an verschiedenen technologischen Problemen, weshalb meistens nur auf einem lokalen, nicht aber internationalen Level gespielt werden konnte. Dazu kam die Sprachbarriere. Yuji Nakas Sonic Team setzt dem durch die Integration innovativer Kommunikationsmodule ein Ende. Die Gamer können mit Mitspielern rund um die Welt interagieren, indem sie entweder ein mit Echtzeit-Übersetzung gekoppeltes Set aus Dialogsequenzen oder ein editierbares, iconbasiertes Sprach-System nutzen. *Phantasy Star Online* besticht darüber hinaus durch seine magisch vibrierende grafische Oberfläche mit Themen aus Hightech-, Science-Fiction- und Fantasywelten, wo die Grenzen zwischen Kunst und Unterhaltung aufgehoben scheinen. Zum Addict wird man spätestens dann, wenn es darum geht, seinen „MAG" zu füttern – eine Art Virtual Pet, das einem in heiklen Situationen zur Seite steht und mit dessen Wohlergehen die Entwicklung des eigenen Characters eng verbunden ist.

Game-Formate verschiedenster Ausprägung – das ist eine der deutlichen Tendenzen im diesjährigen Wettbewerb – werden immer häufiger eingesetzt, um Inhalte, Ideen und Messages effektiv zu transportieren. *Austropolis*, ein politisches Simulationsspiel, nutzt typische Netzelemente (Agenten und Avatars), um eine Form von virtueller Demokratie aufzubauen, während *Fuckedcompany* anhand eines Spiels, in dem man auf Internet-Firmen (bzw. deren Untergang) wetten kann, die Essenz des Web und des Dot-Com-Kollapses einfängt. *Anonymity is king, rumor is truth*. Philip Kaplan ist es gelungen, mit Untergangsgerüchten und Horrorszenarien von US-Internet-Firmen ein Insider-Informationsportal aufzubauen, das man sogar in der Businesswelt scharf im Auge behält. Dem unabhängigen New-Yorker GameLab rund um Eric Zimmerman (dem Mastermind hinter dem schon legendären *Sissy Fight*) gelingt es mit erfrischenden Spielansätzen immer wieder,

attained cult status, is distinguished for the style-setting pioneering character of its work. Finally, *Micromusic* is a digital lifestyle platform for screen kids, joystick jockeys and audio nerds, where the world revolves around game sounds, and lives by the motto, "Low-Tech Music for High-Tech People."

Redesigning the Internet Category

In late 2000, TNC Network accepted the challenge of a total redesign of the Internet category of the Prix Ars Electronica. The mission was to open up the competition category to the full spectrum of current developments on the net, with particular regard to those scenes and sectors previously unrepresented. With over 700 entries, a high number of them first-timers, even the most optimistic expectations were exceeded in the first year. Certainly the most apparent change is the splitting of the net category into two different categories. On the one hand, the Internet has become an established part of our everyday lives, while on the other hand it continues to flourish as a powerful motor for innovation. The two Golden Nicas offer the opportunity to honor both of these aspects equally. Net Excellence distinguishes projects that are compelling because of the originality of their concept, their content, and their creative use of state-of-the-art applications. In contrast to this, the second Golden Nica, Net Vision, distinguishes projects that are striking in their anticipative and innovative way of seeing the potential of the online medium. One Golden Nica and two Awards of Distinction are awarded in each category for outstanding cultural impact on the Internet, as well as 16 Honorary Mentions for the combined categories. Parallel to the redefinition of the category, a nominating committee of internationally recognized Internet professionals and authorities was convened for the first time. The nineteen members of the Nominating Committee made a preselection from the entries in the fields drawing on a wide spectrum of content and format (from gaming, music, animation, film, digital lifestyle, fashion, design and sport, to screen design, net art, cultural heritage, distributed knowledge, literature, urbanism and museums, all the way to e-government, NGOs, digital divide, communities, news services, streaming media, e-commerce, research, P2P

Games einem neuen Publikum nahe zu bringen. *Netbabyworld*, eine der längst kultverdächtigen Game-Plattformen im Netz, wurde für den stilbildenden Pioniercharakter ihrer Arbeit ausgezeichnet. *Micromusic* schließlich ist eine digitale Lifestyle-Plattform für Screen-Kids, Joystick-Lovers und Audio-Nerds, auf der sich nach dem Motto „Low-Tech Music for High-Tech People" alles um Game-Sounds dreht.

Das Redesign der Internetkategorie

Ende 2000 hat TNC Network den Challenge angenommen, das Konzept für das Neudesign der Internetkategorie des Prix Ars Electronica zu entwickeln. Es ging darum, die Wettbewerbskategorie der gesamten Bandbreite gegenwärtiger Entwicklungen im Netz zu öffnen und vor allem auch jene Szenen und Sektoren anzusprechen, die bisher nicht vertreten waren. Mit insgesamt rund 700 Einreichungen und einem hohen Anteil an Ersteinreichern wurden bereits im ersten Jahr selbst die optimistischsten Erwartungen übertroffen. Die auffälligste Neuerung ist sicher die Verdoppelung der bisherigen Netzkategorie. Das Internet hat sich in unserem Alltag etabliert und funktioniert weiterhin als massiver Innovationsmotor. Die zwei neuen Kategorien erlauben es, diese beiden Aspekte gleichwertig zu honorieren. Net Vision zeichnet Projekte aus, die durch antizipativen, innovativen Umgang mit dem Online-Medium überraschen. Im Unterschied dazu zeichnet Net Excellence Sites aus, die durch inhaltliche Originalität und kreativen Umgang mit State-of-the-Art-Anwendungen bestechen. In jeder der beiden Kategorien werden neu eine Goldene Nica und zwei Auszeichnungen für High Cultural Impact im Internet vergeben, sowie für beide Kategorien zusammen bis zu 16 Anerkennungen. Parallel zur Neudefinierung wurde erstmals ein weltweites Netz von Experten und Internetprofessionals mobilisiert. Die neunzehn Mitglieder des Nominating Committee trafen in den inhaltlich jetzt weit geöffneten Bereichen (von Gaming, Musik, Animation, Film, Digital Lifestyle, Fashion, Design und Sport über Screendesign, Net Art, Cultural Heritage, Distributed Knowledge, Literatur, Urbanismus und Museen bis hin zu E-Government, NGOs, Digital Divide, Communities, News Services, Streaming Media, E-Commerce, Research, P2P und Wireless Internet) eine Vorauswahl aus den Einreichungen. Zusätzlich nominierten sie unabhängig von den eingereichten Projekten drei Sites, die in ihrem jeweiligen Spezial-

and wireless Internet). Beyond the submitted projects, each Committee member additionally nominated three sites that set new benchmarks in their respective special fields. This year our panel, experts versed in the scene (such as Gnutella developer Gene Kan; head of the international conference "Museums and the Web", Jennifer Trant; the flash master Peter van den Wyngaert; director of the UNESCO department for the information society, Philippe Quéau; game designer Simon Carless; digital divide specialist Shahidul Alam - to name only a few), guaranteed that projects with a high standard of quality were preselected. The Nominating Committee's shortlist of 114 projects was subsequently presented to the jury for final evaluation.

Are U Free Now?

Another tendency in the net category this year is illustrated by projects, in which the community—as one of the historical elements of the Internet—is recontextualized in the local/global framework
The third nomination in the category Net Vision is a project, in which the old principle of the newsgroup is taken to a deeper level through the platform of mobile technology. *ImaHima*—which roughly means "are you free now?"—is a location-based community service, which enables sending email messages via an Internet cell phone to a group of recipients simultaneously. *ImaHima*—a kind of party-line that makes it easy to locate and contact all your friends who are near-by at the moment—is directly tailored to the local needs and circumstances in Japan, where social networking is of prime value. The service was developed by Neeraj Jhanji from India for the popular Japanese i-mode standard (mobile Internet), and enables adapting private channels to one's own preferences. It has achieved huge popularity among the young urban population of Japan through guerilla marketing and word of mouth. The jury expressly distinguished *ImaHima* as a pioneering project in the context of the current development of the Internet, away from the desktop to pervasive networking.
Also working in the local/global context, but in a radically different field, is *Bytes for All* from Bangladesh. The site—a regional information node for South Asia—informs a worldwide audience about the consequences

gebiet frische Signale setzen. Dieses Jahr garantierten Szenekenner wie etwa der Gnutella-Entwickler Gene Kan, die Leiterin der internationalen Konferenz „Museums and the Web", Jennifer Trant, der Flash-Master Peter van den Wyngaert, der Direktor der UNESCO-Abteilung für die Informationsgesellschaft, Philippe Quéau, der Game-Designer Simon Carless, der Digital-Divide-Spezialist Shahidul Alam – um nur ein paar zu nennen –, dass Projekte mit hohem Qualitätslevel vorselektiert wurden. Die Shortlist mit den vom Nominating Committee ausgewählten 114 Projekten wurde der Jury zur abschließenden Bewertung vorgelegt.

Are U Free Now?

Eine weitere Tendenz in der diesjährigen Netzkategorie illustrieren Projekte, in denen die Community – als einer der historischen Aspekte des Internet – im Spannungsfeld lokal/global neu interpretiert wird. Die dritte Nominierung in der Kategorie Net Vision ist ein Projekt, in dem das alte Prinzip der Newsgroup im Kontext aktueller Mobiltechnologie weitergedacht wird. *ImaHima* – was so viel heißt wie „are you free now?" – ist ein ortsbezogener Community-Service, der es erlaubt, über ein Internet-Handy Emails gleichzeitig an eine Gruppe von Empfängern zu verschicken. *ImaHima* – eine Art Party-Line, dank der es ab sofort ein Kinderspiel ist, alle Freunde, die sich gerade in der Nähe aufhalten, zu orten und zu kontaktieren – ist direkt zugeschnitten auf lokale Bedürfnisse und Gegebenheiten in Japan, wo bekanntlich nichts so wichtig ist wie Social Networking. Der Service wurde vom Inder Neeraj Jhanji für den beliebten japanischen „iMode"-Standard (mobiles Internet) entwickelt und brachte es dank Guerilla-Marketing und Word of Mouth zu großer Popularität in der jungen urbanen Bevölkerung Japans, nicht zuletzt wegen der Möglichkeit, private Channels eigenen Vorlieben anzupassen. Die Jury hat *ImaHima* ausdrücklich als Pionier-Projekt im Kontext der gegenwärtigen Entwicklung des Internet weg vom Desktop zur ubiquitären Nutzung ausgezeichnet. Im Spannungsfeld lokal/global bewegt sich, in einem radikal anderen Bereich, *Bytes for All* aus Bangladesh. Die Site – ein regionaler Informationsknoten für South Asia – klärt ein welt-

of the digital divide and demonstrates, together with NGOs and local associations, what can actually be achieved thanks to widespread networking. Fighting against corruption and for independent media is the aim of *Tehelka*. The Indian online magazine rocked the foundations of the Indian government when it was able to prove through a sting action that leading party representatives were accepting bribes. The degree to which this investigative journalism has upset the powers that be is indicated by the serious threats against the founder Tarun J. Tejpal. A different "divide," this time in the USA, is the subject of *360degrees*. In a web documentary, the authors unite people immediately affected in a frank dialogue about crowded American prisons and the presence of the death sentence in a democratic society. With quiz-like tests, they reveal deep-rooted prejudices in a way that is perceptive, and never moralizing. *Rhizome* and the *Walker Art Center* hardly need to be introduced here. Starting off as a typical grassroots phenomenon, and with the dedication of the international scene, *Rhizome* has grown into an active, much used community resource for media art and theory. Whereas the *Walker Art Center* has long demonstrated how a cultural institution can deal with the net and play an important role in promoting new art forms in the process.

Link Dealer

Is it more interesting to propagate playful, interactive elements that turn exploring a web site into an individualized experience, or is it more valuable to create a highly functional site that will lead the user quickly and efficiently through the information offered? This old controversy is currently undergoing a revival in the discussion of Flash software. As a *Slashdot* user succinctly put it: "Should Flash be blamed for people not having a clue how to use it? Nope. Don't shoot the tool, shoot the people who use it when they shouldn't." The jury took a pragmatic course here: good interface design has to do with both. And thus the highly generalized statement by the usability guru Jakob Nielson, that flash is 99 percent bad, will be ever countered with the response from Joshua Davis: "What Mr. Jakob Nielsen promotes is such a bland

weites Publikum über die Folgen des Digital Divide auf und führt vor, was zusammen mit NGOs und lokalen Vereinigungen dank breiter Vernetzung konkret erreicht werden kann. Die Bekämpfung der Korruption und den Einsatz für unabhängige Medien hat sich *Tehelka* aufs Banner geschrieben. Das indische Onlinemagazin hat die Fundamente der indischen Regierung erschüttert, als dank einer Sting-Aktion führenden Parteivertretern die Annahme von Bestechungsgeldern nachgewiesen werden konnte. Wie ungern dieser Investigationsjournalismus gesehen wird, davon zeugen die massiven Drohungen, denen der Gründer Tarun J. Tejpal ausgesetzt ist. Mit einem anderen „Divide", diesmal in den USA, befasst sich *360degrees*. In einem Web-Documentary vereinen die Autoren Direktbetroffene in einem produktiven Dialog über die überfüllten amerikanischen Gefängnisse und die Todesstrafe in einer demokratischen Gesellschaft und enthüllen anhand von quizartigen Tests auf clevere, nie moralisierende Art tiefsitzende Vorurteile. Kaum vorgestellt werden müssen hier *Rhizome* und das *Walker Art Center*. Als typisches Grassroot-Phänomen entstanden, wuchs *Rhizome* dank des Engagements der internationalen Szene zu einer aktiven, vielgenutzten Community-Ressource für Medienkunst und -theorie, während das Walker Art Center schon seit langem exemplarisch vorführt, wie eine Kulturinstitution mit dem Netz umgehen und dabei eine wichtige Rolle in der Promotion neuer Kunstformen spielen kann.

Link Dealer

Ist es wichtiger, spielerische, interaktive Elemente, die das Erforschen einer Website zu einem individualisierten Erlebnis werden lassen, oder aber Funktionalität und Usability, die einen schnell und effizient durch das Informationsangebot führen, zu privilegieren? Der alte Streit erlebt gegenwärtig durch die Diskussion um die Flash-Software ein Revival. Ein *Slashdot*-User hat ihn so auf den Punkt gebracht: „Should Flash be blamed for people not having a clue how to use it? Nope. Don't shoot the tool, shoot the people who use it when they shouldn't." Die Jury ging hier pragmatisch vor: Gutes Interface-Design hat mit beidem zu tun. Und so wird das pauschalisierende Statement des Usability-Gurus Jakob Nielson, wonach Flash zu 99 Prozent schlecht sei, vor allem in Zusammenhang mit der Antwort von Joshua Davis in die Geschichte eingehen: „What Mr. Jakob Nielsen promotes is such a bland form of standards – that he

form of standards—that he deters this community and society from evolving."

Joshua Davis works as Senior Design Technologist at New York agency Kioken, well known for injecting experimental design in commercial web sites. In his spare time, Joshua Davis tinkers around with *PrayStation*, a showcase for experimental interface design, which was unanimously nominated by the jury for the Golden Nica in the second new category, Net Excellence. With admirable continuity, Joshua pursues the goal of implementing a creative use of technology and design daily, in small modules with *PrayStation*. This one-man research & development web site covers a broad spectrum of action script hacks and Flash pieces. What they have in common is that they deviate from conventional rules, are not easily categorized, and unceasingly explore new paths with their playful approach. Joshua subjects *PrayStation* to a constant process of change. The project started years ago as an homage to video games. Later, he simply wanted to show what a single, independent developer is capable of and thus started posting all his own developments on the site the same day. When he noticed that many designers around the world were following his working process, he refined the calendar-like interface and decided to let the scene in closer to the process by releasing his developments to download as open source. With this, *PrayStation* became one of the most interesting distance-learning communities in the field of web design—true to the motto "Give back to the community what the community has given me". This aspect of passing on skills and experience—far more than just an excellent way of dealing with state-of-the-art technology—is what makes *PrayStation* one of the very few projects that has succeeded in bringing together different scenes (coders, art, design). The influential and "smart" e-zine *Kaliber10000* is also devoted to exchange within the worldwide designer community. Like the ambitious Flash platform *Ultrashock*, moderated by protagonists from the scene, *K10k* belongs to the hyperactive link and info dealers, who contribute on a daily basis, with fresh ways of motivating thousands of creatives around the world to exchange information, and thus take an active part in the permanent state of change that is the medium.

deters this community and society from evolving." Joshua Davis arbeitet als Senior Design Technologist in der New-Yorker Agentur Kioken, die bekannt dafür ist, experimentelles Design auch in kommerziellen Websites einzusetzen. In seiner Freizeit tüftelt er an *PrayStation*, einem Showcase für experimentelles Interface Design, die von der Jury einstimmig für die Goldene Nica in der zweiten neuen Kategorie, Net Excellence, nominiert wurde. Mit faszinierender Kontinuität verfolgt Joshua mit *PrayStation* das Ziel, den kreativen Umgang mit Technologie und Design in täglichen, kleinen Modulen zu implementieren. Die Ein-Mann-Research&Development-Website umfasst ein breites Spektrum an Actionscript-Hacks und Flash-Pieces. Gemeinsam ist ihnen, dass sie von herkömmlichen Regeln abweichen, sich nicht leicht einordnen lassen und mit ihrem spielerischen Nicht-Mainstream-Approach unermüdlich neue Wege erforschen. Joshua unterzieht *PrayStation* einem ständigen Veränderungsprozess. Begonnen hat das Projekt vor Jahren als eine Hommage an Videogames. Später wollte er ganz einfach zeigen, wozu ein einzelner, unabhängiger Developer fähig ist, und begann deshalb, alle seine Entwicklungen am gleichen Tag auf seiner Site zu posten. Als er feststellte, dass viele Designer rund um die Welt seinen Arbeitsprozess mitverfolgten, verfeinerte er das kalenderartige Interface und beschloss, die Szene näher an den Prozess herankommen zu lassen, indem er seine Entwicklungen als Open Source zum Download freigab. Damit avancierte *PrayStation* zu einer der interessantesten Distance-Learning-Communities im Bereich Webdesign – getreu dem Motto „Give back to the community what the community has given me". Dieser Aspekt des Weitergebens von Skills und Erfahrungen – weit mehr als nur ein exzellenter Umgang mit State-of-the-Art-Technologie – macht *PrayStation* zu einem der ganz wenigen Projekte, denen es gelingt, verschiedene Szenen (Coder, Kunst, Design) zu föderieren. Dem Austausch innerhalb der weltweiten Designer-Community hat sich auch das einflussreiche, „smarte" E-zine *Kaliber10000* verschrieben. *K10k* gehört – ähnlich wie die ambitionierte, von Szeneprotagonisten moderierte Flash-Plattform *Ultrashock* – zu jenen

Creative Nodes

Networking the independent scene in the field of streaming is the mission of *Boombox*, a model for a platform that enables its cultural activities through commercial commissions (such as streaming the TV show *Big Brother*). The project is also a good example of the beneficial mutual influence of club and net culture, which is in the broader context of where the second nomination in the category Net Excellence is situated. This nomination goes to the web site of one of the most innovative record labels in the electronic music scene, *Warp Records*. The site is striking because of its style-setting design, the seamless integration of audio and video, and the visceral proximity of the web presence to the product, the music that the label produces. In other words: the *Warp* attitude does not stop at the music. In the form of a micro portal, the site functions as a node in a scene of related labels, projects, designers, graphics artists, and artists (such as Rephlex, Designers Republic etc.), who have come to the forefront in recent years because of their significant contribution to a global electronic culture. The *Warp Records* site was conceived by Kleber.Net, a collective from Sheffield, which developed, among other things, an online shopping system, which makes it possible for small labels to distribute their products with low overhead costs. *Warp* was one of the first independent labels to focus on a strong web presence and demonstrated how efficiently the net can be used by a small label to distribute its music and thus ultimately maintain its independence.

Time Machine

When the whole Prix jury met on the last day for a group photo in an icy church on the Castle Hill in Linz, a rudimentary plan on a wooden panel was passed around, tracing the development of the church over the past centuries. But, quaint as it was, this wooden panel made a poor showing to those, who had seen only a few hours earlier how much more playfully something like this can be realized today. *Manhattan Timeformations*, nominated in the category Net Excellence, demonstrates the significant potential of an intelligent connection between information and architecture—and realizes "information architecture" in the

hyperaktiven Link- und Info-Dealern, die Tag für Tag auf erfrischende Weise dazu beitragen, weltweit Tausende von Creatives zum gegenseitigen Austausch zu motivieren – und die damit aktiv an der permanenten Weiterentwicklung des Mediums mitwirken.

Creative Nodes

An der Vernetzung der unabhängigen Szene im Streaming-Bereich arbeitet Boombox, ein Modell für eine Plattform, die sich ihre kulturellen Aktivitäten über kommerzielle Aufträge (wie etwa das Streaming der TV-Show *Big Brother*) ermöglicht. Das Projekt ist zudem ein gutes Beispiel für die gegenseitige fruchtbare Beeinflussung von Club- und Netzkultur, dem weiteren Kontext, in dem die zweite Nominierung in der Kategorie Net Excellence angesiedelt ist. Sie geht an die Website eines der innovativsten Plattenlabels der elektronischen Musikszene, *Warp Records*. Die Site besticht durch ihr stilbildendes Design, durch die nahtlose Einbindung von Audio und Video und durch die visuelle Nähe des Webauftritts zum Produkt, der Musik, die das Label herausgibt. In anderen Worten: Die *Warp*-Attitude macht nicht bei der Musik Halt. In Form eines Micro-Portals funktioniert die Site als Knoten in einer Szene verwandter Label, Projekte, Designer, Grafiker und Künstler (wie etwa Rephlex, Designers Republic etc.), die sich in den vergangenen Jahren durch ihren bedeutenden Beitrag zur globalen elektronischen Kultur hervorgetan haben. Konzipiert wurde die Warp Records Site von Kleber.Net, einem Kollektiv aus Sheffield, das u. a. ein Online-Shoppingsystem entwickelt hat, das es kleinen Labels ohne großen finanziellen Aufwand ermöglicht, ihre Produkte übers Netz zu vertreiben. *Warp* war auch eines der ersten unabhängigen Labels, das auf eine starke Webpräsenz setzte und demonstrierte, wie effizient das Netz für ein unabhängiges Label zum Vertrieb seiner Musik und damit letztlich zur Wahrung seiner Eigenständigkeit genutzt werden kann.

Time Machine

Als sich die gesamte Prix-Jury am letzten Tag zum offiziellen Fototermin in einer eisigen Kirche auf dem Linzer Schlossberg versammelte, wurde auf einer Holztafel ein rudimentärer Plan herumgereicht, anhand dessen man die Entwicklung der Kirche in den vergangenen Jahrhunderten nachvollziehen sollte. Nun, um ehrlich zu sein, die Holztafel hatte einen schweren Stand ... wenn man ein paar Stunden

true sense of the word. Manhattan Timeformations intuitively allows an insight into the processes that have taken place over the past 370 years in Lower Manhattan. Using multi-layering, the dynamic relationships among the diverse factors of urban development are visualized. The time machine is turned to fast forward in *Chi-Chian*. This online science fiction series takes place in Manhattan in the year 3000 and makes use of the opportunity to reach a wide audience through the distribution channel of the Internet—similar to a completely different production in the field of web fiction, the animation series CUB by Steve Whitehouse. Finally, with his funky interactive music clip DMG:I.O* vs R3:DEV*, Bradley Grosh (aka Gmunk) not only places his faith in the broadband future, he also supplies the high-speed slogan for the 2001 edition of the Internet competition: "And you look at their work, nod your head; you're stoked … inspired—and you get the idea … it never stops … everyone jams … and there's about 20 other artists whom I haven't mentioned who blow my mind as well; I mean, everyone here totally stokes each other, and it pushes us all to become better …" . And it is in this spirit, that we invite you to join the party, and share the fun with the projects of the Prix Ars Electronica 2001!

(Thanks to our jury colleagues Pete Barr-Watson, Tanja Diezmann, Solveig Godeluck and Machiko Kusahara, to Thomas Riha for his invaluable support, and to TNC Network's Kim Danders for editing the English text)

zuvor gesehen hatte, wie viel spielerischer so etwas heute realisiert werden kann. *Manhattan Timeformations*, nominiert in der Kategorie Net Excellence, führt das bedeutende Potenzial einer intelligenten Verbindung von Information und Architektur vor – und realisiert im wahrsten Sinne des Wortes „Information Architecture". *Manhattan Timeformations* verschafft auf intuitive Weise Einblick in die Prozesse, die über die vergangenen 370 Jahre in Lower Manhattan stattfanden. Anhand von Multi-Layering werden die dynamischen Beziehungen zwischen den diversen Faktoren der urbanen Entwicklung visualisiert. Die Zeitmaschine weit nach vorne gedreht hat hingegen *Chi-Chian*. Die Online-Science-Fiction-Serie spielt im Manhattan des Jahres 3000 und nutzt – ähnlich wie eine völlig andere Produktion im Bereich Webfiction, die Animationsserie *CUB* von Steve Whitehouse – die Chance, via den Distributionskanal Internet ein breites Publikum zu erreichen. Bradley Grosh (aka Gmunk) schließlich setzt mit seinem funkigen interaktiven Musikclip *DMG:I.O* vs R3:DEV** nicht nur radikal auf die Breitbandzukunft, er liefert auch die High-Speed-Losung für den Netzjahrgang 2001: „And you look at their work, nod your head; you're stoked … inspired … and you get the idea … it never stops … everyone jams … and there's about 20 other artists whom I haven't mentioned who blow my mind as well; I mean, everyone here totally stokes each other, and it pushes us all to become better …". In diesem Sinn wünschen wir viel Spaß mit den Projekten des Prix Ars Electronica 2001!

(thx an unsere Jurykollegen Pete Barr-Watson, Tanja Diezmann, Solveig Godeluck und Machiko Kusahara sowie an Thomas Riha für seine wertvolle Unterstützung).

PRIX ARS
ELECTRONICA
CATEGORY
NET VISION
NET EXCELLENCE
SUBFIELDS AND
NOMINATING
EXPERTS

ARTS & CULTURE
encompasses the fields
web design, screen design; expert: Taketo Oguchi
net art; *expert: Mark Tribe*
cultural heritage, archives, reference, distributed
knowledge; *expert: Andrea Bandelli*
museums, galleries; *expert: Jennifer Trant*
literature: William Gibson
urbanism, architecture; *expert: Anthony Townsend*

POLITICS
encompasses the fields
cyber democracy, e-government, citizen services;
expert: Philippe Quéau
public campaigning, public opinion, activism,
hacktivism, NGOs, non-profit
organizations; *expert: Kunda Dixit*

SOCIETY
encompasses the fields
education, learning, virtual campus, digital divide;
expert: Shahidul Alam
communities, support groups, gender issues, health;
expert: Will Doherty

BUSINESS & ECONOMY
encompasses the fields
e-commerce, marketing,
global & corporate communication, finance;
expert: Michael Rappa

ENTERTAINMENT
encompasses the fields
gaming, music; *expert: Simon Carless*
animation, film; *expert: Peter van den Wyngaert*
digital lifestyle, fashion, design, sports; *expert: Ora-Ito*

MEDIA
encompasses the fields
magazines, e-zines, net journalism, news services,
chats, forums; *expert: Andrew Leonard*
media convergence, streaming media, TV, radio,
e-publishing; *expert: Lutz Schramm*

SCIENCES
comprises Internet activities in research and science
expert: Hiroaki Kitano

TECHNOLOGY
encompasses the fields
wireless Internet, pervasive computing, broadband,
human computer interface; *expert: Andrea Hoffmann*
information architecture, knowledge management,
P2P, open source, security, privacy; *expert: Gene Kan*

BANJA
Team cHmAn

www.Banja.com
www.cHmAn.com

On the boundary line between a server and an online game, *Banja* proposes a complete world of entertainment contents.

In a screenplay-type adventure game that takes place in a programmed manner in monthly episodes, the user's actions can lead to access to games, animation sequences, media and communal tools.

Varied events continually pop up in the quiet life of Itland, inviting players to live new experiences, discover new areas, meet new characters, and access new contents.

This vast solo adventure, simultaneously played by the whole community of players, calls upon them to cooperate through a forum, to exchange ideas in chats, and solve some games together to make the general common quest evolve.

Banja, das sich an der Grenzlinie zwischen einem Server- und einem Online-Spiel bewegt, bietet dem User eine vollständige Entertainment-Welt. Bei diesem Adventure-Game im Screenplay-Design, dessen Handlung sich auf Basis monatlicher Episoden entwickelt, hat der User je nach seinem persönlichen Engagement Zugang zu Spielen, Animationssequenzen, Medien und Gemeinschaftstools.

Verschiedene Ereignisse durchbrechen die Beschaulichkeit des Lebens auf Itland und laden die Mitspieler ein, neue Erfahrungen zu machen, neue Gebiete zu entdecken, neue Gestalten zu treffen und sich Zugang zu neuen Inhalten zu verschaffen.

In diesem großen Solo-Abenteuer, das simultan von der gesamten Mitspieler-Community gespielt wird, können die einzelnen Teilnehmer über ein Forum kooperieren, ihre Ideen in Chats austauschen und gemeinsam Aufgaben lösen, um das globale Ziel des Spiels zu erreichen.

Presentation of *Banja* on line

A genuine entertainment platform, *Banja* on the web is the first connected universal solution integrating:

– an adventure game with an optimistic spirit in screenplay style distributed in monthly episodes,

– arcade games with online scoring,

– personalisation functions,

– communal areas: chat rooms, forums, messenger service,

– an administrable media area for the distribution of music, contests, the editorial follow-up of texts and advertising insertions.

With colour graphics, engaging characters, electronic music, technological ergonomics, *Banja*'s world is intended for a large public of connected young adults, while remaining accessible to the youngsters. The community born around *Banja* appreciates and shares the same moral values: humour, good nature, frankness, mutual aid, and a whole art of living that one can quietly savour in Itland.

Die Online-Präsentation von *Banja*

Als genuine Unterhaltungsplattform ist *Banja* die erste Connected-Universes-Lösung im Web und integriert:

– ein Abenteuerspiel mit optimistischer Tendenz in Form einer monatlichen Fortsetzungsepisode

– diverse Unterhaltungsspiele mit Online-Zählung

– Möglichkeiten zur individuellen Anpassung

– Gemeinschaftsgebiete: Chat-Rooms, Foren, Nachrichtendienste

– einen administrierbaren Medienbereich für die Verteilung von Musik, Wettbewerbe, redaktionelle Informationen zu Texten und Werbeeinschaltungen.

Farbgrafik, fesselnde Charaktere, elektronische Musik, technologische Ergonomie – *Banjas* Welt richtet sich an ein breites Publikum vernetzter junger Erwachsener, ist aber auch für die Jugendlichen attraktiv. Die Gemeinschaft, die rund um *Banja* entstanden ist, teilt die gleichen Werte: Humor, Friedfertigkeit, Offenheit, gegenseitige Hilfe und eine ganze Lebensart, die man genüsslich in Itland auskosten kann.

[© copyright TEAMcHmAn 1998-2001] ::::::::::::: [any problem ? send a mail to banja@chman.com]

The cHmAn Team

© cHmAn 2000

FOUNDED IN MARCH 1998 BY SÉBASTIAN KOCHMAN AND BERNARD CANDAU, TEAMcHMAN ESTABLISHES ITS ACTIVITIES IN AN OVERFLOWING MULTI-MEDIA CREATIVITY AND ORGANISES ITS GROWTH BY FOLLOWING A VISION: THAT OF A NEW TYPE OF CONTENT, HIGHLY CREATIVE, INTERACTIVE, COMMU-NAL, MAKING OPTIMAL USE OF THE FASCINATING POSSIBILITIES OF THE INTERNET TO DEDICATE THEM TO NEW MODES OF PLANETARY ENTERTAINMENT. SÉBASTIEN KOCHMAN (CEO AND GENERAL MANAGER) IS THE FOUNDER, THE DIRECTOR AND THE CREATIVE VISIONARY OF TEAMcHMAN. A VIDEO GAME FANATIC AND INTERNET MEDIA EXPERT, HIS AMBITION IS TO CREATE ADVANCED FUNNY UNIVERSES, AS INTERACTIVE THEY CAN BE, WITH GRAPHIC ANIMA-TIONS, GAMES, VIDEO, MUSIC AND COMMUNITY. ▬▬ TeamcHmAn (F), im März 1998 von Sébastien Kochman und Bernard Candau gegründet, handelt aus einer übersprudelnden Multimedia-Kreativität heraus und orientiert sein Wachstum an einer Vision: neue hochkreative, interaktive, gemein-schaftsbildende Inhalte zu schaffen, die die faszinierenden Möglichkeiten des Internets optimal ausnützen und neue Arten eines globalen Entertainments eröffnen. Sébastien Kochman ist Gründer und Regisseur und der kreative Visionär von TeamcHmAn. Der Videospiel-Fanatiker und Internet-Medienexperte will ein hochqualitatives lustiges Universum schaffen, so interaktiv wie nur möglich, mit grafischen Animationen, Spielen, Video, Musik und Gemeinschaftserlebnissen.

IMAHIMA
Neeraj Jhanji

ImaHima, Inc. is a Japanese company founded in 1999 focused on providing location-based community services for mobile phone users. The company provides its service to all Japanese Mobile Operators - NTT Docomo, JPhone, KDDI—and has been appointed last year as an official service provider for NTT DoCoMo. The service is unique in Japan and runs on Japanese iMode, WAP platform version 1.1 for KDDI and on a standard web browser. Since its launch in December 1999 on iMode, imaHima has grown to over 250,000 users naturally and receives over a million page requests a day. Within the last 6 months, imaHima experienced a customer growth of more than 200% compared to the Q2 2000 customer base.

With AOL as partner and investor, imaHima is presently accelerating its business development in Japan and the European expansion. For the European market, the company plans to launch a product supporting WAP, iMode, WEB and SMS as communication platforms. "imaHima" is the Japanese expression for "are you free now?"

The basic concept is to utilize the mobile communication facilities, linked with selective Location-Based and Profile Information of mobile customers, and provide the services on a mobile telecommunication and mobile-fixed Internet integrated platform. ImaHima offers a community service, enabling mobile customers to locate and contact their friends, to meet new people and to find information and activities based on their current location from anywhere using mobile phones. The application is scalable and can be customized by the users, either via the Mobile Phone or the web interface.

ImaHima Inc. ist eine 1999 gegründete japanische Firma, die sich auf ortsbasierte Community-Dienste für Handy-Benutzer spezialisiert hat. Das Unternehmen bietet seine Dienste allen japanischen Mobilfunkbetreibern an – NTT DoCoMo, JPhone, KDDI – und wurde im vergangenen Jahr offizieller Dienstleister für NTT DoCoMo. Der angebotene Service ist einzigartig in Japan und läuft auf der japanischen iMode, auf WAP-Version 1.1 für KDDI sowie auf Standard-Webbrowsern. Seit dem Start im Dezember 1999 auf iMode ist *imaHima* auf 250.000 Kunden gewachsen und erhält über eine Million Seitenanfragen täglich. Innerhalb der letzten sechs Monate wurde ein Kundenzuwachs von über 200 Prozent im Vergleich zum zweiten Quartal 2000 verzeichnet.

Mit AOL als Partner und Investor beschleunigt *imaHima* seine Unternehmensentwicklung in Japan und seine Expansion nach Europa. Für Europa ist der Start eines Produktes geplant, das WAP, iMode, Web und SMS als Kommunikationsplattformen unterstützt.

„imaHima" ist der japanische Ausdruck für „Bist du jetzt frei?" bzw. „Hast du jetzt Zeit?" Das Grundkonzept stützt sich auf die Verbindung mobiler Kommunikationseinrichtungen verknüpft mit ausgewählten Orts- und Profilinformationen von Handykunden auf einer ins Internet integrierten gemeinsamen mobil/fixen Plattform. *ImaHima* bietet Gemeinschaftsdienste an, die es dem Handyuser ermöglichen, Freunde aufzuspüren und zu kontaktieren, neue Leute zu treffen sowie Informationen und Aktivitäten in ihrem jeweiligen geographischen Umfeld unabhängig vom Standort schnell aufzufinden. Die Anwendung ist skalierbar und kann von den Anwendern entweder über Handy oder über das Web-Interface angepasst werden.

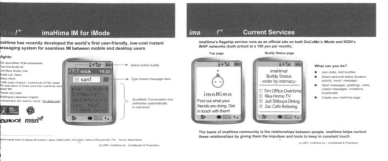

Target groups are the young customer segments and business customers, which require an easy but efficient communication tool for mobile and external employees like sales people, insurance agents and others.

Zielgruppen sind das Segment der jungen Kunden sowie der Business-Kunden, die ein einfaches, aber effizientes Kommunikations-Werkzeug brauchen für ihre Mitarbeiter im Außendienst wie Handelsvertreter, Versicherungsmakler und andere.

NEERAJ JHANJI (RI), AGED 29, FIRST CONCEIVED THE NEED FOR LOCATION-BASED MOBILE GROUP MESSAGING SERVICES IN MARCH '99. BEFORE FOUND-ING IMAHIMA IN DECEMBER 1999, NEERAJ WORKED AS A SENIOR CONSULTANT IN E-COMMERCE STRATEGY FOR ACCENTURE IN TOKYO, PRIOR TO WHICH HE WAS THE FUJITSU ASIA-PACIFIC SCHOLARSHIP RECIPIENT FOR THE MBA PROGRAM CONDUCTED JOINTLY BY UNIVERSITY OF HAWAII, JAIMS AND HITOTSUBASHI UNIVERSITY. HE PREVIOUSLY WORKED IN TECHNICAL AND CONSULTING ROLES FOR SIEMENS AND UNISYS. HE HOLDS AN UNDER-GRADUATE DEGREE IN ELECTRICAL ENGINEERING FROM THE UNIVERSITY OF DELHI AND IS FLUENT IN ENGLISH, HINDI AND JAPANESE. NEERAJ'S CHILD-HOOD DREAM IS TO FLY PLANES. ▬▬▬ Neeraj Jhanhi (RI), 29, hat im März 1999 als erster den Bedarf nach einem ortsbasierten Gruppen-Nachrichten-system für mobile Telephonie erkannt. Vor der Gründung von imaHima im Dezember 1999 war Neeraj als Senior Consultant für E-Commerce-Strategien bei Accenture in Tokio; davor war er Fujitsu Asia-Pacific Stipendiat beim MBA-Programm, das gemeinsam von der University of Hawaii, JAIMS und der Hitotsubashi University durchgeführt wurde. Zuvor war er als Techniker und Berater für Siemens und Unisys tätig. Er hat Elektrotechnik an der Universität Delhi absolviert.

PHANTASY STAR ONLINE
Yuji Naka / Sonic Team / Sega

When we first started designing this online game, we tried to come up with the best way for people to communicate and interact with each other. We decided to create an online game based on the world of Sega's legendary RPG series *Phantasy Star*. That was the moment that the concept of Sega's latest RPG, *Phantasy Star Online* (PSO), was born.

Sega has been trying to create the most exciting game world for players since the 8bit console Sega Mark 3/ Sega Master System was introduced, Events such as a dragon bursting out of the wall will thrill players when they travel in the *Phantasy Star Online* world. The amazing adventure in a realistic 3D world, which Sega has not been able to achieve in the past *Phantasy Star* series, will be available on Dreamcast, Sega's third generation console.

The first worldwide multiplayer online RPG for the console

Explore the online adventure world with other players from around the world through the Internet in *Phantasy Star Online*. Just connect to the Internet, the PSO world is right there 24 hours a day. (24 hours equal 1000 beats.) "Beats" is the worldwide internet time created by SWATCH in Switzerland. The main characters in PSO are the actual players online: meet other people, cooperate with each other or plot against each other ...

Adventure with other people from all over the world!

Other players online won't just be your friends in your neighborhood. There is a chance for all online players to meet other players from around the world.

No language barrier in the game

There aren't many chances to get to know people in other countries, states or even in other cities in real

---

Am Anfang der Entwicklung dieses Online-Spiels stand unser Bemühen, die bestmögliche Form zu finden, in der Leute miteinander kommunizieren und interagieren können. Als Grundlage für das Online-Spiel wollten wir Segas legendäre RPG-Serie *Phantasy Star* verwenden – so entstand das Konzept von Segas neuestem RPG *Phantasy Star Online* (PSO). Schon seit der Einführung der 8-Bit-Konsole Sega Mark 3 / Sega Master System ist Sega bemüht, den Spielern eine möglichst aufregende Spielwelt zu bieten. Ereignisse – wie etwa ein aus der Wand herausbrechender Drache – sorgen für Faszination und Überraschung bei den Spielern auf ihrer Reise durch die Welt von *Phantasy Star Online*. Das fesselnde Abenteuer in einer realistischen 3D-Welt, wie sie Sega in der früheren *Phantasy Star*-Serie nicht zu erzielen vermochte, wird für die Dreamcast/Sega-Spielkonsole der dritten Generation erhältlich sein.

Das weltweit erste Multi-Spieler Online-RPG für die Konsole

Erforschen Sie in *Phantasy Star Online* die Online-Abenteuerwelt mit anderen Spielern aus der ganzen Welt über das Internet. Einfach ins Internet einloggen – die PSO-Welt ist 24 Stunden am Tag da (24 Stunden sind 1000 „Beats", eine weltweite Internet-Zeitmessung geschaffen von SWATCH in der Schweiz). Die Hauptgestalten in PSO sind die Online-Spieler selbst – treffen Sie andere, kooperieren Sie mit anderen oder schmieden Sie Ränke gegeneinander!

Abenteuer mit anderen Menschen aus der ganzen Welt!

Nicht nur die eigenen Freunde aus der Nachbarschaft sind Mitspieler – hier haben alle Online-Spieler Gelegenheit, Freunde aus der ganzen Welt zu treffen.

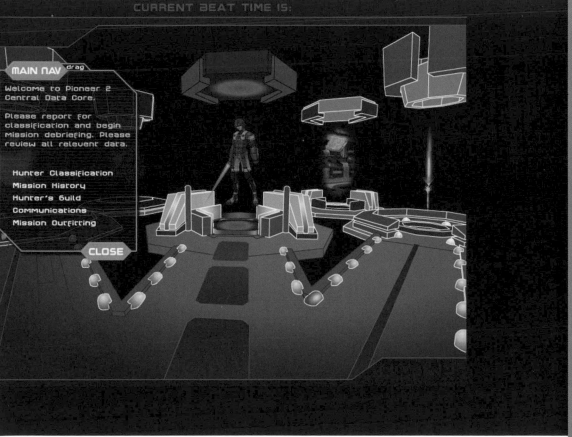

life. Moreover, it's hard to communicate with people from different countries. But relax! The Word Select System in PSO enables players to interact with people of all nationalities.

4-Player Real Time Battle

In PSO, up to four players can make a group with the Real Time Online Battle System. Each player has to be alert and cooperate with each other to fight off the ferocious monsters in the game.

The offline adventure is also fun!

Players don't have to access the Internet to enjoy the game, NPC's (non playerable characters) will support players during the adventure. Battle against the dragon with NPC's, or find items while NPC's are holding the door by pushing a button. Players can enjoy the "play-with-friends" feeling during the game even if they are not using the online play.

These above reasons show why PSO is *the* online Game to give players a brand new experience in gaming.

Keine Sprachbarrieren im Spiel

Man hat nicht so oft die Gelegenheit, Menschen in anderen Ländern und Staaten, ja, nicht einmal in fremden Städten, kennen zu lernen, und außerdem ist es schwer, mit Leuten aus anderen Ländern zu kommunizieren. Aber immer mit der Ruhe! Das Word Select System in PSO erlaubt es den Mitspielern, mit Menschen unterschiedlichster Nationalitäten zu kommunizieren.

Vier-Spieler-Kampf in Echtzeit

Mit Hilfe des Real Time Online Battle Systems können bis zu vier Spieler in PSO eine Gruppe bilden. Jeder der Mitspieler muss aufmerksam mit den anderen kooperieren, um die wilden Monstren des Spiels abzuwehren.

Das Offline-Abenteuer macht auch Spaß!

Man braucht nicht ins Internet zu gehen, um das Spiel zu genießen – NPCs („non playerable characters", „nicht-spielerfähige Gestalten") unterstützen die Mitspieler während des Abenteuers. Mit NPCs kann man gegen den Drachen kämpfen oder Objekte sammeln, während ein NPC den Türöffner drückt. Das Gefühl, mit Freunden zu spielen, wird so auch vermittelt, wenn man nicht online geht.

Aus all diesen Gründen ist PSO *das* Online-Spiel, das den Mitspielern eine völlig neue Spielerfahrung zu bieten hat.

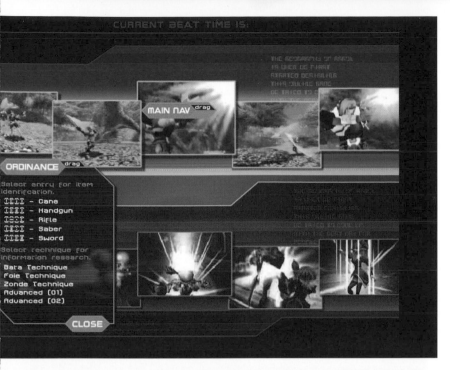

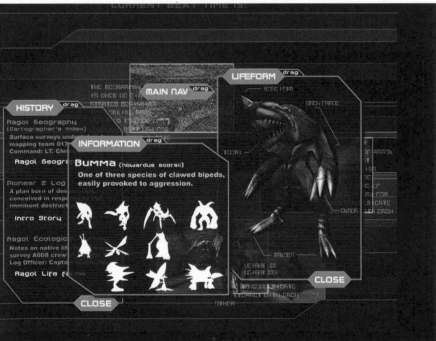

SONIC TEAM (J). ACCLAIMED CONSOLE DEVELOPERS OF SONIC ADVENTURE FOR THE SEGA DREAMCAST, YUJI NAKA'S SONIC TEAM CREATES GAMES FOR A VARIETY OF GENRES INCLUDING RHYTHM AND DANCE, ADVENTURE AND RPG. BASED IN JAPAN, WITH A US BRANCH. ▬▬▬ Sonic Team (J). Als gefeierte Entwickler für die Sega Dreamcast bei Sonic Adventure produziert das Sonic Team unter Yuji Naka Spiele für eine Vielzahl von Genres, darunter Rhythm & Dance, Abenteuer und RPG. Die in Japan ansässige Gruppe unterhält eine Außenstelle in der USA.

MICROMUSIC

Gino Esposto / Michael Burkhardt / Paco Manzanares

Micromusic was initiated in November 98 by Gino Esposto and Michael Burkhardt under the codename "futurelab". After project development and programming, it was finally put on the net in August 1999.

What was originally intended to be a simple tool for low_tech_producers to generate low_tech_music for those who enjoy computer-generated music via the World Wide Web, quickly evolved into a highly complex websound_community_system, with its implemented functions researched and designed using state-of-the-art technology.

In principle, "research" is probably the most appropriate term for the activity that proceeds from micromusic. Although the music produced on consumer PCs is the central theme of micromedia, it involves far more than that. The Internet (in the form as we know it today) is still just at the beginning. The task that micromusic has set for itself is to pursue such questions as how special interest communities may be developed, for instance, or the forms in which communication can take place, what a (perfect?) interface contains (to enable interaction and real-time communication and make audiovisual content consumable). Human perception (including that of the designers!) and audiovisual awareness are currently in the midst of further development.

Since micromusic generates content via the users and assumes the functions of filtering/treatment/moderating/presentation, communication is the primary focus, when it is a matter of building up and maintaining a community. In addition to conventional communication through e-mail (newsletter), there is a microtalk™ function on the homepage, which allows for mutual exchange among the guests. Another function (the "microliner") enables the placement of remarks/statements, which become immediately accessible to the community.

micromusic wurde im November 98 von Gino Esposto und Michael Burkhardt unter dem Codenamen „futurelab" aus der Taufe gehoben, projektiert, programmiert und schließlich im August 1999 ins Netz gestellt.

Was ursprünglich als simples Tool zur Generierung von low_tech_music von low_tech_producern für Liebhaber von computergenerierter Musik via WorldWideWeb erdacht worden war, entwickelte sich rasch zu einem hoch komplexen websound_community_system, dessen implementierte Funktionen unter Verwendung modernster Technologie erforscht und gestaltet worden sind.

Grundsätzlich ist „Forschung" die wohl zutreffendste Bezeichnung der Aktivität, die von micromusic ausgeht. Obwohl die auf Consumer-PCs produzierte Musik das zentrale Thema bei micromusic darstellt, geht es um weit mehr als das. Das Internet (in der Form, wie wir es heute kennen) befindet sich noch in seinen Anfängen. Wie beispielsweise Special-Interest-Communities aufgebaut werden, in welcher Form kommuniziert werden kann, was ein (perfektes?) Interface beinhaltet (das Interaktion und Real-Time-Kommunikation ermöglicht und audiovisuellen Inhalt konsumierbar macht), sind Fragen, denen nachzugehen sich micromusic zur Aufgabe gemacht hat.

Die menschliche Wahrnehmung (auch die der Gestalter!) und deren (audiovisuelles) Bewusstsein sind momentan in Weiterentwicklung. Da micromusic den Content über die User generiert und die Funktionen Filterung/Aufbereitung/Moderation/Präsentation übernimmt, steht Kommunikation an erster Stelle, wenn es darum geht, eine Community aufzubauen und zu pflegen. Nebst der üblichen Kommunikation via E-Mail (Newsletter) findet man auf der Homepage von micromusic beispielsweise eine microtalk™-Funktion, die es den Gästen erlaubt, sich untereinander auszutauschen.

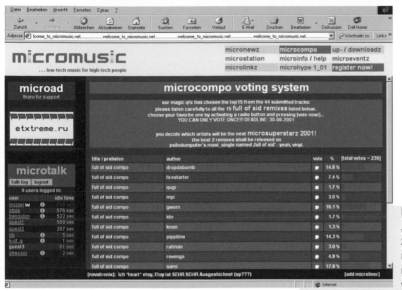

Eine weitere Funktion (der „microliner") ermöglicht die Platzierung von Bemerkungen/Statements, die umgehend der Community zugänglich gemacht werden.

Based on familiar computer games, the interface is designed in such a way that users can influence their microlevel. An individual user's respective level depends on whether the user has actively participated in the further development of the system. For instance, if a user succeeds in having his music accepted by the quality_filter_system (a system that serves to ensure the quality of the content that is introduced), his microlevel is raised by a corresponding number of points. People involved in networking for *micromusic* or who take action in some other form for *micromusic* raise their microlevel. This is rewarded by an increase in permissions at the system level. In this way, it is possible to mutate from a user/nerd to a *micromusic-crew member*.

In less than two years, *micromusic* has succeeded in programming a multimedia interface that is unique on the WWW. An active community of nearly 3500 users has been built up, and the quality of the soundtracks submitted by the users has meanwhile reached a level that has not otherwise been attained in this field. The fact that the success of this project is due entirely to the dedication of talented computer freaks and multimedia artists gives us great pleasure. That results of this kind are even possible exclusively via networking even surprised us.

Das Interface ist in Anlehnung an die bekannten Computerspiele so gestaltet, dass die User Einfluss auf ihren Microlevel haben. Der individuelle Level, dem sich der User jeweils befindet, hängt davon ab, ob er sich aktiv an der Weiterentwicklung des Systems beteiligt. Wer es beispielsweise schafft, dass seine Musik vom quality_filter_system (ein System, das dazu dient, die Qualität des eingebrachten Inhalts zu gewährleisten) akzeptiert wird, erhöht seinen Microlevel um die entsprechende Punktezahl. Leute, die für *micromusic* Networking betreiben oder in irgendeiner Form für *micromusic* tätig sind, erhöhen ihren Microlevel, was mit einer Erhöhung der Zugriffsrechte auf Systemebene belohnt wird. Somit wird es möglich, vom reinen User/Nerd zum Crew-Member von *micromusic* zu mutieren. *micromusic* ist es innerhalb von weniger als zwei Jahren gelungen, ein Multimedia-Interface zu programmieren, das im WWW Seinesgleichen sucht. Eine aktive Community von nahezu 3500 Usern konnte aufgebaut werden, und die Qualität der von den Usern eingereichten Soundtracks hat in der Zwischenzeit ein Niveau erreicht, das auf seinem Gebiet unerreicht ist. Dass dieses Projekt ausschließlich durch den Einsatz von talentierten Computerfreaks und Multimediakünstlern an diesen Punkt gelangen konnte, freut uns ausgesprochen. Dass ausschließlich via Networking ein derartiges Resultat überhaupt möglich ist, hat uns selber überrascht.

GINO ESPOSTO (CH), CEO, PROJECT MANAGEMENT, CODING. BORN 1973, STUDIED IN MANCHESTER. CO-FOUNDER OF ETOY. CONCEPT AND REALIZATION OF "MICROSTATION" FOR THE COMPUTER GAME EXHIBITION "GAME OVER", MUSEUM FÜR GESTALTUNG IN ZURICH. MICHAEL BURKHARDT (CH), WORD, SOUND, COMMUNICATION. BORN 1966. SCHOOL FOR EXPERIMENTAL DESIGN AND NEW MEDIA ZURICH. MEMBER OF VARIOUS FREE JAZZ/HARDCORE BANDS AND LIVE ACTS IN SWITZERLAND AND GERMANY. PACO MANZANARES (CH), ART DIRECTOR, VISUAL DESIGN. BORN 1962, TRAINED AS TYPESETTER. MEMBER OF THE INDUSTRIAL NOISE BANDS "MINI POP BAND" AND "VANDA HAMMA", ORGANIZATION OF WAREHOUSE PARTIES. ACTIVE SINCE 2000 AS ART DIRECTOR FOR MICROMUSIC.NET. ▬▬▬ Gino Esposto (CH), CEO, Projektmanagement, Coding. Geb. 1973. Studien in Manchester. Mitbegründer von etoy. Konzept und Realisation der „microstation" für die Computer-Game-Exhibition „game over", Museum für Gestaltung in Zürich. Michael Burkhardt (CH), Word, Sound, Communication. Geb. 1966. Schule für experimentelle Gestaltung und neue Medien, Zürich. Mitglied verschiedener Freejazz-/Hardcore-Bands und Liveacts in der Schweiz und Deutschland. Paco Manzanares (CH), Art Director, Visual Design. Geb. 1962. Ausbildung als Schriftsetzer. Mitglied der industrial noise bands „mini pop band" und „vanda hamma", Organisation von warehouse parties. Seit 2000 aktiv als Art Director bei micromusic.net.

GAMELAB'S GAMES

gameLab / Ranjit Bhatnagar, Frank Lantz, Peter Lee, Eric Zimmerman

At gameLab, we make games. Digital games are among the most robust vectors of pop culture today. Online communities with tens of thousands of simultaneous players, non-standard computer hardware interfaces, realtime graphics rendering, interactive narratives, artificial life, artificial intelligence, complex systems—are nowhere being explored as energetically as in games. On the other hand, digital games are culturally retarded.

Our mission at gameLab is to explore and expand this undiscovered medium and invent new forms of culture. This mission requires two complementary critical practices: understanding how games work as designed objects and also understanding how they operate within culture at large.

A game is a stylized context where players follow rules in order to experience the game. To play a game of chess, for example, is to limit your behaviors to follow the rules of chess. While rules are an essential component to games, rules by themselves are not fun. They are fixed, rigid, closed, and unambiguous. A paradoxical quality of games is that by following rules, play results. And play is the opposite of rules. Play is improvisational, creative, uncertain, and pleasurable. Like the "free play" of a gear or an automobile steering wheel, play is only possible because of fixed structures. In the example of an automobile, these fixed structures are the wheels, axle, drive shaft, steering wheel, and other utilitarian mechanisms. But at the same time, the "play" of the steering wheel is exactly the place where those structures fail to operate properly. Play exists because of fixed structures of rules, but at the same time play exists despite those structures, emerging in and among the gaps and interstices.

Our challenge at gameLab is to integrate these ideas about rules, play, and games into our work. We rely on a collaborative, interdisciplinary work process focused on iterative design, which means our design decisions are based on our play experience of the game as it is being developed.

Wir von gameLab produzieren Games. Digitale Spiele gehören zu den stärksten Motoren der heutigen Popkultur. Online-Communities mit Zehntausenden von Spielern, die simultan spielen, ungewöhnliche Hardware-Interfaces, Grafikdarstellung in Echtzeit, interaktive Narration, künstliches Leben und künstliche Intelligenz – nirgendwo anders werden diese Bereiche so intensiv untersucht wie im Game-Bereich. Andererseits hinken die Spiele der kulturellen Entwicklung hinterher.

Unsere Aufgabe bei gameLab ist es, dieses unentdeckte Medium zu erforschen und zu erweitern und neue Kulturformen zu entwickeln. Diese Aufgabe erfordert zwei einander ergänzende kritische Analysen: Einerseits muss ein Verständnis dafür erarbeitet werden, wie Spiele als Design-Objekte funktionieren, andererseits ein Verständnis für die Funktion, die sie innerhalb der Kultur als Ganzem erfüllen.

Ein Spiel ist ein stilisierter Kontext, innerhalb dessen Spieler bestimmten Regeln folgen, um das Spiel zu erleben. Um beispielsweise eine Schachpartie zu spielen, beschränkt man sein Verhalten auf die Einhaltung der Regeln des Schachs. Und wenn auch Regeln ein essenzieller Bestandteil der Spiele sind, so machen doch Regeln per se keinen Spaß. Sie sind festgelegt, rigide und eindeutig. Eine paradoxe Eigenschaft von Spielen ist, dass aus der Befolgung der Regeln das Spiel resultiert. „Spielen" bedeutet aber andererseits das Gegenteil von „Regeln befolgen" – es ist improvisatorisch, kreativ, ungewiss und vergnüglich.

Wie beim Leerlauf in einem Getriebe oder beim „Spiel" des Lenkrads im Auto ist Spiel nur auf der Basis fester Strukturen möglich. Beim Auto werden diese Strukturen bzw. Regeln durch Räder, Achsen, Antriebsstrang, Lenkrad und andere Nutzmechanismen vorgegeben. Aber das Lenkradspiel ist genau jener Bereich, in dem diese Strukturen aufhören, ordnungsgemäß zu funktionieren. Spiel existiert auf Grund eines festen Regelwerks, aber gleich-

At the same time, it is crucial that we understand how our game development is a cultural practice—a pop cultural practice, but a cultural practice just the same. We think of our games as interventions in the culture of digital gaming. They intervene by finding new audiences for games, appropriating visual and audio aesthetics from outside the gaming world, constructing narrative and cultural content that isn't normally found in the gaming world, and (especially) by inventing new forms of gameplay.

It's a struggle for us to experiment in a commercial medium like games. At present, the game industry resembles the Hollywood film industry: all center and no margins, without any kind of contexts for the production and reception of independent cinema. By integrating a critical understand of our form with a cultural understanding of our field, our goal is to become the "independent filmmakers" of gaming and change the medium for the better.

Will digital gaming become a more robust cultural form like film or music? Or will it never outgrow its roots in young male adolescent power fantasies. We don't know for sure. But it's why we're making games.

zeitig existiert Spiel *trotz* dieser Strukturen und taucht in den dazwischen liegenden Lücken auf. Bei gameLab bemühen wir uns, diese Gedanken über Regeln, Spiel und Spiele in unserer Arbeit umzusetzen. Wir vertrauen auf einen kooperativen, interdisziplinären Arbeitsprozess, der sich auf interaktives Design konzentriert, das heißt, unsere Design-Entscheidungen basieren auf unseren eigenen Spielerfahrungen während der Entwicklung des Spiels.

Gleichzeitig ist es unabdingbar zu verstehen, dass und wie unsere Spielentwicklung zu den kulturellen Praktiken gehört – zu den Praktiken einer Popkultur, aber nichts desto weniger zu den Kulturpraktiken. Wir verstehen unsere Spiele als Interventionen in der Kultur des digitalen Spielens – sie intervenieren, indem sie neues Publikum für Spiele finden, indem sie sich visuelle und auditive Ästhetik aus Bereichen außerhalb der Welt des Spielens aneignen, indem sie Narrationsformen und kulturellen Inhalt konstruieren, der normalerweise nicht in der Welt der Spiele zu finden ist, und besonders, indem sie neue Formen des „Spiele-Spielens" erfinden.

Es ist anstrengend, in einem kommerziellen Medium wie den Games zu experimentieren. Derzeit ähnelt die Game-Industrie der Filmindustrie in Hollywood: Alles ist Zentrum, es gibt keine Peripherie mit Kontexten, innerhalb derer unabhängiges Kino produziert und rezipiert werden kann. Indem wir eine kritische Haltung sowohl gegenüber der Form, mit der wir arbeiten, als auch gegenüber dem Gebiet, in dem wir tätig sind, einnehmen, wollen wir die „unabhängigen Filmemacher" der Spiele-Welt werden und das Medium zum Besseren verändern.

Wird das digitale Game eine robustere Kulturform werden, wie der Film und die Musik? Oder wird es nie über seine in den Machtfantasien heranwachsender männlicher Jugendlicher verankerten Wurzeln hinauswachsen? Wir sind uns da nicht sicher, aber genau deswegen machen wir Spiele.

ERIC ZIMMERMAN (USA) FOUNDER & CEO OF GAMELAB HAS TAUGHT GAME DESIGN AT MIT, NYU, AND PARSONS SCHOOL OF DESIGN. HE IS CURRENTLY WORKING ON TWO BOOKS ABOUT GAME DESIGN AND GAME CULTURE, TO BE PUBLISHED IN 2002. PETER LEE (USA), FOUNDER & PRESIDENT, CURRENTLY HOLDS AN ADJUNCT PROFESSORSHIP AT NEW YORK UNIVERSITY'S INTERACTIVE TELECOMMUNICATIONS PROGRAM, WHERE HE TEACHES GAME DEVELOPMENT. RANJIT BHATNAGAR (US) HAS BEEN INVOLVED WITH DIGITAL ART ON THE INTERNET BEFORE THE WEB EVER EXISTED. HIS ART AND INSTALLATIONS HAVE APPEARED IN SOLO AND GROUP EXHIBITIONS IN CALIFORNIA AND PENNSYLVANIA. FRANK LANTZ (USA), SENIOR GAME DESIGNER, IS A MEMBER OF THE FACULTY OF NYU'S INTERACTIVE TELECOMMUNICATIONS PROGRAM, WHERE HE TEACHES GAME DESIGN AND INTERACTIVE NARRATIVE. ■■■■ Eric Zimmerman (USA), Gründer und Geschäftsführer von gameLab, hat Spieldesign am MIT, an der New York University und an der Parsons School of Design unterrichtet. Derzeit arbeitet er an zwei Büchern über Spieldesign und Spielkultur, die 2002 erscheinen sollen. Peter Lee (USA), Gründer und Vorsitzender, ist derzeit Adjunct Professor beim Interactive Telecommunications Program der New York University, wo er Spielentwicklung lehrt. Ranjit Bhatnaga (US) war schon im Bereich digitaler Kunst im Internet aktiv, bevor noch das Web überhaupt existierte. Seine Kunstwerke und Installationen wurden in Einzel- und Gruppenausstellungen in Kalifornien und Pennsylvania gezeigt. Frank Lantz (USA), Senior Game Designer, ist Fakultätsmitglied des Interactive Telecommunications Program der NYU, wo er Spieldesign und interaktive Narration unterrichtet.

PRAYSTATION

Joshua Davis

1998/1999—*PrayStation* version I
NoFriendo and VideoGame destruction

The work from these years has been taken offline, to remain a fleeting memory in the minds of those who experienced it. All submissions were related to the effects of classic and modern video games on the minds of Internet designers and artists.

2000—*PrayStation* version II
Calendar based

Its objective was to apply design and technology to a collection of small, sometimes daily, modules. *PrayStation* year I came to a close in October 1999 and was ready to reinvent itself, maintaining the current first-year model.

The millennium was just a breath away and the idea of applying the same concept again for a second year did not seem to sit well. The first year, while it was rewarding, would never be 100 percent original content. So I sought to redefine its concept.

The domain again sat dormant for five months. A new concept was going no where fast. In retrospect, the impending hype of Y2K and its possible technology black out may have left developers thinking "What next?"

On a conceptual level, what hadn't already been done? So *PrayStation* disregarded any heavy, high conceptual theme, believing that "keeping it simple", would yield the best results. The passing of time. What did you do last week ? As adults, with families, paying bills, saving money, thinking of the future, when do we have the time to record the simple events of every day ?

I found myself spending 80 percent of my day on personal introspection and researching building modules. Experiments were placed on the server with the current date affixed to its folder name.

1998/99 – *PrayStation* Version I
NoFriendo und
VideoGame destruction

Arbeiten aus diesen Jahren mussten vom Netz genommen werden und sind nur noch eine schwindende Erinnerung im Geiste derer, die sie erlebt haben. Bei allen Einreichungen ging es darum zu zeigen, welche Wirkung klassische und moderne Videospiele auf den Geist der Internet-Designer und -Künstler ausübten.

2000 – *PrayStation* version II
Kalendergestützt

Das Ziel dieser Version von *PrayStation* war es, Design und Technologie in eine Sammlung von kleinen – fast täglich erscheinenden – Modulen zu formen.

Die *PrayStation* des ersten Jahres lief im Oktober 1999 aus und war bereit, sich selbst neu zu erfinden und das laufende Modell des ersten Jahres beizubehalten.

Die Jahrtausendwende stand damals unmittelbar vor der Tür, und der Gedanke, dasselbe Konzept ein zweites Jahr lang anzuwenden, passte mir nicht. Wenn es auch im ersten Jahr recht lohnend war, so bestand es doch nicht zu 100 Prozent aus Originalinhalten. Deshalb beschloss ich, das Konzept zu überdenken.

Die Domain dämmerte fünf Monate lang vor sich hin – und ein neues Konzept tauchte auch nicht auf die Schnelle auf. Rückblickend könnte auch der Hype rund um das bevorstehende Jahr 2000 und den damit verbundenen Technologie-Blackouts die Entwickler veranlasst haben zu denken: „Und was dann?"

Was war eigentlich auf konzeptueller Ebene noch *nicht* geschehen? Deshalb hat *PrayStation* alle schweren, konzeptuellen Themen außer Betracht gelassen – in der Überzeugung, dass die alte Regel des „So einfach wie möglich" die besten Ergebnisse bringen würde. Die Zeit verfliegt – was haben Sie letzte Woche gemacht? Als Erwachsene – die wir Familie haben, unsere Rechnungen zahlen und sparen müssen, an die Zukunft denken – wann haben wir Zeit, die einfachen Ereignisse eines jeden Tages aufzuzeichnen?

Ich habe bemerkt, dass ich 80 Prozent meiner Zeit in persönlicher Introspektion und mit Überlegungen zum Bau von Modulen verbrachte. Experimente wurden auf den Server geladen,

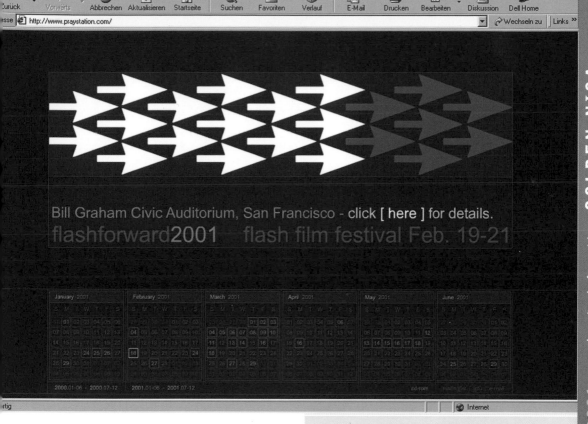

Datei Bearbeiten Ansicht Favoriten Extras ?

Zurück | Vorwärts | Abbrechen | Aktualisieren | Startseite | Suchen | Favoriten | Verlauf | E-Mail | Drucken | Bearbeiten | Diskussion | Dell Home

Adresse http://www.praystation.com/ ▼ Wechseln zu | Links

Fertig | Internet

Welcome to *PrayStation* year II

Its basic foundation is a calendar timeline. The whole year, divided up into three-month increments, is viewed at the bottom in the main navigation menu. You may shift the main timeline by clicking on whatever next set of months you wish to view. In the essence of a developers journal, finished projects, experiments, or general thoughts are posted on the day they are completed.

2001—*PrayStation*
version III—XML residue

PrayStation has always been about the movement of time. It has used a calendar-based system to archive and catalogue events as they happen in the course of a single year. In prior builds, however, content always remained a single untouched module having no relation to what happened before its date of archiving. May 01—releases the new archiving / data visualization system—Joshua Davis and Branden Hall have used Flash 5 and XML to create a tree of visualization. Now entries leave an imprint or residue as you move

wobei jedem Ordner das laufende Datum zugeordnet wurde.

Willkommen zum *PrayStation*-Jahr II

Das Fundament dieser Version von *PrayStation* ist eine Kalender-Zeitleiste. Das ganze Jahr wird, eingeteilt in Drei-Monats-Abschnitte, am unteren Rand im Hauptnavigationsmenü angezeigt. Man kann die Zeitleiste verschieben, indem man auf die nächste Gruppe von Monaten klickt, die man zu sehen wünscht. Wie es sich für ein Entwicklerjournal gehört, werden fertige Projekte, Experimente oder allgemeine Gedanken an dem Tag gepostet, an dem sie abgeschlossen werden.

2001 – *PrayStation*
Version III – XML-Spuren

Bei *PrayStation* ist es immer um die Bewegung der Zeit gegangen. Sie hat ein kalendarisches System zur Archivierung und Katalogisierung von Ereignissen, wie sie während eines einzelnen Jahres passieren, eingesetzt. Aber in den früheren Fassungen blieb der Inhalt immer ein einzelnes unberührtes Modul, das keinen Bezug nahm auf das, was vor seinem Archivierungsdatum passiert ist.

forward in time. New entries might play upon layout and/or space of what has happened before it.

    0 = not currently on stage
  20 = an alpha transparency of 20 % and is the last visible object on the stage
  40 = an alpha transparency of 40 % and is the second to the last visible object on the stage
  60 = an alpha transparency of 60 % and is the middle object on the stage
  80 = an alpha transparency of 80 % and is the second visible object on the stage
100 = an alpha transparency of 100 % and is the top visible object on the stage

This can even be mapped on an interactive level in terms of exploration of space. Interaction can (and will) be explored between multiple dimensions—machines on specific days will interact with machines from previous days—unfolding a little more of the puzzle.
Objects are also aware of their position in the tree—the object on 4–28 displays in multiple colors, but as soon as it drops down (click on 04–29), the same machine runs but a different presentation. In this case all color is stripped. So entries are aware of whether or not they are the "top" visible object and can act or react accordingly.
The artist's canvas that is never complete—as we watch process and form unfold over time, through space and dimension.

Am 1. Mai installierten wir das neue Archivierungs-/Datenvisualisierungssystem. Joshua Davis und Branden Hall haben Flash 5 und XML eingesetzt, um einen Visualisierungsbaum zu erstellen. Neue Einträge hinterlassen einen Rückstand oder eine Spur, wenn sie sich über die Zeit dahinbewegen. Neue Einträge können auf das Layout und/oder den Raum dessen zugreifen, was zuvor geschehen ist.

    0 = derzeit nicht auf der Bühne
  20 = eine Alpha-Transparenz von 20 % und das letzte sichtbare Objekt auf der Bühne
  40 = eine Alpha-Transparenz von 40 % und das vorletzte sichtbare Objekt auf der Bühne
  60 = eine Alpha-Transparenz von 60 % und das mittlere sichtbare Objekt auf der Bühne
  80 = eine Alpha-Transparenz von 80 % und das zweite sichtbare Objekt auf der Bühne
100 = eine Alpha-Transparenz von 100 % und das oberste sichtbare Objekt auf der Bühne

Dies kann in Hinblick auf eine Untersuchung des Raums sogar auf eine interaktive Ebene abgebildet werden. Die Interaktion kann (und wird) auf mehreren Dimensionen untersucht werden – an bestimmten Tagen interagieren Maschinen mit jenen anderer Tage – und somit ein wenig mehr von diesem Puzzle zusammensetzen.
Den Objekten ist auch ihre Position innerhalb des Baums bewusst – das Objekt vom 28. 4. etwa wird in mehreren Farben dargestellt, aber sobald es hinunterrutscht (also wenn man auf den 29. 4. klickt), lädt dieselbe Maschine eine andere Präsentation, bei der die Farbe weggenommen wird. Auf diese Weise „wissen" Einträge, ob sie das „Spitzenobjekt" sind oder nicht, und können dementsprechend reagieren.
Die Leinwand des Künstlers ist niemals fertig – wir beobachten, wie sich Prozess und Form zwischen mehreren Dimensionen über die Zeit und durch Raum und Dimension entwickeln.

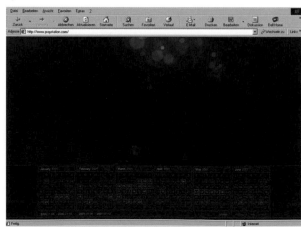

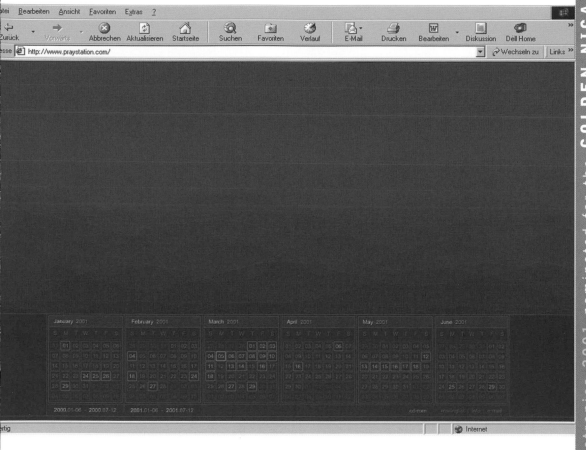

JOSHUA DAVIS (USA) IS A ONE-MAN RESEARCH AND DEVELOPMENT WEB-SITE. ITS OBJECTIVE IS TO APPLY DESIGN AND TECHNOLOGY TO A COLLECTION OF SMALL, SOMETIMES DAILY, MODULES, PRODUCING WORK IN A WORLD THAT IS UNDER CONSTANT FLUX AND CHANGE. HE IS ALSO THE SOLE CREATOR OF *HTTP://WWW.ONCE-UPON-A-FOREST.COM* WHICH IS THE NEMESIS OF WHAT WE PERCEIVE THE WEB TO BE. NO EASY, SHORT DOMAIN NAME. NO EASY TO USE NAVIGATION. NO INSTRUCTIONS. NO FAQ'S. NO ADS, NO LINKS, NO TECH SUPPORT. NO HELP. NO ANSWERS. ▬▬▬ Joshua Davis (USA) betreibt eine Ein-Mann-Forschungs- und Entwicklungs-Website. Sein Ziel ist es, Design und Technologie auf eine Sammlung kleiner, manchmal täglicher Module anzuwenden – Arbeit in einer Welt zu liefern, die in ständiger Bewegung und im Fluss ist. Er ist auch der alleinige Schöpfer von *www.once-upon-a-forest.com*, das die Nemesis dessen darstellt, wie wir das Web erleben. Kein einfacher, kurzer Domain-Name. Keine simple benutzerfreundliche Navigation. Keine Anleitungen. Keine FAQs. Keine Anzeigen. Keine Links. Keine technische Unterstützung. Keine Hilfe. Keine Antworten.

WARP RECORDS

Chris McGrail / Dorian Moore / Dan Sayers / Kleber

The brief was to re-design the Warp Records website, updating both its look and functionality. The label has a very strong musical direction, and the site needed to reflect this. The Designers Republic, who have worked with Warp on many different projects, created the designs. Kleber implemented those designs for the Internet, and built the site structure. The process took two years from start to finish, and the site itself went through two versions of Flash before it was ready.

The Designers Republic designed the site. The Designers Republic's website *http://www.thedesigners republic.com*, also created with Kleber, had 1.5 million hits in its first week. Other recent projects include the acclaimed Funkstörung "Grammy Winners" promo, idents for FilmFour, TV ads for Pringles and the first DR book *3D>2D: The Designers Republic's Adventures. In And Out of Architecture with Sadar Vugar Arhitekti and Spela Mlakar* published in July 2001.

Der Auftrag lautete, die Website von Warp Records neu zu designen und dabei sowohl das Aussehen wie die Funktionalität zu verbessern. Das Label hat eine klare musikalische Ausrichtung, und die Website sollte dies reflektieren. Die Entwürfe stammen von der Gruppe *The Designers Republic*, die schon bei mehreren Projekten mit Warp zusammengearbeitet hat. Kleber hat diese Entwürfe für das Internet implementiert und die Struktur der Site gestaltet – ein Prozess, der insgesamt zwei Jahre gedauert hat, wobei die Site zwei verschiedene Versionen von Flash durchlaufen hat, bevor sie fertiggestellt war.

Das Design der Site stammt von The Designers Republic, deren ebenfalls von Kleber implementierte eigene Website *http://www.the designersrepublic.com* in ihrer ersten Woche bereits 1,5 Millionen Mal aufgesucht wurde. Andere Projekte der letzten Zeit sind die „Grammy Winners"-Promotion für Funkstörung, Logos für FilmFour, Fernsehspots für Pringles und das erste Buch *3D>2D: The Designers Republic's Adventures. In And Out of Architecture with Sadar Vugar Arhitekti and Spela Mlakar*, das im Juli 2001 erscheint.

Datei Bearbeiten Ansicht Favoriten Extras ?

Zurück   Vorwärts   Abbrechen Aktualisieren Startseite   Suchen   Favoriten   Verlauf   E-Mail   Drucken   Bearbeiten   Diskussion   Dell Home

resse http://www.warprecords.com/warp/   Wechseln zu | Links

RED SNAPPER   MAKING BONES   WARP56

ALBUMS

SINGLES

warp-05 INFO-BAR ▶   LOCATION   FORMAT   MEDIA
                                       ▶PREFERENCES   ▶HELP   ▶HOME

ALBUMS   Internet

CHRIS MCGRAIL, DORIAN MOORE AND DAN SAYERS FROM KLEBER WERE THE CONSTRUCTION TEAM THAT PUT THE SITE TOGETHER. BETWEEN THEM THEY HAVE CREATED MANY DIFFERENT WEBSITES UNDER THE KLEBER BANNER, INCLUDING SITES FOR KYLIE, SADE, THE BEATLES, JULIAN COPE AND NINJA TUNE. THE WARP INVADERS GAME HTTP://WWW.WARPRECORDS.COM/INVADERS WAS CREATED BY JAMES TINDELL. ▬▬ Chris McGrail, Dorian Moore und Dan Sayers von Kleber haben die Site als Konstruktionsteam zusammengestellt. Gemeinsam waren sie für zahlreiche Websites unter der Bezeichnung „Kleber" verantwortlich, darunter Sites für Kylie, Sade, die Beatles, Julian Cope und Ninja Tune. Das Warp-Invaders-Spiel <www.warprecords.com/invaders> wurde von James Tindell geschaffen.

MANHATTAN TIMEFORMATIONS
Brian McGrath / Mark Watkins

NET EXCELLENCE

http://www.skyscraper.org/timeformations

Manhattan Timeformations is a computer model which simultaneously presents a layered, cartographic history of the lower half of Manhattan Island, and an exploded time line chronicling the real estate development of high-rise office buildings, which constitute the skylines of Midtown and Downtown Manhattan. The unusual and hybrid character of this computer model allows one to correlate the cartographic history of 370 years of urban development of the island with the peaks and valleys of office building speculation. It is the swarming activity of real estate speculation during concentrated periods of building activity within highly localized districts that characterizes the timeformation of New York City's skyline.

Manhattan Timeformations ist ein Computermodell, das eine kartografische Geschichte der südlichen Hälfte von Manhattan Island in verschiedenen Layern und gleichzeitig eine Zeitlinie präsentiert, die die Entwicklung jener Hochbauten nachzeichnet, die die Skyline von Midtown und Downtown Manhattan ausmachen. Die ungewöhnliche und hybride Darstellungsweise dieses Computermodells erlaubt es, die kartografische Geschichte der 370-jährigen urbanen Entwicklung der Insel mit den Höhen und Tiefen der Grundstücks- und Bauspekulation in Beziehung zu setzen. Gerade die intensive Bodenspekulation während Perioden konzentrierter Bauaktivität in klar umschriebenen Bereichen charakterisiert die zeitlich definierte Herausbildung der Skyline von New York City.

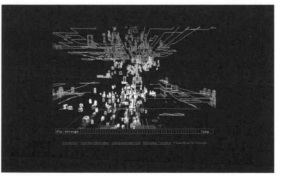

BRIAN MCGRATH (USA) HAS BEEN A PRACTICING ARCHITECT SINCE 1985. HIS WORK HAS BEEN EXHIBITED IN THE QUEENS MUSEUM AND AT PARSONS SCHOOL OF DESIGN. MCGRATH HAS JUST COMPLETED A FULBRIGHT SENIOR SCHOLAR FELLOWSHIP AT CHULALONGKORN UNIVERSITY IN BANGKOK, THAILAND, WHERE HE CONSULTED ON CURRICULA AND COMPUTER TECHNOLO-GIES FOR A NEW MASTER OF URBAN DESIGN PROGRAM FOR THE FACULTY OF ARCHITECTURE. MARK WATKINS (USA) IS A DESIGNER OF WEBSITES FOR THE SKYSCRAPER MUSEUM AND THE DEPARTMENT OF ARCHITECTURE AT PARSONS SCHOOL OF DESIGN AND AN ADJUNCT INSTRUCTOR OF DIGITAL DESIGN COURSES IN ARCHITECTURE, ANIMATION AND WEB DESIGN AT PARSONS SCHOOL OF DESIGN. ▬▬ Brian McGrath (USA) arbeitet seit 1985 als Architekt. Seine Arbeiten wurden im Queens Museum und an der Parsons School of Design ausgestellt. Er hat jüngst einen Fulbright-Senior-Stipendiatenaufenthalt an der Chulalongkorn-Universität in Bangkok abgeschlossen, wo er an der Architekturfakultät als Berater bei der Studien-gangplanung und der Computertechnologie für einen neu zu erstellenden Master-Studiengang zur Stadtplanung tätig war. Mark Watkins (USA) ist der Website-Designer für das Skyscraper Museum und die Architekturabteilung der Parsons School of Design sowie als Lektor für Kurse in Digitalem Architekturdesign, Animation und Webdesign an der Parsons School tätig.

360DEGREES
Alison Cornyn / Sue Johnson

Over the past three years, we have been working with prison inmates, lawyers, judges, corrections officers, parents, victims of crime and others to tell their stories in their own words. Inmates and officers were given tape recorders to keep audio diaries of their experiences in prison. Each story is focused around a specific case and is told through the perspectives of 4—6 people. As you listen to the stories you are immersed in each person's personal space —prison cells, offices, judges chambers and living rooms.

Since 1980 the U.S. prison population has quadrupled to over two million people, most of whom are black or Hispanic, and poor. *360degrees* has grown out of our concern regarding the impact of incarceration on the people directly involved, on their families and on the wider community. Positing that the social policies that sustain this punitive system are based on fear and lack of understanding, this is a project where people with diverse stories of the legal system—from prisoners to judges to the general public—can share their experiences and opinions, and engage in a productive dialogue on the website: www.*360degrees*.org. It is our hope that this site challenges perceptions about who is in prison today and why, and that it will generate ideas, big and small about how we can make positive changes in our communities.

The site tells first person stories through photographs and audio, visually translates statistical information into interactive scenarios and hosts a variety of discussions in the dialogue area. We partnered with a doctoral student at John Jay College of Criminal Justice to write an interactive timeline of the US criminal justice system. We are working with educators and students to develop an educational guide and a Social Action

In den letzten drei Jahren haben wir mit Gefängnisinsassen, Rechtsanwälten, Richtern, Vollzugsbeamten, Eltern, Verbrechensopfern und anderen gearbeitet, damit sie uns ihre Geschichte in ihren eigenen Worten erzählen. Insassen und Beamte erhielten Tonbandgeräte, um im Gefängnis ein Audiotagebuch ihrer Erfahrungen zu führen. Jede Geschichte dreht sich um einen spezifischen Fall und wird aus der Perspektive von vier bis sechs Personen erzählt. Beim Anhören der Stories taucht man in den persönlichen Raum des Erzählers ein – in Gefängniszellen, Büros, Richterzimmer und Wohnräume.

Seit 1980 hat sich die Zahl der Gefängnisinsassen auf über zwei Millionen vervierfacht, von denen die meisten Schwarze oder Hispanos und arm sind. *360degrees* ist aus unserem Interesse an der Auswirkung der Haft auf die Betroffenen, ihre Familien und die Gesellschaft im weiteren Sinne entstanden. Die sozialpolitischen Ansätze, die dieses Strafsystem erhalten, basieren auf Furcht und fehlendem Verständnis. Mit *www.360degrees.org* soll unterschiedlichen Zielgruppen – von Gefangenen über Richter bis zur allgemeinen Öffentlichkeit – eine Plattform gegeben werden, auf der sie ihre Erfahrungen und Meinungen austauschen und einen produktiven Dialog führen können. Wir hoffen, dass diese Site die Wahrnehmung dafür schärft, wer und warum heutzutage in unseren Gefängnissen einsitzt, und dass sie kleinere oder größere Ideen liefert, die dazu beitragen, in unseren Gemeinschaften positive Veränderungen herbeizuführen.

Die Site erzählt anhand von Fotografien und Audio-Geschichten in der Ich-Form, übersetzt statistische Information visuell in interaktive Szenarien und bietet im Dialogbereich eine Anzahl von Diskussionen an. Wir haben uns

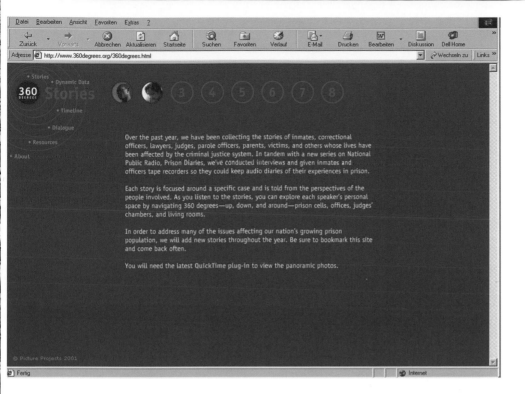

© Picture Projects 2001

Network for schools and communities nationwide. We are partnering with radio producers and journalists across the country as we add new stories.

360degrees has been funded in part by Creative Capital, The Corporation for Public Broadcasting, New York State Council on the Arts, The New York Council for the Humanities and The New York Community Trust. Radio production by Joe Richman and Wendy Dorr, Flash programming by Veronique Brossier and dotsperinch, NY.

mit einem Doktoranden des John Jay College of Criminal Justice zusammengetan, um eine interaktive Zeitleiste des US-Strafrechtssystems zu schreiben. Wir arbeiten mit Erziehern und Studenten an der Erstellung eines Erziehungsführers und eines Sozialarbeits-Netzwerks für Schulen und Institutionen. Wir kooperieren mit Radioproduzenten und Journalisten aus dem ganzen Land bei der Erstellung neuer Stories.

360degrees wird finanziell unterstützt von Creative Capital, The Corporation for Public Broadcasting, New York State Council on the Arts, The New York Council for the Humanities und The New York Community Trust. Die Radioproduktion erfolgte durch Joe Richman und Wendy Dorr, die Flash-Programmierung von Veronique Bossier und dotsperinch, New York.

ALISON CORNYN (US) AND SUE JOHNSON (US) FORMED PICTURE PROJECTS IN 1995 AS A WAY TO USE NEW TECHNOLOGIES AND DOCUMENTARY PHOTOGRAPHY TO EXAMINE COMPLEX SOCIAL ISSUES. OVER THE PAST SIX YEARS THE TEAM HAS BECOME WELL KNOW FOR ITS USE OF INTERACTIVE NARRATIVE. THEY HAVE RECEIVED RECEIVING NUMEROUS AWARDS AND INTERNATIONAL PRESS COVERAGE FOR COLLABORATIVE PROJECTS ABOUT BOSNIA, THE VIETNAM WAR ERA, KURDISTAN AND THE U.S. CRIMINAL JUSTICE SYSTEM. CORNYN AND JOHNSON ARE BOTH WORKING ARTISTS AND HAVE EXHIBITED VIDEO, NEW MEDIA AND INSTALLATION WORKS IN NEW YORK, FLORIDA, MASSACHUSETTS, THE CZECH REPUBLIC, HOLLAND, GERMANY, MACEDONIA, SWEDEN, COLUMBIA AND ITALY. THEY FREQUENTLY PRESENT THEIR WORK ON NEW MEDIA PANELS AND AT INTERNATIONAL FILM FESTIVALS. ■■■ Alison Cornyn (USA) und Sue Johnson (USA) gründeten Picture Projects 1995 mit dem Ziel, neue Technologien und Dokumentarfotografie einzusetzen, um komplexe soziale Fragen zu analysieren. In den letzten sechs Jahren wurde das Team besonders für den Einsatz interaktiver Narration bekannt. Sie haben zahlreiche Preise und internationales Presseecho für ihre kooperativen Projekte über Bosnien, die Zeit des Vietnam-Kriegs, Kurdistan und über das Strafsystem der USA bekommen. Cornyn und Johnson sind beide aktive Künstlerinnen und haben ihre Video-, Neue-Medien- und Installationsarbeiten in New York, Florida, Massachusetts, Tschechien, Holland Deutschland, Mazedonien, Schweden, Kolumbien und Italien ausgestellt. Sie präsentieren ihre Arbeiten häufig bei Mediendiskussionen und bei internationalen Filmfestivals.

BOOMBOX.NET
Laurence Desarzens / Raoul Cannemeijer

Whether it's French hip hop crews, American turntablists, English drum and bass DJs or German electronic wizards: since 1997 *BoomBox.net* streams the best of urban club culture on the net.

But what's the point?

For the two founders Raoul Cannemeijer and Laurence Desarzens, it's a way to show the vitality of urban sounds from anywhere anytime: an alternative to mainstream entertainment. An ever-changing mosaic of styles, constantly evolving for our aural pleasure. Having been involved in club culture themselves for years, and having and still promoting their own club nights (XPD), they decided to share their musical tastes online and play with the beats and bytes. Get in, plug in, and stream. *BoomBox.net* online mixtapes for the streetsmart generation—Pure Dope.

Egal, ob französische Hip-Hop-Crews, amerikanische Turntable-Artisten, englische Drum-and-Bass-DJs oder deutsche Elektronik-Zauberer – seit 1997 bietet *BoomBox.net* das Feinste vom Feinen der urbanen Clubkultur auf dem Netz.

Aber worum geht's?

Für die beiden Gründer Raoul Cannemeijer und Laurence Desarzens ist es eine Möglichkeit, jederzeit die Vitalität urbaner Klänge, egal, woher sie stammen, zu präsentieren – eine Alternative zum Mainstream-Entertainment, ein sich ständig veränderndes Mosaik von Stilen, das sich für unser Hörvergnügen weiterentwickelt. Die beiden sind selbst seit Jahren in die Club-Kultur eingebunden, hatten und haben noch immer ihre eigenen Club Nights (XPD) und beschlossen eines Tages, ihren musikalischen Geschmack online mit anderen zu teilen und mit den Beats und Bytes zu spielen. Reinkommen, einstöpseln, und runterladen – *BoomBox.net* online Mixtapes für die smarte Generation – Pure Dope.

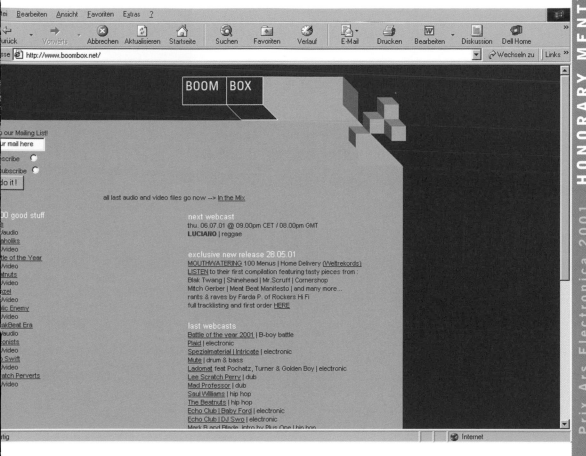

DMG:I.O* VS. R3:DEV*

Bradley Grosh

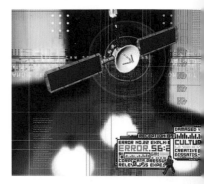

D MG:I.O* vs. R3:DEV* was produced as an explorative graphical and interactive experience representing the evolution of a mentally inept character towards the status of innovative Design Superhero through the assistance of the elite masters of the Innovatechnique ...

It was produced entirely by Bradley Grosh in 3 months using a Powermac G4, a Sony Digital 8 Camcorder, Flash4, SoundEdit 16 and the Adobe Suite (Photoshop, Illustrator, Premiere, AfterEffects, Dimensions).

Upon launching the project from the splash screen, the user will get a loading screen containing a body builder and ornamentation. This screen is loading the front end of the piece. No interactivity.

Next, the first screen will drop in, which is a draggable image strip ornamented with content pertaining to the first half of the piece. Drag this up and down while the remaining portion of the piece is loading.

The first screen is a quicktime interface. The user will see two buttons in the "movie window" labeled "DLF" and "HCF". Rolling over these buttons activates an effect. The user can also pause the playback of the animation by clicking the pause button below.

When finished with the interactivity, the user should roll over the play button and press it.

The user will then be taken to a screen with a satellite and TV screens in the background. Roll over, press and drag the satellite. (Don't release the mouse however!!!) Drag up and down to view a new content block. When finished, release the mouse button to proceed to the next screen.

This screen will be a somewhat hectic and busy blue screen with a stencil of a confused man. At the bottom is another content block with some arrows on the far right side. Roll over, press and drag these arrows to the right, revealing more of the content block. Press on

DMG:I.O* vs. R3:DEV* wurde als experimentelle grafische und interaktive Erfahrung konzipiert, die die Verwandlung einer geistig unfähigen Gestalt in einen innovativen Design-Superhelden darstellt – was nur dank der Unterstützung seitens elitärer Meister der Innovatechnik möglich war ...

DMG:I.O* vs. R3:DEV* wurde von Bradley Grosh innerhalb von drei Monaten fertig gestellt: Zum Einsatz kamen dabei ein Powermac G4, ein Sony Digital 8 Camcorder, Flash4, SoundEdit 16 sowie die Adobe Suite (Photoshop, Illustrator, Premiere, AfterEffects, Dimension).

Wenn der User das Projekt über den Splash-Screen startet, erhält er zunächst einen Lade-Bildschirm mit einem Bodybuilder und Ornamenten. Dieser Bildschirm lädt das Front-End des Stücks und ist nicht interaktiv.

Danach taucht ein erstes Fenster auf, das einen drag-fähigen Bildstreifen zeigt, der mit Inhalten zur ersten Hälfte des Stückes gefüllt ist. Diesen Streifen kann man auf- und zuziehen, während der restliche Teil des Stückes noch lädt.

Der erste Schirm zeigt ein Quicktime-Interface. Der Benutzer sieht zwei Schaltknöpfe im „Filmfenster", die „DLF" und „HCF" heißen. Bewegt sich die Maus über diese Knöpfe, werden bestimmte Effekte aktiviert. Der Anwender kann auch das Abspielen der Animation anhalten, wenn der Pause-Knopf darunter gedrückt wird. Wenn die Interaktivität abgeschlossen ist, drückt man per Rollover die Play-Taste. Der Benutzer kommt dann zu einem Bildschirm, in dessen Hintergrund sich ein Satellit und TV-Schirme befinden. Einmal Rollover, Maustate drücken und den Satelliten ziehen (Maustaste nicht auslassen!). Beim Hinauf- und Hinunterziehen werden neue Inhaltsblöcke angezeigt; wenn man die Maustaste loslässt, kommt man zum nächsten Bildschirm.

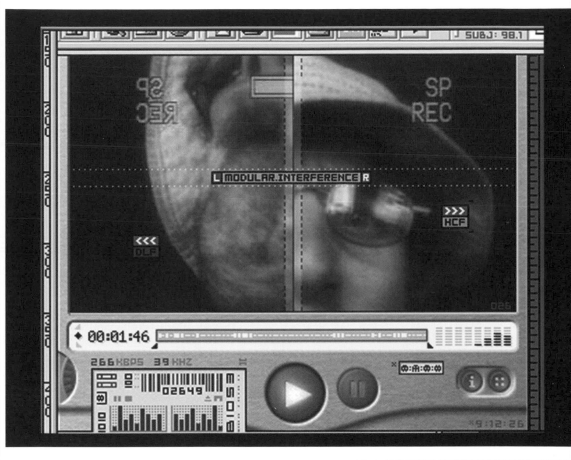

the confused designer in the TV screen on the content block that is now revealed. This will take you through a short animated transition.
The next screen is all black with the text "dmg I.0* Reboot" on the top left. Roll over the text to proceed …

Dieser ist eine etwas hektische, blaue Fläche mit dem Bild eines konfusen Menschen. Am unteren Rand befindet sich eine neue Inhaltsfläche mit Pfeilen an der rechten Seite. Ein Rollover und ein Druck auf die Pfeile enthüllen mehr vom Inhalt. Drückt man nun den konfusen Designer in den Fernsehbildschirm des jetzt dargestellten Inhaltsblocks, so wird man durch eine kurze animierte Übergangssequenz geleitet.
Auf dem nächsten ganz schwarzen Bildschirm steht in der linken oberen Ecke „dmg I.0* Reboot". Um fortzufahren, braucht man nur die Maus über den Text zu bewegen …

BRADLEY GROSH (USA) IS THE CREATIVE DIRECTOR FOR GMUNKSTUDIO, A ONE-MAN PRODUCTION HOUSE SPECIALIZING IN ONLINE NARRATIONS AND VIDEOGRAPHY. BRADLEY IS ALSO AN ARTIST FOR VIR2L TECHNOLOGY IN ROCKVILLE AND MOVED TO LONDON TO WORK IN THE COMPANY'S LONDON DEPARTMENT. BRADLEY GRADUATED SUMMA CUM LAUDE IN FINE ART AND FILM AT HUMBOLDT STATE UNIVERSITY. ■■■■ Bradley Grosh (USA) ist der Creative Director von gmunkstudio, einer Ein-Mann-Produktionsfirma, die sich auf Online-Erzählungen und Videographie spezialisiert hat. Bradley arbeitet auch künstlerisch für Vir2L Technology in Rockville und ist nach London übersiedelt, um in der Londoner Niederlassung der Firma zu arbeiten. Bradley hat sein Studium in bildender Kunst und Film an der Humboldt State University mit Summa Cum Laude abgeschlossen.

FUCKED COMPANY

Philip Kaplan

Your classic deadpool is a game of picking celebrity deaths. Points are generally earned based on odds (which are usually based on the age of the celebrity).

FuckedCompany.com is a game based on the classic deadpool, but instead of betting for (or against) people, you're betting on companies. The lines are a little blurred when dealing with companies, because there is rarely a clean-cut death. To make up for this, *FuckedCompany.com* rates different levels of a company's demise and awards points based on the level of severity. See official rules for more information on scoring.

FuckedCompany.com has also pretty much turned into the source for news about dot-com companies. Bad news, that is.

FuckedCompany.com is free. ~~I don't make—and don't plan to make—any money from it~~. I could maybe make money doing this.

Greetz to waxman, spoon serv, maggot, pseaf, perlgrrl, ftg, and all my other 3l33t homies.

Beim klassischen Spiel „Deadpool" geht es darum, Todesfälle von Berühmtheiten vorherzusagen. Punkte werden normalerweise auf der Basis von Wettquoten vergeben (die ihrerseits auf dem Alter der Stars beruhen).

FuckedCompany.com ist ein Spiel, das auf dem klassischen Deadpool basiert, aber statt auf (bzw. gegen) Leute zu wetten, wird hier auf Firmen gesetzt. Die Grenzen sind bei Firmen insofern etwas schwammig, weil es hier kaum einmal einen eindeutigen „Tod" gibt. Um dieses Manko wettzumachen, bewertet *FuckedCompany.com* verschiedene Ebenen eines Firmenuntergangs und vergibt Punkte je nach der Schwere des Desasters. Nähere Details über die Punktewertung stehen in den offiziellen Regeln.

FuckedCompany.com hat sich ziemlich stark in *die* Quelle für Nachrichten über Dot-Com-Unternehmen verwandelt – für schlechte Nachrichten, versteht sich. ~~Ich verdiene kein Geld mit der Site und plane auch nicht, damit Geld zu verdienen.~~ Ich könnte vielleicht auch Geld verdienen damit.

Grüße an waxman, spoon serv, maggot, pseaf, perlgrrl, ftg und alle meine anderen 3l33t-Homies.

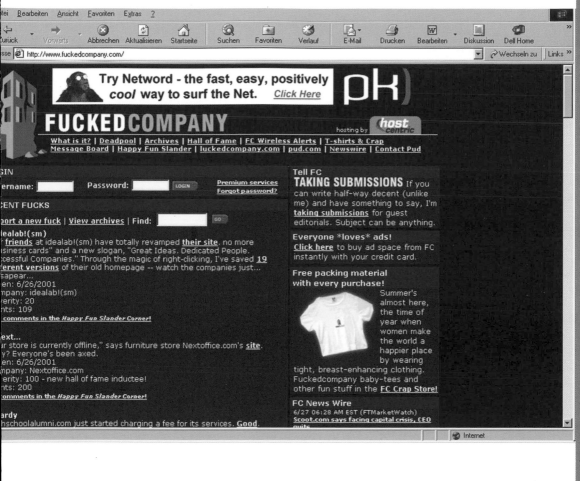

Netbaby World

Netbabyworld is a game community adapted for the Internet and built around a group of characters living on the Nettown-Peninsula. The leading character of *Netbabyworld* is Digger. He was brought up on the moon and moved to Nettown after a successful career as a TV-host.

The *Netbabyworld* philosophy is best described in one word—"fun". We aim to entertain. In consistence with our belief, no product from *Netbabyworld* contains lethal violence or sexual elements.

Netbabyworld.com is the on-line destination for all Netbaby-fun. Our goal is to be the most entertaining experience available on the Internet.

Any game you want to play on *Netbabyworld.com* is for free. You don't have to register to play shockwave games, just say Hi! to Digger and start having fun. To play PlayCom multi-player games, you have to register. On this site you also get a first-hand look at our latest releases as well as updated news about *Netbabyworld* and the citizens of Nettown.

By using our Player Lab you can save, list and compare high scores with other players, both worldwide and nationally. You can also build your own teams and even your own character. It's all for free. Join by registering. If you don't want to use your real name, you're free to choose an alias. When you register at the Player Lab, you also get access to the Netbaby Club, including the *Netbabyworld* Museum and the Media-center. Here you can download high-tech graphics, icons, music packs, movies, 3-D pictures, soundsets etc. to customize your personal desktop.

In 1994, ACNE International, a leading Scandinavian design agency, started to produce Shockwave games. Their first games were small, both in centimeters and in kilobytes—to keep the download time short—and were therefore called Netbabies. The concept grew,

Netbaby World ist eine für das Internet adaptierte Spiele-Community, die rund um eine Gruppe von Figuren aufgebaut ist, die auf der Nettown-Halbinsel leben. Die Hauptgestalt von Netbabyworld ist Digger. Er ist auf dem Mond aufgewachsen und nach einer erfolgreichen Karriere als TV-Moderator nach Nettown übersiedelt.

Die Philosophie hinter *Netbabyworld* lässt sich am besten in einem Wort zusammenfassen: Spaß. Entsprechend unserer Philosophie enthält keines der Produkte aus *Netbabyworld* tödliche Gewalt oder sexuelle Elemente.

Netbabyworld.com ist die Online-Destination für jede Art von Netbaby-Fun. Unser Ziel ist es, die unterhaltsamste Erfahrung zu bieten, die man im Netz machen kann.

Alle Spiele, die man auf *Netbabyworld* spielen kann, sind kostenlos. Man braucht sich nicht registrieren zu lassen, um Shockwave-Games zu spielen, es reicht, einfach Hallo zu Digger zu sagen, und los geht's! Um an PlayCom-Spielen für mehrere Mitspieler teilnehmen zu können, ist allerdings eine Registrierung erforderlich. Auf dieser Site erhält man auch einen Überblick aus erster Hand über unsere jüngsten Releases sowie die neuesten Nachrichten über *Netbabyworld* und die Einwohner von Nettown. Durch Verwendung unseres Player Labs ist es möglich, Punkterekorde zu speichern, aufzulisten und mit anderen Spielern im In- und Ausland zu vergleichen. Man kann auch eigene Teams zusammenstellen und sogar eigene Figuren kreieren – und das alles ist kostenlos und durch eine einfache Registrierung zugänglich. Wer seinen echten Namen nicht angeben will, kann auch ein Alias benutzen. Registrierte Benutzer des Player Labs haben auch Zugang zum Netbaby Club inklusive dem *Netbabyworld*-Museum und dem Media-Center. Dort

and in April of 1999 ACNE founded Netbaby World AB (Incorporated) along with Nightscape Communications, Media and Internet investor, and the domain <www.netbabyworld.com> became an active game community. In the spring of 2000, Netbaby World AB was merged with Game Design Sweden to further enhance its technical strengths.

Today, Netbaby World AB is developing a 3-D game engine that can be modified for several types of games. The goal is to present a perfect mix of multi-player, advanced and smaller games for the Internet as well as games for wireless technology, including a wide range of *Netbabyworld* merchandise.

können Hi-Tech-Grafiken, Icons, Musikpakete, Filme, 3D-Bilder, Sound-Sets usw. heruntergeladen werden, die zur Individualisierung des eigenen Desktops dienen können.

1994 begann ACNE International, eine der führenden skandinavischen Design-Firmen, Shockwave-Spiele zu produzieren. Die ersten Spiele waren recht klein – sowohl in Zentimetern wie in Kilobytes, um die Downloadzeiten kurz zu halten – und wurden dementsprechend „Netbabies" genannt. Das Konzept wuchs, und im April 1999 gründete ACNE gemeinsam mit dem Medien- und Internet-Investor Nightscape Communications die Firma Netbaby World AB. Die Domain <www.netbabyworld.com> wurde zu einer aktiven Spiele-Community. Im Frühjahr 2000 wurde Netbaby World AB mit Game Design Sweden fusioniert, um ihre gemeinsamen technischen Stärken weiter zu verbessern. Heute entwickelt Netbaby World AB eine 3D-Spiele-Engine, die für zahlreiche Typen von Spielen modifiziert werden kann. Ziel ist es, eine perfekte Mischung aus Multi-Player-, leistungsstarken und kleinen Spielen für das Internet sowie für kabellose Technologien zu präsentieren, darunter auch ein breites Spektrum von *Netbabyworld*-Merchandise.

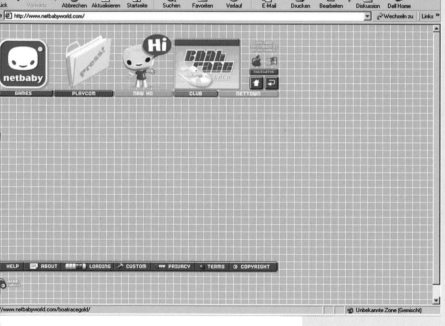

NETBABY WORLD. OUR POLICY IS THAT WE NEVER SPEAK ABOUT THE INDIVIDUALS WHEN WE TALK ABOUT OUR WORK. ▬
Netbaby World. Wir reden grundsätzlich nicht von den Individuen, wenn wir über unsere Arbeit sprechen.

AUSTROPOLIS
Barbara Neumayr

Mach weiter, Du kannst es!
Jedes Kind soll seine eigenen Erfahrungen machen...
Komm doch bitte da runter, das ist gefährlich!

Austropolis is a political multi-user web-game where avatars—artificial creatures representing the users—act and interact independently in their predefined environment. They live in *Austropolis*, a cyber democracy run by the avatars who make new laws, organise demonstrations, opinion polls or plebiscites and elect a new president once a week. The ultimate aim of every avatar is to make a successful career as a politician and maybe even become the president of *Austropolis*. The avatars depend on the users' advice in order to succeed, but they don't always do as they are told.

As a first step, each user creates his own avatar and gives him a specific personality and political orientation by answering several psychological and political questions, and taking a certain attitude toward his avatar in three scenes representing the latter's childhood, as well as a specific visual styling.

Once the user has created his avatar, his virtual alter ego starts living an independent life. He goes to demonstrations, votes in the elections and talks to his fellow avatars. The avatar's actions are determined by his personality and political orientation, as well as by external influences, the user's advice and needs like hunger, thirst, boredom and so on.

The application is active 24 hours a day in order to simulate the life-processes of its virtual creatures and keep the environmental model going. This means that the avatar continues to take actions while the user is off-line and every time the user logs in, he will find an account of the events that have happened to his avatar in the meantime. Whenever two avatars meet and talk to each other, their profiles are matched and one of them might make the other one change his mind about a specific political issue, thereby slightly altering his personality.

Austropolis ist ein politisches Multi-User-Web-Game, bei dem Avatare – künstliche Gestalten als Repräsentanten des Anwenders – unabhängig in einem vorgegebenen Environment agieren und interagieren. Sie leben in Austropolis, einer Cyberdemokratie, die von den Avataren regiert wird, die neue Gesetze erlassen, Demonstrationen organisieren, Meinungsumfragen und Volksbefragungen durchführen und jede Woche einen neuen Präsidenten wählen. Das Ziel eines jeden Avatars ist es, eine erfolgreiche Karriere als Politiker zu machen und möglichst Präsident von Austropolis zu werden. Der Erfolg der Avatare hängt vor allem von den Einflüsterungen der Anwender ab – allerdings folgen sie dem Rat aber nicht immer.

Zunächst schafft jeder User seinen eigenen Avatar und verleiht ihm eine spezifische Persönlichkeit und politische Ausrichtung, indem er etliche psychologische und politische Fragen beantwortet und in drei Szenen, die die Kindheit des Avatars repräsentieren, eine bestimmte Haltung gegenüber diesem einnimmt; außerdem erhält er eine individuelle visuelle Gestalt. Sobald der Anwender seinen Avatar geschaffen hat, beginnt dieses virtuelle *Alter Ego* sein unabhängiges Leben zu führen – er geht zu Demonstrationen und zu Wahlen und unterhält sich mit seinen Mit-Avataren. Seine Handlungen werden durch seine Persönlichkeit und politische Einstellung, durch den Rat des Anwenders und seine Bedürfnisse wie Hunger, Durst, durch Langeweile usw. bestimmt. Die Applikation ist 24 Stunden täglich aktiv, um den Lebensprozess ihrer virtuellen Kreaturen zu simulieren und das Umweltmodell in Betrieb zu halten. Das bedeutet, dass der Avatar auch handelt, wenn sein User offline ist. Jedes Mal, wenn sich der Benutzer einloggt, findet er eine Zusammenfassung von all dem

The game includes features like a daily newspaper reporting on the current political, economic and social situation in *Austropolis*, an in-built mail-box that allows users to contact each other and a discussion forum for direct multi-user interaction.

Austropolis is based on the NetLife platform, which has been developed by sysis in order to implement web-based multi-user simulation games. NetLife is a Java-based platform, which draws on a variety of scientific approaches to simulate social systems and artificial life, including psychological models based on the works of C. G. Jung and Eysenk and artificial intelligence solutions. Unlike most AI solutions, the focus of sysis NetLife is on the individual psyche and social behaviour in the interaction of such artificial beings rather than on their bodily organism.

Austropolis was launched at www.*Austropolis*.at or www.profil.at/*Austropolis* on March 5, 2001.

vor, was seinem Avatar in der Zwischenzeit widerfahren ist. Wenn zwei Avatare sich treffen und sich unterhalten, werden ihre Profile aufeinander abgestimmt, sodass einer der beiden etwa den anderen von einem bestimmten politischen Anliegen überzeugen kann, was wiederum dessen Persönlichkeit leicht verändert.

Das Spiel enthält Details wie eine tägliche Zeitungsberichterstattung über die gegenwärtige politische, ökonomische und soziale Situation in Austropolis, eine eingebaute Mailbox, die einen Kontakt zwischen Usern erlaubt, und ein Diskussionsforum für die direkte Interaktion zwischen mehreren Benutzern.

Austropolis basiert auf einer NetLife-Plattform, die von sysis entwickelt wurde, um webgestützte Multi-User-Simulationsspiele zu erstellen. NetLife ist eine Java-basierte Plattform, die eine Vielzahl wissenschaftlicher Ansätze verwendet, um soziale Systeme und künstliches Leben zu simulieren, darunter psychologische Modelle, die auf den Werken von C.G. Jung und Eysenk sowie KI-Lösungen basieren. Im Unterschied zu den meisten KI-Anwendungen liegt der Schwerpunkt bei Net Life von sysis auf der individuellen Psyche und dem Sozialverhalten in der Interaktion der künstlichen Lebewesen und nicht so sehr auf ihrem körperlichen Organismus.

Austropolis wurde am 5. März 2001 auf *www.Austropolis.at* und *www.profil.at/Austropolis* gestartet.

Technische Voraussetzungen:
PC mit Flash Plugin 4 oder höher, Netscape Navigator bzw. Internet Explorer 4.0 oder höher.

BARBARA NEUMAYR (A), BORN 1969, STUDIED ECONOMICS AND BUSINESS ADMINISTRATION, HAS WORKED FOR SYSIS SINCE 1994; ASSISTANT PROFESSOR AT THE INTERDISCIPLINARY INSTITUTE OF ENVIRONMENTAL ECONOMICS AT THE VIENNA UNIVERSITY; ECONOMICS AND MANAGEMENT FROM 1996 TO MAY 2000. CO-FOUNDER OF SYSIS INTERACTIVE SIMULATION AG AND CURRENTLY WORKING THERE AS MANAGER BUSINESS UNIT NETLIFE. ■■■■ Barbara Neumayr (A), geb. 1969. Studium der Handelswissenschaften. Seit 1994 Mitarbeit bei sysis, zwischen 1996 und Mai 2000 Assistentin am Interdisziplinären Institut für Umwelt und Wirtschaft an der Wirtschaftsuniversität Wien; Gründungsgesellschafterin und derzeit tätig als Leiterin der Business Unit NetLife bei sysis interactive simulations ag.

BYTES FOR ALL
Frederick Noronha / Partha Pratim Sarkar

Realities of the Third World = a modem costs more than a cow + access to telecommunication is a privilege + information by definition is a property of the government.

Welcome to South Asia. This talent-rich, resource-poor, tragic powerhouse of immense software skills, finds its abilities recognized across the globe. And yet millions here can't find the solutions that could make their life a little less of a struggle.

Likewise, software brains from the region are serving some of the biggest companies on the globe. But it also finds itself ironically unable to afford the prices of "legal" software that it very badly needs for itself.

The term "poverty" is most significantly used without addressing its roots to global exploitation. Northern trade interests ensure a conditional access to technology for the urban middle class of the developing nations. For the majority of the world population, IT is a faraway phenomenon let alone a necessary item, as the global village represents the global middle class only. Information, on the other hand, information is strictly denied in the name of state ownership. Imposing huge taxes on VSATs, creating bureaucratic impediments, controlling telephone access are what is rewarded to most of the cases. A fusion of all these create a power structure that fits hand in glove with the interests of local and international elite.

But we simply can't afford to be indifferent to these developments and to let this technology pass by. Here again, IT is the subversive tool that can be effectively used to challenge the whole trend and to reverse the system to the benefits of southern countries in general and of our people in particular. *bytes for all*, an online newsletter from South Asia, stands on this philosophy. It tries to explore the possibilities and examples of

Die Wirklichkeit der Dritten Welt = Ein Modem ist teurer als eine Kuh + Zugang zur Telekommunikation ist ein Privileg + Information ist per definitionem Eigentum der Regierung.

Willkommen in Südasien. Dieses Zentrum immenser Software-Entwicklungsleistung – so reich an Talent und tragischerweise so arm an Ressourcen – wird mit seinen Fähigkeiten auf der ganzen Welt anerkannt. Und dennoch können Millionen hier keineswegs jene Lösungen finden, die ihren Lebenskampf ein klein wenig erleichtern würden. Und wenn auch die Software-Denker dieser Region bei einigen der weltweit größten Firmen unter Vertrag stehen, so ist dieses Gebiet ironischerweise nicht in der Lage, den Preis für die „legale" Software zu bezahlen, die es so dringend bräuchte.

Der Begriff „Armut" wird häufig angewendet, ohne seine Wurzeln in der globalen Ausbeutung zu berücksichtigen. Die wirtschaftlichen Interessen des Nordens sichern der urbanen Mittelklasse der Entwicklungsländer einen bedingten Zugang zur Technologie. Für den Großteil der Weltbevölkerung aber ist IT ein fernes Phänomen und schon gar keine notwendige Einrichtung, zumal das globale Dorf einzige die globale Mittelschicht repräsentiert.

Der Zugang zu Information wird andererseits auch im Namen des staatlichen Informationsmonopols erschwert. Hohe Steuern auf Satellitenschüsseln, die Schaffung bürokratischer Hürden, die Überwachung des Zugangs zur Telefonie – das wird in den meisten Fällen von seiten des Staates geboten. Aus dem Zusammenwirken all dieser Elemente ergibt sich eine Machtstruktur, die sich nahtlos den Interessen der lokalen und internationalen Eliten anpasst.

Wir können es uns einfach nicht leisten, gegenüber diesen Entwicklungen indifferent zu blieben und diese Technologie an uns vorbeige-

such usage. Some of the most relevant software/Internet/computer/IT ventures in South Asia, ironically, fail to get the attention they merit. Showcasing these alternative IT practices may not be perceived as good business sense for the mainstream media.

bytes for all is an attempt to swim against the tide. Through a web site and an e-mail based mailing list, we hope to update interested readers about new and interesting ventures. Attempts that focus on people before profits. This initiative regularly brings articles, news bits and information clips on interesting and people-oriented IT practices in this region. It works as a one-stop information center where people involved in these initiatives can find their collaborators, can discuss issues pertaining to their interests, can know more about the developments and can be aware of other initiatives. It also organizes different campaigns with regard to ICT developments in the third world countries.

hen lassen. Hier ist die Informationstechnologie jenes subversive Werkzeug, das – effizient eingesetzt – diesen Trend stoppen und das System zum Nutzen der südlichen Länder im Allgemeinen und unseres Landes im besonderen umkehren kann. *bytes for all*, ein Online-Magazin aus Südasien, beruht auf dieser Philosophie. Das Projekt versucht, die Möglichkeiten und Beispiele für einen solchen Einsatz zu erforschen. Einige der wichtigsten Software-/Internet-/Computer-/IT-Unternehmen in Südasien erhalten nicht die ihnen gebührende Aufmerksamkeit – eine Darstellung ihrer alternativen IT-Praktiken scheint den Mainstream-Medien nicht zu ihrem Geschäftsauftrag zu passen. *bytes for all* ist ein Versuch, gegen den Strom zu schwimmen. Über die Website und eine E-Mail-basierte Mailingliste hoffen wir, interessierte Leser auf neue und interessante Unternehmungen aufmerksam zu machen, auf Versuche, die den Menschen über den Profit stellen. *bytes for all* dient als zentrales Informationszentrum, wo die in solche Initiativen Involvierten ihre Mitarbeiter finden können, Anliegen im Rahmen ihrer Interessen diskutieren, mehr über die neuesten Entwicklungen erfahren und andere Initiativen kennenlernen können. Darüber hinaus organisieren wir diverse Kampagnen im Zusammenhang mit Informations- und Computertechnologie in Ländern der Dritten Welt.

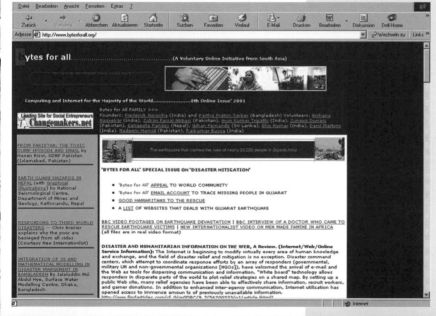

FREDERICK NORONHA (RI), CO-FOUNDER OF *BYTES FOR ALL*, IS A FREELANCE JOURNALIST BASED IN GOA, INDIA INTERESTED IN DEVELOPMENTAL ISSUES. PARTHA PRATIM SARKAR (BANGLADESH), CO-FOUNDER, IS A WEB DEVELOPER AND AN ONLINE ACTIVIST BASED IN DHAKA, BANGLADESH. NOW *BYTES FOR ALL* HAS BEEN EXTENDED TO A 13-MEMBER VOLUNTEER TEAM FROM DIFFERENT COUNTRIES OF SOUTH ASIA, INCLUDING ZUNAIRA IN KARACHI, ZUBAIR IN ISLAMABAD, ARCHANA IN GOA, ARUN-KUMAR IN DARMSTADT, SHIVKUMAR IN MUMBAI, SANGEETA IN NEPAL, DARYL IN CHICAGO, GIHAN IN SRI LANKA AND RAJKUMAR IN MELBOURNE. IT IS A VIRTUAL ORGANISATION WITH NO PHYSICAL PRESENCE OR OFFICE. FINANCES: ZERO RUPEES. ALL BASED ON VOLUNTEER WORK. ■ Frederick Noronha (RI), Mitbegründer von *bytes for all*, ist freier Journalist in Goa (Indien) und interessiert sich für Entwicklungsfragen. Partha Pratim Sarkar (Bangladesh), Mitbegründer, ist Web-Entwickler und Online-Aktivist in Dhaka (Bangladesh). Mittlerweile ist *bytes for all* auf ein 13-köpfiges Team von Freiwilligen aus unterschiedlichen Ländern Südasiens erweitert worden, darunter Zunaira in Karachi, Zubair in Islamabad, Archana in Goa, Arun-Kumar in Darmstadt, Shivkumar in Bombay, Sangeeta in Nepal, Daryl in Chicago, Gihan in Sri Lanka und Rajkumar in Melbourne. Es handelt sich um eine virtuelle Organisation ohne physische Anwesenheit und ohne Büro. Finanzen: Null Rupien – alles basiert auf freiwilliger Arbeit.

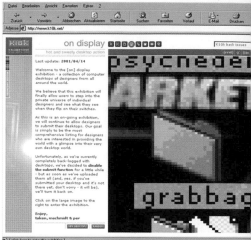

KALIBER10000

Toke Nygaard /
Michael Schmidt /
Per Jørgen Jørgensen

KALIBER10000 is an independent, non-commercial web zine which strives to inspire, to provoke, to allow both others & ourselves the joy of having full creative freedom to give people a break, and re-charge their batteries. We want to put the focus on design, on the whole creative experience, and show everyone out there that not everything has to be streamlined, menu-to-the-left, make-it-look-like-Amazon. Like we say on the site, the things we feature may not always be to your liking, but they're always interesting.

We also want to shoot some holes into some of the more outspoken web design "gurus" who need to get off the lecture circuit and on to the web, so they can actually see what's happening out there—instead of merely theoretizing about it in front of a handful of eat-everything-that-old-men-with-bad-haircuts-say inclined business consultants.

KALIBER10000 is built up around the weekly "issue"—an experiment-like format where anything goes, and where both known and unknown designers/design teams get to strut their stuff, flex their creative muscles, without having to worry about anyone looking over their shoulder or second-guessing their decisions.

To make sure that KALIBER10000 always has a sweet-smelling summery flavor, we have expanded the site over the years with a ton of other goodies, including the massive [on] display exhibition, different forms of special features (games, animated stories, anything that doesn't fit within our issue format), and an almost-hourly updated design news feed, which is kindly supplied by our news-writing buddies from all over the globe.

KALIBER10000 ist ein unabhängiges, nicht-kommerzielles Web-Zine, das inspirieren und provozieren will, das anderen und uns selbst die Freude an vollständiger kreativer Freiheit vermitteln will und zu einer Pause und zum Wiederaufladen der eigenen Batterien einlädt. Unser Schwergewicht liegt auf Design, auf der gesamten kreativen Erfahrung – wir wollen allen Leuten da draußen zeigen, dass nicht alles unbedingt stromlinienförmig glatt sein muss, mit der Menüleiste links im Stil von Amazon. Wie wir auf der Site selbst feststellen, mag vielleicht nicht alles, was wir zeigen, nach jedermanns Geschmack sein – aber interessant ist es auf jeden Fall.

Wir wollen auch ein paar Löcher in einige der lauthals predigenden Web-Design-„Gurus" schießen, die vom hohen Ross herunterkommen und sich ins Web begeben sollten, damit sie sehen, was da draußen wirklich passiert, anstatt nur darüber zu theoretisieren vor einer Hand voll Business-Consultants, die geneigt sind, alles zu schlucken, was die alten Herren mit dem schlechten Haarschnitt so von sich geben.

KALIBER10000 ist rund um die wöchentliche „Ausgabe" aufgebaut – ein experimentelles Format, in dem alles erlaubt ist und wo unbekannte Designer oder Design-Teams ihr Zeug vorstellen, ihre kreativen Muskeln spielen lassen können, ohne befürchten zu müssen, dass ihnen irgendwer über die Schulter schaut und dazwischenredet.

Um sicherzustellen, dass KALIBER10000 immer einen süßen Sommerduft verbreitet, haben wir die Site über die Jahre mit einer Menge anderer Draufgaben garniert: mit einer umfangreichen [on]-Display-Ausstellung, ver-

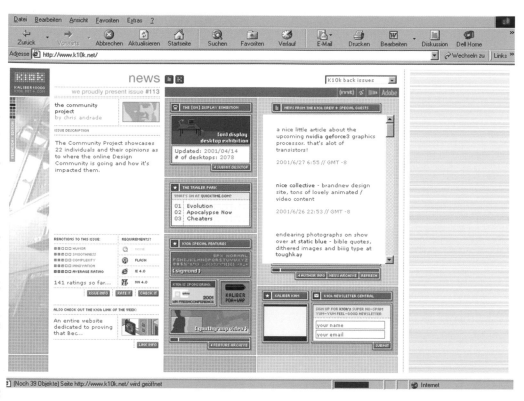

KALIBER10000 has been featured in numerous design magazines & design books, but we try not to let it go to our heads.

The core team behind KALIBER10000 is Toke Nygaard, Michael Schmidt and Per Jørgensen, all originally from Denmark, but now true citizens of the world. We are two-thirds bald, one-third John Lennon's evil twin, and one-third a slight whiff of wet dog. We know that makes four-thirds, but we don't mind.

schiedenen sonstigen Features (Spielen, animierten Stories und allem, was nicht in das Format der Ausgabe passt), und einer fast stündlich aktualisierten Design-News-Leiste, die freundlicherweise von unseren nachrichtenschreibenden Freunden auf der ganzen Welt gespeist wird.

KALIBER10000 wurde in zahlreichen Design-Zeitschriften und -Büchern rezensiert, aber wir sind bemüht, uns dies nicht zu Kopfe steigen zu lassen. Das Kernteam hinter KALIBER10000 besteht aus Toke Nygaard, Michael Schmidt und Per Jørgensen, alle ursprünglich aus Dänemark, jetzt aber echte Weltbürger. Wir sind zu zwei Dritteln kahl, zu einem Drittel der aus der Art geschlagene Zwilling von John Lennon, und zu einem Drittel riechen wir ein wenig nach nassem Hund. Wir wissen, dass das vier Drittel ergibt – aber das ist uns egal.

TOKE NYGAARD (DK), BORN 1973, ATTENDED THE DANISH SCHOOL OF DESIGN; ART DIRECTOR AT ARANEUM, COPENHAGEN 97-99, ART DIRECTOR AT OVEN DIGITAL, LONDON 99-01. CURRENTLY WORKING AT WALLPAPER MAGAZINE. FOUNDING MEMBER OF THE EMBASSY OF CODE AND FORM, CO-FOUNDER OF KALIBER10000. MICHAEL SCHMIDT (DK), BORN 1974, ATTENDED THE UNIVERSITY OF COPENHAGEN, FREELANCED FOR VARIOUS AD AGENCIES, COPENHAGEN 95-96, ART DIRECTOR AT ON-LINE MAGAZINE, COPENHAGEN 96–97, ART DIRECTOR AT ADCORE DBC, COPENHAGEN 97-00, CREATIVE DIRECTOR AT ADCORE LTD., LONDON 00-01, CURRENTLY FREELANCING IN SAN FRANCISCO, CO-FOUNDER OF KALIBER10000. PER JØRGEN JØRGENSEN (DK), BORN 1972, ATTENDED THE UNIVERSITY OF COPENHAGEN (PHYSICS) 91, BACHELOR IN PHYSICS 95, WEB DEVELOPER AT ADCORE DBC, COPENHAGEN 98–00, FREELANCER, COPENHAGEN 00–01, CURRENTLY WORKING AS A GAME DEVELOPER AT THE PLANET, CTO OF KALIBER10000. ■

Toke Nygaard (DK), geb. 1973, besuchte die Danish School for Design. Von 1997 bis 1999 Art Director bei Araneum, Kopenhagen, von 1999 bis 2001 bei Oven Digital, London. Derzeit arbeitet er beim Wallpaper-Magazin. Gründungsmitglied von The Embassy of Code and Form; Mitbegründer von KALIBER10000. Michael Schmidt (DK), geb. 1974, besuchte die Universität Kopenhagen, war 1996 bis 1996 freiberuflich für diverse Werbeagenturen in Kopenhagen tätig; 1996 bis 1997 Art Director beim On-line-Magazin, Kopenhagen; von 1997 bis 2000 Art Director bei Adcore DBC, Kopenhagen; von 2000 bis 2001 Creative Director bei Adcore Ltd., London; derzeit Freiberufler in San Franscisco. Mitbegründer von KALIBER10000. Per Jørgen Jørgensen (DK), geb. 1972, studierte ab 1991 Physik an der Universität Kopenhagen, Bachelor aus Physik 1995; 1998 bis 2000 Web Developer bei Adcore DBC, Kopenhagen; seit 2000 Freiberufler; derzeit als Spielentwickler bei The Planet; Vorstand von KALIBER10000.

TEHELKA.COM
Tarun Tejpal

tehelka.com was conceived as a premier news and views magazine on the Net, which would help push the boundaries of journalism and become the preferred source of credible news and views for Indians all over the world. In a short ten months, it has built up and enjoys a stronger brand equity than most established media houses in India. Two major investigations, several smaller ones, the best Indian writers in the world, and superb design have made *tehelka.com* the most talked about Indian website in the world.

Following the path-breaking investigation, Operation Westend, which led to the resignations of top army and government officials, among them the defence minister George Fernandes, Samata, party chief Jaya Jaitley, and BJP president Bangaru Laxman, *tehelka.com* has been featured extensively in both national and international media ranging from the *BBC*, *CNN*, *Time Magazine*, *The Guardian*, *Newsweek*, *NYT*, and *Daily Telegraph* to hundreds of important papers around the world.

Business Week (US) has recently nominated *tehelka.com* as one of the top ten upcoming e-ventures in the world. Interestingly, it is the only B2C site to be featured in the list. According to the Alexa rankings, it is the fourth largest Indian website in the world in terms of traffic.

tehelka.com first burst into public consciousness in May 2000, with an explosive investigative story on match-fixing in cricket; it has followed that with a performance of sustained excellence. In its short existence, it has broken a number of stories—ranging from the controversy around Point 5353 in Kargil, the Patel Bank robbery, the corruption around the CNG conversion, and Chotta Rajan's Bangkok escape to scooping the fact that Priyanka Gandhi was having a baby boy.

tehelka.com wurde als neuartiges Nachrichten- und Informations-Magazin im Web konzipiert, das die Grenzen des Journalismus weiter stecken und zur *der* Quelle für glaubhafte Informationen und Kommentare für Inder auf der ganzen Welt avancieren will. In nur zehn Monaten hat es sich als Marke besser etabliert als die meisten eingesessenen Medienhäuser Indiens. Zwei größere und mehrere kleinere Untersuchungen, die weltweit besten indischen Autoren sowie ein hervorragendes Design – all das hat *tehelka.com* zur am meisten besprochenen Website Indiens auf der ganzen Welt gemacht.

Im Zuge der bahnbrechenden Recherchen und Reportagen zu „Operation Westend", die zum Rücktritt führender Militärs und Regierungsbeamter – darunter auch des Verteidigungsministers George Fernandes, des Führers der Samata-Partei, Jaya Jaitley, und des BJP-Präsidenten Bangaru Laxman – geführt haben, wurde *tehelka.com* ausführlich in nationalen wie internationalen Medien besprochen, u. a. in *BBC*, *CNN*, *Time Magazine*, *The Guardian*, *Newsweek*, *NYT*, *Daily Telegraph* sowie in vielen weiteren führenden Zeitungen der Welt.

Das amerikanische *Business Week* hat kürzlich *tehelka.com* in die Top-Ten-Liste der Aufsteiger unter den E-Ventures der Welt aufgenommen, wobei auffällt, dass es die einzige B2C-Site unter den Nominierten ist. Laut Alexa-Ranking ist es hinsichtlich der Besucherzahlen die viertgrößte indische Website überhaupt.

Ins öffentliche Bewusstsein trat *tehelka.com* erstmals im Mai 2000, als es mit einer explosiven Geschichte über Schiebereien und Absprachen im Cricketsport herauskam. Diesem Auftakt folgten weitere hervorragend recherchierte Storys. In seiner noch kurzen Geschichte hat das Webmagazin eine ganze Reihe von Storys

It is also known for its comprehensive coverage of national events like the Kumbh Mela, the Gujarat quake, and the ongoing crisis in Kashmir.
Despite this strong news element, what especially distinguishes *tehelka.com* is the unprecedented quality and range of its features and contributors.
tehelka.com posts 20 to 25 new stories everyday on subjects ranging from books, art, entertainment, environment, economics, politics, history, language, society, and culture. Its menu consists of an eclectic and exciting mix of columns, interviews, analyses, essays, stories, profiles and commentaries. Flatteringly, it has often been compared to *Salon*. And now, Operation Westend is deemed as defining a moment in journalism as America's Watergate scandal.

als erstes Medium gebracht – sei es nun die Kontroverse um Point 5353 in Kargil, über den Patel-Bankraub, die Korruption rund um die Konversion der CNG, Chotta Rajans Flucht aus Bangkok bis hin zur Sensationsmeldung, dass Priyanka Gandhi einen Knaben gebar. Das Magazin ist auch bekannt für seine umfassende Berichterstattung über nationale Ereignisse wie das Kumbh Mela, das Erdbeben in Gujarat und die andauernde Krise in Kaschmir.
Trotz dieses starken Nachrichten-Elements zeichnet sich *tehelka.com* vor allem durch seine unvergleichliche Qualität und Bandbreite bei Beiträgen und Beiträgern aus. Täglich werden 20 bis 25 Storys zu Themen wie Bücher, Kunst, Unterhaltung, Umwelt, Wirtschaft, Politik, Geschichte, Sprache, Gesellschaft und Kultur ins Netz gestellt. Sein Angebot besteht aus einer eklektischen, aufregenden Mischung aus Kolumnen, Interviews, Analysen, Essays, Reportagen, Profilen und Kommentaren. Schmeichelhafterweise ist es oft mit *Salon* verglichen worden, und inzwischen wird „Operation Westend" in seiner journalistischen Tragweite durchaus mit dem Watergate-Skandal der USA verglichen.

TARUN J. TEJPAL (INDIA) WAS THE MANAGING EDITOR OF *OUTLOOK*, INDIA'S PREMIER WEEKLY NEWS MAGAZINE. IN AN 18-YEAR CAREER, HE HAS REPORTED FOR *THE INDIAN EXPRESS* AND *THE TELEGRAPH*, AND BEEN AN EDITOR WITH THE *INDIA TODAY* AND *THE INDIAN EXPRESS* GROUPS. HE IS A CO-FOUNDER OF THE PUBLISHING HOUSE INDIAINK, WHICH FIRST PUBLISHED ARUNDHATI ROY'S *THE GOD OF SMALL THINGS*. HE HAS WRITTEN FOR SEVERAL INTERNATIONAL PUBLICATIONS, INCLUDING *THE PARIS REVIEW*, *THE GUARDIAN*, *THE FINANCIAL TIMES* AND *PROSPECT*. AFTER *OUTLOOK* AND INDIAINK, *TEHELKA.COM* IS THE THIRD START-UP PROJECT WITH WHICH HE IS INVOLVED. ■■■ Tarun J. Tejpal (Indien) war Chefredakteur von *Outlook*, Indiens führendem Wochenmagazin. In seiner 18-jährigen Karriere hat er als Reporter für *The Indian Express* und *The Telegraph* gearbeitet, war dann Redakteur bei der *India Today* und der *The Indian Express* Gruppe. Er ist Mitbegründer des Verlagshauses *IndiaInk*, das als erstes Arundhati Roys *The God of Small Things* herausgebracht hat. Er hat für zahlreiche internationale Publikationen geschrieben, darunter *The Parix Review*, *The Guardian*, *The Financial Times* und *Prospect*. Nach *Outlook* und *IndiaInk* ist *tehelka.com* das dritte Projekt, in das er von Anfang an involviert ist.

RHIZOME

Mark Tribe /
Alex Galloway

A rhizome ceaselessly establishes connections between semiotic chains, organizations of power, and circumstances relative to the arts, sciences, and social struggles.
Gilles Deleuze and Felix Guattari,
A Thousand Plateaus

Rhizome is the botanical term for a kind of stem that burrows underground, sending out shoots and roots. Rhizomes connect plants into living networks. Rhizome.org is a non-profit organization that supports the international new media art community through online services and offline events. *Rhizome* was founded in February 1996 in Berlin at a time when the international new media art world was fragmented into local communities and lacked a common platform for the exchange of ideas and information. While festivals such as Ars Electronica and DEAF (the Dutch Electronic Art Festival) did enable people working in this field to share ideas with each other and the public, we saw an opportunity to use the Internet to facilitate a critical dialog that was more accessible, inclusive and ongoing, and to build community across geographical and cultural borders. We began with an email list focused on the intersection of contemporary art and emerging technologies, and email remains at the center of our activities, the glue that binds our community together. Email lists are still among the most important and effective forms of online communication. Our email list is now available in three modes: *Rhizome Raw*, *Rhizome Rare* and *Rhizome Digest*. *Raw* is totally unfiltered. Rare is filtered into four channels from which users may choose. Digest is a weekly filtered newsletter. Our Web site *http://www.rhizome.org* is an online platform for the presentation, interpretation and preserva-

In einem Rhizome [sind] semiotische Ketten-glieder aller Art in unterschiedlicher Codie-rungsweise mit biologischen, ökonomischen etc. Kettengliedern verknüpft ...
Gilles Deleuze und Felix Guattari,
Tausend Plateaus

„Rhizom" ist der botanische Ausdruck für eine Art in der Erde steckender Stamm, von dem aus Triebe und Wurzeln sprießen. Rhizome ver-binden Pflanzen zu lebenden Netzwerken. *Rhizome.org* ist eine Non-Profit-Organisation, die die internationale Medienkunst-Community mit Hilfe von Online-Diensten und Offline-Events unterstützt. *Rhizome* wurde im Februar 1996 in Berlin gegründet – zu einer Zeit, als die internationale Welt der Neuen Medienkunst in lokale Gemein-schaften zersplittert war und keine gemeinsame Plattform für den Austausch von Ideen und Information hatte. Auch wenn Festivals wie Ars Electronica und DEAF (Dutch Electronic Arts Festival) es den auf diesem Gebiet Tätigen ermöglicht haben, ihre Ideen untereinander und mit dem Publikum auszutauschen, sahen wir doch den Bedarf, via Internet einen kritischen Dialog zu ermöglichen, der leichter zugänglich, umfassend und kontinuierlich ist, und damit

art world
internet
read message

narek

ETTERS IN YOUR E-MAILBOX

UR E-MAILBOX
we.net

9, 2001 — Treasure/Crumbs is pleased to announce the launch of the
Service. Not a virus, this feature of World of Awe (WOA) will enable
love letters via email approximately once a month through 2003.

oss-media project since 1995. Conceived by artist Yael Kanarek, it is
on-linear narrative that uses the ancient genre of the traveler's tale
tions between storytelling, memory & technology.

www.worldofawe.net

the Sunset/Sunrise, a desert terrain locked into the mindframe
y, a traveler searches for a lost treasure. According to the website,
and the letters were found on a laptop. An examination of the letters
ey are all addressed to an absent lover, though, both the traveler
bscure in their identities.

scent of 19th century romanticism infused with magical realism.
nt over the absence of the lover or a comical declaration of loyalty
collection of letters portray a wide range of themes joined by the

tion of new media art. It also serves as a resource for
information about Rhizome.org and as a gateway to
our email services. The site's key features are our
artist-created Splash Pages; the TextBase, a library of
indexed texts selected from the email lists; the Art-
Base, an archive of net art projects; and alt.interface,
a series of interface artworks including *Every Image*,
Spiral and *StarryNight*. Our site's use of open source
technology and functional design approach reflect our
overall emphasis on community access and transparency.

Unlike most print and online magazines, which
employ a vertical hierarchy to disseminate content
from a few producers to many consumers, *Rhizome* is
a grassroots community: a horizontally distributed,
many-to-many network. It is in this sense that
Rhizome is indeed rhizomatic.

eine Gemeinschaft über geografische und kulturelle
Grenzen hinweg aufzubauen.

Wir begannen mit einer E-Mail-Liste, die auf die
Schnittpunkte zwischen zeitgenössischer Kunst und
den neuen Technologien abzielte, und E-Mail bleibt
auch der Drehpunkt unserer Aktivitäten – der Leim,
der unsere Gemeinschaft zusammenhält. E-Mail-
Listen gehören noch immer zu den wichtigsten und
effizientesten Formen von Online-Kommunikation.
Unsere Mailing-Liste steht in drei Formen zur Verfügung: Als *Rhizome Raw*, *Rhizome Rare* und *Rhizome Digest*. *Raw* ist komplett ungefiltert; *Rare* ist in
vier Kanäle gefiltert, aus denen der User eine Auswahl treffen kann; *Digest* ist ein wöchentliches gefil-
tertes Nachrichtenbulletin.

Unsere Website *www.rhizome.org* ist eine Online-
Plattform für die Präsentation, Interpretation und
Erhaltung von New-Media-Kunst. Sie dient auch als
Ressource für Informationen über Rhizome.org und
als Zugang zu unseren E-Mail-Diensten. Schlüssel-
Features der Site sind unsere künstlerische Splash-
Seite, die TextBase – eine indizierte Textauswahl der
E-Mail-Listen als Bibliothek –, eine Serie von Interfa-
ce-Kunstwerken, darunter *Every Image*, *Spiral* und
StarryNight. Durch die Verwendung von Open-
Source-Technologie und dank ihres funktionellen
Design-Ansatzes spiegelt die Site unseren Anspruch
auf freien Zugang und Transparenz wider.

Anders als die meisten Print- und Online-Magazine,
die eine vertikale Hierarchie verwenden, um Inhalt
von wenigen Produzenten zu vielen Konsumenten zu
transportieren, ist *Rhizome* eine echte Basis-
Gemeinschaft – eine horizontale Vernetzung vieler
mit vielen. Und in diesem Sinn ist *Rhizome* tatsächlich rhizomatisch.

MARK TRIBE (USA) IS AN ARTIST AND CURATOR WHOSE INTERESTS LIE AT THE INTERSECTION OF EMERGING TECHNOLOGIES AND CON-
TEMPORARY ART. HE IS THE FOUNDER AND EXECUTIVE DIRECTOR OF RHIZOME.ORG. HE RECEIVED A MASTERS OF FINE ARTS IN VISUAL
ART FROM THE UNIVERSITY OF CALIFORNIA, SAN DIEGO IN 1994 AND A BA IN VISUAL ART FROM BROWN UNIVERSITY IN 1990. ALEX
GALLOWAY (USA) LEARNED COMPUTER PROGRAMMING IN 1982 ON AN APPLE II+. SINCE THEN HE HAS PURSUED CAREERS IN BOTH
THE HUMANITIES AND COMPUTING SCIENCES. ALEX RECEIVED A BA IN MODERN CULTURE & MEDIA FROM BROWN UNIVERSITY
(1996), AND IS WORKING ON A PHD IN THE LITERATURE PROGRAM AT DUKE UNIVERSITY. ALEX HAS WRITTEN ON THEORETICAL ISSUES
SURROUNDING DIGITAL TECHNOLOGIES AND IS DEVELOPING NEW INTERFACES FOR NAVIGATING INFORMATION ON RHIZOME.ORG.

Mark Tribe (USA) ist Künstler und Kurator, dessen Interesse auf der Überschneidung der neuen Technologien und der
zeitgenössischen Kunst liegt. Er ist Gründer und Geschäftsführer von *Rhizome.org*. Mark graduierte 1990 an der Brown University
zum BA aus Visual Art und 1994 zum Master of Fine Arts an der University of California, San Diego. Alex Galloway (USA) lernte
1982 auf einem Apple II+ das Programmieren von Computern. Seither hat er eine Karriere sowohl in den Humanwissenschaften
als auch in der Informatik gemacht. Alex erhielt 1996 einen BA aus Moderner Kultur und Medien von der Brown University und ist
derzeit Doktorand am Literaturprogramm der Duke University. Alex hat über theoretische Fragen rund um die digitalen
Technologien geschrieben und entwickelt derzeit neue Interfaces zum Navigieren durch die Information auf *Rhizome.org*.

Prix Ars Electronica 2001 **HONORARY MENTION**

69

ULTRASHOCK.COM

ultrashock.com

Ultrashock, the Ultimate Knowledge Base for Multimedia Developers, is a collaborative effort of professionals within the multimedia and design communities, whose collective goals are centered around sharing knowledge, concepts, and ideas through their own unique explorations and points of view. Providing a wealth of educational content and resources, Ultrashock delivers an environment that is informative, entertaining, and inspirational.

When you enter the site, though, make sure that you don't skip the intro. Otherwise, you'll be missing one of the most stunning sequences around, the opening cartoon of two characters (the site's creators) in space leading into the theme of the site, with the interface and navigation heavily influenced by the great beyond. The intro animation was a collaborative effort between Ultrashock and James Hutchinson (www.crashlander.com). The cartoon characters that you see on the site were actually created from real portraits of the moderators, who help out in the discussion forums on Ultrashock. The whole idea was to create a site that is fun to visit and would simultaneously encourage and inspire our community members to share and learn from one another.

Ultrashock epitomizes where the web should be headed: rich graphics, sumptuous navigation and massive portions of the highest quality content seen nowhere else on the web. It contains links to some fantastic sites and offers Flash tutorials, the latest Flash news, a Flash challenge, interviews, forums and even open source files created by some of the most well known Flash masters.

Ultrashock, die „ultimative Wissens-Datenbank für Mulitmedia-Entwickler", wurde von einigen Profis aus Multimedia- und Design-Communities entwickelt, denen es um den Austausch von eigenen Erfahrungen, Konzepten, Standpunkten und Ideen geht. Durch die Vielfalt an Inhalten und Ressourcen bietet Ultrashock eine Umgebung an, die informativ, unterhaltend und inspirierend zugleich ist.

Beim Besuch der Site sollte man keineswegs das Intro überspringen – man würde eine der beeindruckendsten Sequenzen versäumen, nämlich den Cartoon, der die Figuren der beiden Gründer im Weltraum zeigt und zum Thema der Site hinführt, wobei das Interface und die Navigation stark vom großen Jenseits da draußen beeinflusst wird.

Diese Eröffnungsanimation entspringt den gemeinsamen Anstrengungen von Ultrashock und James Hutchison (www.crashlander.com). Die Cartoon-Figuren entstanden nach realen Protraits der Moderatoren, die in den Diskussionsforen von Ultrashock aushelfen. Zugrunde liegt die Idee, eine Site zu schaffen, die den Besuchern Spaß macht und gleichzeitig die Mitglieder unserer Community anregt, ihr Wissen zu teilen und voneinander zu lernen.

Ultrashock ist exemplarisch für jene Richtung, in die sich das Web entwickeln sollte: aufwendige Grafik, reichhaltige Navigationsmöglichkeiten und vor allem beste Inhalte, die kaum sonst wo im Web zu finden sind. Die Site enthält Links zu einigen fantastischen Websites, das Neueste von Flash, einen Flash-Wettbewerb, Interview, Foren und sogar Open-Source-Files, geschaffen von einigen der bekanntesten Flash-Meister.

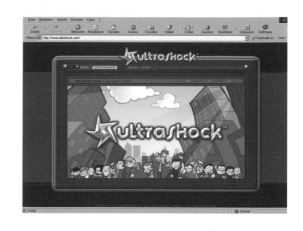

ULTRASHOCK IS A PROFESSIONAL COMMUNITY FOR MULTIMEDIA DEVELOPERS FOCUSED ON SHARING AND EXPLORING IDEAS AND KNOWLEDGE THAT PUSH THE BOUNDARIES OF THE TECHNOLOGIES WE WORK WITH. ULTRASHOCK IS A BLEND OF EDUCATIONAL CONTENT, RESOURCES, AND ENTERTAINMENT PRESENTED IN A PROFESSIONALLY DESIGNED ENVIRONMENT. ■ Ultrashock ist eine professionelle Community für Multimedia-Entwickler, die bereit sind, ihre Ideen und Wissen zu teilen und gemeinsam weiterzuverfolgen und die die Möglichkeiten der Technologien, mit denen sie arbeiten, ausloten. Ultrashock ist eine Mischung aus Weiterbildungscontent, Ressourcen und Entertainment, und das alles in einem professionell designten Environment.

CHI-CHIAN
Voltaire

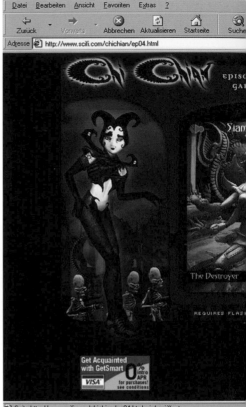

The story of Chi-Chian has lived in the mind of Voltaire for many years. "I was at an outdoor cafe in Harajuku, Tokyo in 1989, when suddenly Chi-Chian jumped out of a near-by skyscraper and landed in my head." Says Voltaire. As he scribbled on the tablecloth in front of him, a young, gentle Japanese Goth girl took form; Chi-Chian was born. As Voltaire developed her character and created a complex history around her, he realized he had to find a way tell her story in a longer, more cohesive form. Over the next 8 years, Chi-Chian appeared in an ID spot for SCIFI Channel as a stop motion character that electrocutes a giant robot with several thousand volts of electricity. She also appeared in a six-issue comic book series published by Sirius Entertainment. This series was released between 1997 and 1999 and found a small but fiercely loyal following in lovers of dark science fiction, organic technology and rich, emotional story telling. Three years after her television debut in that classic station ID, Chi-Chian has found her way back home to SCI FI Channel in an animated, online series at *www.scifi.com/chichian/*.

When first approached to create this animated series using Flash, Voltaire, who had been directing television commercials and station IDs for 15 years, wanted to utilize his experience as a stop-motion animator. So instead of using hand-drawn, vector images, *Chi-Chian* uses photographic, bitmap images of actual stop-motion animation models and sets. This animation style, reminiscent of the minimalist motion seen in Japanese Anime, turns the limitations of Flash technology into a strength. In essence what's been created is a Japanese, animated film shot with stop-motion models! When asked to describe the series in a sentence Voltaire said, "Tim Burton and H. R Giger get together with Ray Harryhausen to create a Japanese Anime."

Die Geschichte von Chi-Chian lebt schon seit vielen Jahren im Kopf von Voltaire. „Ich saß 1989 auf einer Kaffeehausterrasse in Harayuku, Tokio, als plötzlich Chi-Chian aus einem nahe gelegenen Hochhaus sprang und in meinem Kopf landete", sagt Voltaire. Als er auf dem Tischtuch vor sich hinkritzelte, nahm ein junges, nettes japanisches Barbaren-Girl Gestalt an – Chi-Chian war geboren. Als Voltaire ihren Charakter entwickelte und eine komplexe Historie um sie aufbaute, wurde ihm klar, dass er eine Möglichkeit finden musste, ihre Geschichte in einer längeren zusammenhängenden Form zu erzählen.

Im Lauf der nächsten acht Jahre erschien Chi-Chian in einem Trailer für den Scifi-Channel als Puppentrickfigur, die einen gigantischen Roboter mit mehreren Tausend Volt Spannung elektrisch exekutiert. Außerdem erschien sie in einer sechsbändigen Comic-Buchserie bei Sirius Entertainment. Die Bände wurden zwischen 1997 und 1999 publiziert und fanden unter den Liebhabern düsterer Science-Fiction, organischer Technologie und intensiven

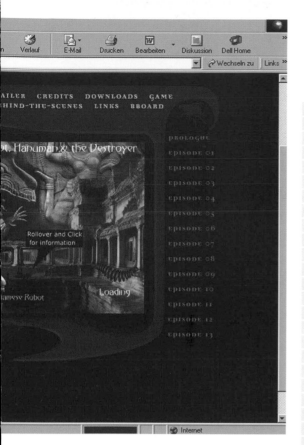

AILER CREDITS DOWNLOADS GAME
HIND-THE-SCENES LINKS BBOARD

t. Hanuman & the Destroyer

PROLOGUE
EPISODE 01
EPISODE 02
EPISODE 03
EPISODE 04
EPISODE 05
EPISODE 06
EPISODE 07
EPISODE 08
EPISODE 09
EPISODE 10
EPISODE 11
EPISODE 12
EPISODE 13

Rollover and Click
for information

rameye Robot   Loading

Chi-Chian the series follows a young, Japanese, Betty Boop-esque Goth girl, who is certainly not your every-day sci-fi heroine. Living in a dark, future Manhattan (destroyed in the New York/New Jersey War that we all knew was bound to happen), Chi-Chian is a gentle soul who respects all living things. But when her friends—a race of six-foot-tall cockroaches—become the target of villainous creeps, she must take up arms to protect the ones she loves. Peppered with sarcasm, tongue-in-cheek humor and a disturbingly original vision of the future, *Chi-Chian* is at its core a story of innocence lost as a child searches for the answer to the age old question, "Why can't people just be nice?" In the process, she experiences first hand the darkness of the human soul.

Geschichtenerzählens eine kleine, aber äußerst loyale Anhängerschaft.

Drei Jahre nach ihrem Debut in jenem mittlerweile klassischen Trailer hat Chi-Chian ihren Weg zurückgefunden zum heimatlichen Scifi-Channel: als animierte Online-Serie unter *www.scifi.com/chichian/*. Als sich Voltaire daran machte, diese Animationsserie mit Flash zu schaffen, wollte er – der seit 15 Jahren als Regisseur für Werbespots und TV-Trailer tätig war – sich seine Erfahrung als Puppentrickanimator zunutze machen. Deswegen verwendet *Chi-Chian* fotografische Bitmap-Bilder von echten Puppentrick-Figuren und -Szenerien anstelle handgezeichneter Vektorbilder. Dieser Animationsstil, der an die minimalistischen Bewegungen im traditionellen japanischen Animé erinnert, verwandelt die Schwächen der Flash-Technologie in Stärken. Im Wesentlichen wird hier ein typisch japanischer animierter Film mit Trickfiguren geschaffen. Auf die Frage, ob er die Serie in einem Satz beschreiben könne, antwortete Voltaire: „Tim Burton und H.R. Giger tun sich mit Ray Harryhausen zusammen, um einen japanischen Animationsfilm zu machen."

Die *Chi-Chian*-Serie folgt einem jungen japanischen Barbaren-Girl im Stile von Betty Boop, die man sicherlich nicht als alltägliche SciFi-Heldin ansehen kann. Sie lebt in einem finsteren Manhattan der Zukunft (das im schon lange absehbaren New-Yorker/New-Jerseyer Krieg zerstört wurde) und ist ein freundliches Wesen, das alle lebenden Kreaturen respektiert. Als aber ihre Freunde – eine Rasse sechs Fuß großer Schaben – zum Ziel hinterhältiger Angriffe werden, muss sie zu den Waffen greifen, um zu verteidigen, was sie liebt. Gewürzt mit Sarkasmus und augenzwinkerndem Humor sowie einer beunruhigend originellen Vision der Zukunft, ist *Chi-Chian* im Grunde eine Geschichte der verlorenen Unschuld, in der ein Kind nach der Antwort auf die uralte Frage sucht: „Warum können die Leute nicht einfach nett sein?" Auf dieser Sucher erlebt sie die Finsternis der menschlichen Seele aus erster Hand.

CHI-CHIAN WAS CONCEIVED AND CREATED BY VOLTAIRE. FILM STAR BAI LING (ANNA AND THE KING, WILD, WILD WEST) VOICED THE CHARACTER OF CHI-CHIAN. MICHAEL LEE OF BROOKLYN, NEW YORK, AND DANIEL GOVAR OF BALTIMORE, MARYLAND ANIMATED THE SERIES. VOLTAIRE MANAGED A CREW WHO DID EVERYTHING FROM MODEL BUILDING TO PHOTO RETOUCHING. THE SCIFI.COM TEAM INCLUDED LEAD PRODUCER ALISSA GORDON AS WELL AS LAURISSA JAMES, SEAN REDLITZ AND RACHEL GIBBS. ■■ *Chi-Chian* wurde von Voltaire konzipiert und geschaffen. Der Filmstar Bai Ling (*Anna and the King, Wild, Wild West*) verlieh der Figur der Chi-Chian ihre Stimme. Michael Lee aus Brooklyn und Daniel Govar aus Baltimore (Maryland) haben die Serie animiert. Voltaire hat eine Crew zusammengestellt, die vom Modellbau bis zur Fotoretusche alles selbst erledigt hat. Zum SCIFI.COM-Team gehörten unter anderem die Produktionsleiterin Alissa Gordon sowie Laurissa James, Sean Redlitz und Rachel Gibbs.

www.walkerart.org
Walker Art Center / New Media Initiatives

The Walker Art Center, based in Minneapolis, Minnesota, USA, is a catalyst for the creative expression of artists and the active engagement of audiences. Its programs span the visual arts, performing arts, film/video, and new media. Walker's online presence is an extension of this mission and includes the Walker site (*http://www.walkerart.org*), a collaborative educational site, ArtsConnectEd (*http://www.artsconnected.org)*, and "Gallery 9" (*http://www.walkerart.org/gallery9/*), devoted to networked digital arts. These efforts are maintained by the department of "new media initiatives," founded in 1996.

NEW

The content of a new medium is always an old medium.
Marshall McLuhan

We take this as a hydra-headed warning. What seems new may simply be putting a camera in the fifth row from the theater's proscenium. Filming a play was not yet cinema.
By the same token, while we may have replaced the idea of a linear, progressing history with notions of cycles, discontinuities, revolution, complexity, and even parallel conspiracies, new is not without history. While acknowledging the fluidity of much contemporary digital activity, we seek to find compelling contexts for it.

MEDIA

Computers both produce the material we experience and allow us to access it. ... To paraphrase Turing, the computer is the medium that can be any medium.
Simon Biggs

Das Walker Art Center in Minneapolis, Minnesota (USA), ist ein Katalysator für den kreativen Ausdruck von Künstlern und für die aktive Einbeziehung des Publikums. Sein Programm umfasst visuelle Kunst, darstellende Kunst, Film, Video und Neue Medien. Die Online-Präsenz des Walker Art Center ist eine Erweiterung dieses Aufgabenbereichs und umfasst die Walker-Site (*www.walkerart.org*), die kooperative Bildungssite ArtsConnectEd (*www.artsconnected.org*) und die „Gallery9" (*www.walkerart.org/gallery9/*), die den netzbasierten digitalen Künsten gewidmet ist. Diese Aufgaben werden in der 1996 gegründeten Abteilung „New Media Initiatives" wahrgenommen.

NEW

Der Inhalt eines neuen Mediums ist immer ein altes Medium.
Marshall McLuhan

Wir verstehen diesen Satz als Warnung vor der Hydra. Was uns als neu erscheint, könnte auch einfach darin bestehen, die Kamera in die fünfte Reihe vor das Proszenium des Theaters zu stellen – aber ein Theaterstück zu filmen, ist noch nicht Kino.
Auch wenn wir die Idee einer linear fortschreitenden Geschichte durch Vorstellungen von Zyklen, Brüchen, Revolutionen, Komplexität und sogar parallelen Verschwörungen ersetzt haben, so ist „neu" deshalb nicht mit „geschichtslos" gleichzusetzen. Wir sind uns zwar bewusst, dass vieles in der zeitgenössischen digitalen künstlerischen Aktivität noch im Fluss ist, aber trotzdem versuchen wir, sie in feste Zusammenhänge zu stellen.

Understanding what constitutes the medium may be even more difficult than defining what is new about it. As a meta-medium, we tend to view new media through the prism of our own experience and knowledge, whether it is video or photography, publishing or visual arts. As a meta-medium, digital media can be like electricity, both object and subject, both what makes things run and something to run with. As a meta-medium, computability may contribute to the breakdown of distinct disciplines while suggesting something distinctive.

INITIATIVES

The effect of concept-driven revolution is to explain old things in new ways. The effect of tool-driven revolution is to discover new things that have to be explored.
　　　Freeman Dyson

The answers to these and other questions cannot be answered only hypothetically. Artists, designers, information architects, interfacers, artificers, screeners, minglers, curators, and producers will use the new tools to create new things that must be explored and, eventually, understood. *(Steve Dietz, Curator of New Media)*

MEDIA
Computer produzieren das Material, das wir erleben, und erlauben uns den Zugang dazu ... Mit Turing könnte man sagen, dass der Computer das Medium ist, das jedes Medium sein kann.
　　　Simon Biggs

Zu verstehen, was ein Medium ausmacht, kann noch schwerer sein als zu definieren, was daran neu ist. Wir neigen dazu, neue Medien, die als Meta-Medien zu verstehen sind, durch das Prisma unserer eigenen Erfahrung und Kenntnisse zu betrachten, sei es nun im Bereich von Video oder Fotografie, Verlagswesen oder visueller Kunst. Als Meta-Medium können die digitalen Medien ähnlich der Elektrizität gleichzeitig Objekt und Subjekt sein: das, was die Dinge zum Laufen bringt, und das, was selbst zum Laufen gebracht wird. Als Meta-Medium kann die Umsetzung mittels Computer zum Zusammenbruch der Einzeldisziplinen beitragen und gleichzeitig selbst zu einer Einzeldisziplin werden.

INITIATIVES
Der Effekt einer konzeptgetriebenen Revolution ist, Altes auf neue Weise zu erklären. Der Effekt einer werkzeuggetriebenen Revolution ist, neue Dinge zu entdecken, die der Erforschung bedürfen.
　　　Freeman Dyson

Die Antworten auf diese und andere Fragen können nicht auf rein hypothetischer Basis gegeben werden. Künstler, Designer, Informationsarchitekten, Entwickler von Interfaces und Artefakten, Screen Designer, Mixer und Mischer, Kuratoren und Produzenten werden die neuen Werkzeuge einsetzen, um neue Dinge zu erschaffen, die erforscht werden müssen, um irgendwann verstanden zu werden. *(Steve Dietz, Kurator Neue Medien)*

TRUDY LANE (US) IS DESIGNER AND PRODUCER, INCLUDING, AMONG OTHER PROJECTS, DESIGN OF ARTSCONNECTED (HTTP://WWW.ARTSCONNECTED.ORG) AND PRODUCER FOR SONIC FLUX (HTTP://WWW.WALKERART.ORG/PA/SONICFLUX/). STEVE DIETZ (US) FOUNDED THE DEPARTMENT OF NEW MEDIA INITIATIVES AND IS CURATOR OF NEW MEDIA. HIS WRITINGS AND ONLINE PROJECTS ARE LINKED FROM (HTTP://WWW.WALKERART.ORG/GALLERY9/DIETZ/). JOE SLAG IS WEBMASTER. LISA MIDDAG IS PROJECT MANAGER FOR NEW MEDIA INITIATIVES. ROBIN DOWDEN, DIRECTOR OF INTEGRATED INFORMATION RESOURCES, IS PROJECT MANAGER FOR ARTSCONNECTED HTTP://WWW.WALKERART.ORG AND LIAISON WITH NATIONAL AND INTERNATIONAL STANDARDS GROUPS, SUCH AS THE CONSORTIUM FOR THE COMPUTER INTERCHANGE OF MUSEUM INFORMATION (CIMI). OCHEN KAYLAN IS MANAGER OF DIGITAL DESIGN AT THE WALKER AND AN ARTIST (HTTP://WWW.WALKERART.ORG/GALLERY9/COMMUNITY/). ▬ Trudy Lane (USA) ist Designerin von u. a. ArtsConnectEd (www.artsconnected.org) und Produzentin für Sonic Flux (www.walkerart.org/ pa/sonicflux/). Steve Dietz (USA) hat die New Media Initiatives-Abteilung gegründet und ist Kurator für Neue Medien. Links zu seinen Schriften und Online-Projekten finden sich auf www.walkerart.org/gallery9/dietz. Joe Slag ist Webmaster. Lisa Middag Projektmanagerin für NMI. Robin Dowden, Leiter der Integrated Information Resources, ist gleichzeitig Projektmanager für ArtsConnectEd und Verbindungsmann zu nationalen und internationalen Normungsgruppen, etwa zum Consortium for the Computer Interchange of Museum Information (CIMI). Ochen Kaylan ist Manager für Digital Design bei Walker und selbst Künstler (www.walkerart.org/gallery9/community/).

CUB
Steve Whitehouse

CUB is a tribute/homage to the awesomely beautiful Japanese comic/movie series *Lone Wolf* & *Cub* … a story about the Shogunate's head executioner Ogami Ito and his son Diagoro …
Ito's wife is murdered in a plot to discredit him so that the Yagyu Clan can take his coveted position …
He decides not only to not commit seppuku (ritual suicide to save face), but vows instead to take revenge on the entire Yagyu clan and restore his family's good name …
he thus goes out with his infant son as an "Assassin at the crossroads of Hell" …
CUB is my take on what would happen after Diagoro has reached manhood, continuing on his fathers mission of justice …

CUB ist eine Hommage an die herausragend schöne japanische Comic/Filmserie *Lone Wolf* & *Cub* – eine Geschichte über den obersten Henker des Shogunats, Ogami Ito, und seinen Sohn Diagoro.
Itos Frau wird ermordet. Er soll dadurch diskreditiert werden, denn der Yagyu-Clan will seine heiß begehrte Position einnehmen. Ito aber beschließt nicht nur, nicht *seppuku* – den rituellen Selbstmord zur Wahrung des Gesichtes – zu begehen, sondern schwört stattdessen, sich am ganzen Yagyu-Clan zu rächen und den guten Namen seiner Familie wiederherzustellen.
So zieht er mit seinem kleinen Sohn aus – als „Mörder am Kreuzweg zur Hölle" …
CUB ist mein Versuch auszumalen, was wohl geschehen wird, wenn Diagoro einmal zum Mann herangereift sein und die Gerechtigkeitsmission seines Vaters fortführen wird …

STEVE WHITEHOUSE (CDN) HAS ALWAYS DRAWN FOR AS LONG AS HE CAN REMEMBER, BUT CARTOONISTS DON'T GET MANY GROUPIES, SO HE TURNED TO MUSIC INSTEAD. HE PLAYED GUITAR FIRST, AND THEN MOVED ON TO THE ALTO SAX. HE HAS WORKED ON NUMEROUS TV SHOWS OVER THE YEARS, INCLUDING: *CARE BEARS*, *BABAR*, *BEETLEJUICE*, *DUCKMAN*, *STICKIN' AROUND* AND *SAM & MAX* (WHICH HE DIRECTED AND WHICH EARNED HIM THE GEMINI FOR BEST ANIMATED SERIES). AS OPPOSED TO TRADITIONAL ANIMATION, WHICH INVOLVES SO MANY PEOPLE, THE CONCEPT OF DOING SOMETHING TOTALLY PERSONAL WAS EXTREMELY APPEALING. SO, AFTER LEARNING NOT TO BE INTIMIDATED BY COMPUTERS ("LOVE 'EM, HATE 'EM"), HE GOT THE FLASH PROGRAM AND BEGAN WORKING! AND HE'S BEEN WORKING AT IT EVER SINCE ... ▬▬▬ Steve Whitehouse (CDN) hat seit jeher gerne gezeichnet, aber weil den Cartoon-Zeichnern die Groupies nicht nachlaufen, ist er stattdessen zur Musik übergegangen. Zunächst spielte er Gitarre, dann Altsaxofon. Er hat im Lauf der Jahre bei zahlreichen TV-Shows mitgearbeitet, darunter bei *Care Bears*, *Babar*, *Beetlejuice*, *Duckman*, *Stickin' Around* und *Sam & Max* (bei dem er Regie führte und das ihm den Gemini-Preis für die beste animierte Serie einbrachte). Im Gegensatz zur traditionellen Animation, bei der sehr viele Leute beschäftigt sind, war das Konzept, etwas ganz Persönliches zu schaffen, äußerst faszinierend. Und deshalb – nachdem er gelernt hatte, sich von den Computern nicht einschüchtern zu lassen („lieb sie, hass sie!") – besorgte er sich das Flash-Programm und machte sich an die Arbeit. Und noch immer arbeitet er daran ...

interactive art

UNDERSTANDING THE WORLD
DIE WELT VERSTEHEN

Masaki Fujihata

This category is entitled "Interactive Art". The objectives of this category relate to "interactivity" but the selection has to be done without any interactive environments; we do not have a chance to interact with a real work or project. When we observe the whole Ars Electronica competition, it is actually strange that only this category deals deeply with real-time interactive processing in digital media, but its selection is done by viewing video documents. In all the other categories, the works are viewed and selected by the real piece which was submitted by artists, in other words CD for Digital Musics, video tape for Computer Animation, and URL for the Web category. The method of selection forces to us to analyze details from documented video, inquiring with the paper, and we need to activate our imagination to understand what happens there. Unfortunately, the quality of the submitted video tape is a very important factor for the selection. This year we had around 50 submissions with CD-ROMs containing digital movie documents or the CD-ROM production itself, instead of documentation of the pieces on video tape. It is clear that it is impossible to see the whole contents of a CD-ROM production and search the files by hand on the fly (although we ultimately took the trouble to do so).

Die Kategorie nennt sich „Interaktive Kunst". Die Ziele dieser Kategorie orientieren sich an „Interaktivität", aber die Auswahl der Werke muss ohne interaktives Environment geschehen – wir haben keine Möglichkeit, mit einem realen Werk oder Projekt zu interagieren. Sieht man den Prix Ars Electronica als Ganzes, so fällt auf, dass nur diese Kategorie sich näher mit interaktiver Echtzeitverarbeitung in digitalen Medien befasst, die Auswahl der Arbeiten aber durch die Betrachtung von Videodokumenten erfolgt. In allen anderen Kategorien werden die tatsächlichen Werke begutachtet und bewertet, wie sie von den Künstlern eingereicht wurden. Mit anderen Worten: CDs bei Digital Musics, Videobänder bei der Computeranimation und URLs in der Web-Kategorie. Diese Auswahlmethode zwingt uns, Details über das dokumentierte Video zu analysieren, die schriftliche Dokumentation zu durchforsten und unsere Vorstellungskraft zu aktivieren, um zu verstehen, was in dem Werk eigentlich vorgeht. Leider spielt die Qualität des eingereichten Videobands eine wichtige Rolle im Entscheidungsprozess. In diesem Jahr erhielten wir rund 50 Einreichungen auf CD-ROMs, die entweder digitale Filmdokumente oder die CD-ROM-Prouktion selbst enthielten, aber keine Dokumentation auf Video. Klarerweise ist es schlichtweg unmöglich, den gesamten Inhalt einer CD-ROM-Produktion schnell und überblicksmäßig zu erkunden und die Dateien von Hand zu laden (obwohl wir das letztlich doch versucht haben). Wir möchten wirklich gut dokumentierte zusammenfassende Videobänder haben, die nur die Essenz der interaktiven Arbeiten enthalten.

Das Interface ist nicht die Schlüsselstelle der Interaktion

Beim Durchsehen der einzelnen Bänder versuchten wir herauszufinden, wie die Arbeit konstruiert ist, welche Art von Schnittstellen verwendet werden, wie Menschen damit spielen können. Dann wurde untersucht, was eigentlich zwischen dem Mitwirkenden und dem

We really want to have well documented, summarized video tapes showing only the essence of the production for your creation of interactivity.

Interface is not a core of interaction

While we viewed the video tapes, we tried to understand the construction of the work, the type of interface used, how people can play. And then what happens between the participant and the system would be considered. Understanding the interface is the main issue for the first stage of the selection. We don't want to misunderstand the interface, which leads us to a wrong understanding of its interaction.

Let us think about what is a good interface. Especially in the field of Computer Human Interfaces, a sophisticated interface is called "transparent", if it connects human and machine without any stress. This type of good interface contains an instruction of usage within it. But when we simply extend this idea to the ultimate user interface, interface will not be seen; it is totally free from the human's body, the interface can be regarded as a part of body. This idea has opened up current serious developments in "Virtual Reality" and "Weareables", and the final goal of these developments is realizing the "transparent" interface.

These transparent interfaces never impose any stress on us. The result is that the man does not need any consciousness for the interface. I think this is a very poor interface, nothing new, nothing creative for the user as a human. I love to use pencils, chalks, and brushes as a medium for expression, however, we need to be trained with these interfaces. Exercising interface is a part of the pleasure of expression. One should be conscious of the interface. I would like to say "interface" must not be invisible. Interface is an object or an icon which sends some signals to the user, which attracts you to do something, which shows what it is connecting to and what you can make possible. Interface is not only an input and output device that determines what you can get. For example, a red chalk prompts you to the possibility of drawing a red line on paper. And then it puts that possibility in your hand. "Red chalk" is more valuable than the red line, because it reminds us of the possibility of drawing a red line. This type of discussion was conducted exten-

System passiert. Das Interface zu verstehen ist die Hauptfrage in der ersten Phase der Bewertung. Wir wollen die Schnittstelle nicht missverstehen, denn dies könnte zu einem falschen Verständnis der Interaktion führen.

Lassen Sie uns kurz erwägen, was ein „gutes" Interface ist. Besonders im Bereich der Mensch-Computer-Schnittstellen (CHI) wird die Schnittstelle als „transparent" bezeichnet, wenn sie Mensch und Maschine völlig stressfrei verbindet. Dieser Typ eines guten Interfaces enthält seine Bedienungsanweisung in sich selbst. Aber wenn wir den Gedanken konsequent fortspinnen, so ist das ultimative Interface nicht sichtbar, es ist völlig frei vom menschlichen Körper, es kann als Teil des Körpers angesehen werden. Dieser Ansatz hat einige ernsthafte Entwicklungen im Bereich der Virtuellen Realität und der „Wearable Interfaces" ausgelöst, deren letztliches Ziel die Realisierung der „transparenten" Schnittstelle ist. Solch transparente Schnittstellen versetzen uns nie in Stress, sodass der Mensch sich des Interfaces gar nicht bewusst sein braucht. Nun halte ich dies aber für eine armselige Form von Interface, für nichts Neues, nichts Kreatives für den Benutzer als Menschen. Ich liebe Bleistifte, Kreide, Pinsel als Ausdrucksmittel, allerdings müssen wir sie als Interface zunächst erlernen. Das Interface zu erleben ist Teil des Vergnügens am Sich-Ausdrücken. Man sollte sich des Interface bewusst sein, ja, ich würde so weit gehen zu sagen, dass ein „Interface" nicht unsichtbar sein darf. Das Interface ist ein Objekt oder ein Symbol, das Signale an den Benutzer sendet und ihn verführt, etwas zu tun, das aber auch aufzeigt, womit es verbunden ist und was es ermöglicht. Das Interface ist nicht nur einfach ein Ein- und Ausgabegerät, das darüber entscheidet, was man letztlich bekommen kann. Eine rote Kreide etwa gibt uns die Möglichkeit, eine rote Linie auf Papier zu ziehen – und dann gibt sie dem Benutzer diese Möglichkeit in die Hand. „Rote Kreide" selbst ist wertvoller als die rote Linie, denn sie erinnert uns an die Möglichkeit, solch eine Linie zu ziehen. Diskussionen dieser Art wurden in den frühen Jahren multimedialer Produktion rund um Desktop-Design, Mensch-Computer-Interface und am häufigsten wohl mit dem Auftreten der CD-ROM-Produktion sehr intensiv geführt. Und auch jetzt ist dies eine wichtige Frage beim Interface-Design. Als wir uns auf das Desktop-Design konzentrierten, gingen wir von der Frage aus, wie die Ikonografie aussehen sollte und

sively in the early years of multimedia productions, such as desktop design, Human Computer Interface, and more popularly with CD-ROM productions, for instance. This is still an important issue now when doing interface design. When we focused on desktop design, the starting point was how the icons should be designed well and link to the contents of databases. There were discussions about how to design interface, but very few discussions about how to connect to the database, how to manipulate the data through the interface. Usually a database is fixed / pre-edited / recorded, and it is impossible for the participant to alter / add to it. All one can do is change the order of appearance on the screen by using Yes / No buttons. These discussions are already long past.

Let us move to the field of real-time interactive art: in some cases the artists have constructed totally new, somehow bizarre, somehow physical, somehow invisible devices as an interface. We saw some good interface design, new devices as an interface. But if it is just about the creation of the interfaces, we were not moved much by it. These new interfaces are just new attractive icons, but what is it for? I recognized that the creation of interface and the creation of interactivity are different issues.

To understand is to invent

What is a new type of creation of interactivity? Through the interface, by interaction, one can reach something which enables us to start understanding it as an object of interaction. This process prompts one's participation and activates one's imagination. When one interacts with it, one starts to imagine what will be happen a few seconds later as a reaction, then it happens in front of him. The order of events must follow a kind of grammar, which shows a certain connection between the icons of the interface and the thing that one will get. This process of reading leads to meaningful action to understand objectives. In an art of interactivity, one must be stimulated by interaction and enjoy having one's imagination activated. Interactivity is a stimulation of the power of imagination. By the power of imagination, one tries to see what will happen a few milliseconds ahead. This brings a future to the present. It is a bridge between a past and a

wie die Symbole mit der Datenbank zu verknüpfen seien. Es gab Diskussionen über das Design des Interface, aber nur selten wurde gefragt, wie die Verknüpfung zur Datenbank aussehen sollte, wie die Daten über das Interface manipuliert werden könnten. Normalerweise ist eine Datenbank vordefiniert und festgelegt und kann seitens des Anwenders nicht verändert werden, einzig die Reihenfolge des Erscheinens auf dem Schirm kann über Ja/Nein-Knöpfe bestimmt werden. Diese Diskussionen sind jedoch schon lange abgehakt. Wenden wir uns dem Feld der interaktiven Echtzeit-Kunst zu: In einigen Fällen haben die Künstler völlig neue, irgendwie bizarre, physische oder unsichtbare Geräte als Schnittstellen entwickelt. Wir haben Einiges an gutem Interface-Design gesehen, z. B. neue Geräte als Schnittstellen. Aber auch wenn es nur um die Schaffung des Interface gegangen wäre – nicht einmal dann wären wir besonders beeindruckt gewesen. Diese neuen Interfaces sind zwar attraktive neue Icons, aber wofür? Ich habe festgestellt, dass die Schaffung von Interfaces und die Schaffung von Interaktivität zwei verschiedene Paar Schuhe sind.

Verstehen ist erfinden

Wie kann also eine neue Art von Interaktivität geschaffen werden?
Durch das Interface, durch die Interaktion kann man etwas erreichen, das uns erlaubt, es als ein Objekt der Interaktion zu verstehen zu beginnen. Dieser Prozess erfordert eine aktive Mitwirkung und aktiviert die Fantasie. Wenn man mit dem Interface interagiert, beginnt man, sich auszumalen, welche Reaktion Sekunden später erfolgen wird, und dann passiert es vor den eigenen Augen. Die Reihenfolge der Ereignisse muss einer gewissen Grammatik folgen, die einen Zusammenhang zwischen den Icons des Interface und dem Ding zeigt, das man bekommen wird. Dieser Leseprozess führt über eine bedeutungsvolle Handlung zum Verständnis von Zielen. In einer Kunst der Interaktivität muss man durch die Interaktion stimuliert werden und Freude daran haben, wenn die eigene Vorstellungskraft angeregt wird. Durch die Kraft der Fantasie versucht man vorherzusehen, was in wenigen Millisekunden passieren

future. Only interactivity can make such a jump, enabling us to escape from the chronological cage. I believe it is a real creation.

It is possible to apply this type of understanding of interactivity not only to human-machine interaction, but also, rather originally, to human and human. We talk, discuss, and love each other. All events are real-time and interactive. It is entirely common to the human that when we are talking to each other, both react interactively. Here we reached the point, though, that talk between humans is not always interesting / delightful / enjoyable / meaningful. What makes it meaningful to talk with someone? It is precisely the same question as to how one can get a splendid personality. Perhaps it is the content of a person. It can not be fixed until their death, but after their death nobody can interact with them. Hopefully, it may be possible for digital media in the future to include / record / store one's life as a digital format, a generative database, which can be accessible through a special interface with good interactivity. This is an important point of the difference from reading a book, when one starts to consider a book as an interactive medium. Up to this point, it is possible to say "interactive art" is an interface medium which can connect one to someone (the author?) at the other end, who can conduct an enjoyable / meaningful discussion with him interactively. The creativity of a system, constructing interactive art, is designing the structure / function of the medium. It is not about creating oneself (content). While creating the system, the person emerges. It is a kind of magic, a participant invents himself in that interactive system. There needs to be an invention of a new language of interactive systems.

The creation of interactivity will be a very popular aspect of the history of art in the very near future as a mixture of computer technology, science, and art.

Remarks from all the jury members regarding the selection criteria:

Hiroshi Ishii wrote: The boundaries between art, design, science and technology are now getting blurry. New forms of interactive expression are emerging at the boundary between physical and digital worlds. My hope in the media arts is to see the *resonance* between the invention of new interactive languages

wird. Dies bringt die Zukunft in unsere Gegenwart, es ist eine Brücke zwischen Vergangenem und Zukünftigem. Nur die Interaktivität kann solch einen Sprung machen und erlaubt uns, dem Käfig der Chronologie zu entfliehen. Und das ist meiner Ansicht nach eine wirkliche „Schöpfung".

Man kann dieses Verständnis von Interaktivität nicht nur auf die Beziehung Mensch-Maschine anwenden, sondern auch – ganz ursprünglich – auf die Interaktion von Mensch zu Mensch. Wir reden, wir diskutieren, wir lieben einander. Alle Ereignisse erfolgen in Echtzeit und interaktiv. Es ist dem Menschen generell zu Eigen, dass z. B. in einem Gespräch beide Partner interaktiv reagieren. Da allerdings kommen wir an den Punkt, dass Gespräche zwischen Menschen nicht immer interessant / erfreulich / erheiternd / bedeutungsvoll sind. Was aber ist es, das ein Gespräch mit einem Menschen inhaltsreich macht? Die Frage ist dieselbe wie die Frage, was eine echte Persönlichkeit ausmacht. Vielleicht hängt es vom Inhalt der Person ab, jedenfalls kann so etwas vor dem Tod einer Person nicht endgültig gesagt werden – und nach dem Tode kann niemand mehr mit ihr interagieren.

Hoffentlich gelingt es den digitalen Medien in Zukunft, das Leben eines Menschen in digitaler Form – in einer Art generativer Datenbank – zu speichern / zu bewahren / aufzuzeichnen, sodass es durch ein spezielles Interface mit guter Interaktivität zugänglich bleibt. Denn das unterscheidet ein wirklich interaktives Medium vom Lesen eines Buches – wenn man ein Buch als interaktives Medium betrachten will. Insofern kann man also sagen, dass „interaktive Kunst" ein Interface-Medium ist, das einen Mitwirkenden mit jemandem am anderen Ende (dem „Autor"?) verbindet und es ermöglicht, mit diesem interaktiv eine bedeutungsvolle und positiv erlebbare Diskussion zu führen. Die Kreativität eines Systems, das Konstruieren interaktiver Kunst, bedeutet, die Struktur und Funktion des Mediums zu konstruieren. Es geht nicht darum, sich selbst (Inhalt) zu schaffen. Beim Schaffen des Systems taucht auch die Person dahinter auf – eine Art von Zauberei, denn der Mitwirkende erfindet sich selbst in diesem interaktiven System. Noch aber bedarf es der Erfindung einer neuen Sprache für interaktive Systeme.

Die Schaffung von Interaktivität wird ein zentraler Aspekt der Kunstgeschichte der allernächsten Zukunft sein – eine Mischung aus Computertechnologie, Wissenschaft und Kunst.

and the experience of a profound message that takes advantage of those new languages. If the resonance becomes strong enough, we will see the breakdown of the walls among old disciplines.

Ulrike Gabriel remarks: Criteria of individuality / uniqueness of artistic approach / imagination. Degree of freedom / radicality in artistic research / exploration. Strength / intensity of artistic concern / content / result / essence. Sensuality. Sensitivity and deepness in questioning and realization. Stringent use of artistic material.

Peter Higgins wrote: I believe that an objective of the jury is to encourage the collaboration of artists and scientists working in the digital domain to create conceptual / tangible opportunities to enable a wide ranging audience to engage with interfaces and processes that extend their cognitive, imaginative, or emotional state.

Joachim Sauter wrote: New media language means that there has been a development of a media language in the last 15–20 years. New paradigms, patterns and principles for how to use this new medium to communicate content (or narration) have been developed, like in the language of film which was developed a hundred years ago, after the invention of the technique of film. Also like the language of film 100 years ago, nearly all the grammar for the new media language has been written down in the last decade. In good media art you see that the artist is able to "speak" with this language and not just stammer. And in very good media art pieces, you see that they are able to break the rules of this grammar and to arrive at unusual results. A lot of so-called media artists don't even know that there is already a language. So I think it is important to look for this new use of media language.

Short comments on the winners
This year, we selected three prize-winning works. Each work has a different type of interactivity.
Polar has a highly complex structure, where the authors are exploring the original concept of the real. This is dealing with the way one's unconsciousness that delivers / affects the globe, slightly changes

unconsciously. We found their interesting approach encouraging.

This year we also found several works / projects that deal with an interactive communication medium. *bump*, does not use a kind of network software, such as C-U-see-me, but constructs a physical interface between distant cities. It realizes one's existence as a ghost in the other place. But when someone else starts to interact with this ghost, he / she realizes it is a shadow of a real person playing at the other location.

The third one, *Remain in Light*, can be seen as an ironical piece for science and art. Traditionally, science approaches nature by using strong technology, such as microscopes, telescopes, nuclear-accelerators to analyze the world precisely. Artists made this system which amplifies / transforms / interprets natural phenomena to visible / audible forms by using special sensors / probes. With this piece, one plays with the metaphor of science by using an insect net as a probe / antenna for catching radio waves and making them visible.

Interactive art is an area of a new creation of medium, which enables us to explore the world in order to know it better, more precisely, or which even changes the world by creating it. Interactive art is not a given form of art, not an established medium yet. The process of creating interactive art is still the process of understanding the world.

---

gute Medienkunstwerke können diese grammatikalischen Regeln sogar brechen, um zu ungewöhnlichen Ergebnissen zu kommen. Eine Vielzahl sogenannter Medienkünstler weiß jedoch nicht einmal, dass es bereits eine Sprache dieses Mediums gibt, und umso wichtiger ist es, nach solchen neuartigen Anwendungen der Mediensprache zu suchen.

Einige Anmerkungen zu den Preisträgern

Auch in diesem Jahr haben wir drei Werke als Preisträger ausgewählt. Jedes von ihnen zeigt eine andere Form von Interaktivität.

Polar hat eine hoch komplexe Struktur, innerhalb derer die Autoren das Ursprungskonzept des Realen erforschen. Hier wird untersucht, wie das eigene Unbewusste, das die gesamte Welt darstellt und betrifft, unbewusst leicht verändert wird – wir haben ihren interessanten Ansatz sehr ermutigend gefunden.

Heuer haben wir auch etliche Werke bzw. Projekte gefunden, die sich mit einem interaktiven Kommunikationsmedium beschäftigen. *bump* verwendet nicht nur Software wie C-U-see-me, sondern konstruiert ein physisches Interface zwischen entfernten Städten. Die Existenz eines Individuums wird dadurch als eine Art von „Geist" in der anderen Stadt erlebt – wer aber mit diesem geisterhaften Abbild zu interagieren beginnt, erkennt bald, dass es der Schatten einer realen Person ist, die am anderen Ort mitspielt.

Das dritte Werk, *Remain in Light*, kann als ironische Arbeit über Wissenschaft und Kunst angesehen werden. Traditionellerweise nähert sich die Wissenschaft der Natur unter großem technologischen Einsatz – mit Mikroskopen, Teleskopen, Teilchenbeschleunigern usw., um die Welt präzise zu analysieren. Dieses System, das über spezielle Sensoren und Messeinrichtungen natürliche Phänomene aufnimmt, verstärkt, interpretiert und in sicht- und hörbare Formen umwandelt, wurde jedoch von Künstlern gebaut. Diese Arbeit spielt mit der Metapher von Wissenschaft, indem ein Schmetterlingsnetz als Antenne zum Einfangen von Radiowellen verwendet wird, die anschließend sichtbar gemacht werden.

Interaktive Kunst ist ein neues Medium, das uns erlaubt, die Welt zu erforschen, um sie besser und genauer kennen zu lernen oder gar schöpferisch zu verändern. Interaktive Kunst ist weder eine vorgegebene Kunstform noch ein etabliertes Medium. Der Prozess der Schaffung interaktiver Werke ist noch immer der Prozess, die Welt zu verstehen.

BUMP
association.creation

**A tactile interface versus
the disembodiedness of network worlds**

Two bridges in public space; the inhabitants of one space cannot see the others, but they can sense them and make contact with them. The deformation of space becomes the interface. The interface is called *bump*, is ready for the masses to come. Every pressure exerted causes resistance that comes through on the other side. There is a knock from underneath, the slats rise, power transmission via network—*sensations on the move*.

"If you move along a city's compact walls, when you least expect it, you see a crack open and a different city appears. Then, an instant later, it has already vanished. Perhaps everything lies in knowing what words to speak, what actions to perform, and in what order and rhythm."
(*Italo Calvino*)

bump creates a crack in the urban interface, a place where there is no more solid ground under your feet.

A crack in the urban surface
"Now there is knocking from below and the boards rise up. Below is another city, reflecting the same irregularity, linked via data transmission line. What is going on there? Undifferentiated mass movements, a stampede of hundreds of feet at rush hour? What about late at night: two or three pairs of feet. A perceptible rhythm. Perhaps a message? Or just a game? We sense the illusion of proximity: directly below the board which raises up, we presume a force which approximates our own.

**Ein taktiles Interface gegen
die Körperlosigkeit der Netzwelten**
Zwei Brücken im öffentlichen Raum, die Bewohner des einen Raumes können die anderen nicht sehen, können diese aber spüren und mit ihnen Kontakt aufnehmen. Die Deformation des Raumes wird zum Interface. Das Interface heißt *bump*, bereit zum Massen-Auftritt. Jeder Druck erzeugt einen Gegendruck, der auf der anderen Seite durchschlägt. Es pocht von unten, die Latten heben sich, Kraftübertragung übers Netz – *sensations on the move*.

„Gehst du die kompakten Wände einer Stadt entlang, so kann es auch geschehen, wenn du am wenigsten darauf gefasst bist, dass sich ein Spalt öffnet und eine andere Stadt zum Vorschein kommt, die im nächsten Augenblick wieder verschwunden ist. Vielleicht liegt alles nur daran zu wissen, welche Bewegungen man in welcher Reihenfolge und welchem Rhythmus machen muss." (*Italo Calvino*)

bump erzeugt einen Spalt im städtischen Interface, eine Stelle, an der es keinen sicheren Boden unter den Füßen gibt.

Ein Spalt in der urbanen Oberfläche
„Es klopft von unten, die Bretter heben sich. Unten ist eine andere Stadt, spiegelbildlich dieselbe Unebenheit, angebunden über eine Datenleitung. Was spielt sich dort ab? Ein gleichgültiger Massen-Auftritt, Getrampel von Hunderten Füßen zur Stoßzeit? Dagegen spät nachts: zwei Paar, drei Paar Füße. Ein wahr-

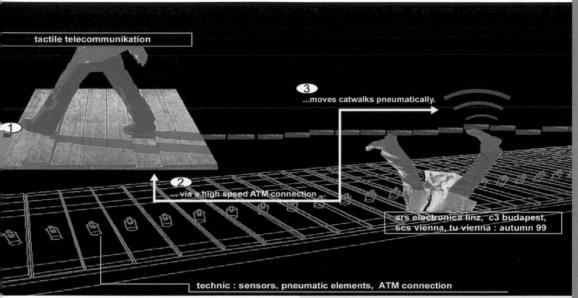

tactile telecommunikation

① ...via a high speed ATM connection...

② ...moves catwalks pneumatically.

③

ars electronica linz, c3 budapest, scs vienna, tu vienna : autumn 99

technic : sensors, pneumatic elements, ATM connection

But there is only the apparatus, the pneumatic piston, the control valve, the sensor. Closeness is only an illusion; the distance is not abolished.
The thin pine board is a wall hundreds of kilometers thick. A casual encounter turns into a lasting irritation of the sense of direction: west is below, below is east. How close can we get together?"
(Christian Kühn)

A catwalk—1.5 by 20 meters—is installed in the public space of each city. If a person steps onto this catwalk their weight triggers an impulse which is transferred to the other city by means of a data-line. There a pneumatic piston raises the corresponding board by a few centimeters. At the same time, the principle of the effect can be grasped through a video conference transmission—and visual contact can be made with the "other side."

How close do we wanna get today?
The free-standing bridge on the street refers to something absent: approaching one another, mutually sensing, sensuously experiencing one another.
The Internet has brought us all closer together, yet with all our fascination with incorporeal, virtual space, we must not forget the quality of what is missing when

nehmbarer Rhythmus, vielleicht eine Botschaft? Oder nur ein Spiel? Wir empfinden die Illusion der Nähe: Direkt unter dem Brett, das sich hebt, vermuten wir eine Kraft, die der unseren gleicht.
Aber dort ist nur der Apparat, der Hubkolben, das Steuerventil, der Sensor. Die Nähe ist nur Schein, die Distanz ist nicht aufgehoben.
Das dünne Fichtenbrett ist eine Wand, Hunderte Kilometer dick. Aus der beiläufigen Begegnung wird eine bleibende Irritation. Wie nah können wir einander kommen?" (Christian Kühn)

In jeder Stadt ist ein eineinhalb Meter breiter und zwanzig Meter langer Holzsteg auf einem öffentlichen Platz installiert. Betritt eine Person diesen Steg, löst sie durch ihr Eigengewicht einen Impuls aus, der mittels Datenleitung in die andere Stadt übertragen wird. Dort hebt ein pneumatischer Hubkolben das entsprechende Brett um Zentimeter. Gleichzeitig kann über eine Video-Konferenzschaltung das Wirkungsprinzip erschlossen und visueller Kontakt mit der „anderen Seite" aufgenommen werden.

Wie nah wollen wir einander kommen?
Die freistehende Brücke auf der Straße verweist auf etwas Abwesendes: Das aufeinander Zugehen, das gegenseitige Fühlen, die sinnliche Erfahrbarkeit.
Das Internet hat uns alle näher gebracht, doch bei aller Faszination für den körperlosen, virtuellen

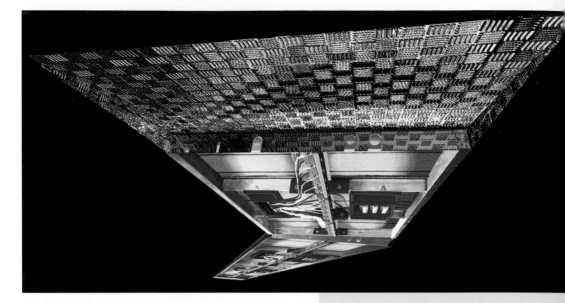

we go into the Internet. The world has become larger for *bump* users.

Sensing as an elemental experience gives us a feeling for distance and closeness. Collective experience is the prerequisite for common impressions and imprints in a game with an anonymous opposite. Interaction becomes communication.

Sensations on the move

"The spacelessness and the disembodiedness of the virtual world returns to the sensuous, tactile world, which means that crossing the border of an 'abstract' medium creates a new actionist reality that would be unimaginable in a reality without a virtual opposite. This enables an intensification of the perception that was previously mourned as loss. Perhaps a new medium is born with this virtu—reality?

bump affords the 'virtual world' a new field of action and the sensuous perception of impulses from previously unimaginable networks." (*Friedrich Achleitner*)

An intelligent urban fixture, accessible

"The telematic arrangement of *bump* is prototypical for intelligent urban fixtures: beyond the specifically local experience in two cities, the interaction and communication of the people in both places through the telematic furnishing are the prerequisite for experiencing telematic simultaneity." (*Gerfried Stocker*)

The telematic bridge is imprinted with logos from companies that enable Internet communication. *bump* as

Raum dürfen wir nicht vergessen, dem Qualität zu geben, was fehlt, wenn wir ins Internet einsteigen. Für *bump*-user ist die Welt größer geworden.

Das Spüren als elementare Erfahrung gibt uns ein Gefühl für Entfernung und Nähe. Kollektives Erleben ist die Vorraussetzung für gemeinsame Eindrücke und Abdrücke in einem Spiel mit einem anonymen Gegenüber. Interaktion wird Kommunikation.

Sensations on the move

„Die Raum- und Körperlosigkeit der virtuellen Welt kehrt in die sinnliche, taktile Welt zurück, das heißt die Grenzüberschreitung eines ‚abstrakten Mediums' schafft eine neue aktionistische Wirklichkeit, die in einer Wirklichkeit ohne virtuellem Gegenüber nicht denkbar wäre. Es eröffnet sich also eine Steigerung jener Wahrnehmung, die bisher als Verlust beklagt wurde. Vielleicht ist mit dieser virtu – reality ein neues Medium geboren?

Mit *bump* bekommt die „virtuelle Welt" ein neues Aktionsfeld und die sinnliche Wahrnehmung Impulse aus bisher nicht denkbaren Vernetzungen." (*Friedrich Achleitner*)

Ein intelligentes Stadtmöbel, begehbar

„Die telematische Anlage von *bump* ist prototypisch für eine intelligente Stadtmöblierung: Über das jeweils lokale Erlebnis in zwei Städten hinaus, sind die Interaktion und Kommunikation der Personen an den beiden Orten durch

das telematische Möbel Voraussetzung für die Erfahrung der telematischen Simultanität." *(Gerfried Stocker)*

Die telematische Brücke ist mit Logos von Firmen bedruckt, die Internetkommunikation ermöglichen. *bump* als ein Abbild und Teil der kommerzialisierten Welt, in der wir leben und der wir uns nicht entziehen können. *bump* als Möbel einer Stadt, durch die du gehst.

bump hat sich als transparentes und funktionierendes Medium bewährt. Die vielen, begeisterten Auftretenden nennen es eine Sensation, die Assoziationen weckt und Verbindungen schafft.

an image and a part of the commercialized world in which we live, and which we cannot elude. *bump* as a furnishing of a city that you traverse.

bump has proven itself as a transparent and functional medium. The many people who have enthusiastically stepped on it call it a sensation that awakens associations and creates connections.

1998 BUMP: Opening of the Ars Electronica 99 by the mayors of Linz and Budapest on the bridge ESTABLISHED in 1997 by: Christian Smretschnig, Michael Bieglmayer, Roland Graf, Werner Schmid. Technical directors: Christian Troger, Elmar Trojer. ac@bump.at, www.bump.at

ASSOCIATION.CREATION (A) IS AN ARTIST COLLECTIVE THAT WORKS ON NETWORKS AND THEIR TRANSITIONS INTO A SENSUOUS CAPACITY FOR BEING EXPERIENCED. WHAT IS ESSENTIAL IS THE "OPEN INTERFACE" THAT ENABLES COMMON EXPERIENCING AND INTERACTING. THE "VIRTUAL WORLD" IS GIVEN A NEW FIELD OF ACTION AND THE SENSUOUS PERCEPTION OF IMPULSES FROM PREVIOUSLY UNIMAGINABLE NETWORKS. ▬▬ association.creation (A) ist ein Künstlerkollektiv, das an Netzwerken und derenÜbergängen in sinnliche Erfahrbarkeit arbeitet. Entscheidend ist die „offene Schnittstelle", die gemeinsames Erleben und Interagieren ermöglicht. Die „virtuelle Welt" bekommt damit ein neues Aktionsfeld und die sinnliche Wahrnehmung Impulse aus bisher nicht denkbaren Vernetzungen.

POLAR
Carsten Nicolai / Marko Peljhan

Artistic Concept and Technical Realization

The work *polar* could be described as an interactive multimedia installation, but its complexity in a way defies this classification. We envisioned the 7m X 7m X 4m, totally connected and tactile space as a complex tactile matrix interface, that enables the visitor to experience the flow of data in the global and local networks in a completely immersive, yet cognitive way. The work was inspired by the notion of the cognitive "ocean" as described in Stanislaw Lem's and Andrey Tarkovsky's *Solaris*. The initial conceptual equation was:

ocean = matrix.

The main outline of the work was based on the creation of two software and hardware "engines", the so-called "polar engine" (with adjacent "poles", "polar", "dictionary" and "knowledge base") and the "change engine" (with adjacent "traceroute visualiser", which consisted of two separate displays). The first was envisioned as the input-analysis and construction zone, the second as the output-syntheses-experience zone. These zones were defined both in conceptual-software and hardware senses and also in the environmental sense.

Künstlerisches Konzept und technische Umsetzung

Das Werk *polar* könnte als interaktive Multi-Media-Installation angesehen werden, aber seine Komplexität spricht gegen eine solch simple Klassifikation.

Wir haben uns den 7 x 7 x 4 Meter großen, vollkommen vernetzten Raum als taktiles Matrix-Interface vorgestellt, das es dem Besucher erlaubt, den Datenfluss im globalen wie in lokalen Netzwerken auf eine völlig immersive und dennoch kognitive Weise wahrzunehmen. Wir wurden in unserer Arbeit auch durch den Begriff des „kognitiven Ozeans" inspiriert, wie er in Stanislaw Lems und Andrej Tarkowskis *Solaris* beschrieben wird.

Die ursprüngliche konzeptuelle Gleichung lautete: Ozean = Matrix.

Das Grundgerüst des Projekts basiert auf der Entwicklung zweier Software- und Hardware-„Maschinen", der sogenannten „Polar-Maschine" (mit zugehörigen Polen, „Polar-Wörterbuch" und „Wissensspeicher") sowie einer „Veränderungsmaschine" (mit einem zugehörigen „Traceroute-Visualisierer" aus zwei unabhängigen Displays). Die Erste wurde als Input-Analyse und Konstruktionszone vorgesehen, die Letzere als Erfahrungsbereich für die Output-Synthese. Die Zonen wurden sowohl in einem

90

We have defined a "zone", in which the biological and physical was directly interacting with the abstract-immaterial.

One main question was posed in this process: How do we construct a cognitive and tactile experience of the seamless and near-abstract matrix with the analysis/ construction transformation of it included in the process?

Basically, we wanted to create an interface between the human body and senses and the matrix, which would, not only through the activities, but even just through the sheer presence of the humans, already transform the structure of the matrix that is observed/ experienced and of the physical space that is inhabited during this process, as well.

The space

The *polar* space is a 7m X 7m X 4m white, 3-dimensional physical space, which includes 4 projection surfaces, 7 speakers, a 3D high resolution tracking system, a microorganism growth module, a wave

konzeptuellen Soft- und Hardware-Sinn wie auch im Sinne eines Environments definiert.

Wir haben eine „Zone" geschaffen, in der das Biologisch-Physische dirckt mit dem Abstrakt-Immateriellen interagiert.

Bei diesem Prozess stellte sich eine Grundfrage: Wie konstruieren wir eine kognitive und taktile Erfahrung der nahtlosen und beinahe abstrakten Matrix, die auch deren Analyse und Transformation im Verlauf des Prozesses enthält?

Wir wollten ein Interface zwischen dem Körper des Menschen mit seinen Sinnen einerseits und der Matrix andererseits schaffen, die nicht nur durch die Aktivitäten, sondern auch durch die schiere Präsenz der Menschen die Struktur der zu beobachtenden/erfahrenden Matrix und des physischen Raums verändert, der während dieses Prozesses begangen wird.

Der Raum

Der „polare" Raum ist ein weißer, dreidimensionaler physischer Raum von 7 x 7 x 4 Metern, der vier Projektionsflächen, sieben Lautsprecher, ein hochauflösendes 3D-Trackingsystem, ein Wachstumsmodul für

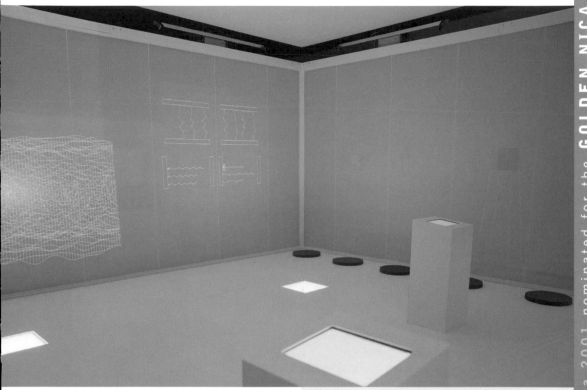

patterning water vibration module, 2 so-called "field" displays—touch input modules—and 7 "pol" zones. The whole construction was modular and also included the ceiling, where a complex system of 32 lights controlled by the main engine of the project also played an active role in the tactile and sensorial experience. One of the main experiential goals of the space design was to minimize the presence of clearly discernible technological elements within it, on one hand, and on the other to approach it from the pragmatic viewpoint of an all-encompassing "human-machine" interface.

Mikroorganismen, ein Wellenmuster-Vibrationsmodul für Wasser, zwei sogenannte „Feld"-Displays – berührungsempfindliche Eingabemodule – und sieben „Pol"-Zonen enthält.
Die ganze Konstruktion ist modular aufgebaut. Dazu gehört auch der Plafond, mit einem komplexen System von 32 Leuchten, das von der Hauptmaschine des Projekts gesteuert wird und eine aktive Rolle in der taktilen und sensorischen Erfahrung spielt. Eines der Hauptziele des Raumdesigns bezüglich der Erfahrung war es, einerseits die Präsenz klar erkennbarer technologischer Elemente innerhalb des Raums zu minimieren, anderseits den Raum aus dem pragmatischen Blickwinkel eines allumfassenden Mensch-Maschine-Interface zu gestalten.

CARSTEN NICOLAI (D) HAS BEEN ACTIVELY WORKING ON "SOUND" AS WAVE-SHAPED DATA, SOUND INSTALLATION THROUGH CRYSTALLIZED STRUCTURES PRODUCED BY NATURAL ECOSYSTEMS, OBJECTS, PAINTINGS, LIVE PERFORMANCE AND CD'S. MARKO PELJHAN (SLO) IS AN ARTIST PIONEERING IN THE FIELD OF RESEARCH INTO TELECOMMUNICATION ENVIRONMENTS, SUCH AS INTERCEPTION/DISPATCHING OF ELECTRIC AND SIGNAL WAVES AND THEIR MAPPING AND REFLECTION. POLAR MARKS THE FIRST TIME THAT CARSTEN NICOLAI AND MARKO PELJHAN HAVE WORKED COLLABORATIVELY ON A FULL-SCALE MEDIA ART PROJECT. ■■■ Carsten Nicolai (D) arbeitet aktiv an „Klang" als wellenförmigen Daten, an Klanginstallationen durch kristalline Strukturen, produziert aus natürlichen Ökosystemen, Objekten, Malerei, Live-Performances und CDs. Marko Peljhan (SLO) ist einer der ersten Künstler, der den Bereich der Telekommunikationsumgebungen erforscht, z. B. den Empfang und das Senden von Signalwellen und ihre Abbildung und Reflexion. Polar ist das erste Medienkunstprojekt in großem Maßstab, bei dem Carsten Nicolai und Marko Peljhan zusammenarbeiten.

REMAIN IN LIGHT
Haruki Nishijima

Remain In Light is a visual representation of ambient analog sound waves, which have been captured using an "electronic insect-collecting kit". The process of collecting these waves begins with a person carrying an insect net, which is attached to a device designed to capture the waves. The net functions as an antenna for catching and accumulating radio-wave data.

Today, it is possible to get a lot of information instantly from great distances without physically moving around. Tune and place move, but have no relationship to the body. Invisible data which we can't see revolves in space and does not appear to be special, because we can't see it.

This work converts bits of analog communication data and allows the viewer to participate in the work by controlling the amount of "time", "air space" and "place" in his/her viewing space. The viewer can see the results of the three processes which were used to capture these "electronic insects" The first is discovering the "electronic insect", the second is capturing the "insect" and the third is converting the analog data and presenting it visually in an interactive environment.

In the past, our world was filled with natural insects. However, in our modern society, there are fewer natural insects, and they have been replaced by "electronic insects", or bits of sound data. In the city, there are numerous opportunities to collect these "electronic insects", but in the countryside there are fewer opportunities to collect them, because there are fewer man-made sounds.

In order to discover and capture these "electronic insects", first we have to look for them in their natural habitat. Clues are necessary in order to find and "cap-

Remain In Light ist die visuelle Wiedergabe analoger Klangwellen aus der Umwelt, die durch ein „elektronisches Insektensammel-Set" eingefangen wurden. Der Prozess des Wellenfangens beginnt damit, dass eine Person ein Schmetterlingsnetz trägt, das mit einem Gerät zum Einfangen der Radiowellen verbunden ist. Das Netz dient als Antenne zum Empfang der Daten der Radiowellen.

Heutzutage ist es möglich, eine große Menge an Information aus weiter Entfernung anzusammeln, ohne sich physisch bewegen zu müssen. Melodie und Ort mögen verschieden sein, aber sie haben keine Beziehung zum Körper. Daten, die wir nicht sehen können, kreisen im Raum und sind für uns nichts Außergewöhnliches – weil wir sie gar nicht wahrnehmen können. Diese Arbeit konvertiert Teile analoger Kommunikationsdaten und erlaubt es dem Betrachter, am Werk teilzunehmen, indem er die Menge an „Zeit", „Luftraum" und „Ort" seines Beobachtungsraums steuert. Der Betrachter kann die Ergebnisse der drei Prozesse, die zum Einfangen der „elektronischen Insekten" dienen, unmittelbar sehen. Der erste Prozess ist das Entdecken des „elektronischen Insekts", der zweite das Einfangen des „Insekts", der dritte schließlich die Umwandlung der analogen Daten und deren visuelle Präsentation in einer interaktiven Umgebung.

Früher war unserer Welt voll von natürlichen Insekten. In unserer modernen Gesellschaft gibt es jedoch immer weniger solche Lebewesen, sie wurden sozusagen durch „elektronische Insekten" ersetzt, durch Teile von Klangdaten. In der Stadt gibt es zahllose Möglichkeiten, diese „Insekten" zu sammeln, aber auf dem offenen Land sind die Gelegenheiten rarer, weil es auch weniger dieser vom Menschen erzeugten Klänge gibt.

ture" them. For example, I select the habitat of a residential area on the basis of places where cars are parked, where there are fragrances coming from dining tables in a home, and the day and time when I'm in the area. These situations lead to and produce certain sounds. However, when I am in a city, I find situations and places which produce very different sounds. I have tried to capture these sounds on the basis of this information.

The viewer will understand that this interactive space is his/her visible environment—a replication of the world outside. This is a modern version of insect collecting.

The "electronic insects" are collected with a net which has been built beforehand, and is similar to those used to capture fireflies. The net is made from a cotton cloth which is often used to cover windows to prevent insects from entering homes. However, my net was designed to bring "insects" inside.

In my interactive presentation, each "electronic insect" is represented by a different color. Each color repre-

Um diese „elektronischen Insekten" aufzustöbern und einzufangen, müssen wir sie zunächst in ihrem natürlichen Lebensraum suchen. Um sie tatsächlich entdecken und einsammeln zu können, benötigt man zunächst einige Hinweise auf ihr Vorhandensein. So suche ich etwa den Wohnbereich eines Siedlungsraums danach aus, ob Autos geparkt sind, ob sich der Duft des Mittagessens durch die Luft zieht, und natürlich auch nach der Tageszeit. Diese Situationen produzieren bestimmte Klänge. Wenn ich jedoch in einer größeren Stadt bin, finde ich Situationen und Orte, die sehr unterschiedliche Klänge ergeben – und ich habe mich bemüht, diese Klänge auf Basis solcher Informationen zu sammeln.

Der Betrachter wird erkennen, dass der interaktive Raum seine eigene Umgebung ist – ein Abklatsch der Außenwelt, eine moderne Form des Insektensammelns.

Die „elektronischen Insekten" werden mit einem Netz eingefangen, das zuvor aufgebaut wurde und das einem „normalen" Insektennetz ähnelt. Der Netzkörper besteht aus einem Baumwollstoff, wie er auch für Mückennetze in Häusern Einsatz findet, nur mit dem Unterschied, dass mein Netz die „Insekten"

sents one frequency. Some sounds, such as radio data, are easy to capture, and therefore the visual representation of that data's color will appear more often. I hope that the viewer will notice that there is a greater amount of data of a certain color, and much less of others—a reflection of the sounds heard in the city. A color chart will be available for viewers to observe.

Will analog data become a thing of the past? Now most communication data is digitized, and the demand for analog data continues to decrease. Actually, data from analog cellular phones became an extinct species of electronic insect in Japan last year. The quality of analog sound data seems to be inferior to that of digital data, but in fact, our real world is filled with analog sounds. I feel it is important to include

nicht abhalten, sondern vielmehr anlocken soll. In der interaktiven Präsentation wird jedes „elektronische Insekt" durch eine andere Farbe dargestellt – jede Farbe entspricht einer Frequenz. Manche Klänge – etwa Radiosendungen – sind leicht einzufangen und scheinen deswegen auch besonders häufig in der visuellen Darstellung auf. Ich hoffe, dass die Häufung einzelner Farben und die relative Seltenheit anderer auch dem Betrachter bewusst wird – sie sind die Reflexion der Klänge, die man in einer Stadt hört. Eine Farbkarte steht den Zusehern zur Verfügung.

Werden analoge Daten bald der Vergangenheit angehören? Heutzutage sind bereits die meisten Kommunikationsdaten digitalisiert, und die Nachfrage nach analogen Daten sinkt weiter. Analoge Daten aus Mobiltelefonen sind in Japan als Spezies elektronischer Insekten beispielsweise bereits vergangenes Jahr ausgestorben. Die Qualität analoger Klangdaten schien jener digitaler Klänge unterlegen zu sein, aber noch immer ist unsere Welt voller analoger

both digital and analog data in our lives, because it is more representative of the real world. Analog data helps you to remember the past. It is my hope that there will be a continued demand for both analog and digital data and that humans will realize the importance of both technological and non-technological interaction.

As for the true insect collecting I experienced in the past, there was always a worldly feeling which I felt was universal. "Electronic insect collecting" is the tool and the means for connecting the technological world to its prototypical experience.

Klänge. Ich glaube, dass es wichtig ist, beide Arten in unser Leben zu integrieren, weil sie gemeinsam viel repräsentativer für die reale Welt sind. Analoge Daten helfen, sich an die Vergangenheit zu erinnern. Ich hoffe, dass auch weiterhin Nachfrage nach analogen wie nach digitalen Daten bestehen wird und dass die Menschen die Wichtigkeit sowohl der technologischen wie der nicht-technologischen Interaktion erkennen.

Meine reale Insektensammlerei hat mir in der Vergangenheit immer ein sehr erdverbundenes Gefühl vermittelt, das, wie ich glaube, universell ist. „Elektronisches Insektensammeln" ist das Werkzeug und Mittel, die technologische Welt mit ihrer prototypischen Erfahrung zu verbinden.

HARUKI NISHIJIMA (JP), BORN IN 1971, HOLDS A MASTER OF FINE ARTS DEGREE IN MURAL PAINTING FROM TOKYO NATIONAL UNIVERSITY OF FINE ARTS AND MUSIC. SINCE 1999 HE HAS BEEN A STUDENT AT IAMAS (INTERNATIONAL ACADEMY OF MEDIA ARTS AND SCIENCE). HE HAS SHOWN HIS WORK IN SEVERAL EXHIBITIONS MAINLY IN JAPAN. ▬▬ Haruki Nishijima (J), geb. 1971, graduierte zum Master of Fine Arts aus Wandmalerei an der Tokyo National University of Fine Arts and Music. Seit 1999 studiert er an der International Academy of Media Arts and Science (IAMAS). Seine Arbeiten wurden vor allem in Japan in zahlreichen Ausstellungen gezeigt.

RAINDANCE
Paul DeMarinis

U.S. Patent Aug. 1, 2000 Sheet 1 of 8 6,095,889

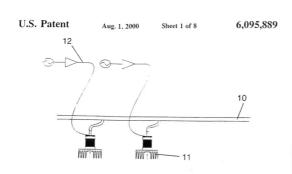

RainDance is an interactive sound installation that uses water to create a variety of non-water sounds. Jets of water droplets modulated by proprietary electronic nozzles carry sound vibrations that are inaudible until the viewer/listener intercepts the stream of water with a large umbrella. The sound is then decoded and resonated from the surface of the umbrella. The umbrella, in effect, becomes the loudspeaker. Diverse electronic and acoustic material is modulated onto the streams so that people strolling along under the water jets can listen to, mix and sequence a variety of sonic material ranging from musical to rhythmic to electronic.

The Experience
The work is attractive and inviting to a wide variety of audiences including children and seniors. The umbrella creates a private zone for listening to the sounds. In

RainDance ist eine interaktive Klanginstallation, die Wasser einsetzt, um damit eine Vielzahl von Nicht-Wasserklängen zu erzeugen. Sprühstrahlen aus kleinen Wassertröpfchen werden durch eigene elektronische Spritzdüsen moduliert und transportieren Klangvibrationen, die unhörbar sind, solange der Betrachter/Hörer nicht den Wasserstrahl mit einem großen Regenschirm unterbricht. Dadurch wird der Klang entschlüsselt und von der Oberfläche des Schirms wiedergegeben – der Regenschirm wird zum Lautsprecher. Verschiedene elektronische und akustische Materialien werden auf die Strahlen moduliert, sodass durchspazierende Menschen jederzeit eine Vielzahl von Klangmaterialien – von musikalisch über rhythmisch bis zu elektronisch – anhören und mischen können.

Die Erfahrung
Das Werk ist für eine Vielzahl von Besuchergruppen attraktiv und einladend – auch für Kinder und Senioren. Der Regenschirm schafft eine private Zone des Hörens und ist in gewissem Sinn ein Talisman-ähnliches Gerät, das den Benutzer gleichzeitig vor dem Wasser schützt und ihm die allgegenwärtigen – aber ansonsten unhörbaren – Klänge aus dem Wasser wiedergibt. Aus einiger Entfernung ist es für Zufallsbetrachter nicht einsichtig, was denn die Menschen mit den Schirmen da tun. Erst wenn sie selbst einen Schirm nehmen und selbst in die Erfahrung eintauchen, beginnen sie diese Welt des feuchten Unhörbaren zu erforschen. Und bei gutem Wetter kann man die Installation auch dazu benutzen, um im Wasser zu planschen, andere Leute anzuspritzen und so weiter.

a sense it is a talismanic device that at once shields the viewers from the water and permits them to hear the ever-present but inaudible sounds contained in the water. From afar, it is not apparent to newcomers what the people with the umbrellas are doing. It is not until they pick up an umbrella and immerse themselves in the experience that they begin to explore this world of the wet inaudible. If the weather is nice there is the additional opportunity for water-play, splashing other people, etc.

PAUL DEMARINIS (USA) HAS BEEN WORKING AS A MULTIMEDIA ELECTRONIC ARTIST SINCE 1971 AND HAS CREATED NUMEROUS PERFORMANCE WORKS, SOUND AND COMPUTER INSTALLATIONS AND INTERACTIVE ELECTRONIC INVENTIONS. HE HAS PERFORMED INTERNATIONALLY, AT THE KITCHEN, FESTIVAL D'AUTOMNE A PARIS, HET APOLLOHUIS IN HOLLAND AND AT ARS ELECTRONICA IN LINZ AND CREATED MUSIC FOR MERCE CUNNINGHAM DANCE CO. HIS INTERACTIVE AUDIO ARTWORKS HAVE BEEN SHOWN AT THE I.C.C. IN TOKYO, BRAVIN POST LEE GALLERY IN NEW YORK AND THE MUSEUM OF MODERN ART IN SAN FRANCISCO. ▬

Paul DeMarinis (USA) arbeitet seit 1971 als Multimedia-Künstler im elektronischen Bereich. Er hat zahlreiche Performances, Sound- und Computerinstallationen sowie interaktive elektronische Projekte entwickelt, die er international präsentiert, z. B. bei The Kitchen, beim Festival d'Automne in Paris, bei Het Apollohuis in Holland und Ars Electronica in Linz. Er schrieb Musik für Merce Cunningham Dance Co. Seine interaktiven Audio-Arbeiten wurden im I.C.C. in Tokyo, in der Bravin Post Lee Gallery in New York und im Museum of Modern Art in San Francisco gezeigt.

YOU THINK THEREFORE I AM
Magali Desbazeille / Siegfried Canto

You think therefore I am (following you) is on anonymity in a public place and the flow of inner thoughts in the closeness of a crowd. The participant walks on a video-projected image. The image presents pedestrians, filmed beforehand from underneath through a transparent floor. When the participant comes into contact with the image of filmed pedestrians, he hears their inner thoughts.

Filmed pedestrians also perhaps passed there, they belong, like the participants, to the memory of the place. The image is like a mirror. The spectator is surprised by these fragmented inner thoughts and smiles to himself. Is he revealed despite himself?

We don't speak as we think and don't think as we speak. Inner thoughts are unrestrained. They jump from one subject to another. They are often linked to banality and daily organisation, but can also be far from this. The inner thoughts are about human communication, anonymity in public space.

How does one pedestrian see another one? How is the city seen by the citizens? So many questions that the inner thoughts try to answer.

There are 130 filmed pedestrians, to which as many thoughts and varying voices correspond. The proportion of various languages can be adapted to the country of presentation.Like most public places, there are many different kinds of filmed pedestrians : men, women, children, old people. Some people are walking fast, some slow, some are waiting.

The projected image is slowed down three times so that the participants can follow the filmed pedestrians and get a chance to hear a longer thought.

Producers/Partnership

Invited writer: Christine Beigel

Le Fresnoy, Studio national des arts contemporains, Ministère de la Culture et de la Communication— Direction Régionale des Affaires Culturelles du Nord-Pas de Calais, Région Île de France, FLIR Systems company, Doublet company, Centre National Chorégraphique de La Rochelle, Théâtre du Nord de Lille, Ryerson University, SURCOUR association and ART-here association.

You think therefore I am (following you) [„Du denkst, also bin ich (dir auf der Spur)"] handelt von der Anonymität im öffentlichen Raum und vom Fluss der innersten Gedanken in der Enge einer Menge.

Der Teilnehmer geht auf einem projizierten Videobild spazieren, das Fußgänger zeigt, die zuvor durch einen transparenten Boden von unten aufgenommen wurden. Wenn der Teilnehmer mit dem Bild gefilmter Passanten in Kontakt kommt, hört er deren innerste Gedanken.

Gefilmte Passanten, die vielleicht zufällig dort vorbeigekommen sind, gehören ebenso zur Erinnerung des Ortes wie die Mitwirkenden. Das Bild ist wie ein Spiegel. Der Beobachter wird von den Fragmenten innerster Gedanken überrascht und lächelt vor sich hin. Wird er etwa ohne sein Wissen bloßgestellt? Wir sprechen nicht, wie wir denken, und wir denken nicht, wie wir sprechen. Die Gedanken sind frei, sie springen von einem Gegenstand zum nächsten, sind oft mit Banalitäten und der Organisation des Tagesablaufes beschäftigt, oft aber auch mit etwas ganz anderem. Die Gedanken betreffen die menschliche Kommunikation, die Anonymität im öffentlichen Raum. Wie sieht ein Fußgänger den anderen? Wie wird die Stadt von den Bürgern gesehen? So viele Fragen, auf die die innersten Gedanken eine Antwort zu geben versuchen.

Insgesamt gibt es 130 gefilmte Fußgänger, denen ebenso viele Gedanken und Stimmen entsprechen. Die Verteilung der einzelnen Sprachen

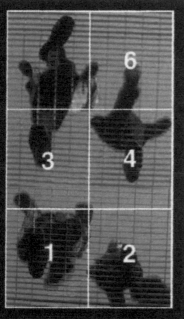

kann dem Aufführungsort angepasst werden.
Wie an den meisten öffentlichen Orten gibt es auch
hier verschiedene Arten von gefilmten Passanten –
Männer, Frauen, Kinder, alte Menschen. Manche
gehen schnell, manche langsam, andere warten. Das
projizierte Bild wird mit einem Drittel der Originalge-
schwindigkeit abgespielt, damit die Teilnehmer den
gefilmten Fußgängern folgen können und die Möglichkeit bekommen, auch längere Gedanken
anzuhören.

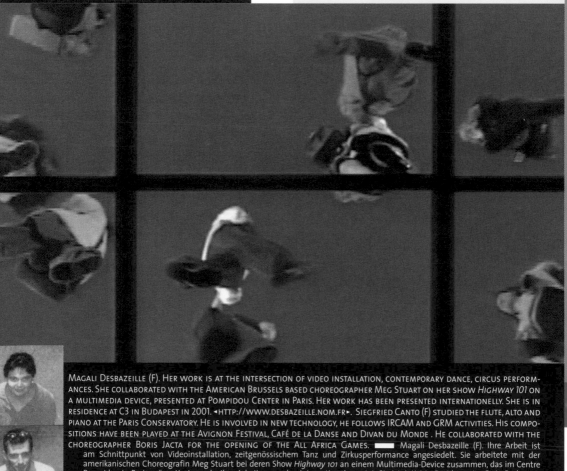

MAGALI DESBAZEILLE (F). HER WORK IS AT THE INTERSECTION OF VIDEO INSTALLATION, CONTEMPORARY DANCE, CIRCUS PERFORM-
ANCES. SHE COLLABORATED WITH THE AMERICAN BRUSSELS BASED CHOREOGRAPHER MEG STUART ON HER SHOW *HIGHWAY 101* ON
A MULTIMEDIA DEVICE, PRESENTED AT POMPIDOU CENTER IN PARIS. HER WORK HAS BEEN PRESENTED INTERNATIONELLY. SHE IS IN
RESIDENCE AT C3 IN BUDAPEST IN 2001. ◄HTTP://WWW.DESBAZEILLE.NOM.FR►. SIEGFRIED CANTO (F) STUDIED THE FLUTE, ALTO AND
PIANO AT THE PARIS CONSERVATORY. HE IS INVOLVED IN NEW TECHNOLOGY, HE FOLLOWS IRCAM AND GRM ACTIVITIES. HIS COMPO-
SITIONS HAVE BEEN PLAYED AT THE AVIGNON FESTIVAL, CAFÉ DE LA DANSE AND DIVAN DU MONDE . HE COLLABORATED WITH THE
CHOREOGRAPHER BORIS JACTA FOR THE OPENING OF THE ALL AFRICA GAMES. ▬▬ Magali Desbazeille (F). Ihre Arbeit ist
am Schnittpunkt von Videoinstallation, zeitgenössischem Tanz und Zirkusperformance angesiedelt. Sie arbeitete mit der
amerikanischen Choreografin Meg Stuart bei deren Show *Highway 101* an einem Multimedia-Device zusammen, das im Centre
Pompidou in Paris präsentiert wurde. Ihre Arbeiten wurden international gezeigt. Sie ist Artist-in-Residence im C3 in Budapest.
<http://www.desbazeille.nom.fr>. Siegfried Canto (F) studierte Flöte, Altsaxofon und Klavier in Paris. Er beschäftigt sich mit neuen
Technologien am IRCAM und GRM. Seine Kompositionen wurden beim Avignon Festival, Café de la Danse und Divan du Monde
aufgeführt. Er arbeitete mit dem Choreografen Boris Jacta für die Eröffnung der All Africa Games zusammen.

CAMERA MUSICA
Gerhard Eckel

The very concept of space became the actual interface to the music and sound in *Camera Musica*. Virtual reality was used for what it can do best and not for mimicking reality. The old dream of looking and moving through walls—something usually avoided by all means in virtual environments—became a central idea of the piece. In an immersive display, where we can actually sense the presence of virtual objects, we can also experience penetrating objects and being penetrated by them. We move through walls, and planes cut through our body (even the most extreme case of a plane cutting right through the middle of our head, so that one eye sees one side of the plane and the other eye the other side, can be experienced).

Description of the Work

Camera Musica is an immersive virtual environment in which the audience explores a musical space. This space is visually defined by a simple virtual architecture. The effortless visual orientation in this architecture is the basis for the navigation through the music. Visitors are visually and auditorily immersed in this space, which they navigate with their body movements and by means of a hand-held steering wand. The *Camera Musica* virtual environment is displayed stereoscopically in a surround-screen display system (e.g. a CAVE). The music is created in reaction to the visitor's movements. It is projected on an 8-channel spatial sound system. Tactile feedback is produced by an active vibration floor. Subsonic vibrations are perceived through feet and legs.

In *Camera Musica* the visitors freely float through spaces delimited by partially transparent cubes, some of them producing sounds when traversed by the head, others marking auditory regions in the soundscape composition. This is how the body becomes an

In *Camera Musica* wird das Raumkonzept an sich zum eigentlichen Interface zu Musik und Klang. Virtuelle Realität wurde für das eingesetzt, was sie am besten kann, und nicht zur Imitation der Wirklichkeit. Der alte Traum, durch Wände sehen und gehen zu können – was in virtuellen Environments normalerweise strikt verpönt ist – wird zu einem Grundgedanken des Stücks. In einem immersiven Display, in dem wir tatsächlich die Präsenz virtueller Objekte spüren können, können wir auch das Eindringen von Objekten erleben und in Objekte eindringen. Wir bewegen uns durch Wände, Ebenen schneiden durch unseren Körper – selbst der Extremfall einer Ebene, die längs durch den Kopf schneidet, kann erlebt werden, wobei beide Augen auf gegenüberliegende Seiten dieser „Wand" gerichtet sind.

Werkbeschreibung

Camera Musica ist ein immersives virtuelles Environment, innerhalb dessen das Publikum einen musikalischen Raum erlebt. Dieser Raum wird durch einfache virtuelle Architektur abgesteckt. Die anstrengungslose visuelle Orientierung in dieser Architektur ist die Basis für eine Navigation durch die Musik. Die Besucher werden visuell und akustisch von diesem Raum umhüllt, durch den sie mit Hilfe ihrer Körperbewegung und eines in der Hand zu haltenden Steuerstabes navigieren. Das virtuelle Environment von *Camera Musica* wird in einem Surround-Scene-Display (etwa einem CAVE) stereoskopisch projiziert. Die Musik wird als Reaktion auf die Bewegung des Besuchers generiert und über ein 8-Kanal-Raumklangsystem abgespielt. Taktiles Feedback wird über einen aktiven Vibrationsboden gegeben. Infraschall-Vibrationen werden über Füße und Beine vom Besucher aufgenommen.

In der *Camera Musica* gleiten die Besucher frei

index in the composition, allowing for a direct experience of formal openness. Whereas the head is the
reference for the rendering of the visual and auditory
scene, the role of the hand is to navigate and interact
with the virtual objects. All objects are surrounded by
invisible force fields which—as long as they are in
equilibrium—keep them in a stable position. The
user's hand holding the navigation wand disturbs this
equilibrium by its own force fields attached to the
wand's 6-degree-of-freedom sensor. This is how the
hand attracts and repulses the other objects and interacts with them through the kinetic simulation which it
becomes part of. This form of interaction highly
increases the sense of presence, because the environment reacts plausibly to the behavior of the visitor.
Camera Musica plays with the different forms of this
type of interaction acknowledging the presence of the
visitor.

durch Räume, die aus teilweise transparenten Würfeln bestehen, wobei einige von ihnen Klänge produzieren, wenn der Kopf in sie eintaucht, andere wiederum markieren Hörregionen in der Komposition der
Klanglandschaft. So wird der Körper zu einem Index
in der Komposition und erlaubt die direkte Erfahrung
formaler Offenheit. Während der Kopf als Bezug für
das Rendering der visuellen und klanglichen Szenerie
dient, ist es Aufgabe der Hand, zu navigieren und
mit den virtuellen Objekten zu interagieren. Jedes
der Objekte ist von unsichtbaren Kraftfeldern umgeben, die es – solange sie im Gleichgewicht sind – in
einer stabilen Position halten. Die Hand des Benut-
zers, die den Navigationsstab hält, stört dieses
Gleichgewicht durch eigene Kraftfelder, die mit dem
Sensor des Stabes gekoppelt sind. So zieht die Hand
andere Objekte an oder stößt sie ab und interagiert
mit ihnen durch die kinetische Simulation, zu deren
Teil sie wird. Diese Interaktionsform erhöht das
Gefühl der Präsenz in starkem Maß, weil die Umgebung plausibel auf das Verhalten des Besuchers rea-
giert. *Camera Musica* spielt mit den verschiedenen
Formen dieses die Anwesenheit des Besuchers zur
Kenntnis nehmenden Interaktionstyps.

GERHARD ECKEL (A), BORN IN 1962, IS A COMPOSER AND RESEARCHER INTERESTED IN THE USE OF NEW TECHNOLOGY FOR MUSIC
COMPOSITION AND PERFORMANCE. AS A RESEARCH SCIENTIST AT GMD, THE GERMAN NATIONAL RESEARCH CENTER FOR INFORMA-
TION TECHNOLOGY, HE IS INVOLVED IN THE DEVELOPMENT OF VIRTUAL ENVIRONMENT APPLICATIONS WHICH CLOSELY INTEGRATE
AUDITORY AND VISUAL SIMULATION. GERHARD ECKEL HAS WORKED AT MAJOR COMPUTER MUSIC CENTERS SUCH AS THE UTRECHT
INSTITUTE FOR SONOLOGY, IRCAM, AND ZKM. ▬▬ Gerhard Eckel (A), geb. 1962, ist Komponist und Forscher, der sich für den Einsatz
neuer Technologien bei der Komposition und Aufführung von Musik interessiert. Als Forscher am GMD – Forschungszentrum
Informationstechnik GmbH ist er in die Entwicklung von Virtual-Environment-Anwendungen eingebunden, die auditive und
visuelle Simulationen eng integrieren. Gerhard Eckel hat an vielen der großen Computermusik-Zentren gearbeitet, darunter am
Utrechter Institut für Sonologie, IRCAM und ZKM.

PROTOTYPE SCHMAROTZER®
(PARASITE)

Frank Fietzek

The *Schmarotzer®-Model A* is based on the phenomenon known as the Seebeck Effect, according to which electrical energy may be obtained through warmth differences (in this case, the body heat of the host and the warmth of the surrounding air). The *Model A* prototype shown here is attached to the skin of the host with adhesive tape and draws the energy needed to maintain or improve the charged state of its batteries directly from the surface of the host's skin. The current energy state of the Model A is displayed by the variable rhythmic blinking of the integrated LED.

Prototype Schmarotzer® (parasite)
Model B, Version 0.3

The *Schmarotzer®-Model B* functions according to the principle of electromagnetic induction: mechanical movement is transformed into electrical energy with a dynamo. The *Model B* prototype shown here is attached to the host's knee and draws the energy needed to maintain or improve the charged state of its batteries from the movement of the host's knee joint, for example when the host walks or rides a bicycle. The current energy state of the *Model B* is shown by a multistage LED charge level display.

Das *Schmarotzer®-Modell A* basiert auf dem als Seebeck-Effekt bekannten Phänomen, nach dem sich elektrische Energie aus Wärmedifferenzen (hier zwischen der Körperwärme des Wirts und der Wärme der Umgebungsluft) gewinnen lässt. Der hier gezeigte Prototyp des *Modells A* wird auf der Haut des Wirts mit Klebeband befestigt und bezieht die Energie zur Erhaltung oder Verbesserung des Ladezustandes seiner Akkumulatoren direkt von der Hautoberfläche des Wirts. Der aktuelle Energiezustand des *Modells A* wird durch das variable rhythmische Blinken der integrierten LED angezeigt.

Prototype Schmarotzer® (parasite)
Model B, Version 0.3

Das *Schmarotzer®-Modell B* arbeitet nach dem Prinzip der elektromagnetischen Induktion: Mit einem Dynamo wird mechanische Bewegung in elektrische Energie umgewandelt. Der hier gezeigte Prototyp des Modells B wird am Knie des Wirts befestigt und bezieht die Energie zur Erhaltung oder Verbesserung des Ladezustandes seiner Akkumulatoren aus der Bewegung des Kniegelenks des Wirts, z. B. beim Gehen oder Fahrradfahren.

Der aktuelle Energiezustand des *Modells B* wird durch eine mehrstufige LED-Ladestandsanzeige angezeigt.

- energy level display

Ni-Cd storage batteries

Tape

LED - energy level display

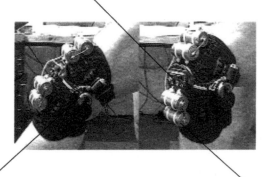

Dynamo

Ni-Cd storage batteries

Frank Fietzek (D), born 1960. 1981–82 studied philosophy at the University of Tübingen; 1983–84 Free Art School Hamburg, 1985–86 studied computer science at the University of Hamburg; 1994/95 guest lecturer at the Merzakademie Stuttgart, College of Design; 1997 lecturer at the Summer Academy of LAG Kunst Schleswig Holstein; 1999/2000 guest lecturer at the Bauhaus University Weimar, media department. Since 1999 project director at LEM—Laboratory for Electronic Media, Hamburg. ▬▬▬ Frank Fietzek (D), geb. 1960. 1981–82 Philosophiestudium, Universität Tübingen; 1983–84 Freie Kunstschule Hamburg, 1985–86 Informatikstudium, Universität Hamburg; 1994/95 Gastdozent an der Merzakademie Stuttgart, Fachhochschule für Gestaltung; 1997 Dozent an der Sommerakademie der LAG Kunst Schleswig-Holstein; 1999/2000 Gastdozent an der Bauhaus-Universität Weimar, Fakultät Medien. Seit 1999 Projektleiter am LEM – Labor für elektronische Medien, Hamburg.

FLOATING EYE

Hiroo Iwata

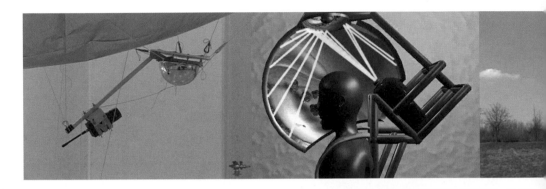

loating Eye is an interactive installation that separates vision from the body. The participant can only see a wide-angle image floating in the air. The wide-angle image is captured by a convex mirror and a video camera. The camera is equipped with a wireless transmitter. The camera-head is attached to an airship. The participant sees the wide-angle image through a wearable dome screen. The display employs a convex mirror. Light from a projector is scattered by the convex mirror. The projected image covers the participant's full field of view. This optical configuration corrects the distortion of the image taken by the camera-head. The system simulates out-of-the-body experience.

The camera-head is designed to capture the image from above. The participant can see his/her body in the captured image. The airship can be maneuvered by pulling the string. Walking around, participants can see themselves as well as the surrounding scene. However, a slight wind disturbs the airship. Thus, the participant is forced to interact with the atmosphere. This installation evokes a new style of self-recognition and the relationship between humans and the atmosphere.

Floating Eye ist eine interaktive Installation, die das Sehen vom Körper abkoppelt. Der Mitwirkende kann nur ein in der Luft schwebendes Weitwinkelbild sehen, das mit einem konvexen Spiegel und einer Videokamera aufgenommen wird. Die Kamera ist mit einem Funksender ausgestattet, das Objektiv ist an einem Luftschiff befestigt. Der Teilnehmer sieht das Weitwinkelbild über einen tragbaren Kuppelbildschirm. Das Display verwendet einen konvexen Spiegel, der den Lichtstrahl des Projektors verteilt, sodass das projizierte Bild das gesamte Blickfeld des Teilnehmers abdeckt. Diese optische Konfiguration korrigiert die bei der Aufnahme durch das Objektiv entstandene Verzerrung und simuliert eine visuelle Erfahrung außerhalb des eigenen Körpers.

Die Kamera nimmt ein Bild aus der Vogelperspektive vom Himmel her auf, und der Teilnehmer kann den eigenen Körper im Bild sehen. Das Luftschiff wird über einen Seilzug gesteuert, der Betrachter kann sich frei bewegen und dabei sich selbst ebenso beobachten wie die umgebende Landschaft. Allerdings wirkt sich jeder Lufthauch auf das Luftschiff aus, was den Betrachter dazu zwingt, mit der umgebenden Atmosphäre mitzureagieren. Diese Installation eröffnet neue Formen der Selbsterkenntnis und erforscht die Beziehung zwischen Mensch und Atmosphäre.

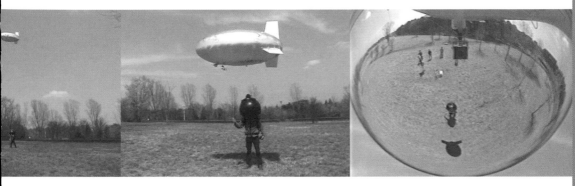

HIROO IWATA (J), BORN 1957, IS ASSOCIATE PROFESSOR AT THE INSTITUTE OF ENGINEERING MECHANICS AND SYSTEMS AT THE UNI-VERSITY OF TSUKUBA, WHERE HE TEACHES HUMAN INTERFACE AND CONDUCTS RESEARCH PROJECTS ON VIRTUAL REALITY. HE RECEIVED B.S., M.S., AND PH.D. DEGREES IN ENGINEERING FROM THE UNIVERSITY OF TOKYO IN 1981, 1983 AND 1986. HE IS ACTIVE IN RESEARCH ON HAPTIC INTERFACES IN VIRTUAL ENVIRONMENTS AND IS INTERESTED IN HOW THE HUMAN ABILITY OF RECOGNITION AND CREATION CAN BE EXTENDED BY HAPTIC INTERFACES. ▬▬ Hiroo Iwata (J), geboren 1957, ist Associate Professor am Institute of Engineering Mechanics and Systems an der Universität Tsukuba, wo er im Bereich Mensch-Maschine-Interfaces lehrt und Forschungsprojekte zur virtuellen Realität leitet. Er hat 1981, 1983 und 1986 die akademischen Grade eines B.S., M.S., und Ph.D. aus Ingenieurwissenschaften an der Universität Tokio erworben. Seine Forschungsaktivitäten konzentrieren sich auf haptische Interfaces in virtuellen Umgebungen und auf die Frage, wie die menschlichen Wahrnehmungs- und Schaffensfähigkeiten durch ein haptisches Interface verbessert werden können.

AUTOPOIESIS
Kenneth Rinaldo

Autopoiesis is an artificial life robotic series commissioned by the Kiasma Museum in Helsinki, Finland. It consists of fifteen musical and robotic sculptures that interact with the public and modify their behaviors based on both the presence of the participants in the exhibition and the communication between each separate sculpture. Autopoiesis is "self making", a characteristic of all living systems. This characteristic of living systems was defined and refined by Francisco Varela and Humberto Maturana. The structures themselves are constructed of cabernet sauvignon grapevines pulled into compression with steel wires. The joints are a custom-molded urethane plastic, which is all tied together using cyanoacrylate and baking soda. The grapevines were selected to create an approachable natural sculpture that exists in the human biological realm.

This series of robotic sculptures talk with each other through a hardwired network and audible telephone tones, which are a musical language for the group. Autopoiesis breaks out of standard interfaces (mouse) and playback methodologies (CRT) and presents an interactive environment, which is immersive, detailed and able to evolve in real time by utilizing feedback and interaction from audience/participant members. The interactivity engages the viewer/participant who in turn affects the system's evolution and emergence. This creates a system evolution as well as an overall group sculptural aesthetic.

Autopoiesis utilizes a number of unique approaches to create this complex and evolving environment. It uses smart sensor organization that senses the presence of the viewer/participant and allows the robotic sculpture to respond intelligently.

Autopoiesis continually evolves its own behaviors in response to the unique environment and viewer/partic-

Autopoiesis ist eine Roboterserie zum Thema Künstliches Leben im Auftrag des Kiasma Museums in Helsinki. Es besteht aus fünfzehn musikalischen Roboterskulpturen, die mit dem Publikum interagieren und ihr Verhalten je nach der Präsenz der Mitspieler wie auch der Kommunikation zwischen den Robotern ändern. Der Begriff „Autopoiesis", wie er von Francisco Varela und Humberto Maturana definiert und weiterentwickelt wurde, bedeutet „Selbstschöpfung" – ein Charakteristikum aller lebenden Systeme. Die Strukturen selbst bestehen aus Cabernet-Sauvignon-Reben, die durch den Zug von Stahldrähten komprimiert werden. Die Gelenke sind eigens aus Polyurethan konstruiert, und das alles wird mit Hilfe von Cyanoacylatkleber und Backsoda zusammengehalten. Die Reben wurden gewählt, um eine zugängliche natürliche Skulptur zu schaffen, die im biologischen Reich des Menschen existiert.

Die Gruppe von Roboterskulpturen kommuniziert untereinander über eine feste Verkabelung und mit Hilfe hörbarer Telefontöne, die für die Gruppe eine musikalische Sprache darstellen. Autopoiesis bricht aus den Standard-Interface- und Wiedergabekonzepten (Maus und Bildschirm) aus und präsentiert eine interaktive, immersive Umgebung, die sich in Echtzeit mit Hilfe des Feedbacks und der Interaktion des Publikums entwickeln kann. Diese Interaktion bezieht den Betrachter ein, der seinerseits die Entwicklung und das Wachstum des Systems beeinflusst, wodurch eine Systementwicklung ebenso entsteht wie eine umfassende skulpturale Gruppenästhetik.

Autopoiesis verwendet eine Vielzahl einzigartiger Ansätze, um dieses komplexe, in steter Entwicklung begriffene Environment zu schaffen. Intelligente Sensortechnik fühlt die Anwesenheit von Betrachtern / Mitwirkenden und

ipant inputs. This group consciousness of sculptural robots manifests a cybernetic ballet of experience, with the computer/machine and viewer/participant involved in a grand dance of one sensing and responding to the other.

Special Thanks to:
Amy Youngs, Dan Shellenbarger, Jesse Hemminger, Jenny Macy, Chris Gose, John Morrow , The Department of Art, and The Kiasma Museum of Contemporary Art for their assistance and financial support in realizing this project.

erlaubt der Roboterskulptur, intelligent zu antworten. *Autopoiesis* entwickelt kontinuierlich eigene Verhaltensmuster als Reaktion auf die Inputs der Umwelt und der Mitspieler. Dieses Gruppenbewusstsein von Roboterskulpturen stellt ein kybernetisches Ballett aus Erfahrung dar, wobei die Computer/Maschinen und die Teilnehmer einen gemeinsamen großen Tanz aus gegenseitigem Fühlen und Reagieren tanzen.

KENNETH RINALDO (USA) IS AN INTERDISCIPLINARY ARTIST AND THEORIST WHO CREATES INTERACTIVE MULTIMEDIA INSTALLATIONS THAT BLUR THE BOUNDARIES BETWEEN THE ORGANIC AND INORGANIC. HE TEACHES INTERACTIVE ROBOTIC SCULPTURE, DIGITAL IMAGING AND MULTIMEDIA IN THE ART AND TECHNOLOGY AREA OF THE DEPARTMENT OF ART AT THE OHIO STATE UNIVERSITY IN COLUMBUS OHIO. HIS WORKS HAVE BEEN COMMISSIONED AND DISPLAYED NATIONALLY AND INTERNATIONALLY AND BEEN REVIEWED AND EDITED IN NUMEROUS PUBLICATIONS AND BOOKS. ▬ Kenneth Rinaldo (USA) ist ein interdisziplinärer Künstler und Theoretiker, der interaktive Multimedia-Installationen schafft, die die Grenzen zwischen dem Organischen und dem Anorganischen verwischen. Er lehrt über interaktive Roboterskulpturen, digitale Bildgestaltung und Multimedia im Bereich Kunst und Technologie des Department of Art der Ohio State University in Columbus, Ohio. Seine Arbeiten, darunter zahlreiche Auftragswerke, wurden national und international ausgestellt und in zahlreichen Publikationen und Büchern rezensiert.

BRAINBALL
Smart Studio

We live in a society where everything seems to move faster and faster. New technology and IT speed up processes of production and communication. The aim of the new technology is to support us in our everyday life. Yet, people in the western world suffer from exhaustion, anxiety and other syndromes related to stress, due to a high-speed lifestyle.

Western society is also a competitive environment, which affects both our professional and private sphere. When it comes to the traditional concept of competing in games, the person who is producing the most adrenaline and is the most active one comes out as the winner.

In *Brainball* the common concept of competition is twisted. Here the winner will be the person who exceeds in passivity and relaxation. *Brainball* can be seen as an interface for the mental state of the two players.

One of the central issues in the Smart Studio is to explore how the development of new technology correlates with our cultural ideological and structural paradigm. In the initial part of the *Brainball* project, we started off with three conceptual preconditions; to create something with a twisted concept, to make a comment on modern life style without moralising and to find new ways of applying new technology in different situations. In this working process, our aim was to find a way to produce a piece in which the very use of the technology would make a comment on the high-speed society. We also found it challenging to try to use an already existing technology in a new context, far from the original purpose.

The preconditions of this specific task, which were put into practice in the full blown version of *Brainball*, naturally correspond to the attitude of the Smart Stu-

Wir leben in einer Gesellschaft, in der sich alles immer schneller und schneller zu bewegen scheint. Neue Technologien – besonders Informationstechnologien – beschleunigen die Kommunikations- und Produktionsprozesse. Ziel dieser Technologien ist es, uns in unserem täglichen Leben zu unterstützen. Und dennoch leiden die Menschen in der westlichen Welt unter Erschöpfung, Ängsten und anderen stressbedingten Symptomen – einfach wegen ihres Hochgeschwindigkeits-Lebensstils.

Die westliche Gesellschaft ist eine Wettbewerbsgesellschaft, was unser Berufsleben ebenso wie unser Privatleben beeinflusst. Wenn es zum traditionellen Konzept des spielerischen Wettkampfes kommt, so wird jener der Sieger, der am meisten Andrenalin ausstößt und am aktivsten ist.

Bei *Brainball* wird das übliche Wettkampfkonzept auf den Kopf gestellt – Sieger wird, wer am meisten Passivität und Entspanntheit zeigt. *Brainball* kann als Interface für den geistigen Zustand zweier Spieler betrachtet werden.

Eines der zentralen Anliegen von Smart Studio ist es, zu erforschen, wie die Entwicklung neuer Technologien mit unseren kulturellen, ideologischen und strukturellen Paradigmen korreliert. Am Anfang der Entwicklung des *Brainball*-Projekts stellten wir uns drei konzeptionelle Bedingungen: Wir wollten ein „verkehrtes" Konzept schaffen, das moderne Leben kommentieren, ohne dabei moralisierend zu sein, und neue Wege in der Anwendung zeitgemäßer Technologie finden. Im Verlauf der Arbeit konzentrierten wir uns darauf, ein Projekt zu entwickeln, bei dem der Einsatz der Technologie selbst zu unserer Hochgeschwindigkeitsgesellschaft Stellung bezieht. Wir fanden es auch spannend, eine bereits bestehende Technologie in einem völlig neuen Kontext fernab

dio as a whole. In the studio's day-to-day activity, we apply a critical perspective on technology. One of the central issues in our work is to explore how the development of new technology correlates with our cultural ideological and structural paradigm. The interdisciplinary approach characterizes our work, of which *Brainball* is an example.

Brainball uses an "off the shelf" biometrics-system from IBVA systems, for the input of the players' brain waves. These signals are analyzed and interpreted by a Macromedia Director application running on an Apple G4 computer. The Director application then sends serial output to an API step motor controller, which in turn controls a linear unit. The unit is mounted below a table surface and a magnet is fixed on the unit's carriage. The ball is placed on the table and is immediately attracted by the magnet below the surface. As the linear unit's carriage moves, the ball moves with it. The buttons are connected to inputs on the API step motor controller to control the Director application.

ihres eigentlichen Einsatzbereiches anzuwenden. Die Voraussetzungen für diese spezifische Aufgabe, die in der Vollversion von *Brainball* gelöst wurde, entspricht auf natürliche Weise der Haltung von Smart Studios als Ganzem. Die Alltagsarbeit im Studio ist durch unseren kritischen Blick auf die Technologie gekennzeichnet. Der interdisziplinäre Ansatz ist charakteristisch für unsere Arbeit, und *Brainball* ist ein gutes Beispiel dafür.

Brainball verwendet ein handelsübliches Biometrie-System von IBVA Systems, um die Gehirnwellen der Mitspieler zu erfassen. Diese Signale werden von einer Macromedia-Director-Anwendung, die auf einem Apple G4 läuft, analysiert und interpretiert. Die Director-Anwendung sendet dann seriellen Output an einen API-Schrittmotor, der seinerseits ein lineares Gerät antreibt. Dieses ist unter einer Tischplatte angebracht und enthält einen Magneten auf einem Transportschlitten. Der Ball wird auf den Tisch gelegt und sofort vom Magneten unter der Tischplatte angezogen. Sobald sich der Schlitten der linearen Einheit bewegt, bewegt sich auch der Ball mit. Die Reglerknöpfe sind mit Anschlüssen der Regeleinheit des Schrittmotors verbunden und dienen zur Steuerung der Director-Anwendung.

THOMAS BROOM (S) IS AN ARTIST WORKING IN PROJECTS FOCUSED ON ARTIFICIAL INTELLIGENCE AND BIOSENSORS. CAROLINA BROWALL (S), BEHAVIOURAL SCIENTIST, WORKS WITH FUTURE LIVING AND ENVIRONMENT, AND GENDER ISSUES. ESBJÖRN ERICSSON(S), ENGINEER, WORKS WITH CONCEPT DEVELOPMENT AND PROJECT MANAGEMENT. SARA ILSTEDT HJELM (S), INDUSTRIAL DESIGNER, WORKS AS A WRITER AND TEACHER. MAGNUS JONSSON (S), ENGINEER, WORKS WITH WORKSHOP AND CREATIVE METHODOLOGY, AND PROJECT MANAGEMENT. ARIJANA KAJFES (S), ARTIST, WORKS WITH IMMATERIAL MEDIA IN REAL SPACE. FREDRIK PETERSSON (S), ENGINEER, WORKS WITH HOMES OF THE FUTURE, SOFTWARE DEVELOPMENT, PROJECT MANAGING. TOBI SCHNEIDLER, (GB) ARCHITECT, WORKS WITH THE INTEGRATION OF PHYSICAL AND MEDIA ENVIRONMENTS IN ARCHITECTURAL DESIGN. INGVAR SJÖBERG (S), ARTIST, PROFESSOR OF FINE ARTS AT VALAND SCHOOL OF FINE ARTS, GOTHENBURG, KONRAD TOLLMAN (S), COMPUTER SCIENTIST, WORKS WITH COMPUTER VISION, DOMESTIC TECHNOLOGIES AND NEW COMMUNICATION MEDIA. LOTTEN WIKLUND (S), CULTURAL SCIENTIST, HAS BEEN WORKING WITH ART AND TECHNOLOGY FROM A THEORETICAL PERSPECTIVE OVER THE LAST FIVE YEARS. THANK YOU: HORREDS FURNITURE PEEKABOO DESIGN. ▬

Thomas Broom (S) ist ein Künstler, der an Projekten mit dem Schwerpunkt Künstliche Intelligenz und Biosensoren arbeitet. Carolina Browall (S), Verhaltensforscherin, beschäftigt sich mit Fragen des zukünftigen Lebens, der Umwelt und des Geschlechts. Esbjörn Ericsson (S), Ingenieur, arbeitet an der Konzeptentwicklung und im Projektmanagement. Sara Ilstedt Jelm (S), Industrial Designer, arbeitet als Autorin und Lehrerin. Magnus Jonsson (S), Ingenieur, arbeitet an Workshop- und kreativer Methodologie sowie im Projektmanagement. Tobi Schneidler (GB), Architekt, arbeitet an der Integration von physischen und medialen Environments ins Architekturdesign. Ingvar Sjöberg (S), Künstler, ist Professor für Bildende Kunst an der Valand-Kunstschule, Göteborg. Konrad Tollman (S), Computerwissenschaftler, arbeitet an Computervision, Haustechnik und neuen Kommunikationsmedien. Lotten Wiklund (S), Kulturwissenschaftler, beschäftigt sich seit fünf Jahren von der Warte des Theoretikers aus mit Kunst und Technologie. Das Team dankt Horreds Furniture Peekaboo Design.

RAKUGAKI

Keiko Takahashi /
Shinji Sasada /
Koichi Nishi

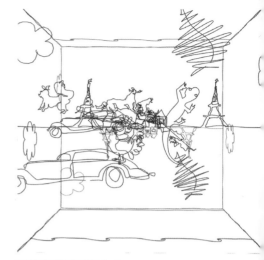

Rakugaki investigates the line between the analog and the digital. The essence of this artwork is about combining the visual effects and the real time interactive nature of computer technology and how it interprets sound and transforms it into a line and animates it. The ultimate aim of this work is to be exhibited in public areas such as subways, shops, and lobbies of buildings, where there is a large open space and an unspecified number of people are able to experience the work.

For this work, I used pictorial representation. Drawing (with a line) is very analog. It is a direct form of expression and has a primal quality. In ancient times, people drew drawings of animals in caves. The first pictorial representation for children is also drawing. I included a device, which transforms a sound created by an instrument into a drawing. An instrument is also analog and one does not need to deal with any complexity.

This idea came from a poetic image of a sound being transformed into a line. When a person plays a toy trumpet, a line will appear. The line starts to bend and wiggle according to the sound of the trumpet, like a snake charmer charming a snake with his flute. The lines start to transform into animals, insects, birds and human forms. They start to become animated and disappear.

By combining the analog, an element of child's play, with computer technology, microphone, projector, and PC, I tried to create a simple yet interactive work

The digital part, a huge cube image, could be projected on a wall, ceiling or floor. The idea of the cube's visual effect came from an image of turning a picture book. Each surface of the cube becomes a screen, and the audience can move it with the sound of drums or maracas. The surface will have an image of land, sky, sea and a line drawn. At the sound of a toy trumpet, it will start wiggling like a spring and transforming into

Rakugaki untersucht die Linie zwischen dem Analogen und dem Digitalen. Essenz dieser Arbeit ist die Kombination der Visual Effects und der Echtzeit-Interaktivität der Computertechnologie, und sie erforscht, wie Klänge interpretiert und in Linien und Animation umgewandelt werden. Der eigentliche Zweck dieses Werks besteht darin, im öffentlichen Raum ausgestellt zu werden – etwa in Unterführungen, Geschäften oder in den Eingangshallen größerer Gebäude, also überall dort, wo ein großer offener Raum zur Verfügung steht und wo eine beliebige Anzahl von Menschen das Werk erleben kann.

Für die Arbeit habe ich eine malerische Darstellungsweise verwendet. Zeichnen (mit einer Linie) ist etwas sehr Analoges, eine direkte Form des Ausdrucks, und es ist ihm etwas Urtümliches zu eigen. Schon in frühester Zeit haben die Menschen Zeichnungen von Tieren in Höhlen gemalt, und auch für Kinder ist die erste bildliche Ausdrucksform die Zeichnung. Ich habe ein Gerät eingebaut, das einen Instrumentalklang in eine Zeichnung umwandelt. Auch das Instrument ist analog, man braucht sich nicht mit komplexeren Dingen herumzuschlagen.

Der Gedanke zum Werk entstand aus dem poetischen Bild eines Klangs, der sich zur Linie wandelt. Wenn eine Person eine Spielzeugtrompete spielt, erscheint eine Linie. Diese beginnt sich zum Klang der Trompete zu biegen und zu wiegen wie die Schlange vor dem Schlangenbeschwörer. Die Linien verwandeln sich in Tiere, Insekten, Vögel und menschliche Gestalten, erwachen zum Leben und verschwinden wieder.

Durch Kombination aus dem Analogen – einem Kinderspiel – und der Computertechnologie samt Mikrofon, Projektor und PC habe ich versucht, ein einfaches, aber doch interaktives Werk zu schaffen.

Der digitale Teil – ein großes Bild eines Würfels – könnte auf eine Wand, einen Plafond oder einen Boden projiziert werden. Jede Fläche des Würfels wird zu einer eigenen Projektionsfläche, und das Publikum kann den Würfel durch den Klang von Trommeln oder Maracas drehen. Auf jeder der Flächen sind Bilder von Land, Himmel oder Wasser sowie eine Linie zu sehen. Beim Klang der Spielzeugtrompete beginnt sich die Linie wie

the most suitable animal for the chosen environment, will become animated.

In addition, when a line is drawn, changes its form or becomes animated, it will generate the sound of a bell, a children's piano and so on. These sounds are something like a rattle to calm a crying baby, or a sound you hear every day bringing back sweet memories of one's past. The warmth, beauty and the approachable aspect of a line drawing promote the audience's participation, as they observe how a line is transformed, interacting with the work.

My aim is to create a piece of work that is enjoyed by people of all ages. They simply see, feel and experience without giving it much thought.

eine Feder zu bewegen und verwandelt sich in ein für die jeweils gewählte Umwelt geeignetes animiertes Tier.

Zusätzlich erzeugt jede Linie, sobald sie gemalt und ihre Form verändert oder belebt wird, einen Klang – eine Glocke, ein Kinderklavier und so weiter. Diese Klänge erinnern an die Kinderrasseln, die man zur Beruhigung schreiender Babys verwendet und rufen in all ihrer Alltäglichkeit Erinnerungen an die eigene Kindheit wach. Die Wärme, Schönheit und der einfache Zugang zu einer Strichzeichnung fördern die Mitwirkung des Publikums, das beobachtet und in der Interaktion mit dem Werk erlebt, wie eine Linie sich verändert.

Mein Ziel ist es, ein Werk zu schaffen, das Menschen aller Altersstufen anspricht – sie sehen, fühlen und erfahren es, ohne viele Gedanken darauf zu verschwenden.

KEIKO TAKAHASHI (J), BORN IN KANAGAWA, JAPAN. 1992 B.A. IN OIL PAINTING, WOMEN'S COLLEGE OF FINE ARTS, TOKYO, JAPAN. SHINJI SASADA (J), BORN 1971 IN EHIME, JAPAN. 1991 GRADUATED FROM JAPAN ELECTRONICS COLLEGE IN TOKYO, JAPAN. KOICHI NISHI (J), BORN 1970 IN OKAYAMA. 1993 B.A. IN VISUAL ARTS, TAMA ART UNIVERSITY, TOKYO, JAPAN. 1997 M.A. IN VISUAL ARTS, TSUKUBA UNIVERSITY, IBARAKI, JAPAN. ■ Keiko Takahashi (J), geb. in Kanagawa, Japan. 1992 B.A. aus Ölmalerei am Women's College of Fine Arts, Tokio. Shinji Sasada (J), geb. 1979 in Ehime, Japan. Graduierte 1991 am Japan Electronics College in Tokio. Koichi Nishi (J), geb. 1970 in Okayama. 1993 B.A. aus Visueller Kunst, Tama Art University, Tokio; 1997 M.A. aus Visueller Kunst, Tskukuba University, Ibaraki, Japan.

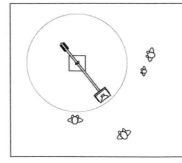

SPATIAL SOUNDS
Edwin van der Heide /
Marnix de Nijs

Spatial Sounds is a purely interactive installation. It's constantly scanning the space for visitors to communicate with.

Spatial Sounds contains two sensors: One Polaroid ultrasonic distance measurement sensor with self developed software and hardware based on a microcontroller. It generates midi output. The sensor is mounted on top of the speaker. It measures the distance of objects in front of the speaker up to 7 meters. One biphase angle measurement sensor with self developed software and hardware based on a microcontroller. It generates midi output. The sensor is mounted on the bottom of the axis. It outputs the current position of the arm in steps of 3 degrees. The information of the sensors is communicated via midi to a Macintosh computer. The computer runs self developed interaction software created within MAX/MSP. The software generates the sound in real-time. The software controls a triphase motorcontroller via a midi to voltage converter. The motorcontroller controls the speed and the direction of the motor. The software controls a lightdesk to change the light settings and incidentally switch on a stroboscope.

It's essential for Spatial Sounds to be able to distinguish the visitors in the space from the space itself. Every time the installation is set up in a new space, the installation first has to learn the shape of the space. This is done in the following way:

The interaction of Spatial Sounds is continuously changing. When there are no people in the space, it becomes very quiet in terms of both movement and sound. The arm slowly spins in one direction waiting for people to enter. The installation shows that it detects the visitor(s) by playing a soft sub-low sound. The installation wants to be sure that the visitor is staying and waits until it detects it/them again. Then it

Spatial Sounds ist eine rein interaktive Installation. Sie sucht ständig den Raum nach Besuchern ab, mit denen sie kommunizieren kann. Die Installation enthält zwei Sensoren. Ein Polaroid-Ultraschall-Entfernungsmesser mit selbstentwickelter Software und Hardware (die auf einem Microcontroller basiert) generiert einen MIDI-Output. Der Sensor ist oben auf dem Lautsprecher angebracht und misst die Entfernung zwischen dem Lautsprecher und Objekten bis auf eine Distanz von sieben Metern.

Ein zweiphasiger Winkel-Messsensor mit eigener Soft- und Hardware (auch auf Microcontroller-Basis) generiert ebenfalls MIDI-Output. Dieser Sensor ist unten an der Achse angebracht und gibt die gegenwärtige Stellung des Arms mit einer Genauigkeit von drei Grad an. Die von den Sensoren ausgegebene Information wird über MIDI an einen Macintosh-Rechner übertragen, der eine selbstgeschriebene Interaktions-Software fährt. Diese Software generiert den Echtzeit-Klang und steuert über einen MIDI-Spannungsregler eine Dreiphasen-Motorsteuerung. Diese regelt ihrerseits die Geschwindigkeit und Richtung des Motors. Die Software steuert ein Lichtmischpult mit variablen Beleuchtungseinstellungen sowie ein fallweise zugeschaltetes Stroboskop.

Spatial Sounds muss in der Lage sein, die Besucher des Raums vom Raum selbst zu unterscheiden – jedes Mal, wenn die Installation neu aufgebaut wird, muss sie zunächst die Form der Raumes „erlernen".

Die Interaktion verändert sich bei Spatial Sounds ständig. Wenn keine Besucher im Raum sind, wird die Installation sowohl hinsichtlich Klang wie hinsichtlich Bewegung sehr ruhig. Der Arm dreht sich langsam in eine Richtung, während auf Besucher gewartet wird.

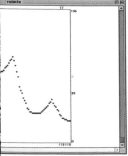

...p of the same room with four people

starts to become more active. The timbre of the sound depends on the distance the person has to the speaker. The visitor is invited to become a participant. The movement of the installation is fully based on where people stand. The installation can follow and/or swing around the participant. It can also deal with multiple people. When there are multiple people, they can really interact together. If people are not very active (if they stay in the same place all the time), the installation will start to ignore them after a certain period. The more you play with the installation, the more active it becomes. However, the installation can get out of control or overexcited.

Die Installation meldet, wenn sie einen eintretenden Besucher erkannt hat, indem sie einen leisen, extrem tiefen Ton spielt. Die Installation will sichergehen, dass der Besucher im Raum bleibt und wartet, bis sie ihn nochmals entdecken kann. Dann fängt sie an, aktiver zu werden. Das Timbre des Klanges hängt vom Abstand zwischen Besucher und Lautsprecher ab. Der Besucher wird eingeladen, zum Mitspieler zu werden. Die Bewegung der Installation hängt ausschließlich von der Distanz zwischen Besucher und Gerät ab; sie kann dem Besucher folgen oder ihn umkreisen. Sie kann auch mit mehreren Personen gleichzeitig interagieren und lädt sie zu gemeinsamer Interaktion ein. Sollten die Besucher nicht besonders aktiv sein, ignoriert sie die Installation nach einiger Zeit. Je mehr man mit ihr spielt, umso aktiver wird die Installation – sie kann allerdings auch außer Rand und Band geraten.

EDWIN VAN DER HEIDE (NL), BORN 1970, STUDIED SONOLOGY AT THE ROYAL CONSERVATORY IN THE HAGUE. HE GRADUATED IN 1992. HE IS A COMPOSER AND PERFORMS PRIMARILY ELECTRONIC MUSIC AND DESIGNS SOUND INSTALLATIONS. MARNIX DE NIJS (NL) IS A ROTTERDAM-BASED ARTIST, WHO EXPLORES THE DYNAMIC CLASH BETWEEN BODIES, MACHINES AND OTHER MEDIA. HIS WORKS INCLUDE MAINLY INTERACTIVE EXPERIENCE MACHINES THAT PLAY WITH PERCEPTION AND CONTROL OF IMAGE AND SOUND. ▬
Edwin van der Heide (NL), Jahrgang 1970, studierte Sonologie am Königlichen Konservatorium in Den Haag und graduierte 1992. Er ist als Komponist vorwiegend elektronischer Musik sowie als Konstrukteur von Klanginstallationen tätig. Marnix de Nijs (NL) ist ein in Rotterdam wohnhafter Künstler, der das dynamische Aufeinanderprallen von Körpern, Maschinen und anderen Medien untersucht. Seine Arbeiten umfassen vor allem interaktive Erfahrungsmaschinen, die mit der Wahrnehmung und der Steuerung von Bild und Klang spielen.

SIGNWAVE AUTO-ILLUSTRATOR

Adrian Ward

$$\pi = 4 \sum_{n=0}^{\infty} \frac{(-1)^n}{2n+1}$$

```
if tools.currenttool=12 then
   // TVifier tool
   tp=newpicture(128,128,16)
   tweens=( sqrt(pow(abs(ldx-dx),2)+pow(abs(ldy-dy),2)) / 8 ) + 1
   tweenx=(dx-ldx)/tweens
   tweeny=(dy-ldy)/tweens

   for tweenv=0 to tweens // Sum of the squares...
      twmx=ldx+(tweenx*tweenv)
      twmy=ldy+(tweeny*tweenv)
      tp.graphics.drawpicture myPict,0,0,128,128,twmx-16,twmy-16,32,32
      tp.graphics.forecolor=tools.forecolor
      for spareint=(-4)+((twmy mod 2)*4) to 128 step 8
         tp.graphics.drawline 0,spareint,128,spareint
      next
      myPict.graphics.drawpicture tp,twmx-16,twmy-16,32,32,0,0,128,128
   next

   drawgfx
end if
```

Although presented much like a traditional piece of graphic design software, *Auto-Illustrator* expresses a vast new way of treating code as a creative extension of the self. The routines of *Auto-Illustrator* have been imbued with coded implementations of the author/artist's creative decision-making process. In effect, this results in a deferred artistic activity, away from the original author, and as it is a computer application, in the hands of the person executing it.

This brings about many questions regarding authorship and authenticity of digital artworks. It poses new possibilities for the valuation of mechanically reproduced artworks, and offers the possibility that programming (a creative act above anything else) becomes more than just a method of production (i.e., a craft)—thus rendering the author as code. This also opens us to the possibility of a real-world implementation of cyborgism. When you run *Auto-Illustrator*, you interact with me, the author of the code. Your final products (despite thinking they are created by you) will actually have been produced in collaboration with the me.

Also presented as a parody of Adobe Illustrator, it mimics certain interface elements in an attempt to highlight the growing inadequacies of modern software. Professional software development is now about

Obwohl sich *Auto-Illustrator* weitgehend wie eine traditionelle Grafikdesign-Software präsentiert, stellt es eine völlig neue Art des Umgangs mit Code als kreativer Erweiterung des Selbst dar. Die Routinen des *Auto-Illustrator* verkörpern die codierten Implementationen des kreativen Entscheidungsfindungsprozesses des Autors/Künstlers. Dies führt zu einer Verlagerung der künstlerischen Aktivität weg vom ursprünglichen Autor und – weil es ja eine Computerapplikation ist – in die Hände der ausführenden Person.

Diese Tatsache zieht zahlreiche Fragen nach der Autorschaft und Authentizität digitaler Kunstwerke nach sich und eröffnet neue Möglichkeiten für die Bewertung mechanisch reproduzierter Kunstwerke – so auch die Möglichkeit, dass das Programmieren (was in erster Linie ein kreativer Akt ist) mehr als nur eine Produktionsmethode (also ein Handwerk) wird, sondern den Autor als Code wiedergibt. Dies gäbe uns auch die Möglichkeit, den Cyborgismus in der realen Welt zu implementieren. Wer *Auto-Illustrator* benutzt, interagiert mit mir, dem Autor des Codes. Selbst wenn der Benutzer denkt, das endgültige Produkt sei von ihm erschaffen, so ist es doch in Zusammenarbeit mit mir entstanden.

Das Programm, das als Parodie auf den Adobe Illustrator präsentiert wird, imitiert gewisse

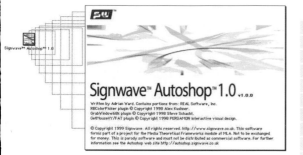

Signwave™ Autoshop™ 1.0 v1.0.0

Written by Adrian Ward. Contains portions from: REAL Software, Inc.
RBColorPicker plugin © Copyright 1998 Alex Kushner.
GrabWindow68k plugin © Copyright 1998 Steve Schacht.
GetMouseXY/FAT plugin © Copyright 1998 PERGAMON interactive visual design.

© Copyright 1999 Signwave. All rights reserved. http://www.signwave.co.uk. This software
forms part of a project for the Media Theoretical Frameworks module at MLA. Not to be exchanged
for money. This is parody software and must not be distributed as commercial software. For further
information see the Autoshop web site http://autoshop.signwave.co.uk

making software for the masses, and not for the professionals. The latest incarnation of Adobe Photoshop typifies this move away from focused professionalism to extreme popularist automation; Photoshop will now render all your web page buttons for you. Hopefully, within a few years, all web pages will conform to Adobe's graphic design specifications!

As an extreme reaction against this, *Auto-Illustrator* deliberately forces the user to experience a slightly jarring and dysfunctional approach to graphic design. Every time you ask it to draw an oval, it tries to draw a psychotic face. It'll never draw the same psychotic face twice, mind you.

Process over Product?

Auto-Illustrator features a great deal of tools and utilities that allow the user to explore different ways of generating artwork. As well as allowing traditional visual design skills, users can automate their own behaviours, and reiterate them on their own artwork, or even on others'. The menus of fitters, transformations and plug-ins reveal that it is possible to codify graphic design skills as code. On a practical level, this makes generating certain visual designs easy (through automation), and yet on a philosophical level, we start to question where a graphic designer's skills may lie. Would it be possible to render yourself purely as code, and then sell your skills as applications?

Interface-Elemente, um die zunehmende Unangemessenheit moderner Software aufzuzeigen. Professionelle Softwareentwicklung beschäftigt sich mit Software für die Massen, nicht für die Profis. Die jüngste Version von Adobe Photoshop demonstriert diese Abwendung von der konzentrierten Professionalität hin zu einer extrem populistischen Automatisierung – Photoshop rendert jetzt all Ihre Webseiten-Schaltflächen für Sie! Hoffentlich werden in wenigen Jahren alle Webseiten den Spezifikationen von Adobes Grafik-Design entsprechen!

Als extreme Reaktion auf diese Tendenzen zwingt *Auto-Illustrator* den Anwender ganz bewusst dazu, einen leicht verschrobenen und dysfunktionalen Zugang zum Grafikdesign zu erleben. Jedesmal, wenn man das Programm auffordert, ein Oval zu zeichnen, versucht es ein psychotisches Gesicht darzustellen – und es zeichnet keine zwei Mal das gleiche Gesicht ...

Prozess vor Produkt?

Auto-Illustrator enthält eine Vielzahl von Werkzeugen und Hilfsmitteln, die es dem Anwender erlauben, verschiedene Arten der Erzeugung von Kunst zu erforschen. Es bietet einerseits alle Möglichkeiten des traditionellen visuellen Designs, daneben aber können die Anwender ihr eigenes Verhalten automatisieren und es immer wieder auf ihre eigenen Werke, aber auch die anderer anwenden. Die Menüs mit Einpassern, Transformatoren und Plug-Ins zeigen, dass es möglich ist, Fertigkeiten, die im grafischen Design gefragt sind, in einen Code zu gießen. Auf der praktischen Ebene erlaubt dies, gewisse visuelle Designs auf sehr einfache Weise zu generieren (durch die Automatisierung), und dennoch hinterfragen wir auf der philosophischen Ebene, wo denn die Fähigkeiten eines Grafikdesigners eigentlich liegen. Wäre es möglich, sich selbst rein als Code darzustellen und dann die eigenen Fähigkeiten als Applikation zu implementieren?

ADRIAN WARD (UK) WORKS AS A SOFTWARE ARTIST, DEVELOPING INTERACTIVE GENERATIVE VISUAL AND AUDIO APPLICATIONS. CONCERNED PRIMARILY WITH ISSUES OF AUTHORSHIP AND THE EXTENSION OF AESTHETIC SUBJECTIVITY INTO CODE, HE IS ENGAGED WITH A NUMBER OF PROJECTS THAT INTEND TO BRING ABOUT A SUBTLE CHANGE IN THE WAY PEOPLE INTERACT WITH TECHNOLOGY. CURRENTLY COLLABORATING WITH A RANGE OF MUSICIANS, CONCEPTUAL AND PERFORMANCE ARTISTS, HE ALSO USES HIS SOFTWARE FOR LIVE MUSICAL PERFORMANCES AND INSTALLATIONS. HE IS INVOLVED WITH A NUMBER OF EDUCATIONAL SOFTWARE PROJECTS THAT ACTIVELY ENGAGE THE USER BY EXPLORING INTERACTIVITY WITHIN A GENERATIVE CONTEXT. ▬▬ Adrian Ward (UK) ist Software-Künstler, der interaktive generative visuelle und Audio-Anwendungen entwickelt. Er beschäftigt sich vor allem mit Fragen des Authorship und der Ästhetik von Codes und arbeitet an Projekten, die eine subtile Veränderung in der Art und Weise, wie Menschen mit Technologie interagieren, bewirken sollen. Zurzeit arbeitet er mit Musikern, Konzept- und Performance-Künstlern und setzt seine Software bei Live-Musik-Performances und Installationen ein. Er entwickelt Software im Bildungsbereich, die den User über Interaktivität in einem generativen Kontext aktiv einbinden.

ZGODLOCATOR

Herwig Weiser /
Albert Bleckmann

Heavy Metal. *zgodlocator* as a techno-visionary phenomenology of material

Granular Hardware

A desert landscape consisting of granulated computer hardware that has been decoupled from an industrial recycling process. Electronic components, such as circuit boards, connectors, integrated circuits or semi-conductors, contain raw material that is valuable to industry, not only in conducting the flow of electricity as a carrier of information, but also in being returned to the flow of capital. *zgodlocator* stages granulated hardware as a desert and the metallurgic circulation of electronic information media in the industrial reproduction machine. Material and information, the real and the symbolic are, in fact, inseparable here, forming instead a deep, haptic surface as a material-force relation.

Sound/Vision Surfaces

The dynamic modulation of hardware is based on a procedure from sound synthesis: granular composition. This is exactly what *zgodlocator* does with electronic hardware itself. Computer media are "sampled", once they have been granulated into the smallest particles. The resynthesis of these granular hardware elements takes place through electromagnetic induction in a landscape surface. Using a controller, the observer and listener gives midi signals for an active-passive sound environment. The controller signals are translated into electromagnetic patterns and generate deep surfaces in the techno-granulate.

Hardware Live Modeling

In *zgodlocator*, software and hardware are conceived the other way around. It is not the hardware that gen-

Heavy Metal. *zgodlocator* als techno-visionäre Phänomenologie der Materie

Granular Hardware

Die Wüstenlandschaft besteht aus granulierter Computerhardware, die aus einem industriellen Recycling-Prozess entkoppelt ist. Elektronische Bauteile wie Leiterplatten, Steckverbindungen, integrierte Schaltkreise oder Halbleiter enthalten für die Industrie wertvolle Rohstoffe, die nicht nur Strom als Träger von Information leiten, sondern auch dem Strom des Kapitals zurückgegeben werden.
zgodlocator inszeniert granulierte Hardware als Wüste und damit die metallurgische Zirkulation elektronischer Informationsmedien in der industriellen Reproduktionsmaschine. Materie und Information, Reales und Symbolisches sind hier eben nicht trennbar, sondern bilden als Materie-Kraft-Relation eine tiefe, haptische Oberfläche.

Sound/Vision-Surfaces

Der dynamischen Modulation von Hardware ist ein Verfahren aus der Sound-Synthese zu Grunde gelegt: granulare Komposition. Genau dies macht *zgodlocator* mit elektronischer Hardware selber. Computermedien sind „gesampelt", insofern sie in kleinste Teile granuliert sind, die Resynthese dieser granularen Hardware-elemente geschieht über elektromagnetische Induktion in einer Oberflächenlandschaft. Über Steuerregler gibt der Betrachter und Zuhörer Midi-Signale für ein aktiv-passives Sound-Environment, die Steuersignale werden in elektromagnetische Muster übersetzt und erzeugen tiefe Oberflächen im Technogranulat.

Hardware-Live-Modeling

Soft- und Hardware sind in *zgodlocator* umgekehrt gedacht. Nicht die Hardware macht spezifische Effekte im Sound, sondern der Sound als in elektromagnetische Felder übersetzter Code induziert und konfiguriert erst die Hardware.
In der elektromagnetischen Interaktion mit Elektronik zeigt sich, dass besonders diejenigen Techno-Granulate eine Tiefe bekommen, die speziell dem Computer als Bildmedium entnommen sind. Die Ablenkspulen von Kathoden-

erates specific effects in sound, but rather the sound as code translated into electromagnetic fields induces and configures the hardware.

In the electromagnetic interaction with electronics, it becomes evident that particularly those techno-granulates derived from the computer as an image medium attain a special depth. The deflection coils from cathode ray tubes are especially sensitive to electromagnetic induction and generate a haptic and deep surface landscape.

zgodlocator thus implies an image theory statement. Electronic images are, in fact, effects of a surface from the start. *zgodlocator* is not only aware of the surface character of electronic images, but even goes beyond this in terms of image theory, as the image is activated via signals as a haptic and deep surface. The signs of electronic media, which are formed on the basis of circuits, can be modulated here as a surface in electromagnetic codes. It is not the images themselves, but rather their technical preconditions as granulated circuit diagrams that are synthesized by sounds. The synopsis of electronics in *zgodlocator* is thus no longer audio-visual, but rather techno-visionary. (*Axel Roch*)

This text by Axel Roch is published by kind permission from Medienturm Graz (www.medienturm.at <http://www.medienturm.at>). First published in CAMERA AUSTRIA Nr. 75, Graz 2001.

With special thanks to:
F. X. Randomitz (NI Reaktor-Input)
Timothy Ingen-Housz, Harald Milchrahm
Kunsthochschule für Medien, Köln
www.native-instruments.de
www.demel.com

zgodlocator

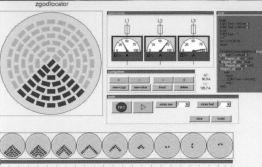

strahlröhren sind besonders sensitiv für elektromagnetische Induktion und erzeugen eine haptische und tiefe Oberflächenlandschaft.

zgodlocator impliziert damit eine bildtheoretische Aussage. Elektronische Bilder sind nämlich von Anfang an Effekte einer Oberfläche. *zgodlocator* ist sich dem Oberflächencharakter der elektronischen Bilder nicht nur bewußt, sondern geht bildtheoretisch darüber noch hinaus, insofern das Bild über Signale als haptische und tiefe Oberfläche angesteuert ist. Die Zeichen elektronischer Medien, die auf der Grundlage von Schaltungen gebildet sind, sind hier als Oberfläche in elektromagnetischen Codes modulierbar. Nicht die Bilder selbst, sondern deren technische Bedingungen als granulierte Schaltpläne werden durch Sounds synthetisiert. Die Synopsis der Elektronik in *zgodlocator* ist damit nicht mehr audiovisuell, sondern techno-visionär. (*Axel Roch*)

HERWIG WEISER (A), BORN 1969, 1990–91 ARCHITECTURE, TECHNICAL UNIVERSITY INNSBRUCK; 1992–94 GERRIT RIETVELD ACADEMY, AMSTERDAM, 1994–98 ART COLLEGE FOR MEDIA COLOGNE, D. EXHIBITION PARTICIPATION: DEAF 98, V2_ROTTERDAM, NL; ZKM KARLSRUHE; MUSEUM LUDWIG KÖLN; TRANSMEDIALE 01, BERLIN ("AWARD-INTERACTIVE"); "CLAASEN-FÖRDERPREIS" FOR PHOTOGRAPHY AND MEDIA ART. ALBERT BLECKMANN (D), BORN 1965, 1984–87 TRAINING AS ELECTRICIAN, TELEKOM COLOGNE; SINCE 1990 HAS STUDIED ELECTRICAL ENGINEERING AT THE SPECIALIZED COLLEGE FH COLOGNE.
Herwig Weiser (A) geb. 1969, 1990–91 Architektur, TU-Innsbruck; 1992–94 Gerrit Rietveld Akademie, Amsterdam, 1994–98 Kunsthochschule für Medien Köln, D. Ausstellungsbeteiligung u. a. bei DEAF 98, V2_Rotterdam, NL; ZKM Karlsruhe; Museum Ludwig Köln; Transmediale 01, Berlin („award-interactive"); „Claasen-Förderpreis" für Fotografie und Medienkunst. Albert Bleckmann (D) geb. 1965, 1984–87 Ausbildung zum Elektromechaniker, Telekom Köln; seit 1990 Studium-Elektrotechnik, FH Köln.

computer animation
visual effects

NO ALLOWANCES NEEDED
KEINE ZUGESTÄNDNISSE

Rick Sayre

Three years ago, Computer Animation was split into two independent categories, Computer Animation and Visual Effects. The continued blurring of the lines between the disciplines has led to a re-unification this year, with the jury considering them together as part of something we don't yet know how to label. "Computer Film" and "Digital Film" are evocative, but reference a dying media. "Computer-Potentiated Linear-Time Visual Media", while semantically accurate, is rather unpleasant. So, for the moment, we continue to use "Computer Animation/Visual Effects".

While the disciplines blur, the need for disparate contexts by which to evaluate the two types of work persists. At least for the present, short-form Computer Animations tend to be the product of small teams and singular visions. We typically judge them as complete works, and if they undertake traditional storytelling, the work must have a good story. While last year's Golden Nica winner was an encouraging departure,

Vor drei Jahren wurde die Kategorie „Computeranimation" des Prix Ars Electronica in zwei unabhängige Kategorien aufgeteilt: in „Computeranimation" und „Visual Effects". Da die Trennlinie zwischen den beiden Kategorien aber nach wie vor unscharf blieb, wurden die beiden Kategorien in diesem Jahr wieder vereint, wobei die Jury diese Doppelkategorie als etwas ansah, was noch kein eigenes Etikett hat. „Computerfilm" und „digitaler Film" sind zwar griffig, berufen sich aber auf ein sterbendes Medium. „Computergestützte zeitlich lineare visuelle Medien" wäre zwar semantisch korrekt, dafür aber ziemlich unschön, deshalb verwenden wir einstweilen weiterhin den Doppelbegriff „Computeranimation / Visual Effects".

Wenn sich auch die Grenzen zwischen den Disziplinen verwischen, die Notwendigkeit für separate Kontextgruppen zur Bewertung der zwei Werktypen bleibt bestehen. Zumindest gegenwärtig scheinen kurze Computeranimationen vorwiegend das Produkt kleiner Teams oder individueller Visionäre zu sein. Wir beurteilen sie typischerweise als Gesamtkunstwerke, und wenn sie sich auf traditionelle Formen der Narration stützen, brauchen sie eine dementsprechend gute Geschichte – die Arbeit des letztjährigen Gewinners der Goldenen Nica, Jakub Pistecky, ist ein gutes Beispiel dafür. Im Gegensatz dazu werden die Visual Effects meistens als Dienstleistung großer Studios zugekauft. Das Werk, dem sie integriert sind, kann darüber hinaus auch Visual Effects von mehreren Produktionsfirmen enthalten, die miteinander nichts zu tun haben. Wenn also die „Story" des großen, teuren, abendfüllenden Films schlecht ist, wenn Sequenzen von anderen Beiträgern schwach sind, wenn der Film selbst ein absoluter Flop ist – darf man das als Argument gegen den Einreicher einer speziellen Visual-Effects-Sequenz vorbringen? Die Jury ist nicht dieser Meinung – bzw. sie findet, dass die Sache so einfach nicht ist. Visual Effects bleiben eine mächtige Kraft in der Medienkultur, und tatsächlich fand die Jury auch unter den kurzen Computeranimationen mehrere, die sich auf

Visual-Effects-Sequenzen vergangener Jahre beziehen. Wenn das Werk innovativ ist, wenn es das Genre erheblich beeinflusst oder wenn es zumindest im Handwerklichen außerordentlich gut gemacht wurde, dann muss es um seines eigenen Wertes willen betrachtet werden, selbst wenn es in ein filmisches Desaster eingebettet ist. Aber vielleicht macht diese Situation auch nur deutlich, dass wir noch immer in der Formierungsphase eines neuen Meta-Mediums stecken.

Die Jury sah sich mit über 250 zu bewertenden Einreichungen konfrontiert. Unser vielleicht etwas byzantinisch anmutender Entscheidungsprozess hat sich kontinuierlich über die vergangenen Jahren entwickelt. Wenn auch eine gewisse Struktur wichtig ist, um eine faire Bewertung einer großen Zahl von Werken in kurzer Zeit sicherzustellen, so waren wir doch bemüht, zu einer Entscheidung zu finden, mit der alle Juroren mit ihren zwar unterschiedlichen, aber sich ergänzenden Hintergründen gut leben konnten. Das Ergebnis eines mathematisch-statistischen Bewertungsprozesses kann daher nur Ausgangspunkt weiterer Überlegungen sein, und wir rechnen es dem Prix Ars Electronica hoch an, dass die einzelnen Jurys ihre eigenen Methoden entwickeln können, die der Zusammensetzung der Gruppe und der Zahl und Qualität der Einreichungen des jeweiligen Jahres gerecht werden.

Zunächst wurden alle eingereichten Werke in einer Phase minimaler Diskussion angesehen. Hier ging es darum, einen Kontext für die spätere genauere Auseinandersetzung zu schaffen. Jeder von uns konnte „Ja" sagen, womit auf eine weitere Betrachtung der Einreichung zunächst verzichtet und das Werk für eine intensivere Analyse vorgemerkt wurde. Um jedoch ein Stück gleich am Anfang auszuscheiden, bedurfte es einer Stimmenmehrheit. So versuchten wir, fesselnde, aber kontroversielle Arbeiten im Bewerb zu halten, wenn es auch nur einem von uns Juroren wichtig erschien, während wir überzeugt waren, dass „Schlechtes" wohl eher allgemein als solches angesehen würde.

Und leider gibt es weiterhin einen durchaus erheblichen Anteil schlechter Werke. Die Jurys vergangener Jahre haben sich bereits zur ungehemmten Vermehrung von „Augäpfeln und Tunneln" in der Kategorie „Schlechte Computergrafik" geäußert, und das heurige Jahr war

Visual Effects are generally sub-contracted as components of vast studio efforts. The work of which they are a portion may further involve Visual Effects from several entirely unrelated production companies. If the "story" of the big-budget feature film sucks, if other sequences from other companies are poor, if the film itself is a hideous failure, can we hold it against the submitter of a particular Visual Effects sequence? This jury thinks not, or rather "it's more complex than that". Visual Effects remain a potent force in media culture;

indeed, the jury saw several short Computer Animation pieces which themselves referenced Visual Effects sequences of previous years. If the work is groundbreaking, clearly influential, or simply done incredibly well, it must be considered on its own merits, even if embedded in a filmic disaster. Perhaps, however, this simply reveals that we are still in the formative stages of a new meta-medium.

The jury was faced with more than 250 entries to consider. Our somewhat Byzantine process represented a continued evolution from years past. While structure is important in order to fairly consider a large number of works in a short time, we also strove to arrive at a decision which felt good to each of us as individuals from disparate yet complementary backgrounds. The result of an arbitrary statistical process could only be a starting point. It is a great credit to the Prix Ars Electronica that the juries may develop their own methods, which suit the makeup of the group and the number and quality of submissions each year.

We first went through all of the pieces submitted, in a phase of minimal discussion. Our goal was to build context for subsequent discourse. Any of us could say "yes," and the piece would be immediately stopped and set aside for later full consideration. In contrast, to terminate a piece early and reject it required a majority vote. We thus attempted to allow compelling yet controversial work to resonate with any individual, while trusting that "badness" would be more universally recognized.

And, unfortunately, there continues to be a fair amount of badness. Juries in years past have commented on the proliferation of "eyeballs and tunnels" in Bad Computer Graphics. This year was no exception. A remarkable new phenomenon became known as the "Bad Character Effect". A piece would open with perfectly reasonable backgrounds, perhaps even develop briefly and lyrically, and then be destroyed by an abysmally designed, modeled or animated character. Often all three. Evidence, perhaps, of the machine using the user, rather than the more desirable obverse.

diesbezüglich keine Ausnahme. Ein bemerkenswertes neues Phänomen wurde bald als der „Schlechte-Gestalten-Effekt" etikettiert: Ein Stück beginnt etwa mit völlig plausiblen Hintergründen, entwickelt sich vielleicht sogar ein Weilchen ganz lyrisch – und wird dann durch eine abgrundtief schlecht designte, modellierte oder animierte Figur (und bisweilen ist sie auch alles gleichzeitig) zerstört. Dies scheint uns ein Indiz dafür zu sein, dass häufig die Maschine den Benutzer bedient statt – wie eigentlich erwünscht – umgekehrt.

Eine andere weit verbreitete Kategorie von Arbeiten, über die wir uns immer wieder ärgerten, wurde bald als „Bildschirmschoner" etikettiert – Stücke, die sich in keiner Weise von Bildschirmschonern, alten SGI-Demos oder WinAmp-Plugins unterscheiden. Es reicht einfach nicht, die Formensprache eines Oskar Fischingers zu kopieren, man braucht auch eine fesselnde Chroeografie. Ähnlich verhielt es sich mit den von uns scherzhaft als „wissenschaftlich" bezeichneten Werken – die bloße Verwendung des Computers reicht nicht aus, ein Werk muss schon auch im Ästhetischen etwas vorzuweisen haben.

Am Ende des ersten Tages waren 47 Werke zur weiteren Bewertung übrig geblieben. Der zweite Tag begann mit einer eingehenden Betrachtung jeder dieser Arbeiten. Um weiter im Bewerb zu bleiben, bedurfte es jetzt zweier Fürsprecher, und in einigen Fällen begann hier bereits eine tief gehende Werkdiskussion, die im Wesentlichen zu Mehrheitsentscheidungen für jedes der Werke führte.

Übrig bleiben zwanzig Arbeiten. Jede war gut, und jede hatte auch ihre Anhänger. Zu diesem Zeitpunkt war klar, dass wir alle zwölf Anerkennungen vergeben würden und – bezeichnend für das heurige Jahr – wir hätten auch mehr vergeben können. Deshalb sollten die mit einer Anerkennung prämierten Werke als *ausgezeichnete* Arbeiten angesehen werden und in keiner Weise als bloße „Adabeis". Wenn auch die Statuten des Prix Ars Electronica eine Maximaldauer von fünf Minuten vorsehen, so werden doch die von uns ausgewählten Werke im Rahmen des Festivals Ars Elec-

Another common annoyance was epitomized by the "Screen Saver" entrants, pieces indistinguishable from screen savers, old SGI demos, and WinAmp plugins. Copying the forms of Oskar Fischinger is not enough, one needs also at least compelling choreography. Similarly, there were pieces jokingly referred to as "scientific". To simply use the computer is not enough, a work must also succeed aesthetically.

At the end of the first day, we had a list of 47 contenders. The next day began with the complete viewing of each work. A piece needed at least two advocates to remain under consideration, and there was in depth discussion of some. This discussion led to essentially majority picks for each of the pieces.

At this stage, we had 20 pieces. They were all strong, and all had their defenders. We therefore decided to award all 12 Mentions. This is significant—we would have awarded more if possible, so please look upon the Honorary Mentions as works of unique merit, not in any sense "also-rans". While the rules state that only five minutes will be considered, the complete pieces are shown at the Ars Electronica if selected. With this consideration, we felt compelled to see the entire works. In some cases, we changed our minds after seeing complete pieces, which was somewhat unsettling.

Rather than prune from the bottom, we decided to concentrate on the top. Our goal was to make the best decision for the Nominees and eventual Golden Nica winner, and for that decision to inform the context of the Mentions. We therefore each voted for our personal three Nominees. This was an agonizing process, as many of us felt there were four very strong contenders. At the end of the vote, we had a short list of eight. This was exactly the goal of our previous endeavors— a short list of works to intensely discuss. We watched them all again, sometimes more than once. We discussed and debated down to four, and used an arcane process to select, from all possible orderings, a personal awards selection. This turned out to be an interesting majority decision, but it was only an intellectual

tronica in voller Länge gezeigt, was uns veranlasste, sie ebenfalls in voller Länge zu betrachten. In einigen Fällen führte dies zu einer Neubewertung nach Betrachtung des Gesamtwerks, was irgendwie beunruhigend war.

Anstatt nun die Liste von unten nach oben zu kürzen, beschlossen wir, uns auf die Spitze zu konzentrieren. Ziel war es, die bestmögliche Entscheidung für die Preisträger – und darunter den Gewinner der Goldenen Nica – zu treffen und uns später um die Anerkennungen zu kümmern. Deshalb gab zunächst einmal jeder seine drei persönlichen möglichen Sieger bekannt – ein schwieriger Entscheidungsprozess, denn viele von uns hatten das Gefühl, es gäbe eigentlich vier Anwärter auf die Goldene Nica. Am Ende der Abstimmung blieb jedenfalls eine Liste von acht Kandidaten übrig.

Und genau das wollten wir mit unseren vorhergegangenen Bemühungen erreichen – eine kurze Liste von Werken, die nun einer eingehenden Diskussion unterzogen wurden. Wir haben sie nochmals alle betrachtet, manche auch mehr denn ein Mal. Wir haben dann diese Liste auf vier reduziert und in geheimer Abstimmung aus allen denkbaren Kombinationen dieser Vier die drei Preisträger ermittelt. Das Ergebnis war eine interessante Mehrheitsentscheidung, aber nicht mehr als eine intellektuelle Übung. Wir wollten zunächst den Abend nutzen, um diese vorläufige Entscheidung auch mit anderen zu diskutieren, darüber zu schlafen und uns das Ergebnis im nüchternen Tageslicht nochmals vornehmen.

Der dritte und letzte Tag führte zu weiteren intensiven Diskussionen. Wir sahen die drei ausgewählten Arbeiten nochmals an und griffen dann nochmals auf unsere Liste von acht Werken zurück, die wir uns dann noch einmal ansahen und durchdiskutierten. Dann beschlossen wir versuchsweise, das Spitzentrio noch einmal in geheimer Abstimmung zu ermitteln, was theoretisch ein breites Feld von Möglichkeiten eröffnet hätte. Erstaunlicherweise ergab sich ein einstimmiges Ergebnis für die drei Preisträger. Bei der Auswahl des Gewinners der Goldenen Nica gab es zunächst Stimmengleichheit, dann eine Mehrheitsentscheidung. Nochmals wurden die Stärken und Schwächen der einzelnen Werke durchargumentiert, letztendlich gelangten wir so zu einer einstimmigen Entscheidung.

exercise. We wanted to have one evening to live with a decision, discuss with others informed by that context, and then to re-evaluate by the harsh light of day. That final day saw more intense discussion. We watched the three we had picked, and then went back to the short-listed eight works. We watched them again. We discussed. It was decided to vote again for the top three Nominees, throwing the list of contenders theoretically wide open. Amazingly, we had unanimous agreement on our three Nominees. Balloting for the Golden Nica led first to a split decision, and then to a majority. We then each argued the merits of the pieces, and came to a unanimous decision.

We used a similar process of voting and discussion to arrive at our list of Mentions. From our list of 17, we knew we must eliminate five. We each voted for the five pieces we would like to see removed, and found we had exactly five majority candidates. We then went back over the full list, allowing for both compelling argument and regretful second thoughts. Any rejected piece could find an advocate for resurrection, if we could agree on which piece would take its sacrificial place.

Wer macht die Kunst von morgen? It is a wonderful irony that we now talk about making allowances for big budget studio work, for 2001 opens the new millennium with a quiet revolution in computer animation and visual effects. There is not a single student piece amongst the Nominees or Mentions for which any "allowances" need be made. The student work competed on an absolutely equal footing with work from the big studios and commercial houses, and was in fact superior in most instances. Two out of three of the Nominees, and most of the Mentions, are student works. This is an occasion to be celebrated—the tools have reached the point at which they are "good enough", and students are acquiring the discipline to undertake works within their means.

The three Prize Winners and every one of the Honorable Mentions represent strong, fully realized work, of commendable maturity and breadth. If any of this

Einen ähnlichen Abstimmungs- und Diskussionsprozess haben wir auch für die Festlegung der Anerkennungen angewendet. Aus unserer Liste von 17 Arbeiten mussten fünf eliminiert werden. Eine individuelle Abstimmung über die „verzichtbaren" Werke ergab tatsächlich eine Mehrheit für fünf Arbeiten, dennoch wurde nochmals die ganze Liste durchgenommen, um uns Gelegenheit zu geben, zwingende Argumente für oder gegen ein Werk vorzubringen. Jedes der ausgeschiedenen Werke konnte in die Liste der Anerkennungen hineinreklamiert werden, wenn man sich darauf einigen konnte, welches andere an seiner Stelle dafür weichen musste.

Wer macht die Kunst von morgen? Es ist eine wundervolle Ironie, dass wir jetzt zum ersten Mal darüber sprechen, ob wir Zugeständnisse an die Arbeiten der großen und finanzkräftigen Studios machen sollen oder nicht, denn 2001 eröffnet das neue Jahrtausend mit einer stillen Revolution in der Kategorie Computeranimation/Visual Effects. Es gibt unter den Preisträgern und Anerkennungen nicht eine einzige studentische Arbeit, bei der wir in irgendeiner Weise „Großzügigkeit" walten lassen mussten. Die studentischen Werke konkurrierten auf absolut gleicher Ebene mit den Produktionen der großen Studios und kommerziellen Anstalten, ja, sie waren ihnen in den meisten Fällen sogar überlegen. Zwei der drei Preisträger und die Mehrzahl der Anerkennungen stammen von Studenten. Und dies verdient, entsprechend gefeiert zu werden – die Tools haben jenen Punkt erreicht, an dem sie „gut genug" sind, und die Studenten haben genug Disziplin, um Werke zu schaffen, die diese Möglichkeiten voll ausschöpfen.

Die drei Preisträger und jede einzelne der Anerkennungen stellen starke, in sich geschlossene Werke von bemerkenswerter Reife und Tiefe dar. Wer auch nur eine dieser Arbeiten nicht kennt, sollte sich unbedingt eine Gelegenheit suchen, sie sehen zu können – sie sind jeder Mühe wert. Die drei Preisträger haben jeder einen unterschiedlichen, aber konsequent umgesetzten „Look". Und wenn auch die Liste der Fünfzehn unleugbar stark

work is unfamiliar to you, seek it out, and watch it! It is all well worthwhile. The three Nominees each have a completely different, fully-realized "look". And yet, while the final list is undeniably strong, we were struck by what seemed to be a strong dichotomy amongst the entrants. The polished, fully realized works tended towards very traditional storytelling. The less polished work bifurcated towards incredibly derivative or utterly pointless. Notably absent were unpolished works which shone with energy, innovation and personal statement. While it may have made our jobs as jury members easier, it left us feeling vaguely uneasy. Why is it that the raw, unpolished work tended to be more derivative than the more "commercial" and "accessible" pieces? Why is the spark missing? The students have demonstrated that the tools really are now good enough. It is up to the visionaries to find them. The innovation to be seen this year comes, by and large, not from big studios, but from small schools and independents. We eagerly await the Takeover.

ist, so war doch auffällig, dass es scheinbar eine starke Dichotomie zwischen den Einreichungen dieses Jahres gab. Die ausgefeilten, durchrealisierten Arbeiten tendierten alle zu eher traditionellem „Geschichtenerzählen", während die weniger ausgefeilten Arbeiten sich in die endlos imitierenden und die absolut inhaltsleeren Arbeiten teilten. Was fehlte, waren „unausgefeilte" Arbeiten, die vor Energie, Innovation und persönlichem Statement strotzen. Auch wenn das unsere Aufgabe als Juroren erleichtert hat, so bleibt doch ein etwas ungutes Gefühl zurück. Warum bloß neigen die rohen, groben, unpolierten Werke dazu, viel imitativer zu sein als die „kommerzielleren" und „zugänglicheren" Arbeiten? Warum fehlt der zündende Funke? Die Studenten haben bewiesen, dass die Werkzeuge jetzt wirklich gut genug sind. Jetzt liegt es an den Visionären, sie zu finden. Was dieses Jahr an Innovationen zu sehen war, stammte im Großen und Ganzen nicht von den großen Studios, sondern von kleinen Schulen und von freien Künstlern. Wir warten sehnsüchtig auf das endgültige Takeover.

LE PROCESSUS

Xavier de l'Hermuzière /
Philippe Grammaticopoulos

I n a society where everyone wears hats, one man loses his hat. From that moment on, he is excluded from the community. To regain his place in this community, he must find his hat again at all costs. This simple event plunges the entire city into a process that seems to have no end ...

This story is a reflection of our time in the form of an allegorical fable. It transports us to a strange, uniform world that has lost its meaning, and in a sense, it mirrors the situation of the modern human being, who lives in isolation and seems to have lost his identity.
In this context, the hat, something completely harmless in itself, becomes the point of crystallization for an absurd ideal of social perfection, which is not called into question. By losing his hat, this man finds himself in a state of abnormality. The man's experiences as he tries to reintegrate himself in this society, reveal the mechanisms that have led to exclusion and prevent integration.

In einer Gesellschaft, in der alle Menschen Hüte tragen, verliert ein Mann seinen Hut. Von diesem Moment an ist er aus der Gemeinschaft ausgeschlossen. Um sich seinen Platz in dieser Gemeinschaft zurückzuerobern, muss er seinen Hut um jeden Preis wiederfinden. Dieses einfache Ereignis stürzt die ganze Stadt in einen Prozess, der kein Ende zu nehmen scheint ...

Diese Geschichte ist eine Reflexion über unsere Zeit in Form einer allegorischen Fabel. Sie versetzt uns in eine entfremdende, uniforme Welt, die ihren Sinn verloren hat und in gewissem Sinn die Situation des modernen Menschen widerspiegelt, der isoliert lebt und seine Identität verloren zu haben scheint.
Der Hut, an sich etwas ganz Harmloses, wird in diesem Kontext zum Kristallisationspunkt für ein absurdes Ideal sozialer Perfektion, die nicht hinterfragt wird. Durch den Verlust des Hutes gerät der Betroffene in einen Zustand der Anormalität. Die Erlebnisse dieses Mannes, der versucht, sich wieder in diese Gesellschaft zu integrieren, legen die Mechanismen offen, die zum Ausschluss geführt haben und eine Integration verhindern.
Paradoxerweise erhebt der Verlust des Hutes den Menschen über die Masse. Selbst dann, wenn er die

Paradoxically, the loss of the hat raises the man above the masses. Even if he were to have an opportunity to become aware of his former state, the gaze of the others forces him to return to this old state as quickly as possible.

The theft of a hat stands for the way people strive for normality. The man has no other choice but to break the "law" in order to regain his place in society. This theft sets an endless cycle in motion: the problem is merely shifted, but no solution is found.

Möglichkeit hätte, sich seines früheren Zustandes bewusst zu werden, zwingt ihn der Blick der Andern dazu, möglichst schnell wieder in den alten Zustand zurückzufinden.

Der Diebstahl eines Hutes steht für das Streben der Menschen nach Normalität. Dem Menschen bleibt nichts anderes übrig, als das „Gesetz" zu übertreten um seinen Platz in der Gesellschaft wiederzufinden. Dieser Diebstahl bringt einen endlosen Zyklus in Gang: Das Problem verschiebt sich nur, es findet keine Lösung.

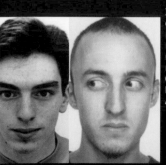

Xavier de l'Hermuzière (F), born 1977. Following a stint at the computer graphics department of CNBDI in Angoulême, he entered Supinfocom in Valenciennes. For Zone 4 (Lille and Paris), he worked on the development of ads for a record label. At Renault Design, he was involved in the production of a film, in which a car of the future—*Vel Satis*—is three-dimensionally integrated into real scenery. He currently works as a computer graphics artist for RF2K Production. Philippe Grammaticopoulos (F) graduated from École Superieure d'Infographie et de Communication (SupInfoCom) with honors. Studied art history/archeology at the Université Libre in Brussels; before that he studied fine art at the Institut d'Enseingement Supérieur Artistique in Brussels with an emphasis on cartoons. ▬ Xavier de l'Hermuzière (F), geb. 1977. Nach einem Zwischenspiel an der Computergrafikabteilung des CNBDI in Angoulême trat er bei Supinfocom in Valenciennes ein. Bei Zone 4 (Lille und Paris) arbeitete er an der Entwicklung von Werbespots für Plattenlabels mit. Bei Renault Design war er mit der Produktion eines Films beschäftigt, in dem ein Auto der Zukunft – „Vel Satis" – dreidimensional in eine reale Szenerie integriert wird. Derzeit ist er als Computergrafiker bei RF2K Production tätig. Philippe Grammaticopoulos (F) hat die École Superieure d'Infographie et de Communication (SupInfoCom) mit Auszeichnung absolviert. Student der Kunstgeschichte/Archäologie an der Université Libre in Brüssel; hat zuvor am Institut d'Enseignement Supérieur Artistique in Brüssel bildende Kunst mit Schwerpunkt Cartoons studiert.

FOR THE BIRDS

Ralph Eggleston

The latest short film by Pixar Animation Studios, *For The Birds*, is a story about a flock of small birds perched on a telephone wire and a larger bird that tries to join them. The unwelcome bird upsets the flock until they decide to get rid of him. *For The Birds* was written, storyboarded, and directed by Ralph Eggleston, the art director for *Toy Story*, Pixar's first feature film, and produced by Karen Dufilho, head of Pixar's shorts department and producer of *Geri's Game*.

The characters and scenes in *For The Birds* were modeled with Alias-Wavefront's Maya and articulated with Pixar's proprietary modeling tools. The 15 little birds in the short film are all the exact same model, except

For the Birds, der neueste Kurzfilm der Pixar Animation Studios, ist eine Geschichte über einen Schwarm kleiner Vögel auf einem Telegraphendraht, zu denen sich ein größerer Vogel hinzugesellen will. Der unwillkommene Eindringling stört die Kleinen, und so beschließen sie, ihn loszuwerden ...

Geschichte, Drehbuch und Regie von *For the Birds* stammen von Ralph Eggleston, dem Art Director bei Pixars erstem abendfüllenden Film *Toy Story*; produziert wurde *For the Birds* von Karen Dufilho, der Leiterin der Kurzfilmabteilung von Pixar und Produzentin von *Geri's Game*.

Die Gestalten und Szenen in *For the Birds* wurden mit Maya von Alias-Wavefront modelliert

for minor variations in the coloring and scratches on their beaks. The biggest technical challenges with this film came in making the contacts between the birds look real as well as animating the feathers. These challenges required the development of some new tools. To address the contact issue, Bill Wise, Supervising Technical Director, created bendable, disc-shaped collision detection widgets he called "contact pads." These made the bodies of the birds realistically change shape as needed throughout the sequences. The film's 50 shots were then animated by 15 animators. Some of these animators were assigned shots rather than characters. They created several layers of animation for the acting poses of the birds, facial ani-

und mit Pixars eigenen Modellierwerkzeugen bewegt. Die 15 kleinen Vögel des Kurzfilms basieren alle auf demselben Modell, einzig die Farbgebung und Details wie Kratzer auf dem Schnabel sind unterschiedlich. Die größte technische Herausforderung bei diesem Film lag in der Animation der Federn und darin, sie beim gegenseitigen Berühren realistisch aussehen zu lassen. Diese Aufgaben verlangten einige neue Werkzeuge. Um dem Berührungsproblem beizukommen, schuf der Supervising Technical Director Bill Wise biegsame, scheibenförmige Kollisions-Detektoren, die er „Contact Pads" nannte. Diese sorgten dafür, dass die Vogelkörper nach Bedarf ihre Form realistisch verändern konnten.

Die 50 Einstellungen des Films wurden dann von 15 Animatoren belebt. Einige der Animatoren waren mit ganzen Einstellungen statt mit Einzelfiguren betraut. Sie schufen etliche Animationsebenen für die „schauspielerischen" Posen der Vögel – Gesichtsanimation, sekundäre Animation, die Berührungen der Vögel, die Federn und den Draht. Hierbei verwendeten sie Pixars selbstentwickelte Animationssoftware Menv. Der letzte Schritt – die Animation der Federn – stellte gleichzeitig das zweite große Problem: Die enorme geometrische Komplexität ließ die Vogelmodelle sehr träge und schwerfällig in den Speicher laden, was bedeutete, dass das Animieren der Vögel sehr langsam vor sich ging und nur für einen oder

mation, secondary animation, the contact between birds, the feathers, and the wire. These animators used Pixar's proprietary animation software, Menv, to create their work. Animating the feathers, while the final step, was also the second technical challenge. The geometric complexity of the feathers made the bird models very slow and difficult to load into memory. This meant that the birds were very sluggish to animate and could only be loaded one or two at a time. To help animators with this problem, several weeks were devoted to optimizing the models and to adding controls to only load a subset of the feathers. Additionally, macro controls were created which enabled animators to animate individual feathers or groups of feathers. The macro controls could move the feathers up or down and could shuffle or puff them. This was an important tool as each bird contains a total of 2873 feathers which all needed to be animated.
For The Birds won the 2000 ASIFA-Hollywood Annie Award for Outstanding Achievement in An Animated Short as well as several other awards from film festivals throughout the world. Pixar continues their tradition of creating short films that explore the creative and technical possibilities of animation.

zwei auf einmal stattfinden konnte. Um den Animatoren zu helfen, wurden mehrere Wochen auf die Optimierung der Modelle verwendet und zur Installation einer Steuerung, die das Laden kleinerer Federgruppen erlaubte. Weiters wurden Makro-Steuerungen eingebaut, die das Animieren einzelner Federn oder Federgruppen ermöglichten – so konnten die Federn gehoben und gesenkt, aufgeplustert und geschüttelt werden. Dies erwies sich als äußerst nützlich, da jeder einzelne Vogel aus immerhin 2873 Federn besteht, die alle animiert werden müssen.
For the Birds hat 2000 den ASIFA-Hollywood Annie Award für herausragende Leistungen in der Kurzfilmanimation sowie zahlreiche andere Preise bei Filmfestivals auf der ganzen Welt gewonnen. Pixar setzt seine Tradition fort, Kurzfilme zu schaffen, die die kreativen und technischen Möglichkeiten der Animation ausloten.

RALPH EGGLESTON (USA) MAKES HIS DIRECTORIAL DEBUT ON PIXAR'S *FOR THE BIRDS*. AFTER WORKING AS ART DIRECTOR FOR *FERN-GULLY* AND CHARACTER COSTUMES DESIGNER FOR *BEVERLY HILLS COP 3*, RALPH JOINED PIXAR IN 1992 AS THE ART DIRECTOR OF *TOY STORY*, THEN WORKED ON THE NEXT FEATURE FILM, *MONSTERS, INC.*, DUE FOR RELEASE HOLIDAY 2001. RALPH IS CURRENTLY WORKING AS PRODUCTION DESIGNER ON ONE OF PIXAR'S FUTURE FEATURE LENGTH FILMS. ■■■ Ralph Eggleston (USA) debutiert als Regisseur in Pixars *For the Birds*. Nachdem er bereits als Art Director an *Ferngully* und als Character Costumes Designer an *Beverly Hills Cop 3* gearbeitet hatte, kam Ralph 1992 als Art Director für *Toy Story* zu Pixar und arbeitete dann am abendfüllenden Film *Monsters, Inc.*, der noch 2001 erscheinen wird. Derzeit arbeitet Ralph als Production Designer an einem der nächsten abendfüllenden Filme von Pixar.

L'ENFANT DE LA HAUTE MER

Laetitia Gabrielli / Max Tourret / Mathieu Renoux / Pierre Marteel

I n a village surrounded by the sea, a little girl lives dreaming from one day to the next. Suddenly, she thinks she has discovered something …
This seven-minute short film was made as a graduation project at the SupInfoCom (School for Infography and Multimedia in Valenciennes, France).
The scenario was inspired by the novel *L'Enfant de la Haute Mer* by Jules Supervielle. "We chose this story, because it conveys a dream-like mood and because there is something compelling about it—that is what we wanted to reproduce in pictures. We worked mostly with the lighting, with light and shadow."

In einem Dorf, das vom Meer eingeschlossen ist, lebt ein kleines Mädchen in den Tag hinein. Plötzlich glaubt es, etwas entdeckt zu haben …
Dieser siebenminütige Kurzfilm wurde als Studienabschlussprojekt an der SupInfoCom (Schule für Infographie und Multimedia in Valenciennes, Frankreich) realisiert.
Das Szenario wurde von der Novelle *L'Enfant de la Haute Mer* von Jules Supervielle inspiriert. „Wir haben diese Novelle ausgewählt, weil sie eine traumähnliche Stimmung vermittelt und weil von ihr eine sehr starke Ausstrahlung ausgeht – und die wollten wir im Bild wiedergeben. Wir haben vor allem mit der Beleuch-

The result of this rendering process merges 3D and 2D: all the textures attached to 3D objects are water-colored.
"We tried to achieve a 'warm' result and to avoid the coldness that is normally associated with computer graphics."
Every stage of the realization (scenario, storyboard, animation and sound) was executed by the group. We relied a lot on painting (Victor Hugo, Turner, Carpeaux) to come to an agreement about the atmosphere and style of the film.
L'Enfant de la Haute Mer has already traveled throughout Europe. It was shortlisted at the "Semaine

tung, dem Licht und den Schatten gearbeitet."
Das Ergebnis dieses Renderingprozesses ist eine Verschmelzung zwischen 3D und 2D: Alle Texturen, die auf die 3D-Objekte aufgebracht wurden, sind aquarelliert.
„Wir haben versucht, ein ‚warmes' Ergebnis zu erzielen und die Kälte, die der Computergrafik normalerweise anhaftet, zu vermeiden."
Alle Etappen in der Realisierung (Szenario, Storyboard, Animation und Ton) wurden in der Gruppe durchgeführt. Wir haben uns stark an die Malerei angelehnt (Victor Hugo, Turner, Carpeaux), um uns über Atmosphäre und Stil des Films zu einigen.

de la critique" of the Cannes Festival and at the "Festival international du film d'animation d'Annecy" in the short film category, and was awarded prizes at "Rencontres Européennes de la jeune création numérique" (Valenciennes) and the "Leaf Awards" of "Digital Media World" (GB) in the student film category.

L'Enfant de la Haute Mer ist bereits durch Europa gereist. Es wurde bei der „Semaine de la critique" des Festival von Cannes und beim „Festival international du film d'animation d'Annecy" der Kategorie Kurzfilm in die Auswahl aufgenommen und bei „Rencontres Européennes de la jeune création numérique" (Valenciennes) sowie bei „Leaf Awards" von „Digital Media World" (GB) in der Kategorie Studentenfilme prämiert.

Laetitia Gabrielli (F) and Max Tourret (F) spent two preparatory years at the SupInfoCom (School for Infography and Multimedia) in Valenciennes (F). Mathieu Renoux (F) spent one year at the Ecole de Communication Visuelle (E.C.V.) in Bordeaux and a preparatory year at the SupInfoCom. Pierre Marteel (F) studied fine art and illustration at the Institut St. Luc de Tournai (B) for three years. At the SupInfoCom, all four of them then specialized in 3D infography. This was the framework, within which L'Enfant de la Haute Mer was produced. ▬▬ Laetitia Gabrielli (F) und Max Tourret (F) haben zwei Vorbereitungsjahre an SupInfoCom (Schule für Infographie und Multimedia) in Valenciennes (F) absolviert. Mathieu Renoux (F) hat ein Jahr an der Ecole de Communication Visuelle (E.C.V.) in Bordeaux und ein Vorbereitungsjahr an der Supinfocom absolviert. Pierre Marteel (F) hat drei Jahre bildende Kunst und Illustration am Institut St. Luc de Tournai (B) studiert. Alle vier haben sich dann an der SupInfoCom auf 3D-Infografie spezialisiert. In diesem Rahmen ist auch L'Enfant de la Haute Mer produziert worden.

KAMI

Julien Charles / Lionel Catry /
Nicolas Launay / Olivier Pautot

Etude d'ambiance pour la sequence finale

Since I wanted to make a computer-animated short film based on cut out paper, I set myself a number of limitations to begin with—from the perspective of animation as well as modeling and rendering—which I was forced to take into consideration from the start. Therefore, I prepared the different colored backgrounds of the film in preproduction and implemented them with oil pastels and other tools (the night scenes were especially important to me). Before the animals were implemented in 3D, they were made in paper to increase their optical credibility.

KAMI now seems very far away—ten months have passed and my plunge into working life marks a new segment. There is no comparison between the working techniques at school and those in a special effects company. Everything has to be learned new, and my impression after these few "post-Supinfocom" months is that it is like a train racing by so fast that it changes time: the weeks seem like hours, the months like days.

And a lot of impressions have to be worked through to be able to deal with the fading feeling that now everything is just beginning …

Da ich einen computeranimierten Kurzfilm auf der Basis von ausgeschnittenem Papier machen wollte, habe ich mir von vornherein eine Anzahl von Beschränkungen auferlegt – sowohl vom Gesichtspunkt der Animation als auch des Modelings und Rendering -, die ich von Anfang an zu beachten gezwungen war. Schon in der Vorproduktion habe ich also die verschiedenen farbigen Hintergründe des Films vorbereitet und mit Hilfe von Ölkreide und anderen Werkzeugen realisiert (wobei mir die Nachtszenen am meisten am Herzen lagen). Die Tiere wurden vor der Umsetzung in 3D zunächst in Papier ausgeführt, um ihre optische Glaubwürdigkeit zu erhöhen.

KAMI ist inzwischen schon wieder weit weg – zehn Monate sind vergangen, und mein Eintauchen in das Berufsleben markiert einen neuen Abschnitt. Die Arbeitstechniken an der Schule und jene in einer Special-Effects-Firma kann man nicht vergleichen. Alles muss neu erlernt werden, und mein Eindruck nach diesen paar „Post-Supinfocom"-Monaten ist, als würde ein Zug so schnell dahinrasen, dass er die Zeit verändert: Die Wochen erscheinen wie Stunden, die Monate wie Tage.

Und eine Menge Eindrücke ist zu verarbeiten, um mit dem verblassenden Gefühl fertig zu werden, dass jetzt erst alles anfängt …

JULIEN CHARLES (F). I HAVE PASSIONATELY LOVED DRAWING SINCE MY EARLIEST YOUTH. I RECOGNIZED THE NECESSITY OF ADDING SOUND TO THE IMAGE AND BRINGING MY "SCRIBBLINGS" TO LIFE IN ORDER TO TELL A STORY WITH THEM. THIS RESULTED IN THE NECESSITY OF FINDING AN APPROPRIATE PATH OF EDUCATION, AND SUPINFOCOM MET THESE CRITERIA. I HAVE EXCELLENT MEMORIES THE SCHOOL AND THE FOUR YEARS IN VALENCIENNES, BOTH BECAUSE OF THE ENRICHING EXCHANGE AND THE STRIVING FOR EMULATION AMONG THE STUDENTS. ▬▬ Julien Charles (F). Ich bin seit meiner frühesten Jugend passionierter Zeichner, habe die Notwendigkeit erkannt, zum Bild noch den Klang hinzuzufügen und „meine Kritzeleien" zu beleben, um mit ihnen eine Geschichte zu erzählen. Daraus ergab sich die Notwendigkeit, einen entsprechenden Ausbildungsgang zu finden, und SupInfoCom entsprach diesen Kriterien. Ich habe die Schule und die vier Jahre in Valenciennes in bester Erinnerung, sowohl wegen des bereichernden Austausches als auch wegen des Wetteiferns unter den Studenten.

TRICK OR TREATS
Candice Clémencet / Jean-Dominique Fievet

It is Halloween night, and as usual, the children are out in their neighborhoods wearing costumes and masks to claim sweets from the neighbors. But woe to those, who don't want to hand anything over - in this case, the most astonishing tricks are allowed!

Our two heroes—real little devils, costumed as a witch and a mummy—are so crazy about bonbons and lollipops, that they take extreme measures to increase the generosity of the more reserved residents. Yet their greed, which they will ultimately regret, finally drives them into a trap …

The idea for this film came to us in 1999. We like the idea of Halloween as a context because of the atmosphere that it implies, a kind of happy, macabre celebration mixed with childish pranks. We took children's books as sources, as well as films like *Beetlejuice* or *The Nightmare Before Christmas* by Tim Burton. For the scenario, we were freely inspired by Hansel and Gretel, where two heroes greedy for sweets end up at a gingerbread house, which turns out to be witch's trap, because she wants to eat them.

The production covered our last year of studies. We spent about three months on preproduction, then six months on the realization with 3D StudioMax 3.1, Character Studio and Photoshop. Montage was done on an Edit-Station. For the soundtrack, we contacted the Supersonic Studio in Paris, where we received friendly and extensive help with the mixing.

This work was a wonderful experience and helped us to further our careers. We are currently working on a series of animated 3D cartoons in Luxembourg.

Es ist Halloween-Nacht, und wie immer sind die Kinder in ihrem Stadtviertel unterwegs, kostümiert und maskiert, um von den Nachbarn Süßigkeiten einzufordern. Aber wehe denen, die nichts herausrücken wollen – in einem solchen Fall sind die erstaunlichsten Streiche erlaubt!

Unsere zwei Helden – wahre Teufelchen, verkleidet als Hexe und Mumie – sind so versessen auf Bonbons und Lutscher, dass sie zu recht extremen Mitteln greifen, um die Freigiebigkeit der zurückhaltenden Anrainer zu erhöhen. Aber ihre Gier, die sie noch sehr bereuen werden, treibt sie zuletzt in eine Falle …

Die Idee zu diesem Film ist uns 1999 gekommen. Halloween als Zusammenhang gefiel uns schon wegen der Atmosphäre, die es impliziert, eine Art fröhlich-makabres Fest vermischt mit kindlichen Lausbübereien. Als Quellen haben wir Kinderbücher ebenso angezapft wie Filme, z. B. *Beetlejuice* oder *Das seltsame Weihnachten des Mr. Jack* von Tim Burton. Hinsichtlich des Szenarios haben wir uns sehr frei von Hänsel und Gretel inspirieren lasen, wo ja auch die beiden nach Süßigkeiten gierenden Helden an ein Knusperhäuschen geraten, das sich als Falle einer Hexe erweist, die sie gerne aufessen würde.

Die Produktion erstreckte sich über unser letztes Studienjahr. Rund drei Monate waren wir mit der Vorproduktion beschäftigt, anschließend sechs Monate mit der Realisierung mit 3D StudioMax 3.1, Character Studio und Photoshop. Die Montage erfolgte auf einer Edit-Station. Für den Soundtrack haben wir uns an das Supersonic-Studio in Paris gewendet, wo man uns freundlich und sehr ausgiebig beim Abmischen geholfen hat.

Diese Arbeit war eine großartige Erfahrung und hat mitgeholfen, uns in unsere Karriere zu befördern. Derzeit arbeiten wir in Luxemburg an einer Serie von animierten 3D-Cartoons.

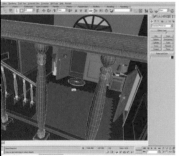 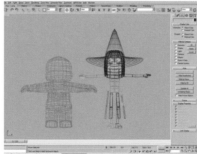 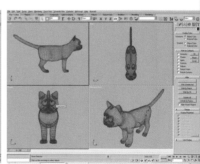

CANDICE CLEMENCET (F), BORN 1976 IN ORLÉANS. AFTER FINISHING SECONDARY SCHOOL, SHE WAS INVOLVED IN FINE ARTS AND FILM CUTTING (16 AND 35 MM) AND ENTERED SUPINFOCOM IN 1998. SHE CURRENTLY WORKS FOR ONIRIA PICTURES IN LUXEMBOURG. JEAN-DOMINIQUE FIEVET (F), BORN 1978 IN CAMBRAI. 1990 TO 1996 SECONDARY SCHOOL IN LILLE, GRADUATED WITH AN EMPHASIS IN NATURAL SCIENCES. 1996 TO 2000: STUDIED 3D COMPUTER GRAPHICS AT SUPINFOCOM, VALENCIENNES. 2000 TO 2001: 3D ANIMATOR FOR ONIRIA PICTURES, LUXEMBOURG. ▬▬▬ Candice Clemencet (F), geb. 1976 in Orléans. Nach ihrer Matura beschäftigte sie sich mit bildender Kunst und Filmschnitt (16 und 35 mm) und trat 1998 bei Supinfocom ein. Arbeitet derzeit bei Oniria Pictures in Luxemburg. Jean-Dominique Fievet (F), geb. 1978 in Cambrai. 1990 bis 1996 Gymnasium in Lille, Matura mit naturwissenschaftlichem Schwerpunkt. 1996 bis 2000: Studium der 3D-Computergrafik bei Supinfocom, Valenciennes. 2000 bis 2001: 3D-Animator bei Oniria Pictures, Luxemburg.

INTRANSIT
Mike Daly

Intransit explores the disturbed mind of a seven-teen-year-old boy, Ben, who is wrestling with guilt after the death of his father in a car accident, in which Ben was the driver. The viewer is plunged into the mind of the protagonist, as opposed to leaving the viewer outside the character to view the happenings from a third person perspective. Digital visual effects are used to blur the boundaries between the real and the psychological. Here are a few selected examples. The city sequence was created using Maya. Photographs of skyscrapers in Sydney were textured onto the geometry and the surfaces were offset using a MEL script that allowed the ray-traced reflections to distort as they normally do on buildings. Streaking car lights, as seen in time-lapse photography, were also added, creating an effect that is impossible with normal cine-matography, as the exposure lengths are far longer than the high frame rate could allow.

After Effects was used to composite the multi-layered memory sequence after the car accident scene, how-ever traditional techniques were also used to achieve the abstract visual style. The footage was shot on reversal 16mm film and cross-processed at the lab. In the telecine stage, the colour cast was removed that was introduced by cross processing the film. This achieved strongly saturated dark colours with offset hues that resulted in a look of slightly altered reality. The footage was then composited in After Effects using time-warping, different transfer modes and travelling soft mattes.

Inferno was used to composite the visual effects that represented an apparent reality. The last shot in the film, where a train collides into the viewer, was creat-

Intransit erforscht die gestörte Psyche eines 17-jährigen Jungen, Ben, der wegen des Todes seines Vaters, der bei einem von ihm verur-sachten Autounfall starb, mit Schuldgefühlen kämpft. Der Betrachter wird in den Geist des Darstellers hineinversetzt – im Gegensatz zu der üblichen Darstellungsweise, bei der der Betrachter außerhalb der Figur bleibt und die Ereignisse aus der Perspektive eines Dritten beobachtet. Digitale Visual Effects werden ver-wendet, um die Grenze zwischen der Realität und den psychischen Ereignissen zu verwi-schen. Hier einige Beispiele:
Die Stadtsequenz entstand unter Verwendung von Maya. Fotos von Hochhäusern in Sydney wurden als Textur auf die Geometrie aufge-bracht und ihre Oberflächen mithilfe eines MEL-Skripts versetzt, das den durch Ray-Tracing konstruierten Reflexionen eine Verzer-rung verlieh, wie man sie normalerweise an Gebäuden beobachtet. Leuchtspuren von Autos, wie man sie von Fotos mit langer Belich-tungszeit kennt, wurden ebenfalls hinzugefügt, um einen Effekt zu erzeugen, der mit normaler Filmtechnik unmöglich ist, weil die Belich-tungszeiten für die erforderliche Kaderzahl viel zu lang wäre.
After Effects wurde zur Komposition der viel-schichtigen Erinnerungssequenz nach der Unfallszene verwendet, aber auch traditionelle Techniken wurden zur Erzielung des abstrakten visuellen Stils eingesetzt. Die Liveaufnahmen entstanden auf 16mm-Umkehrfilm und wurden in einem weiteren Umkehrverfahren im Labor entwickelt. In einem nächsten Schritt wurden die durch den doppelten Umkehrprozess ent-standenen Farbschleier entfernt, was letztlich tief gesättigte Farben mit leicht verschobenen Tönungen ergab, die den Eindruck einer ver-fremdeten Wirklichkeit vermittelt. Das Film-material wurde anschließend in After Effects zusammengesetzt, wobei Time-Warping, ver-schiedene Transfermodi und weiche Maskie-rungsmodi zur Anwendung kamen.
Inferno wurde eingesetzt, um die Visual Effects zu komponieren, die eine scheinbare Wirklich-keit wiedergeben. Für die letzte Einstellung des Films, in der ein Zug den Betrachter überfährt, wurde zunächst ein wegen Bauarbeiten gesperrtes U-Bahn-Gleis aufgenommen. Ein Licht wurde dem Gleisverlauf folgend mehrere

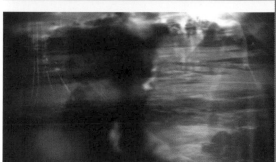

ed by shooting along an underground train track that was closed due to construction. A light was carried several hundred meters down the track towards the camera. In post-production the light was stabilised and separated from the background using a luminance key. A photo of a train was composited in between the background and the light and its size, position and grade was animated to finish off the effect.

The train then passes straight through the viewer. This second half of the shot was created by shooting a single carriage of an unused train on a steady-cam. Several takes were made with the carriage looking slightly different. The shots were stabilised and speed ramped to attain a high velocity and remove the acceleration and deceleration at each end of the carriage. Finally motion blur was added and the reflections of the camera operator removed from the glass at the end of the carriages.

hundert Meter in Richtung auf die Kamera getragen. In der Nachbearbeitung wurde dieses Licht stabilisiert und über eine Luminanzmaske vom Hintergrund getrennt. Das Foto eines Zuges wurde anschließend zwischen Hintergrund und Licht einmontiert und in Größe und Position animiert, um den Fahrteffekt zu vervollständigen.

Dann fährt der Zug direkt durch den Betrachter. Diese zweite Hälfte der Einstellung entstand aus der Aufnahme eines einzelnen unbenutzten U-Bahn-Wagens mithilfe einer Steady-Cam. Es wurden mehrere Aufnahmen gemacht, bei denen das Aussehen des Wagens immer leicht verändert wurde. Diese Aufnahmen wurden stabilisiert und mit hoher Geschwindigkeit animiert, um die hohe Geschwindigkeit zu simulieren und die Beschleunigungseffekte an beiden Enden des Wagens auszugleichen. Abschließend wurden noch Bewegungsunschärfe hinzugefügt und die Reflexionen des Kameramanns von der Glasscheibe am Wagenende getilgt.

MIKE DALY (AUS), BORN 1978, BECAME INVOLVED IN VIDEO PRODUCTION WHEN HE WAS FOURTEEN. AFTER FINISHING HIGH SCHOOL, HE WORKED AS A FREELANCE EDITOR FOR TWO YEARS, THEN STUDIED FOR AN MA IN FILM & TELEVISION, SPECIALISING IN DIGITAL MEDIA AT THE "AUSTRALIAN FILM TELEVISION AND RADIO SCHOOL" (AFTRS). THERE HE MADE THE SHORT FILM INTRANSIT. AFTER FINISHING HIS DEGREE, MIKE WORKED AS A COMPOSITOR AT THE VISUAL EFFECTS COMPANY "ANIMAL LOGIC". MIKE HAS RETURNED TO THE AFTRS TO STUDY FOR AN MA HONOURS DEGREE, ALSO SPECIALISING IN DIGITAL MEDIA, AND HIS NEXT SHORT FILM IS ALREADY IN PRODUCTION. ▬▬ Mike Daly (AUS), geb. 1978, kam mit vierzehn Jahren mit der Videoproduktion in Berührung. Nach Abschluss der High School arbeitete er zwei Jahre als freiberuflicher Cutter, dann studierte er und erwarb einen MA aus Film/Fernsehen mit Schwerpunkt auf Digitale Medien an der Australian Film Television and Radio School (AFTRS). Nach Studienabschluss arbeitete Mike bei der Visual-Effects-Firma „Animal Logic", ist aber mittlerweile an die AFTRS zurückgekehrt, um einen weiteren MA (ebenfalls mit Ausrichtung auf Digitale Medien) zu erwerben.

AP2000

Sébastien Ebzant / Aurélien Delpoux /
Loïc Bail / Benjamin Lauwick

AP200 is one of my most wonderful experiences! For the first time in the course of my studies, I had a chance to concentrate entirely on a ten-month project. Sébastien, Loïc, Benjamin and I were all motivated by a joint project: realizing a short film in 3D, mixing humor, deviousness, mangas and many winking references to our favorite films (*Ghost In The Shell*, *Matrix*, *Blade (!)*, *Star Wars*, *Street Fighter 2* ...) and much more ... An additional motivation was that this kind of manga implementation was something unheard of at our school. In this respect, a certain gap opened up between us and the majority of our professors (who said themselves that they neither knew nor liked this kind of culture very well). For me, the film was a chance to carry out scripting and editing work in a very thorough way (in comparison with my previous work during my art training). This was also my first experience with group work, with the discovery of the advantages and disadvantages that this entails.

But it all ended the way it began: very well, although somewhat tired—there was a certain lack of sleep evident in the final months!

In short—it was very enriching!

One of the happiest days of my life will undoubtedly remain the one of the jury at the end of the year: over 400 people (family, friends, professionals) and stand-

„AP200 ist eine meiner schönsten Erfahrungen! Zum ersten Mal hatte ich Gelegenheit, mich im Zuge der Ausbildung voll und ganz auf ein zehnmonatiges Projekt zu konzentrieren. Sébastien, Loïc, Benjamin und ich waren alle von einem gemeinsamen Projekt motiviert: einen Kurzfilm in 3D zu realisieren, der Humor, Hintergründiges, Mangas und zahlreiche augenzwinkernde Bezüge auf unsere Lieblingsfilme (*Ghost In The Shell*, *Matrix*, *Blade (!)*, *Star-Wars*, *Street Fighter 2* ...) und anderes vermischt ... Eine zusätzliche Motivation war, dass diese Art von „Manga"-Umsetzung an der Schule etwas noch nie Dagewesenes war. Da hat sich übrigens auch eine gewisse Kluft zwischen uns und dem Großteil unserer Professoren aufgetan (die nach eigener Aussage weder besondere Kenner noch Liebhaber dieser Art von Kultur waren). Der Film war für mich die Gelegenheit, eine ziemlich konsequente Drehbuch- und Schnittarbeit durchzuziehen (im Vergleich zu meinen vorherigen Arbeiten während meiner Kunstausbildung). Auch war dies meine erste Erfahrung mit Gruppenarbeit, mit der Entdeckung der Vor- ebenso wie der Nachteile, die sie mit sich bringen kann.

Aber alles hat so geendet, wie es begonnen hat: sehr gut, wenn auch etwas müde – in den letzten Monaten hat schon ein wenig Schlaf gefehlt!

Kurzum – es war sehr bereichernd!

Einer der glücklichsten Tage meines Lebens wird ohne Zweifel jener der Jury am Jahresende bleiben: Über 400 Personen (Familie, Freunde, Profis) und Standing Ovations, die uns wie angewurzelt auf dem Platz gehalten

ing ovations that kept us rooted in place (as though we were not already excited enough)—terrible!

In conclusion, I would like to thank Nicolas Bouvier, who gave me good advice several times during my practical training at DarkWorks (Alone in The Dark 4) for my character design in *AP2000*, and I would also like to take this opportunity to say to the other members of the AP2000 team: friends, it was cool ... I really enjoyed working with you! That is something you can depend on, I think!

For John, Seb, Benj and everyone, who supported us?!"

The Blade (Aurélien Delpoux)

haben (als wären wir nicht ohnedies schon aufgeregt genug gewesen) – schrecklich!

Abschließend möchte ich Nicolas Bouvier danken, der mir während meines Praktikums bei DarkWorks (Alone in The Dark 4) mehrere gute Ratschläge für mein Character Design an *AP2000* gegeben hat, und ich nehme weiters die Gelegenheit wahr, um den andern Mitgliedern des AP2000-Teams zu sagen: Freunde, das war cool ... Ich habe es wirklich sehr genossen, mit euch zu arbeiten! Da kann man sich drauf berufen, glaub' ich!

Für John, Seb, Benj und alle, die uns unterstützt haben ...!"

The Blade (Aurélien Delpoux)

SÉBASTIEN EBZANT (F). FIRST EXPERIENCE AS COMPUTER GRAPHICS ARTIST AT THE AGE OF 19 WITH THE VIDEO GAME *HIGH SIDE*. ENTERED SUPINFOCOM AFTER FINISHING SECONDARY SCHOOL. CURRENTLY CHIEF ANIMATOR FOR ONIRIA PICTURES IN LUXEMBOURG. AURÉLIEN DELPOUX (F), BORN 1976. SECONDARY SCHOOL TRAINING WITH AN EMPHASIS ON FINE ARTS. ENTERED SUPINFOCOM THEREAFTER. CURRENTLY WORKS AS GRAPHICS ARTIST FOR PARTIZAN MIDI-MINUIT TOGETHER WITH LOÏC BAIL. ■■■ Sébastien Ebzant (F). Erste Erfahrungen mit 19 Jahren als Computergrafiker des Videospiels *High Side*. Nach der Matura Eintritt in die SupInfoCom. Derzeit Chefanimateur bei Oniria Pictures in Luxemburg. Aurélien Delpoux (F), geb. 1976. Sekundarausbildung mit Schwerpunkt Bildende Kunst. Anschließend Eintritt in die SupInfoCom. Derzeit gemeinsam mit Loïc Bail als Grafiker bei Partizan Midi-Minuit beschäftigt.

LE CONTE DU MONDE FLOTTANT

Alain Escalle

Hiroshima. On the morning of 6th August 1945, a bright light invaded the edge of the floating world. A man remembers ...
The shock, a violent blast. Bodies that stretched out in pain, dreams of the past in the present, visions of the future in the past.
The child that he was, before ...
Before the flash struck, Before the world was disturbed ...

Production Notes

Le conte du monde flottant is an animation film composed of real characters shot in Japan and a mixture of new and traditional techniques (film, video, photo, illustration and artificial images, etc...). A free evocation and surrealist image of Japan and of the atomic bomb in the form of an imaginary story, cruel and childlike. The dark visions, light, calmness even, agitated by the strange fantasy of a mutated world.

Technical Notes

The director and creative artist wanted to keep a very sensitive feel in all the images from the film: something between classical cinema and traditional film animation. "In computer graphics I like to give a sense of handcraftsmanship."
It took two years of work on the computer graphics (Inferno, Flame and Combustion) to compose all the images and their strong and specific design. The film uses different kinds of computer graphic elements: 2D objects like video (beta & DV), film images or drawings shot with a video camera, and a few 3D images like the little 3D horsemen.

Hiroshima. Am Morgen des 6. August 1945 ergoss sich ein helles Licht über den Rand der schwimmenden Welt. Ein Mann erinnert sich ...
Die Schockwelle, ein gewaltiger Schlag. Körper, im Schmerz hingestreckt, die Träume der Vergangenheit in der Gegenwart, die Visionen der Zukunft in der Vergangenheit.
Das Kind, das er war, bevor ...
Bevor der Blitz einschlug, bevor die Welt in Unordnung geriet ...

Anmerkungen zur Produktion

Le conte du monde flottant ist ein Animationsfilm, der sich aus den in Japan gefilmten realen Darstellern und einer Mischung aus neuen und traditionellen Techniken (Film, Video, Foto, Illustration und künstliche Bilder usw.) zusammensetzt: eine frei gestaltete, surrealistische bildliche Annäherung an Japan und die Atombombe in Form einer imaginären Geschichte, grausam und kindlich zugleich. Dunkle Visionen, Licht, Ruhe und Bewegung, getrieben durch die seltsame Fantasie einer mutierten Welt.

Technische Anmerkungen

Der Regisseur und Künstler wollte in allen Bildern eine sehr sensible Gefühlswelt darstellen, irgendwo zwischen klassischem Kino und traditioneller Film-Animation. „Ich möchte den Eindruck des Handwerklichen in der Computergrafik vermitteln." Zwei Jahre dauerten die Gestaltung der Computergrafiken (Inferno, Flame und Combustion) sowie die Montage der Bilder in ihr starkes spezifisches Design. Der Film verwendet unterschiedliche Arten computergrafischer Elemente: 2D-Objekte wie Video (beta und CD), Filmbilder und Zeichnungen, die über Video aufgenommen wurden, sowie einige 3D-Elemente, z. B. die kleinen Reiter.

The shooting in Tokyo was very short: five days on blue screen with all the actors.
1) For the samurai sequence
2) For the dancers
3) For the women from the past
4) For the ten-year-old boy
5) For the figurants

The director wanted to direct the film on computer graphics, so he made two hours of rendered images to be used as rushes for editing a final cut. For this reason, all the actors were shot with a multi-camera system: some in movement (the samurai sequence), others fixed on the ground; some were shot with a large view of the scenes, some with close-ups. A lot of camera movements are completely digital.

Die Drehzeit in Tokio war dagegen recht kurz – fünf Tage mit allen Schauspielern vor dem Blue Screen
– für die Samurai-Sequenz
– für die Tänzer
– für die Frauen aus der Vergangenheit
– für den zehnjährigen Knaben und
– für die Komparsen.

Der Regisseur wollte den Film über die Computergrafik editieren, deswegen wurden zwei Stunden gerenderter Bilder erzeugt, die als Material für den endgültigen Schnitt dienten. Deshalb wurden auch alle Schauspieler über ein Multi-Kamera-System aufgenommen, das teils in Bewegung (wie bei der Samurai-Sequenz), teils festmontiert war wie bei den Weitwinkelaufnahmen der Gesamtszenen und bei den Nahaufnahmen. Eine Vielzahl von Kamerabewegungen wurden gänzlich digital simuliert.

ALAIN ESCALLE (F). BORN IN 1967, STUDIED APPLIED ARTS IN NIMES, AND CINEMA AND VIDEO IN TOULOUSE FROM 1983 TO 1989. DIRECTOR AND DIGITAL CREATOR SINCE 1991, HE DEVELOPS A VISUAL AND GRAPHIC STYLE USING MOVING PICTURES AND NEW TECHNOLOGIES WITH SOFTWARE SUCH AS *INFERNO* OR *HENRY & HARRY*. HIS PERSONAL RESEARCH HAS OFTEN BEEN BROADCAST ON ARTE AND CANAL+ AND HAS WON MANY PRIZES IN INTERNATIONAL FESTIVALS (IMAGINA, NICOGRAPH, ARS ELECTRONICA, ETC.) ▬
Alain Escalle (F), geb. 1967, studierte von 1983 bis 1989 Angewandte Kunst in Nîmes sowie Film und Video in Toulouse. Als digitaler Künstler und Regisseur entwickelt er seit 1991 einen eigenen visuellen und grafischen Stil, wobei er Filmtechniken und neue Technologien mit Hilfe von Software wie *Inferno* oder *Henry & Harry* kombiniert. Seine persönlichen Arbeiten werden häufig auf Arte und Canal+ ausgestrahlt und haben zahlreiche Preise bei internationalen Festivals gewonnen (Imagina, Nicograph, Prix Ars Electronica usw.).

THE PERFECT STORM
Stefen M. Fangmeier

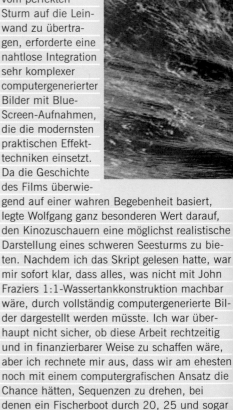

The task of bringing director Wolfgang Petersen's vision for *The Perfect Storm* to the screen required a seamless integration of very complex CG imagery with blue-screen photography which utilized some of the most elaborate practical effects to date. Because the film's story is largely based on a real event, Wolfgang placed a tremendous emphasis on creating a movie-going experience that would provide a highly realistic depiction of a severe storm at sea. After reading the script, I immediately decided that everything which could not be achieved with John Frazier's full-scale watertank setup would be designed by relying entirely on computer generated visuals. While I wasn't at all sure that the work could be done in a timely and financially viable manner, I figured that an all-CG approach would give us the best shot at pulling off sequences which were to show a fishing boat plowing through 70, 80 and even 100+ foot waves. In the end, we produced about 340 visual effects shots for the project, and more than a few of these turned out to be some of the most complex shots ever done at the facility.

R&D and Pre-Production

Creating photo-realistic CG water is undoubtedly one of the more daunting tasks in visual effects, especially when it is to be seen in the context of a raging storm at sea. I directed the R&D team led by Habib Zargarpour in its efforts to identify the essential visual details that needed to be represented and the techniques that should be developed to achieve this. Over a six-month period, new software was written for the water surface itself as well as for the extremely complex particle simulations that would be used to model elements such as spray, crest mist, crest foam, splashes, etc. In parallel to the R&D effort, I was working with Wolfgang Petersen and the production to prepare the film for principal photography.

Die Aufgabe, Regisseur Wolfgang Petersens Vision vom perfekten Sturm auf die Leinwand zu übertragen, erforderte eine nahtlose Integration sehr komplexer computergenerierter Bilder mit Blue-Screen-Aufnahmen, die die modernsten praktischen Effekttechniken einsetzt. Da die Geschichte des Films überwiegend auf einer wahren Begebenheit basiert, legte Wolfgang ganz besonderen Wert darauf, den Kinozuschauern eine möglichst realistische Darstellung eines schweren Seesturms zu bieten. Nachdem ich das Skript gelesen hatte, war mir sofort klar, dass alles, was nicht mit John Fraziers 1:1-Wassertankkonstruktion machbar wäre, durch vollständig computergenerierte Bilder dargestellt werden müsste. Ich war überhaupt nicht sicher, ob diese Arbeit rechtzeitig und in finanzierbarer Weise zu schaffen wäre, aber ich rechnete mir aus, dass wir am ehesten noch mit einem computergrafischen Ansatz die Chance hätten, Sequenzen zu drehen, bei denen ein Fischerboot durch 20, 25 und sogar 30 Meter hohe Wellen pflügt. Letztlich haben wir für das Projekt rund 340 Visual-Effects-Einstellungen gedreht, von denen mehr als nur ein paar zu den komplexesten gehören, die je im Studio gemacht wurden.

Entwicklung und Vorproduktion

Fotorealistisches Wasser darzustellen ist zweifellos eine der größten Herausforderungen im Bereich der Visual Effects, besonders dann,

wenn ein tobender Orkan auf See dargestellt werden soll. Gemeinsam mit dem von Habib Zargarpour geleiteten For-schungs- und Entwicklungsteam versuchte ich, jene visuellen Details herauszufinden, die unbedingt dargestellt werden mussten, und die nötigen Tech-niken hierfür zu entwickeln. Im Lauf von sechs Monaten wurde neue Software für die Wasser-oberfläche selbst sowie für die extrem komplexen Partikel-Simulationen geschrieben, die für die Modellierung von Gischt, Schaumkronen und Wasserspritzern etc. eingesetzt werden soll-te.

Parallel zu der Entwicklungsar-beit arbeitete ich mit Wolfgang Petersen und dem Produkti-onsteam daran, die Hauptdreh-arbeiten vorzubereiten.

Post-Production

In addition to the variety of types of CG water required for shots throughout the film, from calm seas to the most dramatic storm sequences, we constructed highly detailed CG models of the fishing vessel Andrea Gail, the sail boat Mistral, the Coast Guard cutter, a tanker, a container ship, the rescue helicopter and the refuel tanker plane. Full crews of digital stunt doubles were modeled for everything but the tanker and container-ship. Employing these doubles allowed us to continue action established in close-up, non-visual effects shots and also, in a few cases, let us show particular actions that were simply too dangerous to shoot on set.

Post-Produktion

Neben der Vielzahl von CG-Wassertypen – von der ruhigen See bis zum tobenden Orkan –, die wir für den gesamten Film benötigten, konstruierten wir hochdetaillierte CG-Modelle des Fischerbootes Andrea Gail, des Segelbootes Mistral, des Kutters der Küstenwache, eines Tankers, eines Containerschiffs, des Rettungshubschraubers und des Tankflugzeuges. Mit Ausnahme des Tankers und des Containerschif-fes wurde für jedes Einzelne jeweils ein vollständiger Satz von Stunt-Doubles modelliert. Diese Doubles erlaubten uns, Handlungsverläufe fortzusetzen, die in Nahaufnahmen angedeutet worden waren, Non-visual-Effects-Einstellungen zu drehen und in einigen Fällen spezielle Handlungsverläufe zu zeigen, die man, weil sie einfach zu gefährlich gewesen wären, nicht am Set drehen konnte.

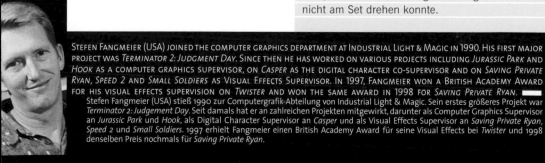

STEFEN FANGMEIER (USA) JOINED THE COMPUTER GRAPHICS DEPARTMENT AT INDUSTRIAL LIGHT & MAGIC IN 1990. HIS FIRST MAJOR PROJECT WAS *TERMINATOR 2: JUDGMENT DAY*. SINCE THEN HE HAS WORKED ON VARIOUS PROJECTS INCLUDING *JURASSIC PARK* AND *HOOK* AS A COMPUTER GRAPHICS SUPERVISOR, ON *CASPER* AS THE DIGITAL CHARACTER CO-SUPERVISOR AND ON *SAVING PRIVATE RYAN*, *SPEED 2* AND *SMALL SOLDIERS* AS VISUAL EFFECTS SUPERVISOR. IN 1997, FANGMEIER WON A BRITISH ACADEMY AWARD FOR HIS VISUAL EFFECTS SUPERVISION ON *TWISTER* AND WON THE SAME AWARD IN 1998 FOR *SAVING PRIVATE RYAN*. ▬

Stefen Fangmeier (USA) stieß 1990 zur Computergrafik-Abteilung von Industrial Light & Magic. Sein erstes größeres Projekt war *Terminator 2: Judgement Day*. Seit damals hat er an zahlreichen Projekten mitgewirkt, darunter als Computer Graphics Supervisor an *Jurassic Park* und *Hook*, als Digital Character Supervisor an *Casper* und als Visual Effects Supervisor an *Saving Private Ryan*, *Speed 2* und *Small Soldiers*. 1997 erhielt Fangmeier einen British Academy Award für seine Visual Effects bei *Twister* und 1998 denselben Preis nochmals für *Saving Private Ryan*.

DICE RAW—
THIN LINE BETWEEN RAW AND JIGGY
One Infinity

The *Dice Raw* project is a 100 percent Flash animated, broadcast-quality music video. By playing the video on the big screen at Resfest 2000, on television via BET, and the Internet on sites such as Sputnik7.com, Shockwave.com, and Heavy.com, One Infinity successfully created one of media history's first convergent entertainment productions.

Dice Raw is an international terrorist operating out of the jurisdiction of worldwide governments. No one knows exactly what Dice's next act of terrorism will be, but reliable sources indicate that he has targeted the Moon.

A rival faction named the Jiggy Clan hastily assembles their best warriors to stop Dice Raw and his renegade posse. Comprised of a highly trained ninja horde led by a mysterious platinum-suited warrior known as The Agent, "Operation: Boxcar" is masterminded from a secret base by the Queenpin, the ruthless leader of the Jiggy Clan.

After losing an arm and one of her eyes in a freestyle battle against Dice Raw, the Queenpin vowed to grow her afro out until she could exact bloody foamy revenge. This rage fueled her swift, brutal ascent to the top of the Jiggy Clan. Now she has the sheer numbers that might be enough to stop Dice Raw.

Fortunately, Dice has assembled his own group of ass-kickers. His field lieutenants Black Thought and Malik B. are superb fighters. Black Thought utilizes his famed Righty-Tighty-Fist technique while Malik B. downs foes with his deft Microphone Nunchuk styles. They have an elite force of Diceheads—animatronic ninjas with dice for heads—programmed with lethal breakdance moves. Weeks of surveillance pay off for the task force—Dice Raw, Black Thought and Malik B. are spotted hurrying towards the North Philadelphia

Das *Dice Raw*-Projekt ist ein zu 100 Prozent in Flash animiertes Musikvideo in Fernsehqualität. Das Video wurde bei Resfest 2000 auf einer großen Projektionsfläche gespielt, im Fernsehen auf BET und im Internet auf Sites wie Sputnik7.com, Shockwave.com und Heavy.com. One Infinity hat also mit dem *Dice Raw*-Projekt eine der ersten konvergenten Unterhaltungsproduktionen der Mediengeschichte geschaffen.

Dice Raw ist ein internationaler Terrorist, der außerhalb der Jurisdiktion der Regierungen dieser Welt agiert. Niemand weiß genau, welches Ziel sein nächster Terrorakt treffen wird, aber verlässliche Quellen deuten an, dass er sich gegen den Mond richten wird.

Eine rivalisierende Fraktion namens Jiggy Clan treibt hastig ihre besten Krieger zusammen, um Dice Raw und sein Aufgebot aus Renegaten zu stoppen. „Operation: Boxcar" besteht aus einer Horde durchtrainierter Ninjas unter der Führung eines mysteriösen platingepanzerten Kriegers – bekannt als The Agent – und wird von der ruchlosen Queenpin, der Herrin des Jiggy Clan, von einer geheimen Basis aus gesteuert.

Nachdem sie in einem Freistilkampf gegen Dice Raw einen Arm und ein Auge verloren hatte, schwor die Queenpin, ihre Afro-Frisur so lange nicht zu schneiden, bis sie blutige Rache genommen hat. Diese Wut war das Motiv hinter ihrem schnellen, brutalen Aufstieg an die Spitze des Jiggy-Clans, und jetzt hat sie endlich die nötige Zahl an Leuten um sich geschart, um Dice Raw stoppen zu können.

Glücklicherweise hat auch Dice seine eigene Gruppe von Arschtretern versammelt. Seine Leutnants Black Thought und Malik B. sind superbe Kämpfer. Black Thought verwendet seine berüchtigte Rechtsganzenge-Fausttechnik,

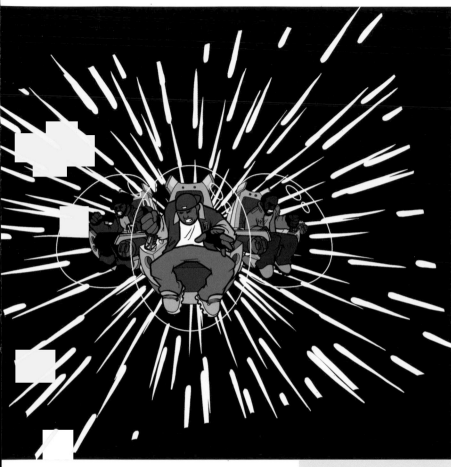

während Malik Gegner mit seinem deftigen Microphone-Nunchuk-Stil unterkriegt. Sie haben eine ausgewählte Armee von Würfelköpfen – animatronische Ninjas mit Würfeln als Köpfen –, die auf tödliche Breakdance-Bewegungen programmiert sind.

Die wochenlange Überwachung hat sich gelohnt – Dice Raw, Black Thought und Malik B.werden erspäht, während sie zur U-Bahn-Station North Philadel-

subway station, a reputed base of operations for the group. The Agent prepares a massive ambush to take care of Dice Raw once and for all, while the Queenpin remotely monitors activities through the Agent's cybernetic eyes.

True hip-hoppers versus phony rappers. The "Thin Line (Between Raw and Jiggy)". This is only the beginning.

phia laufen, die schon lange als Operationsbasis der Gruppe unter Verdacht stand. Der Agent bereitet einen groß angelegten Hinterhalt vor, um Dice Raw ein für alle Mal zu erledigen, während die Queenpin aus der Ferne die Vorgänge durch die kybernetischen Augen des Agents verfolgt.

Echte Hip-Hopper gegen nachgemachter Rapper – „Die dünne Linie (zwischen rau und ungehobelt)" ist erst der Anfang.

ONE INFINITY (USA) IS A DIGITAL ARTIST COLLECTIVE SPECIALIZING IN SUPERIOR INTERACTIVE DESIGN AND MOTION GRAPHICS. SINCE OUR INCEPTION IN 1999, WE HAVE COMPLETED PROJECTS FOR A WIDE RANGE OF CLIENTS, INCLUDING SHOCKWAVE.COM, TOMMY BOY RECORDS, MCA RECORDS, OKAYPLAYER.COM AND MOST RECENTLY, THE FROG'S LEAP WINERY WEBSITE. ■■■ One Infinity (USA) ist ein Kollektiv von Künstlern, die im digitalen Bereich arbeiten und sich auf interaktives Design und Motion-Grafik spezialisiert haben. Seit unserem Start im Jahr 1999 haben wir Projekte für die verschiedensten Kunden gemacht, u. a. für Shockwave.com, Tommy Boy Records, MCA Records, Okayplayer.com und jüngst für die Website der Frog's Leap Winery.

WAKING LIFE
Bob Sabiston / Tommy Pallotta

Waking Life, written and directed by indie icon Richard Linklater (*Slacker*, *Dazed and Confused*), is considered the first independent computer-animated feature film ever made in America—an abstract, psychedelic, digital video improv that takes the Disney/Pixar formula and turns it on its perfectly coiffed head. Sabiston and Pallotta, collaborators for three years, have always had that goal in mind, but the major-league debut of *Waking Life* at the Sundance Film Festival in late January gives them their biggest, most esteemed forum yet: a showcase for an animation style that is unprecedentedly artful. They use computers to paint reality, not mimic it. In that sense alone, *Waking Life*, made with the help of Sabiston's homegrown software, swims against the photo-realistic tide. Sabiston's as-yet-unnamed creation—nicknamed "RotoShop" by some *Waking Life* artists—is so simple that even neophytes can quickly master an otherwise daunting process known as interpolated rotoscoping, in which animators trace over live-action DV footage.

In *Waking Life*, the most linear Sabiston-Pallotta film to date, Wiley Wiggins—the skinny, rubber-faced kid brother in Linklater's *Dazed and Confused*—serves as a kind of floating human consciousness that consorts with street gurus and other entities. The series of seemingly random vignettes follows Wiggins on a dreamlike journey in which shape-shifting characters talk about life and death. Essence is revealed not in the ways that characters remain constant, but in the ways they constantly change.

After the edited footage was loaded onto G4s, a team of Austin artists began the nearly yearlong process of turning video into animation.

Waking Life – Drehbuch und Regie von „Indie"-Ikone Richard Linklater (*Slacker*, *Dazed and Confused*) – gilt als der erste unabhängige computeranimierte abendfüllende Film, der in Amerika je produziert wurde – eine abstrakte, psychedelische, digitale Video-Improvisation, die das Rezept von Disney/Pixar aufgreift und es auf den eigenen perfekt frisierten Kopf stellt. Sabiston und Pallotta, die seit drei Jahren zusammenarbeiten, hatten dieses Ziel seit jeher vor Augen, aber beim Sundance Film Festival Ende Januar, wo *Waking Life* sein Debut hatte, fanden sie ihr bisher größtes und bedeutendstes Forum: ein „Showcase" für einen Animationsstil von bisher unerreichtem künstlerischem Niveau. Sie verwenden Computer, um Wirklichkeit zu malen, nicht um sie zu imitieren. Allein schon in dieser Hinsicht schwimmt *Waking Life* – das mit Hilfe einer von Sabiston selbst geschriebenen Software erstellt wurde – gegen den fotorealistischen Strom. Sabistons noch ungetaufte Kreation, von manchen der *Waking Life*-Mitarbeiter liebevoll „RotoShop" genannt, ist so einfach, dass sogar Anfänger einen ansonsten sehr schwierigen Prozess beherrschen können, nämlich die interpolierte Rotoskopie, bei der Animatoren digitale Video-Live-Aufnahmen übermalen.
Bei *Waking Life*, dem bisher linearsten Sabiston-Pallotta-Film, dient Wiley Wiggins – der knochige, gummigesichtige Junge aus Linklaters *Dazed and Confused* – als eine Art schwebendes menschliches Bewusstsein, das sich mit Straßengurus und anderen Gestalten zusammentut. In einer Serie scheinbar zufälliger Szenen geht Wiggins auf eine traumähnliche Reise, bei der Gestalten, die ständig ihre Form verändern, sich über Leben und Tod unterhalten. Die Essenz wird nicht dadurch präsentiert, dass diese Figuren konstant bleiben, sondern durch die Art und Weise, in der sie sich ständig ändern …
Nachdem das geschnittene Videomaterial in G4-Rechnern geladen war, begann ein Team von Künstlern in Austin, in einem beinahe einjährigen Prozess das Video in eine Animation

Each actor was drawn, or "interpreted," by a different artist, intentionally lending every character a distinctive style

Sabiston and Pallotta had no trouble rounding up a rogue animation crew. In true Austin-indie style, the partners posted flyers in coffee shops and art supply stores, and recruited at University of Texas student art shows. Some of their hires were painters who had no experience with computers, much less computer animation or rotoscoping.

(Richard Baimbridge)

zu transformieren. Jeder Darsteller wurde von einem anderen Künstler gezeichnet bzw. „interpretiert", was jeder Figur auch einen eigenen Stil gab.
Sabiston und Pallotta hatten kein Problem damit, eine wilde Animationscrew zusammenzutreiben. Im für Austin typischen Indie-Stil legten sie Flugblätter in Kaffeehäusern und Künstlerbedarfsläden aus und suchten ihre Mitarbeiter bei studentischen Kunstausstellungen der University of Texas. Manche der angeheuerten Leute waren Maler, die keine Erfahrung mit Computern und noch weniger mit Computeranimation oder Rotoskopie hatten ...

(Richard Baimbridge)

BOB SABISTON (USA) STUDIED COMPUTER GRAPHICS RESEARCH AT MIT MEDIA LAB. BOTH VISUAL ARTS AND COMPUTER PROGRAMMING FIGURE PROMINENTLY IN HIS SHORT FILMS, WHICH HAVE APPEARED IN NUMEROUS FESTIVALS AND HAVE RECEIVED AWARDS, INCLUDING PRIX ARS ELECTRONICA GOLDEN NICA FOR *GOD'S LITTLE MONKEY* (1996). SABISTON COLLABORATED WITH PALLOTTA AND DIRECTOR RICHARD LINKLATER ON THE FEATURE FILM *WAKING LIFE*. TOMMY PALLOTTA (USA) GRADUATED WITH A DEGREE IN PHILOSOPHY. SINCE HIS FIRST FEATURE FILM, *THE HIGH ROAD*, PALLOTTA HAS WORKED EXCLUSIVELY IN VIDEO AND DIGITAL FORMATS. ▬▬ Bob Sabiston (USA) studierte Computer Graphics Research am MIT Media Lab. In seinen bisherigen Kurzfilmen, die bei zahlreichen Festivals präsentiert und preisgekrönt wurden (*God's Little Monkey* gewann z. B. die Goldene Nica des Prix Ars Electronica 96) spielen sowohl visuelle Kunst als auch Computerprogrammierung eine entscheidende Rolle. Tommy Pallotta (USA) hat Philosophie studiert. Seit seinem ersten großen Film, *The High Road*, hat Pallotta ausschließlich in digitalen und Video-Formaten gearbeitet.

LIGHTMARE
Robert Seidel / Michael Engelhardt

A small ... very personal story about loneliness ... and the search for life ... in a housing block filled with people ... who are too old, too drunk ... or too disillusioned ... so you just have to try desperately ... to be positive ...

... *lightmare* ... a free university project ... is based on several of my sketches ... the music, sound and perseverance of michael engelhardt ... nudges of hope from prof. dr. bauer wabnegg, michael flak ... and several others, who have occasionally brightened my surroundings ...

Perceived with concentration, the microcosm of picture and sound condenses into a small "story of survival", where familiar acoustic, visual and temporal patterns appear distorted. The oppressive 3D graphics, specially developed typography, and the little optical kinks grow together with the sound organically. The sound was elaborately produced in Dolby Surround parallel to the pictures.

Making of
Modeling + Animation: discreet 3d studio Max, CEEB's Bunch of Volumes
Textures: Corel Painter, Corel PhotoPAINT
Compositing: Adobe Aftereffects
Sound: Steinberg Cubase + Nuendo

... eine kleine ... sehr persönliche geschichte über die einsamkeit ...und die suche nach leben ... in einem wohnblock voller menschen ... die zu alt, zu betrunken ... oder zu desillusioniert sind ... also muss man ebenso verzweifelt versuchen ... positiv zu sein ...

... *lightmare* ... ein freies uniprojekt ... basiert auf einigen meiner skizzen ... der musik, dem ton und dem durchhaltevermögen von michael engelhardt ... hoffnungsschüben von prof. dr. bauer wabnegg, michael falk ... und einigen anderen, die meine umgebung zeitweilig erhellt haben ...

Der Mikrokosmos aus Bild und Ton ergänzt sich bei konzentrierter Wahrnehmung zu einer kleinen „Überlebensgeschichte", wobei bekannte akustische, visuelle und temporale Muster verzerrt auftreten. Die bedrückende 3D-Grafik, speziell entwickelte Typografie und die kleinen optischen Skurrilitäten wachsen organisch mit dem Ton zusammen, der aufwendig in Dolby Surround und parallel zu den Bildern produziert wurde.

ROBERT SEIDEL (D), BORN 1977, FINISHED SECONDARY SCHOOL 1996, SPENT TWO SEMESTERS STUDYING BIOLOGY AT THE FRIEDRICH SCHILLER UNIVERSITY JENA. CURRENTLY STUDIES MEDIA DESIGN AT THE BAUHAUS UNIVERSITY WEIMAR, SOON TO FINISH HIS DEGREE. FREELANCE AUTHOR AND TRANSLATOR IN THE FIELD OF 2D/3D GRAPHICS, FREELANCE ARTISTIC WORKS IN THE AREA OF ORGANIC DIGITAL GRAPHICS, 3D RECONSTRUCTIONS IN THE FIELD OF BIOLOGY. MICHAEL ENGELHARDT (D), BORN 1976, FINISHED SECONDARY SCHOOL 1994, SECOND FORM DIPLOMA IN CLASSICAL PIANO, CHURCH MUSIC DIPLOMA CLASS C (ORGAN, VOCALS), CURRENTLY STUDIES AT THE FRANZ LISZT MUSIC COLLEGE WEIMAR. GIVES MUSIC SEMINARS, VARIOUS CD PRODUCTIONS. ■ Robert Seidel (D), geb. 1977, Abitur 1996, Abstecher in zwei Semester Biologie an der Friedrich Schiller Universität Jena. Momentan Studium Mediengestaltung Bauhaus Universität Weimar kurz vor dem Diplom. Freier Autor und Übersetzer im Bereich 2D/3D-Grafik, freie künstlerische Arbeiten im Bereich organisch-digitaler Grafik, 3D-Rekonstruktionen im biologischen Bereich. Michael Engelhardt (D), geb. 1976, Abitur 1994, Oberstufenabschluss in klassischem Klavier, Kirchenmusiker Abschluss Stufe C (Orgel, Gesang), momentan Hochschule für Musik Franz Liszt, Weimar. Gibt Musikseminare, diverse CD-Produktionen.

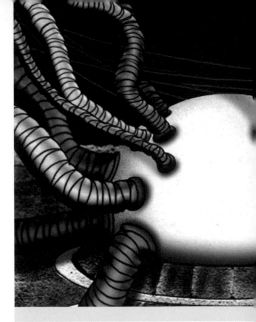

MOVING ILLUSTRATIONS OF MACHINES

Jeremy Solterbeck

I consider *Moving Illustrations of Machines* a revisionist animation. It ignores all of the tenets of traditional animation: color, hypernatural movement, and the depiction of vibrancy and life. The only characters as such are machines. I began work on this film as a commentary on the 1997 cloning of Dolly the sheep. I wanted to visualize a hybrid world where the line between organic machines (such as cells) and their man-made counterparts (such as microchips) begins to blur. There is a duality that has crept into our technological consciousness—first, the idea that any complex mechanism, including a living mechanism such as an ovum, can be described as a "machine". And conversely, the idea that mechanisms with extreme complexity, even man-made mechanisms, must at some point be considered "alive". For instance, the CPU of your average desktop computer can now outperform many insects in terms of information processing power. Does this suggest that microchips are in some way "smarter" or more "alive" than insects? I used this broader paradigm of the machine concept and applied it to a narrative that encompassed many of our emotional perceptions regarding cloning. Setting a provocative tone, the film opens with the mission statement of scientist and entrepreneur Richard Seed: God made man in his own image. God intended for man to become one with God. We are going to become one with God. We are going to have almost as much knowledge and almost as much power as God. Cloning, and the reprogramming of DNA, is the first serious step in becoming one with God.

My film introduces this machine world in a series of images consisting only of the benign spinning and turning of various mechanisms. The world lacks a sense of scale and orientation, is surreal and mysterious, but is also beautiful. The second sequence begins

Ich betrachte *Moving Illustrations of Machines* als eine revisionistische Animation. Sie ignoriert alle Regeln, die für traditionelle Animation gelten – Farbe, hypernatürliche Bewegung und die Darstellung von vibrierendem Leben. Die einzigen Darsteller in dieser Animation sind Maschinen.

Ich begann die Arbeit an diesem Film als Reaktion auf die Klonung des Schafes Dolly – 1997. Ich wollte eine hybride Welt darstellen, in der sich die Grenze zwischen organischen Maschinen (wie Zellen) und ihren von Menschen geschaffenen Gegenstücken (wie Microchips) zu verwischen beginnt. In unser technologisches Bewusstsein hat sich eine Dualität eingeschlichen: die Idee, dass einerseits jeder komplexe Mechanismus, auch ein lebender wie eine Eizelle, als eine „Maschine" beschrieben werden kann, und dass andererseits Mechanismen von extremer Komplexität, selbst wenn sie von Menschen geschaffen sind, an irgendeinem Punkt als „lebendig" anzusehen sind. Die CPU Ihres handelsüblichen Rechners zuhause übertrifft viele Insekten hinsichtlich ihrer Fähigkeit zur Informationsverarbeitung. Aber bedeutet das, dass Microchips irgendwie „intelligenter" oder „lebendiger" sind als Insekten?

Ich habe dieses breitere Paradigma des Maschinenkonzepts auf eine Erzählung angewandt, die viele unserer emotionalen Wahrnehmungen hinsichtlich des Klonens berührt. In einem provokanten Tonfall beginnt der Film mit einem Statement des Wissenschaftlers und Unternehmers Richard Seed: Gott schuf den Menschen nach seinem Abbilde. Gott bestimmte den Men

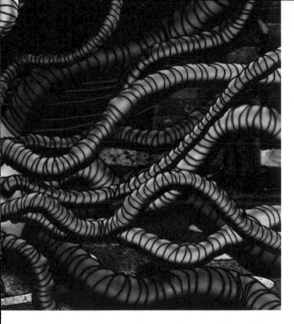

schen dazu, eins mit Gott zu werden. Wir werden eins mit Gott werden. Wir werden fast so viel Wissen und fast so viel Macht haben wie Gott. Das Klonen und die Reprogrammierung von DNA ist der erste ernsthafte Schritt, um mit Gott eins zu werden. Mein Film führt diese Maschinenwelt in einer Serie von Bildern ein, die nur aus dem harmlosen Drehen und Funktionieren diverser Mechanismen besteht. Dieser Welt fehlt ein Gefühlt für Maßstab und Orientierung, sie ist surreal und mysteriös, aber sie ist auch schön. Die zweite Sequenz beginnt mit einem beunruhigenden Bild wurmähnlicher Maschinen. Sie erscheinen komplexer, aber immer noch metallisch und vom Menschen gemacht. Dann werden die Eizellen eingeführt, und der Rest dieser Sequenz schildert die Reise der Eizelle vom „Gezüchtetwerden" über die Befruchtung durch die mechanischen Würmer bis hin zur Informationseingabe durch die Nadel eines unheimlichen Klon-Geräts. Nachdem die restlichen Eier eingegeben wurden, verschmelzen sie langsam, während die Musik sich steigert, und erscheinen am Ende als ununterscheidbare Masse, als organische Oberfläche, die die Akkumulation dieser veränderten organischen Maschinen ist.
Moving Illustrations of Machines möchte hinterfragen, was es heißt zu leben. Haben die Technologie und das Klonen die Definition des Wortes „Maschine" verändert? Ist die menschliche Maschine offen für eine Revision durch die Menschheit selbst? Wenn unsere Technologie immer komplexer und unfassbarer wird, wird da die menschliche Eizelle ebenso für Veränderungen zur Verfügung stehen wie alle unsere mechanischen Gerätschaften? *Moving Illustrations of Machines* beantwortet diese Fragen nicht, es stellt sie nur und fordert den Betrachter auf, sich damit auseinanderzusetzen, jetzt, wo das Klonen und verwandte wissenschaftliche Unternehmungen in den Vordergrund unserer ethischen und moralischen Gewissensfragen rücken.

with an unsettling image of worm-like machines. They appear more complex, but still seem metallic and man-made. Then the ova are introduced and the rest of this sequence details the ova's journey from being "hatched", to being inseminated by the mechanical worms, to being inscribed with information by the needle of an ominous cloning device. After the rest of the eggs have been inscribed, they slowly conglomerate as the music builds, and in the end they appear indistinguishable in a mass, an organic surface that is the accumulation of these altered organic machines.
Moving Illustrations of Machines wishes to reconsider what it means to be living. Has technology and cloning changed the definition of the word machine? Is the human machine open to revision by humanity itself? As our technology becomes unfathomably complex, will the human ovum become as eligible for alteration as any of our mechanical gadgets? *Machines* doesn't propose to answer these questions, only to present them and ask the viewer to consider them, as cloning and related scientific issues continue to surge to the forefront of our ethical and moral quandaries.

JEREMY SOLTERBECK (USA) ATTENDED THE UNIVERSITY OF ALASKA ANCHORAGE AS A FINE ARTS MAJOR AND SAN FRANCISCO STATE UNIVERSITY AS A FILM PRODUCTION MAJOR. HE IS INVOLVED IN MANY ASPECTS OF FILMMAKING: ANIMATION, EDITING, SCORING, AND THE EMERGING FIELD OF DIGITAL FILMMAKING. *MOVING ILLUSTRATIONS OF MACHINES* IS HIS FIRST FILM. ■
Jeremy Solterbeck (USA) schloss die University of Alaska in Anchorage mit einem Fine Arts Major und die San Francisco State University mit einem Film Production Major ab. Er beschäftigt sich mit vielen Aspekten des Filmemachens – Animation, Schnitt, Drehbuch und dem in Entwicklung begriffenen Bereich des digitalen Films. *Moving Illustrations of Machines* ist sein erster eigener Film.

SNYCHRONICITY
Hans Uhlig / Tony Hurd

Synchronicity is an entirely computer-generated ballet and allegory. "It's a story about growing up," says director Hans Uhlig. "The two dancers are born, and as their consciousness dawns they become aware of each other. Their initial reaction is apprehension and fear, and they fight over their identity like teenagers. Their eventual acceptance of each other causes the shell around them to break apart and they're bathed in sunlight."

Synchronicity is also an animated painting. It transitions from the photoreal to the surreal. It begins with an homage to the earliest known films, with art nouveau titles and sepia tones, and as the film and the story progress, a series of stylized film looks underscore the evolution of the characters.

Our intention was to push the envelope. We wanted to create an entirely computer generated short film with photorealistic humans. To make the characters as real and believable as possible, motion capture technology was used. Computer graphics animated by hand has a particular quality. You can see the function curves. You see them ease in and ease out, and you lose the emotion. With motion capture you get all of the subtleties of movement, all of the emotion, for free.

The complex choreography by San Francisco based choreographer Paula Telander was captured using the Vicon 370 optical motion capture system. A ring of seven motion capture cameras and nearly 100 mark-

Synchronicity ist ein vollständig computergeneriertes Ballett und eine Allegorie. „Es ist eine Geschichte, die sich um das Aufwachsen dreht", sagt Regisseur Hans Uhlig. „Die beiden Tänzer werden geboren, und in dem Maße, in dem ihr Bewusstsein erwacht, werden sie sich auch des jeweils anderen bewusst. Ihre erste Reaktion ist Angst, und sie kämpfen wie Teenager um ihre Identität. Als sie aber beginnen, einander zu akzeptieren, zerbricht die Schale, die sie umgeben hat, und sie tauchen ein in ein Bad aus Sonnenlicht."

Synchronicity ist aber auch ein animiertes Gemälde, das vom Fotorealen zum Surrealen hinüberkippt. Es beginnt mit einer Hommage an die ältesten bekannten Filme, mit an Jugendstil erinnernden Titeln und Sepia-Tönen; im weiteren Verlauf des Films bzw. der Geschichte wird die Entwicklung der Charaktere durch die Andeutung verschiedener Filmstile betont.

Unser Ziel war es, das Trägermedium weiterzuentwickeln – wir wollten einen vollständig computergenerierten Kurzfilm mit fotorealistischen Menschen schaffen. Um die Charaktere so glaubhaft wie möglich zu machen, wurde Motion-Capture-Technologie eingesetzt. Handanimierte Computergrafik hat so ihre Besonderheiten – man sieht die Funktionskurven dahinter, man erkennt die Ein- und Ausstiegspunkte und verliert die Emotion im Bild. Bei Motion Capture hingegen bekommt man alle Feinheiten der Bewegung und den emotionalen Inhalt frei Haus geliefert.

Die komplexe Choreografie der in San Francisco lebenden Paula Telander wurde mit einem Vicon 370 Optical-Motion-Capture-Systems aufgenommen. Ein Ring von sieben Kameras und beinahe 100 Markierungspunkte dienten dazu,

ers were used to capture all of the subtleties of the original performance. Vicon, Filmbox, Softimage, and Industrial Light&Magic proprietary software were used to reconstruct and apply the motion capture data to the computer-generated dancers.

The entirely computer-generated environment was created in Softimage, surfaced with Renderman shaders, lit and composited with ILM proprietary software, and ultimately demolished using a Maya rigid body simulation.

The film also has an original score by William Storkson and a 5.1 Dolby SR/D sound mix, courtesy of Skywalker Sound.

alle Details der Original-Performance einzufangen. Software von Vicon, Filmbox, Softimage und Industrial Light&Magic dienten dazu, die Motion-Capture-Daten zu rekonstruieren und sie auf die computergenerierten Tänzer anzuwenden.

Die zur Gänze computergenerierte Szenerie entstand unter Softimage, die Oberflächen wurden mit Renderman-Shadern gestaltet, mit von ILM entwickelter Software zusammengesetzt und letztlich mit Hilfe einer Festkörper-Simulation von Maya demoliert.

Die Musikpartitur zum Film wurde eigens von William Storkson geschrieben, ein Dolby-5.1-SR/D Sound-Mix entstand mit freundlicher Unterstützung von Sykwalker Sound.

HANS UHLIG (D/USA) ATTENDED WILHELM MAYBACH SCHOOL FOR ENGINEERING IN STUTTGART, OBTAINING AN ADVANCED DEGREE IN MECHANICAL ENGINEERING. HE BEGAN WORKING AT INDUSTRIAL LIGHT & MAGIC IN 1996 ON *STAR WARS* TRILOGY SPECIAL EDITION. HE HONED HIS ANIMATION SKILLS ON COMMERCIALS FOR GERMAN TELEVISION, THEN WENT ON TO FOUND DESIGN & MOTION IN MUNICH, FOCUSING ON 3D ANIMATION DESIGN. UHLIG WENT ON TO MUNICH ANIMATION AS MANAGING DIRECTOR, SETTING UP THE 3D DEPARTMENT AND CONTRIBUTING TO WARNER BROS.' *THE FEARLESS FOUR*. TONY HURD (USA) HAS STUDIED AT THE BOSTON UNIVERSITY'S COLLEGE OF COMMUNICATION. HE WORKED AT WGBH IN BOSTON AND AT KQED IN SAN FRANCISCO. IN 1997 HE JOINED INDUSTRIAL LIGHT & MAGIC AS TECHNICAL AREA LEADER IN THE COMPUTER GRAPHICS DIVISION AND IS CURRENTLY THE MANAGER OF PRODUCTION OPERATIONS ADMINISTRATION. ▬▬ Hans Uhlig (D/USA) besuchte die Wilhelm-Maybach-Schule (Fachschulbereich) in Bad Cannstatt und hat ein technisches Diplom aus Maschinenbau. Er begann 1996 bei Industrial Light & Magic mit der Arbeit an der Special Edition der *Star Wars*-Trilogie. Seine Animationsfähigkeiten hat er später an Werbespots für das deutsche Fernsehen ausgefeilt und gründete anschließend Design & Motion in München, wo er sich mit 3D-Animationsdesign beschäftigte. Uhlig war später Geschäftsführer bei Munich Animation, hat dort die 3D-Abteilung eingerichtet und an Warner Bros. *Die Furchtlosen Vier* mitgewirkt. Tony Hurd (USA) hat an der Boston University, College of Communication, studiert. Er arbeitete bei WGBH in Boston und bei KQED in San Francisco. 1997 ging er als Technical Area Leader der Computergrafik-Abteilung zu Industrial Light & Magic und ist zurzeit Manager der Production Operations Administration.

F 8

Jason Wen / Howard Wen / Andrew Jones / Casey Hess / Don Relyea

F8 is a science fiction short animation about one character's attempt to gain a unique identity (both external as well as internal) in a world where such an organic biological norm has virtually been eradicated by technological means.

The concept for this animation was initiated by Jason Wen, whose brother, Howard Wen, then wrote the initial screenplay. Subsequent drafts were written and rewritten by both brothers over a year's time. Jason Wen began initial computer modeling and conceptual design drawings close to the end of 1997. Just before Jason was to graduate from Ringling in 1999, he met Andrew Jones. Andrew became the primary conceptual artist for F8. Through constant collaboration, Andrew designed the looks for all but the main character. Additionally, he rendered illustrations for a blimp inspired aircraft, a slotmachine, a harpoon weapon, interior structure of a building and the alien creature.

Jason used Newtek Lightwave 3D version 5.6 to build all the models which appear in this animation. It took him approximately two years to realize every character, set piece and prop. He then began animation at the very beginning of 2000 using Project:Messiah, a Lightwave character animation plugin. He spent almost the entire year of 2000 on the animation aspect of production.

Rendering was completed with the use of two Intel Pentium III computers and two AMD Athlon machines. The rendered frames were taken into After Effects for compositing, color balancing, correction and 2D effects work. Each scene was output as a DV format video and taken into Premiere for the final edit.

By near the end of 2000, Howard Wen introduced Jason to Casey Hess who, with assistance from bandmate, Don Relyea, became the musician on the project. By the beginning of 2001, Jason began mixing

F8 ist eine Sciencefiction-Kurzanimation über den Versuch einer Figur, eine eigene – eindeutige – Identität (und zwar im externen wie internen Sinn) in einer Welt zu erlangen, in der solch eine organisch-biologische Norm durch technologische Mittel so gut wie ausgerottet worden ist.

Das Ursprungskonzept für diese Animation stammt von Jason Wen, dessen Bruder Howard daraus das erste Drehbuch gestaltete. Im Laufe eines Jahres kamen weitere Entwürfe und Abänderungen dazu, bevor Jason Wen sich gegen Ende 1997 an die ersten Design-Skizzen und Modelle machte. Kurz vor seinem Studienabschluss 1999 lernte Jason Andrew Jones kennen. Andrew wurde zum leitenden Konzeptionist bei F8. In ständiger Zusammenarbeit mit Jason entwarf Andrew das Aussehen aller Gestalten außer der Hauptfigur. Nebenher renderte er das Zeppelin-ähnliche Luftfahrzeug, einen Spielautomaten, eine Harpunenwaffe, die Innenstruktur eines Gebäudes und die außerirdische Gestalt.

Jason verwendete Newtek Lightwave 3D, Version 5.6, für die Erstellung aller Modelle dieser Animation. Er brauchte rund zwei Jahre zur Realisierung von Charakteren, Szenerie und Requisiten. Dann begann er Anfang 2000 mithilfe von Project:Messiah, einem Character-Animation-Plug-in für Lightwave, mit der eigentlichen Animation. Fast das ganze Jahr 2000 verging mit der Animation dieser Produktion.

Das Rendering erfolgte auf zwei Intel-P-III-Computern und zwei AMD-Athlon-Maschinen. Die gerenderten Kader wurden zur Montage, Farbbalance, Korrektur und für die 2D-Effekte auf After Effects transferiert. Jede Szene wurde im DV-Video-Format ausgegeben, die Endmontage erfolgte in Premiere.

Ende 2000 machte Howard Wen Jason mit

the sound for the animation. With the exception of one sound effect, he recorded everything himself using a Sennheiser shotgun microphone and a Tascam portable DAT recorder. The actual sound mix was accomplished from beginning to end with Steinberg Nuendo PC software. To monitor the original 5.1 channel surround mix, Jason used five KRK V8 sound speakers and one KRK SI 2 subwoofer.

Casey Hess bekannt, der – unterstützt von seinem Bandmitglied Don Relyea – der Musiker des Projekts wurde. Anfang 2001 begann Jason mit der Klangmischung für die Animation. Mit Ausnahme eines einzigen Spezialeffekts nahm er alle Klänge mithilfe eines Sennheiser-Richtmikrofons und eines tragbaren Tascam DAT-Rekorders selbst auf. Der endgültige Sound-Mix erfolgte mit Steinberg Nuendo PC-Software. Als Monitorlautsprecher für den 5.1-Kanal-Surround-Mix wurden fünf KRK V8 Boxen und ein KRK SI-2 Subwoofer eingesetzt.

JASON WEN (USA) HAS BEEN PRACTICING COMPUTER ANIMATION FOR APPROXIMATELY SEVEN YEARS. FROM 1995 TO 1999, HE ATTENDED RINGLING SCHOOL OF ART AND DESIGN IN SARASOTA, FLORIDA, U.S.A. WHILE ON SUMMER BREAKS FROM COLLEGE, JASON SPENT HIS TIME INTERNING IN DALLAS, TEXAS AT THE STOKES GROUP (VIDEO POSTPRODUCTION), MESALOGIC (ARCADE GAME DEVELOPER) AND DNA ANIMATION (BROADCAST ANIMATION PRODUCTION.) IN MAY OF 1999, JASON GRADUATED WITH A BFA IN COMPUTER ANIMATION FROM THE RINGLING SCHOOL OF ART AND DESIGN. ■■■ Jason Wen (USA) beschäftigt sich seit etwa sieben Jahren mit Computeranimation. 1995 bis 1999 besuchte er die Ringling School of Art and Design in Sarasota, Florida. Während der Sommerferien arbeitete er als Praktikant in Dallas, Texas, bei der Stokes-Gruppe (Video-Postproduktion), bei Mesalogic (einem Unterhaltungsspiel-Produzenten) und bei DNA Animation (Animationsproduktionen für Fernsehen). Im Mai 1999 graduierte Jason an der Ringling School zum BFA aus Computeranimation.

digital musics

DIGITAL MUSICS DIASPORA
DIE DIASPORA DER DIGITAL MUSICS
Digital Musics Jury

Es ist nicht zu leugnen: Zu Beginn dieses einundzwanzigsten Jahrhunderts kommen die innovativsten, fesselndsten und erstaunlichsten Arbeiten, die im sagenhaft weiten Feld der Digital Musics produziert werden, ausgerechnet von Musikern, deren Werdegang größtenteils außerhalb der akademischen Bildungsgänge und der üblichen Karrieren verlaufen ist. Stattdessen erzählt ihr Werk von einem intensiven autodidaktischen Engagement in den vernetzten Welten postindustrieller Kulturen: konzeptuelle und Performance-Kunst, Installationen und Video-Arbeiten, improvisierte Musik, Öko-Aktivismus, Post-Kolonialismus und nicht zuletzt die Post-Techno/Hiphop/Dub-Grassroots-Diaspora abgestumpfter Beatnuts und der Wohnzimmer-Tüftler.

Ein Teil dieser sozial und kulturell lebendigen offenen Aktivitäten hat die elektronische Musik an die vorderste Front der gegenwärtigen kreativen Anstrengungen katapultiert. Und dies wurde in vielen der Einreichungen zum diesjährigen Prix Ars Electronica deutlich – die drei Preisträger sind ebenso wie die Anerkennungen hervorragende Beispiele für den Kern einer vielfältigen Landschaft voller Ausdruck und voller Suche, die vielleicht noch nie zuvor so vibrierend war. Aber die Tradition und Kultur solcher Preise für elektronische Musik (und eben auch des Prix Ars Electronica) wirkt sich hemmend aus auf die Art von Werken, die im Wettbewerb gehört und prämiert werden. Außerdem hatte die Jury den Eindruck, dass einige der Künstler, die von sich aus eingereicht haben oder die zur Einreichung eingeladen wurden, nicht ihre besten Werke eingesandt haben.

Ein Problem, vor dem die vielschichtige Digital-Musics-Kategorie des Prix Ars Electronica noch immer steht, ist, dass für allzu viele Musiker und Klangkünstler ein „Wettbewerb" als solcher

I t's a fact: on the cusp of the twenty-first century, the most innovative, compelling and startling work being produced in the impossibly broad area of Digital Musics comes from musicians whose backgrounds have largely bypassed academic study and customary career paths. Instead their work speaks of an intense, autodidactic engagement with the hyperlinked worlds of post-industrial cultures: conceptual and performance art, installation and video work, improvised music, post-industrial cultures, eco-activism, post-colonialism, as well as the post-techno/hip hop/dub grass-roots diaspora of blunted beatnuts and bedroom boffins.

Not supported

Some of this socially and culturally vital, open-ended activity has pushed electronic music to the forefront of contemporary creative endeavors. This was apparent in many of the entries in this year's Prix Ars Electronica: the three prize winners along with the honorary mentions are excellent representatives of the core of a vast area of expression and exploration that has perhaps never been so vibrant. But the tradition and culture of electronic music prizes such as the Prix Ars Electronica still mitigate much of this work being heard and celebrated in competition. As well, it was felt by the jury that *some* of the artists who submitted voluntarily or were invited to do so, did not send in their best work.

A problem still facing the Prix Ars Digital Musics tier is that to many of these musicians and sound artists, the notion of competition is either alien or anathema. If they are known at all by the wider musical community, the major music prizes are still seen as the preserve of a musical elite that plies its hermetic art inside the high walls of the world's university music departments and institutions. This is still the case, in spite of the valiant attempts in recent years to broaden the music category. Perhaps many sound artists and music people question the relevance of so-called "contests" and their influence on acts of sonic creation. When laptop pioneers Autechre were initially approached about possibly entering in 1999, they respectfully declined, stating, "I reckon we're no better than anyone else". Curiously enough, the following year there was somewhat of a reconsideration of this stance when the same duo's other project Gescom actually was awarded a distinction, partially because of the jury's acknowledgment of their

entweder unbekannt oder nachgerade der Inbegriff des Bösen ist. Sofern sie überhaupt einer breiteren Öffentlichkeit innerhalb der Musikerschaft bekannt sind, werden die größeren Musikpreise noch immer als das Reservat einer musikalischen Elite betrachtet, die ihre hermetische Kunst innerhalb der hohen Mauern der universitären Musikfakultäten und -institute dieser Welt ausübt. Trotz der tapferen Versuche der vergangenen Jahren, die Musikkategorie auszuweiten, ist diese Ansicht noch immer weit verbreitet. Vielleicht stellen auch viele Klangkünstler und Musikleute die Relevanz so genannter „Wettbewerbe" und ihren Einfluss auf den klanglichen Schöpfungsakt in Frage. Als die Laptop-Pioniere Autechre 1999 im Hinblick auf eine eventuelle Einreichung angesprochen wurden, lehnten sie respektvoll ab mit der Bemerkung: „Ich glaube, wir sind nicht besser als irgendwer anderer." Kurioserweise haben sie diesen Standpunkt im folgenden Jahr überdacht, als das andere Projekt dieses Duos, „Gescom", tatsächlich eine Auszeichnung erhielt, auch teilweise deswegen, weil die Jury die so unterschiedlichen Leistungen des Duos, das in der Öffentlichkeit unter mehreren Identitäten firmiert, anerkannt hat.

Wenn der Prix Ars Electronica weiterhin als eines der wichtigsten und als egalitärer Barometer des gegenwärtigen Zustandes der digitalen Musik im weitesten Sinne anerkannt werden soll, brauchen wir zusätzliche konzertierte Anstrengungen, diesen Anspruch allseits bekannt zu machen – nicht nur in den und über die Akademien, sondern über alle verfügbaren Kommunikationskanäle, von der Musikpresse zur Online-Community. Die meisten Musiker operieren in einem Umfeld, in dem finanzielle Gegebenheiten eine entscheidende Rolle spielen – und wenn schon nichts anderes, so sollte wenigstens der vom Prix Ars Electronica angebotene Geldpreis Anreiz genug sein, um sicherzustellen, dass es sich viele der „elektronischen Außenseiter" doch noch überlegen, zum ersten oder zweiten Mal einzureichen.

diverse achievements under several public identities.

What is needed if the Prix Ars Electronica is to continue to be perceived as one of the world's most crucial and egalitarian barometers of the current state of Digital Musics is an additional concerted effort to broadcast that aspiration far and wide, not just via the academies, but via all available communication conduits, from the music press to the online community. Most musicians operate in a climate compromised by financial imperatives; if nothing else the cash prizes offered by the Prix Ars should be incentive enough to ensure that many of the electronic "outsiders" consider entering for the first or second time.

The war may be over, but there are those remaining who would have the battles linger. As we mulled over the 380 submissions from all sectors of the sonic cybernetic map, some of the questions posed in previous years continue to cause controversy. In last year's "Forward To The World" jury statement, a call went out to the former dominating influence in the competition to "astonish us or fade away". Once again, the reference to the historical hierarchy of the electroacoustic and acousmatic influences on the evolution of the Prix Ars musical wing was reverberating across the conversations of the panel. We would compel any digital musical style to astonish or to try at least. But simply "fading away" seems too easy—as if one wanted to shrink from the demand rather than take it head on and attempt some other angles. It was precisely this challenge that we had our collective ears peeled for.

There was some discussion as to whether the electroacoustic genre should be given special consider-

Der Krieg mag vorbei sein, aber noch gibt es einige, die die Schlacht nicht verloren geben. Als wir die 380 Einreichungen aus allen erdenklichen Sektoren der kybernetischen Klanglandschaft durchforsteten, sorgten einige der in den vergangenen Jahren aufgetauchten Fragen erneut für Kontroversen. Im Jury-Statement des letzten Jahres, *Weiterleiten an die Welt*, erging ein Ruf an die vormals dominierenden Einflüsse im Wettbewerb, uns „entweder zu erstaunen oder zu verschwinden". Auch in den diesjährigen Diskussionen wurde auf die historische Hierarchie der Einflüsse von elektroakustischer und akusmatischer Musik auf die Entwicklung der Musikkategorie des Prix Ars Electronica Bezug genommen. Wir würden jeden musikalischen Stil dazu zwingen, uns aufhorchen zu lassen, oder dies zumindest zu versuchen. Sich einfach nur auszublenden, zu verschwinden, erscheint uns zu simpel – so, als würde man zurückschrecken vor dem, was nachgefragt wird, anstatt sich kopfüber hineinzustürzen und es von einem anderen Blickpunkt aus neu zu versuchen. Und genau nach dieser Herausforderung hielten wir unsere kollektiven Ohren gespitzt.

Es gab einige Diskussion darüber, ob man das elektroakustische Genre in Hinblick auf seine historische Bedeutung vielleicht gesondert betrachten sollte. Es wurde aber beschlossen, diesen Bereich nicht anders zu behandeln. Auch wenn sie die Mehrheit der Einreichungen zum Wettbewerb ausmachten, blieben die meisten elektroakustischen Stücke in seit langem erprobten kompositorischen Strukturen verankert. Die Jury hatte Mühe, frische, unerwartete Ansätze in diesem Gebiet zu finden. Vielleicht ist dieser Mangel an Erneuerung ja auch teilweise auf den Boykott zurückzuführen, der von einigen einflussreichen Mitgliedern die-

ation, given its historical significance. It was decided that it should not be treated differently. While comprising the majority of submissions to the competition, most electroacoustic pieces were anchored in tried-and-true compositional structures. The jury was hard-pressed to find fresh, unexpected approaches in this field. Perhaps this lack of ground-breaking works can be explained in part by the boycott initiated by some influential members of this community. If so, let it be known that this competition is open to everyone, including the scholastically inclined! Of course, the jury is not only looking to reward innovation, and will likely reward exceptionally exciting works, even if they are conceived using traditional techniques. The jury also felt that the competition should reach out to other sonic practitioners, like sound designers in cinema, software programmers, and, of course, people from as many countries as possible. We yearned for real diversity over arbitrary tokenism.

With all the practitioners on even ground, it is remarkable to see how musicians and sound artists from different generations can have so much in common. Many are applying modern real-time laptop techniques that reinvent the slower methodical manner of musique concrète composition. By blurring these former boundaries, the new school will eventually dispense with this digital divide. So if it appears to some the prize has been sold down the river to some commercial backwater, they're going to be perplexed by the lack of mainstream accessibility in any of the chosen 15. We don't want to tar the scene with all the same brush here either. We have to watch out for a new elite taking over past ones, hence falling into simi-

ser Gemeinschaft verhängt wurde. Falls dem so wäre, so sollt ihr wissen, dass dieser Wettbewerb für jedermann offen ist, einschließlich der scholastisch Angehauchten! Natürlich versucht die Jury nicht nur, Innovation zu belohnen, sie wird sicherlich herausragend aufregende Werke auszeichnen, auch wenn sie mit traditionellen Techniken konzipiert wurden. Die Jury hatte auch den Eindruck, der Wettbewerb sollte seine Fühler nach anderen Klangpraktikern ausstrecken, wie etwa nach den Klangdesignern des Kinos, den Softwareprogrammierern und vor allem natürlich nach Menschen aus so vielen Ländern wie möglich. Uns geht es um wirkliche Bandbreite, nicht um Zufälligkeiten und Alibihandlungen.
Stellt man alle Musikpraktiker auf die gleiche Ebene, so erstaunt es zu sehen, wie viel Musiker und Klangkünstler aus unterschiedlichen Generationen doch gemeinsam haben. Manch einer wendet moderne Laptop-Techniken an, die die langsamere methodische Kompositionsweise der Musique Concrète wieder entdecken. Und indem diese früheren Grenzen verwischt werden, wird die neue Schule früher oder später diese Trennung hinwegfegen. Und wer jetzt etwa glaubt, der Prix sei sozusagen den kommerziellen Bach hinunter gegangen oder sonst wie verramscht worden, der wird überrascht sein, wie wenig Mainstream-Zugänglichkeit jedem einzelnen der ausgewählten 15 Werke innewohnt!
Wir wollen andererseits hier auch nicht die gesamte Szene über einen Kamm scheren. Es gilt aufpassen, denn die neue Elite könnte nach der Übernahme früherer Eliten in die gleichen Fallen stolpern. Sicherlich werden uns einige angesichts der heurigen Gewinner und Anerkennungen – etwa des US-Western-Aufgebots rund um kid606 und seine Freunde, J. Lesser, bLecktum from bLechdom und das Tigerbeat6-Kollektiv – der Bevorzugung einer elektronischen „Clique" zeihen. Aber jetzt ist nun einmal deren Zeit angebrochen, und die Jury reagierte eher auf die *Unterschiede* zwischen diesen Individuen,

lar entrapments. There will be those looking at this year's winners and honorary mentions, like the western US posse that surrounds kid606 and friends, J. Lesser, bLectum from bLechdom and the Tigerbeat6 collective and call favoritism toward an electronic "clique". It just happens to be their time right now and the jury responded to the distinctions between these individuals based on musical and sonic impact criteria and less on the fact that they know each other. When the factor of their loose alliance was brought up in discussion, it was considered to be a political imbalance of representation. Though that may be so, each was submitting from different labels, and the jury had to consider what we were actually listening to beyond the personalities involved, while sticking to a musical perspective. We voiced the danger of singling out a particular known group in the results, and this allowed us to consider producers and curators who submit compilations of many various artists to the competition.

Last year, Carsten Nicolai with the Raster-Noton label submitted a multi CD set entitled *20' to 2000* which represented a number of different artists who were acquainted, but working from locations all over Europe and Japan. Carsten Nicolai, as contributor and curator, compiled the project under a unified thematic heading expressing an aesthetic, which brought together a cross-section of important music, and a visual package that caught the eye as well. It seemed that this combination was worthy of the Golden Nica, so this time a sizable number of compilations arrived for scrutiny. The jury took time to discuss the nature of this type of submission that seems to encompass genre gauges or thematic invitationals.

wobei sie die musikalische und klangliche Wirksamkeit als Kriterium hernahm, und weniger darauf, dass sie einander kennen. Die Tatsache, dass sie eine lose Allianz bilden und dass dies nach einem politischen Ungleichgewicht in der Repräsentation der einzelnen Genres aussähe, wurde sehr wohl in die Diskussion geworfen. Das mag seine Richtigkeit haben, allein, jeder hat von unterschiedlichen Labels aus eingereicht, und Aufgabe der Jury war es, das zu Gehör Gebrachte unter musikalischen Gesichtspunkten zu beurteilen, ohne Ansehen der involvierten Personen. Wir haben die Gefahr, eine besonders bekannte Gruppe im Ergebnis auszusondern, erörtert, und dies hat uns erlaubt, auch Produzenten und Kuratoren zu berücksichtigen, die Kompilationen von zahlreichen verschiedenen Künstlern zum Bewerb eingesandt haben.

Im vergangenen Jahr reichte Carsten Nicolai das Multi-CD-Set „20' to 2000" unter dem Label Raster-Noton ein, das eine Anzahl verschiedener Künstler repräsentierte, die einander zwar kannten, aber an unterschiedlichen Orten in ganz Europa und Japan arbeiteten. Als Beiträger und Kurator hat Carsten Nicolai dieses Projekt unter ein gemeinsames Thema gestellt und damit eine Ästhetik zum Ausdruck gebracht, die einen Querschnitt durch wichtige Musik wie auch eine visuell beeindruckende Verpackung zustande brachte. Da diese Kombination einer Goldenen Nica würdig erachtet worden war, erreichte uns heuer eine beträchtliche Anzahl von Zusammenstellungen zur Begutachtung. Die Jury hat sich Zeit genommen, diesen Typ von Einreichung zu diskutieren, der vor allem thematische Einladungswerke und Genre-Querschnitte zu umfassen scheint.

Es ist für Digital Musics von entscheidender

It has become vital for Digital Musics to now recognize new ideas in electronic music in the form of how it is organized, assembled and produced. When labels, galleries or individuals incubate a series or process which demonstrates core methods in which new music is disseminated, distributed and consumed, we should acknowledge the key people behind these manifestations. Without these independent efforts, public exposure to unusual sound art would be far more limited. So with the recent nods to the independent contingents like Mego & Raster-Noton, and this year's honorary mentions to Mille Plateaux, Lucky Kitchen and Tigerbeat6, the Prix Ars jury acknowledges the role of curator as comparable to that of the composer or sound sculptor.

But the prize shouldn't be awarded to someone who decides to gang up their favorite friends' tracks as a convenient arbitrary sampler and take this collection theory as a significant idea without teeth behind it. The artistic concept prior to the compilation becomes the real assessment here. Sometimes a collective context appears to have more of a magnetic pull than solo efforts due to the diversity of varied approaches, but it also makes it harder to judge. Is the compilation being submitted as something convenient to the competition, or with a thematic idea that embraces a consequential substance before the assemblage? Then the whole can be looked at as a singular vision rather than the general pluralistic appellations we had often received.

Another compilation-related dilemma arose when we were given the 2001 retrospective of John Oswald's "Plunderphonics" era, complete with unreleased mixes and untold out-takes. As much

Bedeutung geworden, jetzt auch neue Ideen in der Organisation, Zusammenstellung und Produktion elektronischer Musik anzuerkennen. Wenn Labels, Galerien oder Individuen eine Serie oder einen Prozess ausbrüten, der grundlegende Methoden in der Verbreitung, Verteilung oder im Konsum neuer Musik umfasst, dann sollten wir die entscheidenden Leute hinter diesen Darbietungen auch zur Kenntnis nehmen. Ohne diese unabhängigen Anstrengungen wäre das Publikum wesentlich seltener mit ungewöhnlicher Klangkunst konfrontiert. Mit den vergangenen Verbeugungen vor den Kontingenten der Unabhängigen wie Mego und Raster-Noton und mit den diesjährigen Anerkennungen für Mille Plateaux, Lucky Kitchen und Tigerbeat6 stellt die Jury des Prix Ars Electronica fest, dass die Bedeutung des Kurators durchaus jener des Komponisten oder Klang-Bildhauers gleichkommt.

Aber der Preis sollte natürlich nicht an jemanden vergeben werden, der beschlossen hat, die Tracks seiner besten Freunde als bequemen beliebigen Sampler zusammenzuleimen und diese Sammlungstheorie als signifikante Idee anzusehen, wenn kein Biss dahinter ist. Das künstlerische Konzept *vor* der Kompilation wird hier zum eigentlichen Bewertungskriterium. Manchmal scheint ein kollektiver Zusammenhang wegen der Verschiedenheit der Ansätze eine stärkere Sogwirkung auszuüben als die Anstrengungen Einzelner – was sie andererseits aber schwerer beurteilbar machen. Wird die Kompilation als eine bequeme Form für den Wettbewerb eingereicht oder steckt schon vor der Assemblage eine thematische Idee dahinter, die eine konsequente Substanz mit sich bringt? Nur dann kann das Ganze als eine singuläre Vision angesehen werden und mehr sein als eine der vielen bloß pluralistischen Aussagen, die wir oft erhalten haben.

Ein weiteres kompilationsbezogenes Dilemma tauchte auf, als wir die 2001-Retrospektive von John Oswalds *Plunderphonics*-Ära erhielten, komplett mit

as the panel highly touted the absolute significance of these works that question the notions of copyright, sampling, and appropriation so prevalent in today's MP3 Napster debates, we felt that lifetime achievement awards were not in the province of the Prix Ars Electronica guidelines that each new jury must evaluate for themselves.

And appraise we did! It is always difficult to compare an elaborately composed piece of music with an audio-oriented installation and come to a balanced judgment. The sounds emanating from these installations are usually affected by the parameters of the sculpture itself and not so much the musical compositional structures that "composers" define in the studio. Regardless of the format, we had to come to grips with how one attended the sound, whether it came from horizontal linear or vertical note developments or the interference of found environmental sources. Once these abstracts are extrapolated, more questions arise: what sort of language are we translating, and how does it strike the spirit? These were the criteria beyond the mere skill of the craft. And if something is very simple and realized with rudimentary means, how truly "electronic" does it have to be?

As the distillation process from the enormous range of works became more succinct, the jury thirsted for more quality submissions. Wishing for what wasn't there in this round prompted a lively exchange on how to more effectively attract quality works. How the new MP3 web label coalitions are operating, for example, brings in a realm previously unrecognized in the category and needs further nudging from under the radar. While some presentations could use some fine tuning to more effectively arrest the interest of the panel within the initial 2-3 minutes of quick exposure, the ones that remained managed to instill confidence in the outcome of voluminous listening.

The Golden Nica is a brilliant, clear and exquisite winner, voted unanimously, with the runners up causing some controversy, and yet ultimately sailing through. In the circle of the top three: the Japanese Ryoji Ikeda, with his ultra-minimal and powerful work *Matrix*, explores how we perceive

bisher unveröffentlichen Mixes und zahllosen Out-Takes. So sehr die Juroren die absolute Bedeutung dieser Werke zu schätzen wissen, die die Begriffe von Copyright, Sampling und Aneignung auf den Prüfstand stellen, wie sie in der gegenwärtigen MP3-Napster-Debatte vorherrschen – wir fanden dennoch, dass eine Auszeichnung für ein Lebenswerk nicht in den Rahmen der Richtlinien des Prix Ars Electronica passen, die jede neue Jury für sich neu evaluieren muss.

Denn wir haben genug gefunden, was uns wertvoll erschien … Es ist immer schwierig, ein elaboriert komponiertes Stück Musik mit einer Audio-Installation zu vergleichen und zu einem ausgewogenen Urteil zu kommen. Die Klänge, die von einer solchen Installation ausgehen, werden zumeist von den Parametern der Skulptur selbst determiniert und nicht so sehr von den musikalisch-kompositorischen Strukturen, die die „Komponisten" im Studio definieren. Ungeachtet des Formats mussten wir uns damit auseinandersetzen, wie man den Klang erlebt, ob er aus horizontal-linearer oder aus vertikaler Notenorientierter Entwicklung entsteht oder aus dem Einfluss vorgefundener Umweltquellen. Sobald diese Konzepte abgeklärt sind, tauchen weitere Fragen auf: Welche Art von musikalischer Sprache übersetzen wir und wie spricht sie den Geist an? Dies waren die Kriterien jenseits des rein handwerklichen Geschicks. Und wenn etwas sehr einfach und mit rudimentären Mitteln realisiert wurde – wie „elektronisch" muss es dann eigentlich sein?

Als der Destillierprozess aus der enormen Fülle der Werke voranschritt, begann die Jury nach qualitativ besseren Einreichungen zu dürsten. Der Wunsch nach dem, was in dieser Runde nicht da war, löste einen lebhaften Austausch darüber aus, wie man effizienter gehaltvollere Werke anlocken könnte. Die Art und Weise, wie etwa die neuen MP3-Web-Label-Koalitionen arbeiten, bringt einen ganzen bisher in dieser Kategorie nicht beachteten Bereich ins Spiel und muss noch ein wenig stärker ins Blickfeld gerückt werden. Wenn auch einige Präsentationen durchaus noch etwas Feinschliff vertragen könnten, um das Interesse der Juroren schon innerhalb der ersten zwei bis drei Minuten des ersten Schnelldurchlaufes zu fesseln, so gaben

sound in space, offering us more of his refined and pulsating sine-tone ensembles; Marcus Popp (oval) from Germany, with a corroded sound palette, extracting more melodic and harmonic fragments from his noisy sources, and grounding his explorations in solid theory; and American laptop duo bLectum from bLechdom, who combine a whimsical sense, pop references, and a keen sense of show-womanship to DSP programming, creating both witty and enlivening music. With this trio of winners, there exists an axis from which many compelling musical ideas are emerging. The remaining twelve honorary mentions include an installation from Ted Apel, which uses light-bulbs as sound sources; refined work from the extreme edges of frequency perception by Richard Chartier; abrasive gestures and stripped breakbeats from Louis Dufort; an installation soundtrack from Orm Finnendahl; repetitive, barely-perceived sounds displaced from their usual habitat, and shaped into alluring textures by John Hudak; Lesser and kid606's virtuosic, exciting pop deconstructions, bringing an obsessive use and mastery of sound mangling to the live context; Pan sonic's detailed shaping of sounds, creating stripped-down sonic archery, revealing with this release an increased interest in the use of space/reverb; Alejandra Salinas/Aeron Bergmann/Lucky Kitchen's original merging of field recording materials with synthesized sources to create documentary-like narratives; the sonically rich musique-concrète-meets-vinyl-aberration approach in Janek Schaefer's work; as well as two significant and complimentary compilations from Mille Plateaux and Tigerbeat6.

uns doch die nach der ersten Runde verbleibenden Werke Vertrauen in das Ergebnis der sehr umfangreichen Anhörung.

Der Gewinner der Goldenen Nica ist ein brillantes, klares und exquisites Werk, das einstimmig gewählt wurde, während die beiden Auszeichnungen einige Kontroversen auslösten, sich letztlich aber durchgesetzt haben. Im Zirkel der besten drei: der Japaner Ryoji Ikeda, der mit seinem ultra-minimalistischen und kraftvollen Werk *Matrix* erforscht, wie wir Klang im Raum erleben, und uns dabei mehr von seinen raffinierten und pulsierenden Sinus-Ton-Ensembles bietet; Markus Popp (oval) aus Deutschland mit einer korrodierten Klangpalette, der aus seinen geräuschvollen Quellen eher melodische und harmonische Fragmente destilliert und seine Erforschung auf solider theoretischer Grundlage aufbaut; und das amerikanischen Laptop-Duo bLectum from bLechdom, die mit schrägem Humor, Pop-Bezügen und einem ausgeprägten Sinn für das Show-Frau-Sein in der DSP-Programmierung eine sowohl witzige wie belebende Musik schaffen. Dieses Trio von Siegern verbindet eine Achse, aus der zahlreiche fesselnde musikalische Ideen entspringen. Die zwölf Anerkennungen schließen eine Installation von Ted Apel ein, die Glühbirnen als Klangquellen verwendet; eine raffinierte Arbeit an den extremen Rändern der Frequenzwahrnehmung von Richard Chartier; die abrasiven Gesten und stripped Backbeats von Louis Dufort; einen Installations-Soundtrack von Orm Finnendahl; repetitive, kaum wahrzunehmende Klänge, von John Hudak aus ihrem natürlichen Umfeld herausgelöst und in verlockende Texturen umgeformt; virtuose aufregende Pop-Dekonstruktionen von Lesser und kid606, die geradezu obsessiv die Verwendung und Beherrschung des Sound-Manglings in einen Livekontext stellen; Pan sonics detaillierte Klangformung, die eine Art reduziertes klangliches Bogenschießen schafft und in dieser Ausgabe ein wachsendes Interesse an der Verwendung von Hall und Echo beweist; Alejandra Salinas / Aeron Bergman / Lucky Kitchens originelle Verschmelzung von O-Tönen mit synthetisierten Quellen zu beinahe dokumentarischen Erzählungen; der musikalisch reiche Ansatz in Janek Schaefers Arbeit, der sich nur als „Musique Concrète Meets Vinyl Aberration" umschreiben lässt; und nicht zuletzt die beiden signifikanten Kompilationen von Mille Plateaux und Tigerbeat6.

THE MESSY JESSE FIESTA
bLectum from bLechdom

Oakland, CA, usa: kevin bLechdom and bLevin bLectum from bLectum from bLechdom stumbled upon each other at a gig on halloween 1998. kevin and blevin intersected unintentionally while one faded out and the other faded in; at that moment something happened, both of their musics fit together in a way that made them look deep into each other's eyes and then they nodded.

bLectum and bLechdom began a weekly electronic music series in the basement of the mills college concert hall, called the gLobule. here blectum learned the true joys of playing electronic music in a dusty, dank, occasionally wind-filled snaus-infested hole in the ground, accessed only via stolen key.

to overcome the foul environment, they drank some whiskey. this is how the "messy" part of the *messy jesse fiesta* came to be. they would play live with two loosely-synced rhythmic patterns, constantly having to reset the pattern and adjust the tempo. they reveled in their asynchronicity and un-MIDI confusion. bLectum was just playing music together any old way they wanted to. the messiest part is that bLevin's instruments used BPM to measure time and kevin's instruments used milliseconds to measure time, so they were always off a little, depending on their long division and quality of listening. bLectum's recorded music is highly dependent on their live performances. most of their songs are condensed versions of live shows. they would take a 30 minute live set and keep what they thought was essential and edit the song down to two or three minutes. and then use even smaller edits as source material in future performances.

jesse is a character in Paul Morissey's movie *HEAT*. (produced by Andy Warhol). she is one of kevin's favorite movie characters, and her voice is sampled on the *messy jesse fiesta*. blevin has a favorite song by Jim Copp and Ed Brown, called *messy bess*, telling the sad tale of a woman trapped in her own messy home, doomed to forever watch tv alone. the song goes "how 'bout jesse? worse than jesse! worse than tessy? hesse? jesse? messy messy bess!" and bLectum used this song on a radio show, where they gave away a free trip to costa rica to anyone who could answer the question they would sing: "who was the messiest

Oakland, CA, USA: Kevin bLechdom und bLevin bLectum von bLectum from bLechdom stolperten bei einem Gig zu Halloween 1988 übereinander. Kevin und bLevin überschnitten sich sozusagen unerwarteter Weise gegenseitig, als die eine aus- und die andere einblendete, und in diesem Augenblick passierte etwas – die Musiken der beiden passten auf eine Art und Weise zusammen, die sie veranlasste, tief in die Augen der jeweils anderen zu schauen, und dann nickten sie.

bLectum und bLechdom begannen eine wöchentliche Serie elektronischer Musik im Keller des Konzerthauses am Mills College, das „The gLobule" genannt wurde. Hier lernte bLectum die wahren Freuden kennen, elektronische Musik in einem staubigen, muffigen, manchmal windgefüllten Snaus-belasteten Loch im Boden zu machen, das nur mit einem gestohlenen Schlüssel zugänglich ist.

Um der miesen Umgebung zu entrinnen, tranken sie etwas Whisky – und so wurde der „messy"-Teil, der schlampige Teil von *the messy jesse fiesta* geboren. Sie spielten immer live, mit zwei nur lose synchronisierten rhythmischen Mustern, mussten stets Resets für diese Muster machen und das Tempo einregeln. Sie genossen diese Asynchronizität und die nicht-MIDI-gerechte Konfusion. bLectum spielten gemeinsam Musik auf jede beliebige Art, wie sie gerade wollten. Der konfuseste Teil ist, dass bLevins Instrumente Schläge pro Minute als Maßeinheit für die Zeit verwendeten, während Kevins Instrumente auf Millisekunden zur Zeitmessung eingeregelt waren, weshalb sie immer eine Kleinigkeit auseinander waren, je nach Hörgenauigkeit und wegen ihrer mathematischen Fähigkeiten. bLectums aufgenommene Musik hängt stark von ihren Live-Performances ab. Die meisten ihrer Songs sind eingedampfte Fassungen von Live-Shows. Sie nehmen eine 30-minütigen Liveaufnahme, behalten nur, was sie für essenziell halten, und schneiden den Song auf zwei oder drei Minuten zusammen. Und dann verwenden sie noch kürzere Schnitte als Ausgangsmaterial für zukünftige Performances.

Jesse ist eine Figur in Paul Morissey's Film *HEAT* (produziert von Andy Warhol). Sie ist eine der Lieblingsfilmgestalten von Kevin, und

at the fiesta? bessy? jesse? tessy? or hesse?" because kevin needed a date to her aunt's wedding. but the competition was rigged. so that's the "jesse" part of the *messy jesse fiesta*. and of course the "fiesta."

sound sources used within *messy jesse fiesta*—recordings from inside a pig farm, tearing tree-bark and slapping leaves, broken beatnik banks, Orban testing procedures, Kramer howling like a wolf, home ecstasy experiments caught on video, found 24-track school projects at wrong speeds, disco banghra cassettes, Jad Fair making pig/monster sounds, drum machines, digital synths, original max/msp patches, peak and protools… frustrated musical theater enthusiasts at the stroke of midnight… all dissected, regurgitated, reborn, re-combined, by both bLectums inside and outside of each bLectum separately and simultaneously.

ihre Stimme wurde in *the messy jesse fiesta* eingesampelt. bLevin hat ein Lieblingslied von Jim Copp und Ed Brown, das „Messy Bess" heißt und die traurige Geschichte einer Frau erzählt, die durch ihre Schlamperei im eigenen Heim gefangen ist, auf immer verdammt, alleine fern zu sehen. Der Text dazu lautet „how 'bout jesse? worse than jesse! worse than tessy? hesse? jesse? messy messy bess!" („Und was ist mit Jesse? Schlimmer als Jesse! Schlimmer als Tessy? Hesse? Jesse? Schlampige, schlampige Bess!"), und bLectum verwendeten diesen Song bei einem Radioauftritt, wo sie jedem einen Gratisflug nach Costa Rica versprachen, der die gesungene Frage beantworten konnte: „Who was the messiest at the fiesta, Bessy, Jesse, Tessy, or Hessy?" („Wer war beim Fest am schlampigsten – Bessy, Jesse, Tessy oder Hessy?"), weil Kevin einen Begleiter zur Hochzeit ihrer Tante brauchte. Aber die Komposition stand, und das ist der „Jesse"-Teil der *the messy jesse fiesta*, und natürlich die Fiesta.

Klangquellen, die innerhalb von *the messy jesse fiesta* verwendet wurden: Aufnahmen aus einer Schweinefarm, abbrechende Baumrinde und flatternde Blätter, Orban-Test-Prozeduren, gebrochene Beatnik-Banks, Kramer heulend wie ein Wolf, Videoaufnahmen von Ecstasy-Experimenten zuhause, gefundene 24-Spur-Aufnahmen aus der Schule mit falscher Geschwindigkeit, Disco-Banghra-Kassetten, Jad Fair mit Schweine- und Monstergeräuschen, Drum Machines, digitale Synthesizer, originale Max/MSP-Patches, Peaks und Protools … frustrierte Musiktheater-Enthusiasten um Schlag Mitternacht, alles seziert, wieder ausgespuckt, wiedergeboren, wieder kombiniert, von beiden bLectums innerhalb und außerhalb eines jeden bLectums getrennt und simultan.

KEVIN BLECHDOM AND BLEVIN BLECTUM FROM BLECTUM FROM BLECHDOM WERE BORN ON HALLOWEEN 1998 IN OAKLAND, CALIFORNIA. BLECTUM IS A DIGITAL DUO, OCCASIONALLY JOINED AT THE HIP, WHOSE SPECIALTY IS NOXIOUS, NAUSEOUS AND OBNOXIOUS SUPER MUSIC. THEIR SOUND RANGES FROM MOTIVATIONAL NEW AGE ZONES INTO RAUCOUS COUNTRY JAM-DOWNS OVER TO HYPER-PORNOGRAPHIC SINGING SONGS AND THEN BACK TO EVIL AND PSYCHOTIC DANCE FLOOR BASS-A-THONS. THEY ARE USUALLY CONFUSED AND SUSPENDED BETWEEN OPPOSING FORCES CAUSING THEM INTERNAL ANGST, WHICH FUELS THEIR BAD REPUTATIONS AND UNRULY TEMPERS. THEY ARE NOT WHERE YOU'RE GOING AND HAVE BEEN, BECAUSE THEY WILL BE WHERE YOU WERE WHEN THEY HAD YOU AND WILL CONTINUE TO BE WITH YOU FROM NOW UNTIL YOURS ARE OVER. ■■■ Kevin bLechdom und bLevin bLectum von bLectum from bLechdom wurden zu Halloween 1998 in Okland, Kalifornien geboren. bLectum ist ein digitales Duo, gelegentlich an der Hüfte verbunden, dessen Spezialität ungesunde, schmerzhafte und hartnäckige Super-Musik ist. Ihr Klang reicht von motivbestimmten New-Age-Zones über rauhe Country-Jam-Downs bis hin zu hyperpornografischem Singsang und zurück zu bösartigen und psychotischen Dance-Floor-Bassausbrüchen. Sie sind normalerweise konfus und in Spannung zwischen entgegengesetzten Kräften, die ihnen innerliche Angst verursachen, die ihren schlechten Ruf und ihr unbezähmbares Temperament antreibt. Sie sind nicht dort, wo du hingehst und wo du warst, weil sie sein werden, wo du warst, als sie dich hatten, und werden bei dir sein ab jetzt, bis deine vorbei sind.

MATRIX
Ryoji Ikeda

Ikeda's new release *Matrix* is the final element in a trilogy of CDs that began with +/- in 1996. When it was first released, it came like a bolt out of the white. Nobody had used digital recording processes to produce sound as pure, as intense and as exhilarating. Since releasing *0°* in 1998, Ryoji Ikeda has progressively refined and enhanced the distinctive sonic fields and micro sounds that have strongly influenced post-digital composition, creating sculptural compositions that probe deeply our relationships to time and space, sound and light.

Ikeda's work is fundamentally about perception. The layers of sound that make up *Matrix [for rooms]* transform both the listener and the listening environment into another dimension. The dimensions change as you move about the space, or simply turn your head around the sound, like surveying the angles of a building. Ikeda states that the sound "forms an invisible pattern which fills the listening space," whereby "the listener's movement transforms the phenomenon into his/her intrapersonal music." Ikeda has created an undeniable sound space that one can walk right through and get lost in.

In January 2000, Ryoji Ikeda created an untitled 30-minute performance that toured the UK, selling out at all 5 venues including the Queen Elizabeth Hall in London and Contact Theatre in Manchester*. In live performance, Ikeda combined his high impact sound with video projections synched perfectly to the music by use of time code. Digitally generated graphics, high-speed video sequences and stroboscopic lighting connected with the sound to create a spectacular yet intimate experience for the viewer.

The Wire wrote:

"He began with *Headphonics*, a piece he started working on in 1995. It's perhaps the purest example of his work: constructed from very simple tones, some at the extremes of audible range and beyond, with loops of great simplicity laid over each other to create an extremely affecting interlocked mesh of machine noises…" The video for this opening section was correspondingly simple: X and Y axes flashing across a huge dark screen with a pulsing point at its centre. It was utterly mesmeric.

"Ikeda then moved into +/-. Images of digits ticking

Ikedas neues Album *Matrix* ist das letzte Element in einer CD-Trilogie, die 1996 mit +/- begann. Letztere wirkte bei ihrem Erscheinen wie ein Blitz aus heiterem Himmel – niemand hatte je zuvor digitale Aufnahmeprozesse eingesetzt, um so reinen, so intensiven, so fröhlich stimmenden Klang zu erzeugen. Seit der CD *0°* aus dem Jahr 1998 hat Ryoji Ikeda diese einzigartigen Klangfelder und Mikroklänge, die die post-digitale Komposition so stark beeinflusst haben, weiter verfeinert und damit skulpturenhafte Kompositionen geschaffen, die unsere Beziehung zu Raum und Zeit, zu Klang und Licht so intensiv hinterfragen.

In Ikedas Werken geht es grundsätzlich um Wahrnehmung. Die Klangebenen, aus denen sich *Matrix [for rooms]* zusammensetzt, versetzen sowohl den Hörer wie auch die Hörumgebung in eine andere Dimension. Die Dimensionen verschieben sich in dem Maße, in dem man sich im Raum bewegt; es ist, als würde man den Kopf um den Klang drehen, als wollte man ihn wie ein Gebäude von allen Seiten betrachten. Für Ikeda bildet der Klang „ein unsichtbares Muster, das den Hörraum ausfüllt", wobei „die Bewegung des Hörers das Phänomen in eine Art intrapersonale Musik umformt." Ikeda hat tatsächlich einen Klangraum geschaffen, in den man einfach hineinspazieren und in dem man sich verirren kann.

Im Januar 2000 war Ikeda mit einer unbetitelten 30-Minuten-Performance auf Tournee in Großbritannien, wobei alle fünf Aufführungen – darunter jene in der Queen Elizabeth Hall in London und im Contact Theatre in Manchester – ausverkauft waren.* Bei der Liveperformance kombinierte Ikeda seinen höchst eindringlichen Klang mit Video-Projektionen, die über Time-Codes perfekt mit der Musik abgestimmt waren.Digitale Grafiken, Hochgeschwindigkeits Videosequenzen und stroboskopische Lichteffekte verbanden sich mit dem Klang zu einer spektakulären und für die Besucher doch intimen Erfahrung.

The Wire schrieb dazu:

„Er begann mit *Headphonics*, einem Stück, an dem er 1995 zu arbeiten begann. Es ist vielleicht das reinste Beispiel seiner Arbeit: aus ganz einfachen Tönen zusammengesetzt –

around shot up the screen like a waterfall of numbers in reverse. The passage between musical episodes was marked by intense white flashes that lit up the auditorium. The link between images and music was close and intelligent—as the range of reference in the music grew wider, so the visuals began to depart from abstraction and include fleeting images. It was a powerfully physical event, probing the effect on the body of visual and sonic repetition and sucking the spectator into a vibrant monotone world. While this aspect of the show was intensely private, the feeling of exposure to such large sounds and images gave the music a sense of group involvement. It was more a collective experience than is usually possible in such an auditorium." (*Will Montgomery*)

manche davon sind an der Grenze oder jenseits der Grenze des Hörbaren angesiedelt, mit Schleifen von bestechender Einfachheit, die einander überlagern, um ein extrem fesselndes Netz von Maschinengeräuschen zu knüpfen …" Das Video dieser Eröffnungssequenz war ebenfalls entsprechend simpel konstruiert: X- und Y-Achsen, die über einen großen dunkeln Bildschirm mit nur einem pulsierenden Punkt in der Mitte blitzten – es war nachgerade hypnotisierend. Dann ging Ikeda zu +/- über. Bilder von tickenden Zahlen schossen den Bildschirm hinauf wie ein auf den Kopf stehender Wasserfall von Zahlen. Der Übergang zwischen den musikalischen Episoden wurde durch intensive weiße Blitze markiert, die den Zuhörerraum erhellten. Die Verknüpfung zwischen Bildern und Musik war eng und intelligent – in dem Maß, in dem sich das Spektrum der Bezüge in der Musik erweiterte, verabschiedete sich die Bildwelt zunehmend von der Abstraktion und begann, flüchtige Bilder einzuschließen. Es war ein stark physisch geprägtes Ereignis, das den Effekt klanglicher und visueller Repetition auf den Körper testete und die Zuseher gleichsam in eine vibrierende monotone Welt hineinsaugte. Und obwohl dieser Aspekt der Veranstaltung sich sehr persönlich gestaltete, vermittelte doch das Gefühl, solch großen Klängen und Bildern ausgesetzt zu sein, der Musik ein gewisses Guppenerlebnis – es war eine viel stärkere kollektive Erfahrung, als in solch einem Auditorium normalerweise möglich ist." (Will Montgomery)

* These performances were commissioned and produced by David Metcalfe Associates, with the visuals being developed through collaboration between Ikeda and other members of the Dumb Type art group, Shiro Takatani [video], Hiromasa Tomari [video] and Takayuki Fujimoto [lighting].

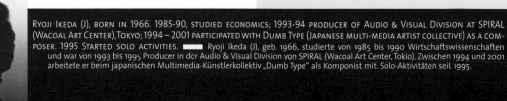

RYOJI IKEDA (J), BORN IN 1966. 1985-90, STUDIED ECONOMICS; 1993-94 PRODUCER OF AUDIO & VISUAL DIVISION AT SPIRAL (WACOAL ART CENTER),TOKYO; 1994 – 2001 PARTICIPATED WITH DUMB TYPE (JAPANESE MULTI-MEDIA ARTIST COLLECTIVE) AS A COMPOSER. 1995 STARTED SOLO ACTIVITIES. ▬ Ryoji Ikeda (J), geb. 1966, studierte von 1985 bis 1990 Wirtschaftswissenschaften und war von 1993 bis 1995 Producer in der Audio & Visual Division von SPIRAL (Wacoal Art Center, Tokio). Zwischen 1994 und 2001 arbeitete er beim japanischen Multimedia-Künstlerkollektiv „Dumb Type" als Komponist mit. Solo-Aktivitäten seit 1995.

OVALPROCESS / OVALCOMMERS
Markus Popp / oval

Ovalprocess is an interdisciplinary, modular, dynamic music project, comprising a software application, a series of audio CDs, a lecture, and (as of April 2001) three interactive sound installation objects of varying size and dimensions. All components are conceptually interwoven and modeled after the unique oval strategies to sound, structure and musical aesthetics.

ovalprocess as a whole is an attempt to suggest a model for one possible alternative approach to audio productivity in contemporary electronic music along the lines of a definition of music-as-software. Formatted as a series of retail CD formats, sound installation objects, concert events and lectures, its ambition is to represent a discursive, engaging and user-centric, potentially controversial effort, in order to propose a new dialogue and to shift the focus of attention to problems and questions of software design, ergonomics and multimedia authoring, in order to suggest additional criteria to electronic music discourse.

ovalprocess and its sequel, commers, are more than just spin-off products, but rather audible milestones, documenting the ongoing development of the oval audio content workflow, the process software application, and its sound installation counterparts.The audio CD releases both represent works in their own right, each pursuing a distinctive, contrasting musical rhetoric. Each CD aims to interpret and at times fundamentally transform the underlying tech specs and formal boundaries of the process concept.

The actual process software application—currently exclusively designed for the MacOS and implemented by programmer Richard Ross, based in San Francisco —is a first attempt to represent a model for a typical workflow in contemporary digital audio productivity, while at the same time precisely delineating the underlying musical strategies behind oval—as applied on the various oval recordings past and present—as well as displaying the inherent deliberate limitations of this particular musical approach.

The process sound installation objects were created in cooperation with architecture company sko-toparc, Berlin, and are designed to serve as a tangible, interactive front-end to the process software and the included original sound-file content. They effectively

ovalprocess ist ein interdisziplinäres, modulares, dnyamisches Musikprojekt, das aus einer Software-Applikation, einer Serie von Audio-CDs, Vorträgen und (seit April 2001) aus drei interaktiven Klanginstallations-Objekten unterschiedlicher Größe und Form besteht. Alle Komponenten sind konzeptuell miteinander verwoben und nach den einzigartigen oval-Strategien für Klang, Struktur und musikalische Ästhetik modelliert.

ovalprocess als Ganzes ist der Versuch, ein Modell für einen möglichen alternativen Ansatz in der Audio-Produktivität der zeitgenössischen Musik zu präsentieren, der auf der Definition von Musik als Software basiert. Formell präsentiert als Serie von CDs, Klanginstallations-Objekten, Konzertereignissen und Vorträgen, versucht ovalprocess auf diskursanregende, fesselnde und benutzerorientierte – wenn auch vielleicht kontroversielle – Weise, einen neuen Dialog vorzuschlagen und das Augenmerk auf Fragen und Probleme des Software-Designs, der Ergonomie und des Multimedia-Authoring im Allgemeinen zu lenken, um dem Diskurs der elektronischen Musik weitere Kriterien anzubieten.

ovalprocess und sein Folgeprojekt commers sind mehr als nur Nebenprodukte, vielmehr sind sie hörbare Meilensteine, die die fortschreitende Entwicklung des oval-Audio-Content-Workflows ebenso dokumentieren wie die process-Softwareapplikation und die zugehörigen Klanginstallationen. Die beiden Audio-CD-Ausgaben stellen eigenständige Werke dar, die jeweils eine eindeutige kontrastierende musikalische Sprache verfolgen. Jede CD zielt darauf ab, die zu Grunde liegenden technischen Spezifikationen und formalen Grenzen des process-Konzepts zu interpretieren und bisweilen grundlegend zu verändern.

Die eigentliche process-Softwareanwendung – derzeit nur für das MacOS verfügbar und vom Programmierer Richard Ross (San Francisco) implementiert – ist ein erster Versuch, ein Modell für den typischen Arbeitsablauf in der zeitgenössischen Audio-Produktion darzustellen und gleichzeitig die musikalischen Strategien hinter oval präzise nachzuzeichnen, wie sie den diversen vergangenen und gegenwärtigen Aufnahmen von oval zu Grunde liegen, sowie die

enable the user to re-structure the latest work-in-progress from the dynamically evolving oval audio research, shifting the overall impetus from a conventional music presentation / distribution format towards a personalized work environment.

Software

In short, the *ovalprocess* software is an interactive authoring environment for personal contemporary desktop audio along the lines of the unique oval approach to electronic music. It is designed to offer an accessible, directly manipulable, fully iconic, object-oriented user interface operating in real time.

The applications' workflow focuses less on the typical sampling, mixing and editing functionality of generic productivity software, but instead offers detailed means for structural changes to the included oval soundfile archive. By effectively enabling the user/audience to configure, layout and perform customized recordings oval-style by radically restructuring the provided sound files via an intuitive, color-coded user interface, process proposes a dialogue on time-based software environments.

inhärenten und gewollten Einschränkungen dieses speziellen musikalischen Ansatzes aufzuzeigen. Die *process*-Klanginstallationsobjekte wurden in Zusammenarbeit mit der Architekturfirma sko-toparc in Berlin konstruiert und sollen als greifbares interaktives Front-End der *process*-Software und des darin inkludierten originalen Klanginhalts dienen. Sie erlauben es dem Benutzer, das jüngste Work-in-progress der sich dynamisch entwickelnden oval-Audio-Research umzustrukturieren und von einem konventionellen Musik-Präsentations- bzw. -Distributionsformat in eine personalisierte Arbeitsumgebung umzuwandeln.

Software

Kurz gefasst, repräsentiert *ovalprocess* ein interaktives Authoring-Environment für zeitgemäßes Personal Desktop Audio sowie einen *oval*-eigenen Zugang zur elektronischen Musik. Sie ist so designt, dass sie ein zugängliches, direkt manipulierbares, völlig auf Icons aufgebautes objektorientiertes User-Interface für Echtzeitverarbeitung anbietet.

Der Workflow der Anwendung konzentriert sich weniger auf die üblichen Sampling-, Mix- und Editier-funktionen der gängigen Produktivitätssoftware, sondern bietet detaillierte Mittel zur strukturellen Veränderung des beigefügten oval-Soundfile-Archivs. Indem dem Benutzer bzw. dem Publikum tatsächlich die Möglichkeit gegeben wird, über das intuitive, farbcodierte Interface eigene Aufnahmen im oval-Stil durch radikale Re-Strukturierung der mitgelieferten Klangfiles zu konfigurieren, designen und aufzunehmen, bringt *process* einen Dialog über zeitbasierte Software-Environments ins Rollen.

MARKUS POPP (D), BORN IN DARMSTADT ON 24.02.1968, LIVES AND WORKS IN BERLIN, GERMANY. ■■■ Markus Popp (D), geboren 1968 in Darmstadt, lebt und arbeitet in Berlin.

POTENTIAL DIFFERENCE
Ted Apel

Piezoelectricity was discovered at the same time that Thomas Edison made his major breakthrough in his work on the incandescent light bulb. The present installation consists of several incandescent light bulbs and corresponding piezoelectric "sound bulbs". The sound levels of the electroacoustic sound bulbs modulate the luminosity of corresponding light bulbs.

The cultural and economic impact of the light bulb has been incomparably greater than that of the piezoelectric element. Yet in both, a small amount of material is activated by electricity, producing two phenomena, the one resulting in sound, the other in light. These sound bulbs allow us to consider the piezoelectric element in the context of the light bulb. By drawing attention to the filament and piezoelectric element, the installation highlights both the technological similarities between them as well as the disparity in their cultural significance.

The light bulb is not meant to be looked at, but to illuminate objects and spaces. The loudspeaker is similarly not designed as a focus of visual or sonic attention. It is designed to invisibly reproduce a sonic environment independent of the loudspeaker. In this installation the filament is the focus of visual attention and the piezoelectric element is the focus of sonic attention. In this way, the meaning of the sounds cannot be separated from how they are transduced. The installation attempts to use the cultural significance of the light bulb and the specific technologies of the filament and the piezoelectric element to expand the context in which we understand and experience sound.

Piezoelektrizität wurde zur gleichen Zeit entdeckt, wie Thomas Edison den Durchbruch in seiner Arbeit an der weißglühenden Glühlampe schaffte. Die Installation *Potential Difference* besteht aus einigen weißglühenden Glühbirnen und entsprechenden piezoelektrischen „Klangbirnen". Die Schallpegel der elektroakustischen Klangbirnen modulieren die Leuchten der entsprechenden Glühbirnen.

Die kulturelle und ökonomische Auswirkung der Glühbirne ist unvergleichbar größer als die des piezoelektrischen Elements. Dennoch: In beiden wurde Material durch Elektrizität aktiviert, was zwei Phänomene produziert: das eine als Ton, das andere als Licht. Die Klangbirnen erlauben uns, das piezoelektrische Element im Kontext der Glühbirne zu betrachten. Indem die Aufmerksamkeit auf den Leuchtfaden der Glühbirne und auf das piezoelektrischen Element gelenkt wird, zeigt die Anlage sowohl die technologischen Ähnlichkeiten zwischen ihnen als auch die Verschiedenheit ihrer kulturellen Bedeutung.

Die Glühbirne ist nicht dazu da, angeschaut zu werden, sondern erhellt Objekte und Räume. Ähnlich ist der Lautsprecher auch nicht als Fokus der Sicht- oder Schallaufmerksamkeit designt. Er ist dazu da, ein Schallklima unsichtbar zu reproduzieren, das vom Lautsprecher unabhängig ist. In dieser Installation ist der Leuchtfaden der Fokus der Sichtaufmerksamkeit und das piezoelektrische Element ist der Fokus der Schallaufmerksamkeit. So kann die Bedeutung der Töne nicht davon getrennt werden, wie sie ausgestrahlt werden. Die Anlage versucht, die kulturelle Bedeutsamkeit der Glühbirne und der spezifischen Technologien des Leuchtfadens und des piezoelektrischen Elements zu verwenden, um den Kontext zu erweitern, in dem wir Ton verstehen und erfahren.

TED APEL (USA) IS A SOUND ARTIST WHOSE SCULPTURES AND INSTALLATIONS FOCUS ON THE AUDIO TRANSDUCING ELEMENT AS THE SOURCE OF VISUAL AND SONIC MATERIAL. HIS SOUND INSTALLATIONS HAVE BEEN SHOWN AT THE AUDIO ART FESTIVAL IN CRACOW, THE SOUND SYMPOSIUM IN ST. JOHN'S NEWFOUNDLAND, AND THE SOUNDCULTURE FESTIVAL IN SAN FRANCISCO. HE STUDIED ELECTROACOUSTIC MUSIC AT DARTMOUTH COLLEGE WITH JON APPLETON, LARRY POLANSKY AND CHRISTIAN WOLFF. HE IS CURRENTLY THE TECHNICAL DIRECTOR OF THE CENTER FOR RESEARCH IN COMPUTING IN THE ARTS (CRCA) AT THE UNIVERSITY OF CALIFORNIA, SAN DIEGO. ▬ Ted Apel (USA) ist ein Klangkünstler, dessen Skulpturen und Installationen auf der Klangleitfähigkeit als Quelle des visuellen und auditiven Materials beruhen. Seine Klanginstallationen wurden beim Audio Art Festival in Krakau, beim Sound Symposium in St. John's (Neufundland) und beim SoundCulture Festival in San Francisco präsentiert. Er hat elektroakustische Musik am Dartmouth College bei Jon Appleton, Larry Plansky und Christian Wolff studiert und ist derzeit technischer Leiter des Center for Research in Computing in the Arts (CRCA) der University of California, San Diego.

HAUNTED FOLKLORE ONE: "RUINAS ENCANTADAS"
Aeron Bergman / Alejandra Salinas / Lucky Kitchen

The title means "haunted ruins", although "encantado" is also what you say in Spanish when you first meet someone, meaning that you have been touched somehow by their presence. Based roughly around the idea of fantasy, we ask: what is folklore? With a healthy belief in the future, based on a continuous dialogue with the past, imagination is totally relevant. Religion, rituals, and future utopia are public fantasies to transcend the empirical world and appreciate the mysteries of being here. Contemporary utopian images are stunted, thus limiting possible change. We offer our ideas of contemporary audio fantasy.

All sounds are based on legends and folk tales.

Brief notes on our use of technology

Using our electronic tools of preference, this work considers the past, while not repeating it. It is not interesting to merely state that we are using the computer. (Businessmen, grandmas, bus drivers, athletes, congresswomen, lawyers, artists, and yes, musicians all over the world have used computers in their daily life for several generations now. Describing computers as "new media" is like saying oil paint is new because it was invented after bone carving.) Instead, we suggest that the folklore of our time is as much online as it is offline.

Basically, we are brewing up a storytelling storm, where the medium is the medium, and not the message itself.

Likewise, Lucky Kitchen presents technology as a commonplace communication medium of secondary importance to the ideas behind it. Lucky Kitchen is as personal as it is technical. Lucky Kitchen presents our own work and the work of others, when we find special qualities somewhere between technique and sentiment ...

Der Titel bedeutet „verzauberte Ruinen", aber „encantado" sagt man im Spanischen auch, wenn man jemandem vorgestellt wird, von dessen Gegenwart man sehr erfreut ist – der einen „verzaubert". Ausgehend vom Konzept von „Fantasie" fragen wir uns: Was ist Folklore? Wenn man einen gesunden Glauben an die Zukunft hat, der auf einem kontinuierlichen Dialog mit der Vergangenheit aufbaut, spielt die Imagination eine ganz große Rolle. Religion, Rituale und Zukunftsutopien sind öffentliche Fantasien, die es ermöglichen, über die empirische Welt hinauszugehen und die dem Mysterium des Hierseins einen neuen Wert beimessen. Zeitgenössische utopische Bilder sind sehr reduziert und beschränken dadurch mögliche Veränderungen. Wir bieten unsere Vorstellung einer zeitgemäßen Audio-Fantasie an.

Alle Klänge basieren auf Legenden und Volkssagen.

Kurze Anmerkungen zum Einsatz der Technologie

Diese Arbeit, bei der wir unsere bevorzugten elektronischen Werkzeuge einsetzen, reflektiert über die Vergangenheit, ohne sie zu wiederholen. Es ist nicht interessant, nur mitzuteilen, dass wir den Computer verwenden (Musiker auf der ganzen Welt verwenden mittlerweile seit mehreren Generation die Computer. Computer als „Neue Medien" zu bezeichnen wäre so, als würde man Ölfarben für neu erklären, bloß weil sie lange nach der Höhlenmalerei erfunden wurden). Wir hingegen sind überzeugt davon, dass die Folklore unserer Zeit genauso online sein sollte, wie sie offline ist. Wir brauen sozusagen einen Geschichten erzählenden Sturm zusammen, bei dem das Medium das Medium ist und nicht die Botschaft. In diesem Sinne fasst Lucky Kitchen die Technologie als ein gewöhnliches Kommunikationsmedium auf, das gegenüber den dahinterstehenden Ideen sekundär ist. Lucky Kitchen ist so persönlich wie technisch. Lucky Kitchen präsentiert unsere Arbeit und ebenso die Arbeit anderer, wenn wir besondere Qualitäten irgendwo zwischen Technik und Gefühl entdecken ...

AERON BERGMAN (USA), STUDIED ART HISTORY AT MICHIGAN STATE UNIVERSITY, THE UNIVERSITY OF TORONTO, AND ART AND TECHNOLOGY AT NEW YORK UNIVERSITY. MARRIED ALEJANDRA SALINAS IN NYC, 1998. FORMED LUCKY KITCHEN WITH DANIEL RAFFEL AND A.S. IN 1997. LIVED IN LONDON AND CURRENTLY LIVES AND WORKS IN LOGRONO, SPAIN. ALEJANDRA SALINAS (E), STUDIED FINE ART AT THE SCHOOL OF VISUAL ARTS, NYC, AND LONDON GUILDHALL UNIVERSITY. MARRIED AERON BERGMAN IN NYC, 1998. FORMED LUCKY KITCHEN WITH DANIEL RAFFEL AND A.B. IN 1997. CURRENTLY LIVES AND WORKS IN LOGRONO, SPAIN. ■ Aeron Bergman (USA) studierte Kunstgeschichte an der Michigan State University und an der University of Toronto sowie Kunst und Technologie an der New York University. Er heiratete Alejandra Salinas 1998 in New York, nachdem er 1997 Lucky Kitchen mit Daniel Raffel und ihr gegründet hatte. Nach einem Aufenthalt in London lebt und arbeitet er in Logrono (Spanien). Alejandra Salinas (E) studierte bildende Kunst an der School of Visual Arts in New York und an der Londoner Guildhall University. 1997 gründete sie mit Aeron Berman und Daniel Raffel Lucky Kitchen, heiratete Bergman 1998, lebt und arbeitet mit ihm in Logrono (Spanien).

SERIES
Richard Chartier

Employing soft, hushed—almost imperceptible—high frequencies, bursts, static and quiet low shifting tones, the compositions of *Series* explore an implied silence that is not silent—a quietness that belies the activity and energy of the sounds. Compositional focus often occurs in the space between the sounds—the duration and meaning, which lay between barely audible events.

The sounds are treated with a sculptural integrity, revealing their aural and visual aspects. Each discrete crackle and hiss is endowed with a physicality, nearly transparent. Between the sound and the silence, the listener can begin to discern patterns in the static or the gentle bass pulses, which at first seem only insinuations of sound.

No narrative is present in these patterns—except that implied by the compositions' existence in time and the levels and plateaus serving as events within that temporal space. In this sense, rhythm is created, thus repetition becomes a predominating compositional quality in a number of the works. Knowable cycles slowly develop, but in that discernment of pattern comes the listeners' variances in perception. In experiencing a stretched out and slowed down serial composition requiring auditory focus, anticipation of the next sound's arrival makes even the faintest change in rhythm or introduction of alternate events significant and the spaces in between sounds concrete.

While separate in creation and capable of isolation, the works on *Series* are interrelated in respect to process and the period of their construction. Dissimilar in some respects, through acts of reduction and structure, each work bears an elemental relationship to the others. *Series*, like much of Chartier's work, explores the interdependence and focus required of sound, silence and the act of listening.

Durch Verwendung von leisen, gedämpften, fast unhörbaren hohen Frequenzen, von Ausbrüchen, Netzrauschen und ruhigen, tiefen wandernden Tönen, erforschen die Kompositionen von *Series* eine scheinbare Stille, die nicht still ist – eine Ruhe, die die Aktivität und Energie der Klänge Lügen straft.

Die Klänge werden mit fast bildhauerischer Akkuratesse bearbeitet, damit sie ihre visuellen und auditiven Aspekte enthüllen können. Jedes einzelne Knacken und Zischen ist mit einer Physis ausgestaltet und dennoch fast transparent. Zwischen Klang und Stille kann der Zuhörer beginnen, Muster im Rauschen und im sanften Pulsieren des Basses zu unterscheiden, das ihm zunächst nur als die Andeutung eines Klangs erschienen sein mag. In diesen Mustern versteckt sich keine Erzählung, abgesehen von jener, die in der zeitlichen Existenz der Komposition und in der Lautstärke und den Plateaus, die in diesem Zeit-Raum-Gefüge Ereignisse sind, impliziert ist. In diesem Sinne entsteht Rhythmus. Langsam entwickeln sich erkennbare Zyklen, aber zu dieser Unterscheidung von Mustern kommen die Variationen in der Wahrnehmung des Hörers.

Wenn man eine weit gedehnte und ganz langsame Komposition hört, die hohe Konzentration verlangt, dann lässt die Erwartung der Ankunft des nächsten Klangs selbst die geringsten Veränderungen im Rhythmus oder die Einführung alternativer Elemente signifikant und die Räume zwischen den Klängen konkret werden.

Wenn die Stücke in *Series* auch unabhängig voneinander entstanden und getrennt hörbar sind, so sind sie doch hinsichtlich des Prozesses und ihrer Entstehungszeit miteinander verknüpft. Trotz der Unterschiedlichkeit in mancher Hinsicht hat jede der Arbeiten eine elementare Beziehung zu allen anderen. Wie viele von Chartiers Arbeiten erforscht *Series* die gegenseitige Abhängigkeit von Klang, Stille und Hören und die erforderliche Konzentration.

RICHARD CHARTIER (USA), MINIMALIST SOUND ARTIST/COMPOSER, PAINTER AND GRAPHIC DESIGNER. HIS WORK EXPLORES THE RELATIONSHIP BETWEEN SOUND, SILENCE AND THE ART OF LISTENING. HIS VISUAL AND SOUND WORKS HAVE BEEN EXHIBITED IN NUMEROUS GALLERIES AND ARTSPACES OVER THE PAST 10 YEARS. SEPTEMBER 2000 MARKED THE BEGINNING OF THE RECORDING LABEL LINE, FOUNDED BY CHARTIER AND TAYLOR DEUPREE AS A SUBLABEL OF 12K FOCUSING NEW, DIGITAL, CONCEPTUAL, ULTRA-MINIMALIST SOUND ART. ■ Richard Chartier (USA), minimalistischer Klangkünstler, Komponist, Maler und Grafikdesigner. Seine Arbeit erforscht die Beziehung zwischen Klang, Stille und der Kunst der Zuhörens. Seine visuellen und auditiven Arbeiten waren in den letzten zehn Jahren in zahlreichen Galerien und Kunsträumen zu hören und zu sehen. Im September 2000 gründeten Chartier und Taylor Dupree das Label LINE als Sublabel von 12k, das seinen Schwerpunkt auf neuer digitaler konzeptueller ultra-minimalistischer Klangkunst hat.

DÉCAP
Louis Dufort

Décap is an extremely dense and eclectic work, both from the perspective of the sound material, and of style. On the morphological level, the work uses Drum & Bass as well as orchestral stamps, the voice of a woman to guttural male voices, while passing by Japanese traditional music to Gregorian chant. On the level of style, we pass by electroacoustic, experimental, industrial and modern music. The goal behind this eclecticism is to recreate a microcosm representing, to some extent, humanity in all its complexity and, more precisely, the horror of the conflicts that have been driving it for centuries. Closer to us, we have to think of the war in Kosovo or confrontations that last forever in Israel. Nowadays, these conflicts are televised and confront us with disconcerting images, where death is shown live on our daily news.

This piece is thus inspired by those bodies wracked by pain, from which the title Décap is taken. This title is actually the diminutive of the word Décapitation, but also Da capo; this musical term means return to beginning, showing the continual loop of violence. This cyclic aspect, represented by rhythmic loops, is very present in the work and leads it to the finale. The use of the voice is also very significant, because it represents the human being so clearly in its softness (voice of the woman), its pain (shouts), and in its animosity (guttural voice). The use of the voices of the No theatre at the beginning of work refers to the evil spirits which have always formed part of our collective unconscious and this independently of the religion or the time. Then there are the disturbed and strongly chopped sounds, which are intended to go into the entrails of the body just like a bullet from a rifle piercing the body.

Décap ist sowohl hinsichtlich des Klangmaterials als auch seines Stils ein extrem dichtes und eklektisches Werk. Auf der morphologischen Ebene verwendet das Werk Drums und Bass ebenso wie orchestrale Klänge, Frauenstimmen ebenso wie gutturale Männerstimmen, und es bewegt sich von traditioneller japanischer Musik bis zum gregorianischen Choral. Auf der stilistischen Ebene wandern wir durch elektroakustische, experimentelle, industrielle Musik. Das Ziel hinter diesem Eklektizismus ist es, einen Mikrokosmos zu erschaffen, der bis zu einem gewissen Grad die Menschheit in all ihrer Komplexität abbildet – genauer gesagt, den Schrecken aller Konflikte, die seit Jahrhunderten die wesentliche Antriebskraft sind. Wir brauchen nur an den Kosovo-Krieg ganz in unserer Nähe zu denken oder an die scheinbar immer während en Auseinandersetzungen in Israel. Heutzutage werden diese Konflikte im Fernsehen gezeigt, sie konfrontieren uns mit den beunruhigenden Bildern, die den Tod live in unseren täglichen Nachrichten zeigen.

Das Stück wird deshalb auch von jenen sich im Schmerz windenden Körpern inspiriert – daher auch der Titel Décap, der sowohl an „Décapitation" (Enthauptung) als auch an „da capo" erinnert, an jenen musikalischen Begriff, der die Wiederholung des Anfangs bezeichnet, die Rückkehr zur ewigen Schleife der Gewalt.

Dieser zyklische Aspekt, der in rhythmischen Schleifen zum Ausdruck kommt, ist im Werk sehr präsent und leitet es bis zum Finale. Auch die Verwendung der Stimme ist signifikant, da sie den Menschen als Lebewesen, sowohl in seiner Weichheit (Frauenstimme) als auch im Schmerz (Schreie) und in seiner Erregung (gutturale Stimme) repräsentiert. Die Stimmen aus dem No-Theater zu Beginn des Werks erinnern an die bösen Geister, die seit jeher Teil unseres kollektiven Unbewussten sind, unabhängig von der Religion oder der Zeit. Und dann gibt es noch die störenden und stark zusammengeschnittenen Klänge, die in die Eingeweide des Körpers eindringen wie eine Gewehrkugel, die ihn durchschlägt.

LOUIS DUFORT (CDN) HAS A BACHELOR'S DEGREE IN ELECTROACOUSTIC COMPOSITION FROM THE FACULTY OF MUSIC OF THE UNIVERSITÉ DE MONTREAL, AS WELL AS A MASTER'S DEGREE FROM THE CONSERVATOIRE DE MUSIQUE DE MONTREAL, WHERE HE RECEIVED A FIRST PRIZE WITH DISTINCTION. HE CURRENTLY DIVIDES HIS TIME BETWEEN COMPOSING FOR THE MARIE CHOUINARD CONTEMPORARY DANCE COMPANY, HIS WORK WITH THE ARTISTIC COMMITTEE OF ACREQ, AND THE CREATION OF HYBRID AND UNBRIDLED MUSICAL EXPERIMENTATION. ■■■ Louis Dufort (CDN) hat einen BFA in elektroakustischer Komposition an der Musikfakultät der Universität Montréal sowie einen Masters-Grad am Conservatoire de Musique de Montréal erworben, wo er auch einen Ersten Preis mit Auszeichnung erhielt. Er komponiert für die Marie-Chouinard-Tanzkompagnie, arbeitet für das künstlerische Komitee des ACREQ und widmet sich hybrider, ungezügelter musikalischer Experimente.

KOMMEN UND GEHEN
Orm Finnendahl

DIGITAL MUSICS

Kommen und Gehen was commissioned by the German pavillion at the World Expo in Hannover last year. It is conceived for violin and tape/live electronics. As the audience is fluctuating permanently through the building, the actual piece was prepared by a "preface" and a sound installation in the hall, which serves two purposes. While permitting people to stay or to leave the building at will, it tries to gain the attention of the audience using a strictly processural setup: The preface consists of a single pitch, played by the violin. This note is recorded and transmitted—electronically transformed—through the loudspeakers. In principle, the installation is a kind of "digestive" process, in which the resulting sounds are repeatedly transmitted through the system, and once again transformed. This recursive process, which is closely related to structures I often use in my compositional work, leads to a densification of sound. In the original version, this process takes about two hours and has been shortened on the CD.

The final piece for Violin and Tape starts with the densified sound, which is abruptly stopped by a Bartok pizzicato on the violin. Like the installation, the piece also transforms sounds originally performed by the violin and refeeds them into the system, thus creating a network of the live violin and the sounds it originated. Since the algorithms used for both the installation and the concert piece model some sort of artificial life, the basic idea is quite simple: the violin is confronted with the "creatures" it created.

All the parts of the tape and the violin have been generated with programs I developed especially for that piece. The transformations mainly use a kind of recursive granular method, which is linked in many ways to contemporary models of communication and perception.

Kommen und Gehen war ein Auftragswerk des Deutschen Pavillons auf der Expo 2000 in Hannover. Es ist für Violine und Tonband/Live-Elektronik konzipiert. Da durch das Gebäude beständig Ausstellungsbesucher strömten, wurde das Stück mit einem „Vorspiel" und einer Klanginstallation im Raum vorbereitet. Obwohl es dem Publikum freisteht, im Saal zu bleiben oder ihn zu verlassen, versucht das Stück, die Aufmerksamkeit der Zuhörer mit seiner streng prozessualen Anlage zu gewinnen: Das „Vorspiel" besteht aus einem einzelnen von der Violine gespielten Ton. Diese Note wird aufgenommen und – elektronisch transformiert – von den Lautsprechern übertragen. In einem rekursiven Prozess wird dieser Klang im Rahmen einer Klanginstallation weiter verdichtet. In der Originalversion erstreckt sich dieser Prozess über zwei Stunden. Für die CD wurde er auf wenige Minuten gekürzt.

Das letzte Stück für Violine und Tonband beginnt mit dem verdichteten Klang, der abrupt von einem Bartok-Pizzicato der Violine angehalten wird. Wie in der Installation werden auch im Stück Klänge, die im Original von der Violine gespielt werden, transformiert und wieder in das System zurückgespeist, so dass eine Vernetzung der Live-Performance mit den von ihr ausgelösten Klangereignissen entsteht. Da die Algorithmen, die für sämtliche Teile der Komposition verwendet wurden, Modellen künstlichen Lebens nachempfunden sind, ist die Grundidee, die Violine mit den von ihr erzeugten „Kreaturen" zu konfrontieren, recht elementar. Alle Teile des Tonbandes und des Violinparts sind mit Programmen generiert worden, die ich speziell für dieses Stück entwickelt habe. Die Transformationen verwenden insbesondere eine Form von rekursiver Granularsynthese, die in vielfacher Weise mit aktuellen Modellen der Kommunikation und Perzeption verbunden ist.

ORM FINNENDAHL (D), BORN 1963, STUDIED COMPOSITION, MUSICOLOGY AND COMPUTER MUSIC IN BERLIN. CURRENTLY ORM FINNENDAHL IS HEAD OF THE INSTITUTE OF CONTEMPORARY MUSIC OF THE HOCHSCHULE DER KÜNSTE IN BERLIN AND TEACHES AT THE INSTITUTE FOR COMPUTER MUSIC AND ELECTRONIC MEDIA (ICEM) OF THE FOLKWANG HOCHSCHULE IN ESSEN. ■ Orm Finnendahl (D), geb. 1963, studierte Komposition, Musikwissenschaften und Computermusik in Berlin. Derzeit ist er Leiter des Instituts für Gegenwartsmusik an der Hochschule der Künste in Berlin und lehrt am Institut für Computermusik und Elektronische Medien (ICEM) der Folkwang-Hochschule in Essen.

HIGHWAY
John Hudak

The Brooklyn-Queens Expressway, which leads to the Brooklyn Bridge, runs beneath the building that my family lives in. We have felt the occasional vibrations of large trucks, especially at night, when there is less traffic and they can travel fast.

Our building sits high above ground level on what would be considered a third shelf of a two-tiered highway: our building sits on top...directly below is one tier of traffic travelling west, and below that one tier travelling east. I found a large support for the shelf that our building sits on, and attached contact microphones to collect the strongest vibrations.

The resultant source recordings were similar to what you would get by recording with an open-air microphone ... harsh and unpleasant. Through a series of filterings, I distilled these sounds down to rhythmic impressions of the highway.

edition ... viii (Atlanta, Georgia USA)
(500 copies)

Der Brookly-Queens Expressway, der zur Brooklyn-Brücke führt, geht gerade an dem Gebäude vorbei, in dem meine Familie lebt. Wir haben immer wieder die Erschütterungen durch schwere Lastwägen gespürt, besonders nachts, wenn wenig Verkehr ist und die Lastautos schnell fahren können.

Unser Gebäude steht hoch über dem Grundniveau auf einer Art Regal in der dritten Etage über einer zweistöckigen Autobahn: Oben also unser Gebäude, darunter eine Fahrbahn in Westrichtung, ganz unten eine Fahrbahn Richtung Osten. Ich habe einen großen Stützpfeiler gefunden, auf dem unser Regal ruht, und Kontaktmikrofone angebracht, um die stärksten Vibrationen aufzunehmen.

Die daraus entstandenen Klangquellen-Aufnahmen ähneln dem, was man auch bei Verwendung eines Luftmikrofons erwarten würde – sie sind grob und unangenehm. Durch eine Serie von Filtern habe ich diese Geräusche zu rhythmischen Impressionen der Autobahn destilliert.

edition ... viii
(Atlanta, Georgia, USA, Auflage: 500).

JOHN HUDAK (US), BORN IN 1958, HAS BEEN INTERESTED IN SOUND AND MUSIC FROM THE AGE OF FOUR, WHEN HE BEGAN TO PLAY A VARIETY OF INSTRUMENTS. AT THE UNIVERSITY OF DELAWARE (BA, ENGLISH 1981) AND NAROPA INSTITUTE FOR THE ARTS (1979), HE STUDIED VIDEO, PHOTOGRAPHY, CREATIVE WRITING AND DANCE. HE THEN BEGAN TO CREATE TAPED SOUNDTRACKS FOR SOLO PERFORMANCE ART PIECES. MOST RECENTLY, HE HAS CONCENTRATED ON SOUND, PARTICULARLY NATURAL SOUNDS. ■ John Hudak (USA), geb. 1958, interessiert sich für Klang und Musik seit seinem vierten Lebensjahr, als er anfing, mehrere Instrumente zu spielen. An der University of Delaware (BA aus Englisch 1981) und am Naropa Institute for the Arts (1979) studierte er Video, Fotografie, kreatives Schreiben und Tanz. Dann begann er, Tonband-Soundtracks für Solo-Performances zu komponieren. In letzter Zeit konzentriert er sich auf Klänge, insbesondere Naturklänge.

Kid 606 originally from Venezuela (now in San Francisco), is a self-described "electronic madman who slices through genres like a rusty knife". His sound is highly electronic and experimental —with an element of ear-splitting noise veering through his own renditions of jungle, hardcore, house, soul, funk , punk, electro, ambient, IDM and everything-else-but-the-kitchen-sink. By this non— embracement of any particular approach he maintains an iconoclastic musical aesthetic that never totally subscribes to bleeding edgers or established sonic trends, provoking intense and often polarized reactions from the listening audiences.

It was as a young teen growing up in Southern California that the Kid (Miguel Depedro) first became interested in electronic music. Many records later, he rejects the notion that there might be a definitive Kid606 style, instead describing his approach in more personal terms "Musically? As long as it's got attitude, I'm not specific as to what the music sounds like— I just want it to sound like ME."

Down With the Scene (on Mike Patton's Ipecac label) is certainly not an easy listen, by any means. With titles like *Punkshit*, *Hardcore*, *It'll Take Millions in Plastic Surgery to Make Myself Black*, and *Luke Vibert Can Kiss My Indie-Punk Whiteboy Ass*, this recording loudly proclaims his something-better-change intent. By giving him the benefit of the doubt, though, one can hear his music as the omnivorous, insatiable frenzy of a restless musical spirit on the prowl.

kid606 stammt ursprünglich aus Venezuela (und lebt jetzt in San Francisco) und beschreibt sich selbst als „elektronischen Verrückten, der durch die Genres schneidet wie ein rostiges Messer". Sein Klang ist sehr elektronisch und experimentell – mit einem ohrenzerreißenden Geräusch, das als Zutat durch seine eigenen Versionen von Jungle, Hardcore, House, Soul, Funk, Punk, Electro, Ambient, IDM und Was-weiß-ich-noch-alles geistert. Indem er einen bestimmten Ansatz eben nicht übernimmt, behält er sich eine bilderstürmerische musikalische Ästhetik bei, die sich niemals irgendwelchen besonders hippen oder etablierten Klangtrends anschließt, was intensive und häufig auch recht geteilte Reaktionen der Zuhörerschaft auslöst.

Schon als Teenager, in Südkalifornien aufgewachsen, begeisterte sich kid606 (Miguel Depedro) für elektronische Musik. In vielen späteren Einspielungen weist er den Verdacht von sich, es gäbe so etwas wie einen typischen kid606-Stil. Seinen Ansatz beschreibt er statt dessen in sehr persönlichen Worten: „Musikalisch … naja, solange sie Haltung bewahrt, kümmert es mich nicht sehr, wie die Musik klingt – Hauptsache, sie klingt nach MIR."

Down With the Scene (auf Mike Pattons Ipecac-Label) ist sicherlich nichts zum Nebenbei-Drüberhören. Mit Titeln wie *Punkshit*, *Hardcore, It'll Take Millions in Plastic Surgery to Make Myself Black* und *Luke Vibert Can Kiss My Indie-Punk Whiteboy Ass* proklamiert diese Scheibe lautstark seine „Irgendwas-muss-sich-ändern"-Einstellung.

Im Zweifel aber kann man seine Musik trotzdem als allesfressenden, unersättlichen Ausbruch eines ruhelosen musikalischen Geistes auf der Pirsch ansehen.

KID606 (USA) IS ONE THAT MANY HAVE BECOME ACQUAINTED WITH. ADORED BY THE CRITICS, HE CAN BE FOUND IN MOST CURRENT MUSIC MAGAZINES AND PERFORMS WORLD-WIDE CONTINUOUSLY. WHETHER IT BE REWORKING *STRAIGHT OUTTA COMPTON*, CHEEKILY STATING THAT *LUKE VIBERT CAN KISS MY INDIE-PUNK WHITEBOY ASS* ON HIS RECENT IPECAC (MIKE PATTON) RELEASE OR RUNNING HIS OWN LABEL TIGERBEAT6, THIS BARELY LEGAL TALENT HAS HAD A DISTINCTIVE EFFECT WITH HIS MUSIC AND IS THE MOST PROMINENT FORCE BEHIND THIS CURRENT WAVE OF LAPTOP TALENT. ■

kid606 (USA) ist einer, mit dem viele vertraut sind – verehrt von den Kritikern, findet man ihn in den meisten Musikmagazinen der Gegenwart und ständig auf Welttournee. Sei es mit der Überarbeitung von *Straight Outta Compton* oder beim vorlaut-witzigen Statement *Luke Vibert Can Kiss Ma Indie-Punk Whiteboy Ass* auf seinem neuesten Ipecac-Album (Mike Patton) oder aber bei seinem eigenen Label Tigerbeat6 – dieses fast schon illegale Talent hat einen höchst bemerkenswerten Effekt mit seiner Musik erzielt und ist wohl die prominenteste Kraft hinter der gegenwärtigen Welle von Laptop-Talenten.

GEARHOUND
J Lesser

Touring extensively with Thrill Jockey's post-rock darlings A Minor Forest, Lesser built up notoriety on the electronic underground. Now the mainstream press is crashing the party: Lesser's side project DISC garnered a rave review from legendary rock critic Richard Meltzer, who called it "the greatest work of electronic sound manipulation since Steve Reich's tape experiments". Lesser's annihilation of drum and bass frameworks has also caught the attention of the in-the-know folks at SPIN magazine, who singled out his "Welcome to the American Experience" release in his profile on the San Diego label Vinyl Communications as an outstandingly fresh and unpredictable work of American electronica. Lesser's newest outing, Gearhound, been called a "detriment to humanity," a title coveted by super villains and world leaders, but seldom realized.

Covering Public Enemy, Merzbow and the Doobie Brothers with equal aplomb, Lesser straddles the division between the drum and bass, IDM and noise scenes. Dropping a fiendish live mixture of beats and improvised freakouts that manages to win over members of all three camps. The wide variety of labels and artists currently seeking tracks (Chicago's Kultbox, Scotland's Diskono! and, ahem, Matador Europe) and remixes (Super Furry Animals, Jr. Varsity) from Lesser indicates the diversity of his approach. Playing guitar in the Metallica cover band Creeping Death, Lesser's got chops for days, and the sense not to put musical muscularity in the way of a good time. Perhaps the hours spent decoding those riffs and solos shows through in the programming finesse, texture and attention to detail you'll find in the average Lesser song—who knows?

J Lesser appears courtesy of Matador Records Europe and prefers to be adressed as "Sir".

Aufgebaut hat Lesser seine Bekanntheit im elektronischen Untergrund bei seinen ausgiebigen Touren mit Thrill Jockeys Post-Rock-Lieblingen „A Minor Forest". Und jetzt stimmt auch die Mainstream-Presse in den Chor ein: Lessers Nebenprojekt DISC hat sich eine überschwengliche Kritik des legendären Rock-Kritikers Richard Meltzer eingefangen, der es „das größte Werk der elektronischen Klangmanipulation seit Steve Reichs Tonbandexperimenten" nannte. Lessers Vernichtung des Drum-and-Bass-Rahmens hat auch bei den hochweisen Leuten des SPIN-Magazin Beachtung gefunden, das Lessers *Welcome to the American Experience*, erschienen bei dem in San Diego ansässigen Labels „Vinyl Communications", als ein herausragend frisches und unvorhersehbares Werk der amerikanischen Elektronikszene apostrophiert hat. Lessers neueste Veröffentlichung, *Gearhound*, wurde als „Schädigung der Menschheit" tituliert, was sonst nur Superverbrechern und Politikern vorbehalten ist, aber selten umgesetzt wird.

Während er Public Enemy, Merzbow und die Doobie Brothers mit gleicher Verve covert, überbrückt Lesser die Trennung zwischen der Drum-and-Bass-, der IDM- und der Noise-Szene. Seine höllische Live-Mixtur aus Beats und improvisierten Freakouts schlägt die Mitglieder aller drei Lager. Die große Bandbreite von Labels und Künstlern, die derzeit auf Lessers Spuren wandeln oder Remixes veranstalten, zeigen die Unterschiedlichkeit seines Ansatzes. Als Gitarrist bei der Metallica-Cover-Band Creeping Death hat Lesser tagelang technische Fertigkeiten eingetrichtert gekriegt und ein Gefühl dafür entwickelt, sich den Spaß nicht mit musikalischem Muskelspiel verderben zu lassen. Vielleicht scheinen diese langen Stunden des Dekodierens von Riffs und Solos ja in der Programmfeinheit, in der Textur und der Liebe zum Detail durch, die man im durchschnittlichen Lesser-Song finden kann – wer weiß?

J Lesser erscheint mit der freundlichen Genehmigung von Matador Records Europe und wünscht, mit „Sir" angesprochen zu werden.

J LESSER (USA) SPENT FORMATIVE YEARS IN THE INDIE-ROCK WASTELANDS OF SAN DIEGO, PLAYING IN BANDS WITH MEMBERS OF HEAVY VEGETABLE, OPTIGANALLY YOURS, CRASH WORSHIP, PHYSICS AND A MINOR FOREST. SOLDERING TOGETHER NEW INSTRUMENTS OUT OF THE REFUSE OF 80'S MIXERS AND SYNTHS, J LESSER AVOIDS THE STANDARD SOUNDS AND STRATEGIES IN FAVOUR OF A CONFRONTATIONAL, SCHIZOPHRENIC AND OFTEN HILARIOUS RETHINKING OF CONVENTIONAL "INTELLIGENT" ELECTRONIC DANCE MUSIC. ■■■ J Lesser (USA) verbrachte seine Lehrjahre in der Indie-Rock-Wüste von San Diego, wo er in Bands gemeinsam mit Mitgliedern von Heavy Vegetable, Obtiganally Yours, Crash Worship, Physics und A Minor Forest auftrat. Indem er neue Instrumente aus den Abfällen der Mischpulte und Synthesizer der 80-er Jahre zusammenlötet, vermeidet J Lesser die Standardklänge und -Strategien zugunsten eines kontroversiellen, schizophrenen und oftmals scherzhaften Überdenkens der konventionellen „intelligenten" elektronischen Tanzmusik.

Prix Ars Electronica 2001 **HONORARY MENTION**

CLICKS AND CUTS 2
Mille Plateaux

DIGITAL MUSICS

Digital machines cover up meaning, disrupt sense, delete historic markings and traces. They do not distinguish, they do calculate. Everything is determined and can be calculated. Sampling already evades the cut-up method which permanently confirms the unity of its system by cutting up and adding texts.

The surfaces of these machines no longer show pictures, but models where music cuts out the aesthetic connotation and becomes purely operational. Only in this way is music able to grow metastatically.

Clicks and Cuts are its symptoms, omnipresent and without reference. Here we can hear the in-between, the leap which links loops, the transitions, and even where clicks simulate the essence of a metronome, the continuous beat, they are also phrase, where the predictable order of emphasis gives way to a permanent shift of emphasis.

Clicks and Cuts are conjunctions as permanent ecstasy, and … and … and …

Their medial implication consists of the permanent ability to connect. Their potential can only develop as the context of an event, a musical event, a consistent coupling with musical forms like Clickhouse, Clicktechno, R&B Click, Glitchfunk, Clickhop, etc. *Clicks and Cuts* works as the either or maybe as the other, as well. Their vagueness is the vagueness of the digital media, which is represented in the trivalent topology of the computer. In the binary logic of connections, there is not only the on and off mode, but also the switch which transfers the connection states. It is the non-representable symbol, the medium or the Ab-Ort which makes the one and zero state possible. *Clicks and Cuts* everywhere connections, shifts, transfers, transductions—trans.

Digitale Maschinen überdecken die Bedeutung, reißen den Sinn auseinander, zerstören historische Spuren und Markierungen. Sie unterscheiden nicht, sie berechnen. Alles ist festgelegt, alles kann berechnet werden. Schon das Sampling flieht aus der Cut-up-Methode, die die Einheit ihres Systems dadurch bestätigt, dass sie Texte auseinanderschneidet und zusammenfügt. Die Oberfläche dieser Maschinen zeigt nicht länger Bilder, sondern Modelle, bei denen die Musik ihre ästhetische Konnotation verlässt und rein operational wird. Nur so kann die Musik metastasenhaft wachsen. *Clicks and Cuts* sind ihre Symptome. Hier können wir das Dazwischenliegende hören, den Sprung, der die Schleifen verbindet, die Übergänge, und selbst dort, wo die Clicks die Essenz eines Metrums simulieren – den durchgängigen Beat –, sind sie gleichzeitig eine Phrase, in der die vorhersehbare Reihenfolge der Gewichtung einer ständigen Gewichtsverlagerung weicht.

Ihre mediale Implikation besteht aus der permanenten Fähigkeit, zu verbinden. Ihr Potenzial kann sich nur als der Zusammenhang eines musikalischen Ereignisses entwickeln, einer ständigen Koppelung mit musikalischen Formen wie Clickhouse, Clicktechno, R&B Click, Glitchfunk, Clickhop und so weiter. *Clicks and Cuts* können als das „Entweder" funktionieren, aber auch als das „Oder". Ihre immanente Unbestimmtheit ist die Unbestimmtheit der digitalen Medien, wie sie in der dreiwertigen Topologie des Computers dargestellt ist. In der binären Logik der Verbindungen gibt es nicht nur den „Ein"- und den „Aus"-Modus, sondern auch den Schalter, der diesen Verbindungsstatus transportiert. Er ist das nicht-darstellbare Symbol, das Medium, der „Ab-Ort", der den „0"- oder „1"-Zustand erst ermöglicht. *Clicks and Cuts* – überall Verbindungen, Verschiebungen, Transfers, Transfigurationen – Trans …

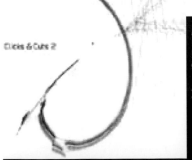

Clicks & Cuts 2

MUSIC TODAY IS MEDIA MUSIC, THE RESULT OF THE INTERPLAY OF NUMEROUS COORDINATES, INCLUDING THE MUSICIAN, THE PROGRAMMER, THE SOFTWARE AND THE HARDWARE. MILLE PLATEAUX AND FORCE INC. POSITION THEMSELVES IN THIS FIELD AND DOCUMENT THE CUT-COPY-PASTE-FUNK OF A GENERATION, FOR WHICH MUSIC ONLY STILL FUNCTIONS AS A PERMANENT DISPERSAL OF MEANING, DATA MANIPULATION AND CONSTANT MUTATION. BREAKS ARE CREATED, LINKS ARE CREATED, THIS IS THE PARADOX THAT MILLE PLATEAUX AND FORCE INC. WANT TO MAKE AUDIBLE. ▬ Musik heute ist Medienmusik, sie ist das Ergebnis aus dem Zusammenspiel zahlreicher Koordinaten, zu denen der Musiker, der Programmierer sowie die Software und Hardware gehören. Mille Plateaux und Force Inc verorten sich in diesem Feld und dokumentieren den Cut-Copy-Paste-Funk einer Generation, für die Musik nur noch funktioniert als permanente Zerstreuung von Sinn, Datenmanipulation und ständige Mutation. Stellt Brüche her, stellt Verbindungen her, diese Paradoxie wollen Mille Plateaux und Force Inc. hörbar machen.

AALTOPIIRI
Pan sonic

A*altopiiri* offers the listener a wide range of flowing, atmospheric sounds and rhythms. Recorded at their studio in Barcelona, the pair choose an improvising approach to recording their music. "When we are in the studio everything is recorded straight on to tape. We might do several takes of a song, but there are no overdubs," explains Mika. They mainly record on analog equipment, some of which is designed and built for them by long time friend, Geri Lehtinen, a physics expert. "For me the most important thing in our music is the sound itself," says Mika. "The structure is secondary. For different kinds of tracks, of course, we're looking for different kinds of sounds. But I still don't know myself what is in a sound that attracts me. There's some kind of nature in the sound itself, some kind of information." *Aaltopiiri* is an album filled with alluring, ambient frequencies and hypnotic rhythms. Tracks like *Kone* and *Kierto* stutter and groove, while elsewhere *Aanipaa* and *Liuos* provide lush, addictive pulses. They are often asked what the track & album titles actually mean when translated into English, but as they often invent or combine Finnish words, the "definitions" become quite vague. For example, a legendary, maybe mythological low creeping mist from a particular area of Finland or a variant technological term for a certain aspect of early radio wave experiments. As Mika says, "There is no theory for Pan sonic. We have no plan. We just make the music."

Aaltopiiri bietet den Hörern ein breites Spektrum fließender atmosphärischer Klänge und Rhythmen. Für die Aufnahmen in ihrem Studio in Barcelona wählten die beiden Musiker einen improvisatorischen Ansatz: „Wenn wir im Studio sind, wird alles direkt auf Band aufgenommen – wir machen zwar manchmal mehrere Aufnahmen von einem Song, aber es gibt keine Überspielungen und Montagen", erklärt Mika. Aufgenommen wird überwiegend auf analogem Equipment, das zum Teil von ihrem langjährigen Freund, dem Physik-Experten Geri Lehtinen entworfen und gebaut wurde. „Für mich ist das Wichtigste an der Musik der Klang selbst", sagt Mika, „die Struktur ist sekundär. Natürlich suchen wir für unterschiedliche Tracks auch nach unterschiedlichen Arten von Klängen. Aber ich könnte nicht sagen, was in einem Klang steckt, der mich anzieht – irgendwie steckt etwas Natürliches im Klang selbst, eine Art von Information."

Aaltopiiri ist ein Album voll von verführerischen Umweltklängen und hypnotischen Rhythmen. Einzelne Nummern wie *Kone* und *Kierto* stottern und grooven, während etwa *Aanipaa* und *Liuos* glatte, süchtig machende Rhythmen liefern. Oft werden sie gefragt, was die Track- und Album-Titel denn übersetzt bedeuten, aber nachdem sie die finnischen Worte oft kombinieren oder gar erfinden, bleiben die „Definitionen" ziemlich vage – sie beziehen sich etwa auf einen mythologischen, niedrig dahinkriechenden Nebel aus einer bestimmten Gegend Finnlands oder auf einen abgewandelten technischen Ausdruck für einen speziellen Aspekt aus der Frühzeit der Radiowellenexperimente.

Wie Mika sagt: „Es gibt keine Theorie für Pan sonic. Wir haben keinen Plan, wir machen nur die Musik."

MIKA VAINIO AND ILPO VAISANEN FORMED AS PANASONIC IN 1994 A HUNDRED MILES WEST OF HELSINKI IN THEIR HOMETOWN OF TURKU, FINLAND. ORIGINALLY A THREE PIECE WITH SAMI SALO, THEY HAVE NOT ONLY LOST A MEMBER BUT ALSO A LETTER IN THEIR NAME. NOW KNOWN AS PAN SONIC, DUE TO INTERVENTION FROM THE JAPANESE ELECTRONIC CORPORATION IN 1997. ▬ Mika Vianio und Ilpo Vaisanen (SF) formierten sich 1994 als „Panasonic" in ihrer Heimatstadt Turku hundert Meilen westlich von Helsinki. Das ursprüngliche Trio zusammen mit Sami Salo hat nicht nur ein Mitglied, sondern auch einen Buchstaben des Namens verloren: Nach einer Intervention des japanischen Elektronikkonzerns 1997 firmieren sie jetzt als Pan sonic.

ABOVE BUILDINGS
Janek Schaefer

The source material for my work with sound has always focused on the use of field recordings, manipulated vinyl and elementary electronics. My emphasis has been on the alteration, abstraction and appropriation of these elements. Prior to this album I had almost exclusively worked live, both in the studio and through performance to create material for my previous releases. For *Above Buildings* I then added the [incredible] control offered by the home computer to create a series of more intricate "found-soundscape" collages. The starting point for the majority of these compositions were recordings sourced travelling around America, England and France. These mostly contact-miked sounds were then broken down, processed live through the studio and re-assembled and edited using basic software.

The scope of my intentions for the album, and my reactions to it were summed up well in these review extracts: "You cannot listen to this music and do something else that requires concentration ...." (*Pitchfork Media*)"... in turns expanding on the familiarity of everyday life and bringing the enormous, infinite universe down to whisper a secret in your ear" (*Forced Exposure*).

Seit jeher liegt mein Schwerpunkt beim Ausgangsmaterial für meine Klangarbeiten auf Vor-Ort-Aufnahmen, manipuliertem Vinyl und elementarer Elektronik. Besonderes Augenmerk habe ich der Veränderung, Abstraktion und Aneignung dieser Elemente geschenkt. Vor diesem Album habe ich fast ausschließlich live gearbeitet, sowohl im Studio als auch bei Performances, um das nötige Material für die früheren Releases zu sammeln. Bei *Above Buildings* habe ich dem die (unglaublichen) Steuerungsmöglichkeiten des Home-Computers hinzugefügt, um eine Serie noch komplexerer „Klangfund-Landschaften" zu erzielen. Ausgangspunkt für den Großteil dieser Kompositionen waren Aufnahmen, die bei Reisen in Amerika, England und Frankreich gesammelt wurden. Diese meist mit Kontaktmikrofonen aufgenommenen Teile wurden zerlegt, im Studio live bearbeitet und mit Hilfe von einfacher Software montiert und geschnitten.

Die folgenden Zitate aus Kritiken fassen mein Ziel für das Album und meine Reaktionen recht gut zusammen: „Man kann nicht dieser Musik zuhören und gleichzeitig etwas anders tun, was Konzentration verlangt..." (*Pitchfork Media*); „... verbreitet sich schrittweise über Bekanntes aus dem Alltag und reduziert das enorme, unendliche Universum darauf, einem ein Geheimnis ins Ohr zu flüstern..." (*Forced Exposure*).

JANEK SCHAEFER (UK). BORN IN MIDDLE ENGLAND TO A CANADIAN SCIENTIST AND A POLISH MODEL, I ENDED UP CREATING "RECORDED DELIVERY" [A SOUND ACTIVATED TAPE RECORDER IN POST] WHILST STUDYING ARCHITECTURE AT THE ROYAL COLLEGE OF ART. I THEN MET PHILIP JECK AND INVENTED THE TRI-PHONIC TURNTABLE [THREE ARM, REVERSE PLAY, MICRO VARI-SPEED, MULTIPLE RECORD, PLAYER] FOR WHICH I WAS VOTED "SOUND DESIGNER OF THE YEAR" BY CREATIVE REVIEW MAGAZINE 1999. THIS IN TURN ENDED UP INSPIRING MY "OFF-AXIS" CUT 7" *Wow.* ▬▬ Janek Schaefer (UK). Geboren in Mittelengland als Sohn eines kanadischen Wissenschaftlers und eines polnischen Models, landete ich bei der Entwicklung von „Recorded Delivery" (einem klanggesteuerten Tonbandgerät in der Post), während ich am Royal College of Art Architektur studierte. Dann lernte ich Philip Jeck kennen und erfand den „Triphonic Turntable" (drei Tonarme, Micro-Vari-Speed, Multiple-Record-Plattenspieler), für den ich vom Creative Review Magazine zum Sound Designer des Jahres 1999 gekürt wurde. Und dies wiederum inspirierte mich zu meiner aus der Achse geschnittenen 7-Zoll-Platte *Wow.*

ATTITUDE
Tigerbeat6

The *Attitude* comp has got a lot of just what it says: attitude! The ubiquitous kid606 rounded up some like-minded electronic terrorists to lace this little 3 inch CD with laptop per-versions of gangsta type rap tunes from the styles of Dr. Dre, NWA and other suspects. Fragments of hip hop hardcore are "covered" here by the likes of Hrvatski, Dat Politics, Matmos, Pimmon, V/VM, Electric Company, Christoph de Babalon, Cex, J Lesser, and kid 606 himself, among others. The material is manic, ridiculous and sounds like demented desecration, but is clearly meant as a twisted tribute to the gangsta pioneers. These unofficial remixes spark a near catastrophic readjustment to the common spine bump of rap beats and voice which has conditioned masses worldwide to expectations of the hip hop experience. This deconstruction will add to the permanent altercation of these preconceptions. As many from the Tigerbeat6 clan of conspirators contributed to this slaughter rap fest, one is left to wonder what would happen if these firebrands confronted the live audiences who frequent the gangsta ghetto circuit. A dangerous and new kind of kick, exceptional in range and rugged in its interior?

Die *Attitude*-Compilation hat viel von dem, was schon der Titel sagt: Attitüde und Haltung. Der allgegenwärtige kid606 hat einige gleichgesinnte elektronische Terroristen zusammengetrieben, um diese kleine Drei-Zoll-CD mit Laptop-Per-Versionen von Rap-Tunes des „Gangsta"-Typs im Stile eines Dr. Der, NWA und anderer zu verzieren. Fragmente von Hiphop-Hardcore werden hier von Leuten wie Hrvatski, Dat Politics, Matmos, Pimmon, V/VM, Electric Company, Christoph de Babalon, Cex, J Lesser und kid606 persönlich sozusagen „gecovert". Das Material ist manisch, lächerlich und klingt wie eine geisteskranke Entweihung, aber es ist eindeutig als eine etwas verquere Hommage an die „Gangsta"-Pioniere gemeint. Diese inoffiziellen Remixes entzünden eine nahezu katastrophale Neuanpassung an den üblichen Spine-Bump der Rap-Beats und Stimme, die die Massen weltweit auf die Erwartung einer Hiphop-Erfahrung konditioniert haben. Diese Dekonstruktion wird den allgemeinen hitzigen Disputen über diese Vorurteile noch eins draufsetzen. Da so viele aus dem Verschwörerclan von Tigerbeat6 zu diesem Rap-Schlachtfest beigetragen haben, fragt man sich, was wohl passieren würde, wenn diese Brandstifter jenem Live-Publikum gegenüberträten, das die „Gangsta"-Ghetto-Kreise bevölkert. Eine gefährliche und neuartige Form von Kick, außergewöhnlich in seiner Bandbreite und grundsolide im Inneren …

SAN FRANCISCO-BASED TIGERBEAT6 IS RUN BY THE ONE AND ONLY KID606. SINCE HE FOUNDED IT IN EARLY 2000, THE KID HAS MOVED TOWARDS ESTABLISHING TIGERBEAT6 AS A TOP PURVEYOR OF THE MORE OFFBEAT SIDE OF ELECTRONIC MUSIC WITH RELEASES SUCH AS A THREE-INCH CD TRIBUTE TO N.W.A. LOOK FOR LOTS MORE TO COME IN THE FUTURE. ■■■ Das in San Franciso ansässige Tigerbeat6 wird von dem einen und einzigen kid606 betrieben. Seit er es Anfang 2000 gegründet hat, hat kid606 viel getan, um Tigerbeat6 als den Top-Lieferanten eher der Offbeat-Seite der elektronischen Musik zu etablieren, mit Releases wie einer 3-Zoll-CD-Hommage an N.W.A. Und noch viel mehr steht zu erwarten!

u19/cybergeneration

A nine-year-old programs a fully functional HTML-Editor with well thought-out short keys and even an integrated, menu-supported VRML Editor.

Within the framework of the competition u19, subtitled "Freestyle Computing", which describes the possibility of operating with the computer outside the range of adult, product-oriented thinking in technical standards, this work—which has been distinguished in the competition, by the way—is representative of a large number of other submissions and raises several questions.

This is even more the case, if this phenomenon is linked with something else that is noticeable: specifically that in the upper age segment of the u19 entrants, in whose work a conceptional approach may frequently be noted, a sometimes limited technical understanding of the computer as a programmable machine becomes a constraining obstacle on the way to implementing an idea.

An unavoidable question arises here: do these technical exercises in style represent a potential, or should they be interpreted as an unfortunate development, an attempt to imitate the adult world and its way of dealing with (computer) reality?

If one assumes that a nine-year-old child does not yet question the value of their work and their exertion (some of the submissions were based on months or even years of developments) and has yet to discover the added value of an idea, one can be optimistic and look forward to exciting things from these young people, even if they are already nineteen.

If one wants to be pessimistic, one can interpret this

Ein Neunjähriger programmiert einen voll funktionsfähigen HTML-Editor, mit gut überlegten Short-Keys und sogar einem integrierten, menügestützten VRML-Editor.

Im Rahmen des Wettbewerbs u19, dessen Untertitel "Freestyle Computing" lautet und der die Möglichkeiten umschreibt, mit dem Computer außerhalb eines erwachsenen, produktorientiertes Denkens in technischen Standards zu operieren, wirft diese – wohlbemerkt ausgezeichnete – Arbeit stellvertretend für eine große Zahl anderer Einreichungen einige Fragen auf. Dies um so mehr, wenn man dieses Phänomen mit einer anderen Feststellung in Verbindung bringt: und zwar damit, dass im oberen Alterssegment der u19-Einreicher, in deren Arbeiten oft ein konzeptioneller Ansatz feststellbar ist, ein zum Teil begrenztes technisches Verständnis des Computers als programmierbare Maschine zu einem beschneidenden Hindernis auf dem Weg zur Umsetzung einer Idee wird. Die Frage, die sich aufdrängt ist: Stellen diese technischen Stilübungen ein Potenzial dar oder sind sie als eine Fehlentwicklung, als ein Nachahmungsversuch der Erwachsenenwelt und deren Umgang mit (Computer)Realität zu interpretieren? Wenn man davon ausgeht, dass ein neunjähriges Kind noch nicht den Wert seiner Arbeit und seiner Anstrengungen (hinter gewissen Einreichungen stehen monate-, ja, gar jahrelange Entwicklungen) hinterfragt und den Mehrwert einer Idee erst noch entdecken wird, kann man optimistisch sein und von diesen Jugendlichen, egal ob sie schon 19 sind oder nicht, noch Spannendes erwarten.

technical obsession among such young people as a lack of imagination—without meaning to mourn the loss of an idealized potential of young people to be creative, cheeky and naive at the same time. This presumed "potential" is probably more of a reflection of the expectations that the adult world has of "youth". While "youth" does much, young people are obviously less concerned with any kind of expectations—and rightly so.

The answer is a matter of belief and it occupied the jury intensively for three days ...

Nevertheless, there are a few key words from this discussion that we would like to pass on to many of the entrants as food for thought:

– more room for hypotheses and unusual ideas
– more courage to experiment
– content before design

There were few projects that held up under these criteria, but—and this must be said—the Honorary Mentions were especially convincing either because of their sometimes unusual implementation or because of a promising idea. Or—as in the case of the three nominations—because of the idea and the implementation.

In the end, the hope predominates that the very young people of today, equipped with the technical capabilities that they have already proven this year, will next year already be able to engage in truly *freestyle computing!*

Will man pessimistisch sein, kann man diese technische Besessenheit bei so jungen Menschen als Fantasielosigkeit interpretieren – ohne damit den Verlust des so idealisierten Potenzials der Jugend, kreativ, frech und naiv zugleich zu sein, beklagen zu wollen. Dieses vermeintliche "Potenzial" spiegelt ja wohl mehr eine Erwartung wider, die die Erwachsenenwelt an "die Jugend" richtet. "Die Jugend" tut vieles, aber kümmert sich offensichtlich wenig um irgendwelche Erwartungen – und das zu Recht.

Die Antwort ist Glaubenssache und hat die Jury drei Tage lang intensiv beschäftigt ...

Vielen Einreichern möchten wir trotzdem – als Denkanstoß – ein paar der Schlagworte dieser Diskussionen nicht vorenthalten:

– Mehr Raum für Hypothesen und ungewöhnliche Ideen
– Mehr Mut zum Experiment
– Inhalt vor Design

Vor diesen Kriterien bestanden zwar wenige, aber – und das muss erwähnt werden – vor allem die Anerkennungen bestachen entweder durch ihre zum Teil außergewöhnliche Umsetzung oder durch eine tragende Idee. Oder – wie bei den drei Nominierungen erkennbar – durch Idee und Umsetzung.

Schlussendlich also herrscht doch die Hoffnung, dass die heute ganz Jungen, ausgestattet mit dem technischen Rüstzeug, das sie in diesem Jahr bereits unter Beweis stellten, schon im nächsten Jahr wirklich freestyle computen!

POWERSPHERE

MARTIN LEONHARTSBERGER

Powersphere is, to put it simply, a remote-controlled vehicle, which differs from conven-tional vehicles available on the market in its form and type of construction. The sphere itself consists of two Plexiglas halves. The two halves are joined through the main axis and the bearing units on the left and right. The sphere draws electricity from two battery blocks. There is a drive controller and a receiver between the two batteries.

A drive unit that hangs from the ball-bearing central axis propels the friction wheel that turns on the inside surface of the sphere. The momentum from the weight of the drive unit moves the sphere. It is steered through the main shaft. The servomechanism moves the two weights out from the center. This shifts the sphere's center of gravity. Consequently, the sphere

Powersphere ist, einfach ausgedrückt, ein ferngesteuertes Gefährt, welches sich in der Form und Art der Konstruktion von regulär am Markt erhältlichen Gefährten unterscheidet. Die Kugel selbst besteht aus zwei Plexiglashälften. Die beiden Hälften werden durch die Haupt-achse und die beiden Lagereinheiten links und rechts zusammengehalten. Den Strom bezieht die Kugel aus zwei Akkublocks. Zwischen den beiden Akkus befinden sich Fahrtenregler und Empfänger.

Eine auf der kugelgelagerten Zentralachse auf-gehängte Antriebseinheit treibt das auf der Kugelinnenfläche laufende Reibrad an. Durch das Gewichtsmoment der Antriebseinheit bewegt sich die Kugel. Die Lenkung erfolgt auf der Hauptwelle. Die beiden Gewichte werden durch den Servo aus der Mitte herausbewegt. Dadurch verschiebt sich der Schwerpunkt der Kugel. Die Folge ist ein Kippen der Kugel.

turns over. Since the sphere always moves around the center of gravity, it rolls a curve.

The project *Powersphere* was originally made as part of construction exercises 1999/2000. The assignment here was to construct a remote-controlled vehicle. Since our group (five people at that time) found this too boring, the idea of the sphere was born. A prototype was built that year in the workshop.

I picked up on this idea again for the competition Cybergeneration u19 Freestyle Computing and constructed the vehicle completely new on the computer using the 3D CAD software Pro/Engineer. My aim was to visualize the ball in 3D and calculate the components. In this way, I got rid of the errors of the first construction and changed the basic technical concept in several places. I also refurbished the prototype.

Da sich die Kugel immer um den Schwerpunkt bewegt, rollt sie eine Kurve.

Das Projekt *Powersphere* entstand erstmals in den Konstruktionsübungen 1999/2000. Hier war die Aufgabenstellung; ein ferngesteuertes Gefährt zu konstruieren. Nachdem dies allerdings unserer Gruppe (damals fünf Mann) zu langweilig schien, wurde die Idee mit der Kugel geboren. Ein Prototyp wurde in diesem Jahr in der Werkstätte gebaut.

Für den Wettbewerb Cybergeneration u19 Freestyle Computing habe ich die Idee wieder aufgegriffen und das Fahrzeug vollständig am Computer mit Hilfe der 3D-CAD-Software Pro/Engineer neu konstruiert. Mein Ziel war hier, die Kugel in 3D zu visualisieren und die Komponenten zu berechnen. Dabei habe ich die Fehler der ersten Konstruktion ausgemerzt und das technische Grundkonzept in einigen Teilen geändert. Weiters wurde der Prototyp wieder auf Vordermann gebracht.

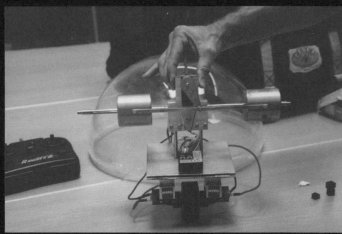

MARTIN LEONHARTSBERGER, BORN 1984, LIVES IN GRAMMASTETTEN NEAR LINZ AND HAS ATTENDED THE TECHNICAL SECONDARY SCHOOL HTBLA II LINZ LITEC SINCE 1998. SUMMER JOB TRAINING 2000 WITH THE PROVINCIAL GOVERNMENT OF UPPER AUSTRIA AT THE COMPUTER CENTER OF THE PROVINCIAL HOSPITAL. EXPERIENCE WITH NUMEROUS PROGRAMMING LANGUAGES AND OPERATING SYSTEMS. HOBBIES: DANCING, SKIING, SWIMMING, MOUNTAIN BIKING, READING, MY COMPUTER, LISTENING TO MUSIC, PLAYING THE TROMBONE, FIDDLING WITH ELECTRONICS (MICRO-CONTROLLER).

MARTIN LEONHARTSBERGER, GEB. 1984, LEBT IN GRAMMASTETTEN BEI LINZ UND BESUCHT SEIT 1998 DIE HTBLA II LINZ LITEC. FERIALARBEIT 2000 BEIM LAND OBERÖSTERREICH IM RECHENZENTRUM DES LKH. ERFAHRUNGEN MIT ZAHLREICHEN PROGRAMMIERSPRACHEN UND BETRIEBSSYSTEMEN. HOBBIES: TANZEN, SCHIFAHREN, SCHWIMMEN, MOUNTAINBIKEN, LESEN, MEIN COMPUTER, MUSIK HÖREN,

PROFESSOR BRÖSL

JOHANNES SCHIEHSL
PETER STROBL
CONRAD TAMBOUR

*P*rofessor Brösl is an interactive 2D point-and-click adventure for the PC, in which you slip into the role of a confused and naive physics professor. The head of the research center where he works commissions him to improve the amount of products manufactured. Professor Brösl finally realizes that machine guns, drug deliveries and counterfeiting money are not part of the normal agenda of physics professors and researchers. In fact, the ZUUM Research Center is a well disguised front for the illegal underground organization ZUUM, whose insane leader of the same name wants to take over the world. After Professor Brösl has helped the staff with their problems and increased the production rate, he gains access to the huge, top secret military base that is located underground, under the research center, where he soon finds himself face to face with Mister ZUUM ...

Professor Brösl ist ein interaktives 2D-Point-and-Click-Adventure für den PC, bei dem Sie in die Rolle eines verwirrten und naiven Physikprofessors schlüpfen. Dieser bekommt vom Leiter des Forschungszentrums, in dem er arbeitet, den Auftrag, die Menge der erzeugten Produkte zu verbessern. Erst spät bemerkt Professor Brösl, dass Maschinengewehre, Drogenlieferungen und Falschgeld-Erzeugung nicht zum normalen Auftragsprogramm von Physikern und Forschern gehören. In Wahrheit ist das ZUUMsche Forschungszentrum nämlich eine gut getarnte Einrichtung der illegalen Untergrundorganisation ZUUM, dessen gleichnamiger, verrückter Anführer die Weltherrschaft an sich reißen will. Nachdem Professor Brösl den Angestellten bei ihren Problemen geholfen und die Produktionsrate gesteigert hat, verschafft er sich Zutritt zu der riesigen, streng geheimen Militäranlage, die sich unterirdisch, unter dem Forschungszentrum befindet, um Mister ZUUM wenig später gegenüber zu stehen ...

The project *Professor Brösl* was made entirely in our free time, in other words on weekends and at night. To begin with, the programmer and background artist Johannes Schiehsl started programming the script engine, which was developed just for this game. Conrad Tambour designed all the persons and figures. First we discussed everything that these figures would have to be able to do and what their position in the room would look like. Then he drew them with a pencil and scanned them in, transforming them into vectors with the program "Streamline" and revising and coloring them in the Adobe Illustrator. In fall 2000, the music student and composer Peter Strobl was hired to compose the soundtrack for Professor Brösl. In early summer 2001, we started cleaning up the game, because it was too slow and boring to play. All the backgrounds were newly rendered, which resulted in intensifying the atmosphere. Then all the puzzles, dialogues and situations that were boring, were removed and replaced with others that were more exciting and bloody. In addition, all the interim sequences were revised and some were shot all over again.

Das Projekt *Professor Brösl* entstand ausschließlich in unserer Freizeit, also an den Wochenenden und in den Nächten. Begonnen wurde zuerst damit, dass der Programmierer und Background-Artist Johannes Schiehsl mit dem Programmieren der nur für dieses Spiel entwickelten Script-Engine begann. Alle Personen und Figuren wurden von Conrad Tambour designt. Zuerst wurde besprochen, was diese Figur alles können muss und wie ihre Position im Raum aussieht. Danach zeichnete er sie mit Bleistift und scannte diese ein, um sie dann mit dem Programm „Streamline" in Vektoren umzuwandeln und im Adobe Illustrator nachzubearbeiten und zu kolorieren. Im Herbst 2000 wurde dann Peter Strobl, ein Musikstudent und Komponist, angeheuert, den Soundtrack für Professor Brösl zu komponieren. Im Frühsommer 2001 wurde mit einer Sanierung des Spiels begonnen, da sich das Spiel zu lahm und langweilig spielte. So wurden sämtliche Hintergründe neu gerendert, was eine Steigerung der Atmosphäre zur Folge hatte. Weiters wurden sämtliche Rätsel, Dialoge und Situationen, die langweilig waren, herausgenommen und durch spannendere, blutigere ersetzt. Außerdem wurden sämtliche Zwischensequenzen überarbeitet und teilweise komplett neu gedreht.

JOHANNES SCHIEHSL, BORN 1984 IN WIENER NEUSTADT, COLLEGE PREPARATORY SECONDARY SCHOOL BERNDORF UNTIL 1998, SINCE THEN SECONDARY SCHOOL INSTITUTE FOR TEACHING AND EXPERIMENTAL GRAPHIC ARTS VIENNA XIV. SPECIAL INTERESTS: PROGRAMMING AND DESIGNING APPLICATIONS, WORKING WITH GRAPHICS, FILM AND SOUND PROGRAMS (PC AND MAC). PETER STROBL, BORN 1977 IN NEUNKIRCHEN/LOWER AUSTRIA, HAS STUDIED SINCE 1997 AT THE J.M. HAUER CONSERVATORY WIENER NEUSTADT (STUDYING INSTRUMENTAL AND VOCAL PEDAGOGY, MAIN SUBJECT PIANO, EMPHASIS ON COMPOSITION AND MUSIC THEORY), HAS WORKED AS A MUSICIAN IN VARIOUS ORCHESTRAS, COMMISSIONS FOR ARRANGEMENTS AND TRANSCRIPTIONS, HAS WORKED AS A STUDIO MUSICIAN. CONRAD TAMBOUR, BORN 1984, ATTENDED THE COLLEGE PREPARATORY SECONDARY SCHOOL AHS AMERLINGSTRASSE, SINCE 1998 SECONDARY SCHOOL INSTITUTE FOR TEACHING AND EXPERIMENTAL GRAPHIC ARTS VIENNA XIV (SECTION GRAPHICS DESIGN). CURRENTLY IN HIS SIXTH SEMESTER. COLLABORATION WORKING IN A TEAM WITH JOHANNES SCHIEHSL.

JOHANNES SCHIEHSL, GEB. 1984 IN WR. NEUSTADT, BUNDESGYMNASIUM BERNDORF BIS 1998, SEITHER HÖHERE GRAFISCHE BUNDES-, LEHR- UND VERSUCHSANSTALT WIEN XIV. BESONDERE NEIGUNGEN: PROGRAMMIERUNG UND DESIGN VON ANWENDUNGEN, ARBEIT MIT GRAFIK-, FILM- UND SOUNDPROGRAMMEN (PC UND MAC). PETER STROBL, GEB.1977 IN NEUNKIRCHEN/NO, SEIT 1997 STUDIUM AM J.M. HAUER KONSERVATORIUM WR. NEUSTADT (STUDIENRICHTUNG INSTRUMENTAL UND GESANGSPÄDAGOGIK, HAUPTFACH KLAVIER, SCHWERPUNKT KOMPOSITION UND MUSIKTHEORIE), TÄTIGKEIT ALS MUSIKER IN MEHREREN ORCHESTERN, AUFTRÄGE FÜR ARRANGEMENTS UND TRANSKRIPTIONEN, TÄTIGKEIT ALS STUDIOMUSIKER. CONRAD TAMBOUR, GEB. 1984, BESUCH DER AHS AMERLINGSTRASSE, SEIT 1998 GRAFISCHE BUNDES- LEHR- UND VERSUCHSANSTALT WIEN (SPARTE GRAFIK-DESIGN). DERZEIT IM SECHSTEN SEMESTER. ZUSAMMENARBEIT IN EINEM ARBEITSTEAM MIT JOHANNES SCHIEHSL.

JIND MARKUS TRISKA

Im Winter 1999 beschäftigte ich mich mit Syntaxanalyse (Parsing). Um herauszufinden, ob ich die in dem Buch *Algorithmen in C* von Robert Sedgewick vorgestellte Methode wirklich verstanden hatte, wollte ich einen Programminterpreter schreiben. Aus gegebenem Anlass nannte ich das in der Programmiersprache „C" geschriebene Programm „Cind" (Christkind). Es stellte sich bald heraus, dass ich die vorgestellten Methoden *nicht* verstanden hatte, doch für den simplen Anwendungsfall des im Labyrinth verirrten Christkinds reichte es allemal (obwohl der Uneingeweihte dem archaischen Schwarz-weiß-Display vielleicht weniger abgewinnen konnte als ich, der stolze Autor).

I n the winter of 1999, I was involved in syntax analysis (parsing). In order to find out whether I had really understood the methods presented in the book *Algorithmen in C* by Robert Sedgewick, I wanted to write a program interpreter. In honor of the occasion, I called the program written in the programming language "C" "Cind" (Christkind). It soon turned out that I had *not* understood the methods presented, but for the simple application case of the Christmas angel lost in a labyrinth, it was still sufficient (although the archaic black and white display may not appeal as much to the uninitiated as it does to me, the proud author).

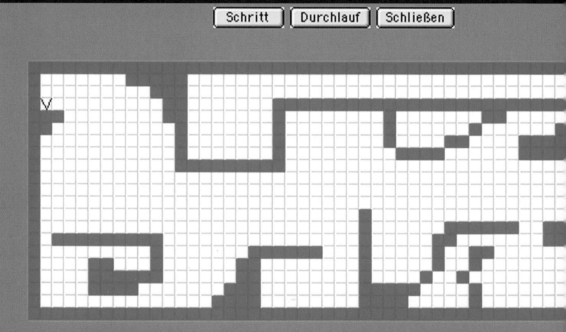

(C) Markus Triska, 20.04.2000 triska@gmx.at

In April of the following year, the student newspaper *In and Online (www.inandonline.x2.nu)* was already running at full speed (and I can proudly say that I contributed to that). In keeping with my position as "chief programmer", when I decided that the time had come, I designed a programming competition.
For this, I needed to pose a problem that everyone could understand and a "programming language" that would be easy to learn. "Cind" seemed to be ideal for this, and I re-implemented the program in the programming language "Java", which is reflected in the new name "Jind" (besides, the Christmas angel is not really appropriate in the spring). This was supplemented by a more colorful surface and nice buttons for operating it – everything the modern surfer desires. I owe the fact that I was able to submit "Jind" at all to a lot of lucky circumstances and a number of people, who have influenced me in many ways.
Many thanks to all of you!

Im April des Folgejahres lief die Schülerzeitung *In and Online (www.inandonline.x2.nu)* bereits auf Hochtouren. (Und ich kann mit Stolz sagen, daran mitgewirkt zu haben.) Als ich die Zeit für gekommen hielt, entwarf ich gemäß meiner Position als „Leitender Programmierer" einen Programmierwettbewerb. Dazu brauchte ich eine Problemstellung, die jeder verstehen konnte, und eine leicht zu erlernende „Programmiersprache". „Cind" schien mir dazu ideal, und ich reimplementierte das Programm in der Programmiersprache „Java", was sich in der neuen Benennung „Jind" widerspiegelt (außerdem ist das Christkind im Frühjahr nicht mehr so aktuell). Dazu kamen eine buntere Oberfläche und schöne Knöpfe zur Bedienung – alles, was sich der moderne Surfer wünscht. Dass ich „Jind" überhaupt einreichen konnte, verdanke ich einer Menge glücklicher Umstände und einer Reihe von Personen, die mich in vielerlei Hinsicht beeinflusst haben.
Vielen Dank an euch alle!

MARKUS TRISKA, BORN 1982 IN KORNEUBURG, ATTENDS THE DE LA SALLE SCHOOL STREBERSDORF (COLLEGE PREPARATORY SECONDARY SCHOOL WITH ENGLISH, FRENCH AND LATIN). 1998: SUMMER JOB TRAINING WITH SIEMENS (PROGRAM AND SYSTEM DEVELOPMENT, CREATING JAVA APPLETS AND CGI PROGRAMS), 1999: SUMMER JOB TRAINING WITH ALLIANZ INVESTMENT BANK (CREATING COBOL AND CLARION PROGRAMS FOR CASH MANAGEMENT). SINCE DECEMBER 1999: COLLABORATOR FOR THE ONLINE STUDENT NEWSPAPER "IN AND ONLINE" (CREATING CGI SCRIPTS, JAVA APPLETS AND C PROGRAMS, DOCUMENTATION AND RELEASE OF THE PROGRAMS UNDER GNU GENERAL PUBLIC LICENSE), AUGUST 2000: SUMMER JOB TRAINING AGAIN WITH ALLIANZ INVESTMENT BANK (DEVELOPING CROSS-PLATFORM INTERNET APPLICATION IN CLARION).

MARKUS TRISKA, GEB. 1982 IN KORNEUBURG, BESUCHT DIE DE LA SALLE SCHULE STREBERSDORF (GYMNASIUM MIT ENGLISCH, FRANZÖSISCH UND LATEIN). 1998: FERIALPRAXIS BEI SIEMENS (PROGRAMM- UND SYSTEM-ENTWICKLUNG, ERSTELLUNG VON JAVA-APPLETS UND CGI-PROGRAMMEN), 1999: FERIALPRAXIS BEI ALLIANZ INVESTMENT BANK (ERSTELLUNG VON COBOL- UND CLARION-PROGRAMMEN ZUM CASH-MANAGEMENT). SEIT DEZEMBER 1999: MITARBEIT BEI DER ONLINE-SCHÜLERZEITUNG "IN AND ONLINE" (ERSTELLUNG VON CGI-SCRIPTS, JAVA-APPLETS UND C-PROGRAMMEN, DOKUMENTATION UND VERÖFFENTLICHUNG DER PROGRAMME UNTER DER GNU GENERAL PUBLIC LICENSE), AUGUST 2000: NOCHMALIGE FERIALPRAXIS BEI ALLIANZ INVESTMENT BANK (ENTWICKLUNG VON PLATTFORMÜBERGREIFENDEN INTERNET-ANWENDUNGEN IN CLARION).

Prix Ars Electronica 2001 nominated for the GOLDEN NICA

RETURN TO SENDER

ANDREA MARIA GINTNER
MICHAELA MARIA PLÖCHL

Bei der Vorbereitung des EDCL-Moduls für Power Point beschlossen einige Schüler unserer Klassen, am Wettbewerb Cybergeneration U19 – Freestyle Computing teilzunehmen. Wir haben dieses Projekt gewählt, weil es uns sehr lustig erschienen ist, einmal selbst eine Liebesgeschichte auf dem Computer entstehen zu lassen.
Das Projekt selbst besteht aus zwölf Folien mit jeweils animierten Cliparts (Strichmännchen). Die Geschichte soll auch beweisen, dass in Sachen Liebe nichts unmöglich ist und dass am Ende doch alles gut wird. Auch wenn es am Anfang nicht so scheint.

During the preparation of the EDCL module for PowerPoint, several of the pupils from our class decided to take part in the competition Cybergeneration U19 – Freestyle Computing. We chose this project, because we thought it would be funny to create a love story on the computer ourselves. The project itself consists of 12 sheets with animated Clipart (stick figures). The story is also supposed to prove that nothing is impossible in love, and it will all turn out well in the end. Even if it doesn't look like it at the beginning.

MICHAELA MARIA PLÖCHL (14) LIVES IN FREISTADT/UPPER AUSTRIA AND ATTENDS THE MIDDLE SCHOOL HAUPTSCHULE 1 THERE. SHE IS ESPECIALLY INTERESTED IN COMPUTER SCIENCE, MATHEMATICS, PHYSICS AND SPORT. ANDREA MARIA GINTNER (14) ALSO LIVES IN FREISTADT AND ATTENDS THE MIDDLE SCHOOL HAUPTSCHULE 1 WITH MICHAELA PLÖCHL.

MICHAELA MARIA PLÖCHL (14) LEBT IN FREISTADT/OBERÖSTERREICH UND BESUCHT DORT DIE HAUPTSCHULE 1. IHRE BESONDEREN INTERESSEN GELTEN DER INFORMATIK, DER MATHEMATIK, DER PHYSIK UND DEM SPORT. ANDREA MARIA GINTNER (14) LEBT EBENFALLS IN FREISTADT UND BESUCHT WIE MICHAELA PLÖCHL DIE HAUPTSCHULE 1.

OMEGA::SHIELD

JÜRGEN HOOG

The security of data and information is very important to me. Unfortunately, however, this security is not always guaranteed. Strangers often penetrate into computer systems and create chaos there.

Now Omega::Shield is intended to provide a new possibility for protection from these kinds of attackers. This is done, as crazy as it sounds, precisely by not protecting yourself, but consciously allowing attackers to penetrate the system.

The trick here is that the attackers do not actually get to see the real system, but only a virtual platform, in order to deceive them.

The supposed "victim" is meanwhile able to observe all the attacker's actions through the Omega::Shield —cutting off the connection if necessary, interacting and even determining the approximate origin of the attack using trace route.

Another feature of Omega::Shield is that the Windows Trace Route command can be started directly from the Omega::Shield-environment. This means that the attacker's position can be traced back through his IP address.

Omega::Shield is flexible software. This means that it is not only possible to use Omega::Shield as a special kind of firewall, but also as a web server, for example, or even a chat server. The Omega::Shield TransferSpy makes it possible to receive and send data directly via TCP, for example, so that you can chat with another Omega::Shield user.

Mir liegt sehr viel an der Sicherheit von Daten und Informationen. Doch leider ist diese Sicherheit nicht immer gewährleistet. Fremde Leute dringen oftmals in Computersysteme ein und verursachen dort ein Chaos.

Omega::Shield soll nun eine neue Möglichkeit schaffen, sich gegen Angreifer zu schützen. Nämlich indem man – so verrückt es auch klingen mag – sich nicht schützt, sondern den Angreifer bewusst in das System eindringen lässt. Der Clou der Sache besteht darin, dass die Angreifer nicht das tatsächliche System zu sehen bekommen, sondern dass ihnen nur eine virtuelle Plattform vorgegaukelt wird, um sie zu täuschen. Das vermeintliche „Opfer" kann einstweilen durch Omega::Shield alle Aktionen des Angreifers mitverfolgen – auch notfalls die Verbindung trennen, interagieren und sogar den ungefähren Herkunftsort des Angriffs mittels Trace Route bestimmen.

Ein weiteres Feature von Omega::Shield ist, dass direkt aus der Omega::Shield-Umgebung heraus der Windows-Trace-Route-Befehl gestartet werden kann. So kann die Position des Angreifers über dessen IP-Adresse zurückverfolgt werden. Omega::Shield ist eine flexible Software. Es ist somit nicht nur möglich, Omega::Shield als spezielle Art von Firewall zu verwenden, sondern z.B. auch als Webserver oder sogar als Chat-Server. Der TransferSpy von Omega::Shield ermöglicht es z.B., direkt Daten über TCP zu empfangen und zu senden, so können Sie z.B. mit einem anderen Omega::Shield-Benutzer chatten.

JÜRGEN HOOG, BORN 1983 IN LINZ, ATTENDS THE GRADUATING CLASS OF THE COLLEGE PREPARATORY SCHOOL ALOISIANUM THERE. SPECIAL INTERESTS ARE OPERATING SYSTEMS, WEB DESIGN, MULTIMEDIA & TELECOMMUNICATION, NETWORKS & SECURITY, SOFTWARE DEVELOPMENT, GENETIC ENGINEERING, NEURAL NETWORKS, QUANTUM PHYSICS, ASTRONOMY, RELATIVITY THEORY, MUSIC AND FILMS.

JÜRGEN HOOG, GEB. 1983 IN LINZ, BESUCHT DORT DERZEIT DIE MATURAKLASSE DES GYMNASIUMS ALOISIANUM. BESONDERES INTERESSE FÜR BETRIEBSSYSTEME, WEBDESIGN, MULTIMEDIA & TELEKOMMUNIKATION, NETZWERKE & SICHERHEIT, SOFTWAREENTWICKLUNG, GENTECHNIK, NEURONALE NETZE, QUANTENPHYSIK, ASTRONOMIE, RELATIVITÄTSTHEORIE, MUSIK UND FILME.

DIGITAL 2001

MARVIN JAGADITS
MICHAEL PAYER

Wir haben die Arbeit mit dem Programm Front-page gemacht, und zwar deshalb, weil ich mich in diesem Programm schon gut zurecht gefunden habe. Wir besorgten uns die paar HTML-Codes aus dem Internet. Das Gleiche gilt für die Grafiken und Melodien. Wir hatten bis zum Einsendeschluss alle Hände voll zu tun, mal ein Fehler hier, dann ein Fehler da, eine Korrekturarbeit am Text, ein Problem mit der Formatierung der Grafiken, das Übliche eben. Aber als wir uns am Samstag die Seite noch mal angesehen haben, bemerkten wir, dass die erste Seite überhaupt keinen „Eye-Catcher" in sich verbarg, und wir strengten noch mal unsere letzten grauen Gehirnzellen an und überlegten. Wir schauten uns im Zimmer um und erspähten die Web-Cam. Ja, das ist es, dachte ich mir, und wir bauten uns ein kleines Studio im Zim-mer auf. Den Text auf die Schranktür geklebt, die man über die Kamera nicht sehen kann, und los ging's. Die erste Aufnahme ging ja in die Hose, wie man auf der Aufnahme unschwer erkennen kann. Diese banden wir dann auch noch in die Seite ein.

We did the work with the program Frontpage, because I already knew how to use it fairly well. We picked up the HTML codes from the Internet. The same is true for the graphics and melodies. Before the deadline, we were very busy fixing an error here, an error there, correcting a text, fixing a problem with the formatting of the graphics, all the usual things. Then when we took one more look at the page on Saturday, we noticed that there was not a single "eye-catcher" there, so we put our brains into gear one more time and thought about it. We looked around the room and noticed the web-cam. That's it, I thought, and we built a small studio for ourselves in the room. We stuck the text on the closet door that you can't see with the web-cam, and off we went. The first shot was a total failure, as you can easily see in the recording. We integrated this into the page, too.

WELCOME
@
DIGITAL 2001

MICHAEL PAYER, BORN 1987 IN VIENNA, FINISHED THE MIDDLE SCHOOL TADTEN AND NOW ATTENDS THE TECHNICAL SECONDARY SCHOOL HTBLA UNGARGASSE IN VIENNA. IN ADDITION TO RIDING, HE IS FASCINATED BY THE COMPUTER AND SURFING THE INTERNET.
MARVIN JAGADITS, BORN 1986 IN VIENNA, CURRENTLY ATTENDS A TECHNICAL SECONDARY SCHOOL IN VIENNA. HE WOULD LIKE TO STUDY COMPUTER SCIENCE AND BIOLOGY AND SEEK A MILITARY CAREER AS PROGRAMMER OFFICER. HE IS ESPECIALLY FASCINATED BY PC STRATEGY GAMES.

MICHAEL PAYER, GEB. 1987 IN WIEN, BESUCHT NACH ABSCHLUSS DER HAUPTSCHULE TADTEN DIE HTBLA UNGARGASSE IN WIEN. NEBEN DEM REITSPORT FASZINIEREN IHN COMPUTER UND DAS INTERNET-SURFEN.
MARVIN JAGADITS, GEB. 1986 IN WIEN, BESUCHT DERZEIT EINE HTL IN WIEN. ER MÖCHTE INFORMATIK UND BIOLOGIE STUDIEREN UND EINE MILITÄRISCHE LAUFBAHN ALS PROGRAMMIERER-OFFIZIER EINSCHLAGEN. BESONDERS FASZINIEREN IHN PC-STRATEGIESPIELE.

GESICHTER - LOGOS

NICOLE KARNER
TANJA PAYERL

At the computer middle school Wieselburg, we can go wild as computer artists in the elective subject PC-Picasso. We liked the many student portraits made with a digital camera. This led to the idea of making a picture out of them. Because our school has a nice logo, we used that as a model. We enlarged a school icon and counted how many photos we would need.
It would have been over a thousand. We didn't even have that many photos. So we cut out only the pictures from 50 photos, colored them yellow and blue with a filter, and copied them as many times as we needed them. We used a grid to put each face where it belonged. You can also send our picture as an e-card from our school homepage (www.hswieselburg.ac.at)!

In der Computerhauptschule Wieselburg können wir uns im Freigegenstand PC-Picasso als Computerkünstler austoben. Uns gefielen die vielen Schülerporträts, die mit der Digitalkamera aufgenommen wurden. Dabei kamen wir auf die Idee, ein Bild daraus zu machen. Weil unsere Hauptschule ein schönes Logo hat, haben wir dieses als Vorlage genommen. Wir vergrößerten ein CHS-Icon und zählten, wie viele Fotos wir brauchen würden.
Es wären über 1000 gewesen. So viele Fotos hatten wir gar nicht. Also schnitten wir nur Gesichter aus 50 Fotos, färbten sie mit einem Filter gelb und blau und kopierten sie, sooft wir sie brauchten. Mit einem Raster brachten wir jedes Gesicht dorthin, wo es hingehörte. Man kann unser Bild auch als E-Card über unsere Schulhomepage (www.hswieselburg.ac.at) versenden!

NICOLE KARNER AND TANJA PAYERL ATTEND THE MIDDLE SCHOOL WIESELBURG TOGETHER.

NICOLE KARNER UND TANJA PAYERL BESUCHEN GEMEINSAM DIE HAUPTSCHULE WIESELBURG.

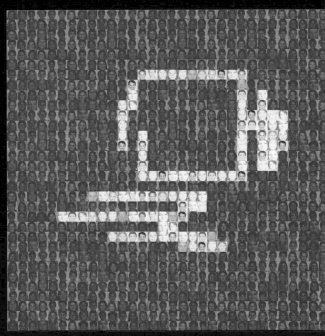

HTML-EDITOR

MARIAN KOGLER

Why I programmed the HTML-Editor:

W I wrote it because of my interest in HTML. Another motivation was that I was looking for a program that would reduce the work of writing. Now I no longer need to enter all the tags by hand!

The Evolution of the Program:

I started working on an HTML editor in February 1999. At that time, it could only generate headings. Then I took a break for half a year. After this half year, I continued working on it, so that the editor became quite a large program over the course of the year 2000. It supports JavaScript, CSS and DHTML and also VRML, if a VRML module is installed.

I am currently working on the following projects:

– a police game
– a disk drive information program
– a rename program
– a batch editor
– a railway simulation (on hold)
– a school simulation

Wieso ich den HTML-Editor programmiert habe:

Ich schrieb ihn aus Interesse an HTML. Ein weiterer Ansporn war, dass ich ein Programm suchte, welches einem Schreibarbeit erspart. Jetzt muss ich nicht mehr alle Tags händisch eingeben!

Die Entstehungsgeschichte des Programmes:

Ich begann im Februar 1999 am HTML-Editor zu arbeiten. Zu diesem Zeitpunkt konnte er zunächst nur Überschriften generieren. Dann machte ich ein halbes Jahr lang Pause. Nach diesem halben Jahr arbeitete ich an ihm weiter, so dass im Lauf des Jahres 2000 aus dem Editor ein ziemlich großes Programm wurde, das Java-Script, CSS und DHTML und, wenn ein VRML-Modul installiert ist, auch VRML unterstützt.

Derzeit arbeite ich an folgenden Projekten:

– ein Polizeispiel
– ein Laufwerksinformationsprogramm
– ein Rename-Programm
– ein Batch-Editor
– eine Eisenbahnsimulation (ruht)
– eine Schulsimulation

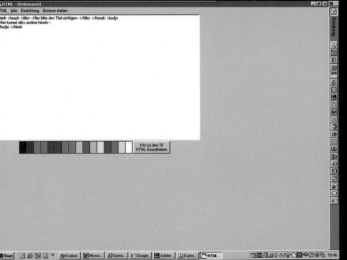

MARIAN KOGLER, BORN 1991 IN VIENNA, EARLY INTEREST IN COMPUTERS (AT THE AGE OF TWO), LANGUAGES, ASTRONOMY, PHYSICS AND NUCLEAR PHYSICS. ATTENDED SECONDARY SCHOOL CLASSES (PHYSICS, CHEMISTRY) EVEN AS A PRIMARY SCHOOL PUPIL. ATTENDED UPPER FORM CLASSES IN COMPUTER SCIENCE AND CHEMISTRY WHEN ATTENDING SECONDARY SCHOOL. UNIVERSITY SEMINAR AT THE INSTITUTE FOR EXPERIMENTAL PHYSICS IN ADDITION. VISITS TO CERN (CH), DESY (D) AND MAX PLANCK INSTITUTE.

MARIAN KOGLER, GEB. 1991 IN WIEN, FRÜHES INTERESSE AN COMPUTERN (MIT ZWEI JAHREN), SPRACHEN, ASTRONOMIE, PHYSIK UND ATOMPHYSIK. SCHON WÄHREND DER VOLKSSCHULZEIT BESUCH VON GYMNASIALKLASSEN (PHYSIK, CHEMIE). IM GYMNASIUM BESUCH VON OBERSTUFENKLASSEN IN INFORMATIK UND CHEMIE. DANEBEN UNIVERSITÄTSSEMINAR AM INSTITUT FÜR

STAY ALIVE
THOMAS LETTNER

I n my game, you go on a bear hunt armed with a bow and arrow. The reason for this is that one night something terrible happened. Your house and half the medieval city were hit by a major fire and destroyed. You stay alive by eating the bear meat you obtain and by selling it and getting something to drink, for example. On the bear hunt, though, you are not spared from injuries either. Therefore you need your catch in order to heal your wounds by selling it. Too great an injury to the head or the chest means the game is over. But very serious injuries on two other parts of your body also lead to a premature end. In addition, you also need to try to earn 850 silver coins, so that you can buy a farm and settle down. The most difficult task in this game, though, is to survive.

In meinem Spiel gehen sie mit Pfeil und Bogen im Gepäck auf Bärenjagd. Eines Nachts passierte nämlich ein schreckliches Unglück. Ihr Haus und die halbe mittelalterliche Stadt sind von einen Großbrand erfasst worden und verbrannt. Am Leben halten sie sich, indem sie das erbeutete Bärenfleisch essen und verkaufen und z.B. ihren Durst löschen. Doch bei der Bärenjagd bleiben ihnen auch Verletzungen nicht erspart. Somit brauchen sie die Beute, um durch Verkauf ihre Wunden zu heilen. Zu großer Schaden an Kopf oder Brust bedeutet das Ende des Spiels. Aber auch zu große Verletzungen an je zwei anderen Körperteilen bringen ein vorzeitiges Ende. Nebenbei müssen sie auch noch versuchen einen Betrag von 850 Silbermünzen zu verdienen um einen Bauernhof zu kaufen und sesshaft zu werden. Das Schwierigste an diesem Spiel jedoch ist zu überleben.

THOMAS LETTNER, 12 YEARS OLD, ATTENDS THE COLLEGE PREPARATORY SCHOOL BRG TRAUN, WITH AN EMPHASIS ON NATURAL SCIENCES. HIS FAVORITE SUBJECTS: PHYSICS, BIOLOGY, MATHEMATICS, SHOP, GEOGRAPHY AND ART EDUCATION. EDUCATIONAL GOAL: TO GRADUATE FROM THE TECHNICAL SECONDARY SCHOOL HTL LEONDING, EMPHASIS: ELECTRONICS. LIKES TO READ HARRY POTTER.

THOMAS LETTNER, 12 JAHRE, BESUCHT DAS BRG TRAUN, NATURWISSENSCHAFTLICHER SCHWERPUNKT. LIEBLINGSFÄCHER: PHYSIK, BIOLOGIE, MATHEMATIK, TECHNISCHES WERKEN, GEOGRAPHIE UND BILDNERISCHE ERZIEHUNG. AUSBILDUNGSZIEL: ABSCHLUSS IN DER HTL LEONDING IM SCHWERPUNKT: ELEKTRONIK. LIEST GERNE HARRY POTTER.

HOUSE-DESIGNER

FABIAN SCHLAGER

Program: Macromedia Flash5
length: 10 -15 minutes
type of game: Drag & Drop (designing a house)
I made this program for computer beginners, who are not very good at using the mouse yet. In this program, you can arrange two blocks into nice houses.
For this, you have:
– different doors
– different windows
– flowers
– street sections
– roofs
– basketball hoop
– and several other possibilities

Programm: Macromedia Flash5
Dauer: 10 – 15 Minuten
Spieltyp: Drag & Drop (Hausgestaltung)
Ich habe dieses Programm für Computereinsteiger gemacht, die noch nicht gut mit der Maus umgehen können. In diesem Programm kann man zwei Blöcke zu schönen Häusern umgestalten. Dazu hat man:
– verschiedene Türen
– verschiedene Fenster
– Blumen
– Straßenstücke
– Dächer
– Basketballkorb
– und noch mehrere Möglichkeiten

FABIAN SCHLAGER, BORN 1988, ATTENDED THE PRIMARY SCHOOL IN ELIXHAUSEN FOR FOUR YEARS, IS NOW IN THE THIRD YEAR AT THE COLLEGE PREPARATORY SECONDARY SCHOOL BRG ZAUNERGASSE IN THE CITY OF SALZBURG.

FABIAN SCHLAGER, GEB 1988, BESUCHTE VIER JAHRE DIE VOLKSSCHULE IN ELIXHAUSEN UND BESUCHT JETZT DIE DRITTE KLASSE AM BRG ZAUNERGASSE IN DER STADT SALZBURG.

TOONPLANET 3D

MARTIN SPAZIERER
DANIEL SPREITZER

I n the beginning, there was ...
A permanent Internet connection. The permanent Internet connection led to the wish for my own homepage. The first trials, in retrospect, were quite primitive. Decorated with copied gifs that everyone has anyway and still without a real concept. Besides, it wasn't really that much fun alone, so I talked it over with my cousin Daniel, who doesn't have an Internet connection, but joined in full of good ideas right away. We discovered the possibilities ...
Then as we were playing around on my laptop one rainy day at my grandparents' house, we rediscovered 3D software, which had been a Christmas present, but seemed too complicated at the time. We lowered our ambitions considerably and tried it with more primitive figures. *Southpark* - that was possible: simple forms and colors, but with completely different characteristics. ... and it worked.

Am Anfang war ...
Ein fixer Internetanschluss. Mit dem fixen Internetanschluss kam auch der Wunsch nach einer eigenen Hompage auf. Die ersten Versuche waren, rückblickend gesehen, schon sehr primitiv. Gespickt mit kopierten Gifs, die ohnehin jeder hat, und noch ohne richtiges Konzept. Außerdem machte es allein gar nicht so richtigen Spaß, und so besprach ich mich mit meinem Cousin Daniel, der zwar ohne Internetanschluss, aber voller guter Einfälle gleich mit dabei war. Wir entdeckten die Möglichkeiten ...
Als wir dann an einem verregneten Tag bei den Großeltern auf meinem Laptop herumspielten, entdeckten wir eine 3D-Software wieder, die ein Weihnachtsgeschenk gewesen war und dann doch zu kompliziert erschien. Wir steckten unsere Ansprüche zurück und versuchten es mit primitiveren Gestalten. *Southpark* – das war möglich: einfache Formen und Farben, jedoch absolut verschiedene Charaktereigenschaften.
... und es klappte.

MARTIN SPAZIERER, BORN 1987 IN VIENNA, ATTENDS THE COLLEGE PREPARATORY SCHOOL GRG 23 ALT ERLAA. HE IS ESPECIALLY INTERESTED IN CREATING HIS OWN HOMEPAGE, AND IN THE INTERNET WITH ALL ITS POSSIBILITIES.
DANIEL SPREITZER, BORN 1986 IN VIENNA, ATTENDS THE COLLEGE PREPARATORY SCHOOL GOETHE-GYMNASIUM, ASTGASSE, IN THE 14TH DISTRICT. PLAYS BASKETBALL, LIKES TO SKATE, AND IS INTERESTED IN COMPUTERS AND HIS PS 2.

MARTIN SPAZIERER, GEB. 1987 IN WIEN, BESUCHT DAS GRG 23 ALT ERLAA, ZWEIG REALGYMNASIUM. SEIN BESONDERES INTERESSE GILT DEM ERSTELLEN EINER EIGENEN HOMEPAGE UND DEM INTERNET MIT SEINEN MÖGLICHKEITEN.
DANIEL SPREITZER, GEB. 1986 IN WIEN, BESUCHT DAS GOETHE-GYMNASIUM IN DER ASTGASSE IM 14. BEZIRK. SPIELT BASKETBALL, SKATET GERNE UND INTERESSIERT SICH FÜR COMPUTER UND SEINE PS 2.

HTTP://

PHILIPP STRAHL

This sound compositing symbolizes the journey of a data packet through the Internet, how it is shifted back and forth by control signals and servers, in order to finally arrive at its destination; extended to a good three minutes.

For this purpose, I downloaded some pictures from various sites and freely accessible data from FTP servers, so that I could open them as WAV files, as sounds, manipulate them and play with them.

Putting them in sequences and sampling them resulted in the rhythm that I like to call the "Pulsation of the Internet". There is a simple, but seemingly random melody flowing along in this, which disappears towards the end. Maybe a kind of "guardian angel" for a data packet?

There were really no bigger problems, except that most of the pictures and files just didn't sound right, so I couldn't use them. So I spent a long time searching, but in my opinion, it was worth it.

I certainly wouldn't call my work "easy listening", because if you listen to it repeatedly, it starts to hurt your ears. However, it is an interesting way of exploring the digital world and its sounds.

Dieses Sound-Compositing symbolisiert die Reise eines Datenpakets durch das Internet, wie es von Steuersignalen und Servern hin und her geschubst wird, um schließlich an seinen Bestimmungsort zu gelangen; verlängert auf gut drei Minuten.

Zu diesem Zweck habe ich aus dem Internet beliebige Bilder von diversen Seiten und frei zugängliche Daten von FTP-Servern heruntergeladen, um sie als WAV-Dateien, als Sounds, zu öffnen, zu bearbeiten und mit ihnen zu spielen. Durch Aneinanderreihen und Samplen entstand der Rhythmus, den ich gerne als das „Pulsieren des Internet" bezeichne. In ihm fließt eine einfache, aber doch irgendwie zufällig wirkende Melodie mit, die gegen Schluss hin verschwindet. Vielleicht eine Art von „Schutzengel" eines Datenpakets?

Größere Probleme gab es eigentlich nicht, nur die meisten Bilder und Dateien klangen einfach nicht richtig, sie ließen sich nicht verwenden. So dauerte meine Suche recht lange, aber ich bin der Meinung, sie hat sich gelohnt.

Ich würde meine Arbeit auf keinem Fall als Easy Listening bezeichnen, da man bei wiederholtem Hören Ohrenschmerzen bekommt, allerdings als interessante Art der Erkundung der digitalen Welt und ihrer Klänge.

PHILIPP STRAHL, BORN 1983, FOLLOWING FOUR YEARS OF COLLEGE PREPARATORY SECONDARY SCHOOL, HAS ATTENDED THE TECHNICAL SECONDARY SCHOOL HTL ORTWEINSCHULE SINCE 1998, IN THE BRANCH AUDIO-VISUAL MEDIA DESIGN IN GRAZ. HOBBIES: LISTENING TO MUSIC AND MAKING MUSIC, FILMS, 3D MODELING AND ANIMATION, COMPOSITING, COFFEE HOUSE, WRITING SCRIPTS. SPECIAL SKILLS: PHOTOSHOP 4.0 AND HIGHER, PREMIERE 5.0 AND HIGHER, 3D STUDIO MAX 2.0 AND HIGHER, COOL EDIT 1.0 AND HIGHER, PRO AUDIO 7 AND HIGHER, DISCREET *PAINT*, AVID ELASTIC REALITY, MACROMEDIA FLASH 4.0, MEDIA 100, GOOD COMMAND OF HTML, SOME KNOWLEDGE OF JAVA.

PHILIPP STRAHL, GEB. 1983, BESUCHT NACH VIER KLASSEN GYMNASIUM SEIT 1998 DIE HTL ORTWEINSCHULE, ZWEIG AUDIOVISUELLES MEDIENDESIGN, IN GRAZ. HOBBIES: MUSIK HÖREN UND MACHEN, FILME, 3D-MODELLIERUNG UND ANIMATION, COMPOSITING, KAFFEEHAUS, VERFASSEN VON DREHBÜCHERN. BESONDERE KENNTNISSE: PHOTOSHOP 4.0 UND HÖHER, PREMIERE 5.0 UND HÖHER, 3D STUDIO MAX 2.0 UND HÖHER, COOL EDIT 1.0 UND HÖHER, PRO AUDIO 7 UND HÖHER, DISCREET *PAINT*, AVID ELASTIC REALITY, MACROMEDIA FLASH 4.0, MEDIA 100, GUTE HTML-KENNTNISSE, EINIGE JAVA-KENNTNISSE.

BILDER FÜR SAM UND SPICE

SONJA ROSA VRISK

There are four parts in this piece:
– single pictures that I made in Paint
– story of roof-mole
– mobile
– calendar

My parents got a computer when I was three and a half. I always watched, and once when my mom was in the bath, I booted it myself and painted something in Paint. After that, I was allowed to use the computer, too. Three years later, we got a new computer and Internet. I like to write emails and sometimes something for school. I still like to draw very much. Naturally I play games, too. My favorite game is "Neverhood". My mother read about this competition in the newspaper. My father is busy with making homepages right now, and I am interested in that, too.

The mobile is like a kind of paper model set, maybe other children would like to try it, too. It's very easy, you just have to save it in Paint first and then mirror it again.
The calendar was actually a present for my grandma. I found a calendar template on the CD "Harry Hops, Workshop für Kids" and made the pictures for it. Then you can print it out and staple it together and hang it up on a string.

Es gibt vier Teile in dieser Arbeit:
– einzelne Bilder, die ich in Paint gemacht habe
– Geschichte vom Dachmaulwurf
– Mobile
– Kalender

Meine Eltern haben einen Computer bekommen, als ich dreieinhalb war. Ich hab immer zugeschaut und einmal, als Mama grade im Bad war, hab ich ihn selber hochgestartet und in Paint was gemalt. Danach durfte ich den Computer auch benutzen. Drei Jahre später bekamen wir den neuen Computer und Internet. Ich schreibe gerne E-Mails und manchmal was für die Schule. Zeichnen tu ich immer noch sehr gerne. Natürlich spiele ich auch. Mein Lieblingsspiel ist „Neverhood". Meine Mutter hat in einer Zeitung von diesem Wettbewerb gelesen. Mein Vater beschäftigt sich grade mit Homepagemachen und das interessiert mich auch.

Das Mobile ist wie eine Art Bastelbogen gedacht, vielleicht mögen andere Kinder auch so was machen, es ist ganz einfach, man muss es nur in Paint zuerst speichern und dann noch mal spiegeln.
Der Kalender war eigentlich ein Geschenk für meine Oma. Ich habe auf der CD „Harry Hops, Workshop für Kids" eine Kalendervorlage gefunden und die Bilder dazugemacht. Man kann's dann ausdrucken und zusammenheften und mit einer Schnur aufhängen.

Archenoa

SONJA ROSA VRISK, BORN 1993 IN KLAGENFURT. BEGINNING 1996 CHILDREN'S GROUP AT THE PARENT-CHILD-CENTER IN KLAGENFURT (MONTESSORI, PAINTING, DANCING), BEGINNING FALL 1996 FIRST EXPERIMENTS ON THE COMPUTER, BEGINNING 1997 PAINTING GROUP "DIE NATÜRLICHE SPUR" WITH SABINE JOBST IN KLAGENFURT, SINCE 1999 ATTENDS PRIMARY SCHOOL NO. 16 IN KLAGENFURT (CURRENTLY SECOND YEAR).

SONJA ROSA VRISK, GEB. 1993 IN KLAGENFURT. AB 1996 KINDERGRUPPE IM ELTERN-KIND-ZENTRUM IN KLAGENFURT (MONTESSORI, MALEN, TANZEN), AB HERBST 1996 ERSTE VERSUCHE AM COMPUTER, AB 1997 MALGRUPPE „DIE NATÜRLICHE SPUR" BEI SABINE JOBST IN KLAGENFURT, 1999 BESUCH DER VOLKSSCHULE 16 IN KLAGENFURT (DERZEIT 2. KLASSE).

FLASH EXPERIMENT

RENÉ WEIRATHER

For two years, I have had my own computer. My mom showed me the programs (Coreldraw, Photopaint and Frontpage—and the Internet, of course, and how to put pages up). So I played around with it. I have games on my PC, too, but only Köpfchen & Co, where you have to solve things. Then one day, I discovered the Flash program on my mom's PC and I wanted it right away. First I looked at all the examples in the program, and then I read all the help topics (there weren't very many), and then I tried making games and cartoons myself. Every day I learned more about Flash, and I have more and more ideas about what else I could make with it. One day I spent a whole eight hours with Flash. I like the actions and variables best. I only put a few of my Flashes on my homepage—the others are all on my PC. I'm glad that I won, because now I can see the computer museum in September, my mom has already told me a lot about it.

Seit zwei Jahren habe ich einen eigenen Computer. Meine Mama zeigte mir die Programme (Coreldraw, Photopaint und Frontpage – und natürlich das Internet und wie man Seiten hinein stellt). Ich hab halt so damit rum gespielt. Spiele habe ich auch auf dem PC meiner Mutter, aber nur Köpfchen und co, wo man Sachen lösen muss. Eines Tages habe ich dann auf dem PC meiner Mama das Flash-Programm entdeckt und wollte es auch sofort haben. Mama gab es mir. Zuerst sah ich mir alle Beispiele in dem Programm an und dann las ich alle Hilfethemen (waren gar nicht so viele) und dann probierte ich, selbst Spiele und Trickfilme zu machen. Von Tag zu Tag lernte ich immer mehr über Flash, und mir fallen immer mehr Ideen ein, was ich noch damit machen kann. Einmal habe ich volle acht Stunden am Tag mit Flash verbracht. Am liebsten sind mir die Aktionen und Variablen. In meine Homepage habe ich nur ein paar meiner Flashs hinein getan – die anderen sind alle auf meinem PC. Ich freue mich, dass ich gewonnen habe, weil dann kann ich mir im September das Computermuseum anschauen, meine Mama hat mir nämlich schon viel davon erzählt.

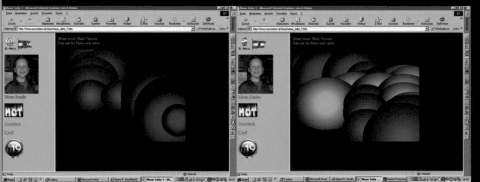

RENÉ WEIRATHER, BORN 1991 IN REUTTE/TIROL. CURRENTLY IN THE 4TH YEAR AT GRAMMAR SCHOOL AND AT SECONDARY SCHOOL STARTING IN THE FALL. FUTURE PLANS STILL UNCERTAIN, MAYBE BECOME AN ANIMAL FILMER OR PROGRAMMER.

RENÉ WEIRATHER, GEB. 1991 IN REUTTE/TIROL. BESUCHT MOMENTAN DIE 4. KLASSE VOLKSSCHULE UND AB HERBST DAS GYMNASIUM. BERUFSWÜNSCHE DERZEIT NOCH UNGEWISS; VIELLEICHT TIERFILMER ODER PROGRAMMIERER.

SMS-NOIFIER

THOMAS WINKLER

The *SMS-Notifier* is a program that permanently checks a web site (e.g. futurezone.orf.at) for new articles and sends the headlines via SMS to all registered users, whenever something comes in. The system consists of two programs. One program (CGI) is responsible for registering users. It enables new users to register via a web interface (see example page <http://tom.shacknet.nu>). The actual message program checks the news site at regular intervals for new articles and then sends these to all the registered users. A working message system can be reached at the URL <http://tom.shacknet.nu>.

Note: <http://tom.shacknet.nu> is my private computer. In principle, it should be reachable 24 hours a day, but unfortunately, sometimes it happens that it is offline briefly. If the URL <http://tom.shacknet.nu> is not working, please just try again later.

Der *SMS-Notifier* ist ein Programm, das eine Website (z. B. *futurezone.orf.at*) permanent auf neue Artikel überprüft und gegebenenfalls die Headlines per SMS an alle registrierten Benutzer verschickt.

Das System besteht aus zwei Programmen. Ein Programm (CGI) ist für die Registrierung der User zuständig. Es ermöglicht es, neue User über ein Webinterface anzumelden (siehe Beispielseite <http://tom.shacknet.nu>). Das eigentliche Benachrichtigungsprogramm überprüft in regelmäßigen Abständen die News-Seite auf neue Artikel und verschickt diese dann an alle registrierten Benutzer. Ein funktionierendes Benachrichtigungssystem ist unter der URL <http://tom.shacknet.nu> erreichbar.

Hinweis: tom.shacknet.nu ist mein privater Rechner. Er sollte zwar grundsätzlich 24 Stunden am Tag erreichbar sein, aber es kann leider auch vorkommen, dass der Rechner zeitweise kurz offline ist. Sollte die URL <http://tom.shacknet.nu> also nicht funktionieren, bitte einfach später nochmals probieren.

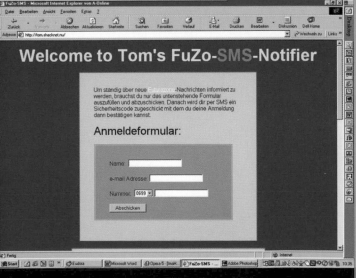

THOMAS WINKLER, BORN 1984 IN OBERWART. GERLITZ MIDDLE SCHOOL, HARTBERG, SINCE 1998 TECHNICAL SECONDARY SCHOOL HTBL PINKAFELD, DEPARTMENT DATA PROCESSING AND ORGANIZATION. EXPERIENCE WITH THE OPERATING SYSTEMS WINDOWS 9x/NT/2000, AND WITH LINUX AND FREEBSD. KNOWLEDGE OF THE PROGRAMMING LANGUAGE C/C++, EXPERIENCE WITH PROGRAMMING PHP AND PERL SCRIPTS, HTML PAGE DESIGN (ADOBE GOLIVE, MACROMEDIA DREAMWEAVER), MULTIMEDIA PAGE DESIGN (MACROMEDIA FLASH), KNOWLEDGE OF INTERNET AND NETWORKING, IMAGE PROCESSING (ADOBE PHOTOSHOP, PAINT SHOP PRO, ...).

THOMAS WINKLER, GEB. 1984 IN OBERWART. GERLITZ-HAUPTSCHULE, HARTBERG, SEIT 1998 HTBL PINKAFELD, ABTEILUNG EDV U. ORGANISATION. ERFAHRUNG MIT DEN BETRIEBSSYSTEMEN WINDOWS 9x/NT/2000 SOWIE MIT LINUX UND FREEBSD. KENNTNISSE DER PROGRAMMIERSPRACHE C/C++, ERFAHRUNG MIT DER PROGRAMMIERUNG VON PHP- UND PERLSCRIPTS, HTML- SEITENGESTALTUNG (ADOBE GOLIVE, MACROMEDIA DREAMWEAVER), MULTIMEDIA-SEITENGESTALTUNG (MACROMEDIA FLASH), INTERNET- BZW. NETZWERKKENNTNISSE, BILDBEARBEITUNG (ADOBE PHOTOSHOP, PAINT SHOP PRO, ...).

jury

Net Vision / Net Excellence Pete Barr-Watson - Tanja Diezmann - Solveig Godeluck - Machiko Kusahara - TNC Network

Interactive Art Masaki Fujihata - Ulrike Gabriel - Peter Higgins - Hiroshi Ishii - Joachim Sauter

...puter Animation / Visual Effects Paddy Eason - Christophe Héry - Barbara Robertson - Rick Sayre - Christian Volckman

Digital Musics Ned Bouhalassa - Reinhold Friedl - Tony Herrington - Naut Humon - Kaffe Matthew

u19 Cybergeneration Sirikit Amann - etoy.TAKI - Florian Hecker - Horst Hörtner - Robert Pöcksteiner

Chairman of the Jury *Hannes Leopoldseder*

NET VISION / NET EXCELLENCE

Pete Barr-Watson (UK)

is co-founder of the cutting edge new media agency *http://www.*

kerb.co.uk, a design-led company creating funky websites in html, Shockwave Director and Flash. Kerb are known especially for their expertise in youth marketing, and viral campaigns. In September 2000 Kerb scooped the prestigious web agency of the year prize at the Future UK Internet Awards.

Tanja Diezmann (D)

is professor for interface design

at the Anhalt College in Dessau. She is a specialist for generic interfaces, modular systems, navigation systems and digital CI. She defined "Navigable Structures" as an interface principle.

Solveig Godeluck (F)

journalist for *Point*, *L'Usine nouvelle*, *L'Express*, *Le Nouvel Observateur*, *Le Monde*, *Le Jour-*

nal de l'Atelier, Capital, Biba, Impact Médecin and others. Author of a book on net economy *Le boom de la netéconomie* (Editions La

Découverte, Paris 2000). Editor for *Transfert*, responsible for the field of net economy.

Machiko Kusahara (J)

has been active as curator of media art and in promoting media art while also doing research on the relationships

between art and such liminal regions in science and technology as telecommunications and artificial life. Her major concern is what digital technology offers the human imagination. Her publications include CG Anthology, CG Access, and the Hyper Image Museum on CD-ROM. Formerly an assistant professor in the Tokyo Institute of Polytechnics' Faculty of Art, she is now an assistant professor in the Graduate School of Science and Technology, Kobe University.

TNC Network (www.tnc.net)

is a Paris-based new-media label dedicated to digital culture & lifestyle. Founded in 1995 by

Tina Cassani and Bruno Beusch, TNC Network has developed ground-breaking concepts and events for the Internet, TV/radio, museums, and festivals in Europe, Japan, and the US. It specializes in the design of new-style conferences & shows for the digital genera-

tion, such as the Electrolobby showroom for digital culture & lifestyle at Ars Electronica. In 2001 TNC was commissioned to redesign the Internet category of the Prix Ars Electronica, where Beusch/Cassani acted also as Jury members.

INTERACTIVE ART

Masaki Fujihata (J)

born 1956; Board member of Japan Animation Film Association, since 1987 Member of ASIFA, since 1990 Associate Professor, Faculty of Environmental Information at Keio University. Since 1998 Professor at Keio

University, Faculty of Environmental Information; since 1999 Professor at National University of Fine Art and Music, Inter Media Art course. Masaki Fujihata's awards include a Golden Nica by the Prix Ars Electronica jury for his entry *Global Interior Project* in the category Interactive Art (1996).

Ulrike Gabriel (D)

media artist, has been developing her own software for interactive installations since the early

nineties. She has studied and worked at the Institute for New Media in Frankfurt a. M. and at the Art College for Media, Cologne, and others. With her own media lab, Codelab Berlin, she cooperates with the College of Arts, Berlin, the Technical University Eindhoven, and will take part in the artist in residence program of Podewil, Center for Current Arts, Berlin, in 2001. Ulrike Gabriel has taken part in exhibitions in Europe, North America, Australia and East Asia.

Peter Higgins (UK)

trained at the Architectural Association and worked as a scenographic designer in West End theatre and for BBC TV. In 1992 he was co founder of Land

Design Studio, who are interpretive designers working with lottery based projects and museums throughout the UK. Most

recently they have been responsible for The Playzone at The Millennium Dome London, which publicly demonstrates the extraordinary potential of interactive digital art.

Hiroshi Ishii (J)

His focus is on media design to augment interactions between humans, computers, and the physical environment. He has

done extensive research on Computer-Supported Cooperative Work [CSCW] and Human-Computer Interaction [HCI]. His team at NTT

Human Interface Laboratories invented TeamWorkStation and ClearBoard. He has been active

in the ACM SIGCHI community. At the MIT Media Lab, he directs the Tangible Media Group.

Joachim Sauter (D)

born 1959, MA in communication design at the University of

the Arts, Berlin, further studies at the German Academy for Film and Television, Berlin. He has been using computers from the

early stages of his work as a designer and filmmaker. Fueled by his interest, he founded Art+Com, an independent design and research group in 1988 together with other designers, scientists and technicians. Today he is head of Art+Com e.V. He has been awarded a Distinction in the Prix Ars Electronica 92 and 97 (Interactive Art), as well as the Los Angeles Interactive Media Festival Impact Award in 1995 and the Prix Pixel INA in 1997.

COMPUTER ANIMATION / VISUAL EFFECTS

Paddy Eason (GB)

is Digital Effects Supervisor. The

films, for which he has been responsible for visual effects, include *Chicken Run*, *Sleepy Hollow*, *The Legend of Ocean Pianist*,

Mission Impossible II and *Little Buddha*. For the digital effects in the ad *Guinness Surfer*, he received an Honorary Mention from the Prix Ars Electronica 1999.

Christophe Héry (F/USA)

joined Industrial Light & Magic in 1993 as a senior technical director on *The Flintstones*. Christophe majored in architecture and electricity at Ecole

Superieure des Travaux Publics, where he received his degree in 1989. While a student in Paris he freelanced as a technical director at BUF, a special effects house, as well as Thomson Digital Images, where he worked on 3D software development in his spare time. After graduation, Christophe took a job as director of research and development at Label 35, a Parisian cartoon studio. Christophe recently completed working as a computer graphics supervisor on *Mission to Mars*.

Barbara Robertson (USA)

has been the West Coast Senior Editor for Computer Graphics World since 1985 and in that capacity has written many award-winning articles on com-

puter animation, visual effects, and graphics technology as she watched the evolution of computer graphics art and technology.

Prior to this work, she was the Editor and Researcher for the

Whole Earth Software Catalog, West Coast Bureau Chief for Popular Computing, and West Coast Editor for Byte Magazine.

Rick Sayre (USA)

joined Pixar Animation Studios in 1987. He developed warping, painting, image processing and shading tools, and served as Technical Director and production software developer as the studio began commercial production. His feature credits

include *Toy Story*, *Toy Story 2* and *A Bug's Life*, for which he was nominated for a British Academy Award. Rick has also been involved

extensively in theater and interactive art, and drew from this experience to develop an innovative animation input device, for which he received a SciTech Academy Award. He is currently Supervising Technical Director on *Monster's, Inc.*, in production for release in 2001.

Christian Volckman (F)

is a filmmaker and graduate of the Ecole Supérieure d'Arts Graphiques. He has made two short films and several animation clips, which reflect his experience as a painter, graphics artist and photographer. At Prix

Ars Electronica 2000 he has been awarded a Golden Nica in the category "Visual Effects" for his film *Maaz*.

DIGITAL MUSICS

Ned Bouhalassa (CDN)

is a studio composer specializing in acousmatic works. His teachers included Kevin Austin and Francis Dhomont. Attracted by cinema, contemporary visual art and science fiction, he tries in his work to balance form and content, while leaving room for emotion and poetry. Presented in concert and on radio in many countries, his works have won him several national and international prizes. Active in the pro-

motion of electroacoustic music in Montréal since 1987, he participates in concerts as a composer and host (ÉuCuE, ACREQ), on radio

as host and performer (CKUT-FM, Radio-Canada), in ommunity work (president and editor for the CEC), and in academic duties (teacher at Concordia University, 1991-96). Recently, he has composed music for a variety of media (cinema, television, Internet).

Reinhold Friedl (D)

Studied piano with Renate Werner, Allan Marks, Alexander von Schlippenbach and others. In Stuttgart and Berlin he studied mathematics and musicology (with C. Dahlhaus, Helga de le Motte, and others). As an interpreter / performer / composer he has received various scholarships, including from eurocréa-

tion Paris France, the Rome Scholarship (Villa Serpentara) of the Academy of Arts Berlin, a working scholarship for STEIM Amsterdam, and also various composition commissions. Reinhold Friedl also heads a seminar together with Prof. Behrends on "Music and Mathematics" in the specialization field of mathematics at the Free University Berlin. He founded and leads the ensembles Piano-Inside-Out and zeitkratzer. In addition, Friedl works regularly as a curator for the Podewil Berlin and directed the Off-ICMC in Berlin in 2000.

Tony Herrington (UK)

is the Publisher & Editor-in-Chief of the British magazine *The Wire*, described by the US Forced Exposure organisation as "the most essential music maga-

zine of the contemporary era". He joined the magazine's staff in 1992 as Deputy Editor, becoming Editor in 1994, Editor &

Publisher in 1996, and Publisher & Editor-in-Chief in 2000. He lives in South London with his partner and daughter.

Naut Humon (USA)

is the director of RECOMBINANT MEDIA LABS which incubates or expands international sonic cinematic projects for mobile performance exhibitions. He conducts, curates and artistically contributes to the facility's orchestral

"dub dashboard" AV system: *Surround Traffic Control*. This spatialized media network recombines sound driven optic image configurations for realtime multichannel audio/video arrays. A number of these operations have been produced for his other San Francisco activity on Asphodel Records during the recent years.

Kaffe Matthew (GB)

has been making and performing new musics via all kinds of digital gadgetry all over the

world for the past ten years. She is now most known for her live sampling performances of events and places in real time: processing in installation, on stage, in galleries, clubs, concert halls, tents, churches, the outback, warehouses, or ambient tea rooms. In her works she is sampling sonic snatches from the venue and around, reprocessing in lines and pulsing slo-tones, playing inside a circle of speakers with the audience. She just released her 4th solo work, "cd dd".

U 19

Sirikit M. Amann (A)

studied political science, theater arts and economics in Austria, Germany and the USA. Since

1987 she has worked for the ÖKS—Austrian Culture Service—

where she is responsible for the concept development and implementation of multimedia projects in schools.

Austrian Culture Service school projects: 1994 "Computer and Games" and 1995 "Speed" (both at the Ars Electronica Festival).

etoy.TAKI

President and founding member of the etoy.CORPORATION. Lives in Zurich and Monza. Since 1995 the etoy.CORPORATION has initiated and cultivated award winning incubations like "the digital hijack" and "TOY-

WAR.com" and controls subsidiary companies like the etoy.HOLDING. Venture capitalists, leading art collections (the Robert Shiffler Foundation and others), institutional investors and many etoy.FANS have invested in this sophisticated corporate structure that generates and increases cultural value by infecting business, entertainment and the art world.

Florian Hecker (A)

is an independent composer in the fields of computer music and digital production. Involved in various sonic projects simulta-

neously, such as recording for labels like Mego and Or, his current activities also include audio publishing and interconnection in new formats, e.g. mp3 via the fals.ch web project, cd_slopper, and visual abstraction with SKOT.

Horst Hörtner (A)

studied telematics at the technical University of Graz and worked as a freelance developer of realtime control systems as well as working for art projects.

Co-founder of the group "x-space". He has worked for EXPO Sevilla, documenta IX, austromir, etc. Since 1995 he is technical director of the Ars Electronica Center in Linz and director of the AEC FutureLab.

Robert Pöcksteiner (A)

born 1971 in Linz. Studied art history in Innsbruck (did not finish). Started working in the

event branch (supervising events in Upper Austria). Has worked for ORF since 1994, ORF Upper Austria events, ORF

Upper Austria radio productions (teasers and promotion until 1999). Since 1999 with ORF Vienna TV—"Willkommen Österreich" (audiovisual design, teasers and promotion). In addition, various special projects (advertisement award presentation EFFIE 2000).

participants

Adriano Abbado
Via Crema 18
20135 Milano
I
adriano@abbado.com

Manuel Abendroth
19 Quai Au Foin
1000 Bruxelles
B
lab-au@lab-au.com

Deanne Achong
303-985 W 14th Ave
V5Z 1R3 Vancouver, BC
CDN
deanne@diamedia.net

Wilfried Agricola De
Cologne
Mauritiussteinweg 64
50676 Köln
D
info@agricola-de-
cologne.de

Flávia Aidar Avenida
Paulista, 149
01311-000 São Paulo
BR
flavia@itaucultural.org.br

Amy Alexander
24700 Mcbean Pkwy F/v
91355 Valencia, CA
USA
amy@plagiarist.org

Eyvind Almquist
Lofotengatan 21
16433 Kista
S
eyvind.almquist
@tietoenator.com

Itae Amit
Po Box 8663
61086 Jaffa
IL
i@b-media.com

Gordana Andelic-Galic
Pruscakova 5/2
71000 Sarajevo
BIH
gosha_gag@hotmail.com

Kestutis Andrasiunas
L. Asanaviciutes
48–49
2050 Vilnius
LT
ke_an@o-o.lt

Ian Andrews
232 Addison Road
Marrickville
2204 Sydney, NSW
AUS
i.andrews@metroscreen.
com.au

Jim Andrews
2313 Esther Pl.
V9B 2E5 Victoria, BC
CDN
jim@vispo.com

Aulestia Armelle
32 Rue Bezout
75014 Paris
F
aulestia@multimania.
com

Anjali Arora
E72 Akash, Bodakdev
380015 Ahmedabad,
Gujarat
INDIA
anjali@artbrush.net

Carsten Aschmann
Am Kleinen Felde 26
30167 Hannover
D
aschmann@mac.com

Nathalie Auzépy
79 Rue Des Archives
75003 Paris
F
nu@n-udesign.com

Wolf Bachschneider
Unertlstr.11
80803 München
D
whb@endorphin-
records.de

Backbone.interactive
Favoritenstr. 9
1040 Wien
A
p.judmaier@myzel.org

Angelo Baiguera
G. Gallina, 4
34100 Trieste
I
angelo.baiguera@luxa.it

Christophe Baillon
80, Rue De Paris
93100 Montreuil
F
cb@iside.net

Ali Bali
297, Rue Fg St. Antoine
75011 Paris
F
flash@3toon.com

Joey Bargsten
198 Lawrence Hall
97403 Eugene, OR
USA
bargsten@darkwing.
uoregon.edu

Stephan Barron
235 Ave Du Puech De
Massane
34080 Montpellier
F
sb@technoromanticism.
com

Kyle Barrow
4-10-4-702 Minamisen-
ba, Chuo Ku
542-0081 Osaka
J

Chris Bassett
3219 Sacramento Str
94702 Berkeley, Ca
USA
chris@robot138.com

Christian Bauer
5724 Stuhlfelden 194
A
chris@well.com

Ricardo Bayer
Tannhäuserpl. 2/5
1150 Wien
A
christoph.schmidt
@create-mediadesign.at

Det Bazelmans
Oeyenbos 8a
5511 LE Knegsel
NL

Wolfgang Beinert
Kaulbachstraße 92
80802 München
D
atelier@beiner.net

Thomas Bell
2518 Wellington Pl.
37128 Murfreesboro
USA
trbell@home.com

Olof Bendt
Po Box 24081
104 50 Stockholm
S
olof.bendt@interactive
institute.se

Kim Binstedt
2-34-1 Uehara,
Shibuya-ku
151-0064 Tokyo
J

Stahlglatt Blumenweich
Benedikt-Schellingerg. 9/8
1150 Wien
A
happypolitics
@stahlglatt.net

Xavier Boissarie
Rue Nollet
75017 Paris
F
biovax@noos.fr

Netsong Bot
24960 Walnut St. #14
91321 Newhall, CA
USA
bot@netsong.org

Sylvie Bourguet
13 Rue Beauvais
56100 Lorient
F
bulot@x-arn.org

Brad Brace
520 3rd St 3rd Flr
94107 San Francisco, CA
USA
bbrace@wired.com

Dar Brady
1665 Pullan Ave
45223 Cincinnati, OH
USA
architexture@earthlink.
net

Bruce Branit
6042 Lee Drive
90630 Cypress, CA
USA

Mez Breeze
1/485 Crown St.
2500 Wollongong
AUS
netwurker@hotkey.net.au

Paul Brown
PO Box 3603
4101 S. Brisbane, QLD
AUS
paul@paul-brown.com

Niels Buenemann
Theodorstr. 42-90/6
22761 Hamburg
D
rieble@form-one.de

Will Bulman
1 Straylands Grove
YO311EB York
UK
qed@enterprise.net

David Buob
Thomas-Müntzer-Platz 9
01307 Dresden
D
daphneb@web.de

Patrick-Henri Burgaud
Zypendaalseweg 75
6814 Ce Arnhem
NL
burgaud@burgaud.
demon.nl

Cup Cake
Pmb #192, 1459 18th
Str
94107 San Francisco, CA
USA
cupcake@sugarand
spice.org

Francois Chalet
Schöneggstr. 5
8004 Zürich
CH
bonjour@francoischalet.
ch

Benjamin Chang
112 South Michigan Ave.
60657 Chicago
USA
bchang@artic.edu

Young-hae Chang
65 Palpan-dong,
Jongno-gu
110-220 Seoul
South Korea
tfa@chollian.net

Olivier Chauvin
24, Rue De Saintonge
75003 Paris
F
ntbcom@noos.fr

Frank Chindamo
775 East Blithedale Ave,
#230
94941 Mill Valley, CA
USA
dctraub@aol.com

Thanasis Chondros
Alli Poli, Konst.
Melenikou 34
54635 Thessaloniki
GR
allipoli@magnet.gr

Curt Cloninger
2409 Baxter Str
36607 Mobile, AL
USA
curt@lab404.com

Daryl Cloran
2 Berkeley St., Suite 305
M5A 4J5 Toronto, Ontario
CDN
rebecca@trapeze.com

Coldcut
#5 205 Mount Royal
West
H2T 2T2 Montreal
CDN
sin@cam.org

Michael Cole
4948 Burnside Road
94572 Sebastopol, CA
USA
colem@ap.net

Jean-Francois Colonna
Route De Saclay
91128 Palaiseau Cedex
F
colonna@cmap.polytech-
nique.fr

Andrew Colquhoun
Santa Madrona 37
08800 Vilanova I
La Geltru, Barcelona
E
dogonefff@dogonefff.org

Jerez Concha
Jesus Y Maria 4
28012 Madrid
E
joseiges@wanadoo.es

Francesco Contin
Contrà S.barbara 19
36100 Vicenza
I
franz@magicflam.com

Frank Cordelle
P.o. Box 4
03442 Bennington, NH
USA

Alison Cornyn
176 Grand Str
10013 New York
USA
suej@picture-
projects.com

Sheila Coronel
107 Scout De Guida
Quezon City
RP

Carlos Correia
Av. Berna, 26-c,8
1069-261 Lisbon
P
citi@mail.telepac.pt

Manuela Corti
Via Zamboni, 7
40126 Bologna
I
manuela.corti@passio-
pea.net

Daniel Cotellessa
Bleichstr. 80
75173 Pforzheim
D
d_cotellessa@UeberDas-
Hoeren.de

Andy Cox
67 29th Str
94110 San Francisco, CA
USA
andycox@twcdc.com

David Crawford
402 Highland Ave #45
02144 Somerville, MA
USA
crawford@lightofspeed.
com

Francesca Da Rimini
Unit 7, 21 Surflen Str
5000 Adelaide, SA
AUS
dollyoko@thing.net

Testing Daemon
Franzensg. 6 / Top 1
1050 Wien
A
manu@web.fm

Sharon Daniel
1156 High Str
95064 Santa Cruz, CA
USA
sdaniel@cats.ucsc.edu

Chiaki Darcy
1186 Broadway #418
10001 New York, NY
USA
chiaki@nicknack.org

Martin Di Costa
Schwertstr.10
67063 Ludwigshafen
D
bunt-und-
chaotisch@gmx.de

Etienne De Bary
Rue Du Pdt Wilson
94250 Gentilly
F
etiennc@debary.nom.fr

Agnès De Cayeux
24, Rue De Saintonge
75003 Paris
F
ntbcom@noos.fr

Joe De Lange
Unit 414, The Studios,
112 Longmarket Str
8001 Cape Town
ZA
joe@redshift.co.za

Jean-François Denis
4580, Avenue De
Lorimier
H2H2 2B5 Montréal, QC
CDN
info@electrocd.com

Laurence Desarzens
Ackerstr. 11
8005 Zürich
CH
laurence@beatmap.com

Dextro Dextro
Lorenz-Mandl-G. 33/1
1160 Wien
A
dextro@dextro.org

Jo Di
Carrer Bruc 56 Pr1
08009 Barcelona
E
jodi@jodi.org

Federico Diaz
Vodickova 36
11602 Prague
CZ
info@e-area.cz,
wdf@wdf.cz

Markus Dietz
Inselkammerstraße 8a
82008 Unterhaching
D
karsten.lauth@marune.de

Viva Digital
Im Mediapark 6d
50500 Köln
D

Dimiter Dimitrov
78, Samokov Blvd.,
Bl.305, Ap.61
1113 Sofia
BG
megaart@otel.net

Christian Dögl
Breite Gasse 3/2
1070 Wien
A
chrid@uma.at

Reynald Drouhin
41 Ave Du General
De Gaulle
94170 Le Perreux Sur
Marne
F
reynald@incident.net

Mac Dunlop
98 Romney Ave.
BS7 Bristol
UK
herenorthere@dial.pipex.
com

Ollivier Dyens
4404 A Fabre
H2J-3V3 Montreal
CDN
odyens@hotmail.com

Jorn Ebner
P.o. Box 25065
G1 5YP Glasgow
CDN
info@mediascot.org

Erational
44 Rue Curiol
13001 Marseille
F
erational@0vs1.com

Dragan Espenschied
Lauffener Strasse 11
74226 Nordheim
D
info@a-blast.org

Gino Esposto
Langsg. 197
8005 Zürich
CH
carl@micromusic.net

Kouichirou Eto
1-10-29 Jingumae
Shibuya-ku
150-0001 Tokyo
J
Kouichirou@Eto.com

Tirtza Even
530 Riverside Dr. #5j
10027 New York, NY
USA
teven12345@aol.com

Exonemo
301 3-15-15 Kichijoji-
minami Musashino-city
180-0003 Tokyo
J
mail@exonemo.com

Aviv Eyal
690 Pennsylvania Av.
#210
94107 San Francisco, CA
USA
shirleys@friskit.com

Alternet Fabric
R. De Langallerie 6
1003 Lausanne
CH
patrick@fabric.ch

Jean Luc Faubert
En Faruselle
31290 Majremont
F
jlf@noname.fr

Kai Festersen
Luederitzstr. 10
13351 Berlin
D

Monika Fleischmann
Schloss Birlinghoven
53754 Sankt Augustin
D
fleischmann@gmd.de

Skawennati Fragnito
725 Grove Str #5
94102 San Francisco, CA
USA
skawennati@yahoo.com

Maria Luiza Fragoso
Colina Bloco A Apt 12
Campus Universitário
70910900 Brasília,
Distrito Federal
BR
malufragoso@hotmail.
com

Tiziano Fratus
Via Palestro N°9
10024 Moncalieri (TO)
I
manifatturae@
manifatturae.it

Fritz
Marlene-Dietrich-Alle 20
14482 Potsdam
D

Johannes Fritz
Langstr. 46a
61276 Hessen
D
jf@helpmaster.com

Mediateca Fundació
La Caixa
Passeig De Sant Joan,
108
08037 Barcelona
E
vfarras.fundacio@lacaixa.
es

Warren Furman
Rr2 Box155
18801 Montrose, PA
USA
wfurman@in.epix.net

D Fuse
3rd Floor, 36 Greville Str
EC1N8TB London
UK
nina@dfuse.com

Franka Futterlieb
Boedeker Str. 85
30161 Hannover
D
franka@sqnc.de

Steven Gan
Jin Bangsar Utama 9
59000 Kuala Lumpur
MAL

Stefan Gandl
Grimmstr. 27
10967 Berlin
D
stefan@designershock.
com

Gerald Ganglbauer
Po Box 522
2012 Strawberry Hills,
NSW
AUS
gerald@gangan.com

Mauricio Garcia
Matamoros
Via Del Falco, 18
00193 Roma
I
magamacol@yahoo.com

Caroling Geary
1031 Crestview Dr.
#318
94040 Mountain View
USA
caroling@wholeo.net

Aleksandra Globokar
Gornji Trg 22
1000 Ljubljana
SLO
aleksia@architectivalia.
org

Doron Golan
414 Broadway #3fl
10013 New York, NY
USA
doron@computer
finearts.com

Carlos J. Gomez De
Llarena
17 W 54th St. Apt. 8-d
10019 New York, NY
USA
informed44@yahoo.com

Jeff Gompertz
60 Berry St.
11211 Brooklyn, NY
USA
fakeshop@thing.net

Judith Gorgone
25 Star Road
02465 Newton, MA
USA
webmaster@planetpals.
com

Jacqueline Goss
76 Day Street
02130 Jamaica Plain
USA
jgoss@massart.edu

Terry Gould
143 Central Drive
L9G 2A3 Ancaster, ON
CDN
flyhigh@globalserve.net

Liliana Gracanin-Vitorovic
Simmeringer Hauptstr.
68-74/4/13
1110 Wien
A
Lilly_Ann1@hotmail.com

Valery Grancher
53 Rue De Seine
75006 Paris
F
vgrancher@nomemory.
org

Bradley Grosh
Flat B,
44-48 Shepherdess Walk
N1 7JP Shoreditch,
London
UK
bradley@gmunk.com

Joris Gruber
Waltherstr. 6
4020 Linz
A
joris@joris.at

Elisabeth Grübl
Bürgerspitalg. 18
1060 Wien
A

Romeo Grünfelder
Auerhofstr. 38
22081 Hamburg
D
gruenfelder@mail.com

Gruppe 51
Promenade 2
3400 Klosterneuburg
A
clemens.appl@blackto-
wer.cc

Carole Guevin
2147 Ave De Vendome,
#20
H4A3M4 Montreal, QC
CDN
carole@soulmedia.com

Shilpa Gupta
Premesh, 6 B Turner
Road
400 050 Mumbai
INDIA
shilpagupta@hotmail.
com

Karen Guthrie
Delfina Studios Trust, 50
Bermondsey Str, London
SE1 3UD London
UK
artists@somewhere.
org.uk

Hermann Josef Hack
Hangweg 11
53757 Sankt Augustin
D
hackhyper@aol.com

Juliane Hadem
111 Sutter St. 16th Floor
94104 San Francisco, CA
USA
aoliver@modemmedia.
com

Marc Haigermoser
Sägewerkstr. 3
83395 Freilassing
D
mc@interrest.net

Martin Haigermoser
Sägewerkstr. 3
83395 Freilassing
D
mt@interrest.net

Usman Haque
557a Leonard Str, #4
11222 Brooklyn, Ny
USA
usman@concentric.net

Malte Haust /
Bionic Systems
Ellerstr. 155
40227 Düsseldorf
D
contact@Bionic-
Systems.com

Sachiko Hayashi
Fridensberg Falerum
597 97 Åtvidaberg
S
mash@epsilon.tele
nordia.se

Carolena Helderman
10/34 Mitford Str
3184 Elwood, Victoria
AUS
carolena@one.net.au

Mario Hergueta
Postfach 1204
64569 Nauheim
D
info@artcart.de

Christian Hochstatter
Inselkammerstraße 8a
82008 Unterhaching
D
taumel@marune.de

Wolfgang Hockenjos
Totentanz 17/18
4051 Basel
CH
who@hyperwerk.ch

Tanja Hoffmann
Kölner Str. 41c
40211 Düsseldorf
D
info@pixelsymphonie.de

Melanie Hofmann
77 Edgecroft Road
94707 Kensington, CA
USA
mel@moonfiredigitalart.
com

Thomas Hofmann
Schwertstr.10
67063 Ludwigshafen
D
bunt-und-
chaotisch@gmx.de

Han Hoogerbrugge
Aleidisstraat 101b
3021 SJ Rotterdam
NL
han@hoogerbrugge

Klaus Hu
Wildenbruch 77
12045 Berlin
D
klaushu@hotmail.com

Leslie Huppert
Hilschbacherstr.31
66292 Riegelsberg
D
info@the-virtual-mine.net

One Infinity
3041 Market St.
94114 San Francisco, CA
USA
seth@oneinfinity.com

Innovation In Digital &
Electronic Arts
Grosvenor Building,
Cavendish Str
M15 6BR Manchester
UK

Takanori Irie
Tomari 394
9390741 Asahi-machi
Simoniikawa-gun,
Toyama-ken
J
tanori@h3.dion.ne.jp

Jessica Irish
2209 Valentine St.
90026 Los Angeles, CA
USA
jirish@onramparts.net

Anita Jedinger
Albrechtstr.56
4600 Wels
A
jedinger.anita@hotmail.
com

Fransje Jepkes
Anjeliersstraat.19
1015 Amsterdam
NL
Fansjej@x84all.nl

Neeraj Jhanji
Ebisu Garden Place
Tower 13f, 4-20-3 Ebisu,
Shibuya-ku
150-6013 Tokyo
J

Tiia Johannson
Mahtra 21-48
13811 Tallinn
EST
xtiiax@online.ee

William David Johnston
4619 Jeanne Mance
H2V 4J5 Montreal, QC
CDN
jhave@vif.com

Guillaume Joire
4, Rue Martel
75010 Paris
F
jp.marron@solotusk.com

Dave Jones
Main Rd.
3409 Natimuk, Vic
AUS
dave@transience.com.au

Yael Kanarek
76 E 7th St #31
10003 New York, NY
USA
yael@treasurecrumbs.
com

Georg Kapeller
Franz-Nabel-Weg 35
8010 Graz
A
Geo@line.at

Philip Kaplan
5 West 31st Str 7th Floor
10001 New York, NY
USA

Carmin Karasic
125 Western Ave
02134 Boston, MA
USA
ben_mayer@wgbh.org

Sampo Karjalainen
Hietalahdenranta 15 A 2
00180 Helsinki
SF
sampo@sulake.com

Raivo Kelomees
Mahtra 21-48
13811 Tallinn
EST
offline@online.ee

Gregory Kennedy
470 West 23rd St. #2a
10011 New York City, NY
USA
greg@m5mobile.com

Andruid Kerne
171 Sullivan St., #2
10012 New York
USA
andruid@creatingmedia.
com

Zsolt Keserue
Nap
2400 Dunaújváros
H
keserue@freemail.hu

Cyril Kestellikian
11, Avenue Des
Coccinelles
13012 Marseille
F
CKestell@aol.com

Rolf-Jürgen Kirsch
Lützowstr. 23
50674 Köln
D
info@koelnlink.de

Ivika Kivi
Tartu Str. 1
10145 Tallinn
EST
ivika@artun.ee

Takuji Kogo
4-34-8, 101 Nishi-
ikebukuro Toshimaku
171-0021 Tokyo
J

The Komtact
Othmarg. 36/5
1200 Wien
afnh@t0.or.at

Rudi Konar
Langg. 9/7
4020 Linz
A
rudor@yahoo.com

Ralf Kopp
Landgraf-Georg-Str. 68
64283 Darmstadt
D
R-Head@T-Online.de

Andreas Korte
Binterimstr. 26
40223 Düsseldorf
D
kurator@mmki.de

Lali Krotoszynski
R. Francisco Perroti, 761
05531-000 São Paulo
BR
lalik@ajato.com.br

Harry Kurz
Grundweg 2
95152 Selbitz
D
harry_kurz@bnhof.de

Michael Kvium
Overgaden Oven
Vandet 96
1415 Copenhagen K
DK
dino@wake.dk

Dídac P. Lagarriga
P.o.box 9142
08080 Barcelona
E
cuitb@ny.com

David Lai
8684 Washington Blvd.
90232 Culver City, CA
USA
david@hellodesign.com

Jean-Luc Lamarque
20 Passage De La Bonne
Graine
75011 Paris
F
lulu@pianographique.
com

Dave Lambard
2934 Keswick Rd.
21211 Baltimore, MD
USA
dave@sqwit.com

Herbert Laner
Buchberg 103
5500 Bischofshofen
A
herbert.laner@gmx.at

Lauranne Lauranne
25 Rue De La Halle
46200 Souillac
F
lauranne@lauranne.net

Thorbjörn Lausten
Plantevej 27
2860 Söborg
DK
lumen@worldonline.dk

Russet Lederman
161 West 75th Str, #11a
10023 New York, Ny
USA
spud@interport.net

Joseph Lefeure
4309 Bordeaux
H2H124 Montreal
CDN
joseph@sat.qc.ca

Miklos Legrady
94 Danforth Rd.
M1L 3W6 Toronto,
Ontario
CDN
miklos@sympatico.ca

Raph Levien
940 Tyler St. Studio 6
94510 Benicia, CA
USA

Lfmi
2518 N.kedzie Blvd #2e
60647 Chicago, IL
USA
dstrak@artic.edu

Lia
Schelleing. 26/2/30
1040 Wien
A
lia@sil.at

Patrick Lichty
355 Seyburn Dr.
70808 Baron Rouge, LA
USA
voyd@voyd.com

Lana Lin
244 East 13th Str,
Apt. 21
10003 New York, NY
USA
lclin@earthlink.net

Norman Lin
Merang. 25/6/19
8010 Graz
A
nlin@linux3dgraphics
programming.org

Christopher Lindinger
Julius-Raab-Str. 1-3
4040 Linz
A
christopher@fl.aec.at

Lizvlx
Hollandstr. 7/19
1020 Wien
A
pr@vote-auction.net

Garrett Lynch
28, Rue St. Lazare
75009 Paris
F
Garrett@asquare.org

Ruediger Mach
Freydorfstr. 3
76133 Karlsruhe
D
ruediger@arteng.de

Calin Man
Enescu 1
2900 Arad
RO
revoltaire@go.ro

Michael Mandiberg
P.o. Box 1390, 350
Canal St.
10013 New York, NY
USA
Michael@Mandiberg

Ken Marchionno
2916 St George St #112
90027 Los Angeles, CA
USA
kmarch99@earthlink.net

Aliyah Marr
119 Hamilton Ave
07022 Fairview, NJ
USA
amarr@radi8.org

Juliet Martin
115 4th Ave, #6i
10003 New York, NY
USA
juliet@bway.net

Fumio Matsumoto
2-11-27-302 Yakumo
Meguro-ku
152-0023 Tokyo
J
matsumoto@plannet-
arch.com

Taizo Matsumura
Ooaza Iwanami 1100,
Yamagata-si
990-2403 Yamagata-ken
J
taizo@cg.tuad.ac.jp

Eva Mattes
Via Avesella 1
40121 Bologna
ITALY
001010100011101110
@0100101110101101.
ORG

Bernd Mattiebe
Vogelsangstr. 101/1
70197 Stuttgart
D
bernd@mattiebe.de

Albert Mayr
Via Tripoli,110
00199 Roma
I
lucamiti@hotmail.com

Marcello Mazzella
20 Cook Str
11206 Brooklyn, NY
USA
marcellomazzella
@digart.net

John McCormick
2 Spenser St.
3182 St. Kilda
AUS
john@companyinspace.
com

Conor McGarrigle
1 Annamount,
Mulgrave St
Dun Laoghaire, Co Dublin
IRL
conor@stunned.org

Chris McGrail
Unit 3b, Leroy House,
436 Essex Road
N1 3QP London
UK
caroline@kleber.net

Brian McGrath
110 Maiden Lane
10005 New York, NY
mark@skyscraper.org

F1.3 Media Attack
Gellertstr. 12
76185 Karlsruhe
D
f1@frestyle.de

Meryl Meisler
345 East 15th Str
NYC 10003
USA
merylart@earthlink.net

Yiannis Melanitis
Velvendou 30
11364 Kipseli, Athens
GR
melanitis@hotmail.com

Marcello Mercado
C/o Peters
Neussestr. 22
50670 Köln
D
marcello@khm.de

Richard Miklos
Schönbrunnerstr. 41
1050 Wien
AUT
rmiklos@werke-dd.co.at

Enrico Mitrovich
Via Milano 53
36100 Vicenza
I
emitrov@goldnet.it

Philipp Mohr
95 Horatio Street 7k
10014 New York, NY
USA
info@metaring.com

Adrian Moore
38 Taptonville Road
S10 5BR Sheffield,
South Yorkshire
UK
a.j.moore@shef.ac.uk

Boris Müller
Franzstr. 12
53111 Bonn
D
boris.mueller@gmd.de

Yuji Naka
C/o Sega.com, Inc.
P.o. Box 7639
94103 San Francisco, CA
USA

Motomichi Nakamura
89-02 70th Rd 3rd Floor
11375 Forest Hills, NY
USA
motomichi@juvenile
media.com

Mark Napier
451 E 14 St #12h
10009 New York, NY
USA

Barbara Neumayr
Josefsplatz 6
1010 Wien
A
bn@sysis.at

Netochka Nezvanova
Achtergracht 19
1071 WI Amsterdam
NL
ecdysone@eusocial.com

Liviu Niculescu
Bvd. Victoriei 44b Sc B
Ap 23,
2400 Sibiu
RO
dvinfo@media-
division.com

Benny Nilsen
Bränningevägen 17-19
10571 Stockholm
S
benny.nilsen@eudora-
mail.com

Ralf Nuhn
89a Rectory Road
N16 7PP London
UK
leislon@ntlworld.com

Andries Odendaal
Unit 4 Tramber Place,
Blake St.
7925 Cape Town
ZA
andries@wireframe.co.za

Aisen Online
Entertainment
Stresemannstr. 128
10117 Berlin
D
behrens@aisen-gmbh.de

Christopher Otto
510 Page Street
94117 San Francisco, CA
USA
rhetoric@email.com

Jim Ovelmen
2924 Bellevue Ave.
90026 Los Angeles
USA
jovel@rampageusa.com

Randall Packer
2332 Huidekoper Pl Nw
20007 Washington
DC
rpacker@zakros.com

Ozlem Paker
269 Varick St. No 5e
07302 Jersey City, NJ
USA
ozlemp@att.net

Eric Paulos
Pmb #192 /
1459 18th Str
94107 San Francisco, CA
USA
paulos@cs.berkeley.edu

Tonya Peck
Bleichen Brücke
20354 Hamburg
D
jessica.nitschke@razor-
fish.com

Margaret Penney
1585 Inlet Court
20190 Reston, VA
USA
info@dream7.com

Michael Perin Wogenburg
Florianig. 31
1080 Wien
A
office@swp.org

Christoph Petersen
Christburger Straße 46
10405 Berlin
D
chris@moccu.com

Tristan Philippe
9 Rue Cavallotti
75018 Paris
F
admin@praktica.net

Martin Pichlmair
Johann-Strauß-G.32/7
1040 Wien
A
martin.pichlmair@xoba-
rap.net

Jörg Piringer
Favoritenstr. 17/14
1040 Wien
A
piringer@monochrom.at

Daniel Pirofsky
Po Box 751
97207-0751 Portland, OR
USA
pirofskyd@pdx.edu

Fee Plumley
Flat 5,
641 Wilbranam Road,
Cnorlton-cum-hardy
Manchester
UK
producer@the-phone-
book.com

Kai Pohl
Dunckerstr. 5
10437 Berlin
D
k.pohl@web.de

Oskars Poikans
11. Novembra
Krastmala 35
1050 Riga
LV
oskars@re-lab.net

Derek Powazek
915 Cole St #356
94117 San Francisco, CA
USA
dmp@fray.com

Pr.future
unit 126; 99-103 Loma-
no Grove
SES7HN London
UK
Futurenatural@ntworld.
com

Gilbertto Prado
Rua Agisse, 172
Apt. 113
05439 010 São Paulo
BR
gttoprado@uol.com.br

Waldek Pranckiewicz
Borowska 202/6
50-557 Wroclaw
PL
czas@free.art.pl

Nikola Prümm
Lehrter Str. 16-17
10557 Berlin
D
pruemm@kei-koo.de

Melinda Rackham
Po Box 1744
2012 Strawberry Hills,
NSW
AUS
melinda@subtle.net

Niels Radtke
Cité Aubry
75020 Paris
F
radtke@nirvanet.net

Nora Raggio
4250 El Camino Real
#c326
94306 Palo Alto, CA
USA
nraggio@visto.com

Rosaria Rainieri
Via San Marco 18
20121 Milano
I
rosy.rainieri@iol.it

Wolfgang Reinisch
Idlhofg. 52
8020 Graz
A
info@reinisch.at

Io Research
26 Clement Str
94118 San Francisco, CA
USA
kris@ioresearch.com

Darren Reynolds
60 Siege House,
Sidney Str
E1 2HQ London
UK
immedia@hotmail.com

Ricardo Ribenboim
Avenida Paulista, 149
01311-000 São Paulo
BR
comunicacao@itau
cultural.org.br

Simone Ricci
Via Milazzo 2
15100 Alessandria
I
simricci@tiscalinet.it

Sergey Rocambol
Lunacharskogo, 38-276
194356 Saint Petersburg
RU
rocambol@lynx.ru

Bernd Rose
Gentzg. 129/1/1/2
1180 Wien
A
Go-@gmx.at

Hubert Roth
Wilhelminaplein 29
3072 DE Rotterdam
NL
mijke.niks@extratain
ment.com

Anthony Rowe
First Floor,
59 Rivington Str
EC2A 3QQ London
UK
dulce@squidsoup.com

Cynthia-Beth Rubin
85 Willow Str #9
06511 New Haven, CT
USA
cbrubin@brainiac.com

Frieder Rusmann
Arndtstr. 35
70197 Stuttgart
D
rusmann@kunsttot.de

Alejandra Salinas
C/ Calvo Sotelo 22
Segundo Izq.
26003 Logrono, La Rioja
E
underwoodwork@yahoo.
com

Ilja Sallacz
Hartmannstr. 6
86159 Augsburg
D
info@oculustemporis.de

Thomas Schmidl
Niehler Straße 180
50733 Köln
D
tomsch@khm.de

Michael Schmidt
Flat 1, 23 Wheler Str
E1 6NR London
UK
m@k10k.net

Cyril Scott
76 Rue Du Faubourg
Du Temple
75011 Paris
F
jimpunk@jimpunk.com

Kochman Sébastien
81 Rue Du Pré Catelan
59110 La Madeleine
F
press@chman.com

Erich Semlak
Auergütlweg 8
4030 Linz
A
erichs@fl.aec.at

Tomoo Shimomura
Room 307, High Home
Kiriyama, 8-2, Kitazawa
1 Chome, Setagaya-ku
155-0031 Tokyo
J
tomoo@tomoo.net

Greg Sidal
89104 Las Vegas, NV
USA
gregsidal@yahoo.com

Julian Simon
Gottfried-v.-Cramm-Weg
35–37
14193 Berlin
D
simon@snafu.de

Simulware
Via S. Caterina 3
34122 Trieste
I
info@simulware.com

Ministry Of Information
And The Arts Singapore
11111 Singapore
Singapore

Gerhard Sinnhuber
Millerg. 41/6
1060 Wien
A
gs@transform.at

Johannes Skala
Am Hausberg 48
3945 Hoheneich
A
hillhouse@gmx.at

Joel Slayton
858 Lincoln Court
95125 San Jose, CA
USA
joel@well.com

Vas Sloutchevsky
630 Ninth Ave,
Suite 605
10036 New York, NY
USA
vaska@firstbornmulti
media.com

Owen Smith
5712 Carnegie Hall
04469 Orono, ME
USA
ofsmith@maine.edu

Barry Smylie
1041 Rathmore Crescent
L1V 5A3 Pickering, ON
CDN
barrysmylie@home.com

Frédéric Sofiyana
5 Bis Rue De L´asile
Popincourt
75011 Paris
F
subakt@subakt.fr

William Louis Sørensen
Grønnemose Allé 21d
2400 Copenhagen Nv
DK
wls@worldonline.dk

Thomas Sperneder
Hollandstr. 11-13
1020 Wien
A
thomas.sperneder@net-
way.ag

Teo Spiller
Ulica Toncke Ceceve 4
1000 Ljubljana
SLO
teo@teo-spiller.org

Louis Spoelstra
Oud Bussummerweg 7
1401SM Bussum
NL
carthago-media@het-
net.nl

Carsten Stabenow
V. Gosen Str. 17
18435 Stralsund
D
cs@osculture.de

Lars Stalling
864 Treat #6
94110 San Francisco, CA
USA
crislars@slip.net

Laurence Arcadias
864 Treat #6
94110 San Francisco, CA
USA
crislars@slip.net

Matej Stefanac
Podplat
3241 Podplat
SLO
sioux_design@email.si

Birte Steffan
Auguststr. 86
10117 Berlin
D
birte22@gmx.net

David Steiner
Bremerstr. 71
10551 Berlin
D
steiner@hdk-berlin.de

Igor Stepancic
Majke Jevrosime 35
11000 Beograd
YU
igor@blueprintit.com

Igor Stromajer
Tabor 7
1000 Ljubljana
SLO
atom@intima.org

Ferenc Studinger
Hunyadi 40.
7625 Pécs, Baranya
H
studing@freemail.hu

Nobuya Suzuki
3-95ryoke-cho
5503-0014 Ogaki City
J
koba@imas.ac.jp

Syndikaton
Alvenslebenstr. 2
66117 Saarbrücken
D
Frau.K@syndikaton.org

S Tanza
92 Lilford Road
SE59HR London
UK
stanza@sublime.net

Joseph Tasnadi
Damjanich U. 52. 2/2.
1071 Budapest
H
oximoris@matavnet.hu

Keystroke Team
Nieuwmarkt 4, De Waag
1012CR Amsterdam
NL
sher@waag.org

Rythmik Team
2 Rue Chabanais
75002 Paris
F
jm@rythmik.com

Lamberto Tedaldi
Via Bellini 2
47100 Forlì
I
lamberto.tedaldi
@officinepixel.com

Andreas Teltscher
Seidlg. 37/15
1030 Wien
A
andreas.teltscher
@chello.at

Diogo Terroso
245 Caledonian Rd.
N1 1ED London
UK
dterroso@hotmail.com

Paul Thomas
6 Hunter St., North Perth
Perth, Western Aus
AUS
prt@visiblespace.com

Henning Timcke
Stadtturmstr. 5
5400 Baden
CH
henning.timcke
@werft22.com

Marc Tinkler
157 Chambers Str
10007 New York, Ny
USA

Andrej Tisma
Modene 1
21000 Novi Sad
YU
aart@eunet.yu

Nancy Tobin
4559, Rue Saint-
Dominique
H2T 1T7 Montreal, QC
CDN
nt.@sympatico.ca

Brad Todd
1125 Ave Lajoie,
Apt.#10
H2V 1N7 Outremont, QC
CDN
bt@mobilegaze.com

Peter Traub
1006 Florence Ln.,
Apt. 4
94025 Menlo Park, CA
USA
ptraub@alum.
dartmouth.org

Atsuko Uda
3-8-13 Nobuto
Chuou_ku
260-0032 Chiba
J
makura@iamas.ac.jp

Igor Ulanovsky
King Shaul Str 1/5
55654 Kiryat-ono
IL
ulanovi@mail.biu.ac.il

Ultrashock.com
3700 Cedar Vista
93110 Santa Barbara,
CA
USA

Stefanie Vandendriessche
Calle Calls 17, 2-1
08002 Barcelona
E
cyberstella@hotmail.com

Andrey Velikanov
Krutitskaya
Naberezhnaya
109088 Moscow
RU
andrey@velikanov.ru

Suzete Venturelli /
Tania Fraga
Campus Universitario
Darcy Ribeiro, Colina,
Bloco C, Ap 15
70910-900 Brasilia, Df
BR
tfraga@unb.br

Verein Mur.at
Leitnerg. 7
8010 Graz
A
verein@mur.at

Voltaire
1230 Ave. Of The Ameri-
cas
10020 New York
USA
rachel@scifi.com

Kerstin Wagener
Nelkenstr. 15
76135 Karlsruhe
D
k@ezaic.de

Michael Wagner
1371 W Blue Ridge Ct
85248 Chandler, Az
USA
michael@geometrek.com

Thomas Wagner
Cusanusstr. 20
67663 Kaiserslautern
D
T.Wagner@design
assembly.com

Marek Walczak
172 East 4th Str #7c
10009 New York, NY
USA
mw@mw2mw.com

Lee Walton
685 25th Ave
94121 San Francisco, CA
USA
bao@silentgallery.com

Hans Wastlhuber
Mozartstr. 21
99423 Weimar
D
wastlhub@uni-weimar.de

Martin Wattenberg
1755 Broadway
10019 New York, NY
USA

David Weil
475 Tenth Ave, 8th Floor
10018 New York, NY
USA
jennifer@egomedia.com

Peggy Weil
411 Lombard Ave
90272 Los Angeles, CA
USA
weilp@earthlink.net

Teresa Wennberg
Idungatan 4
113 45 Stockholm
S
teresa@pdc.kth.se

Steve Whitehouse
225 Clinton St.
M6G 2Y4 Toronto
CDN
whitehouse@halfempty.
com

Michael Wild
Von Hohenborn
Bennauerstr. 53
53115 Bonn
D
kiera@echtzeitraum.com

Evan Williams
350 Townsend St.,
Suite 110
94107 San Francisco, CA
USA
ev@pyra.com

Markus Winkler
Schüttaustr. 1-39/16/7
1220 Wien
A
markus.winkler
@blue-c.com

Maciej Wisniewski
325 W 38th Str
10018 New York, NY
USA

Matthias Wölfel
Wilhelm-Roether-Str.12
76307 Karlsbad
D
Matthias@Wolfel.de

Netbaby World
Majorsgatan 11
11447 Stockholm
S
sara@netbabyworld.com

Judson Wright
223 E 10th St, 7
10003 New York, NY
USA
judson@judson.net

Magnus Wurzer
Rosinag. 9/14
1150 Wien
A
magnus@tivision

Arnon Yaar
225 East 6th St. #3e
10003 New York, NY
USA
arnon@telething.com

Anwar Uz Zaman
16 Sukrabad, Pantha-
path, Mirpur Road
1207 Dhaka
Bangladesh

Andrea Zapp
13 Longford Ave
M32 8QB Manchester
UK
zapp@sniffout.com

Georg Zeitler
Eckperg. 47/2
1180 Wien
A
georgz@aon.at

Jaka Zeleznikar
Gornji Trg 22
1000 Ljubljana
SLO
zeleznikarj@mail.
ljudmila.org

Jody Zellen
843 Bay Str #11
90405 Santa Monica, CA
USA
jodyzel@aol.com

Marina Zerbarini
Teodoro Garcia 1939
P.9 C
1426 Buenos Aires
RA
marinazerbarini@
marina-zerbarini.com.ar

Ga Zhang
452 West 23rd Street
#3a
10011 New York, NY
USA
guide@life.
a-domesticguide.com

Eric Zimmerman
368 Broadway #210
10013 New York, NY
USA

Alexander Zoltan
37 Boulevard
De Sebastopol
75001 Paris
F
zoltan@zoltan2001.com

Marina Zurkow
106 Ridge Str #2b
10002 New York, NY
USA
marina@o-matic.com

Gordana Andelic-Galic
Pruscakova 5/2
71000 Sarajevo
BIH
gosha_gag@hotmail.com

Jan-Erik Andersson
Vuorikatu 7 A B 36
20700 Turku
SF
jan-erik.andersson
@anderssonart.com

Siefert Andreas
Gartenstr. 40
76133 Karlsruhe
D
andy@traumpirat.de

Jim Andrews
2313 Esther Pl.
V9B 2E5 Victoria, BC
CDN
jim@vispo.com

Jussi Angesleva
Kensington Gore
2SW 7EU London
UK
jussi.angesleva
@rca.ac.uk

Marcel.lí Antúnez Roca
C/ La Cera, 27, Baixos
08001 Barcelona
E
marcel-li@marcel-li.com

Adrian Arias
5645 Carlos Ave, Apt #a
94804 Richmond, CA
USA
ariasyaragon@aol.com

Olaf Arndt
Hasenheide 71
10967 Berlin
D
olaf@bbm-ww.de

Plasmatic Arts
2325 Cornell Str
94306 Palo Alto, CA
USA
plasmatic@plasm.com

Florent Aziosmanoff
40, Place Du Forum
51100 Reims
F
aflorent@club-internet.fr

Maribeth Back
3333 Coyote Hill Rd
94304 Palo Alto, CA
USA
back@parc.xerox.com

Joey Bargsten
198 Lawrence Hall
97403 Eugene, OR
USA
bargsten@darkwing.
uoregon.edu

Michele Barker
303/12 Ithaca Rd ,
Elizabeth Bay
2011 Sydney, NSW
AUS
M.Barker@unsw.edu.au

Stephan Barron
235 Ave Du Puech De
Massane
34080 Montpellier
F
sb@technoromanticism
com

Scott Becker
7234 West North Aven
#1102
60707 Elmwood Park,
USA
artscb@interaccess.cor

Iris Benker
Böblingerstr. 9
70178 Stuttgart
D
iris.benker@merz-
akademie.de

Jon Berge
753 Oak Str
43205 Coloumbus, OH
USA
partnersms @aol.com

Claudia Bernett
7 Cornelia Str, Apt. 5a
10014 New York, NY
USA
claudiab@parsons.edu

Rodney Berry
2-2-2 Hikaridai,
Seika-cho, Soraku-gun
619-0288 Kyoto
J
rodney@mic.atr.co.jp

Michael Bielicky
Kubelikova 38
13000 Praha 3
CZ
x@avu.cz

Gabi Bingula
Heusteigstr.33
70180 Stuttgart
D
gbin@klee.architektur.
-stuttgart.de

Kim Binsted
2-34-1 Uehara,
Shibuya-ku
1510064 Tokyo
J
kimb@i-chara.com

Angelika Böck
Adelgundenstr. 21
80538 München
D
angelikaboeck@gmx.d

Sylvie Bourguet
13 Rue Beauvais
56100 Lorient
F
bulot@x-arn.org

Jonah Brucker-Cohen
112 Smith St #4
11201 Brooklyn, NY
USA
jonah@coin-
operated.com

Michael Brynntrup
Hermannstr.64
12049 Berlin
D
brynntrup@mbcc.de

Jeffrey Burns
Krusauer Str. 25
12305 Berlin
D
jeff@snafu.de

Bilbo Mylene Calvez
Manteuffelstr. 5
10997 Berlin
D
Bilbo@berlin.sireco.net

Jose C. Casado
677 Metropolitan Ave,
Apt. 7d
11211 Brooklyn, NY
USA
josecasado@usa.net

Paul Chan
305w.28th, Apt. 19c
10001 New York, NY
USA
mananwichartist
@yahoo.com

Benjamin Chang
112 South Michigan Ave.
60657 Chicago, IL
USA
bchang@artic.edu

Siegfried Canto
70 Rue D' Aubervilliers
75019 Paris
F
magali@desbazeille.nom.
fr

Philippe Chatelain
3-95, Ryoke-cho
503 0014 Ogaki City
J
phhat99@iamas.ac.jp

Shu Lea Cheang
52b Andrews Rd
E84RL London
UK
shulea@earthlink.net

David C.I. Cheung
55 Michael Drive
M2H2A4 Toronto, Ontario
CDN
aocaamw@yahoo.com

Se-lien Chuang
Schaftalbergweg 33
8044 Graz
A
cse-lien@sime.com

Association.creation
Untere Donaustr. 9/2/15
1020 Wien
A
assocreation
@hotmail.com

Eddie D
1e Helmersstraat 152
1054 EJ Amsterdam
NL
d@eddied.nu

Sharon Daniel
1156 High Str
95064 Santa Cruz, CA
USA
sdaniel@cats.ucsc.edu

Anna De Manincor
Via Audinot, 18/2
40134 Bologna
I
anna.dem@libero.it

Paul De Marinis
42433 San Francisco, CA
USA
demarini@well.com

Jordan Detev
P.o.box 15
1712 Sofia
BG
detev@sokerov.com

Dextro Dextro
Lorenz-Mandl-G. 33/1
1160 Wien
A
dextro@dextro.org

Andy Diaz Hope
85 2nd Str
94105 San Francisco, CA
USA
andy@moto.com

Ivor Diosi
Palarikova 4
81105 Bratislava
SK
diosi@luna.sk

Karel Doing
Walenburgerweg 90a
3033 AH Rotterdam
NL
doing@luna.nl

Marc Downie
20 Amest Str
02139 Cambridge, MA
USA
marcd@media.mit.edu

Zhenjun Du
12 Allée Des Lilas
93300 Aubervilliers
F
zjdu@aol.com

Gerhard Eckel
Schloss Birlinghoven
53754 Sankt Augustin
D
eckel@gmd.de

Christa Erickson
Art Dept. Staller Center
2nd Floor
11794-5400 Stony
Brook, NY
USA
christa@christa.art.sunys
b.edu

Tirtza Even
530 Riverside Dr. #5j
10027 New York, NY
USA
teven12345@aol.com

Lennart E. Fahlen
Box 1263
SE16429 Kista
S
lef@sics.se

Paul Farrington
5 Kent House,
Bassano Str
SE22 8RX London
UK
tonne@tonne.org.uk

Sidney Fels
2356 Main Mall
V6T 2G3 Vancouver
CDN
ssfels@ece.ubc.ca

Thomas Feuerstein
Amraserstr. 103
6020 Innsbruck
A
tfeuerstein@t0.or.at

Frank Fietzek
Skalitzerstr. 94 B
10997 Berlin
D
frank.fietzek@t-online.de

Maria Luiza Fragoso
Colina Bloco A Apt 12
Campus Universitário
70910900 Brasília,
Distrito Federal
BR
malufragoso@hotmail.
com

Mathias Fuchs
Sebastianplatz 2/11
1030 Wien
A
fuchs-
eckermann@t0.or.at

Doron Furman
103 Achad Haam St
64253 Tel Aviv
IL
mediaart@netvision.net.il

Pr. Future
Unit 126, 99-103
Lomand Grove
SES 7HN London
UK
futurenatural@ntlworld.
com

Gerard Giachi
28, Rue Des
Convalescents
13001 Marseille
F
giachi@iname.com

Greg Giannis
298 Dandenong Rd
3183 St.kilda East, VIC
AUS
Greg.Giannis@vu.edu.au

Allan Giddy
3/270 Campbell Pde
2026 Bondi Beach, NSW
AUS
agiddy@sysx.
autonomous.org

Piero Gilardi
Corso Casale 121
10132 Turin
I
piero.gilardi@tin.it

Joann Gillerman
950 61st St.
94608 Oakland, CA
USA
viper@metron.com

Mari-F. Giraudon
1640 Darling
H1W 2W5 Montreal
CDN

Nan Goggin
408 E. Peabody
61821 Champaign, IL
USA
n-goggin@uiuc.edu

Doron Golan
414 Broadway #3fl
10013 New York, NY
USA
doron@computer
finearts.com

Rich Gold
3333 Coyote Hill Rd
94304 Palo Alto, CA
USA
richgold@parc.xerox.com

Carlos J. Gomez De
Llarena
17 W 54th St. Apt. 8-d
10019 New York, NY
USA
informed44@yahoo.com

Bogdan Grabuloski
Borka Taleski 103
7500 Prilep
MK
sofija@sonet.com.mk

Tobias Grime
35 London St, Enmore
2042 Sydney, NSW
AUS
toby@kazumichi.com

Tracy Gross
191 East 76th Str #3f
10021 New York, NY
USA
teegross@hotmail.com

Vardit Gross
300 Mercer St. #26b
10003 New York, NY
USA
vardit@vardit.com

Manfred Grübl
Bürgerspitalg. 18
1060 Wien
A
m.gruebl@t0.or.at

Romeo Grünfelder
Auerhofstr. 38
22081 Hamburg
D
gruenfelder@mail.com

Ladislao Pablo Györi
Av. Federico Lacroze
3814 2do. 10
1427 Buenos Aires
RA
lpgyori@sinectis.com.ar

Hanna Haaslahti
Tarkk´ampujankatu 11
Lh 33
00120 Helsinki
SF
hanna@fantomatico.org

Stefan Hager
Arcisstr.39
80799 München
D

Marikki Hakola
Magnusborg Studios
06100 Porvoo
SF
distributor@magnusborg.
fi

Heiko Hansen
47 Rue De La Villette
75019 Paris
F
heiko@heiko.freeserve.
co.uk

Usman Haque
557a Leonard Str, #4
11222 Brooklyn, NY
USA
usman@concentric.net

Cam Harbidge
42 Hallbrook Dr. Sw
T2V 3H4 Calgary, AL
CDN
ccgharbi@ucalgary.ca

Jennifer Harden
Jagowstr. 10
10555 Berlin
D
jha184514@aol.com

Sachiko Hayashi
Fridensberg Falerum
597 97 Åtvidaberg
S
mash@epsilon.tele
nordia.se

Stephan Hechenberger
657 South 6th Str
95112 San Jose, CA
USA
shechenb@cadre.
sjsu.edu

Werner Heisse
Wennerscheider Str. 117
53819 Neunkirchen
D
WHeisse@t-online.de

Stephen Hendee
95-111 N.j.r.r Ave.
07105 Newark, NJ
USA
hendee@ix.netcom.com

Sea-geo Hiraoka
1-11-18-802, Nata,
Higashi-ku
811-0204 Fukuoka-city
J
sea-geo@geocities.co.jp

Perry Hoberman
167 North 9th St
11211 Brooklyn, NY
USA
perry@hoberman.com

Samantha Hodder
369 Sorauren Avenue,
Unit 101, Box 51
M6R 2G5 Toronto, ON
CDN
shodder@cdnfilmcentre.
com

Max Hoffs
Parkstr.1
40477 Düsseldorf
D
x-maxx@2000m.de

Ashley Holmes
North Terrace
5000 Adelaide
AUS
holmbase@iweb.net.au

Tiffany Holmes
112 S. Michigan Ave.
60603 Chicago, IL
USA
tholmes@artic.edu

Beverley Hood
P.o. Box 25065
G1 5YP Glasgow
UK
chris@mediascot.org

Zoe Horsfall
4 The Avenue
3058 Coburg, VIC
AUS
zoehorsfall@yahoo.com

Klaus Hu
Wildenbruch 77
12045 Berlin
D
klaushu@hotmail.com

Markus Huemer
Gereonswall 23b
50688 Köln
D
huemer@khm.de

Joseph Hyde
18 Upper Belgrave Rd
BS8 2XH Bristol
UK
johyde@hotmail.com

Sota Ichikawa
Jingu-mae 3-42-8-405
150-0001 Shibuya-ku,
Tokyo
J
info@d-xx.com

Sanjurjo Rubio Alex
léximal Jélimite
Trav. De Dalt 56,
Esc.b 2º2ª
08024 Barcelona
E
alex.sanjurjo@iua.upf.

Catherine Ikam
4 Rue Elzevir
75003 Paris
F
ikam@club-internet.fr

Haruo Ishii
30-1 Ishibata Narumi-
cho Midori-ku
458-0801 Nagoya
J
MXC00275@nifty.ne.jp

Vicky Isley
19-21 High Str
S043 7BB Southampton,
Lyndhurst
UK
info@boredomresearch.
net

Hiroo Iwata
Inst. Of Engineering
Mechanics And Systems,
University Of Tsukuba
305-8573 Tsukuba
J
iwata@kz.tsukuba.ac.jp

Geoffrey Jones
55 De Bresoles #300
H2Y1V7 Montreal, QC
CDN
geoffj@sympatico.ca

Franklin Joyce
178 27th Ave.
98122 Seattle, WA
USA
franklin@electricbaby.
com

József R. Juhász
L. Fullu 16
841 05 Bratislava
SK
erte@nzamky.sk

Miranda July
P.o. Box 14284
97293 Portland, OR
USA
mjuly@joanie4jackie.com

Eduardo Kac
1167 S. Clarence Ave
60304 Oak Park, IL
USA
ekac@artic.edu

Istvan Kantor
1160a Dundas Str East
M4M 1S1 Toronto, ON
CDN
amen@interlog.com

Aarre Kärkkäinen
Aallonhuippu 5 B 33
02320 Espoo
SF
aarre@karkka.pp.fi

Isato Kataoka
Seika-cho 2-2,
Kyoto Pref.
619-0288 Kyoto
J
isato@sys.i.kyoto-u.ac.jp

Yoichiro Kawaguchi
4-6-1 Komaba,
meguro-ku
153-8904 Tokyo
J
yoichiro@iii.u-tokyo.ac.jp

Shigeo Kawakami
Makami-cho,2-16-36
5691121 Osaka-
hu,takatsuki-shi
J
sige@mb.kcom.ne.jp

Raivo Kelomees
Mahtra 21-48
13811 Tallinn
EST
offline@online.ee

Justin Kent
Bldg N52, Rm. 390, 77
Massachusetts Ave.
02139 Cambridge, MA
USA
jkent@mit.edu,
kimkhanh@mit.edu

Stefan Kernstock
Graf Starhembergg.
30/2/6
1040 Wien
A
gwiku.haizing@hotmail.
com

Zsolt Keserue
Nap
2400 Dunaújváros
H
keserue@freemail.hu

Josef Klammer
Neuholdg. 51
8010 Graz
A
klammer@mur.at

James K-m
16 East Cordova Str,
Suite B
V6A 1K2 Vancouver, BC
CDN
electric@telus.net

Sachiko Kodama
1-5-1, Chofugaoka
182-8585 Chofu-city,
Tokyo
J
kodama@hc.uec.ac.jp

Andreas Korte
Binterimstr. 26
40223 Düsseldorf
D
kurator@mmki.de

Darij Kreuth
Presernova 10
1000 Ljubljana
SLO
uros.korencan@cd-cc.si

Doris Krüger
Märzstr.
1150 Wien
A
dok@i-one.at

Orit Kruglanski
Vila I Vila 82.3.1
08004 Barcelona
E
krugie@bigfoot.com

Olga Kumeger
Bolshaja Fillevskaja
45-1-16
121433 Moscow
RU
kumeger@hotmail.com

Kumiko Kushiyama
518-25,nikaidou
248-0002 Kamakura,
Kanagawa,
J
kushi@ea.mbn.or.jp

Robot Lab
Sachsenstr. 9
76137 Karlsruhe
D
haitz@robotlab.de

Terry Lai
Walden Rd
BR7 5AU London
UK
jurior@usa.net

Herbert Laner
Buchberg 103
5500 Bischofshofen
A
herbert.laner@gmx.at

William Latham
144-146 Buckingham
Palace Rd
SW1W 9TR London
UK
carolyn@artworks.co.uk

Willy Le Maitre
727 6th Avenue,
3rd Floor
10010 New York, NY
USA

Jen Lewin
354 Broadway 10th Floor
10013 New York, NY
USA
jen@blueink.com

Lia
Schelleing. 26/2/30
1040 Wien
A
lia@sil.at

Rigoletti M. / Lotio F.
Scharnweberstr. 31
10247 Berlin
D
ulti_edia@rocketmail.
com

Michael Lutz
Domagkstr. 33, Pf
440143
80750 München
D
michaellutz@lycos.de

Hermen Maat
2e Leeghwaterstraat 7
1018 Ra Amsterdam
NL
maat@xs4all.nl

Dale Macdonald
3333 Coyote Hill Rd
94602 Palo Alto, CA
USA
macdonal@parc.
xerox.com

Desbazeille Magali
70 Rue D' Aubervilliers
75019 Paris
F
magali@desbazeille.nom.
fr

Kristine Malden
52, Boulevard
Beaumarchais
75011 Paris
F
kristine@cybercable.fr;

Gerhard Mantz
Helmstr. 11
10827 Berlin
D
gerhard.mantz@snafu.de

Ken Marchionno
2916 St George St #112
90027 Los Angeles, CA
USA
kmarch99@earthlink.net

Carsten Nicolai
Ane Ziherlove 2
1000 Ljubljana
SLO
marxx@ljudmila.org

Aliyah Marr
119 Hamilton Ave
07022 Fairview, NJ
USA
amarr@radi8.org

Hiroshi Matoba
1-10, Nissin-cho
183-8501 Fuchu, Tokyo
J
matoba@mxb.mesh.ne.jp

Yasushi Matoba
146 Bonsai-cho
330-0035 Omiya
J
matomato@highway.ne.
jp

Steven McCarthy
1985 Buford,
240 McNeal Hall
55104 St. Paul, MN
USA
seminal@earthlink.net

Lisa Mcelligott
Csis Building, Cs2034,
Castletroy, Limerick
IRL
lisa.mcelligott

Yiannis Melanitis
Velvendou 30
11364 Kipseli, Athens
GR
melanitis@hotmail.com

Andrea Messer
203 E 33rd Str #16
10016 New York, NY
USA
amesser@parsons.edu

Katsuya Mikura
3-7-4-507
305-0005 Amakubo
J
s995657@ipe.tsukuba.
ac.jp

Mark Millstein
285 Old Westport Rd
02747 North Dartmouth
MA
USA
mmillstein@umassd.edu

Enzo Minarelli
Via Cremonino 14
44042 Cento (FE)
I
3vitre@iii.it

Reinert Mithassel
Fosswinckelsgt. 43
5008 Bergen
N
reinertm@online.no

Masahiro Miwa
3-95 Ryoke-cho
5030014 Ogaki Gifu
J
mmiwa@iamas.ac.jp

Michel Moglia
1, Rue De Gron Serilly
89510 Etigny
F
orgueafeu@club-
internet.fr

Ken Montgomery
199 Park Place
11238 Brooklyn, NY
USA
kenmontgomery
@earthlink.net

Philippe Monvaillier
15 Rue De Tivoli
21000 Dijon
F
Phil.M@webmail.co.za

Lisa Moren
2308 Tucker Lane
21207 Baltimore, MD
USA
lmoren@umbc.edu

Satoko Moroi
1-25-4,hyakunin-
cho,shinjuku-ku,
169-8522 Tokyo
J
moroi@ts.jec.ac.jp

Kazushi Mukaiyama
2-45-2-8-302
Shirakawadai, Suma
654-0103 Kobe
J
i@kazushi.net

Geert Mul
Exercitiestraat 20b
3034RB Rotterdam
NL
cut-up@v2.nl

Robert Mulder
788 Cedarwood Dr.
K&P 1M7 Kingston, ON
CDN
robmulder@sympatico.ca

Hans Muller
Javakade 360
1019RZ Amsterdam
NL
hmuller@xs4all.nl

Taisuke Murakami
100-55 Kunobe Yasu-cyo
Yasu-gun
520-2353 Shiga-ken
J
taisum98@iamas.ac.jp

Yoko Murakami
Higashi-hashimoto
2-28-22-301
229-1104 Sagamihara,
Kanagawa
J
yoko@murakami.com

Yasohito Nagahara
3-95 Ryoke-cho
503.00414 Ogaki City
J
koba@imas.ac.jp

Yoichi Nagashima
10-12-301, Sumiyoshi-5
430-0906 Hamamatsu,
Shizuoka
J
nagasm@computer.org

Damir Niksic
3202 Circle Hill Rd.
223051 Alexandria, Va
USA
niksicdamir@hotmail.com

Haruki Nishijima
Seikaryou101 2-137
Ryouke-cho
503-0014 Ogaki-City
Gifu
J
haruki99@iamas.ac.jp

Sara Nuytemans
C/ Bailen 149 3-4
08037 Barcelona
E
sara.nuytemans@iua.upf.
es

Sandy Nys
Po Box 106
3200 Aarschot
B
hybryds@planetinternet.
be

Martin Ocko
Litostrojska 32
1000 Ljubljana
SLO
ocko@scientist.com

Julian Oehlenschläger
Iltisstr. 150
50825 Köln
D
Julian.Oehlenschlae-
ger@t-online.de

Yusuke Ohkubo
Hatsudai 2-3-3
151-0061 Shibuya-ku,
Tokyo
J
ponn@fp.catv.ne.jp

Organ-eism (collective)
01
11 Rue De Belloi
13006 Marseille
F
machine@organ-
eism.com

Garth Paine
Seatat Rd 1/13
3931 Mournigton
AUS
garth@activatedspace.
com.av

Ozlem Paker
269 Varick St. No 5e
07302 Jersey City, NJ
USA
ozlemp@att.net

Stephen Partridge
Perth Rd
DD1 4HT Dundee
UK
spartrid@dux.dundee.ac.
uk

Eric Paulos
Pmb #192 /
1459 18th Str
94107 San Francisco, CA
USA
paulos@cs.berkeley.edu

Marko Peljhan
Ane Ziherlove 2
1000 Ljubljana
SLO
marxx@ljudmila.org

Fred Pelon
P/a Korte Prinsengracht
15a
1013 GN Amsterdam
NL
zm@dds.nl

Elisabeth Penker
Ramperstofferg. 52 /13
1050 Wien
A
elpenker@hotmail.com

Liz Phillips
39-39 45th Str
11104-2103 S8nnyside,
NY
USA
ofsound @ eskimo.com

Daniel Pirofsky
P.o. Box 751
97207-0751 Portland,
OR
USA
pirofskyd@pdx.edu

Graham Plumb
1-5 Portpool Lane
EC1 N7UU London
UK
grahamgolden@hotmail.
com

Philip Pocock
Gabelsbergerstr. 1
76135 Karlsruhe
D
philip.pocock@t-
online.de

Paul Poet
Gregoryg. 21-27/3/1
1230 Wien
A
PaulPoet@gmx.net

Alan Price
1000 Hilltop Circle
21250 Baltimore
MARYLAND, USA
bailey@umbc.edu

Paolo Ravalico Scerri
Via Torino 21
34123 Trieste
I
scerri@libero.it

Mark Reaney
Murphy Hall
66045 Lawrence, KS
USA
mreaney@ku.edu

Casey Reas
20 Ames Str, E15-443
02139 Cambridge, MA
USA
creas@media.mit.edu

Daniel Reichmuth
Burgweg 15
4058 Basel
CH
anyaffair@freesurf.ch

The Residents
724 Battery Str
94111 San Francisco, CA
USA
dweissman@vidarts.com

Martin Rieser
20 Elliston Rd Redland
BS6 6QE Bristol
UK
martinrieser@hotmail.
com

Kenneth Rinaldo
146 Hopkins Hall, 128
North Oval Mall
43210 Columbus, OH
USA
rinaldo@cgrg.
ohio-state.edu

Don Ritter
204 15th Str
11215 Brooklyn, NY
USA
ritter@aesthetic-
machinery.com

Lisa Roberts
45 Talbot Rd
7249 Launceston,
Tasmania
AUS
llisa@southcom.com.au

Sergey Rocambol
Lunacharskogo, 38 - 276
194356 Saint Petersburg
RU
rocambol@lynx.ru

Franco Rolle
Via S. Antonio Da Padova
10
10121 Torino
I
francorolle@atelier
nomade.it

Isabel Ron-Pedrique
428 Greenwich Str
10013 New York, NY
USA
irp@sirloin.net

Avi Rosen
Ee Faculty
32000 Haifa
IL
avi@siglab.technion.ac.il

Anthony Rowe
First Floor, 59 Rivington
Str
EC2A 3QQ London
UK
dulce@squidsoup.com

Tania Ruiz
24 Rue St. Bernard
75011 Paris
F
tania@altern.org

Marcin Rupocinski
Ul. A. Mickiewicza 46/2
58-310 Szczawno-zdroj
PL
zizumur@eranet.pl

Tomohiko Saito
3-95, Ryoke-cho
503-0014 Ogaki City,
Gifu
J
tomo2000@iamas.ac.jp

Mika Sakai
3-95, Ryoke-cho
503-0014 Ogaki City,
Gifu
J
mika00@iamas.ac.jp

Ellen Sandor
847 W. Jackson Blvd.
6th Floor
60607 Chicago, IL
USA
artn@artn.com

Veronique Sapin
75, 51e Ave
H8T 2W3 Lachine, QC
CDN
sapin@mail.org

Thecla Schiphorst
1128 Rose Str
V5L4K8 Vancouver, BC,
CDN
schiphorst@techbc.ca

Steven Schkolne
1200 E. California Blvd
91125 Pasadena, Ca
USA
ss@cs.caltech.edu

Lisa Schmitz
Eisenacher Str.73
10823 Berlin
D
lisa.schmitz@snafu.de

Tamar Schori
Hadaga 9
68177 Jaffa
IL
tmr_s@netvision.net.il

Susan Schuppli
500 Emery St. East
N6C 2G1 London, ON
CDN
schuppli@uwo.ca

Jill Scott
Feldegg Str. 54
8008 Zürich
CH
jscott@access.ch

Bill Seaman
Am Kölner Brett 6
50825 Klln
D
mail@235media.com

Stabile Seitenlage
Mauerborg 16a
86152 Augsburg
D
jan@stabile-seitenlage.de

Atsuhito Sekiguchi
3-95, Ryoke-cho, Ogaki
5030014 Ogaki
J
guchi@iamas.ac.jp

Bruce Shapiro
7128 Mark Terrace Dr.
55439 Edina, MN
USA
bshapiro@taomc.com

Ryoji Shibata
Ishizaka, Hatoyama
350-0394 Saitama
J
shibata@ia.dendai.ac.jp

Yuko Shimazaki
8-5-307
659-0023 Daito-cho,
Ashiya, Hyogo
J
u-ko99@iamas.ac.jp

Peter Sinclair
Rte De La Gavotte
13015 Marseille
F
sinclair@aix.pacwan.net

Frédéric Sofiyana
5 Bis Rue De L´asile
Popincourt
75011 Paris
F
subakt@subakt.fr

Kazuo Soma
2-5-29 Otowa-cho
426-0087 Fujieda-shi,
Shizuoka
J
kzs99@iamas.ac.jp

Dani Sperling
Dietrich-Bonhoefferstr. 20
10407 Berlin
D
dani@co-nst.de

Thomas Sperneder
Hollandstr. 11-13
1020 Wien
A
thomas.sperneder
@netway.ag

Louis Spoelstra
Oud Bussummerweg 7
1401SM Bussum
NL
carthago-media
@hetnet.nl

Allucquere Rosanne
(Sandy) Stone
University of Texas at
Austin
CMA 6.118
78712 Austin, TX
USA
sandy@actlab.utexas.edu

Smart Studio
Box 24081
104 50 Stockholm
S
lotten.wiklund@
interactiveinstitute.se

Zoltán Szegedy-Maszák
Orszaghaz U. 9
1014 Budapest
H
marci@c3.hu

Keiko Takahashi
1-25-4 Hyakunin-cyo,
Shinjuku-ku,
169-8522 Shinjuku,
Tokyo
J
keiko@ts.jec.ac.jp

Kentaro Taki
Bancho-haimu
102-0084 Tokyo
J
takiken@netlaputa.ne.jp

S. Tanza
92 Lilford Rd
SE59HR London
UK
stanza@sublime.net

Joseph Tasnadi
Damjanich U. 52. 2/2.
1071 Budapest
H
oximoris@matavnet.hu

Diogo Terroso
245 Caledonian Rd.
N1 1ED London
UK
dterroso@hotmail.com

Florian Thalhofer
Scharnhorststr. 28d
10115 Berlin
D
th@lhofer.de

Tamiko Thiel
Baaderstr. 64
80469 München
D
tamiko@alum.mit.edu

Hiroaki Tobita
Takanawa Muse Bldg. 3-
14-13,
141-0022 Hiagashigo-
tanda Shinagawa-ku,
Tokyo
J
tobita@csl.sony.co.jp

Vladimir Todorovic
Djusina 9
11000 Belgrade
YU
csm@eunet.yu

Naoko Tosa
2-2, Hikari-dai, Seika-cho
6190288 Soraku-gun,
Kyoto
J
tosa@mic.atr.co.jp

Marie-Hélène Tramus
2 Rue De La Liberté
93526 Saint Denis
F
michel.bret@univ-
paris8.fr

Yuki Uesaka
Village-samegai#503, 2
Ganjitsucho, Rokujo
Kudaru, Samagaidori
600-8336 Kyoto,
Shimogyo-ku
J
yukkie@sc4.so-net.ne.jp

Edwin Van Der Heide
Bergstraat 57a
3035 TC Rotterdam
NL
heide@knoware.nl

Mari Velonaki
85 Simmons St,
Newtown
2042 Sydney
NSW/ AUS
mvstudio@alpha.net.au

Bruno Verdi
Güfra
3942 Raron
CH
cie.brunoverdi
@bluewin.ch

Stephen Vitiello
530 Canal Str, Apt. 5e
10013 New York, NY
USA
vitello64@aol.com

Marek Walczak
172 East 4th Str #7c
10009 New York, NY
USA
mw@mw2mw.com

Angie Waller
615 Hudson St. #1
10014 New York, NY
USA
angie@couchprojects.
com

Andreas Walther
Peter-Welter-Platz 2
50676 Köln
D
awa@khm.de

Lee Walton
685 25th Avenue
94121 San Francisco, CA
USA
bao@silentgallery.com

Ade Ward
2nd Floor Nth, Rutland
House, 42-46 New Rd ,
E12AX London
UK
ade@stub.org

Cathy Ward
136 Downham Rd
NI 3HJ Islington London
UK
wanderlustre@trans
romantik.com

Lauren Weinger
239 Chestnut Str
02465 West Newton, MA
USA
lweinger@mediaone.net

Herwig Weiser
Lichtstr. 46
50825 Köln
D
hw@khm.de

Terry Welsh
2274 Howe Hall,
Room 1620
50011 Ames, IA
USA
glindahl@iastate.edu

Monique Wender
114 Rue Petit
75019 Paris
F
mowe@club-internet.fr

Andre Werner
Föhrerstr. 7
13353 Berlin
D
werner.19@t-online.de

Marcel Wierckx
Schalkwijkpad 29
1107JL Amsterdam
NL
marcel.wierckx@www2.
hku.nl

Stephen Wilson
1600 Holloway
94132 San Francisco, CA
USA
swilson@sfsu.edu

Fabian Winkler
Sophienstr. 121
76135 Karlsruhe
D
fwinkler@hfg-
karlsruhe.de

Uli Winters
Mendelssohnstr.13
22761 Hamburg
D
ebener@raumschiff-inter-
active.de

Judson Wright
223 E 10th St, 7
10003 New York
USA
judson@judson.net

Magnus Wurzer
Rosinag. 9/14
1150 Wien
A
magnus@tivision

Arnon Yaar
225 East 6th St. #3e
10003 New York, NY
USA
arnon@telething.com

Takashi Yamaguchi
A-201 Green Plaza 2-17-
47 Futako,takatsu-ku
213-0002 Kawasaki
J
yamag@za3.so-net.ne.jp

Guan Hong Yeoh
P.o Box 856
Wanganui
NZ
yeoh@hyperthesis.com

Jakov Zaper
6114 Normanby Av
3071 Thornbury, VIC
AUS
zapj@ihug.com.au

Guenther Zechberger
Galgenfeldstr. 25
6060 Hall
A
guenther.zechberger
@aon.at

Jody Zellen
843 Bay Str #11
90405 Santa Monica, CA
USA
jodyzel@aol.com

Monika Zielinska
Lwowska 6/15
PL00658 Warsaw
PL
mamzeta@pro.onet.pl

Wolfgang Ziemer
Mozartstr.39
50674 Köln
D
wziemer@netcolognw.de

Adriano Abbado
Via Crema 18
20135 Milan
I
adriano@abbado.com

Gyoerfi Alexander
Alarichstr.18a
70469 Stuttgart
D
gyoerfi@aol.com

Makoto Ando
1-1-32 Shin-urashima-
cho Kanagawa-ku
221-0031 Yokohama
J
and@cg.namco.co.jp

Raf Anzovin
534 Main Street,
Suite C
01002 Amherst, MA
USA
raf@anzovin.com

Sergi Arbones
Ctra. Valldemossa
Km 7.5
07071 Palma
De Mallorca
E
info@studio1.uib.es

Cory Arcangel
468 6th Avenue, #4
10013 New York City, NY
USA
corya@harvestworks.org

Marina Arnaudova
10 Rue Henri Matisse
59300 Aulnoy-les-
Valenciennes
F
wave@freeusrf.fr

Bonnetier Denis
10 Rue Henri Matisse
59300 Aulnoy-les-
Valenciennes
F

Gabriel Arrom
Ctra. Valldemossa Km 7.5
07071 Palma De Mallorca
E
info@studio1.uib.es

John Atkinson
1563 Solano Avenue,
#531
94707 Berkeley, CA
USA
john@atkinson
productions.com

Eric Augier
Le Fort - Av. De
Normandie, Bp 113
59370 Mons-en-Bareul
F
exquise@nordnet.fr

Anna Bacso
Le Fort - Av. De Norman-
die, Bo113
59370 Mons-en-Bareul
F
exquise@nordnet.fr

Loïc Bail
10 Rue Henri Matisse
59300 Aulnoy-les-
Valenciennes
F
wave@freesurf.fr

Eric Barba
300 Rose Avenue
90291 Venice, CA
USA
bhoffman@d2.com

Mathieu Bardon
Le Front - Av. De
Normandie, Bp113
59370 Mons-en-bareul
F
exquise@nordnet.fr

Christophe Barnouin
10 Rue Henri Matisse
59300 Aulnoy-les-
Valenciennes
F
wave@freesurf.fr

Eduard Begusch
Tanbruckg. 8/14
1120 Wien
A
eduard_begusch
@hotmail.com

J.d. Beltran
531 Utah Street
94110 San Francisco, CA
USA
jdbeltrn@pacbell.net

Anat Ben-David
How Street
E179AH London
UK
ben_david_anat
@hotmail.com

Timothy Benedict
2216 Grandview Ave.,
Apt. 3
44106 Cleveland
Heights, OH
USA
tbenedi@hotmail.com

Bello Benischauer
Sackg. 3
3550 Langenlois
A
bello@dada.at

Davy Beunckens
Nijverheidsstraat 8
3740 Bilzen
B
emecstudios@yahoo.com

Agnes Billard
Le Fort - Av. De
Normandie, , Bp113
59370 Mons-en-bareul
F
exquise@nordnet.fr

Sergey Boginsky
323 Geary St.,
Ste. # 617
94102 San Francisco, CA
USA
danielp@creatstudio.com

Nathalie Bonnin
10 Rue Henri Matisse
59300 Aulnoy-les-
valenciennes
F
wave@freesurf.fr

Dar Brady
1665 Pullan Ave
45223 Cincinnati
USA
architexture@earthlink.
net

Günther Brandl
Ibererstr. 15-21
8051 Graz
A
gRue.brandl@styria.com

Claus Arthur
Breda-Gulbrandsen
Nonnegata 28
7014 Trondheim
N
electronamodron
@hotmail.com

Yan Breuleux
4211 B. De Bordeaux
H2H1Z4 Montreal
CDN
ybreuleux@sympatico.ca

Claudius Brodmann
Senefelderstr. 77a
70176 Stuttgart
D
claudius@mark13.com

Michael Buchwald
19 Heisesgade
2100 Copenhagen Ø
DK
michbuch@centrum.dk

Scott Carter
801 Atlantic Drive
30332 Atlanta, GA
USA
viper@cc.gatech.edu

Jose C. Casado
677 Metropolitan Av.,
Apt 7d
11211 Brooklyn, NY
USA
josecasado@usa.net

Gerard Casas
Ctra. Valldemossa
Km 7.5
07071 Palma De
Mallorca
E
info@studio1.uib.es

Yuk Ting Chan
Rm 2528, Tai Yan
House, Tai Yuen Estate,
Tai Po. N.t.
HONG KONG
phnx@parsons.edu

Chris Chapman
22 W. Bryan #325
31401 Savannah, GA
USA
cmchap@gate.net

Olivier Chartoire
Le Fort - Av. De
Normandie, , Bp113
59370 Mons-en-bareul
F
exquise@nordnet.fr

Leïla Chik
10 Rue Henri Matisse
59300 Aulnoy-les-
valenciennes
F
wave@freeusrf.fr

Hanil Cho
59 Rue Ganneron
75018 Paris
F
anilmation@free.fr

Sébastien Chort
10 Rue Henri Matisse
59300 Aulnoy-les-
Valenciennes
F
wave@freesurf.fr

Candice Clemencet
10 Rue Henri Matisse
59300 Aulnoy-les-
Valenciennes
F
wave@freesurf.fr

Jean-Dominique Fievet
10 Rue Henri Matisse
59300 Aulnoy-les-
Valenciennes
F
wave@freesurf.fr

Tim Coe
Brunnenstr. 34
10115 Berlin
D
darkstar@cc4.de

Arno Coenen
Wittenstraat 25
1052Ak Amsterdam
NL
acoenen@hotmail.com

Andy Collen
11900 Sw. 116th Ave.
97223 Portland, OR
USA
HTA@HappyTrails
Animation.com

Couch
Rosenthalerstr. 3
10119 Berlin
D
info@kitty-yo.de

Bruce Currie
1-7 Wynard Street
3205 South Melbourne,
VIC
AUS
alexandra@unreal.
com.au

Stephane Daegelen
Le Fort - Av. De
Normandie, Bp 113
59370 Mons-en-bareul
F
exquise@nordnet.fr

Momoko Daigo
1-1-32 Shin-urashima-
cho,kanagawa-ku
221-0031 Yokohama
J
daigo@cg.namco.co.jp

Mike Daly
Balaclava & Epping
Roads
2113 North Ryde, NSW
AUS
ruths@aftrs.edu.au

Martin Dammann
Cotheniusstr. 13
10407 Berlin
D
MaDammann@aol.com

Luc Degardin
10 Rue Henri Matisse
59300 Aulnoy-les-
valenciennes
F
wave@freesurf.fr

Xavier De L'Hermuzière
10 Rue Henri Matisse
59300 Aulnoy-les-
Valenciennes
F
wave@freesurf.fr

Aurélien Delpoux
10 Rue Henri Matisse
59300 Aulnoy-les-
Valenciennes
F
wave@freesurf.fr

Peter De Lorenzo
Po Box 138
2557 Robertson, NSW
AUS
pdls@ozemail.com.au

Joachim Dennhardt
Appellhofplatz 1
50667 Köln
D
joachim.dennhardt@wdr.
de

Paul Divjak
Hernalser Hauptstr.
43/18
1170 Wien
A
das.pauli.prinzip@gmx.at

Werner Dornik
Sulzbach 149
4820 Bad Ischl
A
w.dornik@utanet.at

Sébastien Ebzant
10 Rue Henri Matisse
59300 Aulnoy-les-
Valenciennes
F
wave@freesurf.fr

Ralph Eggleston
1200 Park Avenue
94608 Emeryville, CA
USA
hart@pixar.com

Alain Escalle
26 Rue Fessart
75019 Paris
F
aescalle@club-internet

Javier Esteban
Ctra. Valdemossa Km 7.5
07071 Palma
De Mallorca
E
info@studio1.uib.es

Tirtza Even
Le Fort- Av. De
Normandie, Bp113
59370 Mons-en-bareul
F
exquise@nordnet.fr

Petra Evers
122 Kaelepulu Drive
96734 Kailua, HI
USA
petra@hawaii.rr.com

Kota Ezawa
876 Vallejo Street
94133 San Francisco, CA
USA
litky@earthlink.net

Stefen Fangmeier
3155 Kerner Blvd
94901 San Rafael, CA
USA
yves@ilm.com

Xeth Feinberg
145 West 28th Street,
Suite 10-sw
10001 New York, NY
USA
xeth@mishmashmedia.
com

Karin Felbermayr
Alfred-Schmidt-Str. 25
81379 München
D
karin.felbermayr@stud.
lrz-muenchen.de

Anne Frédérique Fer
10 Rue Henri Matisse
59300 Aulnoy-les-
Valenciennes
F
wave@freesurf.fr

Mikael Fernstrom
University Of Limerick
Limerick
IRL
mikael.fernstrom@ul.ie

Karine Feron
10 Rue Henri Matisse
59300 Aulnoy-les-
Valenciennes
F
wave@freeusrf.fr

John Fischer
75 Warren Street
10007 New York, NY
USA
jfischer@musicarts.org

Derek Flood
Osterwald Str. 10
80805 München
D
derek@muc.das-werk.de

Bernat Fornes
Ctra. Valldemossa
Km 7.5
07071 Palma
De Mallorca
E
info@studio1.uib.es

Claire Fouquet
121 Rue De Bordeaux
16000 Angoulême
F
m.laval@lin.cnbdi.fr

Isabelle Fournet
Ctra. Valdemossa Km 7.5
07071 Palma
De Mallorca
E
info@studio1.uib.es

Dumoulin François
49 Rue Boissonnade
75014 Paris
F
meumeu@innocent.com

Alessandro Furlan
Via S. Tommaso
D´Aquino 40
00136 Roma
I
infoaltair@altair4.it

D Fuse
3rd Floor, 36 Greville
Street
EC1N8TB London
UK
nina@dfuse.com

Laëtitia Gabrielli
10 Rue Henri Matisse
59300 Aulnoy-les-
valenciennes
F
wave@freesurf.fr

Celestino Gianotti
Basse Di Dora 42
10146 Torino
I
celestino.gianotti
@blisscomedia.com

Mira Gittner
Bayerisches Filmzentrum,
Bavariafilmplatz 7
82031 Geiselgasteig
D
wtpfilm@wtpfilm.de

Harvey Goldman
285 Old Westport Rd.
02747 Dartmouth, MA
USA
hgoldman@umassd.edu

Carlos J. Gomez De
Llarena
17 W 54th St., Apt. 8-d
10019 New York, NY
USA
informed44@yahoo.com

Cécile Gonard
121 Rue De Bordeaux
16000 Angoulême
F
m.laval@lin.cnbdi.fr

François Xavier Gonnet
10 Rue Henri Matisse
59300 Aulnoy-les-
Valenciennes
F
wave@freesurf.fr

Paul Guerillon
10 Rue Henri Matisse
59300 Aulnoy-les-
valenciennes
F
wave@freesurf.fr

Sophie Guillois
10 Rue Henri Matisse
59300 Aulnoy-les-
valenciennes
F
wave@freeusrf.fr

Elisabeth Grübl
Bürgerspitalg. 18
1060 Wien
A
elisag01@hotmail.com

Manfred Grübl
Bürgerspitalg. 18
1060 Wien
A
m.gRuebl@t0.or.at

Andre Gueziec
365 America Ave.
94085 Sunnyvale, CA
USA
gueziec@yahoo.com

Jeanlin Guillaume
10 Rue Henri Matisse
59300 Aulnoy-les-
Valenciennes
F
wave@freesurf.fr

Philippe
Grammaticopoulos
10 Rue Henri Matisse
59300 Aulnoy-les-
Valenciennes
F
wave@freesurf.fr

Daniel Guimard
97 Rue Jean Jaurès
92300 Levallois-Perret
F
emery@trimaran.fr

Sandrine Guyot
Le Fort - Av. De
Normandie, Bp113
59370 Mons-en-Bareul
F
exquise@nordnet.fr

Jonah Hall
3101 Park Boulevard
94306 Palo Alto, CA
USA
amyk@pdi.com

Heath Hanlin
102 Shaffer Art
13244 Syracuse, NY
USA
heath@dynakit.org

Ai Hasegawa
339 Tonbe
436-0224 Kakegawa
City, Shizuoka
J
ai@octodog.com

David Haxton
2036 Sharon Road
32789 Winter Park, FL
USA
haxtond@aol.com

Jose M. Hernandez
Ctra. Valldemossa
Km 7.5
07071 Palma De
Mallorca
E
info@studio1.uib.es

Stéphane Hernoux
10 Rue Henri Matisse
59300 Aulnoy-les-
Valenciennes
F
wave@freesurf.fr

Rob Heyclon
91 Hamilton
M4M-2C7 Toronto
CDN
robheyclon@hotmail.com

Alexander Hoepfner
Paulinenstr. 17
20359 Hamburg
D
alexander.hoepfner@gmx.
de

Max Hoffs
Parkstr. 1
40477 Düsseldorf
D
x-maxx@2000m.de

Daniel Holzwarth
Lindenstr. 25
72074 Tübingen
D
d.holzwarth@gmx.de

In Pyo Hong
280 Marin Blvd. Apt# 7q
07302 Jersey City, NJ
USA
sirknight@hanmail.net

Harald Hund
Hollandstr. 8/1/4
1020 Wien
A
haraldmayr@hotmail.com

Alexander Hupperich
Ryrotzer Ring 3
14627 Elstal
D
alexander.hupperich@t-
online.de

Eunjung Hwang
39-41 60 St. Woodside
11377 New York, NY
USA
hwangeunj@hotmail.com

One Infinity
3041 Market St.
94114 San Francisco, CA
USA
seth@oneinfinity.com

Pawel Janicki
Kuznicza 29a
54-137 Wroclaw 16
PL
paweljanicki@interia.pl

Zbigniew Jaroc
Flat 3, 166 Dyke Road
BN15PU Brighton
GB
z@softloader.com

Geneviève Gauckler /
Jean-Philippe Deslandes
186 Rue Du Château
75014 Paris
F
rxleti@yahoo.fr

Jae-Suk Jo
32f Maple Ave
06019 Canton, CT
USA
jojaesuk@yahoo.com

Philippe Jubard
Le Fort- Av. De Norman-
die, Bp 113
59370 Mons-en-bareul
F
exquise@nordnet.fr

Bernhard Kaeser
Albertstr. 9
8005 Zürich
CH
bkaeser@rom.unizh.ch

Boaz Kaizman
Im Dau 20
50670 Köln
D
kaizman@t-online.de

Katsuyuki Kamei
1-25-4 Hyakunin-cho
169-8522 Shinjyuku-ku,
Tokyo
J
kamei@ts.jec.ac.jp

Kante
Rosenthalerstr. 3
10119 Berlin
D
info@kitty-yo.de

Istvan Kantor
1160a Dundas Street
East
M4M 1S1 Toronto, Ont
CDN
amen@interlog.com

Raphael Kao
Le Fort - Av. De
Normandie, Bp113
59370 Mons-en-bareul
F
exquise@nordnet.fr

Yoichiro Kawaguchi
4-6-1 Komaba,
meguro-ku
153-8904 Tokyo
J
yoichiro@iii.u-tokyo.ac.jp

Omied Khademsaba
Bei Der Osterkirche 3
22765 Hamburg
D
filmgital@aol.com

Hyunsuk Kim
372 Dekalb Ave.,
Apt. #4b
11205 Brooklyn, NY
USA
hyunnat@aol.com

Abbey Klotz
180 Prospect Place. #1b
11238 Brooklyn, NY
USA
ztolka@excite.com

Manuel Knapp
Neilreichg. 64/1/5
1100 Wien
A
manuel.knapp@chello.at

Ralf Kopp
Landgraf-Georg-Str. 68
64283 Darmstadt
D
R-Head@T-Online.de

Gustavo Kortsarz
2 Rue Auguste Poullain
93200 Saint-denis
F
gudako@hotmail.com

Stephan Kozak
Rr#4 542 Conservation
Drive
L6T3S1 Brampton, Ont
CDN
stephankozak@CDN.com

Gerhard Krainer
Günterstr. 5
4040 Linz
A
gerhard.krainer
@fhs-hagenberg.ac.at

Alen Lai
677, Metropolitan Ave,
#6d
11211 Brooklyn, NY
USA
alen_lai@hotmail.com

Lee Lanier
1325 Howard Ave, #524
94010 Burlingame, CA
USA
beezlbug@beezlebugbit.
com

Kai Lappalainen
Hämeentie 135 C
00560 Helsinki
SF
kai.lappalainen@mlab.ui
ah.fi

Mathias Lautour
10 Rue Henri Matisse
59300 Aulnoy-les-
Valenciennes
F
wave@freesurf.fr

Benjamin Lauwick
10 Rue Henri Matisse
59300 Aulnoy-les-
Valenciennes
F
wave@freesurf.fr

Christian Leifelt
Enghavevej 40, 3.
1674 København V
DK
sydow@resonance.dk

Jean Babtiste Lere
120 Rue Danton
92300 Levallois Perret
F
maryle.capmas
@mikrosimage.fr

Jeffrey Lerer
156 Ludlow Street, Loft 4
10009 New York, NY
USA
74073.244@compu
serve.com

Jamyl Lhomme
Le Fort - Av. De
Normandie, Bp113
59370 Mons-en-bareul
F
exquise@nordnet.fr

Jose Manuel Liébana
Ctra. Valldemossa
Km 7.5
01099 Palma
De Mallorca
E
info@studio1.uib.es

Robert Lisek
Bulwar Ikara 18/5
54-130 Wroclaw
PL
robert.lisek@pwn.pl

David Lobser
6875 West David Ave
80123 Littleton
USA
dlobser@hotmail.com

Andrew Lyons
18/13-15 Sturt Ave
2603 Griffith, Act
AUS
alyons@vislab.usyd.edu.
au

Wayne Lytle
317 Nye Rd
13045 Cortland, NY
USA
wayne@animusic.com

Ruediger Mach
Freydorfstr. 3
76133 Karlsruhe
D
Ruediger@arteng.de

Thomas Maier
Ledererg. 38
4020 Linz
A
thomas.maier@ufg.ac.at

Clelia Mandrilly
Le Fort - Av. De
Normandie, Bp113
59370 Mons-en-bareul
F
exquise@nordnet.fr

Land Markfx
10750 E. Mescal St.
85259 Scottsdale, AZ
USA
allen7633@aol.com

Pierre Marteel
10 Rue Henri Matisse
59300 Aulnoy-les-
Valenciennes
F
wave@freesurf.fr

German Martinez
Ctra. Valldemossa
Km 7.5
07071 Palma
De Mallorca
E
info@studio1.uib.es

Javier Martinez
500 Landfair Avenue
90024 Los Angeles, CA
USA
javierMartinez@mac.com

Manel Masia
Ctra. Valdemossa Km 7.5
07071 Palma
De Mallorca
E
info@studio1.uib.es

Henrik Mauler
Rotebühlstr. 159
70197 Stuttgart
D
henrik@konkussion
deluxe.com

Marcello Mercado
C/o Peters,
Neussestr. 22
50670 Köln
D
marcello@khm.de

Dennis H. Miller
360 Huntington Avenue
02115 Boston, MA
USA
dhmiller@mediaone.net

Edward Morin
321 Roosevelt Ave
13210 Syracuse; NY
USA
capsule67@aol.com

Syuhei Morita
9f, 4-2-11, Shirokanedai,
Minato-ku
108 0071 Tokyo
J
pic1@mtvjstaff.com

Eisuke Motomatsu
1-11-17 Miyamae
285-0005 Sakura-shi,
Chiba
J
sakura20@wa2.
so-net.ne.jp

Koichi Mototsuka
4-2-9-105 Nakameguro,
1530061 Meguro-ku,
Tokyo
J
YQD01123@nifty.ne.jp

Norah Mulroney
Balaclava & Epping
Roads
2113 North Ryde, NSW
AUS
ruths@aftrs.edu.au

Jaroslav Ninaj
Vrakunska 29
825 63 Bratislava
SK
wild@wild.sk

Tomoko Nito
1-1-32 Shin-urashima-
cho Kanagawa-ku
221-0031 Yokohama
J
nico@cg.namco.co.jp

Johannes Nyholm
Kaserngatan 26
57595 Eksjö
S
jonas.lowgren@animatio-
nenshus.eksjo.se

Steve Oakes
440 Lafayette St. 6 Fl
10003 New York, NY
USA
vluu@curiouspictures.
com

Klaus Obermaier
Gasserg. 25/17
1050 Wien
A
ko@exile.at

Yasuo Ohba
1-1-32 Shin-urashima-
cho Kanagawa-ku
221-0031 Yokohama
J
ohba@rd.namco.co.jp

Ratsimamanga Olivier
4 Bd Davout
75020 Paris
F
ratsi@emovie.org

Alex Orrelle
105 Palm #10
94118 San Francisco, CA
USA
aorrelle@hotmail.com

Björn Perborg
Godhemsgatan 14c
414 67 Göteborg
S
bjorn.perborg@valand.
gu.se

Florence Pernet
10 Rue Henri Matisse
59300 Aulnoy-les-
valenciennes
F
wave@freesurf.fr

Bernd Pfeiffer
Liebharstalstr.30a
1160 Wien
A
webmaster@bandunion.
at

Van Phan
4644 W 137th Street A
90250 Hawthorne
USA
vanphan75@hotmail.
com

Laurent Pierlot
10 Rue Henri Matisse
59300 Aulnoy-les-
Valenciennes
F
wave@freesurf.fr

Rudy Poat
2160 Hills Avenue,
Suite A
30318 Atlanta, GA
USA
rand@giantstudios.com

Christian Pokorny
Bavaria-Filmplatz 7
82031 München
D
ab@scanline.de

Stuart Pound
34 Blondin Avenue
W5 4UP London
UK
bocadillo@cwcom.net

Matt Pyke
Unit 415, Work Station,
15 Pater Noster Row
S1 2BX Sheffield
U.K.
matt@thedesignersrepu-
blic.com

Edward Quist
East 32.
11234 Brooklyn, NY
USA
edwardquist@aol.com

Mikk Rand
C. R. Jakobsoni 14
10128 Tallinn
EST
info@multifilm.ee

Joan Raspo
440 Lafayette Street 6 Fl
10003 New York, NY
USA
vluu@curiouspictures.co
m

Birgit Rathsmann
851 Manhattan Ave
11222 Brooklyn, NY
USA
brisschitta@earthlink.net

Peter Ratner
6391 W. Donnagail Drive
22846 Penn Laird, VA
USA

Sabine Reiff
Via Torricelli 30
20136 Milano
I
info@pigreca.com

Remi
Leitnerg. 7/5
8010 Graz
A
remi@algo.mur.at

Mathieu Renoux
10 Rue Henri Matisse
59300 Aulnoy-les-
valenciennes
F
wave@freesurf.fr

Nicolas Rey
120 Rue Danton
92300 Levallois Perret
F
maryle.capmas@mikros
image.fr

Gilles Richard
42, Bd. Carnot
21000 Dijon
F
lesrichesdouaniers@free.
fr

Chris Richards-Scully
Balaclava & Epping
Roads
2113 North Ryde, NSW
AUS
ruths@aftrs.edu.au

Nicolas Rivet
10 Rue Henri Matisse
59300 Aulnoy-les-
Valenciennes
F
wave@freesurf.fr

Phil Robinson
2650 18th Street,
2nd Floor
94110 San Francisco, CA
USA
ninar@wildbrain.com

Hubert Roth
Wilhelminaplein 29
3072 DE Rotterdam
NL
mijke.niks
@extratainment.com

Frank Rueckert
Inheidener Str.71
60385 Frankfurt
D
frank@1848uenn.de

Constanze Ruhm
Schöffelg. 6
3002 Purkersdorf
A
con@t0.or.at

Daniel Ruiz
Ctra. Valldemossa
Km 7.5
07071 Palma
De Mallorca
E
info@studio1.uib.es

Tania Ruiz
24 Rue St. Bernard
75011 Paris
F
tania@altern.org

Semi Ryu
4733 Centre Ave,
Apt #5h
15213 Pittsburgh, PA
USA
sryu@andrew.cmu.edu

Bob Sabiston
4204 Ave H
78751 Austin, TX
USA
tommy@mac.com

Mark Sagar
Suite 1015, 7080 Hol-
lywood Blvd
90028 Hollywood, CA
USA
msagar@lifefx.com

Yujiro Sakamoto
1-13-13-201
Higasisinkoiwa
1230023 Katusikaku,
Tokyo
J
yujiros@dj.pdx.ne.jp

Stefano Scarani
Via Bergognone 45
20144 Milano
I
tangatamanu@planet.it

Zach Schlappi
Po Box 1098
10163-1098 New York,
NY
USA
zach@blueskystudios.
com

Marcus Schmahl
Käferbein Str. 24
55270 Essenheim
D
marcus@rauschfaktor.
com

Thomas Schmidl
Niehler Str. 180
50733 Köln
D
tomsch@khm.de

Michaela Schwentner
Stollg. 7/6
1070 Wien
A
jade@rhiz.org

Robert Seidel
Max-Steenbeck-Str. 2
07745 Jena
D
rs@2minds.de

Günther Selichar
Mariahilferstr. 200/14
1150 Wien
A
selichar@t0.or.at

Hideaki Shibayama
2-11-4-203 Sugamo,
1700002 Toshima-ku,
J
hute@104.net

Baba Shinsuke
4-1-13 Honmachi,
Chuo-ku
5410053 Osaka
J
baba.shinsuke
@takenaka.co.jp

Mark Simon
8137 Lk Crowell Circle
32836 Orlando, FL
USA
msimon@cfl.rr.com

Kathy Smith
2639 Monmouth Avenue,
Apt. #1
90007 Los Angeles, CA
USA
kathy@imoods.org   or
kates@usc.edu

Manolo Soler
Ctra. Valldemossa
Km 7.5
07071 Palma
De Mallorca
E
info@studio1.uib.es

Jeremy Solterbeck
615 5th Ave
94118 San Francisco, CA
USA
js7@pacbell.net

Peter Spans
Mühlenkamp 59
22303 Hamburg
D
spans@spans.de

Arthur Stammet
29, Rue Leon Metz
4238 Esch-sur-alzette
L
arthur.stammet@ci.
educ.lu

Suk & Koch
304 Bedford Ave.,
3rd Floor
11211 Brooklyn
USA
martin@sukkoch.com

Dennis Summers
3927 Parkview Dr.
48073 Royal Oak, MI
USA
dennisqdw@home.com

Szm Studios Film-,
TV- und Multimedia-
Produktions Gmbh
Dept. Animation / Vfx
Medienallee 7
85774 Unterföhring
D
justus.engel@szm.de

Marialuisa Tadei
14 Cliveden Place
SW1W8LA London
UK
Marialuisatadei@yahoo.
com

Mio Tagiri
2-8-5-601, Machiya
1160001 Arakawa-ku,
Tokyo
J
mio.t@ma4.justnet.ne.jp

Nobuo Takahashi
1-1-32 Shin-urashima-
cho, Kanagawa-ku,
Yokohama
211-0031 Kanagawa
J
nobuo@vs.namco.co.jp

Kentaro Taki
Bancho-haimu
102-0084 Tokio
J
takiken@netlaputa.ne.jp

Ying Tan
5232 University Of
Oregon
97403 Eugene, OR
USA
tanying@darkwing.
uroegon.edu

Jeans Team
Rosenthalerstr. 3
10119 Berlin
D
info@kitty-yo.de

The Computer Film
Company
19-23 Wells Street
W1P3FP London
UK
martin@cfc.co.uk

Pierre Thomé
Eglistr. 8
8004 Zürich
CH
p.thome@netsurfer.ch

Niels Christian Thornberg
55, Gothersgade
1123 Copenhagen K
DK
dfi@dfi.dk

Toert Toert
Blumenweg 25
2201 Gerasdorf
A
toert_d@yahoo.com

Jan Tomanek
Zdikovska 49
15000 Prague 5
CZ
tomanek@aaa-studio.cz

Bill Tomlinson
E15-320g /
20 Ames Street
02139 Cambridge, MA
USA
badger@media.mit.edu

Max Tourret
10 Rue Henri Matisse
59300 Aulnoy-les-
valenciennes
F
wave@freesurf.fr

Karsten Trappe
Marienstr. 9
38108 Braunschweig
D
karstentrappe@yahoo.de

Selina Trepp
1652 West Division St.
60622 Chicago, IL
USA
selinatrepp@earthlink.net

Isabelle Tripelon
121, Rue De Bordeaux
16000 Angoulême
F
m.laval@lin.cnbdi.fr

Stephan Trojansky
Bavaria-filmplatz 7
82031 München
D
ab@scanline.de

Davide Tromba
121, Rue De Bordeaux
16000 Angoulême
F
m.laval@lin.cnbdi.fr

Gabriel Turkieh
19, Rue Béranger
75003 Paris
F
altomail@worldnet.fr

Hans Uhlig
7 Sky Road
94941 Mill Valley, CA
USA
tony@ilm.com

Anna Ursyn
Department Of Visual
Arts
80639 Greeley, CO
USA
azursyn@bentley.unco.
edu

Christina Vantzos
1400 Mount Royal Ave
21217 Baltimore, ML
USA
ilovepurple9@hotmail.
com

Video Artist Workshop
2f 5-62-8,
mkbuild Nakano
164 0001 Nakanoku,
Tokyo
J
katz@fb3.so-net.ne.jp

Frank Vitz
6315 Yucca Street
90028 Hollywood, CA
USA
santo@kwcc.com

François Vogel
120 Rue Danton
92300 Levallois Peret
F
maryle.capmas@mikrosi-
image.fr

Kerstin Wagener
Nelkenstr. 15
76135 Karlsruhe
D
k@ezaic.de

Yukiko Wakasa
4-20-6 Asahigaoka
2840024 Yotukaido-shi,
Chiba
J
waka2@ma4.justnet.
ne.jp

Diana Walczak
601 West 26th Street,
17 Fl.
10001 New York, NY
USA
amanda@kwcc.com

Alexander Walter
Trierer Str. 40
99423 Weimar
D
alex@alexanderwalter.de

Vincent Wauters
10 Rue Henri Matisse
59300 Aulnoy-les-
Valenciennes
F
wave@freesurf.fr

Holger R. Weiss
Senefelder Str. 77a
70176 Stuttgart
D
holgi@mark13.com

Jason Wen
1801 Lakeland Park Dr.
75043 Garland, TX
USA
jason_wen@yahoo.com

Judith Wesch
Le Fort - Av. De
Normandie,
59370 Mons-en-bareul
F
exquise@nordnet.fr

Ulla West
Fredmansgatan 6b
s-11847 Stockholm
S
west@ettnet.se

Anne Westermeyer
Rotenberg Str. 24
66111 Saarbrücken
D
trykke@hotmail.com

Lennart Westman
Magnus Ladulasgatan 7
118 65 Stockholm
S
sonicart@chello.se

Chel White
440 Lafayette Str. 6 Fl
10003 New York, NY
USA
vluu@curiouspictures.
com

Marie-Laure Wiel
Le Fort- Av. De
Normandie, Bp 113
59370 Mons-en-bareul
F
exquise@nordnet.fr

Marcus Wiesner
Gablenzg. 4/8
1160 Wien
A
oberlinninger@mdw.ac.at

Nina Wild
Engelstr. 64
8026 Zürich
CH
ninawild@yahoo.com

Eddy Wong
54/f Hopewell Centre
183 Queen´s Road East
Wanchai
Hong Kong
ellenho@menfond.
com.hk

Michèle Bokanowski
20 Rue Ernest Cresson
75014 Paris
F
boka@re-voir.com

Achim Bornhoeft
Rappstr. 7
72070 Tübingen
D
achim.bornhoeft@web.de

Tim Bowman
4/31 Daleham Gardens
NW3 5BU London
UK
tbwb@aol.com

Cap N Brainsnatch
74 Marietta St.
L9P1J5 Toronto
CDN
brainsnatch@casa.as

Christopher Brakel
2401 Hwy 6 E. #1605
52240 Iowa City, IA
USA
christopher_brakel
@yahoo.com

Ros Brandt
131-137 Barry Steet
3053 Carlston
AUS
r.brandt@unimelb.edu.qu

Mark Bromwich
12 Spa Terrace
HD8 0BD Huddersfield
UK
m.a.bromwich@hud.
ac.uk

Somna M. Bulist
Po Box 15
15633 Forbes Rd, PA
USA
somna@somna.net

Martin Bürck
Im Hägen 1
72574 Bad
Urachsirchingen
D
Martin_Buerck@gmx.de

Rainer Bürck
Am Samuelstein 9
72574 Bad Urach
D
Buerck_Vihmand
@compuserve.com

Brigid Burke
Po Box 315 Elsternwick
3185 Melbourne
AUS
brigid@alphalink.com.au

Dan Burke
Po Box 681474
60168-
1474 Schaumburg
USA
bzurke@ync.net

Matthew Burtner
Mcfarland 6g, Escondido
Village
94305 Stanford, CA
USA
mburtner@ccrma.
stanford.edu

Christian Calon
3678 Henri-Julien
H2X3H5 Montreal, QC
CDN
klong@sympatico.ca

Stefano Carletti
Via Carlo Pisacane 100
53100 Siena
I
stefaneon@hotmail.com

Massimo Carozzi
Via Audinot 18/2
40100 Bologna
I
massimo.carozzi@libero.
it

Roy Carroll
8 Lisburn Str
D7 Dublin 7
IRL
carrolre@tcd.ie

Emanuele Casale
Via Duca Degli
Abruzzi 52
95030 Trappeto
I
emcasale@infinito.it

Kim Cascone
748 Edgemar Ave
94044 Pacifica, CA
USA

Tim Catlin
28 Clarence Str
3057 East Brunswick
AUS
timc@micronica.com.au

Cd _slopper
Ackerstr. 19 / Remise A
10115 Berlin
D
swx@fals.ch

Werner Cee
Freier Platz 16
35423 Lich / Birklar
D
cee.obrecht@t-online.de

Andrea Cera
Largo Trieste 2
36034 Malo (VI)
I
andreawax@yahoo.it

Paulo C. Chagas
Rolandstr. 74
50677 Köln
D
nc-chagaspa@net
cologne.de

Richard Chartier
1221 N. Courthouse Rd.
#210
22201 Arlington, VA
USA
chartier@3particles.com

Ty Chiu
15f-2, 245, Sec1, Fu-
shin South Rd.
106 Taipei
TAIWAN
djty@ms68.hinet.net

Franz Cibulka
Popelkaring 24
8045 Graz
A
artofcibulka@aon.at

Samuel Claiborne
Po Box 509
12440 High Falls, NY
USA
loons@sonotrope.com

Nick Collins
10 Beechlawns,
Torrington Park,
North Finchley
N12 9PP London
UK
nickcollins@hotmail.com,
adam@spiers.net

William Fowler Collins
1748 Hyde
94109 San Francisco, CA
USA
collins@sirius.com

Mike Cooper
Via Vaglia 34
00139 Roma
I
cooparia@compuserve.
com

Eric Cordier
23 Rue Custine
154 Paris
F
cheveches@free.fr

Couch
Rosenthalerstr. 3
10119 Berlin
D
info@kitty-yo.de

Guillaume Coutu-Dumont
4358 Coolbrook
H4A 3G2 Montréal, QC
CDN
guigui07@hotmail.com

Grant Covell
9 Smith Ave
02143 Somerville, MA
USA
gcovell@c-bridge.com

Royal Cubit
Rue De L´hopital
Militaire
67000 Strasbourg
F
hfourneaux@cus-
strasbourg.net

D_infection
Sant Pere Martir No. 28,
Pal. 2
08012 Barcelona
E
d_infection@yahoo.es

Palle Dahlstedt
Sven Hultins Gata 6
430 85 Göteborg
S
palle@design.chalmers.
se

Riccardo Dapelo
Via Valente 40
16015 Casella (ge)
I
rdapelo@libero.it

Dater Dater
Fuechselbachstr. 12
4060 Leonding
A
christian.eckle@lion.cc

Robin Davies
4209 Drolet
H2W 2L7 Montreal
CDN
robin@music.mcgill.ca

Roderik De Man
1e Tuindwarsstraat 3
1015 RT Amsterdam
NL
rdeman@chello.nl

Markus Decker
Lustenauerstr. 8
4020 Linz
A
maex@firstfloor.org

Shawn Decker
112 S. Michigan
60603 Chicago, IL
USA
sdecker@artic.edu

Franco Degrassi
Via Giovanni Cozzoli 2
70125 Bari
I
degrassi@tin.it

Gordon Delap
University Rd
BT7 Belfast
Northern Ireland
dontmakemelaugh@hot-
mail.com

Christopher Delaurenti
Po Box 45655
98145-0655 Seattle, WA
USA
chris@delaurenti.net

Jim Denley
16/2 St Neot Ave Potts Pt
20111 Sydney, NSW
AUS
splitrec@ozemail.com.au

Miguel Depedro
310 Oakland Ave
94611Oakland, CA
USA
kid606@tigerbeat.com

Le Depeupleur
75 Rue Du Fbg
St. Antoine
75011 Paris
F
kasper@club-internet.fr

Jordan Detev
P.o.box 15
1712 Sofia
BG
detev@sokerov.com

Richard Devine
535 Wheatridge Bluff
30075 Roswell, GA
USA
rdevine@mindspring.com

Agostino Di Scipio
Via Salaria Antica Est
33/a
67100 L'aquila
I
discipio@tin.it

Gary Dibenedetto
Po Box 1296
08502 Belle Mead, NJ
USA
music@garydibenedetto.
com

Paul Divjak
Hernalser Hauptstr.
43/18
1170 Wien
A
das.pauli.prinzip@gmx.at

Roberto Doati
Via Giorgione 66
35020 Albignasego (PD)
I
r.doati@flashnet.it

Jason Doerck (Lesser)
C/o B. Kelly,
862 Vermont Str
94610 Oakland, CA
USA
j@LSR1.com

Oliver Doerell
Obentrautstr.32
10963 Berlin
D
doerell@goldmail.de

Paul Dolden
17 King St
J9H 2K2 Aylmer, QC
CDN
pauldolden@yahoo.com

Wolfgang Dorninger
Freistädterstr. 237
4040 Linz
A
fadi@servus.at

Robert Dow
12 Nicolson Square
EH8 9DF Edinburgh
UK
R.Dow@music.ed.ac.uk

Roger Doyle
Rynville Mews,
Killarney Rd
00 Bray, County Wicklow
IRL
rogerd@eircom.net

R. Luke Dubois
632 W.125th Str,
Rm. 318
10027 New York, NY
USA
luke@music.columbia.
edu

Louis Dufort
2554 Holt
H1Y 1N5 Montreal, QC
CDN
siuol@sympatico.ca

Curd Duca
800 West Ave # 923
33139 Miami Beach, FL
USA

Dudelwurscht
Paulinenstr.17
20359 Hamburg
D
IQ-noise@gmx.de

John Duncan
Fraz. Scrutto 48
33040 San Leonardo
I
info@johnduncan.org

Frank Ekeberg
Ovre Rommesbakken 34
N7300 Orkanger
N
frank@plingplong.com

Ezz Eldin
Wimmerg. 1/21
1050 Wien
A
ezz.3@hotmail.com

Rolf Enström
Helgestavägen 27
12541 Älusjä
S
enstrom.rolf@telia.com

Epy
Neubaug. 45 / Pf 197
1071 Wien
A
office@sixpackfilm.com

Aviv Eyal
690 Pennsylvania Av.
#210
94107 San Francisco, CA
USA
shirleys@friskit.com

John Farrier
6877 Bejay Drive
45371 Tipp City, OH
USA
john.farrier@dynamicdi-
gitalinc.com

Paul Farrington
5 Kent House,
Bassano Str
SE22 8RX London
UK
tonne@tonne.org.uk

Annie Feldmeier
2 College Str
Risd #1983
02903 Providence, RI
USA
mafeldmeier@yahoo.com

Ellen Fellmann
Odersbergerstr.6
10435 Berlin
D
ellen.fellmann@web.de

Christian Fennesz
Dieffenbachstr. 35
10435 Berlin
D
zeitblom@snafu.de

Mikael Fernstrom
University Of Limerick
Limerick
IRL
mikael.fernstrom@ul.ie

Antonio Ferreira
Av. Gaspar Corte Real
N18 4e
2750 Cascais, PA
USA
nop35624@mail.tele-
pac.pt

Massimo Festi
Via Fardella 15
44100 Ferrara
I
avatarcablato@libero.it

Roberto Filoseta
1 Admirals Close
Colney Heath
AL4 0QD Herts
UK
r.l.filoseta@herts.ac.uk

Orm Finnendahl
Seelingstr. 47/49
14059 Berlin
D
fdahl@ifnm.hdk-berlin.de

Giuseppe Finotto
Via Ferrara N.18
10043 Orbassano (to)
I
giuseppefinotto@libero.it

Eduardo Flores Abad
Süvari Caddesi 12/3
35040 Bornova- Izmir
TR
eflores@gmx.net

Fon
Königsegg. 11/7
1060 Wien
A
fon@t0.or.at

Michael Frengel
24 Junction Rd
N19 5RE London
UK
mfrengel@alum.
dartmouth.org

Akemi Fujita
197 Green Str Apt 1
02139 Cambridge, MA
USA
p0esia@lycos.com

Funkstörung
Max-Josefs-Platz 6
83022 Rosenheim
D
funkstorung
@funkstorung.de

Warren Furman
Rr2 Box155
18801 Montrose, PA
USA
wfurman@in.epix.net

Bernhard Gál (a.k.a. Gal)
Große Mohreng. 29/13
1020 Wien
A
gal@gmx.at

Pablo Garcia
72-c Shootup Hill
NW2 3XJ London
UK
pablo@city.ac.uk

Mich Gerber
Altenbergstr. 28, P.o. Box
3000 Bern 13
CH
petra.vongunten@oku-
lar.ch

Stelios Giannoulakis
1 College
LL57 2AL Bangor
UK
mup612@bangor.ac.uk

Mathias Gmachl
Franzensg. 6/1
1050 Wien
A
hiaz@test.at

Gilles Gobeil
1217, Ave Bernard Ouest
#30
H2V 1V7 Outremont, QC
CDN
gobeil@cam.org

Rob Godman
4 Mill Close
GL127LP Wotton -
Under-Edge
UK
rob.godman@virgn.net

Ramon Gonzalez-Arroyo
Sierra Del Agua, 27
28761 Soto De Viñuelas,
Madrid
E
arroyo@mail.ddnet.es

Malcolm Goodman
1 Main St. #11h
11201 Brooklyn, NY
USA
shapeshifter
@schematic.net

Martin Gotfrit
231 14th Ave West
V5Y 1X2 Vancouver, BC
CDN
gotfrit@sfu.ca

Rafael Gondesen
Marktstr. 36
20357 Hamburg
D
stacy_g.2000@gmx.net

Richard Graf
Nelkeng. 115
A- 2821 Lanzenkirchen
A
graf@gitarre.at

Michaela Grill
Neubaug.45/13
1071 Wien
A
office@sixpackfilm.com

Tobias Grime
35 London St, Enmore
2042 Sydney, NSW
AUS
toby@kazumichi.com

Ragnar Grippe
Västerled 5
167 55 Bromma
S
r.grippe@swipnet.se

Elisabeth Grübl
Bürgerspitalg. 18
1060 Wien
A
elisag01@hotmail.com

Gruppe 51
Promenade 2
3400 Klosterneuburg
A
clemens.appl
@blacktower.cc

Sha. & Gtt
Kleeblattg. 11/11
1010 Wien
A
sha.GTT@chello.at

Friedrich Guen
Kurfürstenstr.127
10785 Berlin
D
guen.f@t-online.de

Didier Guigue
Rua Antonio Pessoa
Da Rocha, 90
58945-380 Joao Pessoa,
Paraiba
BR
dguigue@openline.
com.br

Bernhard Günter
Firmungstr. 27
56068 Koblenz
D
info@trenteoiseaux.com

Brent Gutzeit
419 N. Albany
60612 Chicago, IL
USA
bgutzeit@boxmedia.com

Bjørnar Habbestad
Wolffsgate 5
5006 Bergen
N
bjornar@bek.no

Franz Hackl
492 Humboldt Str
11222 Brooklyn, NY
USA
hackl@dackl.com

Georg Hajdu
Kirchplatz 8a
48167 Münster
D
hajdu@uni-muenster.de

Jose Halac
544 Court St
11231 Brooklyn, Ny
USA
jose.interport@rcn.com

Simon Hall
Music Dept
B15 2TT Birmingham
UK
s.t.hall@bham.ac.uk

Usman Haque
557a Leonard Str, #4
11222 Brooklyn, NY
USA
usman@concentric.net

Cam Harbidge
42 Hallbrook Dr.sw
t2v 3h4 Calgary Alberta
CDN
ccgharbi@ucalgary.ca

Thomas Haring
Weichselstr. 13
10247 Berlin
D
hairdressers@gmx.de

Craig Harris
718 SE Sixth Str
55414 Minneapolis, MN
USA
craig@kolmon.com

Alfred Harth
Oeder Weg 128
60318 Frankfurt
D
harth23@yahoo.com

Michael Hartman
3510 W Wrightwood
60647 Chicago, IL
USA
okahart@viet.ws

Will Harvey
40 Lipson Rd
PL4 8PW Plymouth
UK
will@limbomedia.com

Jens Hedman
Sodermalarstrand 61
11825 Stockholm
S
jens.hedman@mail.com

Alex Heimkind
Billhornerbrückenstr. 40
20539 Hamburg
D
hammerbrooklyn@gmx.d
e

Chris Henschke
Po Box 338
3056 Brunswick
AUS
chfactory@netscape.net

Johann Heyss
Caixa Postal 100153
24001 970 Niterói,
Rio De Janeiro
BR
heyss@yahoo.com

Rüdiger Hirt
Gärtnerstr. 86
20253 Hamburg
D
hirt.r@debitel.net

Geert-Jan Hobijn
Po Box 11453
1001GL Amsterdam
NL
staal@euronet.nl

Elizabeth Hoffman
24 Waverly Place
Rm. 268
10003 New York, NY
USA
elizabeth.hoffman@nyu.
edu

Martin Howse
Unit 61, 8 Andrews Rd.
E8 4QL London
UK
paradise@1010.co.uk

Rupert Huber
Laaerbergstr. 2/21
1100 Wien
A
fa.huber@snafu.de

John Hudak
184 Columbia
Heights #1d
11201 Brooklyn, NY
USA
jhudak@pobox.com

Michael Iber
Kaiser-Friedrich-Str. 46
10627 Berlin
D
music@chemie.
fu-berlin.de

Ryoji Ikeda
Po Box 637
NE99 1JF Newcastle
Upon Tyne
UK
dma.1@virgin.net

One Infinity
3041 Market St.
94114 San Francisco, CA
USA
seth@oneinfinity.com

Matt Ingalls
545 Valle Vista #4
94610 Oakland, CA
USA
matt@sfsound.org

Jamie Ingram
24 Siward Str
YO103LW York
UK
jai_uk@hotmail.com

Intelligentsia
346-16 Bushi
358-0053 Irumashi,
Saitama
J
mirai@intelligentsia.nl

Haruo Ishii
30-1 Ishibata
Narumi-cho Midori-ku
458-0801 Nagoya
J
MXC00275@nifty.ne.jp

Miyuki Ito
140 Claremont Ave.
Apt. 5c
10027 New York, NY
USA
mi77@columbia.edu

Ivan Iusco
Via Giustino Fortunato 8/n
70125 Bari
I
Info@Minushabens.com

Toshio Iwai
2-40-17-#301 Chihaya
Toshima-ku
171-0044 Tokyo
J
iwai@gol.com

Chris Janka
Schottenfeldg.78/2
A-1070 Wien
A
blendwerk@t0.or.at

Marius Jarashius
Ziemiu 28a-38
3031 Kaunas
LT
r@delfi.lt

Ramunas Jaras
Ziemiu 28a-38
3031 Kaunas
LT
r@delfi.lt

Zbigniew Jaroc
Flat 3 166 Dyke Rd
bn15pu Brighton
UK
z@softloader.com

Jan Jelinek
Christburger Str. 25
10405 Berlin
D
loop-finding
@scape-music.de

Frédéric Kahn
14, Villa Poissommière
75018 Paris
F
frédéric.kahn@ircam.fr

Klaus Karlbauer
Gymnasiumstr. 71/3
1190 Wien
A
frau-faust@chello.at

Erik Mikael Karlsson
Marietorps Allé 3a
21775 Malmö
S
erik.mikael.karlsson
@telia.com

Dieter Kaufmann
Linke Wienzeile 94/30
1060 Wien
A
kaufmann@mdw.ac.at

Hideko Kawamoto
1700 Dogwood Mile
28352 Laurinburg, NC
USA
hk0008@unt.edu

Keith Kehrer
10097 Maple Leaf Drive
20886 Montgomery
Village, MD
USA
kkehrer@msn.com

Stefan Keller
Haldenstr. 41
5454 Bellikon
CH
stkeller@flutetrends.ch

Edward Kelly
29 Bury Str
NR2 2DJ Norwich
UK
pseudoshark
@netscapeonline.co.uk

Pete Kelly
7 Park View Terrace,
Rawdon
LS19 6ES Leeds
UK
PJPKZ@ukgateway.net

Geoffrey Kidde
9 Sheppard Str
11545 Glen Head, NY
USA
gkidde@ix.netcom.com

Kid606
310 Oakland Ave
94611 Oakland, CA
USA
kid606@tigerbeat6.com

Guttorm Kittelsen
Landoyveien 74
1394 Nesbru
N
guttormk@notam.uio.no

Josef Klammer
Neuholdaug. 51
8010 Graz
A
klammer@mur.at

Petra Klusmeyer
Harpstedterstr. 99
28816 Stuhr
D
pklusmeyer@yahoo.com

Panayiotis Kokoras
E-24 Wood Court
Garrowby Way
YO10 5DJ York
UK
panayiotiskokoras
@hotmail.com

Matej Kolár
Komenskeho 30
586 01 Jihlava
CZ
medved@ji.cz

Joachim Koll
Rosenleiten 16
4101 Feldkirchen
A
joko13@gmx.net

Pavel Kopecky
Smetanovo Nabr. 2
116 65 Prague 1
CZ
kopecky@f.amu.cz

Yuriko Hase Kosima
4-2-c-308 Koyodai
206-0803 Inagi, Tokyo
J
bym01235@nifty.ne.jp

Annja Krautg.r
Pater Schwartz G. 11a
1150 Wien
A
nja@vidok.org

Simon Kunath
Brightling Bungalow,
Burwash, Etchingham
TN19 7DW Etchingham,
East Sussex
UK
sck@unstable.demon.
co.uk

Leo Kupper
23, Ave Albert - Elisabeth
1200 Bruxelles
B
leo.kupper@chello.be

David Kwan
2219 1/2 Stuart Str
94705 Berkeley, CA
USA
kwan@mill8.edu

Eric La Casa
11 Rue Euryale Dehaynin
75019 Paris
F
ascendre@free.fr

Luc Larmor
19, Quai Ille Et Rance
35000 Rennes
F
luc.larmor@wanadoo.fr

Claire Laronde
185 Rue Du Chevaleret
75013 Paris
F
partage.tanzanie
@imaginet.fr

William Latham
144-146 Buckingham
Palace Rd
SW1W 9TR London
UK
carolyn@artworks.co.uk

Steve Law
C1-2/120 Arden St.
3051 Melbourne
AUS
steve@solitary-
sound.com

Sonia Leber
11 Teak Str Caulfield Sth
3162 Vic
AUS
wax@waxsm.com.au

Thomas Lehn
Kalk-Mühlheimer-
Str. 370
51065 Köln
D
ThomasLehn
@compuserve.com

Frank Leipelt
Neue Krugallee 22
12435 Berlin
D
frankleifheit@hotmail.
com

Stan Link
2400 Blakemore Ave
37212-3499 Nashville
TN
USA
stan.b.link@vanderbilt.
edu

Cort Lippe
182 Washington Hwy.
14226 Snyder, NY
USA
lippe@buffalo.edu

Andreas List
Thalhauserfussweg 11
85354 Freising
D
ttmstudio@aol.com

Theodore Lotis
15, Bastwick Str
EC1V 3PE London
UK
T.Lotis@city.ac.uk

Wolfgang Ludewig
Emmendingerstr. 22
79106 Freiburg
D

Matthew Malsky
950 Main St.
01610 Worcester, MA
USA
mmalsky@clarku.edu

Andy Manndorff
Gablenzg. 4/8
1160 Wien
A
oberlinninger@mdw.ac.at

Edgardo Martinez
Esquiú 3026
3000 Santa Fe
ARG
edmar@fafodoc.unl.edu.
ar

Elio Martusciello
Via Montiano, 8b
00127 Roma
I
emartus@tin.it

José Eduardo Mataloni
Silvanstr. 9
50678 Köln
D
mataloni@arnet.com.ar

Stephan Mathieu
Akazienweg 25
66121 Saarbrücken
D
mathieu@bitsteam.de

Ron Mazurek
39 Ross Rd
07057 Wallington, NJ
USA
ronmazurek@home.com

Danny McCarthy
Inis Oirr,
2 Chestnut Drive
Midleton
co Cork
IRL
dannymccarthy1
@ireland.com

Michael McNabb
1378 De Haro St
94107 San Francisco, CA
USA
michael@mcnabb.com

Joao Mendes
Pca Padre Souza, 9
20930-070 Cep Rio De
Janeiro, Rj
BR
jmend@gbl.com.br

Marcello Mercado
Peters,
Neussestr. 22
50670 Köln
D
marcello@khm.de

Chris Mercer
4378 Campus Ave #3
92103 San Diego, CA
USA
camercer@ucsd.edu

Massimiliano Messieri
Via Acquarone 30/12 D
16125 Genova
I
messieri@tin.it

Carol Michelson
Po Box 1051
94920 Tiburon
USA
carol@visualmeditation.
com

Valeriano Migliorati
Via Piane 21
64013 Corropoli (TE)
I
valeriano@itol.it

Ultra Milkmaids
18, Rue Appert
44100 Nantes
F
y@ultra-milkmaids.com

Graeme Miller
28 Commercial Str
El 6ls London
UK
all@artsadmin.co.uk

Roger Mills
34 Claremont Rd,
Bishopston
BS78DH Bristol
UK
roger@devoid.co.uk

Frank Millward
Kingston Hill
KT2 7LB Kingston Upon
Thames
UK
millward@dircon.co.uk

Erik Minkkinen
68 Rue Pelleport
75020 Paris
F
em@pb2.de

Wolfgang Mitterer
Mariahilferstr. 200/14
1150 Wien
A
selichar@t0.or.at

Masahiro Miwa
3-95 Ryoke-cho
5030014 Ogaki Gifu
J
mmiwa@iamas.ac.jp

Werner Möbius
C /o Nikki Dietrich
Taborstr. 51 / 51
1020 Wien
A
wernermoebius
@hotmail.com

Karl Mohr
Bergg. 15/9
1090 Wien
A
info@karlmohr.com

Gordon Monahan
Senefelderstr. 23
10437 Berlin
D
funnyfarmcity
@compuserv.com

Ken Montgomery
199 Park Place
11238 Brooklyn, NY
USA
kenmontgomery
@earthlink.net

Barbara Morgenstern
Kadiner Str. 20
10243 Berlin
D
info@barbara
morgenstern.de

Michael Munson
6 Errol St
3011 Footscray,
Melbourne, VIC
AUS
mgm2@visto.com

Fumitaka Nakamura
Yayoi 2-11-16,bunkyo
113-8658 Tokyo
J
nakamura@nc.
u-tokyo.ac.jp

Netochka Nezvanova
Achtergracht 19
1071 WI Amsterdam
NL
ecdysone@eusocial.com

Stuart Nicefoot
Rue Des Bateliers
67000 Strasbourg
F
dave_de_mille@hotmail.
com

Ken Niibori
Kitamachi 1-18-12-102
1850001 Kokubunji City,
Tokyo
J
nibo@50n0.com

Benny Nilsen
Bränningevägen 17-19
10571 Stockholm
S
benny.nilsen
@eudoramail.com

Hiroki Nishino
Higashi-tyo, 1-45-12
184-0011 Koganei-shi,
Tokyo
J
hn@sfc.keio.ac.jp

Timothy Nohe
2308 Tucker Lane
21207-6638 Baltimore
USA
nohe@umbc.edu

Sbeb Normal
17 Bvd De Nancy
67000 Strasbourg
F
sbeb.normal@caramail.
com

Robert Normandeau
7070, Fabre #1
H2E 2B2 Montréal, QC
CDN
robert.normandeau
@umontréal.ca

Keith O'Brien
18 Palmerston Rd.
6 Dublin
IRL
obrienkm@tcd.ie

Pedro Ochoa
Moreno 1353 4º 24
1091 Buenos Aires
RA
pedroochoa@infovia.com
.ar

Matthias Ockert
Dunckerstr. 62
10439 Berlin
D
ockert.vinzenz
@t-online.de

Paul Oldrige

Camillo Camilliani
90145 Palermo
I
pabigaz@tin.it

Teemu Ontero
Franzeninkatu 22 B 53
00530 Helsinki
SF
tontero@siba.fi

Battery Operated
Bp 14 Les Bigourdins,
Route De Saint Canadet
13770 Venelles
F
beewoo@battery
operated.net

Ed Osborn
Waldstr. 55
10551 Berlin
D
edo@roving.net

Julien Ottavi
12, Rue Jean Jacques
Rousseau
44000 Nantes
F
gossott@canalv.com

John Palmer
Im Kappelfeld 23
70469 Stuttgart
D
J.Palmer@Palmer.
s.shuttle.de

Tae Hong Park
Woolworth Center For
Musical Studies
08544 Princeton, NJ
USA
park@music.princeton.
edu

Michel Pascal
Rue Sainte Croix
13480 Cabries
F
michel.pascal@freesbee.
fr

Peaches
Rosenthaler Str. 3
10119 Berlin
D
info@kitty-yo.de

Joseph Pehrson
P.o. Box 20548 Pabt
10129 New York, NY
USA
jpehrson@rcn.com

Sylvia Pengilly
7480 Bella Vista Rd.
93422 Atascadero, CA
USA
spengilly@jps.net

Elisabeth Penker
Ramperstofferg. 52 /13
1050 Wien
A
elpenker@hotmail.com

Harta Performing
Via Ortigara 17
20052 Monza
I
nicola.frangione@tin.it

Andrian Pertout
257 Mary Str
3121 Richmond, VIC
AUS
apertout@bigpond.com

Angelo Petronella
Trognano 7
27010 Bascape, Milano
I
angelopetronella
@hotmail.com

Jean Piche
4524 Patricia
H4B-1Z1 Montreal, QC
CDN
Jean.Piche@umontreal
.ca

Pimmon
18 Belmont Str
2160 Merrylands, NSW
AUS
pimmon@bRdcast.net

Shawn Pinchbeck
Po Box 35088, Oliver
Postal Outlet
T5K 2R8 Edmonton, AB
CDN
resonate@freenet.edmon-
ton.ab.ca

Michael Pinter
Leitnerg. 7/5
8010 Graz
A
remi@algo.mur.at

Wim Plug
Rijnsburgwerweg 77a
2234 Leiden
NL
polyvinylbigband
@hotmail.com

Franz Pomassl
Po Box 14
3542 Gföhl
A
laton@t0.or.at

Sibylle Pomorin
Arndtstr.18
10965 Berlin
D
SibyllePomorin@aol.com

Markus Popp
Trautenaustr. 16
10717 Berlin
D
popp@snafu.de

Rostislav Prochovnik
Zednická 953
708 00 Ostrava-poruba
CZ
rosta.prochovnik@cbox.
cz

Qwerty Produktions
Mathunistr. 13
80686 München
D
fortschritt90@yahoo.com

Peter Rantasa
Dieffenbachstr. 35
10435 Berlin
D

Giuseppe Rapisarda
Via Ugo Foscolo 34
95047 Paterno (ct)
I
g.rapisarda@musician.
org

Rechenzentrum
Kastanienallee 40
10119 Berlin
D
weiser@rechenzentrum.
org

Eduardo Reck Miranda
83 Boulevard
Saint Marcel
75013 Paris
F
eduardo.miranda@noos.
fr

Michel Redolfi
17, Rue De La Préfecture
06300 Nice
F
michelredolfi
@compuserve.com

Joseph Reinsel
Rm 135 Dcc Basement,
110 8th Str
12180 Troy, NY
USA
reinsj@rpi.edu

Remi
Leitnerg. 7/5
8010 Graz
A
remi@algo.mur.at

Kirsten Reynolds
249 Goswell Rd
EC1V 7JD London
UK
kirsten@projectdark.
demon.co.uk

Alistair Riddell
12 Napier St.
3065 Fitzroy, VIC
AUS
amr@alphalink.com.au

Michael Rieken
Erlenstr.66
28199 Bremen
D
mrieken@gmx.de

Sergey Rocambol
Lunacharskogo, 38 - 276
194356 Saint Petersburg
RU
rocambol@lynx.ru

Anthony Rowe
First Floor
59 Rivington Str
EC2A 3QQ London
UK
dulce@squidsoup.com

Julien Roy
7785 St-Dominique
H2R1X6 Montréal, QC
CDN
julien@artificiel.net

Paul Rudy
1317 E. 97th Terrace
64131 Kansas City, MO
USA
proody@hotmail.com

Marcin Rupocinski
Ul. A. Mickiewicza 46/2
58-310 Szczawno-zdroj
PL
zizumur@eranet.pl

Kiawasch Sahebnassagh
Triester Str. 128a/11
8020 Graz
A
kiawasch@yahoo.com

Alejandra Salinas
C/ Calvo Sotelo 22
Segundo Izq.
26003 Logrono, La Rioja
E
underwoodwork@yahoo.
com

Stefan Saskov
Ilinden 79/10
1000 Skopje
MK
gugu@soros.org.mk

Borut Savski
Kunaverjeva 14
1000 Ljubljana
SLO
borut.savski
@radiostudent.si

Janek Schaefer
34 Crewdson Rd
SW9 0LJ London
UK
janek@audiOh.com

Elisabeth Schimana
Erasinweg 23
2410 Hainburg
A
elise@aon.at

Christof Schläger
Bankwerkerij 1
1021 NS Amsterdam
NL
schlaeger.smit
@wanadoo.nl

Michaela Schwentner
Stollg. 7/6
1070 Wien
A
jade@rhiz.org

Alexander Seitz
Philosophenweg 57
34121 Kassel
D
seitzalexander@hotmail.
com

Evrim Sen
Escher Str. 282
50739 Köln
D
evrim@hackerland.de

Jane Sherratt
Swynnerton
ST15 0QD Stone,
Staffordshire
UK
janesherratt@tesco.net

Johannes Sienknecht
Am Stegkreuz 1a
65719 Hofheim
D
johannes.sienknecht
@gmx.net

Rodrigo Sigal
64 Beverley Court,
Cedar Drive
SL5 0UB Sunningdale,
Berkshire
UK
sigal@city.ac.uk

Pekka Sirén
Kajavankatu 4 B 46
04230 Kerava
SF
agaps@nettilinja.fi

Randall Smith
15 Spencer Ave
M6K 2J4 Toronto, ON
CDN
vertsnd@istar.ca

Nelson Soares
Rua Professor Miguel De
Souza, 305 / 201
30570-150 Belo
Horizonte, Minas Gerais
BR
nelson.bh@zaz.com.br

Rogelio Sosa
75, Rue De Wattignies
75012 Paris
F
ro.sosa@noos.fr

Nikolaos Stavropoulos
1 Vron Square
LL57 2 AL Bangor,
gwynedd
UK
nikosgst@hotmail.com

Ewan Stefani
14 Cromer Terrace
LS2 9JT Leeds
UK
e.j.stefani@leeds.ac.uk

Ian Stewart
Mecklenburgh Square
WC1N 2AB London
UK
artsonics@hotmail.com

Swp
Weserstr.7
60325 Frankfurt
D
ac@force-inc.com

Granular Synthesis
Währingerstr.59
1090 Wien
A
kh@thing.at

Fred J. Szymanski
110 St. Mark's Place,
No.21
10009 New York, NY
USA
fredsz@earthlink.net

Marialuisa Tadei
14 Cliveden Place
SW1W8LA London
UK
Marialuisatadei@yahoo.
com

Jeff Talman
338 Berry Str, Loft 4ne
11211 Brooklyn, NY
USA
jefftalman@mindspring.
com

Nobuyuki Tanahashi
1-58 Muro Machi
503-0906 Ogaki Shi,
Gifu
J
credo99@iamas.ac.jp

Zlatko Tanodi
Perjavica 80/1
10090 Zagreb
HR
zlatkot@piano.muza.hr

Simon Taylor
53 Terry Rd
2114 Denistone, NSW
AUS
smzetaylor@start.com.au

Jeans Team
Rosenthalerstr. 3
10119 Berlin
D
info@kitty-yo.de

Christoph Theiler
Grundsteing. 44/1/5
1160 Wien
A
theiler@t0.or.at

Alain Thibault
1309 Rue Bernard #3
H2V 1W1 Outremont, QC
CDN
alain8@sympatico.ca

Kalev Tiits
Box 86
00251 Helsinki
SF
kalev.tiits@siba.fi

Andreas Tilliander
Ringvägen 158
11631 Stockholm
S
andreas.tilliander@deo.
com

Maciej Toporowicz
97 Crosby St
10012 New York, NY
USA
Noqontrol@aol.com

Trackmark
6 Petite Rue D'Austerlitz
67000 Strasbourg
F
homemade@club-
internet.fr

Mark Trayle
24700 Mcbean Parkway
91355 Valencia, CA
USA
met@shoko.calarts.edu

Pierre Alexandre Tremblay
C.p.934 Succ. Snowdon
H3X3Y1 Montréal, QC
CDN
ora@cam.org

Twins Demon Circuit
Hushimi-haitsu 401,
3-7-16, Minami-kara-
suyama
157-0062 Setagaya-ku,
Tokyo
J
lungs-k@air.linkclub.or.jp

Athanasia Tzanou
47 Chemin De Bellevue
78400 Chatou, Paris
F
Athanasia.Tzanou@ircam
.fr

Music 308 Form And
Analysis Class University
Of Illinois,
Urbana Champaign
1114 W. Nevada
61801 Urbana, IL
USA
g-von@uiuc.edu

Mika Vainio
429 Harrow Rd
W104RE London
UK
stengsmith@aol.com

Luis Valdovino
Fine Arts Department
80309 Boulder, CO
USA
luis.valdovino
@colorado.edu

Mario Verandi
Wielandstr. 18
12159 Berlin
D
mev533@isdugp.bham.
ac.uk

Stephen Vitiello
530 Canal Str, Apt. 5e
10013 New York, NY
USA
vitello64@aol.com

Sándor Von Ivády
Bahnhofstr. 68
88682 Salem
D
andras.ivady@astrium-
space.com

Robert Wacha
Gartenstadtstr. 18
4048 Linz / Puchenau
A
robert_wacha@hotmail.
com

Agnieszka Waligorska
Kajavankatu 4 B 46
04230 Kerava
SF
agaps@nettilinja.fi

Tom Wallace
10 Holmdene Ave
SE24 9LF London
UK
tomw@clara.net

Craig Walsh
Corner Of W. Market And
Mciver
27420 Greensboro, NC
USA
craig341@hotmail.com
and   ctwalsh@uncg.edu

Georg Weidinger
Getreideweg 6a
2301 Wittau
A
mail@klaviermusik.at

Lauren Weinger
239 Chestnut Str
02465 West Newton, MA
USA
lweinger@mediaone.net

Holger Wendland
Prießnitzstr. 21
01099 Dresden
D
edition-raute@t-online.de

Lennart Westman
Magnus Ladulasgatan 7
118 65 Stockholm
S
sonicart@chello.se

Dietmar Wiesner
Gartenstr.14
60594 Frankfurt
D
Dwffm1997@aol.com

Garnet Willis
53 First Ave
M4M 1W7 Toronto
CDN
garnet_willis@goodme-
dia.com

Gerhard E. Winkler
Bründlweg 3
5020 Salzburg
A
winklerg@ping.at

Ryszard Wolny
Zielonogórska 39a/2
66-016 Czerwiensk
PL
wolny@PL.com

Judson Wright
223 E 10th St, 7
10003 New York, NY
USA
judson@judson.net

Shinji Yamamoto
Via Cartoleria 11
40124 Bologna
I
pa14977@iperbole.
bologna.it

Boris Yanachkov
Zk Hipodruma Bl.106
Ap.20
1612 Sofia
BG
borisalexandrov
@hotmail.com

Lo Yeeon
615 Laurel Ave
94025 Menlo Park, CA
USA
acoustic@olagrande.net

John Young
Media Dept.,
Clephan Building
LE1 9BH Leicester
UK
jyoung@dmu.ac.uk

Georg Zeitblom
Dieffenbachstr. 35
10435 Berlin
D

Claus Zimborski
(claustrophobia)
Pfeffenhausener Str. 45a
84032 Pfettrach
D
claustrophobia@t-onli-
ne.de

Andre Zogholy
Makartstr 32
4020 Linz
A
ego@servus.at

Tommy Zwedberg
Dannemoragatan 18,5tr
S 11344 Stockholm
S
tommy.zwedberg
@chello.se

David Aberl
Kronstorfberg 19
4484 Kronstorf
david@guide.at

Linda Ahammer
Glanfeldstr. 34
5020 Salzburg
ahammer@gmx.at

Christian Aigner
5700 Zell Am See
chris.aigner@aon.at

Manuela Aigner
Stadiumstrasse 2 / 1 / 5
3250 Wieselburg

Samuel Ajayi
Meschedeweg 3
4030 Linz
sam.aj@gmx.at

Karl Allerbauer
Schlag 25
8241 Dechantskirchen
karl.allerbauer@mcnon.
com

Hans Altenstrasser
Prarath 42
8443 Gleinstätten

Jelena Alutina
Franz-Plasser-Str.4
5280 Braunau/inn

Matthias Ambrosi
6433 Oetz
ambrosi_matthias
@hotmail.com

Dominik Ameur
Haselgrabenweg 17
4040 Linz
strange888@uboot.com

Sonja Anderle
Spengerg. 44/6
1050 Wien

Stefan Andreas
Messerschmidtg. 34/13
1180 Wien
andreas@flasher-
design.com

Stefan Angel
Ungarg. 69
1030 Wien
sangel@hak.szu.at

Emin Anilmis
Stelzhammerstr. 11/14
5280 Braunau/Inn

Roland Anzenberger
Pestalozzistr. 46
4840 Vöcklabruck

Nadine Art
Redlschlag 41
7434 Bernstein

Diana Atassi
Schloßparkg. 51
8950 Gmünd

Can Attesman
Himmelhofg.
1130 Wien

Markus Auernig
Goppelsberg 12
9771 Berg Im Drautal
thesaint@aon.at

Simon Außerlechner
Weidach 55
6414 Mieming
simon.master@telering.at

Helka Barna
Robinson Club
Ampflwang
4843 Ampflwang

Isabel Baumann
Freistädter Str. 224
4040 Linz

Martin Baumgartner
Biesenfeldweg 4
4040 Linz
martin_baumgartner-
linz@utanet.at

Peter Baumgartner
Obere Hofmark 63a
5282 Ranshofen
p.baumgartner@aon.at

Özgür Bedir
Margaretenstr. 89/1/9
1050 Wien

Martin Bernhard
Zwickenberg 14
9781 Oberdrauburg
motze007@gmx.at

Michael Bernsteiner
Jägerweg 15
8580 Köflach
MB_@gmx.at

Reinhard Binder
Töllerg. 42/2/14
1210 Wien
ReinhardBinder@gmx.at

Andrea Birklbauer
Labach 32
4261 Rainbach/M.
hak@jomo.org

Stefanie Bobory
Jakob-Jonas-Weg 6
6845 Hohenems

Alexandra Bogomolowa
Badg. 34
7434 Bernstein

Sergiu Bontas
C. Flirstr. 10
5280 Braunau/Inn

Peter Bösch
Zur Feldrast 9
6890 Lustenau
peter.boesch.htlr@
schulen.vol.at

Patrick Brandstätter
Bahnhofstr. 36
4550 Kremsmünster
brandstaetter.dach
@gmx.at

Gernot Bukovnik
Bienenweg 11
9241 Wernberg
mavyn@gmx.at

Laura Burger
Kaprun 257
5710 Kaprun
sekretariat@brgzell.
salzburg.at

Manuela Bürger
Ankenreuthe 356
6858 Bildstein

Natascha Burgstaller
Lohbachweg E 110
6020 Innsbruck

Christopher Clay
Gentzg. 52/1/12
1180 Wien
u19@c3o.org

Murat Coskun
Dr.-F.-Kogler-Str. 22
6020 Innsbruck
muratc@gmx.at

Lukas Czerny
Kirschentalg. 27
6020 Innsbruck

Martin Dambauer
Höhenstr. 24
4840 Vöcklabruck
martinda@uboot.com

Victoria Dang
Bräuhausg. 34/112
1050 Wien

Veronika Danzl
Ried 29b
6130 Schwaz

Peter Dely
Aubrunnerweg 33
4040 Linz
peter.d@lion.cc

Andreas Diendorfer
Parmerg. 8
1090 Wien
der_andreas@gmx.at

Dejana Dijanovic
Margaretenstr. 93/2/5
1050 Wien

Fritz Dimmel
Gassnerg. 14
2020 Hollabrunn
fritz@dimmel.at

Thomas Dirschlmayr
Anton Wildgansstr. 2
5026 Salzburg
thomas@dirschlmayr.com

Manuela Djuzel
Kroateng. 29
4020 Linz

Orhan Dönmez
Markt 14
5450 Werfen
orhandoenmez
@yahoo.de

Gregor Dorfbauer
Lebingerstr. 12
4320 Perg
gregor.dorfbauer@aon.at

Markus Dorn
Hockeg. 7/18
1180 Wien
markus.dorn@gmx.at

Florian Dorner
Suttnerweg 14
8041 Graz

Thomas Dornhofer
Schönau 20
8225 Schönegg b. Pöllau
thomasd@a1.net

Claudia Dreer
Spechtweg 20
4030 Linz
claudia_d@a-topmail.at

Christian Dreier
Badidastr. 77
6811 Göfis
christian@cdreier.com

Alexander Duggleby
Ampertalweg 2
D-85395 Thalham
aduggleby@gidion.de

Yvonne Eberhardt
Weinberg 188
7474 Eisenberg
yvonne@eberhardt.at

Magdalena Eberl
Dorfstr.
3250 Schadendorf 16

Sascha Ebner
Unterfarrach 34
8720 Kobenz
Ebner_Toni@a-topmail.at

Johanna Ebner
Faistenau 9
5324 Faistenau

Katharina Eder
Wiesenegg 387
6370 Aurach/Kitzbühel

Harald Egger
Lanzenbichl 27
8813 St. Lambrecht
Harald_Egger
@a-topmail.at

David Eggler
Zürs 126
6763 Zürs
d.eggler@a1.net

Eva-Christina Ehgartner
Franz-Resl-Str.4
5280 Braunau

Tove Elias
Judendorferstr. 28
8700 Leoben
eliast@yline.com

Sebastian Endt
Wallackstr.12
4600 Wels
s.endt@datapool.at

Johanna Enzenhofer
Waldingerstr. 20
4201 Gramastetten

Bastian Enzenhofer
Waldingerstr. 20
4201 Gramastetten

Simon Enzenhofer
Waldingerstr. 20
4201 Gramastetten

David Enzenhofer
Waldingerstr. 20
4201 Gramastetten

Kerstin Erne
Am Neuner 15
6890 Lustenau

Stefan Fahrngruber
Erlaaerstr. 105
1230 Wien
visual.3d@gmx.net

Thomas Fanninger
Himmelreichweg 43
8044 Graz
homepage@fanninger.at

Thomas Fellsner
Plasserstr. 3/14
5280 Braunau

Anna Felnhofer
Dr. Natterergr. 6/3/100
1020 Wien
annaf@chello.at

Lisa Filzmoser
Ottstorf 18
4600 Wels
lisa@filzmoser.at

Gilmar Findeis
Ramperstorferg. 46/2
1050 Wien

Christoph Fink
Josef-Reiter-Str. 37
5280 Braunau

Daniel Fink
Vorderer Sierner 23
4082 Aschach

Christoph Fischer
Vöcklabrucker Str. 5a
4800 Attnang-Puchheim
ChristophFischer@free-way.at

Thomas Flanitzer
Kellerg. 52
2432 Schwadorf
T.Flanitzer@gmx.at

David Flatz
Bahnhofstr. 35
6923 Lauterach
david@upcs.at

Markus Freilinger
Theodor Körnerstr. 21
4050 Traun
m.freilinger@lion.cc

Markus Friedl
Friedrichg. 3
8010 Graz
Sinclair0@hotmail.com

Karin Fritsch
Herderplatz 1
1110 Wien

Belinda Fuchar
8230 Staudach

Roman Gablek
Ziegelofeng. 24-26/2/6/23
1050 Wien
roman.gablek@gmx.at

Wolfgang Gahleitner
Feldweg 5
4202 Hellmonsödt
wolfgang@fancyage.at

Stefan Gahr
Kreuzen 389
5571 Mariapfarr
steve@snowboarding.at

David Gaicher
Afram 55
8410 Wildon

Daniela Gallistl
Schwalbenstr. 24
4240 Freistadt
loggy54@hotmail.com

Patrick Gansterer
Spitalg. 2
7400 Oberwart
patrick@paroga.com

Andreas Gegendorfer
Hubertusg. 5
7350 Oberpullendorf

Matina Germek
Pestalozzistrasse 5/2/9
8605 Kapfenberg
engerl_1982@hotmail
com

Johannes Gerold
Geisslerg. 23
8045 Graz
admin@sge-7a.com

Stefan Gloimüller
Schenkenbrunn 9
3125 Mautern

Christian Gmeiner
Achstr.33a
6922 Wolfurt
mail@visual-page.de

Matthias Gmeiner
Achstr. 33a
6922 Wolfurt
vbgmeiner@vbgmeiner.de

David Gnedt
Voralpenweg 13
3352 St. Peter/Au
d.gnedt@aon.at

Maximilian Gosch
Schönbrunnerstr. 71/3
1050 Wien

Mario Gotthardt
Kainach 69
8410 Wildon

Reinhard Graf
Hauptstr. 31
7344 Stoob
geafrein@aon.at

Christina Gramang
Au 235
3040 Neulengbach
RYC_GRA@aon.at

Peter Gratl
Dölsach 128
9991 Dölsach
p.gratl@hs-nd.tsn.at

Sonja Gratzl
Reinberg-Litschau 38
3861 Eggern
s.m.gratzl@utanet.at

Alexander Grif
Höttinger Au 72/34
6020 Innsbruck
master_of_chaos@gmx.at

Magdalena Grömer
5324 Faistenau

Sabine Grossbauer
Holunderstr. 481
5071 Wals
biggi54@gmx.net

Vera Gruber
Reitlehen 63
5731 Hollersbach/Pzg.
veranita@gmx.at

Martin Grünbart
5324 Faistenau

Andreas Grüneis
Blumenweg 16
4063 Hörsching
grueneis@gmx.at

Georg Gut
Am Hoferfeld 16
6911 Lochau
georg.gut@aon.at

Andreas Gutzelnig
Tobra 40
4320 Perg

Isabella Haas
8230 Staudach

Mario Habenbacher
Pretalstr. 34
8664 Veitsch
mario_h@aon.at

Thomas Haberkorn
Steinböckstraße 10
3340 Waidhofen/Ybbs
tom.hab@gmx.at

Christian Haberl
Josef Schwarzg.
11 - 13/7/18a
1050 Wien

Jürgen Habringer
Steiningerstr. 28
4222 Luftenberg
juergen_habringer
@hotmail.com

Julia Hagen
Am Neuner 26
6890 Lustenau

Martin Hager
8952 Irdning
hager_martin
@hotmail.com

Carmen Hagleitner
Gablerstr. 12
6900 Bregenz

Tobias Haider
Am Damm 10
4470 Enns
thai@uni.de

Franz Haider
Schwindg. 9
1040 Wien
franzhai@yahoo.com

Robert Haider
Schulg. 9
4372 St. Georgen/W.
s411092@eduhi.at

Benjamin Hainbuchner
Oberndorferstr 3
4210 Gallneukirchen
hainbb@schueler.
asn-linz.ac.at

Larissa Halb
Neuhaus 179
8385 Neuhaus
Larissa.Halb@gmx.at

Markus Halbauer
Obere Hauptstr. 28
7162 Tadten
sattler_tadten
@hotmail.com

Sandra Haller
Ötscherg. 9
3252 Petzenkirchen
sandra_13@gmx.at

Martin Harlander
Steinfeldg. 8
7321 Unterfrauenhaid

Florian Hartl
Angererhofweg 51
4030 Linz
hartl@via.at

Elisabeth Hartl
Oberlandshaag 99
4082 Aschach
Melanie_Gahleitner
@i-one.at

Oriana Haselwanter
Lassigg 39
6460 Imst
momo_im@yahoo.com

Alexander Hasslinger
Staudg. 83
1180 Wien
alexander.hasslinger
@gmx.at

Josef Hehenberger
Sindelburg 29
3313 Wallsee

Eva Heidinger
Rettenbach 131
7434 Bernstein

Gerald Heilmann
Mitterweg 8
4222 Gusen
geraldheilmann
@yahoo.com

Katharina Henninger
Amalienstr. 75/4/18
1130 Wien
katrin.henninger@gmx.at

Christian Hinterberger
Waidach 187
5421 Adnet
christian.hinterberger
@gmx.at

Aladin Hochmeier
Sattling 17
4170 Haslach

Eva Hochwimmer
Lengberg
9782 Nikolsdorf
lengberg@asn-netway.at

Gregor Hofbauer
Gentzg. 7/16
1180 Wien
gregor.hofbauer@pilion.at

Florian Hofer
Am Edhügel 46
4115 Kleinzell
flotsch@gmx.at

Wolfgang Hoffelner
Schmiedeg. 17
4040 Linz
level@tm1.at

Nadine Höflinger
Eichenstr. 19
4240 Freistadt

Andreas Hofmarcher
Auf Der Wieden Nr. 9
3270 Scheibbs
anakonda@yline.com

Bernhard Hoisl
Milesstr. 10
9100 Völkermarkt
hoisl@gym1.at

Florian Höll
Langmoos 37a
5621 St. Veit/Pg.
florian.hoell@sbg.at

Ulrike Hollenstein
Am Schlatt 34
6890 Lustenau

Severin Holzer-Graf
St. Lorenz 364
5310 Mondsee
severinhg@edumail.al

Michael Holzinger
Erzb. Gebhard Str. 6
5020 Salzburg
mailfor@fastrun.at

Peter Holzkorn
R. V. Eichtalstr. 5/6
7000 Eisenstadt
p_holzkorn@gmx.at

Jürgen Hoog
Burgstallerstr. 19
4060 Leonding
jhoog@aon.at

Rita Horodecki
Pannaschg. 6/3/13
1050 Wien

Heinz Hösch
Unterweißenbach 174
8330 Feldbach
hoeschdesign@netway.at

Anton Hösch
Unterweißenbach 174
8330 Feldbach

Stefanie Huber
Stuben 116
7434 Bernstein

Patrick Huberth
Raiffeisenstr.
8010 Graz

Martin Humberger
Steinwand 20
4081 Hartkirchen

Waldemar Hummer
Mieders 120
6142 Mieders
waldemar.hummer
@gmx.at

Petra Hunger
M.-Hainischstr.13
4040 Linz
mistake@gmx.at

Amor Ibrisimovic
Kurzwehrhartplatz 4
4082 Aschach

Claudia Iglseder
Pechestr. 12
6020 Innsbruck
claudia@iglseder.at

Karim Jafarmadar
Währingerstr. 160/16
1180 Wien
karim@gmx.at

Franz Janisch-Lang
Reigersberg 11
8262 Ilz
franzjanisch@yahoo.de

Bernhard Jantscher
Ulmg. 14
8570 Voitsberg
berni_jantscher
@hotmail.com

Silvana Jovic
Laabstr. 65
5280 Braunau/Inn

Birgit Jussel
Unterfeld 12 a
6912 Hörbranz

Ahmet Kabaetli
Badg. 13/10
8700 Leoben
ahmet.k@gmx.at

Josef Kaiblinger
Bergg. 5
7350 Oberpullendorf
praetorianX@gmx.net

Verena Kaipel
Redlschlag 96
7434 Bernstein

Albert Kalchmair
Pacherstr. 15
4600 Wels
gustl27@hotmail.com

Thomas Kaltenbrunner
Alpenlandstr. 5
2231 Strasshof
thomas.kaltenbrunner
@aon.at

Lukas Kaltenegger
Flösselg. 9
2391 Kaltenleutgeben
lkaltenegger@surfeu.at

Lukas Kamarad
Bahnstr. 7
2020 Hollabrunn
lukas.kamarad
@bghollabrunn.ac.at

Severin Kampl
Wernbergerstr. 4
9524 St. Ulrich/Villach
skampl@gmx.nt

David Kao
C. Flirstr. 30
5280 Braunau/Inn

Georg Kapeller
Franz-Nabl-Weg 35
8010 Graz
geo@line.at

David Karall
Hauptstr. 13
7302 Nikitsch
david@uboot.com

Nadine Karlinger
Landfriedstetten 24
3252 Petzenkirchen

Nicole Karner
Ebner-Eschenbachg. 5
3250 Wieselburg

Thomas Katzinger
Katzing 7
4150 Rohrbach
games@telering.at

Sebastian Keiler
Rofansiedlung 438
6200 Wiesing
s.keiler@aon.at

Markus Keim
Tiefbrunau 29
5324 Faistenau

Stefan Keller
Obweg 18a
6682 Vils
stefan.keller@telering.at

Bejaze Kelmendi
Höft 1
5280 Braunau/Inn

Markus Kerbler
Hirschentanzstr. 7/3
2384 Breitenfurt

Stefan Kernstock
Graf-Starhembergg.
30/2/6
1040 Wien
gwiku_haizing
@hotmail.com

Dietmar Kerschner
Brunnweg 11/1-2
1100 Wien
didi_post@yahoo.com

Adrienne Kienreich
Eichholzstr. 8
6900 Bregenz

Su-jung Kim
Bräuhausg. 34/2/30
1050 Wien

June Kindel
Ziegelofeng. 12-14
1050 Wien

Erwin Kishore
Grüng. 24/2/10
1050 Wien

Stefan Kitzmantl
Antiesenweg 21
4971 Aurolzmünster
skitzmantl@aon.at

Marco Klammler
Willersdorf 70
8061 St. Radegund
marcoklammler@gmx.at

Sabrina Klaushofer
Faistenau 116
5324 Faistenau

Bianca Klein
Günseck 70
7435 Unterkohlstätten

Benjamin Klemnin
Kettenwerkstr. 18
9371 Brückl
rpgmasterman@i-one.at

Lara Klingler
Hans Murauerstr. 12
84359 Simbach

Patricia Kloiber
Tiefbrunnau 120
5324 Faistenau

Carina Kneidinger
Stiftstr. 20
4082 Aschach

Susanne Koberg
Kainach 70
8410 Wildon

Sabine Kofler
Wildenweg 18
6410 Telfs

Katharina Kögl
Enzelsdorf 6
8072 Fenitz

Sylvia Koglek
Gemmersdorf 171
9421 Eitweg
sylviakoglek@gmx.at

Marian Kogler
Vöscherg. 14
1230 Wien
marian.kogler@vienna.at

Mario Kokalj
8732 Seckau
dylethal@gmx.at

Mathias Kolb
Grünau 14b
6850 Dornbirn
m.kolb@cable.vol.at

Stefan Köppel
Prokesch
Osten 4/3/7
8020 Graz

Philipp Kornfeld
Marieng. 30
7372 Draßmarkt
philippka@a1.net

Ingo Kowatsch
Sattnitzbauerstr. 1
9020 Klagenfurt
ingo.k@aon.at

Rebekka Kranewitter
J.-W.-Klein-Str. 5 / 204
4040 Linz

Stefan Kugler
Mühlstr. 195
2184 Hauskirchen
webmaster
@borgmistelbach.ac.at

Birgit Künz
Vorklosterg. 47
6900 Bregenz

Petra Kupec
Gartenweg 193
2130 Hüttendorf
redButterfly@gmx.at

Katharina Kuschetz
Körösistr. 117a
8010 Graz

Sophia Laabmyr
Faistenau 11
5324 Faistenau

Linda Lam
Rosa-Jochmann-Ring
5/20/9
1110 Wien
lin-chan@gmx.at

Markus Lambauer
Peter Rosegger Str. 14
8073 Feldkirchen

Michael Lampersberger
Biesenberg 57
3912 Oed

Karl Heinz Lampret
Magdalensberg 110
9473 Lavamünd
karllampret
@hotmail.com

Daniel Landauer
Mannswörtherstr. 145
1/2
2320 Mannswörth
landi@aon.at

Katharina Landl
Eichleiten 7
2833 Bromberg

Benjamin Lang
M.-Hainisch-Str. 15
4040 Linz
benjamin.lang@aon.at

Peter Lasinger
Kirchenberg 8
4310 Mauthausen
lasingerpeter@aon.at

Roland Lechner
Mangelberg 8
5165 Berndorf b. Sbg.
cypro@gmx.at

Christoph Ledinek
Schulg. 4
8720 St. Margarethen
cledinek@gmx.at

Thomas Lehninger
Schleifmühlg. 11/22
1040 Wien
Lehninger@chello.at

Martin Leonhartsberger
Freysbergstr. 19
4201 Gramastetten
martin.leonharts
berger@aon.at

Goerg Lerchner
Fichtenweg 8
8054 Gedersberg

Thomas Lettner
Am Nordsaum 20a
4050 Traun
Lettner.herbert@utanet.at

Sandra Leutgöb
Ontlstr. 8
4040 Linz

Marina Leutschacher
Franz-Riepl-G. 27
8020 Graz
minchen00@hotmail.
com

Kurt Lichka
Schöffelg. 15
2320 Schwechat
kurt.l@aon.at

Ines Lindschinger
Jägerweg 23
4082 Aschach

Veronica Theresia List
Tiergartenweg 14
8055 Graz

Judith Machater
Karl-Vogt-Str. 21
5700 Zell Am See
sekretariat
@brgzell.salzburg.at

Bernhard Maier
Burkerring 18
5730 Mittersill
BlairWitch1@sms.at

Gernot Maierhofer
8230 Hartberg

Patrick Gerald Mairbäurl
Höfterstr. 9
5280 Braunau/Inn

Julia Mandl
Pengersdorf 7
2813 Lichtenegg
julia.mandl@gmx.at

Thomas Mandorfer
Ramperstorfferg. 46/15
1050 Wien

Patrick Mannsberger
Wagner-Jauregg-Str. 12
8055 Graz
patrick.mannsberger@uta
.at

Roland Mariacher
Dolomitenstraße 33c
9900 Lienz
rolisenate@gmx.at

Hannes Maritschläger
Ritzbergerstr. 11
4082 Aschach

Sarah Maritschnegg
Klein-Preding 21/2
8504 Preding
sunshine014@uboot.
com

Joachim Marte
Montfortplatz 16a
6923 Lauterach

Cornelia Matt
Tannenstr. 7
6911 Lochau

Claus Matzinger
Untere Dorfstr. 17
4210 Unterweitersdorf
Skateboy3000@sms.at

Philipp Maus
Margaretenplatz 2
2560 Berndorf
kunterbunte.maus@gmx.
at

Thomas Mayr
Gramberg 2
4673 Gaspoltshofen

Florian Mayr
Behamberg 45
4441 Behamberg
florian.mayr
@everymail.net

Ivonne Mayr
Ferdinand-Markl-Str. 1
4040 Linz

Christian Mayr
Aufischerweg 28
4061 Pasching
c.mayr@gmx.at

Bernd Georg Mayr
Krummer Weg 12c
8041 Graz

Mario Meirhuber
Spreitzenberg 4
5222 Munderfing
meih@utanet.at

Daniel Mekisch
Ringstr. 350
8344 Bad Gleichenberg
scotsman@gmx.at

Christian Menkens
Markt 127
5360 St. Wolfgang
christian@menkens.at

Manuel Messerer
Hintermeierstraße 17
3100 St. Pölten
messi666@hotmail.com

Isabell Metzler
Neufeldstr. 14
6890 Lustenau

Christian Michlits
Müllnerg. 6/26
1090 Wien
chris_michlits
@hotmail.com

Christoph Mitasch
Lärchenstraße 25
4210 Gallneukirchen
cmitasch@aon.at

Manuel Mitasch
Lärchenstr. 25
4210 Gallneukirchen
manuel@mitasch.com

Robert Moick
Rustenschacherallee
32/2/7
1020 Wien
m.robi@chello.at

Maximilian Moldaschl
Ziehrerplatz 4 - 5/17
1030 Wien
max.moldaschl@chello.at

Sebastian Moser
Obere Hafnerzeile 16
4240 Freistadt
sebastian@jomo.org

Michaela Moser
Kellnering 29
4081 Hartkirchen
mimo10at@yahoo.de

Emanuel Muckenhuber
Ochsenharing 79
5163 Mattsee
emanuel.muckenhube
@i-one.at

Markus Mühllechner
St. Kollmann 2
4874 Schildorn
Jupitar@a-topmail.at

Bernhard Müllebner
Kühschelmg. 4
2020 Hollabrunn
bernhard.muellebner@bg
hollabrunn.ac.at

Patricia Müllner
Ferdinand-Markl-Str. 19
4040 Linz
muellner.patricia@gmx.at

Martin Murer
Bodendorf 3
8861 St. Georgen o. M.
murx@gmx.at

Andrea Narnhofer
Auwiesenweg 17
8055 Graz
peter.narnhofer
@iic.wifi.at

David Narovec
Hagenau 28
4100 Ottensheim
davidnarovec
@hotmail.com

Mario Neuberger
Wüsterg. 1/8
2401 Fischamend
www.RedIce015@sms.at

Michael Neuhold
Starrein 32
2084 Starrein
fcp@aon.at

Robert Neuner
Mistelbach 6
4613 Mistelbach
zehnerl@crypter.net

Michael Niederer
Oberer Weinberg 4
3150 Wilhelmsburg
office@violette-teufel.at

Thomas Noisternig
Semslach 42
9821 Obervellach
noiste@gmx.at

Bianca Nussbaummüller
Limbach 64
3314 Strengberg

Julia Nußbaummüller
Schaching 69
3312 Oed
julia.nussi@aon.at

Tobias Oberascher
Nelkeng. 6
5204 Straßwalchen
rumblecat@hotmail.com

Nicole Oberkirsch
Voeststr. 27
4060 Leonding
Littlesunshine@gmx.at

Bettina Obermoser
Dellach 123
9772 Dellach/Drau
HS.Dellach@Schule.at

Christoph Obermüller
Leonfeldnerstr. 122
4040 Linz

Ulrike Oberndorfer
Biesenfeldweg 4
4040 Linz

Bianca Obersberger
Laabstr. 117
5280 Braunau/Inn

Christian Olear
Maieraustr. 113
4792 Münzkirchen
webmaster
@webbersmag.com

Markus Oswald
Prof.-Franz-Spath-Ring
13/17
8042 Graz
m_oswald@gmx.net

Andreas Öttl
Linzerstr. 65
4531 Kematen

Lenka Pachta
Erzherzog-Karl-Str. 39 -
47/2/83
1220 Wien
lenka_pachta@mail.com

Verena Pahr
Dreihütten 39
7434 Bernstein

Denise Palkovic
Klausmühle 3
6911 Lochau

Martin Pammer
Schlag 105
4264 Grünbach
martin-pammer@gmx.at

Jakob Papouschek
Einsiedlerg. 15-17/1/5
1050 Wien

Istvan Pataki
G-Grinninger-Str. 63/a 77
4050 Traun
pataki.istvan@gmx.at

Erik Pauer
Spitalstr. 33
7350 Oberpullendorf

Michael Payer
Angerg. 2
7162 Tadten
m.payer@aon.at

Bianca Pechmann
Klausenbachstr. 17
4040 Linz

Melanie Peitl
Buchleiten 165
3312 Oed

Hans Pendl
Dr.-Karl-Widdmann-
Str. 40
8160 Weiz
administration
@bhak-weiz.ac.at

Verena Pertl
Stuben 13
7434 Bernstein

Franziska Petelin
Neufeldweg 8
9586 Fürnitz

Vas Peter
Marcius 15.utca 12/e
2800 Tatabanya
fepeti@elender.hu

Simone Peterseil
Schulg. 38
4311 Schwertberg

Felix Petsovits
Erleng. 13
7312 Horitschon
fpetso@gmx.at

Jakob Petsovits
Erleng. 13
7312 Horitschon
jpetso@gmx.at

Andreas Pfanner
Kehlegg 84
6850 Dornbirn
webmaster@andis-
page.com

Lukas Pilat
Wilbrandtg. 23
1180 Wien
lukas@workmail.com

Michaela Maria Plöchl
Pflanzlstr. 2
4240 Freistadt

Eugeni Polyakov
Estae, 38-10
6370 637000, Pavlodar,
Kasachstan
002@imail.ru

Christoph Posch
Gosau 560
4824 Gosau
christoph.posch@gmx.at

Clemens Pöschko
Hubertusstr. 15
4240 Freistadt
master_71@gmx.net

Andreas Pramhaas
Anton-Föger-Weg 17
6410 Telfs
a.pramhaas@telfs.com

Paloma Preidl
Weizenweg 10
4050 Traun
paloma@traun-stadt.at

Paul Preis
Rudolfstraße 106g
8010 Graz
preis@i-solution.at

David Prem
Kopfing 26
8224 Kaindorf
d.prem@gmx.at

Simon Prentner
Mühlkreisbahnstr. 5
4040 Linz
simon.prentner@aon.at

Christian Prevost
Hetzg. 28/10
1030 Wien
cprevost
@popperschule.at

Stefanie Priewasser
Pfongau 28
5202 Neumarkt
stef@eurotrash.co.uk

Michael Probst
Binderlandweg 14
4030 Linz
slimlimp@aon.at

Katharina Puchner
Kalchgruberstr. 14
4240 Freistadt

Norina Puffer
Stumperg. 64/ 4
1060 Wien

Melanie Puhr
Redlschlag 19
7434 Bernstein

Karin Punz
Gumprechtsfelden 15
3250 Wieselburg

Sarah Putzer
Steinachstr. 2a
6900 Bregenz

Tomislav Radisic
Bucheng. 89/3/9
1100 Wien

Raul Radl
Hochleitenweg 14
8055 Graz

Martin Ras
Bleichhügelstr. 16
9330 Althofen
martin.ras@gmx.at

Kerstin Rebenek
Mühlgraben 121
8385 Neuhaus
kerstin.rebenek@web.de

Andreas Reh
Haidbachstr. 45
4061 Pasching
Rehlien@gmx.at

Thomas Reichhart
Elz 47
4292 Kefermarkt
t.reichhart@edumail.at

Sandra Reif
Dr.-Karl-Widdmann-Str.
40
8160 Weiz
administration
@bhak-weiz.ac.at

Kerstin Reifberger-Dorfer
Ufer 3/4
3313 Wallsee
kerstinreifberger@aon.at

Stephanie Reisinger
Eisenstr. 69
4460 Losenstein

Stephan Reiter
Libellenweg 4
4030 Linz
st_reiter@edumail.at

Christina Reiter
5324 Faistenau

Wolf-Heinrich Reuter
Kirchplatz 7
9210 Pörtschach
wolf.reuter@aon.at

Reiner Ribarics
Erleng. 23
7312 Horitschon
snowball16@utanet.at

Gerald Riegler
Kirchau 65
2831 Warth

Anja Ringhofer
Günseck 65
7435 Unterkohlstätten

Laura Ritter
Schanzweg 11
6900 Bregenz

Valentin Rock
Gralenweg 6
8054 Seiersberg

Alexander Rödhammer
J.-Reiterstr. 6
5280 Braunau/Inn

Christian Rödhammer
J.-Reiterstr. 6
5280 Braunau/Inn

Lukas Roedl
Reihofferplatz 1
2632 Wimpassing
lukas@roedl.at

Gregor Roesler-Schmidt
Lampig. 17/13
1020 Wien
rsg@firmasieben.at

Francesco Rosa
Schönbrunnerstr.
34/1/17
1050 Wien

Stefan Rosenberger
Bahnstr. 41
7210 Mattersb
sekretariat@bsma.at

Andreas Rosenlechner
Tiefbrunau 18
5324 Faistenau

Marco Roß
Traunseerstr. 17
4812 Pinsdorf
marco84@gmx.at

Elisabeth Roth
Rettenbach 75
7434 Bernstein

Christine Rotter
Schiffmühlenstr. 86/14
1220 Wien

Sophia Rüscher
Belruptstr. 26 A
6900 Bregenz

Sergen Sagiroglu
Margaretengürtel
68/58/16
1050 Wien

Angelika Sailnberger
Nappersdorf 5
2023 Nappersdorf

Michael Salcher
Kelchsauerstr. 7
6361 Hopfgarten
michael_salcher
@yahoo.com

Stefan Sallaberger
Weidenstr.4
4701 Bad Schallerbach
s.sallaberger@gmx.at

Jacqueline Salopek
Bacherplatz 4/10/11
1050 Wien

Christoph Saulder
Schulstr. 30
4642 Sattledt
EquinoxOmega
@uboot.com

Helmut Sauseng
Faistenau 12
5324 Faistenau

Martin Schacherl
Paul-Troger-G. 52
2700 Wr. Neustadt
schacherl
@bgzehnwn.ac.at

Ingo Schachner
Eicheng. 1
2354 Neu-Guntramsdorf
punkrock@kabsi.at

Walter Schack
Brockhauseng. 20/4
1220 Wien
w.s.s@gmx.at

Benedikt Schalk
Ing.-Karl-Strycek-Str. 17
2326 Lanzendorf
bschalk@gmx.net

Philipp Schapfl
Kralbergweg 25a
6082 Lans

Thomas Schauer
Tiefbrunau 90
5324 Faistenau

Simon Scheiber
Mitterndorferstr. 16
6330 Kufstein
lobby@visual-noise.com

Johannes Schiehsl
Kreisg. 7
2551 Enzesfeld
joschiehsl@web.de

Dominik Schilcher
Römerstr. 554
5541 Altenmarkt
domsch83@hotmail.com

Mathias Schindler
Josef-Schlesinger-Str. 1
1140 Wien
mschindler
@it-academy.cc

Fabian Schlager
Waldstr .9
5161 Elixhausen
burnItDown@sms.at

Emanuel Schmacher
Zauchen 43
9133 Miklauzhof
emanuel17@gmx.at

Christian Schmid
Aug. 37/14
7350 Oberpullendorf
mundimann@hotmail.
com

Markus Schmid
Feldkirchen 39
5143 Feldkirchen

Florian Schmidt
Maniglweg 6a
4050 Traun
f.schmidt@traun-stadt.at

Silke Schmidt
Kainach 70
8410 Wildon

Marlene Schmidthaler
Laussa 370
4461 Laussa
schmidthaler@freeway.at

Stefan Schnauder
Kopernikusstr. 12
4020 Linz
Steve.Sch@gmx.at

Michaela Schöllhammer
In Der Neupeint 34
4030 Linz

Theresa Schöpp
Tiefbrunau 103
5324 Faistenau

Sandra Schörgenhuemer
Löwengarten 20
4082 Aschach

Maria Schörghuber
Sindellrg 68
3313 Wallsee

Daniel Schranz
Sebastianistr. 17
5280 Braunau
zentralamerika@yahoo.de

Christian Schrei
Borraweg 10
8010 Graz
webmaster
@mexxisdesign.com

Martin Schreiter
Kaprunerstr.22
5671 Bruck
sekretariat
@brgzell.salzburg.at

Paul Schreitl
Nr. 162
2223 Martinsdorf
kaiservonchina@gmx.at

Catharina Schroll
Spengerg. 47/3
1050 Wien

Peter Schüller
Fasangarteng. 55
1130 Wien
peter.schueller@gmx.at

Martin Schürrer
Eckhartweg 14
4020 Linz
schuerrer_martin@gmx.at

Christoph Schuster
Stelzhamerstr. 12
5280 Braunau/Inn

Klaus Schustereder
Pötting 5
4720 Pötting
schusti@utanet.at

Georg Schusterschitz
Grillparzerstr. 27
8010 Graz
georgschusterschitz
@web.de

Thomas Schwarz
Lindeng. 12
2752 Wöllersdorf
tschwarz@hak
wr-neustadt.ac.at

Ralf Schwarz
Pettenbacherstr. 85
4655 Vorchdorf
ralf.schwarz@kirchdorf.
eduhi.at

Silvia Schwarz
Hauptstr. 109
3413 Hintersdorf
silvia-irene@gmx.at

Thomas Schwarz
Lindeng. 12
2752 Wöllersdorf
tschwarz@hakwr-neu-
stadt.ac.at

Christoph
Schwinghammer
Bachweg 8
4502 St.marien
Hippivandatippi@gmx.at

Haris Sehic
Salzburgerstr. 50
4840 Vöcklabruck

Johannes Seifert
Prinz-Eugen-Straße 3b
4061 Pasching
jonny-
seifert@funtastic.net

Gerald Senger
Montanastraße 14
8112 Gratwein
sengergerald@gmx.de

Klaus Seyerlehner
Reisetbauerstr. 44
4020 Linz
seyerlehnerklaus
@yahoo.com

Michael Sick
Leonfeldnerstr. 53
4040 Linz
thematrix02@boot.com

Christoph Sieghart
Mühlg. 32-34/3/1
2380 Perchtoldsdorf
christoph@sieghart.net

Nikola Simonovic
Spengerg. 55/1-2
1050 Wien

Birgit Spalt
Anger 195
5324 Faistenau

Martin Spazierer
Wienerflurg. 68
1230 Wien
flashh@firemail.de

Jakob Sperker
Mittermayerg. 2/10
1130 Wien
sperker@gmx.at

Christof Sperl
Schloßstr. 21/1
5282 Ranshofen
csperl@yline.com

Christoph Sperrer
Hirtstr. 27
4040 Linz

Sabrina Spitaler
Riedstr. 18
6973 Höchst

Martin Stabauer
Irrseeblick 45
4893 Zell Am Moos
martin@stabauer.net

Thomas Steinbach
Mühlbachstr. 37
4451 Garsten
thomas3@lion.cc

Matthias Steinbauer
Columbusg. 104/11
1050 Wien

Sabrina Steiner
Bahng. 30 A
6890 Lustenau

Stefan Steurer
Faistenau 61
5324 Faistenau

Andreas Stickler
G. Festenbergg. 25
2700 Wiener Neustadt
andreas.stickler@gmx.at

Nikolaus Stieldorf
St. Michael 65a
6060 Gnadenwald

Philipp Strahl
Sobothg. 10
8054 Graz
p.strahl@aon.at

Armin Streibl
Sonnleiten 16
8832 Oberwölz

Helga Maria Stubauer
Hofberg 24
4443 Maria Neustift
hestubi@gmx.at

Nicole Stübler
Vorgartenstr. 174/8
1020 Wien

Martin Stückelschweiger
Käserei 22
8713 St. Stefan
stuecki@telering.at

Markus Sucher
Denkmalg. 4
9020 Klagenfurt
upsale@hypo-online.at

Eduard Sydler
Goisern 349
4822 Bad Goisern
edi@sydler.at

Christopher Tafeit
Baumkirchners. 16
8741 Weißkirchen
Christopher.Tafeit@aon.at

Ayse Temur
Einsiedlerg. 60/1/5
1050 Wien

Jürgen Thallinger
Frättingsdorf 26
2132 Frättingsdorf

Luke The Skywalker
Dr.-R.-Griedl-Weg 16
8301 Lassnitzhöhe
lukeskywalker@aon.at

Stefan Toller
Gumppstr. 10
6020 Innsbruck
div2@gmx.at

Patrick Topf
Birkenweg 32
4816 Gschwandt
patrick
@speckdrumm.com

Manuel Treven
Koschatstr. 18
9020 Klagenfurt
m_treven2000
@yahoo.com

Anela Tricic
Im Tal 19
4292 Kefermarkt

Markus Triska
Herbert-Spieß-G. 6
2103 Langenzersdorf
triska@gmx.at

Hava Tulumovic
Ableidingerg. 4/11
2320 Schwechat

Lisa Tureczek
Ramsau 98
5324 Faistenau

Kathrin Ullmann
Franz-Mika-Weg 5/6/14
1100 Wien
sk8ergirly_2000
@yahoo.com

Andreas Ullmann
Winkelfeldsteig 54
6020 Innsbruck/Amras
agi.ullmann-
andreas@gmx.at

Christopher Ulrich
Klosterg. 14
8430 Leibnitz

Dominik Unger
Uranusweg 25
1140 Wien
dj.ferdl@utanet.at

Martin Unger
8384 Minihof-
Liebau 117
hs-neuhaus.klb@bnet.at

Thomas Untereichner
Walzwerkstr. 71
4050 Traun
the-nocturn@gmx.at

Dominic Vanderberg
Margaretenstr. 108/1/18
1050 Wien

Ana-Karolina Vasari
Waltendorfer Hauptstr
101/1
8010 Graz

Gregor Borsi Vedernjak
Delbach 55
9063 Maria Saal
g.b.v.wissenschaft
@chello.at

Christian Viehweider
Oberkoflerweg 220
6073 Sistrans
christian_viehweider
@yahoo.com

Thomas Voglreiter
Dorfstr. 542
5710 Kaprun
tomvogi@gmx.at

Sonja Vrisk
12.-November-Str. 8
9020 Klagenfurt
oe8ymq@oevsv.at

Michael Wagenhofer
Dreihütten 50
7434 Dreihütten

Dominik Wagenknecht
Staufenweg 59
5400 Hallein
dominik_w@gmx.net

Kathrin Wagner
Rettenbach 115
7434 Bernstein

Thomas Walland
Getreideg. 11
9020 Klagenfurt
thomas.walland@aon.at

Lukas Wallentin
Bahnlände 43-45
1100 Wien
Lukas.Wallentin@gmx.at

Markus Wallinger
Torren 132
5440 Golling
markuswallinger@gmx.at

Jenny Waltl
Tulpenweg 8
6974 Gaissau

Thomasz Waluch
8344 Bad Gleichensberg

Teresa Waser
Wallsee 71
3313 Wallsee

Wolfgang Watzinger
Ungarg. 69
1030 Wien
wwatzinger@hak.szu.at

Andreas Weber
Steinamangerg.4
1210 Wien

Daniel Weichselbaum
Galgenbühel 6
4283 Bad Zell

Gerald Weidinger
Im Auholz 19/2
2340 Mödling
d.weidinger
@everymail.net

Richard Weinberger
Haslach 5
6422 Stams
Systemlord@gmx.at

Lisa Weinberger
Höfterstr. 94
5280 Braunau/ Inn

Rene Weirather
Untermarkt 7
6600 Reutte
reneweirather@hotmail.
com

Georg Weissacher
Sperlingweg 17
5023 Langwied
gweissacher@hotmail.
com

Florian Weixelbaumer
F. Plasserstr. 2
5280 Braunau/ Inn

Peter Wernig
Altglandorf
9300 St. Veit / Glan

Sabrina Wernisch
Anton Linderweg 22
9900 Lienz
g.koeck@tirol.com

Daniel Widmar
Maiersdorf 43
8083 St. Stefan

Matthias Wienerroither
St. Lorenz 186
5310 Mondsee
matthias.w@aon.at

Alexander Wienerroither
Südtirolerstr. 23
5280 Braunau
AlexAW@gmx.at

Harald Wieser
Hartlmühl 43
3351 Weistrach
hattio1@gmx.at

Anna Katharina Wilhelm
Südtirolerstr. 55
5280 Braunau/Inn

Peter Willeit
Domplatz 2
6020 Innsbruck
petrizky@uboot.com

Christian Wimmreuter
Stampferg. 472
5541 Altenmarkt
christian@wimmreuter.
com

Manuel Windbichler
Schlag 227
2813 Lichtenegg

Thomas Winkler
Schölbing 221
8230 Hartberg
tomwi@gmx.net

Wolfgang Wipfler
Wienerstr. 72 A
7400 Oberwart
wolfgang_wipfler
@web.de

Irene Wöckinger
Reithweg 14
4210 Unterweitersdorf

Andreas Wolf
Waldsiedlung 124
2823 Pitten
ndee@void.at

Silke Wollinger
Ziegeleistr. 1
4082 Aschach

Bernhard Wurm
Mitterweg 13
4153 Peilstein
wurmbe@gmx.net

Catherine Wurth
Neubaug. 6
3800 Göpfritz/wild

Thomas Würthinger
Dulmading 18
4972 Utzenaich
o8t8o@yahoo.com

Selmani Yaramis
Sonnenhofg. 1/7
1050 Wien

Thore Zahradniczek
Rudolf-Janko-Str. 10
2380 Perchtoldsdorf
thore.zahradniczek
@kabsi.at

Bernhard Zelch
Kleinreithstrasse 10
4694 Ohlsdorf
zelch@virs-media.com

Yi-jun Zhan
Abelstr. 14
4082 Aschach

Alexandra Zinkl
Mariensee 163
2870 Aspang
AZinkl@hakwr-
neustadt.ac.at

Anna Zipperer
Ramsau 41
5324 Faistenau

Roman Zumpf
Dreihütten 61
7434 Bernstein